Medieval Philosophy

Blackwell Readings in the History of Philosophy

Series Editors: Fritz Allhoff and Anand Jayprakash Vaidya

The volumes in this series provide concise and representative selections of key texts from the history of philosophy. Expertly edited and introduced by established scholars, each volume represents a particular philosophical era, replete with important selections of the most influential work in metaphysics, epistemology, moral and political philosophy, and the philosophy of science and religion.

1. *Ancient Philosophy: Essential Readings with Commentary*
Edited by Nicholas Smith with Fritz Allhoff and Anand Jayprakash Vaidya

2. *Medieval Philosophy: Essential Readings with Commentary*
Edited by Gyula Klima with Fritz Allhoff and Anand Jayprakash Vaidya

3. *Early Modern Philosophy: Essential Readings with Commentary*
Edited by A. P. Martinich with Fritz Allhoff and Anand Jayprakash Vaidya

4. *Late Modern Philosophy: Essential Readings with Commentary*
Edited by Elizabeth S. Radcliffe and Richard McCarty with Fritz Allhoff and Anand Jayprakash Vaidya

Medieval Philosophy

Essential Readings with Commentary

Edited by

Gyula Klima
with Fritz Allhoff and Anand Jayprakash Vaidya

Blackwell
Publishing

Editorial material and organization © 2007 by Blackwell Publishing Ltd

BLACKWELL PUBLISHING
350 Main Street, Malden, MA 02148-5020, USA
9600 Garsington Road, Oxford OX4 2DQ, UK
550 Swanston Street, Carlton, Victoria 3053, Australia

The right of Gyula Klima, Fritz Allhoff, and Anand Jayprakash Vaidya to be identified
as the Authors of the editorial material has been asserted in accordance with the UK
Copyright, Designs, and Patents Act 1988.

First published 2007 by Blackwell Publishing Ltd

1   2007

Library of Congress Cataloging-in-Publication Data

Medieval philosophy : essential readings with commentary / edited by Gyula Klima;
with Fritz Allhoff and Anand Jayprakash Vaidya.
      p. cm. — (Blackwell readings in the history of philosophy)
   Includes bibliographical references and index.
   ISBN-13: 978-1-4051-3564-1 (hardback)
   ISBN-10: 1-4051-3564-6 (hardback)
   ISBN-13: 978-1-4051-3565-8 (pbk.)
   ISBN-10: 1-4051-3565-4 (pbk.)
 1. Philosophy, Medieval.   I. Klima, Gyula.   II. Allhoff, Fritz.   III. Vaidya, Anand.

   B721.M458 2007
   189—dc22

                                                                2006025789

A catalogue record for this title is available from the British Library.

Set in 10/12.5pt Dante
by Graphicraft Limited, Hong Kong

For further information on
Blackwell Publishing, visit our website:
www.blackwellpublishing.com

Contents

Text Sources and Credits

The editor and publisher gratefully acknowledge the permission granted to reproduce the copyright material in this book:

Chapter 1: Augustine, bk. 8, chs. 2–12 (pp. 213–224) from *St. Augustine's City of God and Christian Doctrine*, ed. P. Schaff, trans. Rev. M. Dods (New York: The Christian Literature Publishing Co., 1896).

Chapter 2: Anonymous, "Dialectica Monacensis," p. 461 from *Logica Modernorum*, vol. II, part 2, ed. L. M. de Rijk (Assen: Van Gorcum, 1967). Translation © 2007 by G. Klima.

Chapter 3: Thomas Aquinas, ST I, q. 1, aa. 1–10 from *Summa Theologiae*, trans. English Dominican Fathers (London: Burns, Oates, and Washburne, 1912–36; New York: Benziger Bros., 1947–48). Translation revised for this publication by G. Klima with reference to the original Latin text and a new translation by B. Davies.

Chapter 4: Boethius, pp. 90–98 from *Selections from Medieval Philosophers I: Augustine to Albert the Great*, ed. and trans. R. McKeon (New York: Charles Scribner's Sons, 1929). Published in Latin as *Boethius, In Isagogen Porphyrii Commenta*, CSEL, vol. 48, bk. 1, chs. 10–11. Vienna: F. Tempsky, 1906.

Chapter 5: Selections from *The Metalogicon of John of Salisbury*, trans. D. D. McGarry (Berkeley, CA: University of California Press, 1955).

Chapter 6: Lambert of Auxerre, pp. 104–110 from *The Cambridge Translations of Medieval Philosophical Texts*, ed. N. Kretzmann and E. Stump, trans. N. Kretzmann (Cambridge: Cambridge University Press, 1988). © 1998 by Cambridge University. Reprinted by permission of the editors and Cambridge University Press. Text slightly revised and annotated by G. Klima. Published in Latin as "VIII: De suppositionibus et significationibus" in *Logica (Summa Lamberti)*, ed. and trans. F. Alessio. Florence: La Nuova Italia, 1971.

Chapter 7, text 1: William of Ockham, d. 2, q. 8 (pp. 271–274) from *Ordinatio*, ed. G. Gál (New York: St. Bonaventure, 1967). Translation © 2007 by G. Klima; **text 2**: William of Ockham, bk. 1, proem., para. 6 (pp. 351–352) from *Expositio in Librum Peri Hermeneias Aristotelis*, ed.

A. Gambatese and S. Brown (New York: St. Bonaventure, 1978). Translation © 2007 by G. Klima; **text 3**: William of Ockham, bk. 1, chs. 14–16 from *Ockham's Theory of Terms: Part I of the Summa Logicae*, trans. M. J. Loux (Notre Dame, IN: University of Notre Dame, 1974). © 1974 by University of Notre Dame Press. Reprinted by permission of the publisher.

Chapter 8: John Buridan, pp. 103–107 from *Summulae de Dialectica*, trans. G. Klima (New Haven: Yale University Press, 2001). © 2001 by Yale University Press. Reprinted by permission of the publisher.

Chapter 9, text 1: Augustine, pp. 62–63 from *The Essential Augustine*, trans. V. J. Bourke (Indianapolis: Hackett Publishing Company, 1974). © 1974 by Vernon J. Bourke. Reprinted by permission of Hackett Publishing Company, Inc. All rights reserved. Originally published in Latin as *De diversis Quaestionibus octoginta tribus liber unus*, q. 46, 1–2; **text 2**: Augustine, bk. 2, ch. 8 from *On the Free Choice of the Will (De Libero Arbitrio)*, trans. A. S. Benjamin and L. H. Hackstaff (New York: MacMillan/Liberal Arts Press, 1964). © 1964. Reprinted by permission of Pearson Education, Inc., Upper Saddle River, NJ.

Chapter 10: Thomas Aquinas, ST 1, q. 84, a. 5 (pp. 29–33), q. 85, aa. 1–2 (pp. 49–63) and q. 86. a. 1–3 (pp. 91–93) from *Summa Theologiae*, vol. 12 (New York: Blackfriars-McGraw Hill, 1968).

Chapter 11: Thomas Aquinas, bk. 2, lc. 20 (pp. 235–240) from *Commentary on the Posterior Analytics of Aristotle*, trans. F. R. Larcher (Albany: Magi Books, 1970). © 1970 by F. R. Larcher.

Chapter 12: Henry of Ghent, pp. 112–121 from *The Cambridge Translations of Medieval Philosophical Texts*, trans. R. Pasnau (Cambridge: Cambridge University Press, 2002). © 2002 by Cambridge University Press. Reprinted by permission of the translator and publisher. Originally published in Latin as *Summa Quaestionum Ordinariarum*, a. 1, q. 2.

Chapter 13: John Duns Scotus, pp. 120–130 from *Philosophical Writings*, ed. and trans. A. B. Wolter (New York: Nelson, 1962). © 1962 by Allan Wolter. Originally published in Latin as *Opus Oxoniense*, bk. 1, d. 3, q. 4, aa. 4–5.

Chapter 14, text 1: Augustine, from *City of God*, XI, 26, trans. Rev. M. Dods, and reproduced from p. 33 of *The Essential Augustine*, ed. and trans. V. J. Bourke (Indianapolis: Hackett Publishing Company, 1974), with revisions to the translation by V. J. Bourke © 1974 by Vernon J. Bourke. Reprinted by permission of Hackett Publishing Company, Inc. All rights reserved; **text 2**: Augustine, from *On the Trinity*, XV, 12.21–22, trans. Rev. M. Dods, and reproduced from pp. 34–35 of *The Essential Augustine*, ed. and trans. V. J. Bourke (Indianapolis: Hackett Publishing Company, 1974). © 1974 by Vernon J. Bourke. Reprinted by permission of Hackett Publishing Company, Inc. All rights reserved.

Chapter 15: Thomas Aquinas, ST I, q. 17, a. 3 and q. 85, a. 6 from *Summa Theologiae*, trans. English Dominican Fathers (London: Burns, Oates, and Washburne, 1912–36; New York: Benziger Bros., 1947–48). Translation slightly revised for this publication by G. Klima.

Chapter 16: Henry of Ghent, pp. 94–108 from *The Cambridge Translations of Medieval Philosophical Texts*, trans. Robert Pasnau (Cambridge: Cambridge University Press, 2002). © 2002 by Cambridge University Press. Reprinted by permission of the translator and publisher. Originally published in Latin as *Summa Quaestionum Ordinariarum*, a. 1, q. 1.

Chapter 17: Nicholas of Autrecourt, pp. 47–75 from *Nicholas of Autrecourt: His Correspondence with Master Giles and Bernard of Arezzo*, ed. and trans. L. M. De Rijk (Leiden–New York–Köln: Brill, 1994). © 1994. Reprinted by permission of Brill Academic Publishers.

Chapter 18, text 1: John Buridan, bk. 2, q. 1 from *Quaestiones in Aristotelis Metaphysicam: Kommentar zur Aristotelischen Metaphysik* (Paris: 1518; Frankfurt am Main: Minerva, 1964 reprint). Translation © 2007 by G. Klima; **text 2**: John Buridan, bk 8, ch. 4, sect. 4 (pp. 706–711) from *Summulae de Dialectica*, trans. G. Klima (New Haven: Yale University Press, 2001). © 2001 by Yale University Press. Reprinted by permission of the publisher.

Chapter 19: Thomas Aquinas, "De Principiis Naturae," from *Sancti Thomae de Aquino opera omnia* (the "Leonine" edition), vol. 43, ed. Roberto Busa (Rome: Editori di San Tommaso, 1976). Translation © 2007 by G. Klima.

Chapter 20: Thomas Aquinas, "De mixtione elementorum ad magistrum Philippum de Castro Caeli," pp. 155–157 from *Sancti Thomae de Aquino opera omnia* (the "Leonine" edition), vol. 43, ed. Roberto Busa (Rome: Editori di San Tommaso, 1976). Translation © 1997 by Paul Vincent Spade. Reprinted by permission of Paul Vincent Spade.

Chapter 21: Giles of Rome, pp. 386–400 from *Medieval Philosophy: Selected Readings from Augustine to Buridan*, ed. H. Shapiro (Toronto: Random House, 1964). © 1964 by Random House, Inc. Used by permission of Random House, Inc. Published in Latin in *Errores Philosophorum*, ed. J. Koch. Milwaukee: Marquette University Press, 1944.

Chapter 22: From "Condemnation of 219 Propositions," pp. 335–54 from *Medieval Political Philosophy: A Sourcebook*, ed. Ralph Lerner and Muhsin Mahdi, trans E. L. Fortin and P. D. O'Neill (New York: Free Press, 1963). © 1963 by The Free Press of Glencoe, A Division of The Macmillan Company. Reprinted by permission of Ralph Lerner. Published in Latin in the second edition of *Siger de Brabant et l'averroïsme latin au XIIIme siècle, 2me partie, Textes inédites*, ed. P. Mandonnet, pp. 175–191. Louvain, 1908–1911 (2 vols.).

Chapter 23: John Buridan, section 8.2 (pp. 532–538) from Marshall Clagett (ed.), *The Science of Mechanics in The Middle Ages* (Madison: WI: The University of Wisconsin Press, 1959). © 1959 and reprinted by permission of The University of Wisconsin Press. Originally published in Latin as *Questiones super octo physicorum libros Aristotelis*, bk. 8, q. 12.

Chapter 24: Augustine, passages 4, 6, 8–10 (pp. 383–385) from *A Survey of Mediaeval Philosophy*, ed. and trans. Paul Vincent Spade. © 1985 by Paul Vincent Spade. Reprinted by permission of Paul Vincent Spade. This chapter comprises several short selections from various works; the sources for which are indicated in the text.

Chapter 25: Averroës, "The Chapter on the Rational Faculty [Commentary on *De anima* 3.4–8]," pp. 108–117 from *Averroës: Middle Commentary on Aristotle's De Anima*, ed. and trans. A. L. Ivry, from the Arabic text (Provo, Utah: Brigham Young University Press, 2002). © 2002 by A. L. Ivry. Reprinted by permission of A. L. Ivry and Brigham Young University.

Chapter 26: Siger of Brabant, pp. 360–365 from *Medieval Philosophy: From St. Augustine to Nicholas of Cusa*, ed. J. F. Wippel and A. B. Wolter, trans. E. L. Fortin and P. D. O'Neill (New York: The Free Press, 1969). © 1969 by The Free Press. Reprinted by permission of The Free Press, A Division of Simon & Schuster Adult Publishing Group. All rights reserved. Published in Latin as *Tractatus de anima intellectiva*, pp. 145–71 from the second edition of *Siger de Brabant et l'averroïsme latin au XIIIe siècle, 2me partie, Textes inédites*, ed. P. Mandonnet. Louvain, 1908–1911, 2 vols.

Chapter 27: Thomas Aquinas, ST 1, q. 75, aa, 1–2 (pp. 4–13) and q. 76, aa. 1–2 (pp. 38–59) from *Summa Theologiae*, vol. 11 (New York: Blackfriars-McGraw Hill, 1968).

Chapter 28: John Buridan, bk. 3, q. 4 (pp. 252–260) from *John Buridan's Philosophy of Mind: An Edition and Translation of Book III of his Questions on Aristotle's De Anima*, vol. II, ed. and trans. J. A. Zupko (Ann Arbor: University Microfilms International, 1989). © 1989 by Jack Zupko. Reprinted by permission of Jack Zupko. Translation slightly revised for this publication by G. Klima.

Chapter 29: Avicenna, passages 1–5 (pp. 461–462) from *A Survey of Mediaeval Philosophy*, ed. and trans. P. V. Spade. © 1985 by Paul Vincent Spade. Reprinted by permission of Paul Vincent Spade. This chapter comprises several short selections from various works, the sources for which are indicated in the text.

Chapter 30: selections from Thomas Aquinas, *S. Thomae Aquinatis De Ente et Essentia*, 3rd ed., ed. C. Boyer (Rome: Pontifical Gregorian University, 1950). Translation and annotation © 2007 by G. Klima.

Chapter 31: John Buridan, bk. 8, q. 4 from *Quaestiones in Aristotelis Metaphysicam: Kommentar zur Aristotelischen Metaphysik* (Paris: 1518; Frankfurt am Main: Minerva, 1964 reprint). Translation © 2007 by G. Klima.

Chapter 32: Augustine, bk. 5, chs. 2, 4–5, 16 (pp. 119–121, 130–132) from *De Trinitate* [On the Trinity] ed. P. Schaff, trans. A. W. Haddan (New York: The Christian Literature Publishing Co., 1890).

Chapter 33, text 1: Anselm of Canterbury, "Monologion," ch. 1 (pp. 11–12) from *The Major Works*, ed. B. Davies and G. R. Evans (Oxford: Oxford University Press, 1998). Translation © 1998 by Simon Harrison; **text 2**: Anselm of Canterbury, "Proslogion," chs. 2–5 (pp. 87–89), 15 (p. 96) and 22 (pp. 99–100) from *The Major Works*, ed. B. Davies and G. R. Evans (Oxford: Oxford University Press, 1998). Translation © 1965 by OUP; **text 3**: Anselm of Canterbury, "Gaunilo pro Insipiente" [On Behalf of the Fool], ch 6 (p. 109) from *The Major Works*, ed. B. Davies and G. R. Evans (Oxford: Oxford University Press, 1998). Translation © 1965 by OUP; **text 4**: *Anselmi responsio* [Anselm's Reply], chs. 3 (pp. 114–115) and 5 (pp. 116–118) from *The Major Works*, ed. B. Davies and G. R. Evans (Oxford: Oxford University Press, 1998). Translation © 1965 by OUP; all texts reprinted by permission of Oxford University Press.

Chapter 34: Thomas Aquinas, ST 1, qq. 2–3 (pp. 3–43) and q. 13, aa. 1–6 (pp. 138–152) from *Summa Theologiae*, ed. B. Davies and B. Leftow, trans. B. Davies (Cambridge: Cambridge University Press, 2006). © 2006 by Cambridge University Press. Reprinted by permission of the editors and publisher.

Chapter 35: Augustine, chs. 10–13 (pp. 319–320) from *Enchiridion*, ed. P. Schaff (New York: The Christian Literature Publishing Co., 1896).

Chapter 36: Augustine, bk. 8, chs. 2–12 (pp. 326–333) from *St. Augustine's City of God*, ed. P. Schaff, trans. Rev. M. Dods (New York: The Christian Literature Publishing Co., 1896).

Chapter 37: Boethius, "De Hebdomadibus," pp. 299–304 from *Being and Goodness: The Concept of the Good in Metaphysics and Philosophical Theology*, ed. and trans. Scott MacDonald (Cornell: Cornell University Press, 1991). © 1991 by Cornell University. Reprinted by permission of Cornell University Press.

Chapter 38: Thomas Aquinas, ST 1, q. 5, a. 1 from *Summa Theologiae*, trans. English Dominican Fathers (London: Burns, Oates, and Washburne, 1912–36; New York: Benziger Bros., 1947–48). Translation slightly revised for this publication by G. Klima.

Chapter 39: Augustine, bk. VIII, chs. 5, 8–12 (pp. 99–103) from *Confessions*, trans. M. Boulding (New York: New City Press, 1997). © 1997 by the Augustinian Heritage Institute. Reprinted by permission of the Augustinian Heritage Institute, Inc.

Chapter 40: Boethius, bk. V, chs. 2, 3, 6 (pp. 151–156) from *The Consolation of Philosophy* 1st ed., trans. R. H. Green (New York: Macmillan/Library of the Liberal Arts, 1962). © 1962 and reprinted by permission of Pearson Education, Inc., Upper Saddle River, NJ.

Chapter 41: Anselm of Canterbury, "On Free Will," pp. 175–192 from *The Major Works*, ed. B. Davies and G. R. Evans (Oxford: Oxford University Press, 1998). Translation © 1998 by Ralph McInerny. Reprinted by permission of Oxford University Press.

Chapter 42: Henry of Ghent, Quodlibet 1, q. 14 (pp. 25–29) from *Quodlibetal Questions on Free Will*, trans. R. J. Teske (Milwaukee, WI: Marquette University Press, 1993). © 1993 by Marquette University Press. Used by permission of the publisher. All rights reserved, www.marquette.edu/mupress/.

Chapter 43: Boethius, "On the Supreme Good, or on the Life of the Philosopher," pp. 369–375 from *Medieval Philosophy: From St. Augustine to Nicholas of Cusa*, ed. J. F. Wippel and A. B. Wolter, trans. J. F. Wippel (New York and London: The Free Press, 1969). © 1969 by The Free Press. Reprinted by permission of The Free Press, A Division of Simon & Schuster Adult Publishing Group. All rights reserved. Latin version published in M. Grabmann, "Die Opuscula *De Summo Bono sive De Vita Philosophi* und *De Sompniis* des Boetius von Dacien," pp. 287–317 from *Archives d'histoire doctrinale et du Moyen Age* 6 (1931) and reprinted, with some additions to the introduction, in *Mittelalterliches Geistesleben*, 2 (1936), 200–24.

Chapter 44: Thomas Aquinas, ST I–II, q. 2, aa. 7–8 and q. 3, 8 from *Summa Theologiae*, trans. English Dominican Fathers, (London: Burns, Oates, and Washburne, 1912–36; New York: Benziger Bros., 1947–48). Translation slightly revised for this publication by G. Klima.

Chapter 45: Thomas Aquinas, "Question 94: On the Natural Law" and "Question 97: On Revision of Laws" from *Treatise on Law*, ed. and trans. R. J. Regan (Indianapolis: Hackett Publishing Company, Inc., 2000). © 2000 by Hackett Publishing Company, Inc. Reprinted by permission of Hackett Publishing Company, Inc. All rights reserved. Originally published in Latin as *Summa Theologica*, ST I–II, q. 94, aa. 1–6 and ST I–II, q. 97, aa. 1–4.

Chapter 46: John Duns Scotus, "The Decalogue and the Law of Nature," pp. 198–207 from *Duns Scotus on the Will and Morality*, trans. A. B. Wolter (Washington, DC: The Catholic University of America Press, 1997). © 1997 and reprinted by permission of The Catholic University of America Press, Washington, DC. Originally published in Latin as *Opus Oxoniense*, bk. 3, d. 37, *quaestio unica*.

Every effort has been made to trace copyright holders and to obtain their permission for the use of copyright material. The publisher apologizes for any errors or omissions in the above list and would be grateful if notified of any corrections that should be incorporated in future reprints or editions of this book.

Acknowledgments

I owe thanks first of all to my first reader, my son, Greg. Being a student at Fordham University at the time when I compiled the selections, revised the translations, added the footnotes and wrote the introductory essays, he was part of my target audience, so his comments on the content and clarity of presentation, as well as his careful reading of the entire text (catching numerous typos and other infelicities in the process) have been invaluable. I also owe thanks for the same reason to many of my students, who read and gave me feedback on the essays and my translation of Aquinas's *On Being and Essence* in the spring semester of 2006.

Apart from the preliminary feedback I have received from my intended audience, this volume has greatly benefited from the professional advice of the series editors, from the reports of the readers invited by the publisher, and from the comments of my friend and colleague at Fordham, Giorgio Pini. I would also like to thank my graduate assistant, Christopher Rice, for his help with the proofs and the index.

The timely completion of this project was made possible by a generous grant from the Earhart Foundation and two course reductions granted by Fordham University.

But none of the above would have been enough without the loving assistance of my wife, Judit.

G. K.
New York
March 31, 2006

General Introduction

[handwritten: medieval 5th c. AD - 16th cent. 1100 - 1400]

[handwritten: modern phil ↓ 17th - 20th cent.]

[handwritten: Contemp phil end 19th cent - to present]

Medieval Philosophy in Perspective

In the modern mind, the adjective "medieval" has often been associated with ideas of *[handwritten: held as an established opinion]* darkness, dogmatism, oppression, and barbarity. This should not be surprising, if we consider how modernity came to define itself, precisely in opposition to the medieval tradition, as the Renaissance, the re-birth of ancient learning, the Reformation of a corrupt church, the Enlightenment after an age of darkness, an Age of Reason after an age of ignorance and blind faith. Even today, this mentality has its visible effects. To the intellectual reflexes of "the modern mind" referred to above, the very phrase "medieval philosophy" until fairly recently sounded almost like an oxymoron, indeed, so much so that in modern curricula of the history of philosophy the medieval period was barely mentioned, and even nowadays it is skipped by some philosophy departments, boldly leaping from ancient philosophy directly to the study of Descartes (ignoring about two thousand years of Western intellectual history).

To be sure, this situation is happily changing. In the larger scheme of things this is probably due to the fact that we live in a postmodern period, in which the grand, defining ideas of modernity itself have become at least questionable, if not discredited, as a result of modern historical experience (think world wars, industrialized genocides, global exploitation of people and nature, the manipulative uses of "values," ideologies and religions, etc.). This postmodern perspective, by revealing the various limitations of the "grand ideas" of modernity, naturally prompts historical and philosophical reflection on their validity in history, and thus on their emergence from developments in the medieval period.

But, on a smaller scale, recent developments in philosophy as a profession also promoted the growing interest in medieval philosophy. Perhaps the most important of these recent changes is the transformation of mainstream analytic philosophy. Being the descendant of early twentieth-century logical positivism, analytic philosophy used to be strongly anti-metaphysical, secularist, and ahistorical (indeed, sometimes anti-historical: it was not uncommon among analytic philosophers to sneer at the work of their historian colleagues as consisting of book reports, as opposed to serious philosophy). By the 1980s (if not earlier), however, analytic metaphysics emerged as a legitimate philosophical discipline, followed by analytic philosophy of religion and a new interest in analytic historical studies,

[handwritten: Characterized by an emphasis on clarity & argument & a respect for the natural sciences (20th cent. ie. Plato)]

which directly connected the study of historical doctrines and figures to contemporary philosophical concerns (no mere book reports any more!). With this change of interest and attitude of contemporary analytic philosophers, and as a result of the good work of a new breed of analytically minded historians and historically minded analytic philosophers, there arrived a renewed interest in and appreciation of the intellectual achievements of medieval philosophers and theologians even among contemporary analytic philosophers. Indeed, with good reason. For, as the work of this new breed of philosophers made clear, the philosophical interests and style of medieval philosophers were in some respects astonishingly close to those of analytic philosophers. Many of the topics discussed by medieval philosophers and theologians (especially in fields that we would classify as metaphysics, philosophy of mind and language, epistemology, philosophy of religion, and philosophical ethics) could easily find their place in the table of contents of any number of contemporary philosophy journals.

Of course, this should not be taken to mean that any medieval philosophical text could simply be transferred into a contemporary journal for professional engagement by contemporary philosophers. The intervening centuries, after all, brought about such profound conceptual changes that sometimes the very formulation of a problem, let alone the conceptual devices and principles applied in its discussion, would be quite different in medieval and in contemporary philosophy, despite all the obvious agreements in basic philosophical concerns and the methods used in their treatment.

The Boundaries of Medieval Philosophy

Indeed, we should immediately add to these considerations that even in such large-scale (and, therefore, inevitably vague) comparisons, medieval philosophy cannot be treated as a homogenous unit. Stretching from about the last century of the Western Roman Empire to about the period of the religious wars of Europe, or approximately from the time of St. Augustine to the time of Descartes, it encompasses the largest and most varied part of Western intellectual heritage.

It is small wonder, therefore, that the borderlines of this heritage are rather fuzzy and somewhat arbitrary both in time and in space. For example, although it can be claimed with good justification that the first medieval philosopher of note in the history of European philosophy was St. Augustine (354–430), one should immediately observe that Augustine was neither medieval, nor a philosopher; indeed, he was not even European. He was a Roman citizen, born and raised in North Africa, trained as an orator to become a professor of rhetoric first in Carthage, and later in Rome, who, after a stint at the imperial court in Milan and his conversion to Christianity, upon returning to Africa became the bishop of Hippo, earning fame for his wisdom as well as for his sometimes bitter theological debates with the heretics of his time, the Manicheans, Donatists, and Pelagians. At the other end, the borderlines of this heritage are even less clearly defined. For such definitely "non-medieval" philosophers as Francis Bacon (1561–1626), Thomas Hobbes (1588–1679), or René Descartes (1596–1650) were near-contemporaries of such arguably "medieval" philosophers and theologians as Pedro da Fonseca (1528–99), Francisco Suarez (1548–1617), or John of St. Thomas (1589–1644), and a number of others, who, by criteria of doctrine, methodology, mentality, and even terminology, should still be regarded as belonging to the medieval tradition. Yet, as even this remark suggests, there are some unifying characteristics, precisely in doctrine, methodology, mentality, and terminology that can provide some criteria for a more or less *principled* demarcation of the medieval philosophical tradition.

Faith and Reason

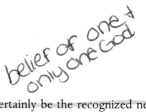
belief of one + only one God

The most prominent of these criteria would certainly be the recognized need for and pre-vailing practice of a systematic reflection on the relationship between humanly attainable knowledge (especially as it is handed down in the authorities of ancient philosophy, primarily Aristotle) and the revealed tenets of the great monotheistic religions, namely, Judaism, Islam, and (predominantly in this tradition) Christianity, or more generally, a systematic reflection on the relationship between faith and reason. In fact, one of the reasons why modern philo-sophers until quite recently may have felt justified in dismissing medieval philosophy as "genuine" philosophy was precisely the practice of this systematic reflection on the relationship between faith and reason, regarded by these modern philosophers as nothing but the *bringing under contro* systematic *subjection* of "pure philosophy" to religious dogma. In a recent article, the noted medievalist Paul Spade aptly countered this sentiment in the following remark:

> The practice is still alive and thriving among quite respectable philosophers in our own day, even if it no longer sets the tone of philosophy generally. Indeed, one of the enduring legacies of medieval philosophy is the development of what we call "philosophy of religion," which can be pursued both by those with and by those without prior doctrinal commitments. Historians of medieval philosophy have sometimes felt a need to defend, or [are] even embarrassed by, this close connection between philosophy and dogma in the Middle Ages, as though it somehow compromised the integrity of their subject. But such concerns are probably misplaced. The popular notion of the philosopher as someone who follows the dictates of "pure reason" wherever they may go, without regard for prior "givens" that have to be accommodated, is something of a naive idealization; throughout its history, philosophy at large has rarely if ever proceeded in this purely autonomous way. One might in fact argue that in our own day it is scientific theory rather than theological doctrine that provides the standard against which much philosophy is measured. Not long ago, for example, some eminent and highly respected philosophers were arguing that [the] distribution laws of classical logic itself must be abandoned because they could not be reconciled with certain interpretations of quantum mechanics (*note*: not that they could not be reconciled with empirical data, but that they were irreconcilable with certain scientific *theories* to interpret those data). Still, just as today there are many areas where one can philosophize freely without fear of trespassing on scientific ground, so too there were many areas of medieval philosophy where one could speculate freely without worrying about theological doctrine. The situations are altogether parallel, so that historians of medieval philosophy need not feel apologetic or defensive about the theological commitments of the philosophy of their period.[1]

One may add to these observations that philosophical reflection on the obvious *limits* of humanly attainable knowledge naturally prompts further considerations of our awareness of what is *beyond* those limits. If philosophical reflection shows that reason may not be the only or even the highest source of reliable information about reality, then it is not unreasonable to accept the legitimacy of some source that is beyond reason, which therefore is not *irrational*, but which might be termed "hyper-rational." So, theology need not be *without* or *against* reason; rather, it deals with something that is *reasonably* believed to be *beyond reason*.

In any case, this is precisely how most (although, as we shall see, definitely not all) medieval philosophers and theologians, from Augustine to Anselm (1033–1109) to Aquinas (1224–74)

---

1   P. V. Spade, "Medieval Philosophy," *The Stanford Encyclopedia of Philosophy* (Fall 2004 edn), ed. Edward N. Zalta, n. 3. <http://plato.stanford.edu/archives/fall2004/entries/medieval-philosophy>.

and beyond, regarded the relationships between faith and reason, or divine revelation and scientifically attainable truth. In their view, scientific and philosophical reasoning can only take us to a certain point in revealing the nature of reality; but the same reasoning can also show us that there definitely *is* something beyond that point. Furthermore, although reason can also show that the nature of that reality (that is, the nature of God) is beyond our philosophical grasp, given the little that we *can* know about it, it is not unreasonable to hold purely by faith what it reveals about itself. Indeed, given what reason can establish on its own (namely, the existence and certain attributes of God), concerning such revelations faith can safely be *presupposed*. Therefore, in the case of statements of faith based on such revelations the task is not to show *whether* what is believed is true (after all, it is already believed to be true), but rather *how* it *can* be true. That is to say, the question is *how it is possible* for these revealed articles of faith to be true, how they can *reasonably* be held to be true without contradicting the principles of reason. On this conception, therefore, faith is obviously not pitted against reason: faith is neither blind to nor oppressive of principles of reason; rather, it is complementary to and meaningfully interpreted by reason. This is precisely the gist of the program of medieval rational (as opposed to mystical) theology initiated by St. Augustine, most fittingly described by St. Anselm's formula: *fides quaerens intellectum* – faith seeking understanding.

This general demand of conflict resolution in this mentality requires meticulous logical analysis, and careful reflection on the language used, and on the thoughts expressed by the language (which is not to say that the use of logical methods in theology itself was regarded as entirely unproblematic). Such reflections, in turn, naturally lead to further, independent philosophical investigations. In fact, even if it may generally be true that in this mentality the prevailing theoretical (and practical) concern is rational inquiry into the meaning of articles of faith, within the whole enterprise of rational theology this concern naturally brings with it an ever-growing autonomous interest in other fields of rational inquiry, which all provide their peculiar input for gaining a better understanding of everything there is for us to understand. Accordingly, the insatiable intellectual curiosity of the medieval mind naturally led it to all fields of inquiry, in the spirit of Hugh of St. Victor's (1096–1141) advice: *omnia disce, videbis postea nihil esse superfluum* – "learn everything, later on you will see nothing is useless" (*Didascalicon* 6, 3).

A Brief Historical Survey of Medieval Philosophy

The Roman (patristic) period

Medieval philosophy grew out of the popular philosophies of late antiquity, especially Stoicism, Neoplatonism, and Aristotelianism. To be sure, with the decline of Greek learning in the Western Roman Empire, these Greek philosophies could only have a somewhat indirect influence through the works of Latin authors such as Cicero (104–43 BC) or Seneca (3 BC–AD 65). Augustine, for example, did learn some Greek, but by his own admission he hated it, and probably never really used it. The last Roman author of note with reliable knowledge of Greek was Boethius (ca. 480–ca. 525). In fact, Boethius himself was quite aware of this situation. In his second commentary on Aristotle's *De Interpretatione* ("On Interpretation"), he announced the overly ambitious project of translating the entire body of Plato's and Aristotle's philosophy and showing in his commentaries and independent treatises their basic agreement with each other. The project was doomed to remain a torso.

But even so it exerted tremendous influence, not only during the soon ensuing Dark Ages, and the emerging monastic culture of the early Middle Ages, but also in the highly sophisticated philosophical culture of the medieval universities, well into the Renaissance. This is even more remarkable given just how little Boethius eventually managed to carry out of his plan. Apparently, he never translated any of Plato's works, and he only managed to translate and comment on some of Aristotle's logical works. Actually, only two of these were in general circulation, namely, the translations of and commentaries on the *Categoriae* ("Categories") and *De Interpretatione*, dealing with terms and propositions, respectively (which are the integral parts of the various sorts of arguments systematically dealt with in the remaining books of the Aristotelian logical corpus). Besides these works, Boethius also translated and commented on the *Eisagoge* (or *Isagoge* – i.e. introduction) to Aristotle's *Categoriae* by the strongly anti-Christian Neoplatonic philosopher, Porphyry (233–309). Owing to Boethius' translation and commentaries, this otherwise deliberately elementary work was to have a tremendous career during the Middle Ages, serving as the starting point of all medieval debates on the fundamental philosophical problem of universals.

Besides these translations and commentaries, Boethius also wrote some independent treatises in logic (transmitting material from Aristotle's dialectic as well as from Stoic logic), and in theology – in Trinitology (discussing the Christian doctrine of the Holy Trinity) and Christology (discussing the doctrine of Christ's divinity and humanity). But the philosophical treatise he is most remembered for even today is the famous *De Consolatione Philosophiae* ("Consolation of Philosophy") he wrote in prison, awaiting execution for high treason, pondering the philosophical issues of man's fate, divine providence, and the choices man makes by free will.

The "Dark Ages" and the Carolingian Renaissance *4th Cont -900 CE*

After Boethius' time, there followed a period that by and large deserves the (otherwise often over-used and abused) name of "Dark Ages", although even in the relative (intellectual) darkness of about five centuries there were glimmering lights here and there, mainly in monasteries and in the courts of the occasional enlightened ruler. The most outstanding example of the latter was the court of Charlemagne (742–814), Charles the Great, or in Latin, Carolus Magnus, whose name is duly preserved in the phrase "Carolingian Renaissance." The leading scholar of Charlemagne's court was the English monk Alcuin of York (735–804). Aiding the king's efforts in the revival of learning, he produced a number of didactic works (*didascalia*), mainly on grammar and logic (covering the material he could gather from Boethius), but also on astronomy and theology, for example, a work on the Trinity primarily based on Augustine. Originality was certainly not his greatest virtue, but neither was it his goal, as was typical in the period.

Nevertheless, even this period produced a truly original author in John Scottus Eriugena (ca. 800–ca. 877). Eriugena, an Irishman well versed in the liberal arts and, quite uniquely in this period, with good knowledge of Greek, brought unmatched erudition to the court of Charles the Bald (823–77). At the request of the king he produced translations of the writings of the mysterious (Pseudo-)Dionysius the Areopagite, mistakenly thought at the time to have been St. Paul's convert in Athens (Acts 17: 34). In fact, these Neoplatonic Christian writings, showing a strong influence of pagan Neoplatonic philosophers such as Plotinus and, especially, Proclus (411–85), come from an author who was probably a native of Syria, lived around the turn of the fifth and sixth centuries, and assumed in these writings the identity

A Christian Neoplatonist

of Paul's convert, which lent enormous authority to his works. Thus, owing to Eriugena's translation, the Pseudo-Dionysian writings exerted tremendous influence in later medieval theology, especially by their emphasis on *apophatic* or negative theology, in which the incomprehensible divine nature is characterized by denying it all creaturely attributes (God is *not* material, spatial, temporal, finite, thus, He is *not* a body, etc.). But Eriugena's originality consisted especially in his unique combination of the theological doctrines of Greek (e.g., Maximus Confessor, Gregory of Nyssa, Gregory of Nazianzus) as well as Latin (e.g., Ambrose, Jerome, and above all Augustine) Church Fathers with his extensive knowledge of the Roman liberal arts tradition (Martianus Capella) and earlier encyclopedists (late Roman or early medieval authors who produced encyclopedic accounts of ancient learning, such as Cassiodorus or Isidore of Seville). Eriugena did not hesitate to bring his erudition and dialectical skills to bear upon his theological investigation, which was looked upon with a jaundiced eye by his critic Prudentius (d. 861), who at one point snidely remarked: "Your Capella has led you into a labyrinth, because you have tied yourself more to the meditation of his work than to the truth of the Gospel" (*PL* CXV 1294a). In fact, Eriugena's originality, most prominent in his unique, encyclopedic work *De Divisione Naturae* ("On the Division of Nature") may have been too much for his contemporaries. Both because of this work and because of a work on the issue of free will and predestination (God's predetermination of who will be saved or damned) he was subjected to ecclesiastical censure.

The early medieval period

But the trend of applying dialectical methods in theology, already quite tangible in Eriugena's work, only became stronger over time in the monastic educational culture of subsequent generations. This is the context in which the work of St. Anselm of Canterbury (1033–1109) emerged, exhibiting such subtlety and sophistication that it has kept theologians and philosophers intrigued to this day. Anselm, an unassuming Benedictine monk of the monastery of Bec in Normandy, who was later to become the archbishop of Canterbury, invented what is perhaps the single most debated piece of reasoning in the history of philosophy, the "ontological argument" for the existence of God (so named only in modern times, according to the classification of all possible proofs for God's existence provided by Immanuel Kant [1724–1804]). Anselm's original argumentation, as well as his ensuing debate with his confrere Gaunilo of Marmoutier, shows dialectical skills and sophistication that can only be the result of serious training in logic, and participation in actual disputations. Indeed, besides his important theological works, Anselm also wrote a piece on a purely logical problem stemming from Aristotle's *Categoriae*, in the form of a dialogue between a master and student, which may very well reflect some of the actual discussions Anselm and his brethren were engaged in. But Anselm never got censured for his use of dialectic in theology. To be sure, his former master, the more "conservative" Lanfranc, taking the side of the "anti-dialecticians" of the contemporary debates on the use of dialectic in theology, strongly cautioned him against relying too much on dialectical argumentation. But Anselm's unquestionable Augustinian orthodoxy, coupled with his genuine personal humility, saved him from any serious trouble.

A generation later, the brilliant Peter Abelard (1079–1142) was to prove his exact opposite in this latter regard. In his characteristically titled autobiography, *Historia Calamitatum* ("The Story of my Adversities"), he describes how he decided to pursue philosophy in the following way:

gladly leaving to my brothers the pomp of glory in arms, the right of heritage and all the honors that should have been mine as the eldest born, I fled utterly from the court of Mars that I might win learning in the bosom of Minerva. And, since I found the armory of logical reasoning more to my liking than the other forms of philosophy, I exchanged all other weapons for these, and to the prizes of victory in war I preferred the battle of minds in disputation.

Abelard may have left the court of Mars, but he did not leave behind his pugnacious character, which, coupled with his unmatched dialectical skills, landed him in trouble after trouble both in his personal and in his professional life. But despite all the animosity it generated, Abelard's work, which is undoubtedly the culmination of early medieval philosophy, simply could not be ignored. Working basically from the same resources as anybody else before him since the time of Boethius, he produced some truly original, insightful work in logic, ethics, and theology. In logic, he worked out a unique, nominalist theory of universals (a theory that denied the existence of universal things common to several particulars), along with an innovative theory of the signification of whole propositions (i.e., declarative sentences expressing truth or falsity), reconstructing from Boethius much of Stoic propositional logic (i.e., a theory of logical validity based on the structure of complex propositions); in ethics, he is still referred to as the main historical authority for emphasizing the importance of the agent's intention in establishing responsibility; and in his theological work *Sic et Non* ("Yes and No"), he established the paradigm of later scholastic disputations, searching for answers through weighing opposing arguments.

As is beautifully testified by the account of his student, John of Salisbury (ca. 1115–76), Abelard's time was a period of intellectual fervor in the Latin West. It was this already explosive brew of ideas that was catalyzed, not even a full generation later, by the influx of new and newly recovered old philosophical and scientific literature, leading to an explosion of intellectual activity in the subsequent two centuries, a period often referred to as High Scholasticism.

High Scholasticism

Institutional developments

In fact, there were two fundamentally important, and certainly not unrelated, developments in the second half of the twelfth century that led to this boom by the thirteenth century. Besides the above-mentioned influx of newly recovered ancient ideas, there was the most important, characteristically medieval institutional development, the rise of the universities. As mentioned earlier, during the previous period, most learning was confined to the court of an enlightened ruler (as Charlemagne's) or to monasteries (such as St. Anselm's in Bec, or the famous monastery of Saint Victor, organized by one of Abelard's many opponents, William of Champeaux [ca. 1070–1121]). By Abelard's time, however, it was not unusual for famous masters to establish their own schools in the growing medieval cities. As Paul Spade insightfully remarks, "perhaps the closest analogue to this arrangement would be the modern 'martial arts' schools one often finds in present-day cities." Another form of education was provided by cathedral schools, where masters and students worked under the auspices of a bishop. William of Champeaux, for example, was the master of the cathedral school of Paris, until his student Abelard drove him out with his criticisms and took over. Another important school was associated with the cathedral of Chartres, and with such influential figures as Bernard of Chartres (d. ca. 1130), Thierry of Chartres (d. ca. 1150), and Gilbert of Poitiers (ca. 1085–1154).

But the most important institutional development of the period was the emergence of the medieval universities. The medieval universities started out as any other *universitates* of medieval society, that is, as *guilds*, or trade unions. The oldest university, the University of Bologna, which came to be a famous center for legal studies, started out from a student union, as a *universitas studentium*, whereas the universities of Paris and Oxford, famous for their faculties of arts and theology, were started as teachers' unions, *universitates scholarium*. The universities were commonly organized into Faculties, among which the *Facultas Artium*, the rough equivalent of a modern Faculty of Arts and Sciences, took care primarily of "undergraduate" instruction, i.e., the instruction of younger students in grammar, logic, and in various philosophical and scientific disciplines, which prepared most of them for entering the equivalents of modern graduate or professional schools, the Faculties of Law, Medicine and Theology.

Doctrinal developments: the recovery of Aristotle

There would have been no need for this specialization and organization had it not been for the exponential growth in the number of students and teachers as well as in the amount of material to be studied. As mentioned earlier in connection with Abelard, during his lifetime the authoritative philosophical, theological, and scientific texts were about the same as those that had been available since Boethius' time. About a generation later, this situation changed radically. Owing to new contacts with the Muslim world and Byzantium (especially after the First Crusade, started in 1095), new translations of previously unavailable texts started pouring in from the Kingdom of Sicily (where mostly translations of mathematical and scientific works were prepared), from Constantinople (where most importantly James of Venice prepared translations of Aristotle's logical and other works from the Greek in the 1120s), and from Toledo in Spain (then a booming Islamic city, where Muslim and Jewish scholars worked together with Christians preparing the Latin translations of Greek works, sometimes through intermediary Syriac and/or Arabic translations, and of original works of Muslim and Jewish thinkers).

The most important and influential among the newly recovered texts were Aristotle's writings, which provided medieval thinkers with a comprehensive philosophical system, based on a carefully crafted logical methodology that surveyed everything that was humanly knowable about the natural world, its ultimate principles and causes, as well as man's place and destiny in this universe – all this, without the aid of divine revelation! No wonder Aristotle soon achieved the status of "the Philosopher," as he was commonly referred to, among the authorities to be reckoned with. But it was not just the whole system of Aristotelian logic, natural science, metaphysics, psychology, ethics, and politics that started exerting its influence. Aristotle's works arrived with commentaries by Muslim thinkers, along with some very influential Neoplatonic works (such as the *Liber de Causis*, "The Book of Causes," an excerpt of the *Elementatio Theologica* of the pagan Neoplatonic philosopher, Proclus), and original Muslim and Jewish medical, mathematical, scientific, philosophical, and theological literature. The European "Dark Ages" had been the period of flourishing of a highly sophisticated Islamic culture, and now the fruits of that flourishing suddenly became available to the already busy minds of the Latin West.

The assimilation and integration of this enormous amount of new material, coming from a radically different cultural background into the existing philosophical-theological framework of Western Christianity, was a huge enterprise that necessarily led to some deep-seated tensions and conflicts within this framework.

The tension between faith and reason especially had to re-emerge in this context on a new level. For at this point the issue was not merely the conflict between "dialecticians" and "anti-dialecticians," as was fundamentally the case, for instance, in the conflict between Abelard and Bernard of Clairvaux (1090–1153), but rather the multiple conflicts between philosophy and theology, between Aristotelianism and Platonism (especially, as it survived in medieval Augustinianism), and between Christian theological considerations and Muslim and Jewish interpretations of Aristotle, on top of all the new empirical and scientific information to be assimilated, concerning which the Church Fathers could not give much guidance. The task of sorting out and systematically organizing this material required extraordinary minds that were capable of integrating all of these considerations into huge, comprehensive systems of thought, the intellectual equivalent of the gothic cathedrals of the period. In fact, the simile is far from superficial. For just as the cathedrals are built up from finely chiseled blocks that all serve an overarching structure designed to elevate the spirit, so are the finely crafted arguments and distinctions of the huge volumes of medieval philosophical and theological literature designed to fit into an overarching system of thought, to elevate human understanding.

Main figures, literary genres

So who were the architects of these cathedrals of thought, and what sorts of works embody the cathedrals themselves? In theology, the historically most important systematic work was the *Libri Quattuor Sententiarum* ("Four Books of Sentences") of Peter Lombard (ca. 1100–60), in which the author, cautiously proceeding in the footsteps of his master, Abelard, collected and collated the main theses and arguments of the Church Fathers, in order to provide a systematic survey of the theological doctrine of the Church. As a teacher at the cathedral school of Notre Dame, Peter soon established his work as a standard textbook for those who came there to study theology. But the work gained real importance in the subsequent three centuries when, with the rise of the universities (especially the universities of Paris and Oxford), the *Sentences* became the set reading for theology students and the text to be commented on by future masters of theology. In fact, it soon became the general practice in the course of acquiring the licentiate in theology to write one's commentary on the *Sentences*. This practice, then, gave rise to an entire literary genre in scholastic theology, the "commentaries on the *Sentences*."

Despite the fact that commentaries are usually supposed to provide mere elucidations, helping students to get a firmer grasp on the doctrine of the author, these commentaries were by no means mere slavish repetitions of some old, trite doctrine. This was well served by Peter's original style, which (following Abelard's *Sic et Non*), collated several apparently opposing authorities, sometimes providing his own resolution, but sometimes leaving a question open for further discussion. The great commentaries of the subsequent centuries formally accepted this invitation for further discussion in their peculiar literary form: the *question-commentary*. A question-commentary is not a mere running commentary offering clarifications of the text (in the form of lectures, *lectiones*); rather, it is a systematic, thoroughgoing discussion of the main problems raised by the text in the form of yes/no questions, to be decided on the basis of an array of opposing arguments. In these arguments, the text commented on eventually provides a mere opportunity to raise the question and to supply some authoritative quotes, but the discussion itself draws on the whole range of knowledge available to the commentator. This knowledge, by the thirteenth century, especially after the work of Robert Grosseteste (ca. 1170–1253) and St. Albert the Great (1206–80), comprised the entire Aristotelian corpus, as well as the works of the Islamic and Jewish thinkers it inspired.

The first and foremost among these was Alfarabi (Al Farabi, ca. 870–950), known to the Arabs as "the second master" (i.e., second only to Aristotle). He was followed by Avicenna (Ibn Sina, 980–1037), who famously claimed that he could not understand Aristotle's *Metaphysics* even after reading it 40 times until he read Alfarabi's commentary on it. But then, among other works concerning logic, psychology and medicine, he wrote his own *Metaphysics*, which had a great impact on the thought of Albert's student, St. Thomas Aquinas. Another important non-Christian source was Avicebron (Ibn Gabirol, 1021–58), the Jewish author of a work known in Latin as *Fons Vitae* ("Fountain of Life"), which combined Aristotle's hylomorphist metaphysics with biblical doctrine. The great Muslim jurist and theologian, Algazel (Al-Ghazali, 1058–1111), used philosophy (criticizing especially Alfarabi and Avicenna) to refute philosophy and to affirm the certainty of faith. In the West, his *occasionalism* (the doctrine that attributes all activity to the first agent, God, and denies all activity to secondary agents) was strongly criticized by Aquinas, but was embraced by late medieval Ockhamist theologians, and had long-lasting (at least indirect) influence in early modern philosophy. But the most influential Muslim author was Al-Ghazali's first and foremost Aristotelian critic, Averroës (Ibn Rushd, 1126–98), who was soon recognized in the Latin West as 'the Commentator' for his penetrating understanding of and illuminating commentaries on Aristotle's works. Finally, one should mention Moses Maimonides (1135–1204), also known to Latin theologians as Rabbi Moyses, whose theological considerations concerning negative theology (according to which our finite concepts only allow us to say truly what the infinite God *is not*, and not what He is) also directly influenced Albert, Aquinas, and the famously subtle Franciscan theologian, John Duns Scotus (1266–1308).

Given this vast and varied philosophical, theological, and scientific tradition to deal with, the masters of theology of the thirteenth and fourteenth centuries, especially at the two great universities of Paris and Oxford, were expected to provide comprehensive systems of thought, not only in their commentaries on the *Sentences*, but throughout their usually long and extremely prolific academic careers. By modern standards, the volume and range of their output are nothing short of staggering. The works of a medieval master of theology besides his commentary on the *Sentences* typically include two sets of disputed questions, the *ordinary* and *quodlibetal* disputations. The *ordinary* disputations collect records of regular disputations on a related set of questions discussed by a designated opponent and respondent, presided over and determined by the master. Such are, for example, the disputed questions of Aquinas *De Veritate* ("On Truth"), *De Anima* ("On the Soul"), or *De Potentia* ("On Power"). The quodlibetal questions are collections of records of solemn disputations held before Christmas and Easter, when the master determined questions *on any topic* (the literal meaning of the Latin phrase *de quolibet*) raised by the audience and answered any objections to his position. Such questions ranged from issues about whether God can make two bodies occupy the same place or make one body present in two places at the same time to current issues in ecclesiastic policy, such as whether confession has to be made orally or may be provided in writing. (The importance of the former topic, besides its obvious relation to the issue of what is possible by divine omnipotence, is its not so obvious contribution to the metaphysical problem of individuation. The importance of the latter topic can be appreciated if we recall the role written *indulgences* played in the late Middle Ages in triggering the Protestant Reformation.)

The disputations complemented the ordinary lectures (*lectiones*), which usually resulted in running commentaries on authoritative texts, such as books of the Scriptures or the philosophical works of Aristotle. But in the later Middle Ages it was not uncommon for masters of theology as well as of arts to produce question-commentaries, sometimes without a running commentary, resulting in sets of *Quaestiones* on various works of Aristotle.

Besides these commentaries, masters of theology often produced their own systematic treatises, the great *summae*, or "summaries," systematically surveying an entire field. Outstanding examples of this genre are Aquinas's *Summa Theologiae*, written in question format, and *Summa contra Gentiles*, written in the form of a polemic, apologetic treatise. But sometimes even collections of ordinary questions were organized into systematic *summae*, as is the case with the *Summa Quaestionum Ordinariarum* of Henry of Ghent (ca. 1217–93), the great "secular" theologian of the University of Paris (meaning simply that he did not belong to a religious order, as did the Dominican Albert or Aquinas, or the Franciscan Bonaventure or Scotus). However, it is not only in theology that such architectonic works gained prominence. In logic, from the time of Abelard's monumental *Dialectica*, the masters of subsequent generations produced their own comprehensive textbooks, some of which gained such importance that they remained in general use for centuries. Perhaps the most important of these was the realist logic of the *Summulae Logicales* of Peter of Spain (questionably identified with the Portuguese pope, John XXI), written sometime in the first half of the thirteenth century, and the great nominalist theories of the *Summa Logicae* of William Ockham (ca. 1287–1347), and the *Summulae de Dialectica* of John Buridan (ca. 1300–58/61).

In all fields, ranging from logic to natural philosophy, metaphysics, theology, as well as moral, political, and legal philosophy, the commentary literature and the great systematic works are surrounded by various genres of shorter treatises. In theology, short meditations of the sort exemplified by St. Anselm's *Proslogion* continued to flourish in the thirteenth century. A beautiful example is provided by the *Itinerarium mentis in Deum* ("The Mind's Journey to God") of St. Bonaventure (1221–74). In natural philosophy, in metaphysics, and in ethics, it was usually the short, polemic treatises (which allowed authors to express their original views in a particularly pointed fashion) that generated the most dispute, sometimes followed up by direct responses from other authors (or the occasional ecclesiastical censure), pretty much like contemporary journal articles generate disputes over several issues. This sort of polemical treatise is best exemplified by the controversial works of Latin Averroists, such as Siger of Brabant (fl. 1260–77) or Boethius Dacus (fl. 1240–d. 1280) on the eternity of the world or on the unity of the human intellect, and Aquinas' pointed responses to them in his own similarly titled short treatises (*opuscula*).

But the real proliferation of short treatises occurred in the Arts Faculties, especially in logic, where the practice of writing, teaching, and studying such short treatises, generally referred to as *summulae*, earned the name *summulistae* for those involved in this activity. The *summulae*-literature in logic in the High Scholastic (roughly, thirteenth century) and the Late Scholastic (roughly, after 1320) periods is particularly important. These little treatises embody the specifically medieval contribution to Aristotelian logic. Abelard still worked with just the so-called *Logica Vetus*, the Old Logic, which comprised the Boethian translations of and commentaries on Porphyry's *Isagoge*, Aristotle's *Categoriae* and *De Interpretatione*, and Boethius' short logical treatises (on division, categorical and hypothetical syllogisms, and topics). This was completed by the arrival of the remaining books of the Aristotelian *Organon*, collectively referred to as the *Logica Nova*, the New Logic: the two *Analytics* (containing Aristotle's theories of syllogistic and demonstration), the *Topics* (dealing with probable reasoning), and *Sophistic Refutations* (dealing with logical fallacies). This body of writings together, i.e., the *Logica Vetus* and the *Logica Nova*, was known as the *Logica Antiqua*, or Ancient Logic. It is to this core of Aristotelian (and in some parts Stoic) logical doctrine that the work of the *summulistae* from around the second half of the twelfth century through the mid-fifteenth century added their own original contribution (generally referred to as the *logica modernorum*, "the logic of the moderns"), providing the conceptual tools that yielded the unprecedented (and after the decline of scholasticism until the twentieth century unparalleled) analytic precision of scholastic argumentation. Among these treatises, the treatises on the (semantic) properties of terms and treatises on the signification of propositions were especially significant, for they articulated the basic principles for understanding the relationships between language, thought, and reality, which, as it were, laid down the basic rules of the "language games" (to use Wittgenstein's fitting metaphor) to be played in all sorts of argumentation in any particular field. In fact, what provided much of the unity of scholastic thought (besides the obvious unity of a common stock of authorities and shared ideas) despite all the disputes, disagreements, and diversity of opinions in particular fields was precisely this fundamental agreement concerning the most general principles that govern the rationality of any disagreement in any rational disputation, along with a shared image of the basic relations between language, thought, and reality.

Major issues

The basic ideas of this shared image were laid down for the medievals by Augustine's Neoplatonic Christianity together with its Aristotelian refinements provided by Boethius, especially in his logical works. The most fundamental idea of this image is that the *words* of our language are meaningful by virtue of expressing significant units of our thoughts, our *concepts*, which are applicable to the reality we conceive by them in virtue of their *conformity* to the *objects* of this reality. So, the words expressing our concepts are true of the things we conceive on account of those things' being informed by the *same forms* that inform our minds.

To be sure, this *sameness of form* cannot be understood as strict numerical identity. When we say that two billiard balls have the *same* shape or form, we do not mean that the shape of this ball is numerically *one* and the same thing as the shape of that ball. If there are two balls, then they are informed by *two*, numerically distinct, round shapes, for the shape of *this* ball, informing it *here*, cannot be the same thing as the shape of *that* ball, informing it *there*.

Yet, it makes good sense to say that these distinct round shapes are just numerically distinct *instances of the same shape*, as opposed to another, say, cubical or tetrahedral shape. But then what is this "same shape" that is supposed to exist in two distinct instances? And how can this "same shape" inform the mind of someone thinking of round things? Just because I am thinking of round things, this should not mean that my mind thereby becomes round!

This is one way to introduce the notorious *problem of universals*. The medieval problem of universals originated in ancient philosophy, with Plato's answer to the question of the possibility of universal knowledge. How is it possible for us to know *universally*, concerning

[margin note: fusion of Christianity & Platonicism & Platonicism]

all things of a certain kind that they have some property? For example, how can we know that *all* triangles inscribed in a semicircle are right-angled? It is certain that we do not know this from experience, for the claim concerns a potential infinity of individuals, of which we obviously have not seen (and will not see) *all*. To be sure, we know this universal theorem on account of a geometrical proof, using a simple diagram. But that diagram contains only a single triangle inscribed in a semicircle, whereas the theorem concerns all such triangles. Indeed, if we take a closer look at the diagram itself, we can soon realize that what is drawn there is not really what the proof is about. For in the proof we are talking about a perfect circle, all of whose points are perfectly equidistant from a given point, and about a triangle with perfectly straight one-dimensional edges meeting in unextended points on the circumference of the circle, but the diagram consists of visibly extended chalk or ink marks, roughly overlapping on the circumference of what is only more or less a circle, but is certainly not the perfect geometrical shape we have in mind as we construct the proof. In fact, the proof is about that ideal object we have in mind, and it is precisely on account of the fact that we have that object in our mind that we know exactly what the shortcomings of our diagram are. The diagram merely serves as a *visible reminder* for us to keep track of what we are supposed to have in mind in constructing the proof. But what we have in mind is the common Form or Idea of *all* triangles inscribed in a semicircle, and thus we know concerning *all* visible figures that resemble this Form that they will have the properties of this Form insofar as and to the extent that they resemble this Form. So, what we mentally grasp in this diagram and in any other resembling it is this common Form, which serves as their common exemplar, a model for the construction of all.

It is easy to appreciate the appeal of this answer if we consider the fundamental role Forms played in Plato's philosophy in all major fields of inquiry. Forms as the universal exemplars of all kinds of particular things are the principles that determine for all sorts of things *what they are* insofar as they *imitate* or *participate in* their Form. So, Forms in their role of being the universal exemplars of particulars are the primary constituents of Plato's *ontology*, the study of *being* as such (from the Greek words *on* for "being" and *logos* for "reason, account, reasoning, method, study"). But the same Forms, insofar as they account for our universal knowledge of all particulars of the same kind (because they all imitate the same Form), are also the primary items in Plato's *epistemology*, his theory of *knowledge* (from the Greek word *episteme* for "knowledge"). Finally, insofar as the Ideas or Forms set the *ideal* standards of perfection, determining for us what we ought to do to realize these standards in our lives, they are the basis of Plato's *ethics* and *theory of value* in general.

Despite all its appeal, however, the theory could not be maintained in its original form, as it turned out to be inconsistent. The inconsistency of the "naive" theory of Forms (the theory as stated in Plato's *Republic* and *Phaedo*, for example) was realized already by Plato himself in his *Parmenides*. (This late dialogue contains the first formulation of the famous "Third Man" argument, conclusively showing the inconsistency of the theory, at 132a1–b2.) But it was even more relentlessly criticized by Plato's brilliant student, Aristotle, who even provided an alternative solution to the question of the possibility of universal knowledge, in his theory of *abstraction*. This theory could dispense with Plato's Forms as the principles of universal knowledge by claiming that the human mind has the natural ability to form universal concepts from singular experiences by abstracting from the peculiarities of these experiences. Thus the human mind does not have to have some direct (according to Plato, pre-natal) access to universal entities in order to have universal knowledge. But the appeal of Plato's theory was still hard to resist, so later generations of his followers, the Neoplatonic philosophers, first in Hellenistic, then in Roman, and later in medieval times, kept coming up with ever more refined versions of Plato's ideas, trying to reconcile his teachings first with those of Aristotle, and later with Christian religious doctrine.

The common framework of the ever more refined solutions to the resulting problem of universals in medieval philosophy from Augustine through Boethius to Duns Scotus (and beyond) can be intuitively described in the following manner. Individuals of the same kind are informed by numerically distinct instances of the same common form, in the way in which several copies of the same book carry numerically distinct copies of the same information. In physical reality, there are only these individual copies. There is no numerically one, common, "universal book" over and above, and yet somehow existing in, the numerically distinct individual copies of the same book. As Boethius' careful argument in his commentary on the *Isagoge* showed, it is absurd to suppose the existence of some numerically one thing that is common to many numerically distinct things, informing them at the same time, for then this one thing itself would also have to be many distinct things, which is impossible. So, there is no such thing as "the book" over and above the individual copies. Still these copies are copies of the *same book*, for they are all copies of the same original exemplar, first conceived and written by the author. And readers of these copies who understand the author's intention will gain the *same information* informing their own minds, which they can then creatively use to form their own ideas to produce further works of art that may again be published in several copies, indeed, in various different media. In the same way, Augustine would say, natural (as opposed to artificial) things of the same kind belong to the same kind because they are all modeled after the same original Idea conceived by the Author of Nature, i.e., after an Idea of the Divine Mind. On the other hand, the human mind learning about the things of nature will be informed by the *same information*, which it can again creatively use to produce things with forms it invented, namely, the forms of human artifacts.

Using this analogy, then, we may quite plausibly understand the perhaps mysterious-sounding notion of "the sameness of form in several instances and in the mind" as being no more mysterious than having the same information encoded in several copies, possibly in several different media, whether in several physical manifestations or in informing the mind of a thinking subject, where, in turn, they can even serve as the exemplars of further physical manifestations, if the thinking subject uses them as the guiding principles of its productive activity.

So, in this framework, Plato's Forms are preserved in a way, namely, in their role as universal exemplars of particulars of the same kind; however, they are not preserved as independently existing "abstract entities," but as the creative Ideas of God. Indeed, for Augustine, Plato's Forms are preserved not only in their ontological role, as the exemplars of individuals of the same kind, but also in their epistemological role, as the principles of cognition of individuals of the same kind, and in their ethical (value-theoretical) role, as the standards of perfection for these individuals (in particular, standards for perfection in human action, virtue, and character, and so, as the objective standards for judging the *lack* or *privation* of some requisite perfection, i.e., for judging the presence of some evil). Thus, for Augustine, Divine Ideas are the principles of Being, Truth, and Goodness of all creation.

This general framework, which clearly avoids the inconsistencies of a "naive" theory of Platonic Forms, nevertheless yields its own problems. These were precisely the problems that prompted the ever more sophisticated refinements of this framework in scholastic philosophy and theology.

An obviously emerging ontological problem was the conflict between the plurality of divine ideas and the unity and simplicity of divine essence. Of course, the problem presupposes the thesis of divine simplicity as stemming from God's absolute perfection. A simple piece of reasoning establishing this conclusion, which would be commonly endorsed in this tradition, may be formulated as follows. Anybody who properly understands the name "God" has to understand by that name an absolutely perfect being. And an absolutely perfect being has to be absolutely simple, indivisible into a multitude of parts. For a thing that is composed of several parts has to have those parts either essentially or accidentally. If it has those parts accidentally, i.e., not necessarily, so that it may or may not have them without its own corruption, then it is changeable with respect to those parts. But a thing that is changeable cannot be absolutely perfect, for an absolutely perfect thing cannot become more or less perfect; whereas anything that changes becomes more or less perfect by its change. So, God cannot have any accidental parts. But God cannot have any essential parts either, i.e., parts without which He cannot exist. For anything that has several essential parts is dependent for its being on those parts. But an absolutely perfect being cannot be dependent for its existence on anything, for dependency is an imperfection and an absolutely perfect being cannot have any imperfection whatsoever. So God has to be absolutely simple. But then the question arises as to how He can have a plurality of ideas. The ideas, being the archetypes of creation, cannot themselves be creatures. Therefore, since anything is either a creature or their creator, the ideas cannot be entities other than God. But how can a plurality of ideas be the same as the one, simple, indivisible God? (The gist of the solution provided in ever more refined forms by thirteenth-century theologians was that the multiplicity of ideas is just the infinite multiplicity of the ways in which God conceives of the infinite perfection of His own essence as imitable by the limited perfection of any finite, created essence. But the multiplicity of the ways of conceiving of something does not have to imply any multiplicity of the things conceived: conceiving of Plato now as the student of Socrates, now as the teacher of Aristotle does not have to imply conceiving of several things.)

Another commonly discussed problem concerned divine ideas as the potential sources of universal knowledge, a Platonic theme preserved in Augustine in the form of his doctrine of *divine illumination*. The Platonic solution to the problem of how universal knowledge of a potential infinity of individuals of a given kind is possible was to assume that the human mind has direct access to the common exemplar of all these individuals. Therefore, knowing what all these individuals are modeled after, the mind obviously knows all these individuals, insofar as they resemble this common exemplar. In Augustine's Christian version of the same conception, it is God who provides this access to His creative ideas, especially for those souls that are "holy and pure." The problem generated by this conception is that it turns what one would normally assume to be a *natural* ability of the human mind, namely, attaining universal knowledge and understanding, into a *supernatural* gift, which would leave the existence of wise pagans or evil geniuses quite inexplicable, and the specific, natural ability of humans as such apparently useless and futile. Indeed, in the face of the competing Aristotelian conception (explaining universal knowledge and understanding in terms of the natural abilities and activities of perception, memory, experience, abstraction, induction, and deduction), illumination is apparently not needed for the explanation. Many Aristotelians, such as Aquinas and Duns Scotus, therefore, opted for keeping divine illumination only "nominally" as it were, attributing its function to the natural faculty of the active or agent intellect (*intellectus agens, nous poietikos*, the faculty of the human mind forming universal concepts from sensory experiences by abstraction) posited by Aristotle. Their

Augustinian opponents, however, such as Bonaventure, or Henry of Ghent, insisted on the necessity of genuinely *supernatural* illumination for true wisdom, i.e., some intellectual light directly coming from God, complementing, as it were, the *natural* functioning of the agent intellect. In this way, the epistemological controversy naturally paralleled the controversy in moral theology concerning the role of *supernatural* grace and the *natural* acts of human free will (weighed down as it is by *original sin*) in determining morally relevant human action. For in both cases the issue was to find out about the actual mechanisms of, and the balance between, supernatural and natural determinations of some specifically human activity, the theoretical activity of the intellect or the practical activity of the will.

But the conflict between Augustinian and Aristotelian theologians over the epistemological issue of the mechanisms of intellectual cognition was even further complicated by the ostensible ontological implications of the Aristotelian conception as it was conceived by the radical Aristotelian philosophers of the Arts Faculty of the period, the Latin Averroists, such as Siger of Brabant and Boethius Dacus. Having argued on the basis of Aristotle's remarks (in the third book of his *De Anima*, 429a10–b5) that since the intellect is capable of receiving all material forms, it cannot have a material form of its own, just as the pupil of the eye, being capable of receiving all colors, cannot have any color of its own, they adopted Averroës' position that this immaterial intellect cannot be an inherent form of the material body, so it has to be a separate substance, existing separately from matter. And since the immaterial intellect exists separately from matter, it cannot be multiplied in several material bodies in the way material forms, such as shapes or colors, are multiplied with the multiplicity of bodies. The inevitable conclusion seems to be that all human beings share one common intellect. This is the famous Averroistic doctrine of *the unity of the intellect*, which can perhaps best be understood by the modern analogy of conceiving of the separate intellect as a mainframe computer to which individual humans are related as the terminals of the mainframe, providing it with input and accessing it for data, but where the processing of all the input provided by the terminals takes place in the same mainframe only.

This conception generated several problems, both philosophical and theological. For, as Aquinas argued against Siger, if all thinking takes place in the allegedly separate intellect, then it seems impossible to hold that the intellect is that by which a human being thinks, despite the fact that this is supposed to be the definitive character of the human intellect. Furthermore, if there is one separately existing intellect for all humans, and it is only this intellect that survives the death of each, then belief in a *personal* afterlife, and personal reward and punishment in that afterlife becomes pointless.

But these were not the only problems caused by the teachings of the Latin Averroists. Relying strictly on Aristotelian metaphysical principles, they argued for such claims as the eternity of the world or the impossibility of the existence of accidents without their subject, as inevitable philosophical conclusions. But the first of these obviously contradicts the article of faith that the world had a beginning in time with its creation, while the second contradicted the theological doctrine of the Eucharist, according to which in the transubstantiation of the bread (i.e., the substance of the bread turning into the substance of the body of Christ), its sensible qualities and dimensions cease to inhere in a substance, for its substance is miraculously replaced by the substance of the body of Christ, which is not informed by these qualities and dimensions.

To be sure, the Latin Averroists insisted that their conclusions are not *absolute truths*, but rather they are merely inevitable conclusions of philosophical principles; so, they are truths *of philosophy* that are only to be regarded as truths *with the assumption of philosophical principles*. However, as Aquinas argued, this defense would have to lead to conceding the absolute falsity of those philosophical principles from which these conclusions followed. For if the conclusions are merely true with the assumption of those principles, but they are to be taken to be false on account of their conflict with the absolute truth of the faith, then, inevitably, the principles that entail them also have to be taken to be absolutely false. So, not wanting to give up the absolute truth of philosophical principles (and, of course, granting the absolute truth of articles of faith revealed by the First Truth, i.e., God), Aquinas rather argued for the claim that whenever there is a perceived conflict between philosophical and theological conclusions, then this has to be the result of some *rationally corrigible error*. For true principles can validly entail only true conclusions, and truths cannot contradict truths, so the valid conclusions of two sets of true principles (i.e., the principles of philosophy and articles of faith) can never contradict each other. Therefore, their perceived conflict is merely the result of some (logical) error, whether in the interpretation of the conclusions (judging them to be contradictory when they are not), or in the reasoning leading to these conclusions (using some fallacious argument), or in the interpretation of the principles themselves. So, in this way, Aquinas' defense of the necessary harmony between faith and reason was actually a defense of the absolute truths of philosophy and the philosophical enterprise in general, charging philosophers as well as theologians with the *philosophical* task of elaborating their respective doctrines whenever a perceived conflict between them emerges.

But Aquinas' conciliatory reaction to the challenge posed by Latin Averroism was not the official response. The official administrative reaction to the problem of Latin Averroism came in the form of the famous condemnation of 1277 issued by the bishop of Paris, Etienne (Stephen) Tempier, advised by a group of theologians, the most influential among them being the formidable Augustinian opponent of Thomas Aquinas, Henry of Ghent. The sweeping condemnation, therefore, generally asserted not only the authority of theology over philosophy, but in fact a strongly Augustinian theological position over Aristotelian tendencies in theology as well. To be sure, the main target of the condemnation was definitely the "radical Aristotelianism" of the Averroists, which is shown by the fact that condemned theses involved their positions in all major fields, not only in epistemology, metaphysics, and natural science (including the philosophy of the mind), but also in moral philosophy. But the theses certainly touched on several Aristotelian positions held by theologians, in particular, some positions explicitly held by Aquinas. For example, besides condemning such characteristic theses of the Averroists as the eternity of the world, or the unity of the intellect, or the thesis that happiness consists in living a philosophical life (all of them heavily criticized by Aquinas himself), it also condemned typical theses of Aquinas, such as the thesis of the impossibility of the multiplication of immaterial substances in the same species (Aristotle's separate forms, identified with Judeo-Christian angels), based on the Aristotelian conception of individuation Aquinas shared with the Averroists, according to which the multiplication of a specific form is only possible through its several numerically distinct instances being imprinted on distinct parcels of matter.

To be sure, some of the theses themselves represented rather unfairly the positions they condemned. Thus, the Averroistic distinction between the absolute truths of faith and the relative truths of philosophy (assuming the ordinary course of nature, when it is not overruled by divine omnipotence), in the condemnation becomes the contrived "theory of double truth" (*veritas duplex*), as if the philosophers of the Arts Faculty ever subscribed to the absurd claim that two contradictory propositions can equally be true, one according to philosophy and the other according to faith.

But it also has to be kept in mind that the sweeping condemnations were rather far removed from the much more sophisticated discussions of the same issues, both before and after the condemnation itself. Thus, Henry of Ghent's own position on the problem of the multiplication of immaterial substances was based on his decidedly non-Aristotelian conception of individuation in terms of the existence of creatures, whether material or immaterial, which then opened up the field for the even more influential alternative conception of John Duns Scotus, in terms of an ultimate *individual substantial difference*, his famous "haecceity" (*haecceitas*, "this-ness," which distinguishes individuals within the same lowest species, just as a *specific difference* distinguishes several species of the same genus).

In general, the March 7, 1277 Paris condemnation of 219 propositions, and the near-simultaneous (March 18, 1277) Oxford condemnation of 30 related propositions issued by Robert Kilwardby (ca. 1215–79), archbishop of Canterbury, just as well as previous condemnations meant to restrict the influence of Aristotelianism (in 1210, 1215, 1231, and 1270), did not result in the suppression of the study of Aristotle or the use of logic and philosophy in theology, let alone in natural science or other disciplines. Rather, these condemnations had the impact of influencing the general character of further, ever more sophisticated, discussions. In particular, the Paris and Oxford condemnations of 1277, placing their emphasis on divine omnipotence (and thus on the limited validity of the principles of Aristotelian philosophy based on natural necessity), started a new and growing trend in metaphysics and natural philosophy, considering hypothetical scenarios that would have been regarded as impossible by Aristotelian natural necessity, but possible by *God's absolute power*, freely choosing among possible plans for creation, not constrained by the natural necessities of the actual creation. Thus, creating several worlds, moving the world along a straight line, sustaining quantity without a substance, creating a vacuum, or two bodies occupying the same place, which were all thought to be impossible by the lights of Aristotelian metaphysics and natural philosophy, now were seriously considered as genuinely realizable at least by the absolute power of God, which opened up new conceptual possibilities, such as the possibility of an empty, absolute space, paving the way for modern, mechanistic conceptions of physics. Furthermore, the rejection of the Aristotelian conception of individuation through matter (implicit in the condemnation of the thesis about the impossibility of the plurification of immaterial substances in the same species) opened the way for radically different ways of thinking about individuation, as illustrated by the alternative theories of Henry of Ghent and Duns Scotus.

The discussions exploring such and similar conceptual possibilities were couched in an ever more refined, increasingly technical language, as the disputants made ever more sophisticated distinctions to express their precise positions. Indeed, with these refinements, even the distinctions themselves had to be distinguished. For besides the obvious numerical distinction that there is between two distinct things, these conceptual developments demanded the distinction of other sorts of distinctions as well. Earlier we touched on the distinction of different ways of conceiving of the same thing in connection with the solution to the problem of the apparent conflict between the multiplicity of divine ideas and the simplicity of divine essence. But the same type of solution applied to the apparent conflict between the multiplicity of true divine attributes and the simplicity of divine essence. Aquinas' way of formulating his solution involved the distinction between a merely conceptual distinction or distinction of reason (*distinctio rationis*) and the real distinction between two things (*distinctio realis*). But Aquinas also used this distinction in explaining his famous theory of the *unity of substantial forms*. The point of the theory, with far-reaching consequences in philosophical anthropology and the philosophy of mind, is that a substance can only have one substantial form to account for all its essential characteristics. Thus, all essential predicates of the same substance, such as "human," "rational," "animal," "sensitive," "living," "body," that are true of this particular human being, signify in her the same, unique substantial form that accounts for her being a human, being able to reason, etc., as well as being extended in three dimensions in space. Therefore, if Aquinas' theory is right, then we must say that what these predicates signify in this human being, say, her humanity, rationality, animality, corporeity, etc. are distinct merely *conceptually*, on account of the different concepts that we formed of the same thing, but not *really*, in the thing in itself.

On the other hand, Aquinas also argued that in many cases we have to recognize a real distinction between the *significata* of our predicates that apply to the same things. Most importantly, he argued that what the predicate "exists" signifies in a creature, namely, the creature's act of existence, cannot really be the same as what its essential predicates signify in it, namely, its essence. It is only God whose absolute simplicity excludes the composition of His essence with a distinct existence, so it is only God whose essence is His existence, whereas all creatures have an act of existence distinct from their essence. This is Aquinas' famous and famously controversial *thesis of the real distinction of essence and existence in creatures*, which for him is the foundation of the radical contingency of all creaturely existence. Indeed, it is this radical contingency of creaturely existence that provides the ultimate evidence for God's existence: for if creaturely existence is radically contingent, then it is not self-explanatory; but then the fact that creatures exist calls for a sufficient explanation, which can only be provided ultimately in terms of the existence of a cause the existence of which calls for no further explanation.

No matter how appealing this position may be, Henry of Ghent and others raised several serious objections to it. (One obvious objection is that if creaturely essence and existence are really distinct items, then one could be created without the other, which is clearly absurd, for how could there *exist* a thing of a certain kind, i.e., of a certain *essence*, without having *existence*?) So, Henry argued for the real identity of essence and existence in all things, while at the same time admitting between them a new type of distinction, a so-called intentional distinction (*distinctio intentionis*), which he conceived to be midway between a full-fledged real distinction and a mere distinction of reason, based on God's creative *intention* in producing a creature, realizing in its existence a certain kind of essence.

Clearly inspired by Henry's ideas, Duns Scotus introduced an even further type of distinction, the so-called "formal distinction on the part of the thing" (*distinctio formalis a parte rei*), which he sometimes characterized as a "less-than-numerical distinction." He argued, for example, that this is the kind of distinction that there is between a thing's specific nature (say human nature, as such) and its "haecceity," its principle of individuation.

Such and similar subtleties rendered metaphysical disputations toward the turn of the fourteenth century increasingly difficult to follow; so much so that some critics denounced them as not only needless, but utterly nonsensical. For example, an early defender of Aquinas' views against Henry's and Scotus' criticism, Thomas Sutton (ca. 1250–1315), a Dominican theologian in Oxford, flatly rejected Henry's and Scotus' distinctions, arguing that only the two kinds of distinctions (real and conceptual) used by Aquinas can make any good sense.

It should also be noted here that besides their substantive philosophical and theological motivations, some personal and institutional rivalries also colored these disputations. For despite the famous friendship between the Dominican Aquinas and the Franciscan Bonaventure (who became the minister general of his order), there was the equally famous competition between Franciscans and Dominicans in general for university chairs, combined with the further competition from "secular" theologians, such as Henry of Ghent. Thus, when, emboldened by the 1277 condemnation, the Franciscan theologian William de la Mare (d. ca. 1290) published his *Correctorium Fratris Thomae* ("Corrective of Brother Thomas") in 1278, it was soon adopted by the order as the official corrective of Aquinas' teachings to be read together with Aquinas' *Summa Theologiae*. To be sure, the Dominicans did not wait long with their response: in a couple of years several treatises appeared under the title *Correctorium Corruptorii Fratris Thomae* ("Corrective of the Corruptor of Brother Thomas" – the different treatises were usually distinguished by adding their opening word to the title). One of these was even (spuriously) attributed to a non-Dominican, an Augustinian Hermit, Giles of Rome (ca. 1243–1316), who may have been a student of Aquinas, and certainly endorsed many of his doctrines, but was generally a rather independent mind.

But even apart from such "sociological" factors complicating the situation, by the early fourteenth century philosophy and theology became highly complex, sophisticated, technical subjects, considering arcane questions concerning the distinction or identity (or quasi-distinction and quasi-identity) of all sorts of entities (or quasi-entities) allegedly corresponding to our different ways of conceiving (and therefore signifying by means of our words) the various items considered in these subjects.

Apparently, this situation served as the main motivation for the radical program of the Franciscan theologian William Ockham, intending to "wipe the slate clean" of all these obscure entities and quasi-entities.

Late Scholasticism and the emergence of Renaissance and early modern philosophy

Ockham's program of eliminating these unwanted entities from his ontology is sometimes characterized as a sweeping metaphysical program to establish a strictly nominalist ontology in which he eliminated universal entities by wielding his famous Razor (the methodological principle that if the existence of certain entities is not required for the best explanation of something, then their existence can safely be denied, often cited in the form *entia non sunt multiplicanda praeter necessitatem* – "entities are not to be multiplied beyond necessity"). But this general characterization is acceptable only with a number of important qualifications.

In the first place, even if Ockham did deploy several arguments against the existence of universal entities (assuming each of these putative entities to be some numerically one substance that is somehow common to many particulars), these and similar arguments were in common stock even before him, and since the time of Boethius nobody held this crude view of universals. (Indeed, some late medieval authors argued that Plato himself may not have held his theory of Forms in this crude form.) So, Ockham's genuine contribution to the debate was rather his rejection of the Scotistic notion of formal distinction required for a much subtler view of real universals, arguing for the intrinsic inconsistency of this view, and outlining an alternative view that explains the obvious universality of our common terms and concepts without any need to invoke such universal entities.

Thus, in the second place, Ockham often used his Razor principle only in addition to his direct argumentation against what he took to be Scotus' inherently inconsistent view of individualized universal natures being merely formally distinct from their principle of individuation, their "haecceity." Therefore, the logical role of his Razor can be fitted into the general structure of his argumentation only as a last step, roughly in the following way: "The assumption of these entities leads to such and such inconsistencies, and, given my alternative theory, they are not even needed for the explanation of universality; therefore, they do not exist, and we are better off without them."

In the third place, Ockham himself did not immediately break with "all sorts of quasi-entities." His first theory of universals, developed in his *Commentary on the Sentences*, characterized universals as mere objects of thought, the so-called *ficta*, which are not really existing entities, but rather the universal thought-contents of our universal acts of thought, whereby we conceive of several individuals at once in a universal manner. It was only later that, convinced by the arguments of his confrere, Walter Chatton (d. 1343), Ockham abandoned his *fictum* theory and embraced the mental act theory, which identifies universals simply with universally representing mental acts. These mental acts are universal only in their mode of representation, but in their being they are just as ordinary singular qualities as is the color of this particular apple or the heat of that particular flame.

Finally, Ockham's "program of ontological reduction" is rather a *logical* program to work out his alternative theory of universality, and in general, his new, alternative theory of how language and thought can be mapped onto a parsimonious, nominalist ontology containing only two distinct categories of entities, namely, singular substances and their singular qualities. It is especially in this logical theory that Ockham valiantly wields his Razor, showing that he can provide a coherent, subtle, logical theory without any need for the complex, obscure ontology required by the "realist" conception: he can account for the semantic properties of terms in the ten distinct Aristotelian categories without having to assume a corresponding tenfold classification of entities in extra-mental reality. Indeed, Ockham claims that the opposite opinion is rooted in the erroneous view of his contemporaries, who would "multiply entities according to the multiplicity of terms," i.e., who would try to establish a one-to-one mapping between linguistic, conceptual, and ontological categories.

Ockham's charge, stated in this form, is rather unjustified. To be sure, the thirteenth-century *modistic grammarians* argued for a strict parallelism between *modi essendi, intelligendi et significandi*, i.e., between the ways things are, are understood, and are signified, in order to establish the theoretical foundation of a universal, *speculative grammar* common to all languages. But generally speaking, even philosophers who endorsed the idea of such overall parallelism did so with all sorts of (quite obviously necessary) provisos. For example, all medieval philosophers rejected universally existing substances, yet none rejected universal concepts or universal words universally representing and signifying singular substances. But, especially in finer details, the idea of a one-to-one mapping between items of language (whether written, spoken, or mental) and reality was definitely not endorsed or demanded. We have seen this already in the case of Aquinas' doctrine of the unity of substantial forms, where different terms, signifying different concepts in the mind, signify the same individualized forms in the same substances conceived differently by these different (more or less universal) concepts. It was also quite commonly allowed that terms in different categories can signify the same items in reality; for example, relying on Aristotle's authority, it was commonly held that a particular action of a given agent is the same motion as the passion caused by the agent in the patient, although action and passion were taken to be distinct genera in the Aristotelian system of categories.

But then, what is Ockham's novelty? It is not so much his "reduced ontology" (since others before him also argued for a reduced number of real categories corresponding to the ten logical categories) as it is the radically revised picture involved in his alternative theory of the relations among items in language, thought, and reality. For, especially in his mature, mental act theory, Ockham radically revised the Aristotelian notion of abstraction accounting for the universality of our concepts. In his view, abstraction is not to be regarded as the intellectual grasp of some common intelligible content informing singulars of the same kind (in the way the common intelligible content of a book informs its singular copies), for distinguishing this common content from the individuals themselves would, in his opinion, just give rise to the problems of formal distinction he criticized in Scotus' (and his followers') view.

So, instead, Ockham claims that the universality of our concepts is simply due to their *indifference* in representation. The concept of cats represents all cats simply because it no more distinctly represents this cat than that one, although, of course while it represents this cat and that cat it does not represent this dog, which is why it is a specific concept representing only cats but not dogs. By contrast, the concept of animals is an indifferent representation of all cats and all dogs and all other animals, but it is not a representation of any non-animals. But this universality of representation is not due to our intellects' being informed by the same common information content that informs or organizes the matter of cats and dogs; rather it is simply the result of the *indifference*, i.e., the non-distinctive character of this representation. Accordingly, our common terms should not be regarded as primarily signifying such a common intelligible content in the individuals grasped by means of our intellectual concepts; rather, they should be regarded as signifying the singulars themselves, indifferently represented by the concepts expressed by these terms.

To be sure, these innovations in themselves may seem to be minor. But they are tremendously significant, particularly for two reasons. In the first place, they radically break with the idea of the pervasive formal unity that was supposed to constitute both metaphysical structures of reality (the kinds of things there are) and conceptual structures of the human mind (the order of concepts reflecting the kinds of things there are), both structures being modeled after the creative ideas of the Divine Mind, the universal archetypes of all creation. Indeed, for Ockham, divine ideas are no longer to be conceived as universal archetypes: God's ideas for Ockham are but God's singular creatures as He intuitively preconceives each in its singularity from eternity. But this is a radical departure from the fundamental idea that provided much of the conceptual cohesion of the entire medieval tradition from Augustine to Scotus and beyond. In the second place, Ockham's innovations gain their significance in particular in the entire system of a consistently nominalist logic that shows how his alternative conception can really "work" without any commitment to the pervasive intelligible structures assumed by the earlier view.

Indeed, Ockham's ideas eventually got serious traction only somewhat later, when they were put to work in the comprehensive nominalist logic and philosophy of the Parisian Master of Arts, John Buridan, especially in his architectonic *Summulae de Dialectica*. To be sure, Ockham himself had already composed a comprehensive system of logic in his *Summa Logicae*, and his ideas immediately provoked vehement reactions from various quarters, in logic, natural philosophy and metaphysics, and in theology. But he was generally regarded with suspicion, especially in theology, as being not only controversial, but potentially heretical. And it certainly did not help his cause that, after an investigation of his works at the papal court in Avignon turned hostile (not over his nominalism, but over his defense of the Franciscan doctrine of apostolic poverty), in 1328 he fled the court to seek asylum in the imperial court of Louis of Bavaria. After that time until his death in 1347, Ockham lived and worked under imperial protection, and wrote exclusively about politics.

Buridan, on the other hand, never had similar conflicts with authority. He prudently stayed as a professor at the Arts Faculty, instead of following the usual career path of his peers, who would normally move on to the "higher" (and, just as nowadays, higher-salaried) positions at the Faculties of Theology, Law, or Medicine. But in the Arts Faculty he became a highly regarded *magister* (master), who served twice as rector of the university (and one who was exceptionally highly paid for an Arts Master).

Buridan's prudence in his practical dealings is also reflected in his theoretical work. He never picked a fight he could not win; instead, he quietly and effectively worked out the details of a comprehensive and thoroughgoing nominalist system of logic, metaphysics, natural philosophy (including his naturalistic philosophy of the soul), and ethics, earning well-deserved fame as a teacher, churning out scores of students, many of whom would become influential professors at Paris (for example, Nicholas Oresme [1323–82], teacher of the Dauphin, who became Charles V) or at the new universities sprouting up all over the Continent at the time (for example, Albert of Saxony, probably not a student, but a younger colleague of Buridan's, yet clearly influenced by his doctrines, the first rector of the University of Vienna [1365], or Marsilius of Inghen, rector of the University of Heidelberg [1386]).

In this way, Ockham's nominalism in Buridan's hands turned from what was at first regarded as a radical and potentially dangerous innovation into a sound and simple, alternative way of doing logic, philosophy, science, and, eventually, even theology, without all the metaphysical complications and "obscurities" of the old way of dealing with these subjects. Indeed, through the work of his students, Buridan's nominalism by the fifteenth century even institutionally emerged as the "new way" (*via moderna*), as opposed to the "old way" (*via antiqua*), of dealing with these subjects. The separation of the two *viae* was in many ways comparable to the recent separation of "analytic" and "Continental" philosophy at modern American universities: some universities, after some bloody in-fighting among faculty members and their students (which has even earned the distinctive moniker *Wegestreit* – "the battle of the ways" – in the German historical literature of the period), exclusively adopted one or the other approach, whereas other universities opted for peaceful coexistence, acknowledging both ways in their statutes, and requiring students to engage both. But regardless of the outcome of the *Wegestreit* in any particular place, what was symptomatic about this separation everywhere was the emergence of a characteristically *modern phenomenon*, namely, the emergence of *paradigmatically different conceptual schemes*. In such a situation the disagreements no longer concern mere differences of opinion about particular questions (e.g., What is the principle of individuation?), but rather the very legitimacy of the questions raised by the other party (Why should there be a principle of individuation at all?) or the methods, terminology and conceptual apparatus used by the other party in answering it (a formal distinction between the alleged common nature and a presumed principle of individuation makes no good sense).

This was a radically new conceptual development that resulted from the nominalists' rejection of the fundamental intuition of the *via antiqua* concerning the pervasive formal unity of real and conceptual structures. Indeed, this denial, combined with the post-1277 emphasis on God's absolute power, opened up conceptual possibilities that *had not been there before*. One such possibility was that of an extreme form of skepticism allowing a subject's complete cognitive isolation from an extramental, physical reality, at least by divine omnipotence. (That this is in fact a genuine possibility is by now taken for granted to such an extent that even a movie trilogy, *The Matrix*, was based on this premise.) This possibility was soon realized by Buridan's contemporary, Nicholas of Autrecourt (d. 1369). Although Autrecourt himself may not have been the skeptic he was later made out to be (or even as Buridan may already have believed him to be), his realization of the logical possibility of complete cognitive isolation is one of those thoughts that (paraphrasing Thomas Paine's famous remark in *The Rights of Man*, part 13) once thought, cannot be "unthought." Indeed, it was probably due at least in part to Buridan's reply to the implied skeptical challenge (in terms of a naturalistic reliabilism rediscovered or reinvented in modern philosophy by Thomas Reid) that the idea remained in circulation in various forms until it made its appearance in Descartes' famous "Demon Argument." The particular historical details of these developments are obscure, and are still to be recovered from the immense and largely unstudied late medieval output. But even the little we know about these developments allows us some glimpses into the intrinsic mechanisms of those conceptual tensions between the older realist and the new nominalist *viae* that eventually led to the breakdown of scholastic discourse and to the new, primarily epistemological and methodological, questions of early modern philosophy.

But besides the intrinsic conceptual tensions *within* scholastic philosophy as it was practiced in late medieval academia, there were also several extrinsic factors that accelerated the breakdown of its conceptual unity. Most important among these were the emergence of humanism, the rebirth (*renaissance*) of classical Greek and Latin learning (bringing about the emergence of the corresponding sense of superiority on the part of humanists, who routinely reviled the "barbarities" of the highly technical, austere Latin of "the schoolmen"), and the emergence of Protestantism, challenging the authority of the Catholic Church as well as the validity of scholastic theological doctrine, which according to Protestant theologians had too much immersed itself in the philosophy of Aristotle, or rather in a distorted "medieval" version of his philosophy (as the pre-humanist period, the period between ancient learning and its revival, now came to be called).

All these factors eventually led to the near-extinction of scholasticism by the seventeenth century. At any rate, by that time scholastic philosophy certainly ceased to be "mainstream," although it survived in the Catholic Church well into the twentieth century in the form of neo-scholasticism. But, perhaps more importantly from the point of view of the history of ideas, scholastic philosophy was still very much "in the air" in the early modern period, when scholastic categories and distinctions still tended to inform the thought of even those philosophers whose starting point was precisely a deliberate break with the scholastic tradition. After all, much of Descartes' philosophy is completely unintelligible without the scholastic distinction between objective and formal reality, or the notion of eminent causation. But these are just the most obvious examples. Further research will certainly bring out even more evidence of the fundamental continuity between late medieval and early modern thought, highlighting the paradoxical fact of intellectual history that the connections rendering these developments continuous in their details are at the same time responsible for those large-scale discontinuities that separate one major period from another.

About This Volume

If there is one thing the foregoing survey ought to have made clear, it is the fact that no standard modern anthology can do justice to the wealth, complexity, and breadth of the medieval philosophical output. Indeed, several of the authors, works, and ideas mentioned in this survey could not make it into the selection, and several selections could not be discussed in this survey. The latter defect will be remedied by the brief introductions preceding the main parts. The former, however, can only be taken care of by further study, especially given the fact that several interesting authors and topics are simply beyond the scope of this volume. To help with this task, this volume also contains a selective bibliography with pointers to further information about the authors and works only mentioned here, but not selected for this volume.

The selections are organized doctrinally (as opposed to, say, around persons or topics), adhering to the medievals' own conception of the division of philosophical disciplines (presented in the first section). Thus, the three main parts of the volume present selections from the three major philosophical disciplines as Augustine (clearly influenced by the Stoic tradition) conceived of them: logic (including what we would call epistemology, in general, the discipline reflective on and regulative of the operations of reason in its search for the knowledge of Truth); physics/metaphysics (in general, the pure theoretical reflection on the first principles of Being); and ethics (or in general, practical philosophy, reflecting on the principles that ought to guide our actions toward what is truly and ultimately Good).

Each part contains several sections, each dealing with some salient problems of its discipline through an array of chronologically arranged selections. The sections generally strive to cover the chronological range between early and late medieval philosophy (as much as this is possible within the confines of the allotted space), giving a taste of the developments in the ever more sophisticated treatments of the same topics. The introductions preceding each part place the selections in their proper theoretical context in relation to the foregoing survey, occasionally providing some pointers to directly relevant secondary literature.

Part I

Logic and Epistemology

Introduction

As indicated in the General Introduction, logic in medieval philosophy was not as narrowly construed as it tends to be in contemporary philosophy. Logic was regarded not merely as the study of the validity of arguments, but rather as the universal instrument of reason (which is why the name *Organon* – Greek = "tool," "instrument" – was given to the collection of Aristotle's logical works), the universal discipline that reflects on and regulates the activity of reason in all disciplines in its search for knowledge. This conception conferred on logic (or dialectic) a particularly important status in medieval learning. Considered "the art of arts, the science of sciences" (*ars artium, scientia scientiarum*), logic had within its scope detailed reflections on the relationships between language, thought, and reality, reflection on all forms of rational argument (including fallacious arguments, in order to detect logical errors), and on all sorts of epistemic and methodological considerations, including problems of the acquisition and justification of the first principles of scientific demonstrations, and the organization of arguments, their premises, and conclusions into scientific disciplines. Accordingly, it was also taken to be the task of logic to consider the divisions of various scientific disciplines, their distinctions and interdependencies, and thus their organization into the entire body of humanly attainable knowledge.

It is in accordance with this broad medieval conception of logic that in this part we have selections discussing such diverse topics as the division of sciences (in particular, the status of theology as a science, obviously bearing on the general issue of faith and reason discussed in the General Introduction above), selections concerning the problem of universals (the primary issue in medieval logical semantics, explaining the relationships between our common terms, common concepts, and singular items of reality), the foundations of scientific knowledge both according to the Augustinian "illuminationist" and the Aristotelian "abstractionist" account, and the issue of knowledge and skepticism.

The first set of selections, therefore, deals with the methodological considerations involved in the distinction of philosophical and scientific disciplines, and their relation to religious faith and rational theology. The first selection, from Augustine, presents the three-fold distinction of the three major philosophical disciplines that also served as the rationale for organizing the selections of this volume into three main parts. Augustine's discussion, which forms part of a larger discussion in his monumental work *De Civitate Dei* ("The City of God"), provides a brief survey of the history of philosophy, culminating, according to Augustine, in Neoplatonic philosophy, which laid the foundations of the three major philosophical disciplines: logic, metaphysics, and ethics. For Augustine, Neoplatonic philosophy elevates human understanding just about as high as it can get on its own, and this is precisely what allows it to realize its need for supernatural help in the form of illumination (to aid failing human reason) and grace (to provide proper direction to human will, corrupted by original sin).

The anonymous twelfth-century author of the next selection, in the introductory discussion of an elaborate treatise on logic from the booming post-Abelard period, takes his cue from the same conception of human nature, but has much more this-worldly material to accommodate and organize into a coherent system of philosophical and scientific disciplines. It is with remarkable smoothness that the author integrates the basic threefold division we find in Augustine with the disciplines of the Seven Liberal Arts (*Septem Artes Liberales*) of late antiquity and with the Aristotelian system.

Finally, the last selection of this section provides Aquinas' discussion of his conception of theology as a science, which differs methodologically from secular science only in that it takes its principles from a supernatural source, i.e., divine revelation. It is also here that we can find Aquinas' main argument (already presented in the main introduction) for the necessary concordance between faith and reason.

The section on the problem of universals surveys the issue from Boethius to Buridan, as it formed part of logical discussions prompted by the opening remarks of Porphyry's *Isagoge*, i.e., introduction to Aristotle's *Categoriae*. The selection from Boethius' second commentary on this work sets the stage for all later medieval discussions. His solution provided in terms of Aristotle's theory of abstraction recurs in ever more refined forms e.g., in Abelard,[1] John of Salisbury,[2] and Aquinas.[3]

Unfortunately, Abelard's sophisticated discussion (his detailed refutation of contemporary alternative theories and the presentation of his own original theory) proved to be too long for this volume, but it is easily available in Spade's excellent translation cited above, along with other longer selections from Porphyry, Boethius, Scotus, and Ockham. In the present volume Abelard's period could only be represented by the short, but vivid, description provided by John of Salisbury in his *Metalogicon*.

The selection from the *Summa Lamberti* (dubiously attributed to Lambert of Auxerre, a Dominican author who flourished in the mid-thirteenth century) illustrates the way the moderate realist theory of universals that prevailed in the thirteenth century was put to work in logical semantics, in discussions of the so-called *properties of terms*, which describe the various semantic functions terms have in various propositional contexts.[4]

---

1 In his *Logica "Ingredientibus,"* see *Five Texts on the Mediaeval Problem of Universals: Porphyry, Boethius, Abelard, Duns Scotus, Ockham*, tr. P. V. Spade (Indianapolis and Cambridge: Hackett, 1994), p. 48.

2 *Metalogicon*, bk 2, c. 20, 877c7–878a9.

3 *Summa Theologiae* I, q. 85, a. 1, ad 1-um.

4 A larger selection from the same work is available in the source of this brief selection: see Text Sources and Credits on p. viii above. The Suggestions for Further Reading also provides a sampling of the vast and fast-growing modern literature on the subject. An excellent survey article is easily available online: Stephen Read, "Medieval Theories: Properties of Terms," *The Stanford Encyclopedia of Philosophy* (Spring 2002 edn), ed. Edward N. Zalta, <http://plato.stanford.edu/archives/spr2002/entries/medieval-terms/>.

The selections from Ockham present his arguments against Scotus' version of the moderate realist position, and his alternative accounts, first in terms of his *ficta*, and then in terms of his *mental act* theory, discussed in the General Introduction.

Finally, the short selection from Buridan (ostensibly written in the form of a commentary on Peter of Spain's corresponding treatise, but in fact presenting Buridan's own ideas) illustrates how Buridan puts to use Ockham's nominalist conception, simply identifying universals with the predicables of Porphyry, i.e., with the common terms of various written and spoken human languages and the language of thought that is the same for all human beings (i.e., our common concepts).[5]

The selections in the next section deal with the epistemological aspect of the problem of universals, insofar as universal intellectual cognition is the precondition of the possibility of acquiring scientific, i.e. universal, necessary knowledge. Of the two short selections from Augustine, the first presents the link between his conception of Divine Ideas and his theory of illumination; the second presents Augustine's main argument for the necessity of divine illumination for the formation of our intellectual concepts. This is the argument that is fundamentally challenged by the Aristotelian conception of the possibility of forming our intellectual concepts *without* the need for supernatural illumination in the natural process of abstraction, as explained in the subsequent selections from Aquinas' *Summa Theologiae*. The next selection, from Aquinas' commentary on Aristotle's *Analytica Posteriora* ("Posterior Analytics"), explains how abstraction can ground universal scientific knowledge in the process of the induction of the first principles of scientific demonstrations.

It is this Aristotelian conception that is further challenged by the selection from Henry of Ghent, who (while granting the role of abstraction in the formation of our mundane universal concepts) argues that the attainment of "pure truth" is not possible without the supernatural help of divine illumination.

Finally, the selection from Scotus argues against Henry's solution, and presents the Aristotelian position that came to dominate late medieval philosophy until the arrival of an "Augustinian backlash" against the dominant Aristotelianism of the late Middle Ages, in the form of Cartesian Rationalism.[6]

The selections in the last section of part I deal with the epistemological problems of the very possibility of acquiring knowledge. The short selections from Augustine present his reaction to the challenges of ancient skepticism, in terms of the absolute certainty of self-knowledge, serving as the starting point of his "introspective theology," most aptly summarized in his oft-quoted admonition: *Noli foras ire, in teipsum redi; in interiori homine habitat veritas* – "Do not want to go outside, return into yourself; truth dwells in the inner man" (*De Vera Religione* 39, 72). It is important to note that the same idea of the absolute certainty of self-knowledge would be put to a very different systematic use by Descartes,

---

5   Of course, the selection presented here provides only a tiny fragment of Buridan's logical theory. For those who are interested in pursuing the intricacies of his nominalist logic, his entire *Summulae* is now available in English translation: John Buridan, *Summulae de Dialectica*, an annotated translation with a philosophical introduction, tr. Gyula Klima, New Haven: Yale University Press, 2001.

6   An easily accessible survey of the problem of the ontological, logical, and epistemological aspects of the medieval problem of universals is available online: Gyula Klima, "The Medieval Problem of Universals," *The Stanford Encyclopedia of Philosophy* (Winter 2004 edn), ed. Edward N. Zalta. <http://plato.stanford.edu/archives/win2004/entries/universals-medieval/>.

who made it the "Archimedean point" of his system in grounding all knowledge, including the scientific knowledge of physical reality.

The question from Aquinas' *Summa Theologiae* illustrates Aquinas' radically different, abstractionist foundation for the possibility of acquiring certain knowledge about physical reality, namely, the idea that since simple intellectual apprehension consists in the conformity of the intellect and its objects, the simple concepts of the mind are necessarily related to their proper objects, and so such simple intellectual apprehensions must always be veridical (i.e., they must represent the true nature of the things they apprehend), and the judgments apprehended to be true on the basis of such simple apprehensions are also necessarily true and known to be such without error. (Error arises in judgment by taking the nature of one thing apprehended by some concept to be that of another, or by constructing an at least implicitly inconsistent definition, e.g., "the greatest prime number.")

The selection from Henry of Ghent presents his unique combination of Aristotle and Augustine in his response to the challenges of ancient skepticism that he learned about mainly from these two sources. Henry's response still reflects the characteristic epistemological confidence of the period in the veridicality of our cognitive powers with respect to their proper objects and our ability to sort out veridical from non-veridical cognitive acts in a reliable, rational process.

It is this sort of confidence that is undermined by the radical skepticism reflected in the selection from Nicholas of Autrecourt, obviously paving the way for Descartes' "Demon-skepticism." The fundamental novelty of this new kind of skepticism (grounded in the post-1277 emphasis on God's absolute power and by the post-Ockham possibility of abandoning the idea of the formal unity of the knower and the known) is that it allows for the possibility of the complete cognitive isolation of a thinking subject from an external physical reality. Accordingly, in contrast to ancient skepticism, which merely doubted whether we are ever reliably able to distinguish our veridical cognitive acts from our non-veridical cognitive acts, this sort of skepticism allows for the possibility of our having *no* veridical cognitive acts whatsoever that would faithfully represent the nature of external physical reality as it is.

Finally, the selection from John Buridan represents his "pragmatic" nominalist reaction to this sort of radical skepticism in terms of a surprisingly "modern" naturalistic reliabilism, which (while granting the abstract possibility of absolute deception by an omnipotent agent) argues that the mere logical possibility of this sort of "supernatural deception" should not suffice for undermining the reliability of our scientific or ordinary knowledge-claims, given the various degrees of certainty and various kinds of evidence that can reasonably be demanded in different fields and disciplines.

Philosophy, Theology, Logic, and the Sciences

1

Augustine on Ancient Philosophy

Book VIII

Chapter 2
Concerning the Two Schools of Philosophers, That Is, the Italic and Ionic, and their Founders

As far as concerns the literature of the Greeks, whose language holds a more illustrious place than any of the languages of the other nations, history mentions two schools of philosophers, the one called the Italic school, originating in that part of Italy which was formerly called Magna Græcia; the other called the Ionic school, having its origin in those regions which are still called by the name of Greece. The Italic school had for its founder Pythagoras of Samos, to whom also the term "philosophy" is said to owe its origin. For whereas formerly those who seemed to excel others by the laudable manner in which they regulated their lives were called sages, Pythagoras, on being asked what he professed, replied that he was a philosopher, that is, a student or lover of wisdom; for it seemed to him to be the height of arrogance to profess oneself a sage.[1] The founder of the Ionic school, again, was Thales of Miletus, one of those seven who were styled the "seven sages," of whom six were distinguished by the kind of life they lived, and by certain maxims which they gave forth for the proper conduct of life. Thales was distinguished as an investigator into the nature of things; and, in order that he might have successors in his school, he committed his dissertations to writing. That, however, which especially rendered him eminent was his ability, by means of astronomical calculations, even to predict eclipses of the sun and moon. He thought, however, that water was the first principle of things, and that of it all the elements of the world, the world itself, and all things which are generated in it, ultimately consist. Over all this work, however, which, when we consider the world, appears so admirable, he set nothing of the nature of divine mind. To him succeeded Anaximander, his pupil, who held a different opinion concerning the nature of things; for he did not hold that all things spring from one principle, as Thales did, who held that principle to be water, but thought that each thing

---

1   *Sapiens*, that is, a wise man, one who had attained to wisdom.

springs from its own proper principle. These principles of things he believed to be infinite in number, and thought that they generated innumerable worlds, and all the things which arise in them. He thought, also, that these worlds are subject to a perpetual process of alternate dissolution and regeneration, each one continuing for a longer or shorter period of time, according to the nature of the case; nor did he, any more than Thales, attribute anything to a divine mind in the production of all this activity of things. Anaximander left as his successor his disciple Anaximenes, who attributed all the causes of things to an infinite air. He neither denied nor ignored the existence of gods, but, so far from believing that the air was made by them, he held, on the contrary, that they sprang from the air. Anaxagoras, however, who was his pupil, perceived that a divine mind was the productive cause of all things which we see, and said that all the various kinds of things, according to their several modes and species, were produced out of an infinite matter consisting of homogeneous particles, but by the efficiency of a divine mind. Diogenes, also, another pupil of Anaximenes, said that a certain air was the original substance of things out of which all things were produced, but that it was possessed of a divine reason, without which nothing could be produced from it. Anaxagoras was succeeded by his disciple Archelaus, who also thought that all things consisted of homogeneous particles, of which each particular thing was made, but that those particles were pervaded by a divine mind, which perpetually energized all the eternal bodies, namely, those particles, so that they are alternately united and separated. Socrates, the master of Plato, is said to have been the disciple of Archelaus; and on Plato's account it is that I have given this brief historical sketch of the whole history of these schools.

Chapter 3
Of the Socratic Philosophy

Socrates is said to have been the first who directed the entire effort of philosophy to the correction and regulation of manners, all who went before him having expended their greatest efforts in the investigation of physical, that is, natural phenomena. However, it seems to me that it cannot be certainly discovered whether Socrates did this because he was wearied of obscure and uncertain things, and so wished to direct his mind to the discovery of something manifest and certain, which was necessary in order to the obtaining of a blessed life, – that one great object toward which the labor, vigilance, and industry of all philosophers seem to have been directed, – or whether (as some yet more favorable to him suppose) he did it because he was unwilling that minds defiled with earthly desires should essay to raise themselves upward to divine things. For he saw that the causes of things were sought for by them, – which causes he believed to be ultimately reducible to nothing else than the will of the one true and supreme God, – and on this account he thought they could only be comprehended by a purified mind; and therefore that all diligence ought to be given to the purification of the life by good morals, in order that the mind, delivered from the depressing weight of lusts, might raise itself upward by its native vigor to eternal things, and might, with purified understanding, contemplate that nature which is incorporeal and unchangeable light, where live the causes of all created natures. It is evident, however, that he hunted out and pursued, with a wonderful pleasantness of style and argument, and with a most pointed and insinuating urbanity, the foolishness of ignorant men, who thought that they knew this or that, – sometimes confessing his own ignorance, and sometimes dissimulating his knowledge, even in those very moral questions to which he seems to have directed the whole force of his mind. And hence there arose hostility against him, which ended in his being calumniously impeached, and condemned to death. Afterwards, however, that very city of the Athenians, which had publicly condemned him, did publicly bewail him, – the popular indignation having turned with such vehemence on his accusers, that one of them perished by the violence of the multitude, whilst the other only escaped a like punishment by voluntary and perpetual exile.

Illustrious, therefore, both in his life and in his death, Socrates left very many disciples of his philosophy, who vied with one another in desire for proficiency in handling those moral questions which concern the chief good (*summum bonum*), the possession of which can make a man blessed; and because, in the disputations of Socrates, where he raises all manner of questions, makes assertions, and then demolishes them, it did not evidently appear what he held to be the chief good, every one took from these disputations what pleased him best, and every one placed the final good[2] in whatever it appeared to himself to consist. Now, that which is called the final good is that at which, when one has arrived, he is blessed. But so diverse were the opinions held by those followers of Socrates concerning this final good, that (a thing scarcely to be credited with respect to the followers of one master) some placed the chief good in pleasure, as Aristippus, others in virtue, as Antisthenes. Indeed, it were tedious to recount the various opinions of various disciples.

Chapter 4
Concerning Plato, the Chief Among the Disciples of Socrates, and his Threefold Division of Philosophy

But, among the disciples of Socrates, Plato was the one who shone with a glory which far excelled that of the others, and who not unjustly eclipsed them all. By birth, an Athenian of honorable parentage, he far surpassed his fellow-disciples in natural endowments, of which he was possessed in a wonderful degree. Yet, deeming himself and the Socratic discipline far from sufficient for bringing philosophy to perfection, he travelled as extensively as he was able, going to every place famed for the cultivation of any science of which he could make himself master. Thus he learned from the Egyptians whatever they held and taught as important; and from Egypt, passing into those parts of Italy which were filled with the fame of the Pythagoreans, he mastered, with the greatest facility, and under the most eminent teachers, all the Italic philosophy which was then in vogue. And, as he had a peculiar love for his master Socrates, he made him the speaker in all his dialogues, putting into his mouth whatever he had learned, either from others, or from the efforts of his own powerful intellect, tempering even his moral disputations with the grace and politeness of the Socratic style. And, as the study of wisdom consists in action and contemplation, so that one part of it may be called active, and the other contemplative, – the active part having reference to the conduct of life, that is, to the regulation of morals, and the contemplative part to the investigation into the causes of nature and into pure truth, – Socrates is said to have excelled in the active part of that study, while Pythagoras gave more attention to its contemplative part, on which he brought to bear all the force of his great intellect. To Plato is given the praise of having perfected philosophy by combining both parts into one. He then divides it into three parts, – the first moral, which is

2   *Finem boni.*

chiefly occupied with action; the second natural, of which the object is contemplation; and the third rational, which discriminates between the true and the false. And though this last is necessary both to action and contemplation, it is contemplation, nevertheless, which lays peculiar claim to the office of investigating the nature of truth. Thus this tripartite division is not contrary to that which made the study of wisdom to consist in action and contemplation. Now, as to what Plato thought with respect to each of these parts, – that is, what he believed to be the end of all actions, the cause of all natures, and the light of all intelligences, – it would be a question too long to discuss, and about which we ought not to make any rash affirmation. For, as Plato liked and constantly affected the well-known method of his master Socrates, namely, that of dissimulating his knowledge or his opinions, it is not easy to discover clearly what he himself thought on various matters, any more than it is to discover what were the real opinions of Socrates. We must, nevertheless, insert into our work certain of those opinions which he expresses in his writings, whether he himself uttered them, or narrates them as expressed by others, and seems himself to approve of, – opinions sometimes favorable to the true religion, which our faith takes up and defends, and sometimes contrary to it, as, for example, in the questions concerning the existence of one God or of many, as it relates to the truly blessed life which is to be after death. For those who are praised as having most closely followed Plato, who is justly preferred to all the other philosophers of the Gentiles, and who are said to have manifested the greatest acuteness in understanding him, do perhaps entertain such an idea of God as to admit that in Him are to be found the cause of existence, the ultimate reason for the understanding, and the end in reference to which the whole life is to be regulated. Of which three things, the first is understood to pertain to the natural, the second to the rational, and the third to the moral part of philosophy. For if man has been so created as to attain, through that which is most excellent in him, to that which excels all things, – that is, to the one true and absolutely good God, without whom no nature exists, no doctrine instructs, no exercise profits, – let Him be sought in whom all things are secure to us, let Him be discovered in whom all truth becomes certain to us, let Him be loved in whom all becomes right to us.

Chapter 5
That It Is Especially with the Platonists that We Must Carry on our Disputations on Matters of Theology, their Opinions Being Preferable to Those of All Other Philosophers

If, then, Plato defined the wise man as one who imitates, knows, loves this God, and who is rendered blessed through fellowship with Him in His own blessedness, why discuss with the other philosophers? It is evident that none come nearer to us than the Platonists. To them, therefore, let that fabulous theology give place which delights the minds of men with the crimes of the gods; and that civil theology also, in which impure demons, under the name of gods, have seduced the peoples of the earth given up to earthly pleasures, desiring to be honored by the errors of men, and by filling the minds of their worshippers with impure desires, exciting them to make the representation of their crimes one of the rites of their worship, whilst they themselves found in the spectators of these exhibitions a most pleasing spectacle, – a theology in which, whatever was honorable in the temple, was defiled by its mixture with the obscenity of the theatre, and whatever was base in the theatre was vindicated by the abominations of the temples. To these philosophers also the interpretations of Varro must give place, in which he explains the sacred rites as having reference to heaven and earth, and to the seeds and operations of perishable things; for, in the first place, those rites have not the signification which he would have men believe is attached to them, and therefore truth does not follow him in his attempt so to interpret them; and even if they had this signification, still those things ought not to be worshipped by the rational soul as its god which are placed below it in the scale of nature, nor ought the soul to prefer to itself as gods things to which the true God has given it the preference. The same must be said of those writings pertaining to the sacred rites, which Numa Pompilius took care to conceal by causing them to be buried along with himself, and which, when they were afterwards turned up by the plough, were burned by order of the senate. And, to treat Numa with all honor, let us mention as belonging to the same rank as these writings that which Alexander of Macedon wrote to his mother as communicated to him by Leo, an Egyptian high priest. In this letter not only Picus and Faunus, and Æneas and Romulus or even Hercules, and Æsculapius and Liber, born of Semele, and the twin sons of Tyndareus, or any other mortals who have been deified, but even the principal gods themselves,[3] to whom Cicero, in his Tusculan questions,[4] alludes without mentioning their names, Jupiter, Juno, Saturn, Vulcan, Vesta, and many others whom Varro attempts to identify with the parts or the elements of the world, are shown to have been men. There is, as we have said, a similarity between this case and that of Numa; for the priest being afraid because he had revealed a mystery, earnestly begged of Alexander to command his mother to burn the letter which conveyed these communications to her. Let these two theologies, then, the fabulous and the civil, give place to the Platonic philosophers, who have recognized the true God as the author of all things, the source of the light of truth, and the bountiful bestower of all blessedness. And not these only, but to these great acknowledgers of so great a God, those philosophers must yield who, having their mind enslaved to their body, supposed the principles of all things to be material; as Thales, who held that the first principle of all things was water; Anaximenes, that it was air; the Stoics, that it was fire; Epicurus, who affirmed that it consisted of atoms, that is to say, of minute corpuscles; and many others whom it is needless to enumerate, but who believed that bodies, simple or compound, animate or inanimate, but nevertheless bodies, were the cause and principle of all things. For some of them – as, for instance, the Epicureans – believed that living things could originate from things without life; others held that all things living or without life spring from a living principle, but that, nevertheless, all things, being material, spring from a material principle. For the Stoics thought that fire, that is, one of the four material elements of which this visible world is composed, was both living and intelligent, the maker of the world and of all things contained in it, – that it was in fact God. These and others like them have only been able to suppose that which their hearts enslaved to sense have vainly suggested to them. And yet they have within themselves something which they could not see: they represented to themselves inwardly things which they had seen without, even when they were not seeing them, but only thinking of them. But this representation in thought is no longer a body, but only the similitude of a body; and that faculty of the mind by which this similitude of a body is seen is neither a body nor the similitude of a body; and the faculty which judges whether the representation is beautiful or ugly is without doubt

---

3   *Dii majorum gentium.*

4   Book i. 13.

superior to the object judged of. This principle is the understanding of man, the rational soul; and it is certainly not a body, since that similitude of a body which it beholds and judges of is itself not a body. The soul is neither earth, nor water, nor air, nor fire, of which four bodies, called the four elements, we see that this world is composed. And if the soul is not a body, how should God, its Creator, be a body? Let all those philosophers, then, give place, as we have said, to the Platonists, and those also who have been ashamed to say that God is a body, but yet have thought that our souls are of the same nature as God. They have not been staggered by the great changeableness of the soul, – an attribute which it would be impious to ascribe to the divine nature, – but they say it is the body which changes the soul, for in itself it is unchangeable. As well might they say, "Flesh is wounded by some body, for in itself it is invulnerable." In a word, that which is unchangeable can be changed by nothing, so that that which can be changed by the body cannot properly be said to be immutable.

Chapter 6
Concerning the Meaning of the Platonists in that Part of Philosophy Called Physical

These philosophers, then, whom we see not undeservedly exalted above the rest in fame and glory, have seen that no material body is God, and therefore they have transcended all bodies in seeking for God. They have seen that whatever is changeable is not the most high God, and therefore they have transcended every soul and all changeable spirits in seeking the supreme. They have seen also that, in every changeable thing, the form which makes it that which it is, whatever be its mode or nature, can only *be* through Him who truly *is*, because He is unchangeable. And therefore, whether we consider the whole body of the world, its figure, qualities, and orderly movement, and also all the bodies which are in it; or whether we consider all life, either that which nourishes and maintains, as the life of trees, or that which, besides this, has also sensation, as the life of beasts; or that which adds to all these intelligence, as the life of man; or that which does not need the support of nutriment, but only maintains, feels, understands, as the life of angels, – all can only *be* through Him who absolutely *is*. For to Him it is not one thing to *be*, and another to live, as though He could *be*, not living; nor is it to Him one thing to live, and another thing to understand, as though He could live, not understanding; nor is it to Him one thing to understand, another thing to be blessed, as though He could understand and not be blessed. But to Him to live, to understand, to be blessed, are *to be*. They have understood, from this unchangeableness and this simplicity, that all things must have been made by Him, and that He could Himself have been made by none. For they have considered that whatever *is* is either body or life, and that life is something better than body, and that the nature of body is sensible, and that of life intelligible. Therefore they have preferred the intelligible nature to the sensible. We mean by sensible things such things as can be perceived by the sight and touch of the body; by intelligible things, such as can be understood by the sight of the mind. For there is no corporeal beauty, whether in the condition of a body, as figure, or in its movement, as in music, of which it is not the mind that judges. But this could never have been, had there not existed in the mind itself a superior form of these things, without bulk, without noise of voice, without space and time. But even in respect of these things, had the mind not been mutable, it would not have been possible for one to judge better than another with regard to sensible forms.

He who is clever, judges better than he who is slow, he who is skilled than he who is unskillful, he who is practised than he who is unpractised; and the same person judges better after he has gained experience than he did before. But that which is capable of more and less is mutable; whence able men, who have thought deeply on these things, have gathered that the first form is not to be found in those things whose form is changeable. Since, therefore, they saw that body and mind might be more or less beautiful in form, and that, if they wanted form, they could have no existence, they saw that there is some existence in which is the first form, unchangeable, and therefore not admitting of degrees of comparison, and in that they most rightly believed was the first principle of things which was not made, and by which all things were made. Therefore that which is known of God He manifested to them when His invisible things were seen by them, being understood by those things which have been made; also His eternal power and Godhead by whom all visible and temporal things have been created.[5] We have said enough upon that part of theology which they call physical, that is, natural.

Chapter 7
How Much the Platonists Are To Be Held as Excelling Other Philosophers in Logic, i.e. Rational Philosophy

Then, again, as far as regards the doctrine which treats of that which they call logic, that is, rational philosophy, far be it from us to compare them with those who attributed to the bodily senses the faculty of discriminating truth, and thought, that all we learn is to be measured by their untrustworthy and fallacious rules. Such were the Epicureans, and all of the same school. Such also were the Stoics, who ascribed to the bodily senses that expertness in disputation which they so ardently love, called by them dialectic, asserting that from the senses the mind conceives the notions (ἔννοιαι) of those things which they explicate by definition. And hence is developed the whole plan and connection of their learning and teaching. I often wonder, with respect to this, how they can say that none are beautiful but the wise; for by what bodily sense have they perceived that beauty, by what eyes of the flesh have they seen wisdom's comeliness of form? Those, however, whom we justly rank before all others, have distinguished those things which are conceived by the mind from those which are perceived by the senses, neither taking away from the senses anything to which they are competent, nor attributing to them anything beyond their competency. And the light of our understandings, by which all things are learned by us, they have affirmed to be that selfsame God by whom all things were made.

Chapter 8
That the Platonists Hold the First Rank in Moral Philosophy Also

The remaining part of philosophy is morals, or what is called by the Greeks ἠθική, in which is discussed the question concerning the chief good, – that which will leave us nothing further to seek in order to be blessed, if only we make all our actions refer to it, and seek it not for the sake of something else, but for its own sake. Therefore it is called the end, because we wish other things on account of it, but itself only for its own sake.

5 Rom. 1: 19, 20.

[handwritten notes: Summum Bonum / Chief good~happiness / That for the sake of which / (Teleological)→virtue ethics]

This beatific good, therefore, according to some, comes to a man from the body, according to others, from the mind, and, according to others, from both together. For they saw that man himself consists of soul and body; and therefore they believed that from either of these two, or from both together, their well-being must proceed, consisting in a certain final good, which could render them blessed, and to which they might refer all their actions, not requiring anything ulterior to which to refer that good itself. This is why those who have added a third kind of good things, which they call extrinsic, – as honor, glory, wealth, and the like, – have not regarded them as part of the final good, that is, to be sought after for their own sake, but as things which are to be sought for the sake of something else, affirming that this kind of good is good to the good, and evil to the evil. Wherefore, whether they have sought the good of man from the mind or from the body, or from both together, it is still only from man they have supposed that it must be sought. But they who have sought it from the body have sought it from the inferior part of man; they who have sought it from the mind, from the superior part; and they who have sought it from both, from the whole man. Whether therefore, they have sought it from any part, or from the whole man, still they have only sought it from man; nor have these differences, being three, given rise only to three dissentient sects of philosophers, but to many. For diverse philosophers have held diverse opinions, both concerning the good of the body, and the good of the mind, and the good of both together. Let, therefore, all these give place to those philosophers who have not affirmed that a man is blessed by the enjoyment of the body, or by the enjoyment of the mind, but by the enjoyment of God, – enjoying Him, however, not as the mind does the body or itself, or as one friend enjoys another, but as the eye enjoys light, if, indeed, we may draw any comparison between these things. But what the nature of this comparison is, will, if God help me, be shown in another place, to the best of my ability. At present, it is sufficient to mention that Plato determined the final good to be to live according to virtue, and affirmed that he only can attain to virtue who knows and imitates God, – which knowledge and imitation are the only cause of blessedness. Therefore he did not doubt that to philosophize is to love God, whose nature is incorporeal. Whence it certainly follows that the student of wisdom, that is, the philosopher, will then become blessed when he shall have begun to enjoy God. For though he is not necessarily blessed who enjoys that which he loves (for many are miserable by loving that which ought not to be loved, and still more miserable when they enjoy it), nevertheless no one is blessed who does not enjoy that which he loves. For even they who love things which ought not to be loved do not count themselves blessed by loving merely, but by enjoying them. Who, then, but the most miserable will deny that he is blessed, who enjoys that which he loves, and loves the true and highest good? But the true and highest good, according to Plato, is God, and therefore he would call him a philosopher who loves God; for philosophy is directed to the obtaining of the blessed life, and he who loves God is blessed in the enjoyment of God.

Chapter 9
Concerning that Philosophy which Has Come Nearest to the Christian Faith

Whatever philosophers, therefore, thought concerning the supreme God, that He is both the maker of all created things, the light by which things are known, and the good in reference to which things are to be done; that we have in Him the first principle of nature, the truth of doctrine, and the happiness of life, – whether these philosophers may be more suitably called Platonists, or whether they may give some other name to their sect; whether, we say, that only the chief men of the Ionic school, such as Plato himself, and they who have well understood him, have thought thus; or whether we also include the Italic school, on account of Pythagoras and the Pythagoreans, and all who may have held like opinions; and, lastly, whether also we include all who have been held wise men and philosophers among all nations who are discovered to have seen and taught this, be they Atlantics, Libyans, Egyptians, Indians, Persians, Chaldeans, Scythians, Gauls, Spaniards, or of other nations, – we prefer these to all other philosophers, and confess that they approach nearest to us.

Chapter 10
That the Excellency of the Christian Religion Is Above All the Science of Philosophers

For although a Christian man instructed only in ecclesiastical literature may perhaps be ignorant of the very name of Platonists, and may not even know that there have existed two schools of philosophers speaking the Greek tongue, to wit, the Ionic and Italic, he is nevertheless not so deaf with respect to human affairs, as not to know that philosophers profess the study, and even the possession, of wisdom. He is on his guard, however, with respect to those who philosophize according to the elements of this world, not according to God, by whom the world itself was made; for he is warned by the precept of the apostle, and faithfully hears what has been said, "Beware that no one deceive you through philosophy and vain deceit, according to the elements of the world."[6] Then, that he may not suppose that all philosophers are such as do this, he hears the same apostle say concerning certain of them, "Because that which is known of God is manifest among them, for God has manifested it to them. For His invisible things from the creation of the world are clearly seen, being understood by the things which are made, also His eternal power and Godhead."[7] And, when speaking to the Athenians, after having spoken a mighty thing concerning God, which few are able to understand, "In Him we live, and move, and have our being,"[8] he goes on to say, "As certain also of your own have said." He knows well, too, to be on his guard against even these philosophers in their errors. For where it has been said by him, "that God has manifested to them by those things which are made His invisible things, that they might be seen by the understanding," there it has also been said that they did not rightly worship God Himself, because they paid divine honors, which are due to Him alone, to other things also to which they ought not to have paid them, – "because, knowing God, they glorified Him not as God: neither were thankful, but became vain in their imaginations, and their foolish heart was darkened. Professing themselves to be wise, they became fools, and changed the glory of the incorruptible God into the likeness of the image of corruptible man, and of birds, and fourfooted beasts, and creeping things;"[9] – where the apostle would have us understand him as meaning the Romans, and Greeks, and Egyptians, who

6 Col. 2: 8.
7 Rom. 1: 19, 20.
8 Acts 17: 28.
9 Rom. 1: 21–3.

gloried in the name of wisdom; but concerning this we will dispute with them afterwards. With respect, however, to that wherein they agree with us we prefer them to all others namely, concerning the one God, the author of this universe, who is not only above every body, being incorporeal, but also above all souls, being incorruptible – our principle, our light, our good. And though the Christian man, being ignorant of their writings, does not use in disputation words which he has not learned, – not calling that part of philosophy natural (which is the Latin term), or physical (which is the Greek one), which treats of the investigation of nature; or that part rational, or logical, which deals with the question how truth may be discovered; or that part moral, or ethical, which concerns morals, and shows how good is to be sought, and evil to be shunned, – he is not, therefore, ignorant that it is from the one true and supremely good God that we have that nature in which we are made in the image of God, and that doctrine by which we know Him and ourselves, and that grace through which, by cleaving to Him, we are blessed. This, therefore, is the cause why we prefer these to all the others, because, whilst other philosophers have worn out their minds and powers in seeking the causes of things, and endeavoring to discover the right mode of learning and of living, these, by knowing God, have found where resides the cause by which the universe has been constituted, and the light by which truth is to be discovered, and the fountain at which felicity is to be drunk. All philosophers, then, who have had these thoughts concerning God, whether Platonists or others, agree with us. But we have thought it better to plead our cause with the Platonists, because their writings are better known. For the Greeks, whose tongue holds the highest place among the languages of the Gentiles, are loud in their praises of these writings; and the Latins, taken with their excellence, or their renown, have studied them more heartily than other writings, and, by translating them into our tongue, have given them greater celebrity and notoriety.

Chapter 11
How Plato Has Been Able to Approach So Nearly to Christian Knowledge

Certain partakers with us in the grace of Christ, wonder when they hear and read that Plato had conceptions concerning God, in which they recognize considerable agreement with the truth of our religion. Some have concluded from this, that when he went to Egypt he had heard the prophet Jeremiah, or, whilst travelling in the same country, had read the prophetic scriptures, which opinion I myself have expressed in certain of my writings.[10] But a careful calculation of dates, contained in chronological history, shows that Plato was born about a hundred years after the time in which Jeremiah prophesied, and, as he lived eighty-one years, there are found to have been about seventy years from his death to that time when Ptolemy, king of Egypt, requested the prophetic scriptures of the Hebrew people to be sent to him from Judea, and committed them to seventy Hebrews, who also knew the Greek tongue, to be translated and kept. Therefore, on that voyage of his, Plato could neither have seen Jeremiah, who was dead so long before, nor have read those same scriptures which had not yet been translated into the Greek language, of which he was a master, unless, indeed, we say that, as he was most earnest in the pursuit of knowledge, he also studied those writings through an interpreter, as he did those of the Egyptians, – not, indeed, writing a translation

---

10   *De Doctrina Christiana*, ii. 43. Comp. *Retract*. ii. 4, 2.

of them (the facilities for doing which were only gained even by Ptolemy in return for munificent acts of kindness,[11] though fear of his kingly authority might have seemed a sufficient motive), but learning as much as he possibly could concerning their contents by means of conversation. What warrants this supposition are the opening verses of Genesis: "In the beginning God made the heaven and earth. And the earth was invisible, and without order; and darkness was over the abyss: and the Spirit of God moved over the waters."[12] For in the *Timæus*, when writing on the formation of the world, he says that God first united earth and fire; from which it is evident that he assigns to fire a place in heaven. This opinion bears a certain resemblance to the statement, "In the beginning God made heaven and earth." Plato next speaks of those two intermediary elements, water and air, by which the other two extremes, namely, earth and fire, were mutually united; from which circumstance he is thought to have so understood the words, "The Spirit of God moved over the waters." For, not paying sufficient attention to the designations given by those scriptures to the Spirit of God, he may have thought that the four elements are spoken of in that place, because the air also is called spirit.[13] Then, as to Plato's saying that the philosopher is a lover of God, nothing shines forth more conspicuously in those sacred writings. But the most striking thing in this connection, and that which most of all inclines me almost to assent to the opinion that Plato was not ignorant of those writings, is the answer which was given to the question elicited from the holy Moses when the words of God were conveyed to him by the angel; for, when he asked what was the name of that God who was commanding him to go and deliver the Hebrew people out of Egypt, this answer was given: "I am who am; and thou shalt say to the children of Israel, He who *is* sent me unto you";[14] as though compared with Him that truly *is*, because He is unchangeable, those things which have been created mutable *are* not, – a truth which Plato zealously held, and most diligently commended. And I know not whether this sentiment is anywhere to be found in the books of those who were before Plato, unless in that book where it is said, "I am who am; and thou shalt say to the children of Israel, *who is* sent me unto you."

Chapter 12
That Even the Platonists, though They Say These Things Concerning the One True God, Nevertheless Thought that Sacred Rites Were to Be Performed in Honor of Many Gods

But we need not determine from what source he learned these things, – whether it was from the books of the ancients who preceded him, or, as is more likely, from the words of the apostle: "Because that which is known of God, has been manifested among them, for God hath manifested it to them. For His invisible things from the creation of the world are clearly seen, being understood by those things which have been made, also His eternal power and Godhead."[15] From whatever source he may have derived this knowledge, then, I think I have made it sufficiently plain that I have not chosen the Platonic philosophers undeservedly as the parties with whom to discuss; because the question we have just taken up concerns the

---

11   Liberating Jewish slaves, and sending gifts to the temple. See Josephus, *Ant.* xii. 2.
12   Gen. 1: 1, 2.
13   *Spiritus.*
14   Ex. 3: 14.
15   Rom. 1: 20.

natural theology, – the question, namely, whether sacred rites are to be performed to one God, or to many, for the sake of the happiness which is to be after death. I have specially chosen them because their juster thoughts concerning the one God who made heaven and earth, have made them illustrious among philosophers. This has given them such superiority to all others in the judgment of posterity, that, though Aristotle, the disciple of Plato, a man of eminent abilities, inferior in eloquence to Plato, yet far superior to many in that respect, had founded the Peripatetic sect, – so called because they were in the habit of walking about during their disputations, – and though he had, through the greatness of his fame, gathered very many disciples into his school, even during the life of his master; and though Plato at his death was succeeded in his school, which was called the Academy, by Speusippus, his sister's son, and Xenocrates, his beloved disciple, who, together with their successors, were called from this name of the school, Academics; nevertheless the most illustrious recent philosophers, who have chosen to follow Plato, have been unwilling to be called Peripatetics, or Academics, but have preferred the name of Platonists. Among these were the renowned Plotinus, Iamblichus, and Porphyry, who were Greeks, and the African Apuleius, who was learned both in the Greek and Latin tongues. All these, however, and the rest who were of the same school, and also Plato himself, thought that sacred rites ought to be performed in honor of many gods.

2

Dialectica Monacensis
(Anonymous, Twelfth Century)

On the Division of Science

As we are going to deal with dialectic, which is, as it were, the pathway to all the other arts, at the beginning of this treatise we provide the division of science.

We should know, therefore, that human nature is plagued by three scourges. The first is ignorance, on the part of the soul, the second is indigence, on the part of the body, and the third is vice, on the part of the substance composed of these two. Against these plagues three remedies were given to man: against ignorance the capability to acquire the liberal sciences, against indigence the mechanical arts, and against vices the capability to acquire virtues.

Furthermore, science is divided into rational, natural and moral philosophy. Natural philosophy is divided into metaphysics, mathematics and physics. Metaphysics or theology deals with God and with the supreme and divine substances and things, and the principles of other sciences.

Mathematics is divided into arithmetic, music, geometry and astronomy. . . .

Physics is handed down to us in Aristotle's *Physics*, *On Heaven and Earth*, *On Coming to Be and Passing Away*, *Meteorology*, *On Plants and Animals*, *On the Soul*, and *On Sleeping and Being Awake*. The first of these deals with moving bodies absolutely speaking, the second with bodies that move by locomotion, the third is about the generation, corruption and mixing of bodies absolutely speaking, the fourth is about their generation and corruption in the air, the fifth about plants, the sixth about animals, the seventh about the human soul, insofar as it is naturally connected to the body and about its powers, and the eighth about sleeping and being awake.

Furthermore, moral science is divided into three parts; politics, economics and monastics. The first consists in the government of society, the second concerns managing family matters, and the third regards one's own proper conduct.

Furthermore, rational science is divided into three parts: grammar, rhetoric and logic. Grammar teaches the proper arrangement of letters into syllables, syllables into words and words into phrases. Rhetoric deals with three kinds of causes, namely demonstrative, deliberative and judicial. Dialectic deals with syllogism absolutely speaking, as in the *Prior Analytics*, and its subjective parts, as in the *Posterior Analytics*, in the *Topics* and in the *Sophistic Refutations*; while its integral parts are dealt with in the *Categories* and the *Perihermeneias (On Interpretation)*.

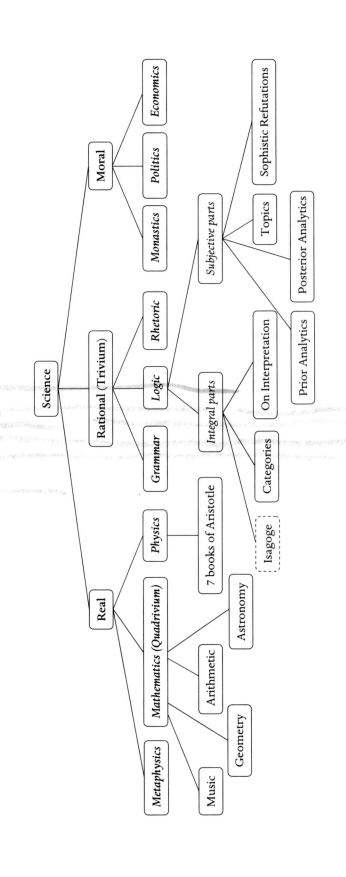

3

Thomas Aquinas on the Nature and Scope of Sacred Doctrine

Summa Theologiae

Part I, Question 1. The Nature and Extent of Sacred Doctrine

To place our purpose within proper limits, we first endeavor to investigate the nature and extent of this sacred doctrine. Concerning this there are ten points of inquiry:

 1 Whether it is necessary?
 2 Whether it is a science?
 3 Whether it is one or many?
 4 Whether it is speculative or practical?
 5 How it is compared with other sciences?
 6 Whether it is the same as wisdom?
 7 Whether God is its subject-matter?
 8 Whether it uses arguments?
 9 Whether it should use metaphorical or figurative language?
 10 Whether the Sacred Scripture of this doctrine may be expounded in different senses?

Article 1. Whether, besides philosophy, any further doctrine is required?

Objection 1: It seems that we need no teaching beyond the philosophical disciplines. For man should not seek to know what is beyond reason: "Seek not the things that are beyond you."[1] But whatever is not beyond reason is sufficiently dealt with in the philosophical disciplines. Therefore any other teaching beyond the philosophical disciplines seems to be superfluous.

Objection 2: Further, knowledge can be concerned only with being, for nothing can be known, except what is true; and being and truth are convertible. But the philosophical disciplines deal with all beings – even God Himself; so there is a part of philosophy that is called theology, or divine science, as Aristotle has proved.[2] Therefore there is no need for any teaching other than what can be gained from the philosophical disciplines.

1 Ecclesiasticus 3: 22.
2 Aristotle, *Metaphysics* VI, 1, 1026a19.

On the contrary, "All Scripture inspired by God is profitable for teaching, for reproof, for correction, and for training in righteousness."[3] Now Scripture, inspired by God, is no part of philosophical disciplines, which are the invention of human reason. Therefore it is useful to have a divinely inspired science besides the philosophical disciplines.

I answer that, It was necessary for man's salvation that there should be a doctrine based on divine revelation besides the philosophical disciplines pursued by human reason. Primarily, because man is directed to God, as to an end that surpasses the grasp of his reason. As Isaiah says, 'Without you, God, no eye has seen what you have prepared for those who love you.'[4] But the end must first be known by those who are to direct their thoughts and actions to the end. Hence it was necessary for the salvation of humans that certain truths which surpass human reason should be made known to them by divine revelation. Indeed, it was necessary that man should be taught by a divine revelation even those truths about God which human reason could have discovered; because the truth about God that reason could discover would only be known by a few, and that after a long time, and with the admixture of many errors. But man's whole salvation, which is in God, depends upon the knowledge of this truth. Therefore, in order that the salvation of humans might be brought about more aptly and more surely, it was necessary that they should be taught divine truths by divine revelation. It was therefore necessary that besides the philosophical disciplines pursued by reason there should be a sacred doctrine obtained through revelation.

Reply to Objection 1: Although those things which are beyond man's knowledge may not be pursued by man through reason, nevertheless, once they are revealed by God, they must be accepted by faith. Hence, the same passage continues, "You are shown many things that are above the understanding of human beings."[5] And sacred doctrine consists in these things.

Reply to Objection 2: Sciences are differentiated according to the different formal aspects under which they consider their subjects. For the astronomer and the physicist both may prove the same conclusion, for instance, that the earth is round. But the astronomer does so by means of a mathematical middle term,[6] i.e. one that abstracts from matter, whereas the

---

3   2 Timothy 3: 16.

4   Isaiah 64: 4.

5   Ecclesiasticus 3: 25.

6   The "middle term" in question is a term shared by the premises of a demonstrative syllogism. A syllogism is an argument consisting of two premises that share one term, the middle term, and whose conclusion is formed by joining the other two terms, the so-called "extremes", of the premises. For example, in the demonstration "Every body whose all projections are circular is round; but the earth is a body whose all projections are circular (as is clear from its shadow cast on the moon); therefore, the earth is round", the middle term is "a body whose all projections are circular", and it is obviously a geometrical middle term, which abstracts from matter (since it applies to any body on account of its shape, regardless of its matter, whether it is ivory or resin (as in billiard balls), or any other solid matter. On the other hand, in the syllogism "A body whose all parts gravitate toward the same point on account of their gravity is round, but the earth is a body whose all parts gravitate toward the same point on account of their gravity; therefore, the earth is round", the middle term is obviously a physical middle term that involves in its meaning the consideration of the gravitating matter of the earth. These demonstrations have been widely referred to in medieval philosophy as illustrations of typical scientific demonstrations (used by Aristotle in his *Physics* and *On the Heavens*). So much for the Enlightenment propaganda, still being taught in American high schools, that medievals believed the earth was flat.

physicist by means of a middle term that involves the consideration of matter. So there is no reason why those things that the philosophical disciplines deal with insofar as they are knowable by the light of natural reason should not also be dealt with by another doctrine, insofar as they can be learned by the light of divine revelation. Hence the theology that pertains to sacred doctrine differs in kind from that theology which is a part of philosophy.

Article 2. Whether sacred doctrine is a science?

Objection 1: It seems that sacred doctrine is not a science. For every science proceeds from self-evident principles. But sacred doctrine proceeds from articles of faith which are not self-evident, since their truth is not admitted by all. As *2 Thessalonians* says, "not all have faith."[7] Therefore, sacred doctrine is not a science.

Objection 2: Further, there is no science of singulars. But sacred doctrine is about singulars, such as the deeds of Abraham, Isaac and Jacob and the like. Therefore, sacred doctrine is not a science.

On the contrary, Augustine says that "to this science alone pertains that which generates, nourishes, protects, and strengthens the faith that saves us."[8] But this can be said of no science except sacred doctrine. Therefore sacred doctrine is a science.

I answer that, Sacred doctrine is a science. We must bear in mind that there are two kinds of sciences. There are some which proceed from principles known by the natural light of understanding, such as arithmetic and geometry and the like. There are some which proceed from principles known by the light of a higher science: thus the science of perspective proceeds from principles established by geometry, and music from principles established by arithmetic. Sacred doctrine is a science in this second way, because it proceeds from principles established by the light of a higher science, namely, the science of God and the blessed. Hence, just as music relies on principles taught by arithmetic, so sacred science relies on principles revealed by God.

Reply to Objection 1: The principles of any science are either in themselves self-evident, or reducible to the recognition of a higher science; and such, as we have said, are the principles of sacred doctrine.

Reply to Objection 2: Sacred doctrine deals with singulars, not because it is concerned with them principally, but they are introduced rather as examples to be followed in our lives (as in moral sciences) and in order to establish the authority of those men through whom the divine revelation, on which this sacred scripture or doctrine is based, has come down to us.

Article 3. Whether sacred doctrine is one science?

Objection 1: It seems that sacred doctrine is not one science; for according to the Philosopher "that science is one which deals with subjects of one and the same genus."[9] But creator and creature, which are both dealt with in sacred doctrine, are not subjects of one and the same genus. Therefore sacred doctrine is not one science.

7   2 Thessalonians 3: 2.
8   St Augustine, *De Trinitate* XIV, 7. PL 42, 1037.
9   *Posterior Analytics* I, 28, 87a38.

Objection 2: Further, in sacred doctrine we deal with angels, corporeal creatures and human morality. But these belong to separate philosophical sciences. Therefore sacred doctrine cannot be one science.

On the contrary, Holy Scripture speaks of it as one science: "Wisdom gave him the science of holy things."[10]

I answer that, Sacred doctrine is one science. The unity of a faculty or habit is to be gauged by its object, not materially, but with regard to the formal aspect under which it is the object. For example, people, donkeys and stones all agree in the same formal aspect of being colored; and color is the formal object of sight.[11] Therefore, because Sacred Scripture considers things precisely under the formal aspect of being divinely revealed, all divinely revealed things share the same formal aspect of the object of this science, and therefore they are subsumed under sacred doctrine as under one science.

Reply to Objection 1: Sacred doctrine does not deal with God and creatures equally, but with God primarily, and with creatures only insofar as they are related to God as their origin or end. Hence the unity of this science is not compromised.

Reply to Objection 2: Nothing prevents lower faculties or habits from being diversified by something that falls under a higher faculty or habit as well; because the higher faculty or habit regards the object under a more universal formal aspect. For example, the object of common sense [*sensus communis*] is anything that affects the senses, including, therefore, everything that is visible or audible. Hence, although the common sense is one faculty, it extends to all the objects of the five senses.[12] Likewise, objects that are the subject-matter of different philosophical sciences can yet be dealt with by one and the same sacred science under the same formal aspect, namely, insofar as they are divinely revealed. So, in this way, sacred doctrine is like an imprint of the knowledge God itself, which is one and simple, yet extends to everything.

Article 4. Whether sacred doctrine is a practical science?

Objection 1: It seems that sacred doctrine is a practical science; for according to the Philosopher "a practical science has action as its end."[13] But according to the letter of *James*, sacred doctrine is directed to action: "Be doers of the word and not only hearers."[14] Therefore sacred doctrine is a practical science.

10   Wisdom 10: 10.
11   That is to say, all these very diverse subjects fall under the same cognitive faculty, namely, sight, insofar as they are all colored, i.e., visible, perceivable by sight. These subjects are diverse "materially" as opposed to the same "formal" aspect they all share, namely, their being colored (and hence visible), just as all bearing balls and billiard balls and other round objects share the same form, namely, round shape, even if they are materially diverse, for some are made of steel, others of ivory or resin, etc.
12   In Aristotelian psychology, the common sense is an inner sense, the sensory faculty that has the task of monitoring the activity of the five external senses, making us aware of our perceptions, distinguishing, organizing, and further processing the "raw input" of the external senses. Therefore, the objects of the common sense are all sensible objects, insofar as they are sensible in general, comprehending all the more specific objects of the external senses, namely, all visible, audible, tangible, etc. objects.
13   Metaphysics II, 1, 993b21.
14   James 1: 22.

Objection 2: Furthermore, sacred doctrine is divided into the Old and the New Law. But law pertains to moral science which is practical. Therefore sacred doctrine is a practical science.

On the contrary, Every practical science is concerned with what humans can do or make; as moral science is concerned with human actions, and architecture with buildings. But sacred doctrine is chiefly concerned with God, who makes people [rather than is made by them]. Therefore, sacred doctrine is a theoretical science, rather than a practical one.

I answer that, As I have already said,[15] sacred doctrine, while it is one and the same, extends to things which belong to different philosophical sciences, because it considers each under the same formal aspect, namely, insofar as they can be known through divine revelation. Hence, although among the philosophical sciences one is theoretical and another practical, nevertheless sacred doctrine covers both; just as God knows both Himself and His works, by one and the same knowledge. Still, sacred doctrine is theoretical rather than practical, because it is concerned with divine things rather than with human actions. It deals with the latter insofar as they lead us to the perfect knowledge of God in which eternal bliss consists. And from this the answer to the objections is clear.

Article 5. Whether sacred doctrine is nobler than any other science?

Objection 1: It seems that sacred doctrine is not nobler than other sciences; for the nobility of a science depends on the certitude it establishes. But other sciences, the principles of which cannot be doubted, seem to be more certain than sacred doctrine; for its principles – namely, articles of faith – can be doubted. Therefore other sciences seem to be nobler.

Objection 2: Furthermore, a lower science depends upon a higher; as music depends on arithmetic. But sacred doctrine does in a sense depend upon philosophical sciences. As Jerome observes: "the ancient doctors so enriched their books with the ideas and phrases of the philosophers, that you do not know which to admire more: their secular erudition or their scriptural learning."[16] Therefore sacred doctrine is inferior to other sciences.

On the contrary, Other sciences are called the handmaidens of this one: "Wisdom sent her maids to invite to the tower."[17]

I answer that, Since this science is partly speculative and partly practical, it transcends all others, speculative and practical. One speculative science is said to be nobler than another, either by reason of its greater certitude, or by reason of the higher worth of its subject-matter. This science surpasses other speculative sciences in both of these respects: in certitude, because other sciences derive their certitude from the natural light of human reason, which can err, whereas this derives its certitude from the light of divine knowledge, which cannot be misled; in the higher worth of its subject-matter, because this science deals with those things that by their sublimity transcend human reason; while other sciences consider only those things that are within reason's grasp. Among practical sciences that one is nobler which is ordained to a further purpose, as politics is nobler than military strategy; for the good of the army is subordinated to the good of the state. But the purpose of this science, in so far as it is practical, is eternal bliss; to which the purposes of every practical

15 Ia. 1: 3.
16 St Jerome (c. 345–420), *Epistola* 70. PL 22, 668.
17 Proverbs 9: 3.

science are subordinated as to their ultimate end. Hence it is clear that from every stand-point, sacred doctrine is nobler than all other sciences.

Reply to Objection 1: It may well happen that what is in itself the more certain appears to us the less certain on account of the weakness of our intelligence "which is dazzled by the clearest objects of nature; as the owl is dazzled by the light of the sun."[18] Hence the fact that some happen to doubt the articles of faith is not due to the uncertain nature of those truths, but to the weakness of human intelligence. Still, even the slightest knowledge that may be obtained of the highest things is more desirable than the most certain knowledge obtained of lesser things.[19]

Reply to Objection 2: This science can in a sense depend upon the philosophical sciences, not as though it stood in need of them, but only in order to make its teaching clearer. For it accepts its principles not from other sciences, but immediately from God, by revelation. Therefore it does not depend upon other sciences as upon higher sciences, but makes use of them as subsidiaries and as handmaidens, even as the master arts make use of their subordinate arts, as politics uses military strategy. That it thus uses them is not due to its own defect or insufficiency, but to the defect of our intelligence, which is more easily led by what is known through natural reason (from which the other sciences proceed) to things that are beyond reason (as are the teachings of this science).

Article 6. Whether this doctrine is wisdom?

Objection 1: It seems that this doctrine is not wisdom. For no doctrine that borrows its principles from elsewhere is worthy of the name of wisdom; given that "the office of the wise is to govern others, and not to be governed by them."[20] But this doctrine borrows its principles, as was said earlier.[21] Therefore this doctrine is not wisdom.

Objection 2: Furthermore, it pertains to wisdom to prove the principles of other sciences. Hence it is called "the chief of the sciences."[22] But this doctrine does not prove the principles of other sciences. Therefore it is not wisdom.

Objection 3: Furthermore, this doctrine is acquired by study, whereas wisdom is acquired by divine inspiration, so that it is numbered among the seven gifts of the Holy Spirit (as is clear from Isaiah[23]). Therefore this doctrine is not wisdom.

On the contrary, at the beginning of the Torah *Deuteronomy* says "This is our wisdom and understanding in the sight of the peoples."[24]

I answer that, This doctrine is wisdom above all human wisdom; not merely in any one field, but absolutely. Since it belongs to the wise man to command and to judge, and since lesser matters should be judged in the light of some higher principle, he is said to be wise in any field who considers the highest principles of that field. For example, in architecture, the artist who plans the form of the house is called wise and the architect, as opposed to

---

18   *Metaphysics* II, 1, 993b10.
19   *On the Parts of Animals* I, 5, 644b31.
20   *Metaphysics* I, 2, 982a18.
21   Ia. 1: 2.
22   *Nicomachean Ethics* VI, 7, 1141a16.
23   Isaiah 11: 2.
24   Deuteronomy 4: 6.

the subordinate craftsmen who hew the timbers and cut the stones: "Like a wise architect, I have laid the foundation."[25] Again, in matters of human life, the prudent man is called wise, inasmuch as he directs his acts to a fitting end: "Prudence in a person is a form of wisdom."[26] Therefore, he who considers absolutely the highest cause of the whole universe, namely God, is called wise most of all. Hence wisdom is said to be the cognition of divine things, as Augustine says.[27] But sacred doctrine most appropriately deals with God as the highest cause; not only with regard to what can be known about Him through creatures, which philosophers have recognized (see *Romans*: "What is known of God is plain to them"[28]), but also with regard to what only He knows about Himself and communicates to others by revelation. Hence, sacred doctrine is especially called wisdom.

Reply to Objection 1: Sacred doctrine takes its principles not from any human knowledge, but from divine knowledge, through which, as through the highest wisdom, all our knowledge is set in order.

Reply to Objection 2: The principles of other sciences either are self-evident and cannot be proved, or are proved by natural reason in some other science. But the knowledge that is proper to this science comes through revelation and not through natural reason. Therefore it has no concern to prove the principles of other sciences, but only to judge of them. So, anything that in the other sciences is found contrary to any truth of this science must be condemned as false "destroying counsels and every height that rears itself against the knowledge of God."[29]

Reply to Objection 3: Since judgment pertains to wisdom, there are two kinds of wisdom, corresponding to two kinds of judgment. A man may judge in one way by inclination, as anyone who possesses some virtue correctly judges what should be done in accordance with that virtue on account of his very inclination to do it. This is why Aristotle says that the virtuous person sets the measure and standard for human acts.[30] In another way, man may judge by knowledge, just as a man educated in moral science might be able to judge correctly about virtuous acts, though he may not have the virtue. The first manner of judging divine things belongs to that wisdom which is set down among the gifts of the Holy Spirit: "The spiritual person judges all things."[31] And Dionysius says that "Hierotheus was taught by the experience of divine things, not only by learning about them."[32] The second manner of judging belongs to this doctrine insofar as it is acquired by study, though its principles are obtained by revelation.

Article 7. Whether God is the subject of this science?

Objection 1: It seems that God is not the object of this science. For every science has to presuppose the knowledge of what its subject is, according to Aristotle.[33] But this science

---

25 1 Corinthians 3: 10.
26 Proverbs 10: 23.
27 *De Trinitate* XII, 14. PL 42, 1009.
28 Romans 1: 19.
29 2 Corinthians 3: 10.
30 *Nicomachean Ethics* X, 5, 1176a17.
31 1 Corinthians 2: 15.
32 Dionysius the Areopagite (c. 500), *De divinis nominibus* II, 9. PG 3, 648.
33 *Posterior Analytics* 1, 4, 71a13.

cannot presuppose knowledge of the essence of God, since, as Damascene remarks, "In God's case, it is impossible to say what he is." So, God is not the subject of this science.[34]

Objection 2: Furthermore, anything concerning which a science determines certain truths must be comprised under the subject of that science. But Sacred Scripture determines truths not only concerning God, but also concerning many other things, such as creatures and human morality. Therefore God is not the subject of this science.

On the contrary, The subject of a science is what this science is talking about. But this science is talking about God, because it is called *theology*, that is, "talk about God".[35]

I answer that, God is the subject of this science. For a science is related to its subject as a habit or faculty to its object. Now strictly speaking, that is the object of a faculty or habit under the formal aspect of which all things are referred to that faculty or habit, as man and stone are referred to the faculty of sight insofar as they are colored. Hence the proper object of sight is something colored [as such]. But in sacred science, all things are dealt with under the aspect of God; either because they are God Himself or because they refer to God as their beginning and end. Hence it follows that God is truly the subject of this science. This is clear also from the principles of this science, namely, the articles of faith, for faith is about God. But the subject of the principles is the same as that of the whole science, since the whole science is virtually contained in its principles. Some people, however, looking at the diverse things dealt with in this science, and not at the aspect under which they are dealt with, have assigned differently the subject of this science – that is, either as things and signs; or as the works of salvation; or as the whole Christ, as the head and members. For this science does deal with all these things; however, it deals with all of them insofar as they are related to God.

Reply to Objection 1: Although we cannot know what God is, nevertheless in this science we use His effects (whether of nature or of grace) in place of a definition to demonstrate what we consider about God within this doctrine; even as some philosophical sciences demonstrate something about a cause from its effect, by taking the effect in place of a definition of the cause.

Reply to Objection 2: Any other things determined in this sacred doctrine are comprised under God, not as parts or species or accidents, but as things that are in some way related to Him.

Article 8. Whether sacred doctrine uses arguments?

Objection 1: It seems that this doctrine should not use arguments. For Ambrose says: "Cast arguments aside where faith is sought."[36] But in this doctrine, faith especially is sought: "But these things are written that you may believe".[37] Therefore, sacred doctrine should not use arguments.

Objection 2: Further, if it does use arguments, then the argument is either from authority or from reason. If the argument is from authority, then the reasoning seems to be unbefitting

34   St John Damascene (c. 655–c. 750), *De fide orthodoxa* I, 4. PG 94, 797.
35   The word 'theology' has as its roots the Greek words 'theos' meaning 'God' and 'logos' meaning 'talk, reason, reasoning, discipline'.
36   St Ambrose (c. 339–397), *De fide catholica* I, 13. PL 16, 370.
37   John 20: 31.

the dignity of this doctrine, for according to Boethius authority is the weakest ground of proof.[38] But if it is from reason, then the process is unbefitting its end, because, for according to Gregory, "Faith has no merit where the reason presents actual proof from experience."[39] So, sacred doctrine does not use arguments.

On the contrary, The Scripture says that a bishop should "embrace that faithful word which is according to doctrine, that he may be able to exhort in sound doctrine and to convince the gainsayers".[40]

I answer that, Just as other sciences do not argue to prove their principles, but argue from their principles to demonstrate other truths in these sciences: so this doctrine does not argue to prove its principles, which are the articles of faith, but it goes on to prove something else from them; as the Apostle argues to prove the general resurrection from the resurrection of Christ.[41] However, we should bear in mind in regard to the philosophical sciences that the inferior sciences neither prove their principles nor dispute with those who deny them, but leave this to a higher science; whereas the highest of them, viz. metaphysics, can dispute with someone who denies its principles, if only the opponent will make some concession; but if he concedes nothing, it can have no dispute with him, although it can answer his objections. Hence Sacred Scripture, since it has no science above itself, can dispute with one who denies its principles, if the opponent admits some at least of the truths obtained through divine revelation; thus we can argue with heretics from texts in Holy Scripture, and against those who deny one article of faith, we can argue from another. But if the opponent believes nothing of divine revelation, there is no longer any means of proving the articles of faith by reasoning, but only of answering his objections – if he has any – against faith. However, since faith rests upon infallible truth, and since the contrary of a truth can never be demonstrated, it is clear that the arguments brought against faith cannot be demonstrations, but are difficulties that can be answered.

Reply to Objection 1: Although arguments from human reason cannot avail to prove what must be received on faith, nevertheless, this doctrine argues from articles of faith to other truths.

Reply to Objection 2: This doctrine especially draws on arguments from authority, inasmuch as its principles are obtained by revelation: thus we ought to acknowledge the authority of those to whom the revelation has been made. Nor does this take away from the dignity of this doctrine, for although the argument from authority based on human reason is the weakest, yet the argument from authority based on divine revelation is the strongest. But sacred doctrine makes use even of human reason, to be sure, not to prove faith (for that would take away the merit of faith), but to make clear other things that are put forward in this doctrine. Therefore, since grace does not destroy nature but perfects it, natural reason should assist faith, just as the natural inclination of the will serves charity. This is why St. Paul speaks of "bringing into captivity every understanding into the service of Christ."[42] And this is also why sacred doctrine uses even the authority of philosophers, insofar as they have been able to perceive the truth by natural reason – as when St. Paul quotes Aratus: "As

38 Boethius (c. 480–c. 524), *In Topicis Ciceronis* I. PL 64, 1166.
39 St Gregory the Great (c. 540–604), *In Evangelium* II, 26. PL 76, 1197.
40 Titus 1: 9.
41 1 Corinthians 15: 12.
42 2 Corinthians 10: 5.

some of your poets have said, we are God's offspring."[43] Nevertheless, sacred doctrine makes use of these authorities as providing extraneous and probable arguments. It uses the authority of the canonical Scriptures as its own when it argues with necessity, and it also properly uses the authority of other doctors of the Church, but then it argues only with probability. For our faith rests upon the revelation made to the apostles and prophets who wrote the canonical books, and not on the revelations (if any such there are) made to other doctors. Hence Augustine says: "Only those books of Scripture which are called canonical have I learned to hold in such honor as to believe their authors have not erred in any way in writing them. But other authors I so read as not to deem everything in their works to be true merely on account of their having so thought and written, no matter how saintly and learned they were."[44]

Article 9. Whether sacred doctrine should use metaphorical or figurative language?

Objection 1: It seems that sacred doctrine should not use metaphors. For that which is proper to the lowest discipline seems not to befit this doctrine, which holds the highest place of all, as I have already said. But to proceed by the aid of various similitudes and figures is proper to poetry, the lowest of all the disciplines. Therefore it is not fitting that this doctrine should make use of such similitudes.

Objection 2: Further, this doctrine seems to be intended to make truth clear. Hence a reward is held out to those who do so: "Those who explain me shall have everlasting life."[45] But by such similitudes truth is obscured. Therefore, it does not befit this science to teach divine things by likening them to corporeal things.

Objection 3: Further, the higher creatures are, the nearer they approach to the divine likeness. If therefore any creature is to be taken to represent God, this representation ought chiefly to be taken from the higher creatures, and not from the lower; yet this is often found in Scriptures.

On the contrary, Hosea writes, "I have multiplied visions, and I have used similitudes by the ministry of the prophets."[46] But to teach something by means of similitudes is to use metaphors. Therefore, sacred doctrine may use metaphors.

I answer that, Sacred Scripture fittingly teaches divine and spiritual truths by means of comparisons with material things. For God provides for everything according to the capacity of its nature. Now it is natural to man to attain to intellectual truths through sensible objects, because all our knowledge originates from the senses. Hence in Sacred Scripture, spiritual truths are fittingly taught under the likeness of material things. This is what Dionysius says: "The divine rays cannot enlighten us except wrapped up in many sacred veils."[47] Again, sacred Scripture is intended for all of us in common; as we read in *Romans*: "I am a debtor both to the learned and the ignorant".[48] So, Sacred Scripture fittingly teaches spiritual truths by means

---

43   Acts 17: 28. Aratus was a celebrated Hellenistic poet, who lived in the late fourth and early third centuries B.C., and was famous for his poem *Phaenomena*.

44   *Epistola* 82, 1. PL 33, 277.

45   Ecclesiastes 24: 31.

46   Hosea 12: 10.

47   *De caelesti hierarchia* I, 2. PG 3, 121.

48   Romans 1: 14.

of the imagery of corporeal things, so that even uneducated persons (who are unable to grasp intellectual truths in their own terms) may be able to understand them.

Reply to Objection 1: Poetry makes use of metaphors to produce a representation, for it is natural to man to be pleased with representations. But sacred doctrine makes use of metaphors because they are both necessary and useful, as I have just explained.

Reply to Objection 2: The ray of divine revelation is not extinguished by the sensible imagery by which it is veiled, as Dionysius says, and its truth remains, so that it does not allow the minds of those to whom the revelation has been made, to rest in the images, but raises them to the cognition truths; and through those to whom the revelation has been made others also may receive instruction in these matters. Hence those things that are taught metaphorically in one part of Scripture, in other parts are taught more explicitly. Indeed, the very hiding of truth in imagery is useful as a challenge for inquisitive minds and as a defense against the ridicule of the impious, in accordance with the words "Do not give what is holy to dogs."[49]

Reply to Objection 3: As Dionysius says, Sacred Scripture more fittingly teaches divine truths using the imagery of less noble than of nobler bodies, for three reasons.[50] In the first place, this provides better safeguards against error for the human mind. For it is clear that these things cannot apply literally to God, which might be open to doubt had they been expressed by using the imagery of nobler bodies, especially for those who could think of nothing nobler than bodies. In the second place, this way of talking is more befitting the knowledge that we have of God in this life. For it is clearer to us what He is not than what He is. Therefore, the similitudes drawn from things farthest away from God make us better appreciate how far God is above whatsoever we may say or think of Him. In the third place, divine matters are in this way better shrouded from the unworthy.

Article 10. Whether in Sacred Scripture a passage may have several senses?

Objection 1: It seems that in Sacred Scripture a passage cannot have several senses, namely, the historical or literal, allegorical, tropological or moral, and anagogical. For several different senses in one text produce confusion and deception and destroy all force of argument. Hence no argument, but only fallacies, can be drawn from propositions having several senses. But Sacred Scripture should effectively state the truth without any fallacy. Therefore the same passage in it should not have several senses.

Objection 2: Furthermore, Augustine says "we can divide the Scripture which we call the Old Testament into history, etiology, analogy, and allegory."[51] Now these four seem altogether different from the four divisions mentioned in the first objection. Therefore it does not seem fitting to explain the same passage of Sacred Scripture according to the four different senses mentioned above.

Objection 3: Furthermore, besides these senses, there is the parabolic sense, not included among the senses just listed.

---

49   Matthew 7: 6.
50   *De caelesti hierarchia* II, 2. PG 3, 136.
51   *De utilitate credendi* 3. PL 42, 68.

On the contrary, Gregory says that "sacred Scripture transcends all other sciences by its very style of expression, in that one and the same discourse, while narrating an event, also reveals a mystery."[52]

I answer that, The author of Sacred Scripture is God, in whose power it is to signify His meaning, not by words only (as man also can do), but also by things themselves. So, whereas in every other science things are signified by words, this science has the distinctive property that the things signified by the words in it also have a signification. Therefore that first signification whereby words signify things belongs to the first sense, the historical or literal. That signification whereby things signified by words also have a signification is called the spiritual sense, which is based on the literal, and presupposes it. Now this spiritual sense has a threefold division. For, as the Apostle says, "The Old Law is a figure of the New."[53] And, as Dionysius says, the New Law is itself "a figure of the glory to come."[54] Again, in the New Law, what our Head (Christ) has done is a sign of what we ought to do. Therefore, according to the allegorical sense, the things of the Old Law signify the things of the New Law. According to the moral sense, the things done by Christ or by those who prefigure Christ are the signs of what we ought to do. But according to the anagogical sense they signify what relates to eternal glory. However, since the literal sense is that which the author intends, and since the author of Sacred Scripture is God (who comprehends all at once by His understanding), it is not unfitting, as Augustine remarks, that even the literal sense of the same passage of Scripture conveys several meanings.[55]

Reply to Objection 1: The multiplicity of these senses does not produce equivocation or any other kind of multiplicity of meanings, given that these senses are not multiplied because one word signifies several things, but because the things signified by the words can themselves be the signs of other things. Thus no confusion results in Sacred Scripture, for all the senses are founded on one – the literal sense. An argument can be drawn only from this sense, and not, as Augustine remarks in his letter to Vincent the Donatist, from things said by allegory.[56] Nevertheless, nothing of Holy Scripture perishes on account of this, since nothing necessary for faith is contained under the spiritual sense that is not elsewhere put forward by the Scripture in its literal sense.

Reply to Objection 2: These three – history, etiology, analogy – are grouped under the literal sense. For as Augustine explains in the same place, we have history whenever something is simply related; we have etiology when its cause is assigned, as when Our Lord gave the reason why Moses allowed the putting away of wives – namely, on account of the hardness of men's hearts; and we have analogy whenever the truth of one text of Scripture is shown not to contradict the truth of another. Of the four senses listed in the objection, allegory alone stands for the three spiritual senses. Thus Hugh of St. Victor included the anagogical sense under the allegorical, and he enumerated just three senses – the historical, the allegorical, and the tropological.[57]

---

52 *Moralia* XX, 1. PL 76, 135.
53 Hebrews 7: 19.
54 *De ecclesiastica hierarchia* V, 2. PG 3, 501.
55 *Confessiones* XII, 31. PL 32, 844.
56 *Epistola* 93, 8. PL 33, 334.
57 Hugh of St Victor (d. 1142 AD), *De sacramentis* I, prol. 4. PL 176, 184.

Reply to Objection 3: The parabolical sense is contained under the literal, for words signify things strictly or figuratively. The literal sense is not the figure of speech itself, but what it stands for. When Scripture speaks of God's arm, the literal sense is not that God has such a physical limb, but only what is signified by such a limb, namely operative power. Hence it is plain that nothing false can ever underlie the literal sense of Sacred Scripture.

The Problem of Universals

4

Boethius Against Real Universals

[. . .]

10. But Porphyry remembered that he was writing an introduction, and he does not depart from the form of treatment which is the manner of instruction. He says in fact that *he abstains from the knots of the more lofty questions, but resolves the simple ones with ordinary interpretation.* Moreover he sets down what the more lofty questions are which he promises to put aside, thus:

> At present, he says, I shall refuse to say concerning genera and species whether they subsist or whether they are placed in the naked understandings alone or whether subsisting they are corporeal or incorporeal, and whether they are separated from sensibles or placed in sensibles and in accord with them. Questions of this sort are most exalted business and require very great diligence of inquiry.

I pass over, he says, the more lofty questions, lest by pouring them intemperately into the mind of the reader I disturb his beginnings and first efforts. But lest he should make the reader wholly negligent, and lest the reader think that nothing more is hidden than what he had said, he adds the very thing whose question he promised he would put off pursuing, that he might spread no confusion before the reader by treating of these things obscurely and completely, and yet that the reader, strengthened by knowledge, might recognize what could be inquired into rightly. The questions, however, concerning which he promises to be silent are extremely useful and secret and have been tried by wise men but have not been solved by many. The first of them is of this sort. The mind, whatever it understands, either conceives by understanding and describes to itself by reason that which is established in the nature of things, or else depicts to itself in vacant imagination that which is not. It is inquired therefore of which sort the understanding of genus and of the rest is: whether we understand species and genera as we understand things which are and from which we derive a true understanding, or whether we deceive ourselves, since we form for ourselves, by the empty cogitation of the mind, things which are not. But even if it should be established that they are, and if we should say that the understanding of them is conceived from things which are, then another greater, and more difficult question would occasion doubt, since the most grave difficulty is revealed in distinguishing and understanding the nature of genus itself. For since it is necessary that everything which is, be either corporeal or incorporeal, genus and species will have to be in one of these. Of what sort then will that which is called genus be, corporeal or incorporeal? Nor in fact can attention be turned seriously to what it is, unless it is known in which of these classes it must be placed. But even when this question has been solved, all ambiguity will not be avoided. For there remains something which, should genus and species be called incorporeal, besets the understanding and detains it, demanding that it be resolved, to wit, whether they subsist in bodies themselves, or whether they seem to be incorporeal subsistences beyond bodies. Of course, there are two forms of the incorporeal, so that some things can be outside bodies and perdure in their incorporeality separated from bodies, as God, mind, soul; but others, although they are incorporeal, nevertheless cannot be apart from bodies, as line, or surface, or number, or particular qualities, which, although we pronounce them to be incorporeal because they are not at all extended in three dimensions, nevertheless are in bodies in such fashion that they cannot be torn from them or separated, or if they have been separated from bodies, they in no manner continue to be. These questions although they are difficult, to the point that even Porphyry for the time refused to solve them, I shall nevertheless take up, that I may neither leave the mind of the reader uneasy, nor myself consume time and energy in these things which are outside the sequence of the task I have undertaken. First of all I shall state a few things concerning the ambiguity of the question, and then I shall attempt to remove and untie that knot of doubt.

Genera and species either are and subsist or are formed by the understanding and thought alone. But genera and species cannot be. This moreover is understood from the following considerations. For anything that is common at one time to many cannot be one; indeed, that which is common is of many, particularly when one and the same thing is completely in many things at one time. Howsoever many species indeed there are, there is one genus in them all, not that the individual species share, as it were, some part of it, but each of them has at one time the whole genus. It follows from this that the whole genus, placed at one time in many individuals, cannot be one; nor in fact can it happen that, since it is wholly in many at one time, it be one in number in itself. But if this is so, no genus can possibly be one, from which it follows that it is absolutely nothing; for everything which is, is because it is one. And the same thing may properly be said of species. Yet if there are genus and species, but they are multiplex and not one in number, there will be no last genus, but it will have some other genus superposed on it, which would include that multiplicity in the word of its single name. For as the genera of many animals are sought for the following reason, that they have something similar, yet are not the same, so too, since the genus, which is in many and is therefore multiplex, has the likeness of itself, which is the genus, but is not one, because it is in many, another genus of this genus must likewise be looked for, and when that has been found, for the reason which has been mentioned above, still a third genus is to be sought out. And so reason must proceed *in infinitum*, since no end of the process occurs. But if any genus is one in number, it cannot possibly be common to many. For a single thing, if it is common, is common by parts, and then it is not common as a whole, but the parts of it are proper to individual things, or else it passes at different times into the use of those having it, so that it is common as a servant or a horse is; or else it is made common to all at one time, not however that it constitute the substance of those to which it is common, but like some theatre or spectacle, which is common to all who look on. But genus can be common to the species according to none of these modes; for it must be common in such fashion that it is in the individuals wholly and at one time, and that it is able to constitute and form the substance of those things to which it is common. For this reason, if it is neither one, because it is common, nor many, because still another genus must be sought for that multitude, it will be seen that genus absolutely is not, and the same conclusion must be applied to the others. But if genera and species and the others are grasped only by understandings, since every idea is made either from the subject thing as the thing is constituted itself or as the thing is not constituted – for an idea cannot be made from no subject – if the idea of genus and species and the others comes from the subject thing as the thing itself is constituted which is understood, then they are not only placed in the understanding but are placed also in the truth of things. And again it must be sought out what their nature is which the previous question investigated. But if the idea of genus and the rest is taken from the thing not as the thing is constituted which is subject to the idea, the idea must necessarily be vain, which is taken from the thing but not as the thing is constituted; for that is false which is understood otherwise than the thing is. Thus, therefore, since genus and species neither are, nor, when they are understood, is the idea of them true, it is not uncertain that all this must be set forth relative to the care which is needed for investigating concerning the five predicables aforementioned, seeing that the inquiry is neither concerning the thing which is, nor concerning that of which something true can be understood or adduced.

11. This for the present is the question with regard to the aforementioned predicables, which we solve, in accord with Alexander, by the following reasoning. We say that it is not necessary that every idea which is formed from a subject but not as the subject itself is constituted, seem false and empty. For false opinion, but not understanding, is in only those ideas which are made by composition. For if any one composes and joins by the understanding that which nature does not suffer to be joined, no one is unaware that that is false, as would be the case should one join by the imagination horse and man and construct a centaur. But if it be done by division and by abstraction, the thing would not be constituted as the idea is, yet for all that, the idea is still not in the least false; for there are many things which have their being in others, from which either they cannot at all be separated, or if they should be separated they subsist by no reason. And in order that this be shown to us in a well known example, the line is something in a body, and it owes to the body that which it is, namely, it retains its being through body. Which is shown thus: if it should be separated from body, it does not subsist; for who ever perceived with any sense a line separated from body? But when the mind receives from the senses things confused and intermingled with each other, it distinguishes them by its own power and thought. For sense transmits to us, besides bodies themselves, all incorporeal things of this sort which have their being in bodies, but the mind which has the power to compound that which is disjoined and to resolve that which is composite, so distinguishes the things which are transmitted by the senses, confused with and joined to bodies, that it may contemplate and see the incorporeal nature in itself and without the bodies in which it is concrete. For the characteristics of incorporeal things mixed with bodies are diverse even when they are separated from body. Genera therefore and species and the others are found either in incorporeal things or in those which are corporeal. And if the mind finds them in incorporeal things, it has in that instance an incorporeal understanding of a genus, but if it has perceived the genera and species of corporeal things, it bears off, as is its wont, the nature of incorporeals from bodies, and beholds it alone and pure as the form itself is in itself. So when the mind receives these incorporeals intermixed with bodies, separating them, it looks upon them and contemplates them. No one,

therefore, may say that we think about the line falsely because we seize it by the mind as if it were outside bodies, since it cannot be outside bodies. For not every idea which is taken from subject things otherwise than the things are themselves constituted, must be considered to be false, but, as has been said above, that only is false which does this by composition, as when one thinks, joining man and horse, that there is a centaur; but that which accomplishes it by divisions, and abstractions, and assumptions from the things in which they are, not only is not false, but it alone can discover that which is true with respect to the characteristic of the thing. Things of this sort therefore are in corporeal and sensible things, but they are understood without sensible things, in order that their nature can be perceived and their characteristic comprehended. Since genera and species are thought, therefore their likeness is gathered from the individuals in which they are, as the likeness of humanity is gathered from individual men unlike each other, which likeness conceived by the mind and perceived truly is made the species; again when the likeness of these diverse species is considered, which cannot be except in the species themselves or in the individuals of the species, it forms the genus. Consequently, genera and species are in individuals, but they are thought universals; and species must be considered to be nothing other than the thought collected from the substantial likeness of individuals unlike in number, and genus the thought collected from the likeness of species. But this likeness when it is in individual things is made sensible, when it is in universals it is made intelligible; and in the same way when it is sensible, it remains in individuals, when it is understood, it is made universal. Therefore, they subsist in sensibles, but they are understood without bodies. For there is nothing to prevent two things which are in the same subject from being different in reason, like a concave and a convex line, which things, although they are defined by diverse definitions and although the understanding of them is diverse, are nevertheless always found in the same subject; for it is the same line which is convex and concave. So too for genera and species, that is, for singularity and universality, there is only one subject, but it is universal in one manner when it is thought, and singular in another when it is perceived in those things in which it has its being.

Once these distinctions are made, therefore, the whole question, I believe, is solved. For genera and species subsist in one manner, but are understood in another; and they are incorporeal, but they subsist in sensible things joined to sensible things. They are understood, to be sure, as subsisting through themselves and not as having their being in others. Plato, however, thinks that genera, and species, and the rest not only are understood as universals, but also are and subsist without bodies; whereas Aristotle thinks that they are understood as incorporeal and universal, but subsist in sensibles; we have not considered it proper to determine between their opinions, for that is of more lofty philosophy. But we have followed out the opinion of Aristotle very diligently for this reason, not in the least because we approved of it, but because this book has been written for the *Categories*, of which Aristotle is the author.

5

John of Salisbury on the Controversy over Universals

In what a pernicious manner logic is sometimes taught; and the ideas of moderns about [the nature of] genera and species.

To show off their knowledge, our contemporaries dispense their instruction in such a way that their listeners are at a loss to understand them. They seem to have the impression that every letter of the alphabet is pregnant with the secrets of Minerva. They analyze and press upon tender ears everything that anyone has ever said or done. Falling into the error condemned by Cicero, they frequently come to be unintelligible to their hearers more because of the multiplicity than the profundity of their statements. "It is indeed useful and advantageous for disputants," as Aristotle observes, "to take cognizance of several opinions on a topic." From the mutual disagreement thus brought into relief, what is seen to be poorly stated may be disproved or modified. Instruction in elementary logic does not, however, constitute the proper occasion for such procedure. Simplicity, brevity, and easy subject matter are, so far as is possible, appropriate in introductory studies. This is so true that it is permissible to expound many difficult points in a simpler way than their nature strictly requires. Thus, much that we have learned in our youth must later be amended in more advanced philosophical studies. Nevertheless, at present, all are here [in introductory logical studies] declaiming on the nature of universals, and attempting to explain, contrary to the intention of the author, what is really a most profound question, and a matter [that should be reserved] for more advanced studies. One holds that universals are merely word sounds, although this opinion, along with its author Roscelin, has already almost completely passed into oblivion. Another maintains that universals are word concepts, and twists to support his thesis everything that he can remember to have ever been written on the subject. Our Peripatetic of Pallet, Abelard, was ensnared in this opinion. He left many, and still has, to this day, some followers and proponents of his doctrine. They are friends of mine, although they often so torture the helpless letter that even the hardest heart is filled with compassion for the latter. They hold that it is preposterous to predicate a thing concerning a thing, although Aristotle is author of this monstrosity. For Aristotle frequently asserts that a thing is predicated concerning a thing, as is evident to anyone who is really familiar with his teaching. Another is wrapped up in a consideration of acts of the [intuitive] understanding, and says that genera and species are nothing more than the latter. Proponents of this view take their cue from Cicero and Boethius, who cite Aristotle as saying that universals should be regarded as and called "notions." "A notion," they tell us, "is the cognition of something, derived from its previously perceived form, and in need of unravelment." Or again [they say]: "A notion is an act of the [intuitive] understanding, a simple mental comprehension." They accordingly distort everything written, with an eye to making acts of [intuitive] understanding or "notions" include the universality of universals. Those who adhere to the view that universals are things, have various and sundry opinions. One, reasoning from the fact that everything which exists is singular in number, concludes that either the universal is numerically one, or it is non-existent. But since it is impossible for things that are substantial to be non-existent, if those things for which they are substantial exist, they further conclude that universals must be essentially one with particular things. Accordingly, following Walter of Mortagne, they distinguish [various] states [of existence], and say that Plato is an individual in so far as he is Plato; a species in so far as he is a man; a genus of a subaltern [subordinate] kind in so far as he is an animal; and a most general genus in so far as he is a substance. Although this opinion formerly had some proponents, it has been a long time since anyone has asserted it. Walter now upholds [the doctrine of] ideas, emulating Plato and imitating Bernard of Chartres, and maintains that genus and species are nothing more nor less than these, namely, ideas. "An idea," according to Seneca's definition, "is an eternal exemplar of those things which come to be as a result of nature." And since universals are not subject to corruption, and are not altered by the changes that transform particular things and cause them to come and go, succeeding one another almost momentarily, ideas are properly and correctly called "universals." Indeed, particular things are deemed incapable of supporting the substantive verb, [i.e., of being said "to be"], since they are not at all stable, and disappear without even waiting to receive names. For they vary so much in their qualities, time, location, and numerous different properties, that their whole existence seems to be more a mutable transition than a stable status. In contrast, Boethius declares: "We say that things 'are' when they may neither be increased nor diminished, but always continue as they are, firmly sustained by the foundations of their own nature." These [foundations] include their quantities, qualities, relations, places, times, conditions, and whatever is found in a way united with bodies. Although these adjuncts of bodies may seem to be changed, they remain immutable in their own nature. In like manner, although individuals [of species] may change, species remain the same. The waves of a stream wash on, yet the same flow of water continues, and we refer to the stream as the same river. Whence the statement of Seneca, which, in fact, he has borrowed from another: "In one sense it is true that we may descend twice into the same river, although in another sense this is not so." These "ideas," or "exemplary forms," are the original plans of all things. They may neither be decreased nor augmented: and they are so permanent and perpetual, that even if the whole world were to come to an end, they could not perish. They include all things, and, as Augustine seems to maintain in his book *On Free Will*, their number neither increases nor diminishes, because the ideas always continue on, even when it happens that [particular] temporal things cease to exist. What these men promise is wonderful, and familiar to philosophers who rise to the contemplation of higher things. But, as Boethius and numerous other authors testify, it is utterly foreign to the mind of Aristotle. For Aristotle very frequently opposes this view, as is clear from his books. Bernard of Chartres and his followers labored strenuously to compose the differences between Aristotle and Plato. But I opine that they arrived on the scene too late, so that their efforts to reconcile two dead men, who disagreed as long as they were alive and could do so, were in vain. Still another, in his endeavor to explain Aristotle, places universality in "native forms," as does Gilbert, Bishop of Poitiers, who labors, to prove that "native forms" and universals are identical. A "native form" is an example of an original [exemplar]. It [the native form, unlike the original] inheres in created things, instead of subsisting in the divine mind. In Greek it is called the *idos*, since it stands in relation to the idea as the example does to its exemplar. The native form is sensible in things that are perceptible by the senses; but insensible as conceived in the mind. It is singular in individuals, but universal in all [of a kind]. Another, with Joscelin, Bishop of Soissons, attributes universality to collections of things, while denying it to things as individuals. When Joscelin tries to explain the authorities, he has his troubles and is hard put, for in many places he cannot bear the gaping astonishment of the indignant letter. Still another takes refuge in a new tongue, since he does not have sufficient command of Latin. When he hears the words "genus" and "species," at one time he says they should be understood as universals, and at another that they refer to the *maneries* of things. I know not in which of the authors he has found this term or this distinction, unless perhaps he has dug it out of lists of abstruse and obsolete words, or it is an item of jargon [in the baggage] of present-day doctors. I am further at a loss to see what it can mean here, unless it refers to collections of things, which would be the same as Joscelin's view, or to a universal thing, which, however, could hardly be called a *maneries*. For a *maneries* may be interpreted as referring to both [collections and universals], since a number of things, or the status in which a thing of such and such a type continues to exist may be called a *maneries*. Finally, there are some who fix their attention on the status of things, and say that genera and species consist in the latter.

6

The *Summa Lamberti* on the Properties of Terms

[1. General Introduction]

(205) Because the logician considers terms, it is appropriate for him to give an account of the term itself and its properties, for the person who is to consider something as a subject must consider its properties also. [. . .] because *signification* is, as it were, the fulfillment of a term, and the properties of terms are founded on signification, for the sake of clarity in what follows we must at the outset consider what the *signification* of a term is, and how it differs from *supposition*.

[2. Signification]

[2a. Definition of signification]

The signification of a term is the concept of a thing, a concept on which an utterance is imposed by the will of the person instituting the term. For, as Aristotle maintains in the first book of *De interpretatione* [*On Interpretation*] (16a3–5), utterances are signs of states in the soul – i.e., in the understanding – but concepts are the signs of things.

[2b. Explanation of the definition]

In order to understand this, it is essential to know that four things are required for an utterance to be significant: a thing, a concept [or some understanding, *intellectus*] of the thing, an utterance, and the union of the utterance with the concept of the thing. What we are calling the thing is something existing outside the soul, which is apprehended by the soul by means of an idea of it – e.g., a man, or a stone. What we call the concept of the thing is the idea [*species*] or likeness of the thing, which exists in the soul; for according to Aristotle in the third book of *De anima* (III, 8, 431b30–432a1), not the stone but rather an appearance [*species*] of the stone is in the soul; and it is by means of the appearance that the soul grasps the thing. The utterance is that which is put forward along with the concept [or understanding] of the thing; in that case [i.e., when the utterance is made with some understanding of a thing] a signification is united to the utterance and the utterance is made significant.[1] And although both the concept of the thing and the utterance are natural in the same way (since they are formed by natural sources), the utterance is nevertheless said to signify by the will of the person instituting it, because the union of the concept of the thing with the utterance is effected by the will, and it is in that [action] that the imposition of the utterance consists.[2]

In this way, therefore, an utterance is primarily – in itself – and directly the sign of a concept of the thing; but in addition it is indirectly the sign of the thing. For just as we say that whatever is a cause of the cause is a cause of the thing caused, so we can say that in its own way whatever is a sign of the sign is a sign of the thing signified. Thus, since an utterance is a sign of a concept, and a concept is a sign of a thing, in this way [the utterance] is a sign of the thing as well. An utterance that is a sign of a sign – of the concept – will be a sign of the signified – i.e., of the thing; it is, however, a sign of the concept directly but a sign of the thing indirectly.[3]

[2c. The difference between signification and supposition]

Now signification differs from supposition in that signification is prior to supposition. For the signification is the concept of the thing represented by means of the utterance, and before the union of it with the utterance there is no term; rather, a term is constituted in the union of that concept of a thing with an utterance. Supposition, on the other hand, is a certain property of a term that has been constituted in that way.

There is another difference, because signification extends only to the thing the term is imposed to signify; supposition, however, extends not only to the thing signified by means of the term but can extend to supposita contained under that thing. For example, the signification of 'man' extends only to *man*, not to the things contained under *man*; for 'man' signifies *man*, not Socrates and not Plato. 'Man' can, nevertheless, supposit for Socrates, and for Plato, and for *man*.[4]

---

1   The point here simply is that a meaningful utterance, such as 'man' or 'stone' in English, is different from some meaningless articulate sound, such as 'biltrix' (Boethius' classic example of a meaningless utterance), precisely on account of the fact that the former is uttered with some understanding that it is supposed to convey, whereas the latter is not.

2   That is to say, although both the utterance and the concept are natural things (the utterance is some sound produced by speech organs and the concept is an act of understanding of the mind), it is only the concept that represents the thing conceived by it naturally, the utterance signifies it only on account of being related to the concept by convention, as a result of voluntarily imposing the name on the thing conceived by the concept.

3   This is a classic statement of the Aristotelian "semantic triangle": words signify things, but they do so only through the mediation of concepts, for they only signify the things that are represented by the concepts they directly signify.

4   Clearly, *man* here, as opposed to the individual humans, such as Socrates or Plato, is the universal nature signified by the term 'man' and represented by the concept that his term directly signifies. So, the signification (or meaning) of this term extends only to this universal nature, the direct object of the concept of humans, although, on account of this signification, it can be used in a sentence to stand for the individual humans who have this nature. The function of the term of standing for these individuals in a sentence is its property that is called "supposition" (which is why this property is often compared to the modern notion of reference, as it is contrasted with meaning).

[3. Supposition]

[3a. On 'supposition']

Next, as regards supposition. [. . .]⁵ Supposition is said to be the acceptance of a term for itself, for its [signified] thing, for some suppositum contained under its [signified] thing, or for more than one suppositum contained under its [signified] thing.

[3b. Broad and Strict Supposition]

It is important to know, however, that the supposition meant here is talked about in two ways: broadly and strictly. Supposition broadly speaking is, as has already been said, the acceptance of a term for itself, or for its [signified] thing (as when one says 'Man is a species,' 'White dazzles'), or the acceptance of a term for some suppositum or for supposita belonging to its [signified] thing (as when one says 'A man is running,' 'A white thing is running'). For when one says 'Man is a species,' [the term] 'man' is taken for itself or for its [signified] thing, and not for any suppositum; whereas if one says 'A man is running,' it is taken for a suppositum. Likewise, when one says 'White dazzles,' then [the term] 'white' is taken here for itself or for its [signified] thing; for that predicate applies to white not by reason of a suppositum but by reason of its form. When, however, one says 'A white thing is running,' it is taken for a suppositum.

Supposition broadly speaking is divided into supposition strictly speaking and copulation. For broadly speaking both substantival and adjectival terms supposit; strictly speaking, however, supposition is attached to substantival terms and copulation to adjectival terms.

Supposition strictly speaking is the acceptance of a term representing a thing that is stable and stands on its own, an acceptance in accordance with which the term can be taken for its [signified] thing or⁶ for a suppositum or any supposita contained under its [signified] thing.

[3c. Copulation]

Copulation is the acceptance of a term representing a dependent thing, an acceptance in accordance with which it can be taken for its [signified] thing or⁷ for a suppositum or supposita contained under its [signified] thing. [. . .]

[3d. Syncategorematic words]⁸

Some words, such as syncategorematic words, neither supposit nor copulate.

5   In the omitted passage, the author distinguishes four different senses of the term 'suppositio' as it was used in contemporary grammar and logic. Since the other three senses he dismisses as irrelevant, it is only his description of the fourth sense that is provided here.
6   The Latin text contains 'non' here, which is correctly rendered by Norman Kretzmann's translation as 'not'. However, for doctrinal reasons, a 'vel', that is, 'or' is more fitting here. For the text as it stands would *exclude* the possibility of a substantive standing for its individual *supposita*, which is certainly not what the author means. Also, the correction seems to be quite justified by the parallel construction of the immediately following paragraph, which is characteristic of this type of texts.
7   This is the clear parallel of the construction of the previous passage.
8   Such are words that taken in their proper significative function cannot be subjects or predicates of sentences, but rather have the function of affecting the semantic functions of subjects and predicates or other units of speech, such as 'not', 'or', 'and', 'every', 'to', 'for', etc.

[3e. Signification and property of a term]

From the things already said it is clear that supposition is both the signification of a term and a property of a term, and copulation likewise. Nevertheless, 'supposition' is taken differently (om. *supponitur vel*) depending on whether it is the signification of a term or a property of a term, and so is copulation, as we have seen. And our concern here is with the supposition and copulation that are properties of terms, not insofar as they are the significations of terms.[9]

[3f. Supposition and substantives, copulation and adjectives]

Again, if anyone asks why supposition is appropriate to substantives and copulation to adjectives, it is clear from the things that have been said what we must say. For suppositing belongs to what stands on its own and to what represents its stable [signified] thing, but to stand on its own and to represent its stable [signified] thing is a property of substantives. Copulating, on the other hand, belongs to what adjoins [something else] and to what represents a dependent thing, but to adjoin and to represent a dependent thing is a property of adjectives. Therefore, speaking strictly, supposition belongs to substantives, but copulation to adjectives.

[3g. Divisions of supposition]

[3g(i). Natural and accidental]

Supposition is divided first in this way: One sort of supposition is natural, the other accidental.

Natural supposition is what a term has on its own and by its nature. A term is said to have this sort of supposition when it is used by itself – i.e., when it is not joined to any other. But a term having that sort of supposition supposits not only for the things that share its form, but instead for all the things that share, [have shared, and will share] its form – i.e., for present, past, and future things [of that form]. And this supposition is called natural because it is not an extrinsic but an intrinsic propensity; for whatever has an internal source is natural.[10]

Accidental supposition is what a term has from what is adjoined to it, and a term supposits in this supposition in keeping with the requirement of that to which it is adjoined. For if someone says 'A man exists,' ['man'] supposits for present things because it is adjoined to a present-tense verb; if someone says 'A man existed,' for past things; if someone says 'A man will exist,' for future things. And this supposition is called accidental because it inheres in a term extrinsically; for what inheres extrinsically in something is accidental to it.

---

9   In this passage, the author relates the difference between supposition and copulation as they are the properties of terms to the difference between substantival and adjectival signification (i.e., the kind of signification whereby substances are signified and the kind of signification whereby accidents are signified) distinguished in a previously omitted passage.

10   Note that this remark is not in conflict with the conventionality of the signification of an utterance: for a term is conventionally constituted from an utterance and its relation to a naturally representative concept. Once the conventional connection between utterance and concept is established, however, the term constituted by this connection naturally has the ability to stand for whatever is naturally represented by the concept.

[3g(ii). Simple and personal]

One sort of accidental supposition is simple, the other personal.

Simple supposition is the kind according to which a term is taken for itself or for its [signified] thing, without relation to the supposita contained under it. The supposition that is in the term by reason of its form is called simple; and it is because form is of itself simple and indivisible that the supposition that is in a term as a result of form is called simple. [. . .]

It should be noted, however, that [a term's] having no relation to the supposita can occur either in such a way that there is no sort of relation to them, neither determinately nor indeterminately, or in such a way that there is a relation to them, not determinately, but indeterminately. It is on that basis that one can say that there is a certain sort of simple supposition in which the term is in no way related to the supposita but is interpreted only for its [signified] form. The term 'man' has this sort of supposition when one says '*Man* is a species,' and this is simple supposition speaking strictly. But there is another simple supposition in which a common term is not related to the supposita determinately and yet has a relation to them indeterminately. The term 'man' has this sort of supposition when one says 'I know there is a man in England'; similarly, the term 'pepper' when one says 'Pepper is sold here and in Rome.' This, however, is called simple supposition less strictly than the first sort.[11]

Personal supposition is [the sort] according to which a term is interpreted for a suppositum or for supposita. It is called personal for the following reason, however: in the case of rational substance a suppositum or individual is the same as a person. For Boethius (*Against Eutyches and Nestorius*) defines person in this way: a person is an individual substance belonging to rational nature; for an individual in the case of rational substance is a person. And because in the case of other things individuals are picked out in accordance with an analogy drawn from rational things, the supposition in which a term is interpreted for supposita or individuals is called personal – not because all individuals are persons (for only individuals that have to do with rational substance are persons, certainly not other sorts of individuals); but all individuals either are persons or are picked out by analogy with those that are persons.

11   In these sentences, the terms in question apparently cannot be taken to stand for the individuals falling under them. For no singular man is a species, and it may not be true of this man that I know him to be in England, and it is not true of that man, etc., listing all singulars (if I know nobody in England), and it is not true of any single pepper that it is sold both here and in Rome. At any rate, these were classic examples that realist logicians took to illustrate the cases when terms are taken to stand not for singulars but for universals. Nominalists, on the other hand, provided different interpretations for these sentences. In the first place, they would claim that the term 'species' applies to singular acts of understanding representing several singular things indifferently. Likewise, they claimed that even if it is not true of this man that I know him to be in England, and it is not true of that man that I know him to be in England, and so on for all singular men, it is still true that I know this man or that man or that man, etc. to be in England, where there is no need to refer to a universal. Again, they would say that although it is not true of a single pepper that it is sold both here and in Rome, it may be true that some pepper is sold here and some pepper is sold in Rome, and this is the sense of the sentence, without reference to any sort of universal entity. In brief, the nominalists following Ockham interpreted cases of simple supposition in the strict sense as reference to concepts (understood as singular acts of understanding), and they treated the "less strict" cases of simple supposition presented here and elsewhere in realist logic as analyzable in terms of personal supposition, eliminating the apparent reference to universals. This strategy of "elimination by paraphrase" is also the "weapon of choice" of the nominalists of 20th-century philosophy (for example, Goodman, Quine), when they seek to eliminate unwanted reference to "abstract entities." But these 20th-century developments are historically unrelated to the similar medieval developments.

7

William Ockham on Universals

Ockham's First Theory: A Universal is a *Fictum*

One can plausibly say that a universal is not a real thing inherent in a subject [*habens esse subiectivum*], whether in the soul or outside the soul, but it exists only as an object of the soul [*habet esse obiectivum in anima*].[1] And it is a sort of mental image [*fictum*] that in its existence as an object of the soul [*in esse obiectivo*] is like an external thing in its real existence [*in esse subiectivo*]. And I mean this in the following sense: The intellect seeing some thing outside the soul makes up a similar one in the mind in such a way that if it had the power to make it just as it has the power to make it up, then it would produce a thing in real existence that is numerically distinct from the first one; and this would be analogous to the activity of a craftsman. For similarly to the case of a builder who, upon seeing a house or a building outside, makes up a similar one in his soul, and later builds a similar one outside that is only numerically different from the first, in the case under consideration, the figment [*fictum*] in the mind taken from the sight of the external thing would serve as a certain exemplar [a "blueprint"]; for in this way, just as the house imagined is an exemplar for the builder, so that figment would be an exemplar for the person who forms it, if he had the power to

This selection, coming from Ockham's early (and unfinished) *Commentary on the Sentences* (*Ordinatio*, d. 2, q. 8, pp. 271–4), presents Ockham's first theory of universals, which he later abandoned, convinced by the arguments of his confrere, Walter Chatton, that it is needless to posit such dubious entities to explain universal cognition.

1 The distinction is between having something in mind, as an object of the mind, i.e., as that which we are thinking of and which may not exist in reality at all, on the one hand, and the existence of a really existing thing, especially a form that really inheres in a subject, whether it is being thought of or not, on the other. The former kind of object is said to have a mere objective existence [*esse obiectivum*], while the latter kind of things are said to have real existence in a subject of inherence, or subjective existence [*esse subiectivum*]. This distinction, which is quite the reverse of the contemporary colloquial understanding of the contrast between 'objective' [mind-independent, real] and 'subjective' [mind-dependent, unreal, arbitrary] was quite commonly made already in the second half of the 13th century, and it still influenced Descartes' distinction between the mere objective reality and the formal or subjective reality of ideas.

produce it in reality. And it can be called a universal, for it is an exemplar and it relates indifferently to all external singulars. And because of this similarity in its existence as an object [of the intellect] [*in esse obiectivo*], it can refer to [*supponere pro*] the things that have a similar existence outside the intellect. And so in this way a universal does not come to be by generation, but by abstraction, which is nothing but a sort of imagination [*fictio*].

I first show that there is something that has this mere objective existence [*esse obiectivum*] in the soul, without any real existence [*esse subiectivum*].

This is clear first from the following: According to philosophers, being [*ens*] is first divided into being in the soul and being outside the soul; and beings outside the soul are sorted into the ten categories. And then I ask: How is 'being in the soul' to be taken here? It is either taken for something that has mere objective existence (and then we have what we wanted to prove) or for something that has real existence [*esse subiectivum*], but this is not possible. For something that has real existence inhering in the soul as its subject is contained precisely among the beings sorted into the ten categories, because it is some quality, since a thought and universally all accidents informing the soul are true qualities, just as are heat or whiteness, and thus these [accidents] are not contained under that member of the division that is divided against the beings that are sorted into the ten categories.[2]

Again, figments [*figmenta*] are in the soul, and not subjectively, for then they would be real things, and so a chimera or a goat-stag and the like would be real things; therefore, there are things that have mere objective existence.

Likewise, propositions, syllogisms and the similar items that logic is about do not have subjective existence; therefore, they only have objective existence, so that for them to be is for them to be cognized. Therefore, there are such things that have only objective existence.

Likewise, artifacts do not seem to have subjective existence in the mind of the craftsman, as neither do creatures in the divine mind before the creation.

Likewise, relations of reason[3] are commonly admitted by professors. Then I ask: Do these relations only have subjective existence? – If so, then they are genuine and real things [which is impossible]; or do they have mere objective existence? – If so, then we have what we wanted to prove.

[. . .]

2   So, the inherent qualities of the soul are to be understood as being among those entities that are sorted into the ten categories, but those are precisely the things that are classified as beings outside the soul, as opposed to beings in the soul. Therefore, the beings in the soul in the sense of this phrase required by the first division are not the inherent qualities of the soul, but the mere thought-objects of the soul, its *ficta*.

3   Relations of reason are relations that pertain to a thing only on account of some act of the mind and do not have real inherence in the thing, so their coming to be or ceasing to be in the thing does not amount to a real change in the thing. For example, Socrates's relational property of being admired by Plato is a relation of reason, because it pertains to him only on account of Plato's mental act of admiring him. And of course Socrates's coming to be admired by a modern day student does not amount to a real change in Socrates, for only an actually existing thing can undergo real change, and Socrates, being dead, does not actually exist. For more on relations of reason, and beings of reason in general in Aquinas and Ockham, see G. Klima, "The Changing Role of *Entia Rationis* in Medieval Philosophy: A Comparative Study with a Reconstruction", *Synthese* 96 (1993), pp. 25–59.

Likewise, virtually everybody distinguishes second intentions from first intentions, while not calling second intentions real qualities of the soul; therefore, since they [the second intentions] cannot really exist outside the soul, they can only exist objectively in the soul.

In the second place, I say that this mental image [*fictum*] is that which is primarily and immediately denominated by the intention of universality, has the nature of an object, and it is that which immediately terminates an act of understanding when no singular is understood, and which is such in objective existence as the singular is in subjective existence; this is why it can, on account of its nature, supposit for the singulars of which it is a sort of similitude.

And I say that just as an utterance is a universal and a genus or a species, but only by convention, so a concept thus formed [*conceptus sic fictus*] and abstracted from the singular things cognized earlier is a universal by its own nature.

Ockham's Later Theory: A Universal Is an Act of Understanding[4]

Another opinion could be that a 'passion of the soul' [that Aristotle is talking about][5] is the act of understanding itself. And since this opinion seems to me to be more probable than all the other opinions that take these passions of the soul to be subjectively inhering and really existing in the soul as its true qualities, therefore, I first explain the most plausible way of interpreting this opinion. [. . .]

I say, therefore, that someone who wants to hold this opinion can assume that the intellect apprehending a singular thing elicits in itself an act of cognition about only that singular thing, which is called a passion of the soul, and which, on account of its own nature, is capable of referring to [*supponere pro*] that singular thing. So, as the utterance 'Socrates' refers to the thing it signifies by convention, in such a manner that someone hearing the utterance 'Socrates runs' will not think that the utterance he hears, namely, 'Socrates', is running, but that the thing signified by that utterance is running, in the same way, he who would see or understand something affirmed about that singular intellection of that singular thing, would not understand that affirmation to apply to that intellection, but to the thing itself that the intellection is about; in this way, just as the utterance refers to that thing by convention, so the intellection would, by its own nature, without any convention, refer to the thing it is about.

But besides this intellection of that singular thing the intellect forms other intellections as well, which are no more about this thing than about another, just as the utterance 'man' signifies Socrates, but no more than it does Plato, and so it refers to Socrates, but no more than it does to Plato, and the same would go for this intellection, namely, that Socrates is no more understood by it than is Plato, and so on for all other men. And thus there would also be another intellection, by which this animal would be understood, but not more than that animal, and so on for the rest.

---

4   This is the opinion Ockham eventually settled on, abandoning his earlier *ficta* as being superfluous, and therefore eliminable by his Razor, the famous methodological principle according to which in the explanation of certain phenomena that theory is preferable which assumes the existence of fewer entities. This selection comes from Ockham's *Commentary on Aristotle's "On Interpretation"* (Per Hermeneias), bk. 1, proem., para. 6, pp. 351–2).

5   The phrase 'passion of the soul' derives from Aristotle's remark in his *On Interpretation*, expressing his idea of the "semantic triangle" (often referred to as such in the secondary literature) according to which meaningful words signify the passions of the soul (where 'passion' is to be taken in the broad sense of some sort of affection) and by their mediation the extramental things.

In short, it is the intellections of the soul themselves that are called the passions of the soul, and they refer by their own nature to things outside the soul or to other things in the soul, just as utterances refer to things by convention.

＊　＊　＊

On Universals: *Summa Logicae*, Part I

Chapter 14: On the universal

It is not enough for the logician to have a merely general knowledge of terms; he needs a deep understanding of the concept of a term. Therefore, after discussing some general divisions among terms we should examine in detail the various headings under these divisions.

First, we should deal with terms of second intention and afterwards with terms of first intention. I have said that "universal," "genus," and "species" are examples of terms of second intention. We must discuss those terms of second intention which are called the five universals, but first we should consider the common term "universal." It is predicated of every universal and is opposed to the notion of a particular.

First, it should be noted that the term "particular" has two senses. In the first sense a particular is that which is one and not many. Those who hold that a universal is a certain quality residing in the mind which is predicable of many (not suppositing for itself, of course, but for the many of which it is predicated) must grant that, in this sense of the word, every universal is a particular. Just as a word, even if convention makes it common, is a particular, the intention of the soul signifying many is numerically one thing a particular; for although it signifies many things it is nonetheless one thing and not many.

In another sense of the word we use "particular" to mean that which is one and not many and which cannot function as a sign of many. Taking "particular" in this sense no universal is a particular, since every universal is capable of signifying many and of being predicated of many. Thus, if we take the term "universal" to mean that which is not one in number, as many do, then, I want to say that nothing is a universal. One could, of course, abuse the expression and say that a population constitutes a single universal because it is not one but many. But that would be puerile.

Therefore, it ought to be said that every universal is one particular thing and that it is not a universal except in its signification, in its signifying many things. This is what Avicenna means to say in his commentary on the fifth book of the *Metaphysics*. He says, "One form in the intellect is related to many things, and in this respect it is a universal; for it is an intention of the intellect which has an invariant relationship to anything you choose." He then continues, "Although this form is a universal in its relationship to individuals, it is a particular in its relationship to the particular soul in which it resides; for it is just one form among many in the intellect." He means to say that a universal is an intention of a particular soul. Insofar as it can be predicated of many things not for itself but for these many, it is said to be a universal; but insofar as it is a particular form actually existing in the intellect, it is said to be a particular. Thus "particular" is predicated of a universal in the first sense but not in the second. In the same way we say that the sun is a universal cause and, nevertheless, that it is really and truly a particular or individual cause. For the sun is said to be a universal cause because it is the cause of many things (i.e., every object that is generable and corruptible), but it is said to be a particular cause because it is one cause and not many. In the same way the intention of the soul is said to be a universal because it is a sign predicable of many things, but it is said to be a particular because it is one thing and not many.

But it should be noted that there are two kinds of universals. Some things are universal by nature; that is, by nature they are signs predicable of many in the same way that the smoke is by nature a sign of fire; weeping, a sign of grief; and laughter, a sign of internal joy. The intention of the soul, of course, is a universal by nature. Thus, no substance outside the soul, nor any accident outside the soul is a universal of this sort. It is of this kind of universal that I shall speak in the following chapters.

Other things are universals by convention. Thus, a spoken word, which is numerically one quality, is a universal; it is a sign conventionally appointed for the signification of many things. Thus, since the word is said to be common, it can be called a universal. But notice it is not by nature, but only by convention, that this label applies.

Chapter 15: That the universal is not a thing outside the mind

But it is not enough just to state one's position; one must defend it by philosophical arguments. Therefore, I shall set forth some arguments for my view, and then corroborate it by an appeal to the authorities.

That no universal is a substance existing outside the mind can be proved in a number of ways:

No universal is a particular substance, numerically one; for if this were the case, then it would follow that Socrates is a universal; for there is no good reason why one substance should be a universal rather than another. Therefore no particular substance is a universal; every substance is numerically one and a particular. For every substance is either one thing and not many or it is many things. Now, if a substance is one thing and not many, then it is numerically one; for that is what we mean by "numerically one." But if, on the other hand, some substance is several things, it is either several particular things or several universal things. If the first alternative is chosen, then it follows that some substance would be several particular substances; and consequently that some substance would be several men. But although the universal would be distinguished from a single particular, it would not be distinguished from several particulars. If, however, some substance were to be several universal entities, I take one of those universal entities and ask, "Is it many things or is it one and not many?" If the second is the case then it follows that the thing is particular. If the first is the case then I ask, "Is it several particular things or several universal things?" Thus, either an infinite regress will follow or it will be granted that no substance is a universal in a way that would be incompatible with its also being a particular. From this it follows that no substance is a universal.

Again, if some universal were to be one substance existing in particular substances, yet distinct from them, it would follow that it could exist without them; for everything that is naturally prior to something else can, by God's power, exist without that thing; but the consequence is absurd.

Again, if the view in question were true, no individual would be able to be created. Something of the individual would pre-exist it, for the whole individual would not take its existence from nothing if the universal which is in it were already in something else. For the same reason it would follow that God could not annihilate an individual substance without destroying the other individuals of the same kind. If He were to annihilate some individual, he would destroy the whole which is essentially that individual and, consequently, He would destroy the universal which is in that thing and in others of the same essence. Consequently, other things of the same essence would not remain, for they could not continue to exist without the universal which constitutes a part of them.

Again, such a universal could not be construed as something completely extrinsic to the essence of an individual; therefore, it would belong to the essence of the individual; and, consequently, an individual would be composed of universals, so that the individual would not be any more a particular than a universal.

Again, it follows that something of the essence of Christ would be miserable and damned, since that common nature really existing in Christ would be damned in the damned individual; for surely that essence is also in Judas. But this is absurd.

Many other arguments could be brought forth, but in the interests of brevity, I shall dispense with them. Instead, I shall corroborate my account by an appeal to authorities.

First, in the seventh book of the *Metaphysics*, Aristotle is treating the question of whether a universal is a substance. He shows that no universal is a substance. Thus, he says, "It is impossible that substance be something that can be predicated universally."

Again, in the tenth book of the *Metaphysics*, he says, "Thus, if, as we argued in the discussions on substance and being, no universal can be a substance, it is not possible that a universal be a substance in the sense of a one over and against the many."

From these remarks it is clear that, in Aristotle's view, although universals can supposit for substances, no universal is a substance.

Again, the Commentator in his forty-fourth comment on the seventh book of the *Metaphysics* says, "In the individual, the only substance is the particular form and matter out of which the individual is composed."

Again, in the forty-fifth comment, he says, "Let us say, therefore, that it is impossible that one of those things we call universals be the substance of anything, although they do express the substances of things."

And, again, in the forty-seventh comment, "It is impossible that they (universals) be parts of substances existing of and by themselves."

Again, in the second comment on the eighth book of the *Metaphysics*, he says, "No universal is either a substance or a genus."

Again, in the sixth comment on the tenth book, he says, "Since universals are not substances, it is clear that the common notion of being is not a substance existing outside the mind."

Using these and many other authorities, the general point emerges: no universal is a substance regardless of the viewpoint from which we consider the matter. Thus, the viewpoint from which we consider the matter is irrelevant to the question of whether something is a substance. Nevertheless, the meaning of a term is relevant to the question of whether the expression "substance" can be predicated of the term. Thus, if the term "dog" in the proposition "The dog is an animal" is used to stand for the barking animal, the proposition is true; but if it is used for the celestial body which goes by that name, the proposition is false. But it is impossible that one and the same thing should be a substance from one viewpoint and not a substance from another.

Therefore, it ought to be granted that no universal is a substance regardless of how it is considered. On the contrary, every universal is an intention of the mind which, on the most probable account, is identical with the act of understanding. Thus, it is said that the act of understanding by which I grasp men is a natural sign of men in the same way that weeping is a natural sign of grief. It is a natural sign such that it can stand for men in mental propositions in the same way that a spoken word can stand for things in spoken propositions.

That the universal is an intention of the soul is clearly expressed by Avicenna in the fifth book of the *Metaphysics*, in which he comments, "I say, therefore, that there are three senses of 'universal.' For we say that something is a universal if (like 'man') it is actually predicated of many things; and we also call an intention a universal if it could be predicated of many." Then follows the remark, "An intention is also called a universal if there is nothing inconceivable in its being predicated of many."

From these remarks it is clear that the universal is an intention of the soul capable of being predicated of many. The claim can be corroborated by argument. For every one agrees that a universal is something predicable of many, but only an intention of the soul or a conventional sign is predicated. No substance is ever predicated of anything. Therefore, only an intention of the soul or a conventional sign is a universal; but I am not here using the term "universal" for conventional signs, but only for signs that are universals by nature. That substance is not capable of functioning as predicate is clear; for if it were, it would follow that a proposition would be composed of particular substances; and, consequently, the subject would be in Rome and the predicate in England which is absurd.

Furthermore, propositions occur only in the mind, in speech, or in writing; therefore, their parts can exist only in the mind, in speech, and in writing. Particular substances, however, cannot themselves exist in the mind, in speech, or in writing. Thus, no proposition can be composed of particular substances. Propositions are, however, composed of universals; therefore, universals cannot conceivably be substances.

Chapter 16: Against Scotus' account of the universal

It may be clear to many that a universal is not a substance outside the mind which exists in, but is distinct from, particulars. Nevertheless, some want to claim that the universal is, in some way, outside the soul and in particulars; and while they do not want to say that a universal is really distinct from particulars, they say that it is formally distinct from particulars. Thus, they say that in Socrates there is human nature which is contracted to Socrates by an individual difference which is not really, but only formally, distinct from that nature. Thus, while there are not two things, one is not formally the other.

I do not find this view tenable:

First, in creatures there can never be any distinction outside the mind unless there are distinct things; if, therefore, there is any distinction between the nature and the difference, it is necessary that they really be distinct things. I prove my premise by the following syllogism: the nature is not formally distinct from itself; this individual difference is formally distinct from this nature; therefore, this individual difference is not this nature.

Again, the same entity is not both common and proper, but in their view the individual difference is proper and the universal is common; therefore, no universal is identical with an individual difference.

Again, opposites cannot be attributed to one and the same created thing, but *common* and *proper* are opposites; therefore, the same thing is not both common and proper. Nevertheless, that conclusion would follow if an individual difference and a common nature were the same thing.

Again, if a common nature were the same thing as an individual difference, there would be as many common natures as there are individual differences; and, consequently, none of those natures would be common, but each would be peculiar to the difference with which it is identical.

Again, whenever one thing is distinct from another it is distinguished from that thing either of and by itself or by something intrinsic to itself. Now, the humanity of Socrates is something different from the humanity of Plato; therefore, they are distinguished of and by themselves and not by differences that are added to them.

Again, according to Aristotle things differing in species also differ in number, but the nature of a man and the nature of a donkey differ in species of and by themselves; therefore, they are numerically distinguished of and by themselves; therefore, each of them is numerically one of and by itself.

Again, that which cannot belong to many cannot be predicated of many; but such a nature, if it really is the same thing as the individual difference, cannot belong to many since it cannot belong to any other particular. Thus, it cannot be predicable of many; but, then, it cannot be a universal.

Again, take an individual difference and the nature which it contracts. Either the difference between these two things is greater or less than the difference between two particulars. It is not greater because they do not differ really; particulars, however, do differ really. But neither is it less because then they would admit of one and the same definition, since two particulars can admit of the same definition. Consequently, if one of them is, by itself, one in number, the other will also be.

Again, either the nature is the individual difference or it is not. If it is the difference I argue as follows: this individual difference is proper and not common; this individual difference is this nature; therefore this nature is proper and not common, but that is what I set out to prove. Likewise, I argue as follows: the individual difference is not formally distinct from the individual difference; the individual difference is the nature; therefore, the nature is not formally distinct from the individual difference. But if it be said that the individual difference is not the nature, my point has been proved; for it follows that if the individual difference is not the nature, the individual difference is not really the nature; for from the opposite of the consequent follows the opposite of the antecedent. Thus, if it is true that the individual difference really is the nature, then the individual difference is the nature. The inference is valid, for from a determinable taken with its determination (where the determination does not detract from or diminish the determinable) one can infer the determinable taken by itself; but "really" does not express a determination that detracts or diminishes. Therefore, it follows that if the individual difference is really the nature, the individual difference is the nature.

Therefore, one should grant that in created things there is no such thing as a formal distinction. All things which are distinct in creatures are really distinct and, therefore, different things. In regard to creatures modes of argument like the following ought never be denied: this is A; this is B; therefore, B is A; and this is not A; this is B; therefore, B is not A. Likewise, one ought never deny that, as regards creatures, there are distinct things where contradictory notions hold. The only exception would be the case where contradictory notions hold true because of some syncategorematic element or similar determination, but in the same present case this is not so.

Therefore, we ought to say with the philosophers that in a particular substance there is nothing substantial except the particular form, the particular matter, or the composite of the two. And, therefore, no one ought to think that in Socrates there is a humanity or a human nature which is distinct from Socrates and to which there is added an individual difference which contracts that nature. The only thing in Socrates which can be construed as substantial is this particular matter, this particular form, or the composite of the two. And, therefore, every essence and quiddity and whatever belongs to substance, if it is really outside the soul, is just matter, form, or the composite of these or, following the doctrine of the Peripatetics, a separated and immaterial substance.

8

John Buridan on the Predicables

2.1   Chapter 1. On the Predicables

2.1.1   Several senses of the term 'predicable'

[The term] 'predicable' is sometimes taken strictly, sometimes broadly. A predicable, strictly speaking, is what is predicated of many [things]; a predicable, taken broadly, is what is predicated whether of only one or of many things; of only one thing, as 'Socrates' is predicated only of him [i.e., Socrates], when we say: 'Socrates is Socrates', of many things, as when 'animal' is predicated of man and horse, and 'man' of Socrates and Plato, and so forth.

The second treatise deals with predicables. It contains seven chapters: the first is about a distinction concerning the name 'predicable', the second is about genus, the third is about species, the fourth is about difference, the fifth is about property, the sixth is about accident, and the seventh is about the proper and common characteristics of predicables. The first chapter contains three parts: the first is the distinction concerning the name 'predicable', the second is about the accord between the names 'predicable' and 'universal', and the third is the division of predicables. Concerning the first part, and the whole treatise, we should note that the terms 'predicate' and 'predicable' do not differ in their significations, except with respect to actuality and potentiality. And although we may say that Porphyry discussed predicables and Aristotle, in the *Topics*, discussed predicates, we should not think that Aristotle and Porphyry wanted to draw a distinction in their discussions between these with respect to actuality and potentiality; indeed, both of them call that which is predicated . . . etc., that is, what can be predicated . . . etc., a genus. Second, we should note that although every conventionally significative utterance when taken materially can be the subject or the predicate in a proposition, not all such utterances when taken significatively can thus be the subject or the predicate. But here we intend to consider only terms that can be predicated when taken significatively. Third, we should note that the things that exist without any operation of the soul, such as stones or plants, are neither predicates nor subjects in propositions, but the concepts in the mind, insofar as they occur in mental propositions, can be [subjects or predicates], as can vocal or written terms, which are rendered significative by the mediation of

predicate - declare, assert, imply

these concepts, as has been said elsewhere. And these are called predicables insofar as they are apt to be predicated of certain subjects in certain propositions; and they could likewise be called subjectible, insofar as they can also be subjected to certain predicates in certain propositions.

Therefore, we should note with reference to the author's distinction that some terms are predicated, or are apt to be predicated, of many things, and some only of one thing, as he himself illustrates; and broadly speaking both [kinds] are called 'predicable'. But strictly speaking, the name 'predicable' is restricted to supposit only for terms predicable of many things, and it is in this strict sense that Porphyry intends to discuss the predicables. But then a serious doubt arises as to whether any term is predicable only of one thing. And it appears not. For such would be the term 'Socrates' or some other term that we call 'singular', or 'discrete'; but this is not the case, for the term 'Socrates' is predicable of many things. Proof: for a thing is not predicated of a thing, speaking about things that exist without the operation of the soul, such as stones or trees; but it is [only] a significative term that is predicated of another significative term, as was said above. Now it is obvious, however, that the term 'Socrates' is predicated of a great number of terms, as for example, of 'Socrates', 'man', 'animal', 'risible[1] [animal]', 'white [thing]', 'educated [person]', etc.; for a man is Socrates, an animal is Socrates, a risible [animal] is Socrates, a white [thing] is Socrates, and so forth for many others.

Now, without any doubt I believe that the objection is valid in its own way, and that every term truly predicable or subjectible in a true affirmative proposition is truly predicable not only of one, but of many, i.e., of each and every one of many different terms. Therefore, [the distinction] should be expounded in such a manner that a singular term, such as 'Socrates', is not apt to be predicated of many things, meaning that it cannot supposit for many things dividedly, i.e., for each and every one, in the sense that if we mark one thing for which it supposits, it cannot supposit for another. Indeed, even if we mark several things for which it supposits conjunctively [supponit coniunctim], as does the term 'this people', it cannot supposit for any others, unless this happens by equivocation, or it happens because it denominates the whole on account of a principal part, or on account of the unity resulting from the continuity of several parts succeeding each other in something, as in a river, or in some such manner (which is not to be discussed here, but elsewhere, namely, where the question will be raised about the identity of parts [taken together] with their whole); as, e.g., how the term 'Seine' is a singular term, although it is not the same water that is now the Seine and that was the Seine last year.[2] Therefore, a 'predicable', strictly speaking, in the sense intended here, is described as a term apt to be predicated of many things, i.e., apt to supposit for many things, and not for only one thing in the way we just described concerning singular terms.

Supposit - suppose assume

---

1   Obviously, 'risible' here and throughout should not be taken in the modern vernacular sense of 'ridiculous', but in the somewhat outmoded, but still quite commonly recognized sense of 'capable of laughter'. In any case, in this sense, the term *risibilis* (risible) was taken to be the stock example of a *proprium* (property) of man, in the technical sense of 'property' to be explained by Buridan in more detail below.

2   See J. Buridan, *Quaestiones super octo Physicorum libros Aristotelis: Kommentar zur Aristotelischen Physik* (Paris, 1509; reprint, Frankfurt am Main: Minerva, 1964), bk. 1, q. 10.

2.1.2 The difference and agreement between 'predicable' and 'universal'

Therefore, a predicable, strictly speaking, is the same [thing] as a universal, but they differ because a predicable is defined as something that is apt to be predicated of many things, and a universal as something that is apt to be in many things.

The second part is in accordance with [the formulation of] our author,[3] but is not true, properly speaking [*de proprietate sermonis*]; for if A is the same [thing] as B, then the one does not differ from the other. Therefore, I abandon his text, and I say that the terms 'predicable' and 'universal' are not the same, but they are convertibly said to be [the] same [thing] [*dicuntur idem convertibiliter*], so that every predicable is a universal and conversely, and thus the predicate '[the] same [thing]' is truly affirmed of them taken significatively. For every predicable and universal are [the] same [thing], and, conversely, every universal and predicable are [the] same [thing].[4] But the terms 'predicable' and 'universal' are said to be diverse in their concepts, for they were imposed according to different concepts to signify the same things. For the terms 'predicate' and 'subject' are predicated correlatively, and thus also are the terms 'predicable' and 'subjectible'; for a term is said to be predicable, because it can be predicated of a subject, and subjectible, because it can be subjected to a predicate in a proposition. But the same term is called a universal because it indifferently signifies many things, and is apt to supposit for many things, as has been said, whether as a subject or as a predicate. Nor should we think that a universal term is *in* the terms contained under it, except taking 'being in' [*inesse*] for being truly predicated affirmatively, so that 'being predicated' and 'being in' would not differ, except verbally [*secundum vocem*]. And we should note that although sometimes something is said to be a universal with respect to causation, because it is a cause of many things, as is God, or a universal on account of distribution, as when a proposition is said to be universal, or in some other ways, nevertheless, 'universal' is here taken only for a common term because it signifies many things, or rather, to put it better, because it supposits for many, as was said earlier.

2.1.3 The division of predicables

Predicables, taken strictly, are divided into genus, species, difference, property and accident.

The third part divides the term 'predicable' into its species. For, since something is called a predicable because it is apt to be predicated of many things, it is reasonable to distinguish the species or modes contained under the term 'predicable' according to the different modes of predication. Therefore, everything that is predicated of something is either predicated essentially, so that neither term adds some extraneous connotation to the signification of the other, or it is predicated denominatively, so that one term does add some extrinsic connotation to the signification of the other. This division is clearly exhaustive, for it is given in terms of opposites. If, therefore, something is predicated essentially, in the above-described manner, then it is either predicated in [reply to the question] 'What [is it]' [*in quid*] or in [reply to the question] 'What [is it like?]' [*in quale*]; and if *in quale*, then it is a difference, and if *in quid*,

---

3   See Peter of Spain, *Tractatus*, ed. L. M. de Rijk (Assen: van Gorcum, 1972), p. 17.
4   This is in fact the explication of the phrase *dicuntur idem convertibiliter* (are convertibly said to be the same thing).

then, if it is predicated of many things differing in species, then it is called 'genus', but if it is predicated of many things differing only numerically, then it is called 'species', or even if it is predicated of many things differing in species and has a superior genus, it is still called a 'species', as will be explained later. If, however, it is predicated denominatively, then it is either predicated convertibly with that of which it is predicated, or it is not; if so, then with respect to that it is called 'property'; if not, then with respect to that it is called 'accident'. Thus it is obvious that every predicable, with respect to that of which it is predicable, has to be called either a genus, or a species, or a difference, or a property, or an accident.

[Some] doubts concerning this division will be considered, when its individual members will have been discussed in particular. But some people want to draw the distinctions in another way, saying that every predicable is predicable either *in quid* or *in quale*; if *in quid*, then it is either a genus or a species, and if *in quale*, then either essentially or accidentally; and then, if accidentally, then either convertibly or not. But this whole [division] is wrongly stated, for there are many predicables that are neither predicated in reply to the question 'What is it?' [*in quid*] nor in reply to the question 'What is it like?' [*in quale*], but in reply to the question 'How much?' [*in quantum*], [i.e., 'How big?', 'How long?', etc.] as 'two-cubits-long' or 'three-cubits-long', or in reply to the question 'How many?' [*in quot*], as 'three', 'four', or in reply to the question 'When?' [*in quando*], as 'yesterday', 'tomorrow', or in reply to the question 'Where?' [*in ubi*], as 'in the house', 'outside the house', etc.

Illumination vs. Abstraction, and Scientific Knowledge

9

Augustine on Divine Ideas and Illumination

Divine Ideas as Prototypes

Plato is known as the first to have named the Ideas. Not that if this name were nonexistent before he established it, the things that he called Ideas would not have existed, or would not have been understood by anyone – but they were probably called by different names by different people. It is permitted to give to any known thing that lacks an accepted name, whatever name one wishes. . . . But enough has previously been said about the name; let us examine the thing which is principally to be considered and understood, leaving each person free, as far as the terms are concerned, to give whatever name he wishes to the object of his knowledge.

So, in Latin we may call Ideas forms or species, to make it clear that we are translating word for word. But, if we call them "reasons," we are departing somewhat from a strict translation; reasons are called *logoi* in Greek and not Ideas. However, if a person chose to use this term, he would not be far from the real meaning. In fact, Ideas are the primary forms, or the permanent and immutable reasons of real things, and they are not themselves formed; so they are, as a consequence, eternal and ever the same in themselves, and they are contained in the divine intelligence. And since they never come into being or go out of it, everything that can come into being and go out of it, and everything that does come into being and goes out of it, may be said to be formed in accord with them.

It is denied that the soul can look upon them, unless it be rational, in that part whereby it excels, that is, in its mind and reason, as it were in its face or interior and intellectual eye. And for this vision not everyone is suitable but only that rational soul which is holy and pure, that one which keeps the eye in which such objects are seen, healthy, clear, serene and like unto those objects to which its view is directed. What religious man, infused with the true religion, even though not yet able to contemplate these objects, would nevertheless dare to deny and even refuse to confess that all things that are – that is, whatsoever things are constituted with a nature of their own in their proper kinds – were created by God as their source, so that they might exist? And that all living things are alive by virtue of the same source? And that the whole of things is preserved, and the very order in which they change, as they manifest their temporal courses according to a definite pattern, is maintained and governed, by the laws of the highest God? When this is established and admitted, who will dare to say that God established all things in an irrational manner? Now if this cannot be said or accepted in any proper sense, the conclusion remains that all things were founded by means of reason. Not that a man is based on the same reason as a horse; this would be an absurd notion. So, each one of these is created in accord with its own reason. Now, where would we think that these reasons are, if not in the mind of the Creator? For He did not look to anything placed outside Himself as a model for the construction of what he created; to think that He did would be irreligious.

Now, if these reasons for all things to be created, or already created, are contained in the divine mind, and if there can be nothing in the divine mind unless it be eternal and immutable, and if Plato called these primary reasons of things Ideas – then not only do Ideas exist but they are true because they are eternal and they endure immutably in this way; and it is by participation in these that whatever exists is produced, however its way of existing may be.

★ ★ ★

Book II, Chapter VIII
The Order of Numbers, Known as One and Unchangeable,
Is Not Known by the Bodily Senses

AUGUSTINE: Come! Listen and tell me whether we may find anything that all reasoning men see with their reason and mind in common with all others, while what is seen is present in all and, unlike food or drink, is not transformed into some use by those to whom it is present, instead remaining uncorrupted and complete whether or not men discern it. Perhaps you think that nothing like this exists?

EVODIUS: On the contrary, I see that many such things exist, one of which is quite enough to mention: the order and the truth of number [*ratio et veritas numeri*] are present to all who think. Everyone who calculates tries to understand the truth of number with his own reason and understanding. Some can do this rather easily; others have more difficulty. Yet the truth of number offers itself to all alike who are able to grasp it. When a man understands it, it is not changed into a kind of nourishment for him; when he fails to grasp it, the truth of number does not disappear; rather, it remains true and permanent, while man's failure to grasp it is commensurate with the extent of his error.

AUGUSTINE: Correct! I see that you are not inexperienced in this, and have quickly found your answer. If someone were to say to you that numbers were impressed upon our spirit not as a result of their own nature, but as a result of those objects which we experience with the bodily senses, what answer would you make? Or do you agree with this?

EVODIUS: No, I do not. Even if I did perceive numbers with the bodily senses, I would not be able to perceive with the bodily senses the meaning of division and addition. It is with the light of the mind that I would prove wrong the man who makes an error in addition or subtraction. Whatever I may experience with my bodily senses, such as this air and earth and whatever corporeal matter they contain, I cannot know how long it will endure. But seven and three are ten, not only now, but forever. There has never been a time when seven and three were not ten, nor will there ever be a time when they are not ten. Therefore, I have said that the truth of number is incorruptible and common to all who think.

AUGUSTINE: I do not disagree with your answer, for you spoke truly and clearly. But you will easily see that numbers themselves are not drawn from the bodily senses, if you realize how any number you please multiplied by one is that number. For example, two times one is two; three times one is three; ten times one is ten; any number times one is that number. Anyone who really thinks about the number one realizes that he cannot perceive it through the bodily senses, for whatever we experience through a sense is proven to be many, not one. This follows because it is a body and is therefore infinitely divisible. But I need not concentrate upon each small and indistinct part; however small such a bodily part may be, it has a right, left, upper, and lower side, or a farther and nearer side, or ends and a middle. These, we admit, must be in a body, however small it is; thus, we concede that no body is truly and purely one. Yet all these parts could not be counted, if they had not been distinguished by the concept of one. When, therefore, I look for one in a body, I do not doubt that I will not find it. I know what I am seeking there and what I shall not find there. I know that I cannot find one, or rather that it does not exist in a body at all. How do I know that a body is not one? If I did not know what one is, I could not count the many parts of the body. Moreover, however I may know one, I do not know it through the bodily senses, because through the bodily senses I know nothing except a body which, we have proven, is not really and simply one. Furthermore, if we have not perceived one through a sense of the body, we have not perceived by a sense any number of those numbers which we discern only through the understanding. There exists no number which does not get its name from the number of times it contains one. The perception of one does not occur through any bodily sense. The half of any body whatsoever, although the whole body consists of two halves, also has its own half; therefore, there are two parts of a body which are not simply two. Moreover, the number which is called two because it is twice what is irreducibly one, cannot be two parts of one, in other words, that which is simply one cannot again have a half or a third or whatever part you please, since it is simply and truly one. In observing the order of numbers, we see after one the number two, which is twice one. Twice two does not follow next in order; rather, three comes next, and then four, which is twice two. This order [ratio] continues throughout all the rest of the numbers by a fixed and unchangeable law. Thus after one, the first of all numbers, when one itself is excepted, the first number is the double of one, for two comes next. After this second number, that is, after two, when two is excepted, the second number is the double of two; for after two the first number is three, and the second number is four, the double of two. After the third, that is, after the number three, when it is itself excepted, the third number is the double of three; for after the third number, that is, after three, the first number is four, the second five, and the third six, which is the double of three. So after the fourth number, when it is itself excepted, the fourth number is the double of four; for after the fourth number, after four, the first number is five, the second is six, the third is seven, and the fourth number is eight, which is the double of four. Through all of the rest of the numbers you will find the same thing that is found in the first pair of numbers, one and two, namely, the double of any number is as many times after this number as such a number is from the beginning.

How do we discern that this fact which holds for the whole number series is unchangeable, fixed, and incorruptible? No one perceives all the numbers by any bodily sense, for they are innumerable. How do we know that this is true for all numbers? Through what fantasy or vision do we discern so confidently the firm truth of number throughout the whole innumerable series, unless by some inner light unknown to bodily sense?

Men to whom God has given ability in argument, and whom stubbornness does not lead into confusion, are forced to admit that the order and truth of numbers have nothing to do with the bodily senses, but are unchangeable and true and common to all rational beings.

Therefore, although many other things could occur to us that are common and, as it were, public for rational beings, things that are seen by each individual with his mind and reason and still remain inviolate and unchanged, nevertheless, I am not unwilling to accept the fact that the order and truth of number are the best possible examples that you could have given when you wished to answer my question. Not without reason was number joined to wisdom in the Holy Scriptures where it is said, "I and my heart have gone round to know and to consider and to search out wisdom and number" [Eccles. 7:26].

Thomas Aquinas on Illumination vs. Abstraction

Summary Theologiae

Part I, Question 84. How the Soul, while Joined to the Body, Knows Material Things

Here there are eight points of inquiry:

1. whether the soul knows material things through the intellect;
2. whether it understands them through its own essence or through species; *(forms)*
3. if by means of species, whether the species of all intelligible objects are inborn in the soul's nature;
4. whether these species come to the soul through the influence of non-sensible immaterial forms;
5. whether the things our soul understands are all seen in the divine ideas;
6. whether the soul acquires intellectual knowledge from the senses;
7. whether, using only the species it has, without turning to sense images, the intellect can actually understand;
8. whether intellectual discernment is impeded when the sense faculties are impeded.

[...]

Article 5. Does the intellectual soul know material things in the divine ideas?

The first point:[1] 1. It would seem that the intellectual soul does not know material things in the divine ideas. For there must be prior and better knowledge of that in which a thing is known. Now the intellectual soul of man, in his earthly life, does not know the divine ideas

---

1   Cf. 1a. 12, 11 ad 3.

– for it does not know God, in whom these ideas exist, but is, according to Dionysius,[2] *united to him as to the unknown.* Therefore the soul does not know everything in the divine ideas.

2. Again, in Scripture[3] it is said that *the invisible things of God are there for the mind to see in the things he has made.* But among the invisible things of God are the divine ideas. Thus these divine ideas are known through material created things and not the other way around.

3. Again, the divine ideas are precisely that – ideas. For Augustine says,[4] that *ideas are the patterns of things existing unchanged in the divine mind.* Therefore if we say that the intellectual soul knows everything in the divine ideas, we revive the opinion of Plato who held that all knowledge is derived from Ideas.

On the other hand, there is Augustine's saying,[5] *If we both see that what you say is true, and if we both see that what I say is true, where, I ask, do we see it? Certainly I do not see it in you, nor you in me, but both in the unchangeable truth itself, which is above our minds.* But the unchangeable truth is contained in the divine ideas. Therefore the intellectual soul knows all truths in the divine ideas.

Reply: As Augustine says,[6] *If those who are called philosophers said by chance anything that was true and consistent with our faith, we must claim it from them as from unjust possessors. For some of the doctrines of the pagans are spurious imitations or superstitious inventions, which we must be careful to avoid when we renounce the society of the pagans.* Accordingly Augustine, who was steeped in the doctrines of the Platonists, whenever he found anything in their statements consistent with the Faith he accepted it, but amended what he found hostile.

Now Plato, as was said above, held that the forms of things subsist of themselves separate from matter. He called these Ideas and said that our intellects know everything by participation in them; thus, as corporeal matter becomes stone by participation in the Idea of stone, so, by participation in the same Idea, our intellects know stone. However, since it seems alien to the Faith that the forms of things should subsist of themselves, outside things and without matter – as the Platonists held, saying that 'life as such' and 'wisdom as such' are creative substances (according to Dionysius[7]) – Augustine substituted[8] in place of these Ideas which Plato posited the ideas of all creatures existing in the divine mind. All things are formed according to these, and in addition the human soul knows everything according to them.

Thus when the question is asked: Does the human soul know everything in the divine ideas?, the reply must be that one thing can be spoken of as known in another in two ways: first, as in an object itself known, for instance, when one may see in a mirror things whose images are reflected there. In this sense the soul, in its earthly state of life, cannot see everything in the divine ideas; on the other hand, the blessed who see God and everything else in God do thus know everything in the divine ideas. Secondly, a thing is spoken of as known in another as in a principle of knowledge; for instance, we might say that things seen by

2 *De mystic. theol.* 3. PG 3, 1001.
3 Romans 1: 20.
4 *Lib. 83 quæst.* 46 PL 40, 30.
5 *Confessions* XII, 25. PL 32, 840.
6 *De doctrina christiana* II, 40. PL 34, 63.
7 *De divinis nominibus* 11. PG 3, 956. lect. 6.
8 *Lib. 83 quæst.* 46. PL 40, 30.

sunlight are seen in the sun. In this sense we must say that the human soul knows everything in the divine ideas, and that by participation in them we know everything. For the intellectual light in us is nothing more than a participating likeness of the uncreated light in which the divine ideas are contained.

Many say: Who will give us sight of happiness?[9] and the Psalmist replies to the question, *The light of your face, Lord, is signed upon us,* as if to say, by the seal of the divine light in us everything is made known to us.

Nevertheless, since besides the intellectual light which is in us, species taken from things are required for our knowledge of material things, we do not have this merely by participation in the divine ideas in the way in which Platonists held that mere participation in the Ideas sufficed for knowledge. And so Augustine asks,[10] *For pray, because philosophers dispute most truly, and persuade us by most certain proofs, that all things temporal are made after ideas that are eternal, are they therefore able to see clearly in these ideas, or to collect from them, how many kinds of animals there are, what are the seeds of each in their beginnings? Have they not sought out all these things through the actual history of places and times?*

Moreover, that Augustine did not understand everything to be known *in the divine ideas* or *in the unchangeable truth* in the sense that the divine ideas themselves were seen is clear from what he writes,[11] *Not any and every rational soul can be called worthy of that vision,* namely of the divine ideas, *but only one that is pure and holy* – such as are the souls of the blessed.

From all this the replies to the objections are evident.

[...]

Part I, Question 85. The Mode and Order of Understanding

Next to be considered are the mode and order of understanding, and with respect to these there are eight issues for discussion:

1. whether our intellect understands by abstracting species from sense images;
2. whether the species abstracted from images are related to our intellect as *what* is understood or as *that whereby* things are understood;
3. whether our intellect naturally understands first the more universal;
4. whether our intellect can understand more than one thing at a time;
5. whether our intellect understands by combining and separating;
6. whether the intellect can be in error;
7. whether, with respect to the same reality, one can have a better understanding than another;
8. whether our intellect knows the indivisible before the divisible.

9   Psalms 4: 6–7.
10   *De Trinitate* IV, 16. *PL* 42, 902.
11   *Lib. 83 quæst.* 46. *PL* 40, 30.

Article 1. Does our intellect understand material, corporeal realities by abstraction from sense images?

The first point:[12] 1. It would seem that our intellect does not understand material and corporeal realities by abstraction from sense images. For if one understands an object otherwise than as it really is then he is in error. But the forms of material things are not abstract, set apart from the particulars represented by sense images. Therefore if we understand in abstraction species from sense images, our intellect will be in error.

2. Again, material things are natural things, requiring matter in their definition. Now nothing can be understood without something which is required for its definition. Hence material things cannot be understood without matter. But matter is the principle of individuation. Therefore material things cannot be understood by abstracting the universal from the particular, which is the same as abstracting species from sense images.

3. Again, Aristotle says[13] that sense images have the same relation to the intellectual soul that colour has to sight. But seeing does not take place by abstracting images from colours, but by colours being impressed on the sight. Neither, therefore, does understanding happen by way of something being abstracted from sense images, but by an impression made on the intellect by sense images.

4. Again, as Aristotle says,[14] in the intellectual soul there are two faculties: namely, the possible and the agent intellects. But the function of the possible intellect is not that of abstracting species from images but of receiving species already abstracted. Neither, however, does it seem to be the function of the agent intellect: it has the same relation to sense images that light has to colours, which is not that of abstracting anything from colours but rather of streaming out to them. Therefore in no way do we understand by abstracting from sense images.

5. Again, Aristotle says[15] that the intellect *thinks the forms in the images*. Not therefore, by abstracting them.

On the other hand, Aristotle says[16] that *as realities are separable from matter, so is it with their being understood.* Therefore material realities must be understood precisely as abstracted or set apart from matter and from material likenesses such as sense images.

Reply: As was said earlier,[17] knowable objects are proportioned to knowing faculties, and there are three levels of such faculties. First, one kind of cognitive faculty is the form of a corporeal organ: such is sense. Accordingly, the object of every sense faculty is a form existing in corporeal matter, and so, since this sort of matter is the principle of individuation, all the faculties of the sense part of man only know particulars.

A second kind of cognitive faculty is neither the form of a corporeal organ nor in any way joined to corporeal matter; such is an angel's intellect. Accordingly, its object is a form subsisting without matter, for although angels can know material things, they see them only in something immaterial, namely either in themselves or in God.

---

12   Cf. 1a. 12, 4, *CG*, II, 77. *In Meta.* II, lect. 1.
13   *De Anima* III, 7. 431a14.
14   *De Anima* III, 5. 430a14.
15   Ibid III, 7. 431b2.
16   Ibid III, 4. 429b21.
17   1a. 84, 7.

The human intellect stands in the middle. It is not the form of an organ, although it is a faculty of the soul which is the form of a body, as is clear from what was said earlier.[18] Accordingly, it is proper for it to know forms which, in fact, exist individually in corporeal matter, yet not precisely as existing in such or such individual matter. Now to know something which in fact exists in individuated matter, but not as existing in such or such matter is to abstract a form from individual matter, represented by sense images. Thus we have to say that our intellect understands material things by abstraction from sense images.

Through material things known in this way we come to a limited knowledge of immaterial realities, just as, in the contrary way, angels know material realities by way of the immaterial.

Now Plato, paying attention only to the immateriality of the human intellect and not to the fact that it is somehow joined to a body, held that the object of the intellect is immaterial Ideas, and that we understand, as we have mentioned,[19] not by abstraction, but by participation in abstract entities.

Hence: 1. Abstraction occurs in two ways: one, by way of combining and separating, as when we understand one not to be in another or to be separate from it; two, by way of a simple and absolute consideration, as when we understand one without considering the other, at all.

And so although for the intellect in the first way to abstract objects which in reality are not abstract is not without falsehood, it is not in the second way, as clearly appears with sensible realities. For example, were we to understand or say that colour does not exist in a coloured body, or that it exists apart from it, there would be falsehood in the opinion or statement. Whereas were we to consider colour and its properties, without any consideration of the apple which has colour, and go on to express verbally what we thus understand, the opinion or statement would be without falsehood. For being an apple is not part of the definition of colour, and thus nothing prevents colour from being understood apart from the apple being understood.

I claim likewise that whatever pertains to the definition of any species of material reality, for instance stone or man or horse, can be considered without individuating conditions which are no part of the definition of the species. And this is what I mean by abstracting the universal from the particular, the idea from sense images, to consider the nature of a species without considering individuating conditions represented by sense images.

Therefore when it is said that that understanding is false, which understands a thing other than as it is, the statement is true if 'other than' refers to the thing understood. For the understanding is false whenever one understands a thing to be other than it is; hence the understanding would be false if one should so abstract the species of stone from matter that he would understand it to exist apart from matter, as Plato held.

The proposition, however, would not be true if 'other than' were taken as referring to the one understanding. For there is no falsity if the mode of understanding in the one who understands is different from the mode of existing in the thing – a thing understood is in the one who understands in an immaterial way, according to the mode of the intellect, and not in a material way, according to the mode of a material reality.

18   1a. 76, 1.
19   1a. 84, 1.

2. Some have thought that the species[20] of a natural thing is all form, that matter is not a part of the species; but if this were so, matter would not be included in definitions of natural things.

Another way of speaking is thus required, distinguishing between two kinds of matter, *common* and *designated* or *individual: common* would be, for instance, flesh and bones, and *individual* this flesh and these bones. The intellect abstracts the species of a natural thing from individual sensible matter, but not from common sensible matter. Thus it abstracts the species of man from this flesh and these bones which do not pertain to the definition of the specific nature – they are, rather, as Aristotle says, parts of the individual. The specific nature therefore can be considered without them. However, the species of man cannot be abstracted by the intellect from flesh and bones as such.

Mathematical species, on the other hand, can be abstracted by the intellect from both individual and common *sensible matter* – though not from common (but only individual) *intelligible matter*. For *sensible matter* means corporeal matter as underlying sensible qualities – hot and cold, hard and soft, etc. – whereas *intelligible matter* means substance as underlying quantity. Now it is obvious that quantity inheres in substance, before sensible qualities do. Hence quantities – numbers, dimensions, shapes (which are boundaries of quantities) – can be considered apart from sensible qualities, and this is precisely to abstract them from sensible matter. They cannot, however, be considered apart from an understanding of *some* substance as underlying quantity – which would be to abstract them from common intelligible matter – though they can be considered apart from this or that substance – which is to abstract them from individual intelligible matter.

Finally, some things – such as being, oneness, potentiality and actuality, etc. – can be abstracted even from common intelligible matter, as is evident in immaterial substances.

Plato, however, since he gave no consideration to the two modes of abstraction mentioned above, held that all the things we have spoken of as abstracted by the intellect exist in reality as abstract entities.

3. Colours, as existing in individual corporeal matter, have the same mode of existence as the faculty of sight. Consequently, they can impress their likeness on sight. Sense images, on the contrary, since they are likenesses of individuals and exist in corporeal organs, do not have the same mode of existence as the human intellect – as is obvious from what has been said. Consequently, they cannot, of their own power, make an impression on the possible intellect.

However, in virtue of the agent intellect and by its turning to sense images (which, in turn, represent the realities of which they are images), a likeness is effected in the possible intellect, but only with respect to the specific nature. And it is thus that species are said to be abstracted from sense images, and not as though a form, numerically the same as the one that existed before in the sense images, should now come to exist in the possible intellect in the way in which a body is taken from one place and transferred to another.

4. Sense images are illuminated by the agent intellect and further, by its power, species are abstracted from them. They are illuminated because sense images, by the power of the agent intellect, are rendered apt to have intellectual intentions or species abstracted from them, just as man's sense part receives heightened power from being joined to his intellectual part. The agent intellect, moreover, abstracts species from images, in that by its power

---

20   As an incidental characteristic, an *accidens* or 'accident'.

we can consider specific natures without individuating conditions, and it is by likenesses of these natures that the possible intellect is informed.

5. Our intellect both abstracts species from sense images – in so far as it considers the natures of things as universal – and yet, at the same time, understands these in sense images, since it cannot understand even the things from which it abstracts species without turning to sense images, as mentioned before.[21]

Article 2. Do species abstracted from sense images stand in relation to our intellect as what is understood?[22]

The first point:[23] 1. It would seem that species abstracted from sense images do stand in relation to our intellect as *that which* is understood. For what is actually understood exists in the one who understands; it is, in fact, identical with the intellect as actualized. But of the thing understood there is nothing in the intellect which understands except the abstracted species. Therefore this species is what is actually understood.

2. Again, what is actually understood must exist in something, or else it would simply not exist. But it does not exist in anything outside the soul, for, since things outside the soul are material, nothing in them can be what is actually understood. Therefore it follows by exclusion that what is actually understood is in the intellect, and thus that it is nothing other than the species mentioned.

3. Again, Aristotle says[24] that *spoken words are the symbols of things experienced in the soul.* But words signify things understood, since we use words precisely to signify what we understand. Therefore things experienced in the soul, namely species, are the things actually understood.

On the other hand, a species has the same relation to the intellect as a sensible image to the senses. But sensible images are not *what* is sensed; they are rather *that by which* sensation takes place. Therefore the species is not *what* is understood, but *that by which* the intellect understands.

Reply: Some have held that our cognitive faculties know only what is experienced within them, for instance, that the senses perceive only the impressions made on their organs. According to this opinion the intellect understands only what is experienced within it, i.e., the species received in it. Thus, again according to this opinion, these species are *what* is understood.

The opinion, however, is obviously false for two reasons. First, because the things we understand are the same as the objects of science. Therefore, if the things we understand were

---

21 1a. 84, 7.

22 St Thomas is now turning to a consideration of 'representationalism' – the theory that the objects of our knowledge are ideas or images impressed on the mind of the knower. He implicitly attributes the idea to the 'ancients', a term usually reserved for the Presocratics, and to a lesser extent (and only in a very limited way) to Plato. Since these historical attributions are very uncertain, however, it seems likely that the article is to be explained historically in one of two ways. Either the opinion was held by some of St Thomas's contemporaries, otherwise unidentified; or else he raises the question as a possibility to be derived from other doctrines that were being held.

23 Cf. *De veritate* x, 9, *CG* iv, 11. *In De anima* iii, *lect.* 8.

24 *Peri Hermeneias* i, 1. 16a3.

only species existing in the soul, it would follow that none of the sciences would be concerned with things existing outside the soul, but only with species existing in the soul. (It may be recalled how the Platonists held that all the sciences are concerned with Ideas, which they said were things actually understood.)

Second, because a consequence would be the error of the ancient philosophers who said that *all appearances are true*,[25] implying that contradictory opinions could at the same time be true. For if a faculty knows only what is experienced within it, that only is what it can discern. Now a thing 'appears' in accord with the way a cognitive faculty is affected. Therefore the discernment of a cognitive faculty will always judge a thing to be what it discerns, namely, what is experienced within it, and accordingly every judgment will be true.

For instance, if the sense of taste perceives only what is experienced within it, then when a man whose sense of taste is healthy discerns that honey is sweet, his judgment will be true. Similarly, if a sick man, whose sense of taste is affected, experiences honey as bitter, his judgment will be true. For each makes his judgment as his sense of taste is affected. It will thus follow that every opinion – and indeed every perception of any kind – has an equal claim to truth.

We must say, therefore, that species stand in relation to the intellect as *that by which* the intellect understands. To make the matter clear: although there are two kinds of activity[26] – one that remains within the agent (e.g., seeing or understanding), and one that passes over into a thing outside (e.g., heating or cutting) – nevertheless each is produced in accord with a form. Now just as the form from which an activity extending to a thing outside proceeds is like the object of the activity (for instance, the heat of a heater is like that of the thing heated), so also, in a similar way, the form from which an activity remaining within an agent proceeds is a likeness of the object. Thus it is according to a likeness of a visible thing that the faculty of sight sees, and likewise a likeness of a thing understood, i.e., a species, is the form according to which the intellect understands.

However, since the intellect reflects upon itself, by such reflection it understands both its own understanding and the species by which it understands. Thus species are secondarily that which is understood. But what is understood first is the reality of which a particular species is a likeness.

This is, in fact, already evident in the opinion of the ancient philosophers who held that *like is known by like*.[27] For they held that the soul would know solids that are outside it by means of solids within it, etc. Thus if we understand the species of a solid instead of actual solid materials – according to Aristotle's teaching,[28] *it is not the stone which is present in the soul but its form* – it will follow that by means of species the soul knows things which are outside the soul.

Hence: 1. What is understood is in the one who understands by means of its likeness. This is the meaning of the saying that what is actually understood is identical with the intellect as actualized, in so far as a likeness of the thing understood is the form of the intellect, just as a likeness of a sensible reality is the form of a sense when actualized. Hence it does not follow that an abstracted species is what is actually understood, but only that it is a likeness of it.

---

25 Aristotle, *Metaphysics* III, 5. 1009a8.
26 Aristotle, *Metaphysics* VIII, 8. 1050a23.
27 Aristotle, *De Anima* I, 2 & 5. 404b17; 409b25.
28 Ibid III, 8. 431b29.

2. The phrase 'what is actually understood' involves two points: namely, the thing which is understood and the being understood. And likewise in the term 'abstracted universal' there are two, namely, the nature of a thing and its state of abstraction or universality. Thus the nature, to which 'being understood' and 'being abstracted' (or the intention of universality) are applied, exists only in individuals, whereas 'being understood' and 'being abstracted' (or the intention of universality) exist in the intellect.

We can more easily see this by comparison with the senses. For instance, the sense of sight sees the colour of an apple but not its characteristic scent. Thus if one asks: Where does this colour, which is seen apart from the scent, exist?, it is obvious, on one hand, that the colour seen exists only in the apple, but on the other that being perceived without the scent can be attributed to it only with respect to sight, in so far as in the sense of sight there is a likeness of the one but not of the other.

Similarly, humanity, when understood, exists only in this or that human being, but its being apprehended without individuating conditions (i.e., its 'being abstracted' and the consequent intention of universality) can be attributed to humanity only as perceived by the intellect where there is a likeness of the specific nature, but not of individuating conditions.

3. In the sense part of man there are two kinds of activity. One takes place by way of a change effected from outside, thus the activity of the senses is fully carried out through a change effected by sensible objects. The other activity is a 'formation' by which the faculty of imagination formulates for itself a model of something absent or even of something never seen.

Now both of these activities are joined in the intellect. For, first, there is indeed an effect produced in the possible intellect in so far as it is informed by a species; and then, secondly, when it is thus informed, it formulates either a definition or else an affirmative or negative statement, which is then signified by words. Thus the meaning which a name signifies is a definition, and an enunciation or proposition signifies the intellect's combining or separating. Therefore words do not signify the effects produced in the possible intellect but those things which the intellect formulates for itself in order to understand things outside.

Part I, Question 86. What our Intellect Knows with Respect to Material Realities

What our intellect knows with respect to material realities is next to be considered, and in this regard there are four points of inquiry:

1. whether it knows singulars;
2. whether it knows the infinite;
3. whether it knows contingent things;
4. whether it knows the future.

Article 1. Does our intellect know singulars?

The first point:[29] 1. It would seem that our intellect does know singulars. For whoever knows a combination knows the terms in the combination. But our intellect knows the combina-

---

29   Cf. IV *Sent.* 50, 1, 3. *De veritate* II, 5–6; X, 5. *In De anima* III, *lect.* 8. *Quodl.* XII, 8. *De principio individuationis.*

tion, *Socrates is a man* – it is, in fact, its function to formulate such a proposition. Therefore our intellect knows this singular, for instance Socrates.

2. Again, since it is directive of activities, and activities are concerned with singulars, the practical intellect must know singulars.

3. Again, our intellect understands itself. But it is something singular or else it could not act, since activities are of individuals. Therefore our intellect knows the singular.

4. Again, since a higher power can do whatever a lower one can, and the senses know singulars, therefore *a fortiori* the intellect must also.

On the other hand, Aristotle says[30] *the universal is more knowable in the order of explanation, the particular in the order of sense.*

Reply: Directly and immediately our intellect cannot know the singular in material realities. The reason is that the principle of singularity in material things is individual matter, and our intellect – as said before[31] – understands by abstracting species from this sort of matter. But what is abstracted from individual matter is universal. Therefore our intellect has direct knowledge only of universals.

Indirectly and by a quasi-reflection, on the other hand, the intellect can know the singular, because, as mentioned before,[32] even after it has abstracted species it cannot actually understand by means of them except by a return to sense images in which it understands the species, as Aristotle says.[33]

Therefore, in this sense, it is the universal that the intellect understands directly by means of the species, and singulars (represented in sense images) only indirectly. And it is in this way that it formulates the proposition, 'Socrates is a man'.

Hence: 1. The first solution is evident.

2. The choice of a particular thing to be done is, as it were, the conclusion of a syllogism in the practical intellect.[34] But a singular proposition cannot be deduced from a universal proposition directly, but only on the assumption of a mediating singular proposition. Hence a universal argument in the practical intellect has no motivating force except by means of an apprehension of the particular in the sense part of man.[35]

3. The singular's repugnance to being intelligible is not because it is singular, but because it is material – since only the immaterial can be understood. Thus if there is such a thing as an immaterial singular – and the intellect is such – then it has no repugnance to being intelligible.

4. A higher power can do whatever a lower one can, but in a superior way. Thus what the senses know materially and concretely the intellect knows in an immaterial and abstract way, which is to know the universal.

[. . .]

---

30   *Physics* I, lect. 5. 189a5.
31   1a. 85, 1.
32   1a. 84, 7.
33   *De Anima* III, 7. 431b2.
34   *Nicomachean Ethics* VII, 3. 1147a28.
35   *De Anima* III, 11. 434a16.

Article 3. Does the intellect have knowledge of contingent things?

The first point:[36] It would seem that our intellect does not have knowledge of contingent things. For, as Aristotle says,[37] insight, wisdom, and demonstrative knowledge are concerned, not with contingent things, but with necessary things.

2. Again, Aristotle also says:[38] *Those things which at one time exist, at another do not, are measured by time.* But the intellect abstracts from time as from other material conditions. Therefore since it is proper to contingent things that they at one time exist, at another do not, it would seem that contingent things cannot be known by the intellect.

On the other hand, all demonstrative knowledge is in the intellect. But some of the demonstrative sciences – for instance, the moral sciences (which are concerned with human acts governed by free will), and even the natural sciences (where they treat of realities subject to generation and corruption) – are concerned with contingent things. Therefore the intellect has knowledge of contingent things.

Reply: Contingent things can be considered in two ways: precisely as contingent, and according as an element of necessity is found in them – for nothing is so contingent that it has nothing necessary in it. For instance, the fact that Socrates is running is of itself contingent, but the relationship between running and motion is necessary, for it is necessary that, if Socrates is running, he is also moving.

Now anything contingent is such by reason of matter, since the contingent is what has the potentiality to be or not be and potentiality pertains to matter. Necessity, on the other hand, is a natural consequence of form, since the requirements of form are necessary properties. But matter is the principle of individuation, whereas the universal is such because it is received in the abstraction of a form from particular matter. Moreover, as said before, the direct and essential object of the intellect is universals; whereas singulars are the object of the senses, though also, as we have noticed, of the intellect indirectly.

Therefore contingent things, as contingent, are known by the senses directly, by the intellect indirectly; but universal and necessary aspects of contingent things are known by the intellect.

Thus if we look at the universal aspects of the objects of demonstrative knowledge, all the demonstrative sciences are concerned with necessary things. If, on the other hand, we look at things in themselves, some sciences are concerned with necessary things, others with contingent things.

This makes the solution of the difficulties clear.

36   Cf. *In Ethic,* VI, *lect.* 1.
37   *Nicomachean Ethics* VI, 6. 1140b31.
38   *Physics* IV, *lect.* 12. 221b29.

11

Thomas Aquinas on our Knowledge of the First Principles of Demonstration

Lecture 20
(99b18–100b17)
How the First Principles of Demonstration Are Known By Us

After showing how that which is the principle of demonstration in the sense of a middle comes to be known, the Philosopher now shows how the first common principles come to be known. First, he states his intention. Secondly, he pursues it (99b20).[1] He says therefore first (99b18), that from what follows it will be clear concerning indemonstrable principles both how we come to know them and by what habit they are known. However, the plan we shall observe calls for us first to propose certain problems touching this matter. Then (99b20) he pursues his plan. Concerning this he does two things. First, he raises the problem. Secondly, he settles it (99b32). In regard to the first he does three things. First, he prefaces something from which the need for an inquiry of this kind is indicated. Secondly, he raises the questions (99b23). Thirdly, he objects to a question (99b26).

He says therefore first (99b20), that it has already been established above that nothing is scientifically known through demonstration, unless the first immediate principles are known beforehand. Therefore, in order to have scientific knowledge of demonstration, it is useful to know how the first principles are acquired.

Then (99b23) he raises three questions touching this knowledge of the principles. The first question is whether the knowledge of all immediate principles is the same or not. The second is whether there is a science of all immediate principles or of none; or is there science of some, and some other type of knowledge of the others. The third question is whether the habitual knowledge of those principles comes to exist in us after previously not existing, or have they always been in us but escaped our notice.

Then (99b26) he objects to the last question to which the others are ordered. First, he objects to the second side, saying that it is absurd to claim that we have the habitual knowledge of these principles but they escape our notice. For it is obvious that those who

---

1 'The Philosopher . . . (99b20)': all references are to Aristotle, *Posterior Analytics*. Gk.

have knowledge of the principles have a knowledge which is more certain than that which is acquired through demonstration. But knowledge through demonstration cannot be had such that it escapes the notice of the one having it. For it was established in the beginning of this book that a person who has scientific knowledge of something knows that it is impossible for it to be otherwise. Therefore, it is far less possible for someone having a knowledge of the first principles to have it escape his notice. Yet this absurdity would follow, if habitual knowledge of this kind were in us but escaped our notice.

Secondly (99b28), he objects to the other side. For if a person states that we acquire these habits or principles *de novo* after previously not having them, we are left with the further problem of how we can know and learn such principles *de novo* without some previous knowledge existing in us: for it is impossible to learn anything save from pre-existing knowledge, as we have established above in regard to demonstration. But the reason why we cannot learn the immediate principles from pre-existing knowledge is that pre-existing knowledge is more certain, since it is a cause of certitude of the things which are made known through it. But no knowledge is more certain than the knowledge of these principles. Hence it does not seem that we can begin to know them, when previously we did not know.

Thirdly (99b30), he concludes from the above two arguments that it is neither possible always to have had the knowledge of these principles but it escaped our notice, nor possible that such knowledge is generated *de novo* in us to supplant a state of absolute ignorance in which no other habitual knowledge was possessed.

Then (99b32) he solves these questions. First, he solves the last one. Secondly, he solves the first two (100b5). In regard to the first he does three things. First, he proposes that some principle of knowing must pre-exist in us. Secondly, he shows what it is (99b34). Thirdly, he shows how from a pre-existing principle of knowing we attain the knowledge of principles (100a4).

He says therefore first (99b32), that there must be in us from the beginning a certain cognitive power that exists previously to the knowledge of principles, but not such that it is stronger as to certitude than the knowledge of principles. Hence the knowledge of principles does not come about in us from pre-existing knowledge in the same way as things which are known through demonstration.

Then (99b34) he shows what that pre-existing cognitive principle is. Apropos of this he posits three grades among animals. The first of these is something which seems to be common to all animals, namely, that they have a certain connatural faculty [i.e., potency, i.e., power] for estimating about sense-perceptible things. This faculty, which is not acquired *de novo* but follows upon their very nature, is called *sense*.

Then (99b36) he mentions the second grade, saying that although sense is found in all animals, in some of them a sensible impression remains after the sense-object is removed, as happens in all the perfect animals. But in certain others this does not occur, as in certain imperfect animals; say in those which are not capable of progressive local movement. And it might perhaps be that in regard to some animals an impression remains in regard to certain sense-objects which are more vigorous, and not in regard to those which are weaker. Therefore, those animals in which no impression of sensible objects remains at all have no knowledge except when they are sensing. Similarly, in regard to animals in which such an impression is apt to remain, if it does not remain in them in the case of certain sensible objects, they cannot have any knowledge of them except while they are sensing. But animals, in which a trace of such an impression remains, are capable of having some knowledge in the mind beyond sense; and these are the animals which have *memory*.

Then (100a1) he shows, in view of the foregoing, how the knowledge of first principles comes about in us; and he concludes from the foregoing that from sensing comes remembrance in those animals in which a sensible impression remains, as has been stated above. But from remembrance many times repeated in regard to the same item but in diverse singulars arises *experience*, because experience seems to be nothing else than to take something from many things retained in the memory.

However, experience requires some reasoning about the particulars, in that one is compared to another: and this is peculiar to *reason*. Thus, when one recalls that such a herb cured several men of fever, there is said to be experience that such a herb cures fevers. But reason does not stop at the experience gathered from particulars, but from many particulars in which it has been experienced, it takes one common item which is consolidated in the mind and considers it without considering any of the singulars. This common item reason takes as a principle of art and science. For example, as long as a doctor considered that this herb cured Socrates of fever, and Plato and many other individual men, it is *experience*; but when his considerations arise to the fact that such a species of herb heals a fever absolutely, this is taken as a *rule of the art of medicine*.

This, then, is what he means when he says that just as from memory is formed experience, so from experience or even from the universal resting in the mind (which, namely, is taken as if it is so in *all* cases, just as experience is taken as being so in certain cases. This universal is said to be resting in the mind, inasmuch as it is considered outside the singulars which undergo change. Furthermore, he says that it is *one outside the many*, not according to an autonomous existence but according to the consideration of the intellect which considers a nature, say of man, without referring to Socrates and Plato. But even though it is one outside the many according to the intellect's consideration, nevertheless in the sphere of existents it exists in all singulars one and the same: not numerically, however, as though the humanity of all men were numerically one, but according to the notion of the species. For just as *this white* is similar to *that white* in whiteness, not as though there were one numerical whiteness existing in the two, so too Socrates is similar to Plato in humanity, but not as though there were numerically one humanity existing in the two.) the principle of *art* and *science* is formed in the mind.

And he distinguishes between art and science, just as he did in *Ethics* VI, where it is stated that art is right reason in regard to things to be made. And so he says here that if from experience a universal in regard to generation is taken, i.e., in regard to anything that can be made, say in regard to healing or husbandry, this pertains to *art*. *Science*, however, as it is stated in the same place, is concerned with necessary things; hence if the universal bears on things which are always in the same way, it pertains to *science*; for example, if it bears on numbers or figures. And this process which has been described is verified in regard to the principles of all sciences and arts. Hence he concludes that there do not pre-exist any habits of principles in the sense of being determinate and complete; neither do they come to exist anew from other better known pre-existing principles in the way that a scientific habit is generated in us from previously known principles; rather the habits of principles come to exist in us from pre-existing sense.

And he gives as an example a battle which starts after the soldiers have been beaten and put to flight. For when one of the soldiers shall have taken a stand, i.e., begun to take a battle position and not flee, another takes his stand next to him, and then another, until enough are gathered to form the beginning of a battle. So, too, from the sense and memory of one particular and then of another and another, something is finally reached which is the principle of art and science, as has been stated.

But someone could believe that sense alone or the mere remembrance of singulars is sufficient to cause intellectual knowledge of principles, as some of the ancients supposed, who did not discriminate between sense and intellect. Therefore, to exclude this the Philosopher adds that along with sense it is necessary to presuppose such a nature of mind as cannot only suffer this (i.e., be susceptible of universal knowledge, which indeed comes to pass in virtue of the *possible intellect*) but can also cause this in virtue of the *agent intellect* which makes things intelligible in act by abstraction of universals from singulars.

Then (100a4) he elucidates something asserted in the preceding solution, namely, that the universal is taken from *experience* bearing on singulars. And he says that what was stated above, albeit not clearly – namely, how from the experience of singulars the universal is formed in the mind – must now be discussed again and explained more clearly. For if many singulars are taken which are without differences as to some one item existing in them, that one item according to which they are not different, once it is received in the mind, is the first universal, no matter what it may be, i.e., whether it pertains to the essence of the singulars or not. For since we find that Socrates and Plato and many others are without difference as to whiteness, we take this one item, namely, white, as a universal which is an accident. Similarly, because we find that Socrates and Plato and the others are not different as to rationality, this one item in which they do not differ, namely, rational, we take as a universal which is an essential difference.

But how this one item can be taken he now explains. For it is clear that sensing is properly and *per se* of the singular, but yet there is somehow even a sensing of the universal. For sense knows Callias not only so far forth as he is Callias, but also as he is this man; and similarly Socrates, as he is this man. As a result of such an attainment pre-existing in the sense, the intellective soul can consider man in both. But if it were in the very nature of things that sense could apprehend only that which pertains to particularity, and along with this could in no wise apprehend the nature in the particular, it would not be possible for universal knowledge to be caused in us from sense-apprehension.

Then he manifests this same point in the process which goes from species to genus. Hence he adds: "Again in these," namely, in man and horse, "the mind lingers in its consideration, until it attains to something indivisible in them, which is universal." For example, we consider such an animal and another one, say a man and a horse, until we arrive at the common item, "animal," which is universal; and in this genus we do the same until we arrive at some higher genus. Therefore, since we take a knowledge of universals from singulars, he concludes that it is obviously necessary to acquire the first universal principles by induction. For that is the way, i.e., by way of induction, that the sense introduces the universal into the mind, inasmuch as all the singulars are considered.

Then (100b5) he solves the first question, namely, whether the knowledge of first principles is science, or some other habit. In regard to this he accepts, from what has been stated above, that the knowledge of principles pertains to the intellect whose function is to know the universal: for he says that the universal is a principle of science. But in regard to the intellect there are two genera of habits, and these are not related to the true in exactly the same way. For some are always true, whereas others sometimes receive what is false, as in opinion and in those cases of reasoning which can be of the true and of the false. Again, there are certain erroneous habits, namely, which bear on the false. But because principles are most true, it is clear that they do not pertain to habits which are always of the false, or even to habits which now and then receive falsity, but only to habits which are always of the true. But these are *science* and *understanding* [i.e., intuition]. (In *Ethics* VI a third one is added, namely, *wisdom*: but because wisdom, as it is stated there, comprehends within itself both science and understanding – since it is a science and the chief of the sciences – he omits it here). Therefore, leaving this one aside, no other genus of knowledge but understanding is more certain than science.

Now it is plain that the principles of demonstrations are better known than the demonstrated conclusions, as was established in Book I. Moreover, it cannot be through science that we have those principles, because science is the result of reasoning, namely, demonstrative, whose principles are the very things about which we are speaking. Therefore, because nothing can be truer than science and understanding (for wisdom is included in them), what follows from our consideration of the foregoing is that, properly speaking, the knowledge of principles is understanding.

He also proves this with another reason, namely, because a demonstration is not of necessity a principle of a demonstration; otherwise there would be an infinite process in demonstrations, and this was disproved in Book I. Since, therefore, demonstration causes science, it follows that science cannot be the principle of science, as though the principles of the sciences were made known through science. Therefore, if we have no other type of knowledge except science which is always true, it follows that understanding will be the principle of science, namely, because the principles of the sciences are made known through understanding, so far forth, namely, that this understanding which is the principle of science is cognoscitive of the principles from which science proceeds. But this, namely, science, is *all*, i.e., a whole, which is related to every thing (i.e., to the entire matter with which science is concerned) in the way that understanding is related to the principles of science.

Henry of Ghent on Divine Illumination

[II.] Reply

[A. Knowledge in a broad sense]

Consider all the objects of cognition, standing in an ordered relation to each other so that the last is always suited to be cognized through a preceding one. If a cognition of the first of those could be attained through intellect by purely natural means without any special divine illumination, then likewise a cognition of all the later ones could be attained in the same way. For if a human being by purely natural means without any special divine illumination could attain a cognition of the first theoretical principles, then likewise by purely natural means without any special divine illumination he could attain a cognition of all the conclusions following from those principles. For although the cognition of principles is a kind of illumination toward the cognition of conclusions, nevertheless if someone could attain such a cognition by purely natural means then there is not said to be any special divine illumination in cognizing conclusions through those principles.

In contrast, if in the case of some interrelated objects of cognition the first of them cannot be attained by someone by purely natural means, but only through a special divine illumination, then likewise neither can any of those that come later. For the later ones are cognized only by reason of the first. But now it is undoubtedly true that in the case of some objects of cognition, the first of them cannot be cognized or known by purely natural means, but only by a special divine illumination. This is so in the case of those that are held by the faith in themselves, unconditionally (*per se et simpliciter credibilia*). And so in such cases, it ought to be granted unconditionally and absolutely that it is not possible for a human being to know anything by purely natural means, but only by a special divine illumination. We will establish this later [*Summa* art. 5, q.3].

But some want to extend this mode of knowing to everything that is knowable: They say that nothing true can be known by a human being by purely natural means, without a special divine illumination infused by some supernatural light. And they believe this to be Augustine's view in all his works, wherever he claims that whoever sees something true sees it in the first truth, or in the eternal rules, or in the eternal light. As he says in *City of God* XI.x,

> It is not inappropriate to say that the soul is illuminated by the incorporeal light of God's simple wisdom, just as a body of air is illuminated by a bodily light.

Those who speak in this way greatly degrade the worth and perfection of the created intellect. For matched with every natural thing that is perfect in its form there ought to be some natural action or operation that is proper to it and through which by purely natural means it can attain the good natural to it. This is clear in the case of all other natural things. In keeping with this, Damascene says in *Sentences* Bk. I that of things whose natures are different, their operations are also different. For it is impossible for a substance to lack its natural operation. And in the *Liber de duplici natura et voluntate Christi*, ch. 4: It is impossible for a nature to be established outside of those natural characteristics that are proper to it – e.g., living, rational, voluntary. For someone that does not reason is not a human being, since no human being has been made that does not reason, either well or badly. But as is said in *De anima* I [403a8], knowing and understanding are the intellect's proper operation, "above all else." For this reason, then, if knowing is not possible for someone by purely natural means, then neither is any operation at all; such a person would hence be inferior to all creatures, which is absurd. As the Philosopher says in *De caelo* II [292a22–b12], a thing well completed by the whole of goodness does not need an operation by which it is good, and it is the first cause of everything from which every other thing receives its goodness. So [every other thing] needs its proper operations, through which it is moved toward that [first cause] so as to participate in its divine existence insofar as it can. For all things desire it, and whatever they do by nature they do because of it.

At this point, perhaps it will be said in defense of the above view that it clearly is true that understanding and knowing what is true are the proper and natural operation of intellect and the human soul, and that through which it acquires its goodness. Still, because of that act's eminence and worth, one needs a special illumination for it, even though other beings carry out their actions by purely natural means. For they do so because of the imperfection of those actions – and it is not absurd that one thing should need more to carry out a more perfect action, whereas another thing needs less to carry out a less perfect action.

It is utterly absurd to say this, and is highly derogatory to the worth of the rational soul. For if other inferior things are by purely natural means capable of some operation corresponding and proportionate to their nature, then it is absurd to deny this of the rational soul. The result would be not just that it is not capable by purely natural means of an eminent operation exceeding its nature, but also that it would not even be capable of some operation agreeing with and proportionate to its nature. For it is highly absurd that God would have made the human soul among natural things and not have prepared for it the natural instruments by which it would be capable of any natural operation suited to it, given that he prepared those instruments for other inferior things. For God, much more than nature, does not do anything pointless, or fail to provide a thing with what is necessary for it. But the proper natural operation of the human soul is nothing other than knowing or cognizing. Therefore it must absolutely be granted that a human being through its soul without any special divine illumination can know or cognize something, and can do so by purely natural means. For to hold the contrary is highly derogatory to the worth of the soul and of human nature.

(When I say 'by purely natural means,' I am not excluding the general influence of the first intelligence – which is the first agent in *every* intellectual and cognitive action. Just as in every movement of every natural thing, the first mover produces the movement, so too the general influence that helps with cognition does not preclude that cognition's being said to be brought about by purely natural means. For a human being has that influence assisting him while he cognizes all the things he cognizes naturally, and for this reason it should be said that he attains by purely natural means the cognition of all the other subsequent things that he attains through that influence.)

So if we take 'to know' broadly for every certain cognition (*notitiam*) of a thing, so that it includes even sensory cognition (*cognitionem*), then (as was said in the preceding question) to the extent that it comes from the senses and sensory cognition, it is clear that we ought to say unconditionally and absolutely that one can know and cognize something through a sensory cognition that is certain, as was shown in the preceding question. Further – and this pertains to the present question – this can occur by purely natural means, because the primary sensible objects make an impression on the senses by purely natural necessity, and it is through these sensibles, again by natural necessity, that all subsequent sensible objects make an impression on both the external and internal senses.

[B. Knowledge of the truth]

A distinction must be drawn, however, with respect to intellect and intellective cognition: It is this cognizing, strictly, that is called knowing. For although nothing is known unless it is true (according to Augustine in his *Book of 83 Questions* [Q54]), still it is one thing to know of a creature what is true with respect to it, and another to know its truth. So there is one cognition by which a thing is cognized, another by which its truth is cognized. For every cognitive power that through its cognition apprehends a thing just as it has existence in itself, outside the cognizer, apprehends what is true in it. But through this it does not apprehend the thing's truth. For the senses even in brute animals apprehend well enough concerning a thing what is true in it – for instance, a true human being, true wood, a true stone, and especially the proper objects with respect to which the senses are necessarily true. But still they apprehend or cognize the truth of no thing, because they cannot judge regarding any thing what it is in actual truth – e.g., concerning a human being, that it is a true human being, or concerning a color, that it is a true color.

So through the intellective cognition of something created, one can have two kinds of cognitions. By one, someone knows or cognizes through a simple understanding solely what a thing is. By the other, someone knows and cognizes the truth of the thing itself, through an understanding that composes and divides. In the case of the first cognition our intellect entirely follows the senses, and there is no concept in intellect that was not first in the senses. Insofar as it is of this sort, then, such an intellection certainly can be true – by conceiving or cognizing the thing as it is – just as the sense that it is following can be. But it doesn't conceive or understand the thing's very truth through a certain judgment by perceiving of it what it is – for instance, that it is a true human being or a true color.

There are two reasons for this, one pertaining to the intellect itself, another pertaining to what is intelligible. The reason that pertains to the intellect is that it conceives the truth not by a simple understanding, but only by composition and division (as the Philosopher claims in *Metaphysics* VI [10727b18–32] and as will be explained below). Hence just as a sense is called true because of grasping a thing as it is, not because of grasping its truth, so too a simple understanding following a true sense is called true because of grasping a thing as it is, not because of grasping its truth.

The reason that pertains to what is intelligible is that the intention of the thing by which it is that which it is and the intention by which it is called true are two different things, even though – since every being is true and vice versa – these intentions coincide in each and every thing and are convertible with one other. For as the first proposition of the *Liber de causis* says, the first of created things is existence, and so the first intention capable of being grasped by intellect is the notion *being (ratio entis)*. One can understand this notion without understanding any other intention pertaining to *being*, because it includes none of the others in itself, and is included in all the others. For although the intention *being* is understood only under the notion *true*, which is the per se object of intellect, it is nevertheless not the case that *true*, as the notion from which *being* is understood, is the object of intellect in the way that *being* is. For the notion *true* is the notion of intelligibility in all things. But the object [of intellect] is *true being*, or *true good*, and so on for the other intentions of things. Hence, the intention *being* is included in all the other intentions of things, both universal and particular, because what is not a being is nothing. For this reason, the Commentator claims regarding the first proposition of the *Liber de causis* that existence is characterized by its adhering to the thing more vehemently than do the other intentions in that thing.

The next most proximate intentions in the thing, after the intention *being*, are these universal intentions: *one*, *true*, and *good*. This is so in various ways, in order, because anything existing under the intention *being* can be considered in three ways:

- First, insofar as it has in its nature a determinate existence by which through its form it is in itself undivided but divided from everything else. In this way the intention *one* holds of it. For everything is one insofar as it is, in itself, formally undivided, but divided from everything else. For as the Philosopher says in *Metaphysics* III [999b33], something is one that exists by itself and alone.
- Second, insofar as it has in its own existence what its corresponding exemplar represents it as having. In this way the intention *true* holds of it. For each thing is true insofar as it contains in itself what its exemplar represents.
- Third, insofar as it holds of the end to which it is directed. In this way the intention *good* holds of it. For every thing is good insofar as it aims toward an end that is good.

So *true* indicates an intention concerning the thing relative to its exemplar. And since this is not first but secondary, whereas *being* indicates the first, discrete intention concerning the thing, it follows that the intellect can indeed apprehend that which is a being and is true in the thing, without apprehending the intention of its truth. For the intention of truth in a thing can be apprehended only by apprehending its conformity to its exemplar. The intention *being*, on the other hand, is apprehended in the thing discretely, without such a relation. But in a second cognition, by which the truth of the thing itself is known or cognized (without which it is not a complete human cognition of the thing), the cognition and judgment of intellect altogether exceed the cognition and judgment of the senses, since (as has been said) the intellect cognizes something's truth only by composing and dividing, which a sense cannot do. Hence such an intellection can cognize a thing in a way that the senses cannot, nor can even an intellection that is an understanding of simples: Such an intellection can apprehend by a certain judgment concerning a thing that in actual truth it is such or such – for instance, [that it is] a true human being, a true color, and so on.

[C.   Different kinds of exemplars]

So with respect to this mode of knowing and cognizing something through intellect, by which the truth of the thing is known (this is knowing in the strict sense), it is still in doubt whether a human being can know anything by purely natural means, without any special divine illumination. We should say the following. It was said already [II.B] that the truth of a thing can be cognized only by cognizing the conformity of the cognized thing to its exemplar. For as Augustine says in *De vera religione* [xxxvi.66], "true things are true insofar as they are like their one source." Also, Anselm says in *De veritate* [ch. 7] that "truth is the conformity of a thing to its most true exemplar" and, in the same passage: "What is, truly is, insofar as it is what is there." For this reason, then, inasmuch as there are two kinds of exemplars of a thing, a thing's truth has two ways of being cognized by a human being, with respect to two exemplars. For according to what Plato holds in the *Timaeus* [27d–29a], there are two exemplars: one kind made and constructed, the other kind perpetual and unchangeable. The first exemplar of a thing is its universal species existing within the soul, through which the soul acquires a cognition of all the individuals it stands for. This exemplar is caused by the thing. The second exemplar is the divine art containing the ideal formulations of all things. Plato says that God established the world from this exemplar (just as an artisan builds a house from an exemplar of the artistry in his mind) and not from the first exemplar.

We should know, then, that in examining that first exemplar, there are two ways in which a human being can go about it:

- First, so as to examine the cognized object depicted outside the cognizer – as by examining a person's image painted on a wall in order to recognize that person;
- Second, so as to examine the basis (*rationem*) of cognizing depicted in the cognizer – in that the species of sensible things are depicted in the senses and the species of intelligible things in the intellect.

In the first way it is impossible to cognize a thing's truth by examining its exemplar. One can have only an imaginary apprehension of the thing, an apprehension of whatever sort someone's imaginative power happened to be able to form for him. Thus, as Augustine says in *De trinitate* VIII [v.7], someone would marvel if a person he had imagined but never seen were to appear before him [just as he imagined]. Also, through that imaginary apprehension taken from a painted image, if someone were to learn the name of the person in the image, then he could come to an estimative judgment of that person – if that person were to appear before him. At that point he could for the first time, on the basis of the thing itself seen in its own form, cognize its truth, and on that basis make a judgment as to whether that image is a true one, corresponding to the person seen. It was in this way, one reads, that Queen Candace had a painted image of Alexander made for herself before she had ever seen him, and she recognized him immediately when she saw him, even though he pretended to be someone else.[1]

---

1   *Historia Alexandri Magni*, III. 19–22.

So in the second way – that is, by examining the exemplar taken from the thing itself, so as to examine the basis of cognizing in the cognizer himself – the truth of the thing itself can indeed be cognized in a way: by forming a mental concept of the thing, conforming to that exemplar. It was in this way that Aristotle held that human beings acquire knowledge of things and a cognition of truth by purely natural means – and this with respect to natural, changeable things. Aristotle held that such an exemplar is acquired from things through the senses as the primary basis of art and knowledge, according to what he says at the start of the *Metaphysics* [981a5–7]: "Art results when from many things understood through experience, one universal judgment is made regarding similar cases." And in *Posterior Analytics* II [100a4–8]:

> Memory is produced from sense, and from a memory often produced, experience. And from experience – a universal existing in the soul – the one [is produced] over the many. That is the basis of art and knowledge.

This accords with what Augustine says in *De trinitate* XI.iii [6]:

> If the species of a body that is sensed by a body is taken away, its likeness remains in the memory. Through this the will turns the mind's attention so that it is formed internally by that, just as it was formed externally by the body that was its sensible object.

And so, as he says in *De trinitate* VIII.v [7], things we have not seen we think of according to generic or specific cognitions, either naturally innate or gathered from experience. So through the universal cognition that we have within ourselves, acquired from different species of animals, we form a cognition, regarding whatever appears to us, of whether it is an animal or not, and through the specific cognition of a donkey we form a cognition, regarding whatever appears to us, of whether it is a donkey or not.

[D. Infallible knowledge of the truth requires illumination]

But through such an exemplar, acquired within us, it is altogether impossible for us to have an altogether certain and infallible cognition of the truth. There are three reasons for this: The first draws on the thing from which such an exemplar is abstracted, the second on the soul in which such an exemplar is received, the third on the exemplar itself that is received in the soul from the thing.

The first reason is that such an exemplar, because it is abstracted from a changeable thing, necessarily has some of the characteristics of a changeable thing. So since natural things are more changeable than mathematical things, the Philosopher claimed that our knowledge of mathematical things has more certainty than our knowledge of natural things, through their universal species. This can be only because of the changeability of the species themselves existing within the soul. Hence Augustine, taking up this cause of the incertitude of the knowledge of natural things (the cause due to sensibles), says in his *Book of 83 Questions* Q9 that "pure truth shouldn't be sought from the bodily senses" and that

> We are warned for our own sake to turn away from this world and toward God – that is, toward the truth that is understood and apprehended in the inner mind, and that always remains and is of the same nature – and to make this turn with all haste.

The second reason is that because the human soul is changeable and undergoes error, nothing that is equally changeable or more so can correct it so that it is not bent by error, and so that it persists in the correctness of truth. Therefore, every exemplar that the soul receives from natural things, since it is of a lower grade of nature than the soul, is necessarily equally changeable as the soul or more so. It therefore cannot correct the soul so that it persists in infallible truth. This is the argument of Augustine in *De vera religione* [xxx.56] by which he proves that the unchangeable truth through which the soul has certain knowledge is above the soul:

> It is clear enough that the law of all arts, since it is utterly unchangeable – whereas the human mind, to which it has been granted to see such a law, can suffer the changeability of error – is the law above our mind that is called the truth.

Only this is sufficient to correct our changeable and bendable mind with infallible cognition. The mind does not have the ability to judge this law, but through that it judges everything else. For the mind is more able to judge anything lower than itself than it is able through that to judge another, as Augustine concludes in the same passage.

The third reason is that an exemplar of this sort, since it is an intention and species of a sensible thing abstracted from a phantasm, has a likeness with the false as well as with the true. So as far as the species is concerned, they cannot be distinguished. For it is through the same images of sensible things that (a) we judge in sleep and in madness that the images are the things themselves, and (b) when awake we judge the things themselves. But the pure truth is not perceived unless it is discerned from what is false. Therefore it is impossible through such an exemplar to have certain knowledge and a certain cognition of the truth. Thus if we are to possess certain knowledge of the truth, the mind must turn away from the senses and sensible things and from every intention, no matter how universal and abstracted from the senses, and turn toward the unchangeable truth existing above the mind. This truth "does not have an image of the false from which it cannot be discerned," as Augustine says in his *Book of 83 Questions* Q9, where he discusses this argument.

13

Duns Scotus on Divine Illumination

[Article IV. Concerning Henry's Conclusion]

In the fourth article I argue against the conclusion of [Henry's] view as follows: What, I ask, is meant by certain and unadulterated truth? Either it means infallible truth, that is, a truth which excludes all doubt and deception. And in this case, we have proved and declared already in the second and third articles that such truth is possible on purely natural grounds. Or by such truth he means truth as an attribute of "being". In which case, since we can know "being" we can also know its attribute "true". And if we know "true" we can also know truth by a kind of abstraction. For any form that can be recognised in a subject can also be known in itself and in the abstract apart from the subject. Or truth is to be understood in still another way, as truth of conformity to an exemplar. If the exemplar in question is taken to be created, we have what we seek to prove. If conformity to an uncreated exemplar is meant, why such conformity cannot be recognised unless the exemplar itself is known, for unless the term of a relation is known the relation itself cannot be known. Consequently, it is false to assume that an eternal exemplar is the reason why we know something when this exemplar itself remains unknown.

Secondly, I argue further that simple intelligence can know by way of definition all that it knows in a confused manner by the simple expedient of discovering the definition of the thing known by way of division. This definitive knowledge seems to be the most perfect kind of knowledge that pertains to simple intelligence. From this most perfect knowledge of the terms, however, the intellect can understand the principle most perfectly; and from the principle, the conclusion. Intellectual knowledge seems to be complete with this, so that no further knowledge of truth over and above the aforementioned truths seems necessary.

In the third place, either the Eternal Light, which you say is necessary in order to have unadulterated truth, causes something naturally prior to the act or not. If it does, then this thing is produced either in the object or in the intellect. But it cannot be produced in the object, because the object, in so far as it exists in the intellect, has no real existence but only intentional existence. Therefore, it is incapable of any real accident. If this thing is produced in the intellect, then the Eternal Light transforms [the mind] to know pure truth only through the medium of its effect. If this be the case, then it seems that common opinion attributes knowledge to the Uncreated Light to the same extent as does this, for the common view assumes that knowledge is seen in the active intellect, which is the effect of the Uncreated Light, and indeed is a more perfect effect than this accidental created Light would be. If this Uncreated Light does not cause anything prior to the act, then either the Light alone causes the act [of knowledge], or the Light with the intellect and object do so. If the Light does so alone, then the active intellect has no function whatsoever in knowing pure truth. But this seems inconsistent because the latter is the most noble function of our intellect. The active intellect, then, which is the most noble [faculty of knowledge] in our soul, must concur in some way in this action.

And the inconsistency here inferred also follows from the aforesaid opinion in another way. For according to the one who holds this opinion, any agent using an instrument is incapable of performing an action which exceeds the action of the instrument. Therefore, since the power of the active intellect could not arrive at the knowledge of pure truth, the Eternal Light using the active intellect could not produce this knowledge or have anything to do with the act whereby pure truth is known and still have the active intellect function as an instrument. And if you say that the Uncreated Light causes this unadulterated truth together with the intellect and the object, this is the common opinion which assumes that the Uncreated Light acting as the remote cause produces all certain truth. Consequently, either this opinion [of Henry] is inconsistent or it is not at variance with the common view.

[Article V. Solution of the Question]

As to the question, then, I say that because of what Augustine has said, one should concede that infallible truths are seen in the eternal rules, where the term "in" can be taken in the sense of "in an object". There are four ways in which this could be done: (1) either as in a proximate object, or (2) as in that which contains the proximate object, or (3) as that in virtue of which the proximate object moves [the intellect], or (4) as in a remote object.

[The first way]

In explanation of the first, I say that all the intelligibles have an intelligible being in virtue of the act of the divine intellect. In these intelligibles all the truths that can be affirmed about them are visible so that the intellect knowing these intelligibles and in virtue thereof understanding the necessary truths about them, sees these truths in them as in an object. Now these intelligibles inasmuch as they are secondary objects of the divine intellect are "truths" because they are conformed to their exemplar, viz. the divine intellect. Likewise, they are a "light" because they are manifest. And there they are immutable and necessary. But they are eternal only in a qualified sense, because eternity is characteristic of something really existing, and these intelligibles "exist" only in a qualified sense. This then is the first way in which we can be said to see in the Eternal Light, i.e. as in the secondary object of the divine intellect, which object is truth and eternal light in the sense explained.

[The second way]

The second way is also clear, because the divine intellect contains these truths like a book, as Augustine testifies in *De Trinitate*, BK. XIV, c. xv: "These rules are written in the book of Eternal Light", that is, in the divine intellect inasmuch as it contains these truths. And although this book itself is not seen, nevertheless those truths are seen which are written in this book.

And to this extent, our intellect could be said to see truths in the Eternal Light, i.e. to see things which are in that book as in something which contains the object.

And Augustine's statement in *De Trinitate*, BK. XII, c. xiv, that the meaning of "square body" remains incorruptible and immutable, and so on, can be understood seemingly in either of these two ways. For the meaning of a square body remains incorruptible and immutable only inasmuch as it is a secondary object of the divine intellect.

But there is a doubt about this first way. We do not see these truths as they are in the divine intellect, because we do not see the divine intellect itself. How then can we be said to see things in the Uncreated Light – things, which exist indeed in the Uncreated Light as objects known by that intellect, but which we see only in something which is the eternal light in a qualified sense. To this the third way gives the following answer.

[The third way]

These intelligibles in so far as they are secondary objects of the divine intellect have existence only in a qualified sense. But something that exists only in a qualified sense, to the precise extent that it "exists" in this way, is incapable of any truly real operation. If such an operation pertains to it at all, it does so only in virtue of something which exists in an unqualified sense. Therefore, these secondary objects do not enjoy the power to move the intellect, to speak precisely, except by virtue of the existence of the divine intellect, which exists in an unqualified sense and through which the intelligibles have existence in a qualified sense. And so we see in the eternal light in a qualified sense as in the proximate object. But according to this third way we see in the Uncreated Light as in the immediate cause by virtue of which the proximate object moves [the intellect].

We can also be said to see in the Eternal Light in this third way inasmuch as this Light is the cause of the object itself. For the divine intellect produces this intelligible in existence and by its act gives to this object one type of being and to another a second type of being. Consequently, the divine intellect gives them such intelligible content as they possess as objects of knowledge. Now it is through their intelligible content that they afterward move the intellect to certain knowledge. And, properly speaking, it could be said that our intellect sees in the Light, because the Light is the cause of the object. This is clear from a simile: for we are said to understand properly in the light of the active intellect, although this light is nothing more than the active cause (i.e., that which makes the [potential] object actual, or that in virtue of which the object moves, or both).

The fact then that the divine intellect, the true Uncreated Light, has a twofold causality (viz. that it produces objects in intelligible being and that it is also that in virtue of which the secondary objects produced actually move the intellect) – this fact can supply as it were a third type or mode of interpretation as to how we can be said to see truly in the Eternal Light.

But suppose someone should object to these two ways of supplying a third interpretation on the following grounds. We should rather be said to see in God willing or in God in so far as He is will, for the divine will is the immediate principle of every act directed towards something outside Himself.

I reply that the divine intellect, as far as it is in some way prior to the act of the divine will, produces these objects in intelligible being, and thus the intellect seems to be a purely natural cause in their regard. For God is not a free cause of anything unless volition as an elicited act somehow precedes the thing in question. Now, inasmuch as the intellect produces objects in intelligible being prior to the act of the will, it would seem to co-operate as a prior cause with these intelligibles in the production of their natural effect – which effect consists in this: Once these intelligibles are grasped and formulated in a pro-position they cause the conformity of what is grasped [viz. the proposition] to themselves [as terms]. Consequently, it seems to involve a contradiction that an intellect should form such a proposition and still not have this proposition conform to the terms even though it is possible that the intellect should not grasp the terms or formulate them in a proposition. For even though God freely co-operates with the intellect when it combines or does not combine these terms, still once the terms have been formed into a proposition, the conformity of the latter with the terms seems to follow as a necessary consequence from the very meaning of the terms – a meaning which they have by reason of the fact that the intellect of God has naturally produced these terms in intelligible being.

From all this, it is clear why a special illumination is not required in order to see in the eternal reasons, for Augustine assumes that we see in them only such truths as are necessary in virtue of their terms. Now it is in just such truths that we have the greatest necessity between the effect and both its proximate and remote causes (that is, both on the part of the divine intellect in its relation to the objects which move [our intellect] and on the part of the objects in relation to the truth of the propositions about them). Even though the necessity of perceiving such a truth is not so great that not to perceive it would include a contradiction, still there is a necessity present which arises from the proximate cause [viz. the intelligibility of the terms] assisted by the remote cause [viz. the divine intellect which gives such ideas their intelligibility]. For once the terms are grasped and formed into a proposition, they are naturally able to make evident the conformity that exists between the proposition and its terms even though it be granted that God co-operates with these terms in producing their effect, not by a natural necessity, but by a general [free] influence. But whether it be by a general influence, or what is more, by a natural necessity, that God co-operates with the terms in producing their effect, it is quite clear that no special illumination is required.

The assumption as to what Augustine meant is clearly justified by what he says of the infidel philosophers in *De Trinitate*, BK. IV, c. xxxv: "Some of them have been able to see through and beyond all creation and with their mind's eye to reach at least in some degree the light of immutable truth, a thing which they ridicule many Christians, who live meanwhile by faith alone, for not being able to do." He wishes to say, therefore, that Christians do not see in the eternal rules the things they believe and yet the philo-sophers see many necessary truths therein. And the same with *De Trinitate*, BK. IX, c. vi: "Not of what sort the mind of one particular man happens to be, etc." – as if he were to say: "It is not contingent but necessary truths that are seen there". And in the same work he argues against those philosophers: "Just because they argue most truly that all that hap-pens in time takes place on account of eternal reasons, are they therefore able to perceive therein how many kinds of animals exist or how many seeds of each there were in the begin-ning, and so on. . . . Have they not sought all these things not by that unchangeable know-ledge, but by the history of places and times, and have they not believed the written experience of others?" Consequently, he means that contingent truths known by the senses alone or believed on the account of others are not known through the eternal rules. And yet special illumination is required even more for what must be believed than for necessary truths. Indeed, this special illumination is least needed in the case of the latter; general illumination alone suffices.

On the contrary. Why then does Augustine say in *De Trinitate*, BK. XII, c. xiv: "It is only for the few to attain the intelligible reasons with their mind's eye", and in the *Eighty-three Questions*, q. xlvi: "Only the pure of soul reach them"? I reply that he does not mean by this purity a freedom from vices, for in *De Trinitate*, BK. XIV, c. xv, he holds that the unjust man sees in the eternal rules what a just man must do and how he must regard things in their light. And in the fourth book, in the chapter cited above, he maintains that the philosophers saw truth in the eternal reasons even though they lacked faith. And in the same question, he holds that no one can be wise without a knowledge of the ideas in the way, for instance, that they would concede Plato to be wise. But this purity must be understood of the elevation of the intellect to the contemplation of these truths as they are in themselves and not as they appear in the sense image.

Here we must remember that the sensible thing outside causes a confused sense image, something with only an incidental unity in the faculty of imagination, which represents the thing according to its quantity, colour and other sensible accidents. And just as the sense image represents things only confusedly and according to an incidental unity, so many perceive only such incidental combinations. Now, primary truths are primary precisely because their terms are grasped in their proper nature and apart from all that is merely incidental to them. Now this proposition, "The whole is greater than its part", is not primarily true of the whole as realised in a stone or in wood, but of "whole" in the abstract, i.e. apart from everything with which it merely happens to be joined. Consequently, the mind which never conceives totality except in an incidental concept such as the totality of a stone or the totality of wood, never really understands the pure truth of this principle, because it never grasps the precise nature of the terms to which the principle owes its truth. It is only within the power of the few to attain the eternal reasons, because it is only the few that have an understanding of the essentials, whereas the many grasp things merely in incidental concepts such as those mentioned above. But these few are not said to be distinguished from the others by a special illumination, but by better natural powers, since they have a sharper and more abstractive mind, or because of greater research which enables one person to know those essences which another equally talented individual does not discover because he does not investigate them.

And in this way we can understand Augustine's statement in *De Trinitate*, BK. IX, c. vi, regarding the individual on the mountain who sees the pure light above and the mist below. For whoever grasps nothing but incidental notions in the way that the sense image represents such objects, viz. as a kind of accidental aggregate, is like one in a valley surrounded by mist. But by grasping just what things are of themselves, a person separates the essences from the many additional incidental features associated with them in the sense image. Such a one, as it were, has the sense image in the mist beneath him, but he himself is on the mountain to the extent that in virtue of the uncreated intellect, the Eternal Light, he knows this truth and sees what is true from above, as a more universal truth.

[The fourth way]

And finally, we can concede that pure truths are known in the Eternal Light as in a remotely known object. For the Uncreated Light is the first source of speculative things and the ultimate end of practical things. The first speculative and practical principles, then, are derived from it. Hence, the knowledge of speculative and practical things by means of principles derived from the Eternal Light, where the latter is known, is more perfect and prior to knowledge derived from principles from the respective class of things as such, as has been pointed out in the question on the subject of theology. Such knowledge is more eminent than any other. Now it is in this way that the knowledge of all things pertains to the theologian. In this way pure truth is said to be known, since truth alone without admixture of anything else is known, for it is known through the First Being. And once this Being is known, the principles for knowing in this perfect way are derived therefrom. But any other thing from which principles of knowing something in kind are derived is defective truth.

Only God knows all things purely in this perfect way, for as we have said in the question on the subject of theology. He alone knows all things precisely through His essence. Nevertheless, every intellect can be moved by some object to know that something is true in virtue of Him, and in this way the knowledge of all things pertains to the theologian, as has been said in the question on the subject of theology. For to know that a triangle has three [angles equal to two right angles], in so far as this is a kind of participation of God and that it has such an order in the universe that it expresses more perfectly as it were the perfection of God, – this is a nobler way of knowing a triangle has three [angles, etc.] than to know this truth from the notion of a triangle itself. Similarly, to know that one should live temperately in order to attain the supreme happiness, which consists in attaining the essence of God in Himself, is a more perfect way of knowing this practical truth than to be aware of it through some principle in the class of mores, for instance, through the principle that one is obliged to live uprightly.

And in this manner Augustine speaks of the Uncreated Light as known in *De Trinitate*, BK. XV, C. xxvii, where addressing himself, he says: "You have seen many things and these you have discerned through that Light in which you saw them shining forth to you. Turn your eyes to the Light itself and fasten them upon it, if you can, for in this way you will see how the nativity of the Word of God differs from the procession of the Gift of God." And a little later: "This and other things this Light has revealed to your inner eyes. What then is the reason with fixed glance you are unable to see the Light itself, if it is not indeed your weakness? . . ."

Knowledge and Skepticism

14

Augustine on the Certainty of Self-Knowledge

If I Am Deceived, I Exist[1]

26. For we both *are*, and *know* that we are, and *take delight* in our being and knowing. Moreover, in these three things no true-seeming illusion disturbs us; for we do not come into contact with these by some bodily sense, as we perceive the things outside us – colors, e.g., by seeing, sounds by hearing, smells by smelling, tastes by tasting, hard and soft objects by touching – of all which sensible objects it is the images resembling them, but not themselves, that we perceive in the mind and hold in the memory, and which excite us to desire the objects. However, without any delusive representation of images or phantasms, I am most certain that I am, that I know, and that I delight in this. On none of these points do I fear the arguments of the skeptics of the Academy who say: what if you are deceived? For if I am deceived, I am. For he who does not exist cannot be deceived; and if I am deceived, by this same token I am. And since I am if I am deceived, how am I deceived in believing that I am? For it is certain that I am, if I am deceived. Since therefore I, the person deceived, should be, even if I were deceived, certainly I am not deceived in this knowledge that I am. Consequently, neither am I deceived in knowing that I know. For, as I know that I am, so I know this also, that I know. And when I love these two [being and knowing], I add to them a third, that is, my love, which is of equal importance. For neither am I deceived in this, that I love, since in those things which I love I am not deceived; even if these were false, it would still be true that I loved false things. For how could I justly be blamed and prohibited from loving false things, if it were false that I loved them? Since these facts are true and real, who doubts that, when these things are loved, the love of them is itself true and real?

I Know That I Am Alive[2]

21. First, of what sort and how great is the very knowledge itself that a man can attain, be he ever so skillful and learned, by which our thought is formed with truth, when we speak

1   *City of God*, XI, *26*.
2   *On the Trinity*, XV, 12.21–2.

what we know? For to pass by those things that come into the mind from the bodily senses, among which so many are otherwise than they seem to be, that he who is overmuch pressed down by their resemblance to truth, seems sane to himself, but really is not sane – whence it is that the Academic philosophy has so prevailed as to be still more wretchedly insane by doubting all things – passing by, then, those things that come into the mind by the bodily senses, how large a proportion is left of things which we know in such manner as we know that we live? In this, indeed, we are absolutely without any fear lest perchance we are being deceived by some resemblance of the truth; since it is certain that he too who is deceived, yet lives. And this again is not reckoned among those objects of sight that are presented from without, so that the eye may be deceived in it; in such way as it is when an oar in the water looks bent, and towers seem to move as you sail past them, and a thousand other things that are otherwise than they seem to be: for this is not a thing that is discerned by the eye of the flesh. The knowledge by which we know that we live is the most inward of all knowledge, of which even the Academic cannot insinuate. Perhaps you are asleep, and do not know it, and you see things in your sleep. For who does not know that what people see in dreams is precisely like what they see when awake? But he who is certain of the knowledge of his own life does not therein say "I know I am awake" but "I know I am alive"; therefore, whether he be asleep or awake, he is alive. Nor can he be deceived in that knowledge by dreams; since it belongs to a living man both to sleep and to see in sleep. Nor can the Academic again say, in confutation of this knowledge, "Perhaps you are mad, and do not know it": for what madmen see is precisely like what they also see who are sane; but he who is mad is alive. Nor does he answer the Academic by saying "I know I am not mad" but "I know I am alive." Therefore he who says he knows he is alive, can neither be deceived nor lie. Let a thousand kinds then of deceitful objects of sight be presented to him who says "I know I am alive"; yet he will fear none of them, for he who is deceived yet is alive. But if such things alone pertain to human knowledge, they are very few indeed; unless that they can be so multiplied in each kind, as not only not to be few, but to reach in the result to infinity. For he who says "I know I am alive" says that he knows one single thing. Further, if he says "I know that I know I am alive," now there are two; but that he knows these two is a third thing to know. And so he can add a fourth and a fifth, and innumerable others, if he holds out. But since he cannot either comprehend an innumerable number by additions of units, or say a thing innumerable times, he comprehends this at least, and with perfect certainty, viz. that this is both true, and so innumerable that he cannot truly comprehend and say its infinite number. This same thing may be noticed also in the case of a will that is certain. For it would be an impudent answer to make to any one who should say "I will to be happy" that perhaps you are deceived. And if he should say, "I know that I will this, and I know that I know it," he can add yet a third to these two, viz. that he knows these two; and a fourth, that he knows that he knows these two; and so on *ad infinitum*. Likewise, if any one were to say, "I will not to be mistaken," will it not be true, whether he is mistaken or whether he is not, that nevertheless he does will not to be mistaken? Would it not be most impudent to say to him "Perhaps you are deceived?" when beyond doubt, whereinsoever he may be deceived, he is nevertheless not deceived in thinking that he wills not to be deceived. And if he says he knows this, he adds any number he chooses of things known, and perceives that number to be infinite. For he who says, "I will not to be deceived, and I know that I will not to be so, and I know that I know it," is able now to set forth an infinite number here also, however awkward may be the expression of it. And other things too are to be found capable of refuting the Academics, who contend that man can know nothing. But we must restrict ourselves, especially as this is not the subject we have undertaken in the present work. There are three books of ours on that subject [*Against the Academics*], written in the early time of our conversion, which he who can and will read, and who understands them, will doubtless not be much moved by any of the many arguments which they have found out against the discovery of truth. For whereas there are two kinds of knowable things – one, of those things which the mind perceives by the bodily senses; the other, of those which it perceives by itself – these philosophers have babbled much against the bodily senses, but have never been able to throw doubt upon those most certain perceptions of things true which the mind knows by itself, such as is that which I have mentioned, "I know that I am alive." But far be it from us to doubt the truth of what we have learned by the bodily senses; since by them we have learned to know the heaven and the earth, and those things in them which are known to us, so far as He who created both us and them has willed them to be within our knowledge. Far be it from us too to deny that we know what we have learned by the testimony of others: otherwise we know not that there is an ocean; we know not that the lands and cities exist which most copious report commends to us; we know not that those men were, and their works, which we have learned by reading history; we know not the news that is daily brought us from this quarter or that, and confirmed by consistent and conspiring evidence; lastly, we know not at what place or from whom we have been born: since in all these things we have believed the testimony of others. And if it is most absurd to say this, then we must confess, that not only our own senses, but those of other persons also, have added very much indeed to our knowledge.

22. All these things, then, both those which the human mind knows by itself, and those which it knows by the bodily senses, and those which it has received and knows by the testimony of others, are laid up and retained in the storehouse of the memory; and from these is begotten a word that is true, when we speak what we know, but a word that is before all sound, before all thought of a sound. For the word is then most like to the thing known, from which also its image is begotten, since the sight of thinking arises from the sight of knowledge, when it is a word belonging to no tongue, but is a true word concerning a true thing, having nothing of its own, but wholly derived from that knowledge from which it is born. Nor does it signify when he learned it, who speaks what he knows; for sometimes he says it immediately upon learning it; provided only that the word is true. *i.e.* sprung from things that are known.

15

Thomas Aquinas on whether the Intellect Can Be False

Summary Theologiae

Part I, Question 17. Concerning Falsity

Article 3. Whether falsity is in the intellect

Objection 1: It seems that falsity is not in the understanding. For Augustine says (*Questions 85*, q. 32), "Anyone who is deceived does not understand that in which he is deceived." But falsity is said to be in some cognition in so far as we are deceived in that cognition. Therefore, falsity does not exist in the intellect [i.e., understanding].

Objection 2: Further, the Philosopher [Aristotle] says (*De Anima* iii, 51) that the intellect is always right. Therefore there is no falsity in the intellect.

On the contrary, It is said in *De Anima* iii, 21, that "where there is composition of objects understood, there is truth and falsehood." But such composition is in the intellect [i.e., understanding]. Therefore truth and falsehood exist in the intellect.

I answer that, Just as a thing has being by its proper form, so a cognitive faculty has cognition by the likeness of the thing cognized. Hence, just as natural things cannot fail to have the existence that belongs to them by their form, but may fail to have some things consequent upon or accidental to them, even as a man may fail to possess two feet, but may not fail to be a man; so a cognitive faculty may not fail in the cognition of the thing the likeness of which informs it, but may fail with regard to something consequent upon or accidental to that form. For it has been said that sight is not deceived about its proper sensible, but about common sensibles that are consequent upon that object or about accidental objects of sense.[1] Now just as the sense is directly informed by the likeness of its

---

1 If I see a white sugar cube, I properly see something white, because my sight is properly receptive of color. I also see something cubical, because the color my sight receives is the quality of cubical surface. But this shape is not the proper object of my sight, because I could also sense it by touch. Finally, I also see something that is coincidentally (*per accidens*) sweet, but of course I do not see it insofar as it is sweet, because its taste does not affect my sight at all; so, this sweet thing is a merely

proper object, so is the intellect by the likeness of the essence of a thing. Hence the intellect is not deceived about the essence of a thing, as neither is the sense about its proper object. But in affirming and denying the intellect may be deceived, by attributing to the thing the essence of which it understands something which is not consequent upon it or is opposed to it. For the intellect is in the same position as regards judging of such things, as sense is as to judging of common, or accidental, sensible objects. There is, however, this difference, as mentioned earlier regarding truth, that falsity can exist in the intellect not only because its cognition is false, but also because the intellect cognizes its falsity, just as it cognizes its truth; whereas the senses do not cognize their falsity, as was stated above.[2]

Although falsity of the intellect can occur properly only in the composition of the intellect, falsity nevertheless can also occur accidentally in that operation of the intellect whereby it knows the essence of a thing, insofar as it is mixed up with some composition of the intellect. This can take place in two ways. In one way, when the intellect attributes the definition of one thing to another thing; as when it attributes the definition of circle to a man. For the definition of one thing is false of another. In another way, when it constructs an inconsistent definition. For in this way the definition is not only false of some thing, but it is false in itself. For example, if it were to form the definition "rational four-footed animal," the intellect would be false in making it, because it is false in forming the composition: "some rational animal is four-footed." For this reason the intellect cannot be false in its knowledge of simple essences; but it is either true, or it understands nothing at all.

Reply to Objection 1: Because the essence of a thing is the proper object of the intellect, we are properly said to understand a thing when we reduce our judgment about it to its essence, as we do in demonstrations, in which there is no falsity. This is how Augustine's words must be understood that anyone who is deceived does not understand that in which he is deceived, and not in the sense that no one is ever deceived in any operation of the intellect.

Reply to Objection 2: The intellect is always right concerning first principles; since it is not deceived about them for the same reason that it is not deceived about the essence of a thing. For self-evident principles are those that are known as soon as their terms are understood, because their predicate is contained in the definition of their subject.[3]

---

coincidental or accidental object of my sight. Under good conditions, and with clear eyesight, I cannot be deceived that what I see is something white, but under the same conditions I may rashly judge that what I see is a sugar cube, whereas it may actually be a slightly elongated prism of salt viewed from the wrong angle.

2   That is to say, when I clearly see something white, my sight truly represents the white thing I see, for it truly conforms to the whiteness of the thing, encoding its proper color in the natural process of color vision. Still, it is not by my sight that I know that what I see is truly white. This requires the intellectual operation of forming the judgment 'This thing is white' of which I can only intellectually know that it is true. For I do not literally see its truth with my bodily eyes or hear its truth with my bodily ears, etc., because truth, consisting in the conformity of the intellect to the thing understood, is simply not a sensible quality. And similar considerations apply to falsity.

3   Note that the understanding of the terms here is supposed to be not the mere linguistic understanding of the meanings of the words used (the understanding of the *nominal definition* of the terms), but rather the understanding of the quiddity or essence of the thing signified by those terms. So, the point is that our cognition of the first principles of demonstration depends primarily on our understanding of the nature of things, as was explained by Aquinas in his *Commentary on Aristotle's Posterior Analytics*, bk. 2, lc. 20.

Question 85. The Mode and Order of Understanding

Article 6. Whether the intellect can be false?

Objection 1: It would seem that the intellect can be false; for the Philosopher says (*Metaph.* vi) that "truth and falsehood are in the mind." But the mind and intellect are the same, as was shown above. Therefore falsehood is in the mind.

Objection 2: Further, opinion and reasoning belong to the intellect. But falsehood exists in both. Therefore falsehood can be in the intellect.

Objection 3: Further, sin is in the intellectual faculty. But sin involves falsehood: for "they err who work evil" (Prov. 14: 22). Therefore falsehood can be in the intellect.

On the contrary, Augustine says (*Questions* 83, q. 32), that "anyone who is deceived does not understand that in which he is deceived." And the Philosopher says (*De Anima* iii, 10), that "the intellect is always true."

I answer that, The Philosopher (*De Anima* iii, 6) compares intellect with sense on this point. For sense is not deceived in its proper object, as sight with regard to color, except accidentally, on account of some fault in the sense organ – for example, when the taste of a fever-stricken person judges a sweet thing to be bitter, because his tongue is vitiated by ill humors. Sense, however, may be deceived with regard to common sensible objects, as size or shape; when, for example, it judges the sun to be only a foot in diameter, whereas in reality it is larger than the earth. And it is even more deceived concerning accidental sensible objects, as when it judges that bile is honey because of their similar color. The reason for this is evident; for every faculty, as such, is *per se* directed to its proper object; and things of this kind are always related to one another in the same way. Hence, as long as the faculty exists, its judgment concerning its own proper object does not fail. Now the proper object of the intellect is the quiddity of a material thing; and hence, properly speaking, the intellect is not deceived concerning this quiddity; whereas it may go astray as regards the surroundings of the thing's essence or quiddity, in relating one thing to another, by affirmation or negation, or also in the process of reasoning. For this reason, the intellect cannot err with regard to those propositions that are apprehended [to be true] as soon as the quiddities of their terms are apprehended, as in the case of first principles from which arises infallible truth in the certitude of scientific conclusions.

The intellect, however, may be accidentally deceived in the quiddity of composite things, not by the defect of its organ, for the intellect is not a faculty that uses an organ; but on account of the composition effecting the definition, when, for instance, the definition of a thing is false of something else, as the definition of a circle applied to a triangle; or when a definition is false in itself, because it involves the composition of incompatible things; for instance, taking "a rational winged animal" as the definition of something. Therefore, as regards simple objects, whose definitions cannot be effected by composition, we cannot be deceived, but we fail by totally not attaining to them, as is said in *Metaph.* ix.

Reply to Objection 1: The Philosopher says that falsehood is in the intellect in regard to affirmation and negation. The same answer applies to the *Second Objection* concerning opinion and reasoning, and to the *Third Objection*, concerning the error of the sinner, who errs in the practical judgment of the desirable object. But in the absolute consideration of the quiddity of a thing, and of those things which are known through it, the intellect is never deceived. And this is what the authorities quoted in the argument *on the contrary* say.

Henry of Ghent on whether a Human Being Can Know Anything

Summa Quaestionum Ordinariarum a.1 q.1

I. Arguments that a Human Being Cannot Know Anything

1. Based on the mode of knowing, it is argued as follows. Whatever a human being knows he knows from something prior and better known to him (*Posterior Analytics* I [71b20–23]; *Physics* I [184a10–20]). But a human being can know something in this way only by knowing it through something prior and better known than it, and (for the same reason) by knowing this through something else that is prior and better known than it, and so on to infinity. But one can know nothing at all by approaching knowledge in this way, according to the Philosopher in *Metaphysics* II [994a1–b30]. Therefore, etc.

2. Based on the means by which a thing is known, it is argued as follows. All human intellective cognition has its origin in the senses (*Metaphysics* I [980a26]; *Posterior Analytics* II [100a11]). But "pure (*sincera*) truth shouldn't be sought from the bodily senses," according to Augustine (*Book of 83 Questions*, Q9). Therefore a human being cannot know pure truth through intellective cognition. But one can know only by knowing pure truth, since nothing is known but what is true (I *Posterior Analytics* [71b25]) and according to Augustine (*Book of 83 Questions*, Q1) it is not the truth unless it is pure – that is, clear (*pura*) of falseness. Therefore, etc.

3. From the same premise, those who denied knowledge argued as follows (as is said in *Metaphysics* IV [1009b1–10]). The senses apprehend nothing of what is certain concerning a thing. For if something appears to one person concerning some thing, its contrary appears to another concerning that same thing. And when something appears to a given person at a given time and in a given condition, its contrary appears to the same person at a different time and in a different condition. Therefore, since the intellect apprehends nothing if not through the senses, it can apprehend nothing of what is certain concerning anything at all. But there can be knowledge only by apprehending something certain and determinate, according to the Philosopher in *Metaphysics* VI. Therefore, etc.

4. Based on the knowable, according to *Metaphysics* IV [1010a7–14], they have a similar argument, as follows. There is knowledge only of what is fixed and stable, according to Boethius in *Arithmetic* I [ch. 1]. But there is nothing fixed or stable in the sensible things from which, by means of the senses, all human cognition is drawn. This is so according to Augustine,

who says in his *Book of 83 Questions* Q9 that "what is called the sensible changes without any intervening time." Therefore, etc.

5. Based on the knower, there is the argument of the *Meno*, at the beginning of the *Posterior Analytics* [71a29], by which he denied that there is knowledge. As the Commentator says on *Metaphysics* IX [5], no one learns unless he knows something. This accords with Augustine, in *Contra academicos* III [iii.5], and with the Philosopher, in *Metaphysics* IX [1046b35]. But someone who knows something isn't learning, because learning is a movement toward knowing. Therefore there is no one who learns anything. But no one who has not learned anything can have learning, according to Augustine in the same passage. Therefore, etc.

6. From the same premise, by forming the argument in another way, it is argued as follows. Someone who knows nothing learns nothing; but someone who learns nothing cannot have learning; therefore someone who knows nothing cannot have learning. Every human being at first knows nothing, because the human intellect, before it receives species, is like a blank slate on which nothing has been drawn, as is said in *De anima* III [430a1]. Therefore, etc.

7. Based on the object, it is argued as follows. One who doesn't perceive the essence and quiddity of a thing, but only its image, can't know (*scire*) the thing. For one who has seen only a picture of Hercules doesn't know (*novit*) Hercules. But a human being perceives nothing of a thing, except only its image – that is, a species received through the senses, which is an image of the thing and not the thing itself. For "it is not the stone but a species of the stone that is in the soul."[1] Therefore, etc.

II. Arguments to the Contrary

1. The Commentator's argument on the beginning of *Metaphysics* II [1] goes as follows. A natural desire is not pointless. But according to the Philosopher in *Metaphysics* I [980a21], a human being desires by nature to know. Therefore a human being's desire to know is not pointless. But it would be pointless if he were unable to know. Therefore, etc.

2. From the same premise, by forming the argument in another way, it is argued as follows. It is possible for what a person naturally desires to come to him, according to what Augustine says in *Contra Julianum* IV [PL 44, 747]: "Nor would all human beings wish by natural impulse to be blessed unless they could be." A human being naturally desires to know. Therefore, etc.

3. From basically the same premise, there is this further argument. Anyone can attain the perfection to which he is naturally ordered, because [his being so ordered] would otherwise be pointless. Knowing is the perfection of a human being to which he is naturally ordered, because according to the Philosopher, in *Ethics* X [1177a17], one's happiness consists in speculative knowledge. Therefore, etc.

4. The Philosopher says in *Metaphysics* III [999b9–12] and IV and in *De caelo* II [292b17–21] that it is impossible for what cannot be completed to be begun by an agent through nature or reason, because every movement has an end and a completion on account of which it exists. But according to the Philosopher, in *Metaphysics* I [982b20–27], human beings philosophized and first began to investigate prudence for the sake of knowing and understanding and escaping ignorance. Therefore, it is possible for a human being to know and to understand.

---

1 Aristotle, *De anima* III 8, 431b29.

5. According to Augustine, in *De vera religione* [xxxix.73], anyone who doubts whether someone can know something doesn't doubt whether he is doubting – he is certain of that. But he is certain only of something true that he knows. Therefore anyone who doubts whether he knows must necessarily concede that he knows something. But this wouldn't be so unless he happened to know something when he happens to doubt. Therefore, etc.

6. Along basically the same lines, the Philosopher and his Commentator argue as follows in *Metaphysics* IV [1008a7–b31, 1012b14–22]. Anyone who denies that there is knowledge says by this that he is certain there is no knowledge. But he is certain only of something that he knows. Therefore anyone who denies that there is knowledge and that a human being can know must necessarily concede that there is knowledge and that a human being can know something. And this argument is similar to the argument by which the Philosopher concludes in *Metaphysics* IV that anyone who denies that there is speech must necessarily concede that there is speech.

[III. Reply]

If 'to know' is taken broadly for every certain cognition (*notitiam*) by which a thing is cognized as it is, without any mistake or deception, and if the question is understood and proposed in this way, then it is manifest and clear – contrary to those who deny knowledge and every perception of truth – that a human being can know something and can do so in every mode of knowing and cognizing. For someone can know something in two ways: either through another's external testimony or through one's own internal testimony.

That one can know something in the first way Augustine says in the *Contra academicos* and in *De trinitate* XV.xii [21]:

> Let it be far from us to deny that we know what we have learned from the testimony of others. Otherwise we do not know of the ocean, nor do we know there to be the lands and cities that famous reports describe. We know of the existence neither of the people nor of the deeds of those people which we have learned about through historical reading. Finally, we don't know from what place or what people we came, since we have learned all these things through the testimony of others.

But that in the second way one can know something and perceive a thing as it is is clear from things we experience within ourselves and around ourselves, through both sensory and intellective cognition. For in sensory cognition a thing is truly perceived as it is, without any deception or mistake, by a sense that during its own action of sensing its proper object is not contradicted by a truer sense or by an intellection received from a different truer sense, whether in the same or in another [person].[2] Nor concerning something that we perceive in this way should one be in doubt whether we perceive it as it is. Nor need one search in this matter for any further cause of certainty. For as the Philosopher says,[3] it is a weakness of intellect to search for reason in cases where we have sensation, since one should not search for a reason for the thing we possess that is more valuable (*dignius*) than reason. For the test of true words is that they agree with what is sensed. Hence Augustine says, in the same place:

---

2   Compare Aristotle, *De somno* 3, 461b3.
3   Perhaps the reference is to *Physics* II 1, 193a2–9.

Let it be far from us that we doubt to be true those things that we have learned through the bodily senses. For through them we have learned of the sky and earth, and the things in them that are known by us.

Hence also Cicero, in his *Academics* [II.vii.19], wanting to prove against the Academics that one can know something with certainty, says the following:

Let us begin with the senses, from which judgments are so clear and certain that, if one were allowed to choose one's own nature, I do not see what more would be sought. In my judgment truth exists in the senses above all. And if they are healthy and in good condition and all the things are removed that oppose and impede them, then a glance itself engenders faith in their judgment.

Concerning faith in intellective cognition, however, since through it one can in this way truly know something as it is, he immediately continues the same passage [vii.21]:

These things that we say are perceived by the senses are such that others follow that are not said to be perceived by the senses – for example, *This one is white*, [therefore] *This one is old*. Then greater claims follow, for example, *If something is a human being then it is an animal*. On the basis of claims of this sort the cognition of things is given to us.

So through intellective cognition, as has already been said about sensory cognition, a thing is truly perceived as it is, without any deception or falseness, by an intellection that in its proper action of intellective cognition is not contradicted by a truer intellection, or by one received from a truer sense. Nor should there be any more doubt regarding such an intellection than there is regarding the senses. Thus Augustine, in the same passage as before [*De trinitate* XV.xii.21]:

Since there are two genera of things that are known, one of which the mind perceives through the bodily senses, the other through itself, those philosophers (i.e., the Academics) raised many complaints against the bodily senses, since they were utterly unable to call into doubt certain perceptions of true things that in themselves are most firm. Of this sort is 'I know that I live.'

With respect to this we don't need to worry that we are deceived by some likeness of what is true. For it is certain that anyone who is deceived is alive. Thus nor can an Academic say that perhaps you are asleep and do not know it, and are seeing in your dreams. For no one can be mistaken in that knowledge through dreams, since sleeping and seeing in dreams both belong to the living. Nor can that Academic say that perhaps you are crazy and don't know it, because the visions even of the crazy are like those of the sane. For anyone who is crazy is alive, nor does the Academic dispute this. Therefore someone who said that he knows he is alive is not deceived, nor can he be lying.

Nor concerning this should another proof be required beyond that which is used for training the intellect, and through evident *a posteriori* signs, of the sort that will be set out later.

Seven errors have endured from ancient times against this view, based on both the senses and intellect. The Philosopher refutes five of these in *Metaphysics* IV, in particular the error of those who deny knowledge by denying this principle of knowledge: For any thing, either its affirmation or negation is true, and not both at the same time in the same respect.

The sixth error, from the *Meno*, denies that a human being can learn. Aristotle refutes this at the start of the *Posterior Analytics* [71a25–b9]. The seventh belonged to the Academics who denied perception of the true. Augustine and Cicero refute this in their books on the Academics.

But as for those whose errors the Philosopher argues against in *Metaphysics* IV, some said that all things are false, whereas others said that all things are true. Still others said that all things are true and false at the same time. Of those who said that all things are false, some based their view on the things themselves, as for example Anaxagoras and Xenocrates,[4] who said that everything is mixed with everything, since they saw that everything is made from everything. They said that that mixture is neither being nor nonbeing and, in a way, neither of the extremes, but rather, by cancellation, a medium between them. Hence they said that it is impossible to judge something truly; rather, all judgments are false. And for this reason they said that there is no knowledge of anything, since knowledge is only of things that are true (as is said in *Posterior Analytics* I [71b25]). These men erred by not distinguishing potential from actual being. For contraries and contradictories exist at the same time potentially, but not actually. This is because the distinction among contraries and contradictories holds only for beings in actuality. Only here, in other words, is something determinately this and not that. Through this, there is determinate truth and knowledge that a thing is what it is and not something else.

But others said that all things are false, taking their argument from the senses. Democritus and Leucippus, for example, said that the same thing is sensed by some people as sweet, and by others as bitter, and that these groups differ only in that the one is larger, the other smaller, since there are many healthy people to whom it seems sweet, and a few sick people to whom it seems bitter. Therefore nothing, as they said, is in actual truth determinately this or that. Rather, each thing is neither this nor that, and for that reason nothing is true; instead, all things are false, and there is no knowledge at all. The reason for their error was their judging that the intellect and the senses are the same, and that knowledge is grasped by the senses. So when they saw that sensible things have different conditions within the senses, and that nothing of what is certain is sensed, they believed that nothing is known with certainty.

Associated with their views was the view of the Academy. Augustine says that they affirmed that human beings can perceive nothing true or certain, but not that human beings ought to stop inquiring into the truth. They did say, however, that either God alone knows the truth, or perhaps also the disembodied soul of a human being. They directed these remarks only to things pertaining to philosophy, not caring about other things. Their reasoning, according to what Augustine recounts [in *Contra academicos*], was this: They said that what is true can be recognized only by signs that cannot have the character (*rationem*) of what is false [II.v.11], so that "the true is discerned from the false by distinct marks" [II.vi.14] and "does not have signs in common with what is false" [III.ix.18]. Thus what is true "cannot appear false" [III.ix.21]. But they believed it impossible that such signs could be found [III.ix.19, 21], and so they concluded that, "because of a certain darkness on the part of nature," the truth either does not exist or, "obscured and confused" [II.v.12], is hidden from us. Thus Democritus, as *Metaphysics* IV [1009b12] recounts, said that either nothing is entirely true or else it is not shown to us.

---

4   Though this is the manuscript reading, and though Aristotle occasionally discusses Xenocrates, his contemporary, the correct reference is to the pre-Socratic Xenophanes (cf. *Met* IV 5. 1010a6).

Others, such as Protagoras and his followers, said that everything true and false exists simultaneously. They said that there is no truth outside the soul, and that what appears outside is not something that exists in the thing itself at the time at which it appears; instead, it exists in the one apprehending. Thus they completely denied that things have existence outside the soul, and so they had to say that two contraries are true at the same time: not only relative to different people apprehending through the same sense but also relative to the same person through different senses and through a [single] sense in different conditions. For what appears sweet to one person through taste will appear not sweet to another through taste; what appears sweet to someone through sight will appear not sweet to that same person through taste; what appears to be a single thing to the eyes will appear to be two things when the position of the eyes is changed. From this they concluded that nothing appears determinate, that nothing is determinately true, and that therefore there is absolutely no knowledge.

Still others, such as Heraclitus and his followers, said that all things are true and false at the same time, since they supposed that only sensible things are beings and that they are not determinate in their existence, but constantly changed. For this reason they said that nothing about them remains the same in actual fact; rather, being and nonbeing belong to them at the same time and in the same respect. For motion is composed of being and nonbeing, and every change goes between being and nonbeing. Accordingly, they further said that one needn't reply yes or no to a question. And thus Heraclitus[5] at the end of his life believed that he needn't say anything, and he moved only his finger. From this they were led to say that there is nothing a human being can acquire knowledge of.

The view of the *Meno* and of certain of the Platonists was that no one can learn anything, and that therefore no one can know anything, as was said above in the fifth and sixth arguments [I.5–6]. The defect in the reasoning of these views will be clear at once when we solve the arguments.

To deny knowledge is to destroy all faith and the whole of philosophy, as the Philosopher says in *Metaphysics* IV. For this reason it is impossible to dispute their main view by demonstrating that there is knowledge and that something can be known, because they deny all the principles of knowing. The only thing that should be used against them in defense of knowledge is true and extremely well established (*probabilibus*) assertions that they cannot deny. So it was by means of such assertions that Cicero refutes them in his *Academics* through three obvious absurdities that follow from their claim. The first of these is taken from craft-based knowledge, the second from acts of virtue, the third from the conduct of human affairs. Cicero explains the first in this way:

> Every craft is based on many perceptions. If you were to take these perceptions away, how would you distinguish a craftsman from someone who is ignorant? For what is it that can be accomplished through craft if the one who is to practice the craft has not perceived many things? [II.vii.22]

Thus Augustine says in *De vera religione* [xxx.54] that "common craft is nothing other than the memory of things experienced." Cicero explains the second in this way:

> How can that good man who has decided to endure every torture rather than neglect his duty or faith, how can it happen that he accepts every suffering unless he has assented to things that cannot be false? [II.viii.23]

---

5 In fact, the reference should be to *Cratylus*; see *Metaphysics* IV, 1010a12.

He explains the third in this way:

> How will someone dare to undertake anything or to act with assurance, if nothing of what follows is certain to him, and he is ignorant of the ultimate good by which all things are reckoned? [II.viii.24]

The Philosopher gives a good example of this in *Metaphysics* IV [1008b15–19]: Someone who is walking walks and does not stop, because he believes that he should be walking. And along the way he does not fall into a well that stands in his path, but he avoids it. For he knows that falling into a well is bad.

[IV.   Reply to the Initial Arguments]

So the arguments proving that someone can know something [II.1–6] should be granted. But we should reply individually to the arguments for the other side [I.1–7].

To the first – that all knowledge comes from something prior and better known, etc. – one ought to say that that mode of acquiring knowledge should be understood to apply only to the knowledge of conclusions. For principles are cognized first, immediately, and through themselves, not through other things, because they don't have anything else better known than themselves. Therefore, the infinite regress and nothing's being known is an issue for no one other than those who don't distinguish what is known through itself from what is known through another.

To the second – that pure truth shouldn't be sought from the bodily senses – one ought to say that this is true everywhere and in all things, when one follows the senses' judgment. This is because of two claims based on which Augustine argues that certain judgment is not established in the senses: first, the changeability of sensible things; second, the fallibility of the senses themselves. But from an apprehension made through the senses, by turning away from the senses so that a judgment is made in reason (which Augustine urges us to do especially when inquiring into the truth), pure truth should indeed be sought from the senses. This is so to the extent that it can be discerned either by purely natural means through the judgment of reason in a pure, natural light, or else absolutely through the judgment of intellect in the clarity of the eternal light. Augustine speaks in these very terms of this purity in the judgment of reason following the senses, as we will see below with regard to the two ways of examining the truth.

So pure truth certainly should be sought from the senses in a certain way, as the origin of truth. For a proper sense has the most certain cognition of its proper object, unless it is impeded either in itself, by the medium, or by something else. But when every impediment is lifted, there is no chance (*nec contingit*) that it will err or apprehend its proper object otherwise than as it is – though such a cognition is not stable, because of changeability on the part of either the object or the sense itself. Hence truth that is certain can't be grasped for long by depending entirely on the judgment of the senses. Nevertheless, truth that is entirely certain is grasped through the senses, by abstracting that which was apprehended by an undeceived sense and forming a judgment in intellect where what was apprehended remains as if unchanged, unable to be obscured by truthlike species of phantasms. And for us the most certain knowledge is that of sensible things, when we can trace it back to sensory experience.

Hence those letting go of the senses and thoroughly denying their judgment, deceived by sophistical arguments, frequently fell into the most absurd errors of intellect. Take Zeno, for example, who said that nothing can move, and all those who said that all things are moved by a single motion. Thus one should always believe a particular sense when it is not impeded, unless it is contradicted by some other worthier sense (either in the same person at a different time or in a different person at the same time) or by a higher power perceiving that the sense is impeded. For the senses are not in equal good condition in everyone or in the same person at different times, and so one should not believe their judgments equally – as is clear with the healthy and the sick. For we should believe the taste of someone healthy more than the taste of someone sick, and someone who sees something up close more than someone who sees it from a distance, and someone who sees a thing through a uniform medium more than someone who sees it through a varying medium, and so on for other conditions of this sort.

To the third – that the same thing often appears in different ways to the same person or to different people – one ought to say that it doesn't follow from this that no sense should be believed. For, as was said, in a case in which one [sense] is deceived, another frequently indicates what is true; or in a case in which [a sense] is deceived in one condition, in another condition it indicates what is true. It's clear in this way how the reasoning of Democritus was deficient. For though sensible things have different conditions within the senses, a thing is still determinately perceived through an undeceived sense, at the time at which it is not deceived. And sensations differ not only as there are fewer and more who sense it [that way], but also according to the greater and lesser worth of the senses when it comes to sensing.

The defect in the reasoning of the Academics is similarly clear. For their claim is not true, that nothing is determinately perceived through signs and that signs do not show what is true in things. Instead, those signs that are the proper sensibles of a given sense display that which they are to their proper sense, assuming that sense is neither deceived nor impeded, and can bring intellect to a determinate cognition of a thing's truth. And hence the Academics themselves, more than others, were devoted to inquiring into the truth through signs of this sort, although their view was that they could never find the truth. In this respect their view was like that of someone who runs to grasp a thing he never will grasp – this is how the Philosopher reproves them in *Metaphysics* IV. Other issues concerning their view will be spelled out further in the next question.

It's clear for the same reason that the assumption of Protagoras – that things follow the appearances of the senses – is false, because sensations, whether true or deceived, can be derived only from things, since a sense is a passive power. So even though the same thing appears in different ways to the same or different [senses], this happens only on account of a sense's being deceived or impeded. In this case one needn't believe that sense. But one should not, on this account, say that no sense is to be believed, because an undeceived sense ought to be believed completely. As for which sense is such, the intellect above all else has to judge this on the basis of many prior experiences concerning what the senses can be deceived or impeded by.

To the fourth – that all sensible things are in constant change – one ought to say that the Heracliteans, whose argument this was, believed that only sensible things are existent. And this was the error of all the philosophers up to the time of the Italians: They unanimously denied that there is knowledge, on account of the changeability of natural sensible things. Perceiving their error, later philosophers asserted that there is knowledge and that something can be known of natural sensible things. But they were divided as to how one knows and acquires knowledge. Pythagoras, the first of the Italians, believed with his predecessors that one can't have knowledge of natural things through the things themselves, because of their changing. But to preserve in some way the knowledge of natural things, he brought mathematical facts into nature, proposing them as the principles and causes of natural things both in existence and in cognition. For mathematical facts are in a certain way unchangeable, through their abstraction from sensible and changeable matter.

But Plato, coming after Pythagoras, saw that in reality mathematical facts inhere in natural things. So however much they are abstracted from natural things, mathematical facts are really changed along with them, and no fixed knowledge of natural things can be had through them. Plato proposed ideal Forms as the causes and principles of natural things, both in existence and in cognition, entirely separate from natural things and without any change. In this way, through them, there can be unchangeable knowledge of what is changeable.

Aristotle, however, saw that a thing has existence and can be cognized only through something that exists within it (*in re*). And he saw that, due to their changing, there cannot be knowledge of singulars through themselves. So he claimed that universals – that is, genera and species – are abstracted by intellect from the singulars where they have true existence. For a universal is one in many and of many. And though they are changeable as they exist in singulars, they are unchangeable as they exist in intellect. Accordingly, he claimed that we do have fixed knowledge of changeable, particular, sensible, natural things, through their universals existing within intellect.

Augustine was imbued with the philosophy of Plato. If he found in it things suitable to the faith, he took them into his own writing. The things he found that were adverse to the faith he interpreted in a better light to the extent that he could. Now as Augustine says in his *Book of 83 Questions*, Q46, it seemed to be "sacrilege" to believe that the ideas of things are located outside the divine mind – ideas that the divine mind contemplates so as to establish what it establishes. So for this reason, even though Aristotle attributed this view to Plato, Augustine said that Plato located these ideas in the divine intelligence and that they subsist there. As he says in *City of God* VIII.iv,

> What Plato thought about these matters – that is, where he thought or believed that the end of all actions, the cause of all natures, and the light of all reasons exist – I don't believe should be rashly decided. For it may be that those celebrated by fame who praise Plato above all others perceive something about God so as to find in God the cause of subsisting, the reason for understanding and the direction for living.

Thus Augustine, interpreting Plato's pronouncements more soundly than Aristotle did, claims that the principles of certain knowledge and of cognizing the truth consist in eternal, unchangeable rules or reasons existing in God. It is by participating in them, through intellective cognition, that one cognizes whatever pure truth is cognized in creatures. Consequently, just as by his being he is the cause of the existence of all things insofar as they exist, so too by his truth he is the cause of the cognition of all things insofar as they are true. In this way there can be certain and fixed knowledge of changeable things no matter how changeable they are. Accordingly, Augustine says in *De trinitate* XII [xiv.23]:

> It is not only for sensible things located in space that intelligible and incorporeal reasons endure, apart from local space. Those same intelligible, nonsensible reasons stand, apart from any

passing of time, for the motions that pass by in time. Few attain these through keenness of mind, and when they are attained insofar as they can be, the one who has attained them does not endure there. Hence a transitory thought is formed of a thing that is not transitory. Nevertheless this transitory thought is committed to memory through the training by which the mind is educated, so that there is someplace to where a thought can return after it is forced to pass away. For if the thought were not to return to memory and find what it had placed there, then as if never educated it would once again be led just as it once had been, and would find it where it had first found it, in the incorporeal truth. And from there it would again, as if written down, be formed in memory.

[. . .]

To the fifth and sixth – that one can't know because one can't learn – one ought to say that the assumption is false. For one can indeed learn, as will be clear below.[6] But it should be realized that 'to learn' can be taken in two ways. In one way, generally, learning extends to every new acquisition of knowledge. In this way it needn't be the case that every learner knows something. For someone learning to cognize first principles acquires this through no preceding cognition. In another way, strictly, learning extends to a cognition only of conclusions, which one acquires in actuality from a prior cognition of principles in which the conclusion lies hidden, in potentiality (as will be clear below). In this way, someone who is learning knows something.

To the seventh – that a human being perceives nothing of the thing to be cognized except the image alone – it should be replied that one can perceive a thing's image in two ways. In one way, it can be perceived as the object of cognition. In this way it is true that someone perceiving only the thing's image does not cognize the thing: For example, someone seeing an image of Hercules painted on a wall does not thereby either see or cognize Hercules. In another way, it can be perceived as the basis (*ratio*) of cognizing, and in this way the claim is not true. For a thing is truly cognized through just a perceived species of it – as a stone is truly seen through its sensible species alone, received in the eye, and is truly understood through its intelligible species alone, received in intellect.

But perhaps you will say that that species is something sensible received by a sense and that therefore, because it is an accident and the likeness of only an accident, it doesn't lead to a cognition of the thing's quiddity and substance. To this one should reply that even if the intellect first receives intelligible species of sensible and corporeal things as they are sensible, and first understands them through those species, nevertheless secondarily, out of those species of sensible things, by means of the investigation of natural reason, it conceives cognitions of nonsensible things through itself. These are the quiddities of substances, for instance, and others of the same sort that don't have their own species in intellect. And this is what Augustine says, in *De trinitate* IX.iii [3]:

> That power by which we discern through the eyes, whether it is rays or something else, we are not able to discern with the eyes, but we seek with the mind, and (if possible) we comprehend with the mind. The mind itself, then, just as it collects cognitions of corporeal things through the bodily senses, so it collects cognitions of incorporeal things through itself.

6   See *Summa* 1.6: "Can one human being acquire knowledge through the teaching of another human being?"

He calls things corporeal inasmuch as they are sensible, and calls incorporeal whatever is not sensible, whatever it is – such as mathematical things, the quiddities of substances, [composed of] matter and form, and others of this sort. The mind, through the efforts of natural reason, puts together a cognition of such things from out of the species of sensible things, on the basis of a natural connection between the sensible and the nonsensible – as if by digging under the species something sensible presents to it. It's in this way that a sheep by natural instinct makes an estimation through a sensed species about something not sensed – as when through the sensible species of a wolf, imagined or seen, it makes an estimation that the wolf is harmful and hostile. And so one speaks of understanding (*intelligere*), as if it were reading from within (*ab intus legere*).

Nicholas of Autrecourt on Skepticism about Substance and Causality

I The First Letter to Bernard

1 With all the reverence which, considering the worthiness of the Friars, I feel obligated to show to you, most amiable father Bernard, I wish in the present letter to unfold some points of doubt – or rather as it seems to some people, some obviously inconvenient sequels that appear to follow from what you are claiming – so that, by their resolution, the truth may be more clearly revealed to me and to others. For in a certain report of the lectures that you have delivered in the school of the Friars Minor and released as authentic to whomever wished to have it, I read the following propositions.

2 The first (which is set forth by you in your commentary on the first Book of the *Sentences*, dist. 3, q. 4) is this:

> Clear intuitive cognition is that by which we judge a thing to be, whether it is or is not.

Your second proposition (which is laid down in the place mentioned above) runs as follows:

> The inference 'The object is not; therefore it is not seen' is not valid, nor does this hold 'This is seen; therefore it is'.

What is more, there is a fallacy in either of them, just as in these inferences 'Caesar is thought of; therefore Caesar is', 'Caesar is not: therefore Caesar is not thought of'. The third proposition (put forward in the same place) is this:

> Intuitive cognition does not necessarily require something existent.

3 From these propositions I infer a fourth one <saying> that

> Every impression we have of the existence of objects outside our minds can be false,

since, according to you, it can exist, whether or not the object is. And still another proposition, which is the fifth one and runs as follows:

In the natural light we cannot be certain *when* our awareness of the existence of external objects is true or false,

because, as you say, no matter whether a thing is or is not, it represents it as being in one and the same manner.

4 And, thus, since anyone who posits the antecedent must also posit the consequent that, by formal implication, is inferred from that antecedent, it follows that because you do not have evidential certitude as to the existence of external objects, you must also concede anything that follows therefrom. *That* you do not have evident certitude of the existence of sensorial objects, is clear, because no one has certitude of any consequent through an inference in which manifestly a fallacy is committed. Now, such is the case here, for, according to you, there is a fallacy here: 'Whiteness is seen; therefore there is whiteness.'

5 But perhaps you want to say, as it seems to me you wished to suggest in a certain disputation at the Black Friars', that although from the act of seeing it cannot be inferred, when the seeing has been produced or is conserved by a supernatural cause, that the object seen exists, even so when it has been produced by causes that are purely natural, with <only> the general influence of the First Agent concurring, – then it can be inferred.

6 But to the contrary: When from some antecedent, if produced by some agent, a certain consequent could not be inferred by a formal and evident implication, then from that antecedent, no matter by what other <agent> it be produced, that consequent could not be inferred either. This proposition is obvious by example and by reason. By an example: In the same way as, if whiteness had been produced by some agent A and it could not be formally inferred then 'There is whiteness; therefore there is colour' – likewise this inference could not be made even if it had been produced by another, no matter which, agent. It is also clear by reason, because the antecedent as such does not vary according as the respective agents vary, nor does the state of affairs signified by the antecedent.

7 Furthermore. Since from that antecedent it cannot be inferred evidently by way of intuitive cognition 'therefore there is whiteness', one must add, then, something to the antecedent, namely what you suggested above, viz. that the whiteness has not been produced or conserved supernaturally. But from this it is clear that I have proved my point. For: When somebody is certain of some consequent only in virtue of some antecedent of which he is not evidently certain whether or not the case is such as <the antecedent> states <it to be>, because that antecedent is not known by the meaning of its terms, nor by experience, nor deduced from such knowledge, but is only believed, – such a person is not evidently certain of the consequent. <Now>, this is the case, if that antecedent is considered together with its modification, as is clear to everybody. Therefore *etc.*

8 Furthermore. In line with your reply <it can be remarked>: Whoever makes an inference from that antecedent taken without that modification added, makes an invalid inference. But the philosophers, such as Aristotle and others, did not add this to the antecedent, because they did not believe that God could impede the effects of natural causes. It follows, therefore, that they were not certain of the existence of sensible things.

9 Furthermore. I ask you if you know all natural causes that are and those that are possible and how much they can do; and how you know evidently, by evidentness reducible to the certitude of the first principle, that there is anything such that its coming into being does not involve a contradiction and which, all the same, can only come into being by God. On these questions I would gladly be given certitude of the kind indicated.

10 Furthermore. You say that, as long as the natural order is intact, there can be an incomplete intuitive cognition of a non-existent thing. I now ask you about your intuitive knowledge, how you are certain, with an evidentness as described before, *when* your intuitive knowledge is perfect to such a degree that, the natural order being intact, it cannot be of a non-existent thing. I would also be gladly taught about this.

11 Thus, it is clear, it seems to me, that from your claims it follows that you have to admit that you are not certain of the existence of the objects of the five senses. But what might be even harder to stomach: you must say that you are not certain of your own acts, for example, that you are seeing, or hearing; and what is worse, that you are not certain that anything is, or has been, perceived by you. For, in the passage cited above, the first book of the *Sentences*, dist. 3, you say that our intellect does not have intuitive cognition of our actions. And you adduce this argument as a proof: 'Every intuitive cognition is clear; but the cognition our intellect has of our own acts, is not a clear one; therefore *etc.*' Now, in keeping with this reasoning, I argue thus: The intellect that is not certain of the existence of things of whose existence it has a clear cognition, will also not be certain about those things of which it has a less clear cognition. But (as was said) you are not certain of the existence of objects of which you have a clearer cognition than you have of your own acts. Therefore.

12 And if you, should say that sometimes some abstractive cognition is as clear as an intuitive cognition (e.g. 'Every whole is greater than its part'), this will not do you any good, because you expressly say that the cognition we have of our own acts is not as clear as an intuitive cognition, and yet intuitive cognition, at least that which is incomplete, does not, within the natural order, yield evident certitude (this is clear from what you say). And thus it follows evidently that you are not certain of the evidentness of your impression. And, consequently, you are not certain whether anything appears to you at all.

13 And it also follows that you are not certain whether a proposition is true or false, because you are not evidently certain whether there is, or has been, any proposition. And what is worse, it follows that if you were asked about the articles of faith whether you believe them, you would have to say 'I am in doubt', because, according to your position, you could not be certain of your act of believing. And I corroborate this as follows: If you were certain of your act of believing, this would be either by means of the act itself and, in that case, the direct and the reflexive act would be identical, which you do not wish to concede, – or else by another act, and in that case, according to your position, you would not be absolutely certain, because, then, there would be no more contradiction involved than when there is vision of whiteness without there being whiteness.

14 And thus, reviewing and summing up your position, it appears that you have to admit that you are not certain of those things which are outside of you. And so you do not know if you are in the sky or on earth, in fire or in water. And, consequently, you do not know whether today's sky is the same one as yesterday's, because you do not know whether or not there was any sky. Just as you do not know if the Chancellor or the Pope exists and, if they exist, whether they are not, perchance, different persons in any given moment of time. Similarly, you do not know what things are in your direct surroundings, as whether you have a head, a beard, hair and the like. Hence it follows *a fortiori* that you are not certain of things which now belong to the past, as whether you have been reading, or seeing, or hearing. Furthermore, your position seems to lead to the destruction of civilian and political life, because if witnesses testify of what they have seen, it does not follow 'We have seen it; therefore it has happened'. Likewise, reasoning along these lines, I ask you how the Apostles were sure that Christ suffered on the cross, that He has risen from the dead, and so on.

15 I wish that your mind would declare itself on all these questions. Indeed, I wonder very much how you can say to be evidently certain even of some theses that are still more

obscure, such as the one concerning the existence of the Prime Mover, and the like, and yet you art not certain of these things and the other ones I have discussed. Furthermore, considering in the light of your position, it is a mystery to me how you propose to show that a cognition is distinct from what is cognised, because you are not certain either, if reasoning along your lines, that there is any cognition or that there are any propositions, and, consequently, nor that there are propositions that are contradictory, since (as I have shown) you do not have certitude as to the existence of your own acts, still according to your position. Moreover, you will not have certitude about your own mind either and, thus, you do not know whether it exists. And, as it seems to me, from your position there follow things that are more absurd than follow from the position of the Academics. And, therefore, in order to avoid such absurdities, I have upheld in disputations in the Aula of the Sorbonne that I am evidently certain of the objects of the five senses and of my own acts.

16 I state these objections against your claims, and many others, so many, indeed, that there is, so to speak, no end to them. I pray you, Father, to instruct me, who, however ignorant, am nevertheless yearning when it comes to acquiring knowledge of the truth. May you abide in Him, who is the Light, and in whom there is no darkness.

II The Second Letter to Bernard

1 Reverend father, brother Bernard, the admirable depth of your subtlety would be duly recognised by me, if I knew you to possess evident cognition of the immaterial substances; and not only if I were really certain, but even if I could convince myself without too strong an effort of belief. And not only if I believed that you have true cognition of the immaterial substances but also if I deemed you to have cognition of those conjoined to matter. And therefore to you, Father, who claim that you have evident cognition of such sublime objects of knowledge, I wish to lay bare my doubtful and anxious mind, so that you may have the opportunity to lead the way and make me and others partners in your knowledge of such magic things.

2 The first thing that presents itself for discussion is this principle: 'Contradictories cannot be simultaneously true'. Concerning which, two things suggest themselves. The first is that this is the first principle, expounding 'first' negatively as 'than which nothing is prior'. The second is that this principle is first in the affirmative or positive sense as 'that which is prior to any other'.

3 These two statements are proved by means of one argument, as follows: Every certitude we possess is resolved into this principle. And it is itself not resolved into any other in the way a conclusion would into its premise(s). It therefore follows that the principle in question is first by a twofold primacy. This implication is well-known as following from the meaning of the term 'first' according to either of the expositions given. The antecedent is proved with respect to both of its parts. First, as to its first part (to wit, that all our certitude falling short of this certitude is resolved into this principle): Regarding anything proven whatsoever, which falls short of <the evidentness of> this principle, and which you assert you are certain of, I propose this inference: 'It is possible, without any contradiction following therefrom, that it will appear to you to be the case, and yet will not be so. Therefore, you will not be evidently certain that it is the case.' It is clear to me that if I admitted the antecedent to be true, I would <thereby> admit the consequent to be true. And, consequently, I would not in the unqualified sense be evidently certain of that of which I said I was certain. From this it is clear that it is into our said principle that our certitude is resolved. And that it is not itself resolved into another one in the way a conclusion would into its principle is clear from the fact that all <arguments> are resolved into this one, as has been said. And so it follows 'this one is prior to any other than itself; therefore nothing is prior to it'. And thus it is first with the aforesaid twofold primacy.

4 The third point that presents itself is that a contradiction is the affirmation and negation of one and the same <attribute> . . . *etc.*, as the common formula runs.

5 From this I infer a corollary, namely 'The certitude of evidentness that one has in the natural light, is certitude in the unqualified sense', since it is the certitude that is held in virtue of the first principle, which neither is nor can be contradicted by any true law. Therefore, what is proved in the natural light, is proved unqualifiedly. And, thus, just as there is no power which can make contradictories simultaneously true, so there is no power by which it can happen that the opposite of the consequent simultaneously obtains with the antecedent.

6 The second corollary I infer on this score is: 'The certitude of evidentness has no degrees'. For example, if there are two conclusions of each of which we are evidently certain, we are not more certain of one than of the other. For (as has been said) all certitude is resolved into the same first principle. Either, indeed, those conclusions are resolved into the same first principle with equal immediacy – in which case we have no reason for being more certain of one than of the other –, or else one is resolved mediately and the other immediately, and, then, this still is no objection <to my thesis>, because, once the reduction to the first principle has been made, we are equally certain of the one as of the other; just as the geometrician claims that he is as certain of a second conclusion as of the first, and similarly of a third one, and so on, – although, because of the plurality of the deductions, he cannot be, on first consideration, as certain of the fourth or third as of the first.

7 The third corollary I infer, on the basis of what has been said, is: 'With the exception of the certitude of faith, there is no other certitude but the certitude of the first principle, or the one that can be resolved to the first principle.' For there is no certitude but that which is not founded on falsity, because: If there were any certitude that could be based on falsity, let us suppose that it *is* actually based on falsity. Then, since (according to you) that certitude remains, it follows that somebody will be certain of something whose contradictory opposite is true.

8 The fourth corollary is this: 'Every syllogistic scheme is immediately reduced to the first principle', because the conclusion which has been proved by means of it, either is immediately reduced (and, then, I have made my point), or else mediately; and, then, either there will be an infinite regress, or one must arrive at some conclusion that is immediately reduced to the first principle.

9 The fifth corollary is: 'In every inference that is reduced immediately to the first principle, the consequent, and the antecedent either as a whole or in part, are factually identical', because, if this were not so, then it would not be immediately evident that the antecedent and the opposite of the consequent cannot simultaneously be true, without contradiction.

10 The sixth corollary is this: 'In every evident inference, reducible to the first principle by as many steps as you please, the consequent is factually identical with the antecedent, or with part of what is signified by the antecedent.' This is shown as follows: Suppose that some conclusion is reduced to the certitude of the first principle by three steps, then in the first consequence, which is evident with the evidentness reduced to the certitude of the first principle, the consequent will be factually identical with the antecedent, or with part of what is signified by the antecedent (in virtue of the fifth corollary); and similarly in the second inference (by the same corollary), and in the third one as well (by the same corollary). And, thus, since in the first inference the consequent is factually identical with the antecedent, or with part of what is signified by the antecedent, and likewise in the second, and similarly in the third, – so it follows, from the first to the last, that in this series of inferences, the last consequent will be factually identical with the first antecedent, or with part of what is signified by the first antecedent.

11 In accordance with these statements, I have laid down elsewhere, among others, this thesis: 'From the fact that some thing is known to be, it cannot be inferred evidently, by evidentness reduced to the first principle, or to the certitude of the first principle, that there is some other thing.' Among other arguments (which were quite numerous) I brought forward this argument: 'In such an inference in which from one thing another thing would be inferred, the consequent would not be factually identical with the antecedent, nor with part of what is signified by the antecedent. It therefore follows that such an inference would not be evidently known with the aforesaid evidentness of the first principle. The antecedent is conceded and posited by the opponent. The implication is plain from the definition of "contradiction", which runs "an affirmation and a negation of one and the same <attribute> . . . etc." Since, then, in this case the consequent is not factually identical with the antecedent, or with part of the antecedent, it is manifest that, assuming the opposite of the consequent, and the antecedent to be simultaneously true, there still would not be an "affirmation and negation of one and the same <attribute> . . . etc." '

12 But Bernard replies, saying that although in this case there is no formal contradiction, for the reason given, yet there is a virtual contradiction; he calls that contradiction virtual from which a formal one can be evidently inferred.

13 But against this you can argue manifestly, on the basis of the fifth and the sixth of the above corollaries. For in these it has been shown that in every inference either mediately or immediately reducible to the certitude of the first principle, it is necessary that the consequent, – whether the first one given or the last – be factually identical with the antecedent first given, or with part of it.

14 It can also be manifestly refuted on the basis of another argument, namely as follows: He says that, although in an inference in which from one thing another thing is inferred, there is not a formal contradiction, yet there is a virtual one from which a formal one can be evidently inferred. Well, let us propose, for example, the following inference: 'A is; therefore B is'. If, then, from the propositions 'A is' and 'B is not', a formal contradiction could be evidently inferred, this either would be the case by assuming one or more consequents of one of these propositions, or else of each of these propositions. But whichever way it is, the point is not made. For these consequents would either be in fact identical with their antecedents, or they would not. If identical, then: just as there will not be a formal contradiction between those consequents, because there would not be an affirmation and a negation of one and the same <attribute>, – likewise this would not be the case between the antecedents either. Just as, if there is no formal contradiction in saying that a man is and a horse is not, so there would not be a formal contradiction either in asserting a rational animal to be and a neighing animal not to be; and this for the same reason.

15 If it be said, however, that these consequents differ from their antecedents, then (just as before) the implication is not evidently known, with the evidentness reduced to the certitude of the first principle, because the opposite of the consequent would be compatible with whatever is signified by the antecedent, without contradiction. And if one should say that there is a virtual contradiction from which a formal can be inferred, we will go on as before. And, thus, it <either> would be an infinite process, or else it will be necessary to say that in an inference that is evident in an unqualified sense, the consequent is identical in its meaning with the antecedent or part of what is signified by the antecedent.

16 What this father has said with regard to this matter, is true, <viz.> that it would not be correct to say that, in an inference which is evident in an unqualified sense, it is required that the opposite of the consequent, and the antecedent contradict. For he says that here is a plain counter-instance: 'Every animal is running; therefore every man is running'; indeed, the contradictory of the consequent, and the antecedent can simultaneously be false, and are, therefore, not opposed as contradictories.

17 In actual fact, however, this by no means impedes <what I am maintaining>. For I do not mean to say that the opposite of the consequent must be the contradictory of the antecedent, for in many inferences the antecedent can signify more than does the consequent, albeit that the consequent signifies part of what is signified by the antecedent, as is the case in the inference that has been put forward: 'There is a house; therefore there is a wall'. And on this account the opposite of the consequent, and the antecedent can be both false. But what I mean to say is that in an evident inference, the opposite of the consequent, and the antecedent, or part of what it signifies, are opposed as contradictories.

18 It is obvious that this is the case in every valid syllogism. For since no term occurs in the conclusion without occurring in the premises, therefore the opposite of the conclusion, and something of what is signified by the premises, are opposed as contradictories. So it must also be in every valid enthymeme, because an enthymeme is only conclusive in virtue of some withheld proposition; and thus it is a sort of mental syllogism.

19 Furthermore. As to my main thesis I presented the following argument: 'Never, in virtue of any implication, can there be inferred a greater mutual identity between the extreme terms than that which existed between the extremes and the middle term, because the former is only inferred in virtue of the latter. But the opposite of this would happen, if from the fact that one thing is a being, it could evidently be inferred that something else is a being, because the predicate and the subject of the conclusion signify what is in fact identical, whereas they are not in fact identical with the middle term, by which some other thing is posited.'

20 But Bernard counter-instances against the proposed rule: 'It follows evidently, with the evidentness reduced to the certitude of the first principle, "There is whiteness; therefore there is something else", because there can only be whiteness if some substrate sustains it in being. Likewise it follows "A is now for the first time; therefore there was something else <before>"; similarly, "Fire is brought into contact with the hemp; and there is no impediment; therefore there will be heat."'

21 To these counter-instances I have elsewhere given many answers. But for the present I claim that if he came up with a thousand such counter-instances, either he would have to admit that they are not to the point, or else, if relevant, yet they argue nothing conclusively against me, since in such inferences as he states, the consequent is in fact identical in its meaning either with the antecedent as a whole, or with part of the antecedent, and, therefore, the argument is not to the point, because in that case I would admit the inferences to be evident, and this would not be inconsistent with my position. But if it should be said that the consequent is not identical with the antecedent, or with part of it, then, too, if I admit the opposite of the consequent, and the antecedent to be simultaneously true, it is patently clear that I am not admitting contradictories, because a contradiction concerns one and the

same <attribute> ... etc., even so such an inference is not evident either with the evidentness of the first principle, since, it was said, one speaks of 'evidentness of the first principle' when, if to admit that the opposite of the consequent is compatible with the antecedent would amount to admitting that contradictories are simultaneously true. For although someone who, with regard to this inference 'There is a house; therefore there is a wall', admits that there is a house and there is not a wall, does not <thereby> admit that contradictories are simultaneously true (because the propositions 'There is a house' and 'There is not a wall' are not contradictories, for they can be simultaneously false), – yet he does admit contradictories for another reason, <viz.> because someone who indicates that there is a house indicates that there is a wall; and then the contradiction occurs that there is a wall and that there is not a wall.

22 From this rule, thus made plain to whoever is gifted with intellect, I infer that Aristotle never possessed evident knowledge about any substance other than his own soul – taking 'substance' as a thing other than the objects of the five senses, and other than our formal experiences. And this is so, because he would have possessed knowledge of such a thing prior to all discursive thought – which is not true, since they are not perceived intuitively, and <if they were> also rustics would know that there are such things. Nor are they known by discursive thought, namely as inferred from what, prior to any discursive thought, is perceived to be – for from one thing it cannot be inferred that there is another thing, as the above thesis states. And if he did not possess evident knowledge of conjoined substances, *a fortiori* he had no such knowledge of abstract ones.

23 From this it follows – whether you like it or not, and let they not impute it to me, but to the force of argument! – that Aristotle in his entire natural philosophy and metaphysics possessed such certitude of scarcely two conclusions, and perhaps not even of one. And father Bernard, who would not put himself above Aristotle, possesses an equal amount of certitude, or much less.

24 And not only did Aristotle possess no evident knowledge, but, worse than that, – although I do not hold this as a tenet, I have an argument that I am unable to refute, to prove that he did not even possess probable knowledge. For nobody possesses probable knowledge of a consequent in virtue of an antecedent of which he is not absolutely certain whether the consequent has once obtained simultaneously with the antecedent. For, if one considers it properly, it is in this way that probable knowledge is acquired, For example, because it was once evident to me that when I put my hand toward the fire, I was hot, therefore it seems probable to me that if I should do it now, I would be hot. But from the rule stated above it follows that it was never evident to anyone that, if these things which are apparent before any discursive thought existed, there should be some other things, that is, which are called substances. From this it follows that we do not possess probable knowledge of their existence. I am not committed to this conclusion. Let anyone who can think up a solution refute this argument.

25 And that we do not possess certitude concerning any substance conjoined to matter other than our own soul is clear: When a log or a stone has been pointed out, it will be most clearly deduced that a substance is there, from a belief accepted simultaneously. But this cannot be inferred from a simultaneous belief evidently. For, even if all kinds of things are perceived prior to such discursive thought, it can happen, by some power, namely the divine, that no substance is there. Therefore in the natural light it is not evidently inferred from these appearances that a substance is there. This inference is apparent from what has been explained above. For it was said that an inference which is evident in the natural light is evident in an unqualified manner, so that it is a contradiction that by some power it could occur that the opposite of the consequent would be compatible with the antecedent. And if he says that the inference *is* evident when it is added to the antecedent that 'God is not performing a miracle', this is disproved along the same line of argument as is found in a similar case in the first letter to Bernard.

26 Please, Father, take notice of these doubts and give counsel to my lack of wisdom. I believe that I will not be obdurate in evading the truth for which I am gasping with all my strength.

18

John Buridan on Scientific Knowledge

Whether It Is Possible to Comprehend the Truth about Things

Concerning the second book we ask *whether it is possible for us to comprehend to truth about things.*

It is argued first that it is not, on the part of the senses. [Some standard skeptical arguments from the relativity of sense-perception, optical illusions and the like are omitted here.]

The senses can be deceived, as it is commonly said, and it is certain that the species of sensible things can be preserved in the sense organs in the absence of these things, as it is stated in [Aristotle's] *On Sleep and Waking.* And then we judge that which is not there to be there, and that is why we err on account of the senses. And the difficulty is greatly increased by what we believe in our faith; for God can form in our senses the species of sensible things without these sensible things, and can preserve them for a long time, and then[, if He did so,] we would judge those sensible things to be present. Furthermore, you do not know whether God, who can do such and even greater things, wants to do so. Hence, you do not have certitude and evidentness about whether you are awake and there are people in front of you, or you are asleep, for in your sleep God could make sensible species just as clear as, or even a hundred times clearer than, those that sensible objects can produce; and so you would formally judge that there are sensible things in front of you, just as you do now. Therefore, since you know nothing about the will of God, you cannot be certain about anything.

Next, it is argued on the part of the intellect that our intellect is dependent on the senses for its understanding; therefore, if we do not have certitude by means of the senses, as has been argued, then we do not have it by the intellect either.

Furthermore, the intellect has to be moved by external things if it is to understand them, but this is impossible, because the mover has to be nobler than the thing moved, as stated in Book 3 of the *De Anima.* And the species of sensible things, before they could reach the intellect, have to pass through a number of intermediaries, such as the interior senses, the common sense and imagination. And it is quite possible that in these intermediaries they become distorted, and so they cannot represent things to the intellect with certitude.

Again, it is argued with regard to the [first] principles that these principles become known through experience; but experiences are deceptive as is clear from Hippocrates. And we prove in the second place that they *are* deceptive. Experiences do not have the force to conclude a universal principle, unless by means of induction over many [singular cases]. But a universal proposition never follows by induction, unless the induction covers all singular cases of that universal, which is impossible. Indeed, let us assume that whenever you touched fire, you always felt it to be hot; therefore, by experience you judge the next fire, which you have never touched, to be hot too, etc., and so finally you judge that every fire is hot. Let us assume, then, that by God's will whenever you touched a piece of iron, then you felt it to be hot. It is clear by parity of reasoning that when you next see a piece of iron that is in fact cold, you will judge it to be hot, and that finally you will judge every piece of iron to be hot. And these would be false judgments, although at that point you would have just as much experience about iron as you now in fact have about fire.

Again, by Plato's reasoning, if the intellect never knew a first principle, and it happened on it, it would no more assent to it than to its opposite, in accordance with his example about the fugitive slave and his master [who would not be able to recognize his slave if he had never seen him]; therefore, we shall not be certain about the first principles.

[...]

Again, a conclusion or an effect cannot be known through its cause, or a cause through its effect, because the cause is not contained essentially or virtually in its effect. And an effect cannot be known through its cause, because causes are lesser known to us. And if you say that they are better known by nature, then that is beside the point, because we are inquiring about our learning and not about nature's. But it seems that we can never have evident knowledge about one thing through another, because there is no evidentness, except by reduction to the first principle, which is grounded in contradiction.[1] However, we can never have a contradiction concerning two diverse things: for let us assume that they are A and B; then it is not a contradiction that A exists and B does not exist, or that A is white and B is not white. Therefore, there will never be an evident inference concluding that A exists from the fact that B exists, and so on for other cases.

[...]

The opposite is argued by [the authority of] Aristotle, who says that [the comprehension of truth] in one way is easy and in another way is difficult, and so he regards it as possible. And the Commentator argues as follows: that for which we have a natural desire is possible; for nothing that is founded in nature is in vain. But we do have a natural desire for knowledge, and consequently for the certain comprehension of truth, as Aristotle said in the preface of this work; therefore, etc.

To clarify the question, we have to explain its terms. I will discuss incomplex truth in detail in connection with the other books. But here I am only concerned with complex truth, on account of which a proposition is said to be true. And we can disregard spoken and written propositions, for these are said to be true or false only because of the true or false mental propositions they represent, just as a urine sample is said to be healthy or sick because it signifies the health or sickness of an animal.

---

1 "The first principle" in question is the principle of non-contradiction: nothing can both be [an F] and not be [an F] at the same time.

Furthermore, I assume for the time being that the truth of a mental proposition is nothing other than the true mental proposition itself, although the name "true" and "truth" connote that a proposition of this sort conforms to the things it signifies in the way explained elsewhere.

Next we should see what we are supposed to understand by the comprehension of truth. And in view of the foregoing it should be clear that the comprehension of truth is the comprehension of a true proposition.

The comprehension of truth can be taken in three ways. In one way the comprehension of truth is nothing but the formation or existence of a proposition in the soul, and then again the comprehension of a true proposition is nothing but the true proposition itself, and it is clear that this is possible. Thus we have to conclude that in this way the comprehension of truth is possible for us.

In another way the comprehension of truth is taken for the adherence or assent by which we assent or adhere to a true proposition, and it is again obvious that this is possible for us to do. Indeed, we can not only assent to true propositions, but we often assent to false ones as well, namely, when we stubbornly persist in a false opinion. Therefore, we should conclude that the comprehension of truth is still possible for us in this way.

However, on the basis of the foregoing objections one might wonder if this sort of assent to the truth would be possible for us with certitude. And then we should note that assent to the truth with certitude requires the firmness of truth and the firmness of assent.

Now the firmness of truth is possible; in one way absolutely, as in the case of the proposition "God exists," which can in no situation [*in nullo casu*] be falsified. But there is also firmness of truth with the assumption of the common course of nature [*ex suppositione communis cursus naturae*], and in this way it is a firm truth that the heavens are moving and that fire is hot, and so on for other scientific conclusions, notwithstanding the fact that God would be able to make cold fire, which would falsify the proposition that every fire is hot. Thus it is clear that the firmness of truth is possible.

But the firmness of assent is that whereby we adhere and assent to a proposition without fear of the opposite [*absque formidine ad oppositum*] and this can take place in three ways.

In one way, [it proceeds] from the will, and in this way Christians assent and adhere firmly to the articles of Catholic faith, and even some heretics adhere to their false opinions, so much so that they would rather die than deny them, and such is the experience of the saints who were willing to die for the faith of Christ. And so it is clear that in this way the firmness of assent is possible for us.

In the second way, firmness proceeds in us from natural appearances by means of reasoning, and in this way it is still possible for us to assent not only to truth but also to falsity. For many people believing and holding false opinions take themselves to have firm scientific knowledge, just as Aristotle says in Book 7 of the *Ethics* that many people adhere to what they opine no less firmly than to what they know.

In the third way, firmness proceeds in us from evidentness. And it is called the evidentness of a proposition absolutely, when because of the nature of the senses or the intellect man is compelled, though without necessity, to assent to a proposition so that he cannot dissent from it. And this is the sort of evidentness that the first complex principle [the principle of non-contradiction] has, according to Aristotle in the fourth book of this work. Evidentness is taken in another way not absolutely, but with the assumption that things obey the common course of nature, as was said earlier. It is in this way that it is evident to us that every fire is hot or that the heavens are moving, although the opposite is possible by

God's power. And this sort of evidentness is sufficient for the principles and conclusions of natural science. Indeed, there is an even weaker kind of evidentness that suffices for acting morally well, namely, when someone, having seen and investigated all relevant facts and circumstances that man can diligently investigate, makes a judgment in accordance with these circumstances, then his judgment will be evident with the sort of evidentness that suffices for acting morally well, even if the judgment is false, because of some insurmountable ignorance of some circumstance. For example, it would be possible for a magistrate to act well and meritoriously in hanging a holy man because from testimonies and other legal evidence it sufficiently appeared to him concerning this good man that he was an evil murderer.

Therefore, we conclude as a corollary that some people speak very wrongly [*valde mali/male dicunt*], wanting to destroy the natural and moral sciences on the grounds that their principles and conclusions are often not absolutely evident, but can be falsified by supernaturally possible situations. Because such sciences do not require absolute evidentness, but the above-mentioned kinds of non-absolute or conditional [*secundum quid sive ex suppositione*] evidentness suffice. Therefore, Aristotle correctly points out in the second book of this work that mathematical exactitude is not to be sought in all sciences. And since it has become clear that the firmness of truth and firmness of assent are possible for us in all the ways discussed above, therefore, we should conclude what was sought, namely, that the comprehension of truth is possible for us with certitude. And then we should respond to the objections [. . .]

In response to [the argument about the deceptiveness of the senses] I say that if the senses are naturally deceived, then the intellect has to investigate whether there are people there or not, and it has to correct the judgments of illusion; but if God absolutely miraculously intervened, then we should conclude that he can do so; therefore there is only conditional evidentness here, which, however, suffices for natural science, as has been said.

In response to the next objection I concede that the intellect depends on the senses for its first, simple apprehension. But later on the intellect can form complex concepts, such as affirmations and negations [*potest componere et dividere*], and can discern beyond the discernment of the senses. Thus, to what was said, namely, that the thing cannot move the intellect because the mover has to be nobler than the thing moved, I respond that this has to be understood as concerning the principal mover, such as the agent intellect, but it is not true for all movers. And to the claim that the species passing through several media can be distorted, I reply that in a well-disposed medium they are not distorted [*non alienantur in peius*]; rather, they are refined in the inner senses, in order to represent their objects better or more clearly [*ad minus/melius vel purius*].

To the next objection, which says that experiences are not sufficient for concluding a universal principle, I reply that this is not a formally valid inference, but the intellect, on account of its natural inclination to the truth, predisposed by experiences, assents to a universal principle. And one may concede that experiences of this sort are not sufficient for absolute evidentness, but they are good enough for the type of certainty that suffices for natural science. Furthermore, there are also other principles, which, based on the inclusion or incompatibility of their terms, do not need experience [for their verification], such as the first principle; indeed, this is evidently true: "A chimera exists or it does not" or "A goatstag exists or it does not" or "Man is an animal," provided the signification of the terms is known.

To the other objection I reply that the effects are known by means of their causes as to the reason why [*propter quid*] the effect is, because the cause is better known even to us than

~~the reason why the effect~~ is. Likewise, a cause is known through its effect as to whether it is [*quia est*], because the effect bears some similitude to the cause, and so it can represent its cause along with the natural inclination of the intellect to the truth. And when it is said that a thing cannot conclusively be known from another, I deny this, and I say that there is a virtual infinity of self-evident principles [*principia per se nota*], through the senses, or through experience, or through the inclusion of terms without having to be proved by means of the first principle. Indeed, in the *Posterior Analytics* Aristotle proves that there are nearly as many indemonstrable principles as there are demonstrable conclusions.

★ ★ ★

The Differences between Knowledge and Opinion

8.4.4   Their differences

(1) Now, then, in order to bring out the differences between knowledge and opinion, we say that knowledge differs from opinion first because every [act of] knowledge has to occur with certainty and evidentness, as is clear by its nominal definition, but it is not possible for opinion to be like this. (2) The second difference is that every [act of] knowledge has to be of a true proposition, but not every opinion is such. (3) The third difference is that we cannot have knowledge of first principles by demonstration, but we can have opinion concerning them based on dialectical argument.

The fourth part is about the differences between knowledge and opinion. It contains three sections. (1) The first states the difference that knowledge [but not opinion] has to occur with certainty and evidentness. I say, therefore, first, 'with certainty'. For certainty requires two things, one on the part of the proposition that is assented to, namely, that it be true; for it is not certain belief on the basis of which we assent to something false, but rather it is uncertain and deceptive; and it is clear that, taken in this way, certainty is required for knowledge, for that which is false we do not know. Another thing is required on our part, namely, that our assent be firm, i.e., without doubt or fear of the opposite side; and this is also required for knowledge, since a doubtful and fearful assent does not transcend the limits of opinion. For if someone assents to a proposition fearing [that] the opposite [may be true], he would never say that he knows that it is true, but rather that he takes it or believes that it is.

And I also say 'with evidentness' so as to indicate that difference [between knowledge and] that credulity that we believers ought to have concerning the articles of Catholic faith, e.g., that God is triune. That credulity has the greatest degree of certainty on the part of the proposition, for it is a maximally true proposition that God is triune. And it should also be the firmest, without any fear on our part, in accordance with the Athanasian Creed [*Symbolum*], at the end: "This is the Catholic faith. Everyone must believe it, faithfully and firmly; otherwise he cannot be saved."[2] But it is compatible with this perfect certainty that because

---

2   *Symbolum "Quicunque"* ("Athanasianum"), in *Enchiridion symbolorum*, ed. H. Denzinger and K. Rahner (Barcelona: Herder, 1957), chaps. 39–40, pp. 17–18. Inc.: "Quicunque vult salvus esse, ante omnia opus est, ut teneat catholicam fidem, quam nisi quisque integram inviolatamque servaverit, absque dubio in aeternum peribit. Fides autem catholica haec est, ut unum Deum in Trinitate, et Trinitatem in unitate veneremur. . . . Expl.: Haec est fides catholica, quam nisi quisque fideliter firmiterque crediderit, salvus esse non potest."

of the lack of evidentness we do not properly have knowledge of [the content of] these articles. Improperly speaking, however, there is evidentness, because the cognitive power by its nature, along with its concurrent circumstances, is disposed to assent to the truth.

That a man can have firm credulity even concerning nonevident, unknown things, without any fear [of the opposite alternative], is clear from Aristotle, who in bk. 7 of the *Ethics* says: "Some people are no less convinced of what they opine than others of what they know."[3] And this firmness of assent without any fear of the opposite arises in us in three ways: first, by evidentness, and this is scientific assent; in another way on the basis of will, backed by the authority of the Sacred Scripture, and this is the Catholic faith of the saints who choose to die to sustain it; and in the third way, [the firmness of assent arises] from some false appearance, along with the will's being confined by it, as is the case with stubborn heretics, who also choose to die to sustain their false opinion.

It is true that, because of the aforementioned requirements demanded by the concept [*ratio*] of knowledge, some people, wanting to do theology, denied that we could have knowledge about natural and moral [phenomena].[4] For example, we could not know that the sky is moving, that the sun is bright and that fire is hot, because these are not evident. God could annihilate all these, and it is not evident to you whether He wills to annihilate them or not; and thus it is not evident to you whether they exist. Or God could put the sky to rest or remove light from the sun or heat from fire. And finally, they say that it is not evident to you concerning the stone you see as white that it is such that it is white, for even without the whiteness and the stone God can create in your eye an image [*species*] entirely similar to the one you have now from the object; and thus you would make the same judgment as you do now, namely, that there is a white stone here. And the judgment would be false, whence it would not be certain and evident; and, consequently, it would not be evident even now, for it is not evident to you whether God wills it so or not.[5]

But these objections are solved on the basis of bk. 2 of the *Metaphysics*. For there Aristotle says: "Mathematical exactitude is not to be demanded in all cases, but only in the case of those things that do not have matter; for this reason this is not the method of natural science."[6] And consequently the Commentator remarks on this passage[7] that one need not demand the kind of belief in natural demonstrations [found] in mathematics. We shall therefore declare that there are many diverse kinds of certainty and evidentness.

For there is the certainty and evidentness of divine wisdom, to which no created cognition can attain.

And in the genus of human cognition there are several kinds of certainty as well as of evidentness. For as far as we are concerned, certainty or assent should not be called that

3　Aristotle, *Nicomachean Ethics* VII.3.1146b29–30.

4　The allusion is clearly to Nicholas of Autrecourt.

5　Nobody could demand a clearer statement of the demon argument made famous in modern philosophy by Descartes. For the conceptual relationships between the demon argument and fourteenth-century nominalism see G. Klima, "Ontological Alternatives vs. Alternative Semantics in Medieval Philosophy," S. *European Journal for Semiotic Studies* 3–4 (1991); 587–618.

6　Aristotle, *Metaphysics* IV.3.1005b19–22.

7　*Aristotelis Metaphysicorum libri XIIII cum Averrois Cordubensis variis in eosdem commentariis*, in Averroes, *Aristotelis Opera cum Averrois Commentariis* (Venice, 1562–74; reprint, Frankfurt am Main: Minerva, 1962), f. 35vb K: "Et non oportet hominem quaerere ut modus fidei demonstrationibus naturalibus sit sicut modus fidei in mathematicis." The critical text's *sit nec* here obviously has to be emended to this edition's *sicut*. Indeed, this reading also appears in several codices according to the critical apparatus.

of knowledge, unless it is firm, without any fear [of falsity]. But as far as the proposition is concerned one sort of certainty is that which pertains to a proposition so firmly true that it, or one similar it, can by no power be falsified. And in this way we should certainly concede, as they have argued, that it is impossible for us to have such certainty about an assertoric categorical affirmative proposition, unless it consists of terms suppositing for God, or, perhaps if we admit natural supposition, of which we spoke elsewhere. But this sort of certainty is not required for natural sciences or metaphysics, nor even in the arts or morality [*prudentia*]. Another sort of human certainty on the part of the proposition, however, is that of a true proposition that cannot be falsified by any natural power and by any manner of natural operation, although it can be falsified by a supernatural power and in a miraculous way. And such certainty suffices for natural sciences. And thus I truly know, by natural science [or knowledge, *scientia*] that the heavens are moved and that the sun is bright.

Accordingly, it seems to me to be possible to conclude as a corollary that supernaturally it is possible for my [act of] knowledge, while it remains the same, to be converted into non-knowledge. For as long as the sun and the sky are moving in accordance with all their natural ways, the assent by which I firmly and with certainty assent to the proposition 'The sun is bright' is true, evident, and certain natural knowledge [*scientia*], endowed with the evidentness and certainty appropriate to natural science [*scientia*]. I posit, then, that if this [act of] assent, which is knowledge at the present time, remains in me for the whole day, and at nine o'clock God removes light from the sun without my knowing this, then that [act of] assent of mine will no longer be knowledge after nine o'clock, for it will no longer be true, nor will it have a true proposition as its object.

An analogous distinction can be made concerning evidentness as well as concerning certainty. For some human evidentness is such that in accordance with it the cognitive power is compelled either by its own nature or by some evident argument to assent to a truth or a true proposition that cannot be falsified by any power; but this is not required for natural science. Another [type of evidentness] is such that in accordance with it the cognitive power is compelled either by its own nature [or by some evident argument][8] to assent to a truth or a true proposition that cannot be falsified naturally, although it could be falsified super-naturally. And this is what is required for natural science.

But that no opinion is of this kind is clear, because this much is signified or connoted by [the term] 'opinion', namely, being short of knowledge in not meeting some of these requirements. But then you would ask whether, when I clearly see Socrates running, I know that Socrates is running or whether I merely opine this. And I reply that then I do not opine this, but I know. For everybody speaks in this way: "I know that this iron is hot, for I clearly feel that it is hot," and "I certainly know that Socrates was running yesterday, for I saw him running." But this knowledge is not knowledge in the second, the third, or the fourth of the modes distinguished above,[9] but in the first mode. Nevertheless, that mode is correctly dis-tinguished universally from opinion. And if the assent by which I assent [to the claim] that Socrates runs when I see him running will remain even after Socrates gets out of my sight, this will no longer be knowledge, but opinion. Therefore, this mode of knowledge soon and easily can be changed into opinion.

---

8   This clause does not appear in the text, but both symmetry and Buridan's doctrine clearly require it.
9   Aristotle, *Posterior Analytics* I.33.89a39–b9.

(2) The second section states that every [act or habit of] knowledge is [the knowledge] of a true proposition, but not every opinion [is such], since what is false is not known but may well be opined.

(3) The third and final section states that of the first principles one cannot have knowledge by demonstration, for it was said earlier that by 'first' and 'immediate' we mean 'indemonstrable'. But one can have opinion about them by dialectical argumentation. And this is true of many principles that at first had been doubted, until they were made evident by the senses, memory, and experience. For these can be taken to be false, and later opined, on the basis of insufficient evidence, and finally evidently known, when experience has sufficiently been made complete.

Still, lest on account of certain of Aristotle's remarks someone should have an occasion for error in this chapter, it is asked whether it is possible for the same person to have knowledge and opinion of the same thing at one and the same time. And Aristotle responds that in one way this is possible, and in another it is not. In brief, this should be understood so that with respect to that which is immediately knowable and opinable, which is a proposition, it is impossible for the same person to have knowledge and opinion about the same thing at the same time; for it is not possible that you assent to the same proposition with certainty and evidentness and without certainty and evidentness at the same time, although this may be possible successively. But when talking about the remote object of knowledge and opinion, which is a term of which the proposition is composed, or the thing signified by this term, it is possible for me to have knowledge and opinion at the same time about the same thing, for I can so possess a true and necessary proposition, for example, that every man is an animal, and an impossible or a contingent proposition, for example, that every man is a stone or that every man is awake; one I know, whereas the other perhaps I opine. And this is obvious.

Part II

Philosophy of Nature, Philosophy of the Soul, Metaphysics

Introduction

This part comprises selections that pertain to the second main philosophical discipline in Augustine's division, which in the *Dialectica Monacensis* (selection number 2) comprehends all "real sciences," i.e., all disciplines that theoretically study the nature of reality, as opposed to the self-reflective/regulative study of the operations of reason in logic, and to the practical/normative considerations in ethics.

Accordingly, the first section contains selections that present the generally presumed conceptual framework for studying the nature of reality in medieval philosophy, namely, Aristotelian hylomorphism, and the discussion of some important problems related to this general framework in connection with natural philosophy. The selections of the second section deal with the nature of the human soul, an entity of particular importance, not only because it constitutes our nature, but also because of its peculiar place in the overall scheme of reality, situated as it is on the (presumed) borderline between material and immaterial reality. The selections of the third section deal with this overall scheme of reality, as it is the proper subject of the most universal metaphysical considerations. Finally, the selections of the last section deal specifically with what we can know by natural reason about the origin and end of this reality, i.e., the existence and nature of God.

The first selection of the first section is the complete text of Aquinas' *De Principiis Naturae* ("On the Principles of Nature"). This short treatise provides an ideal introduction to the basic concepts and principles of Aristotelian hylomorphist metaphysics and philosophy of nature. Besides its obvious virtues of succinctness and clarity, what is truly remarkable about Aquinas's presentation is that it makes quite clear how the principles and conceptual distinctions introduced here are generally applicable regardless of our particular scientific, physical explanations of the phenomena that we think instantiate them. For example, it is always universally true that a substantial change results in the ceasing to be of one thing and the coming to be of another, whereas in an accidental change the same thing persists, only in a different state than it was before the change.

The universal applicability of the conceptual apparatus developed here renders it a powerful tool in the analysis of all sorts of natural phenomena regardless of our theories concerning the particular mechanisms that account for those phenomena. For the level of generality in these considerations concerns any possible natural change and its conditions as such, abstracting precisely from the particular mechanisms that account for the specific characteristics of this or that phenomenon. This is the reason why Aquinas's solution to a problem of Aristotelian natural philosophy presented in the next selection (concerning the presence of elements in mixed bodies or what we would call compounds) is equally applicable whether we take the elements in question to be the four Aristotelian elements or the elements of the modern Periodic Table. Indeed, this is also why the same conceptual apparatus is equally applicable to phenomena we still do not understand in detail, such as psychological phenomena.

However, this apparently unlimited universal applicability of these principles invites their application to phenomena concerning which religious doctrine makes some explicit claims, such as the creation of the world *ex nihilo* (from nothing), or the possibility of various miracles by divine omnipotence that are apparently excluded by the principles of Aristotelian metaphysics and natural philosophy. This inevitably leads to the conflicts between Aristotelian philosophy and religious dogma cataloged in the next selection, which come from *De Erroribus Philosophorum* ("The Errors of Philosophers") dubiously attributed to Aquinas' student, Giles of Rome. Whether or not it is the authentic work of Giles, the systematic presentation, useful summaries of the main doctrinal points criticized, and their reduction to their principles make this short treatise a particularly useful source for studying the doctrinal conflicts of the period. The selection in this volume only reproduces the critique of Aristotle, Avicenna, and Averroës (although the complete work also deals with Algazel, Alkindi, and Maimonides).

However, the most important document of the "official reaction" to these conflicts is still the text of the 1277 Paris Condemnation, reproduced in part in the next selection. As has already been indicated in the General Introduction, the sweeping Condemnation primarily targeted the radical Aristotelianism of the Latin Averroists, but it also touched on some of the theses of Aquinas, especially those connected to his conception of matter as the principle of individuation. The relevant theses of the Condemnation are indicated by an 'A' added to their number in the present selection.

By the late medieval period, Aristotelian physics came to be criticized for more than only theological or arcane metaphysical reasons. The last selection of this section presents Buridan's criticism of the Aristotelian principle that motion requires the activity of an actual mover, which does not appear to be the case in the motion of projectiles (i.e., in cases that we would characterize in modern physics as *inertial motion*). Buridan produces a barrage of arguments against Aristotle's own solution to the problem (provided in terms of the motion of the surrounding air), based on keen observation and careful reasoning. Buridan's own solution, in terms of the postulation of an impressed force, the so-called *impetus*, proved to be enormously influential, up until Galileo's time. Although this seems to be just a particular problem for Aristotelian physics, Buridan's solution has far-reaching implications for metaphysics and natural theology. For if motion can be present without an actual mover (as is clearly the case if its *impetus* can move a body long after the mover has let it go), then the existence of motion in the universe cannot provide evidence for the actual existence and activity of the ultimate source of this motion. Therefore, Buridan's *impetus* theory poses a serious challenge to the Aristotelian argument for the existence of a prime mover, adapted by many (indeed, practically all) thirteenth-century theologians and philosophers for proving the existence of God.

The selections of the second section deal with human nature and the human soul. The brief selections from Augustine are meant to illustrate his Platonic conception of human nature, according to which a human person is nothing but a soul ruling a human body. That the soul and body are two distinct entities and a human being is a composite of the two is not something Augustine feels the need to argue for. As a result, he has to deal with something like the modern, post-Cartesian "interaction problem," the problem of how the material body can act on the immaterial soul (in sense perception), and how the immaterial soul can act on the material body (in voluntary action). It is quite telling, however, that Augustine only has the first half of this problem: what he finds problematic is the body's action on the soul; the soul's ability to move the body is not an issue for him. The reason is that he does not have among his assumptions the idea of the causal closure of a (mechanistic) physical universe usually assumed in post-Cartesian thought. After all, for him all physical phenomena are just manifestations of God's continuous creative and sustaining activity, and so, just as God rules the material world in the macrocosm of nature, so does the soul rule its body in the microcosm of human nature. Thus, voluntary acts are just manifestations of the soul's power to move the body, just as the movement of the heavenly bodies is a manifestation of God's power to move the entire universe. But perception poses a problem precisely because of this conception of causality in terms of ruling or dominance. For that which is subordinate in this asymmetrical relation cannot affect that which dominates it. Augustine's solution in terms of the soul's attention required by the resistance of the body to its rule quite elegantly deals with this problem, but his rather skeletal conception leaves a great deal unanswered. So it is no wonder that after the arrival of Aristotle's detailed and sophisticated theory of the soul in general and of the human soul in particular, Augustine's conception exerted a somewhat oblique influence within a generally Aristotelian conceptual framework, in the form of Augustinian theologians' endorsement of the idea of a plurality of substantial forms in the same individual (i.e., the doctrine that the same individual substance has several substantial forms; say, in a human person there would be a form accounting for her corporeal features, such as being extended in space, another one accounting for her vegetative functions, a vegetative or nutritive soul, another accounting for her sensitive functions, a sensitive soul, and yet another accounting for her rationality, a rational soul, although some authors would take only two or three of these to be really distinct from each other).

In the Aristotelian framework, the soul (in Latin, *anima*) is simply the principle of life: that which *animates* any living – that is, *animate* – being. So the soul is that on account of which a living being is alive. And since for a living being to live is for it to be, absolutely speaking, to have its substantial being, and since that on account of which something has its substantial being is its substantial form, it follows that the soul of a living being is its substantial form. Note how this conception can get around the "interaction problem": since the soul and body are not two distinct entities acting on each other, but are rather the essential, integral parts of primary substances (which are the primary agents in causal relations), the question is not what sort of causal mechanisms can account for the interaction between body and soul; rather, the question will be what sort of causal powers living bodies informed by their peculiar substantial forms must have in order to perform their vital functions. So, plant-souls obviously need to have powers for nutrition, growth, and self-reproduction, more developed brute animal souls must have in addition powers of perception, memory, and imagination, and, finally, rational human souls must possess in addition the rational powers of intellect and will. However, this picture raises a peculiar problem in connection with the rational soul in particular: the nature of the intellect, which enables human beings informed by this sort of soul to perform the specific human activity of thinking.

Aristotle, in his *De Anima* ("On the Soul"), argued that thinking is simply not the kind of activity that can take place in a material medium: given that the intellect is able to think all material natures, the intellect itself cannot have a material nature, for otherwise its material nature would prevent it from thinking any other material nature, in the way any color in the eye itself would prevent it from seeing any other colors.[1]

To be sure, medieval philosophers and theologians certainly welcomed this conclusion, along with the further conclusion that the intellect is therefore immortal, for if the intellect is immaterial, then it is naturally capable of surviving the death (i.e., the disintegration of the material organization) of the body. But then the inevitable question is just how this immaterial intellect is related to the material body, indeed, to the material substantial form of this body, the rational soul.

The following selections from Averroës and Siger of Brabant, respectively, address this issue in the manner already indicated in the General Introduction. Accepting Aristotle's conclusion about the immateriality of the intellect, Averroës and Siger conclude that it cannot be a form inherent in matter; so, it must be a subsistent form (a form for which to be is not for it to inform matter); therefore, it must be a separate substance. Indeed, if the intellect is a form existing separately from matter, then, given the Aristotelian conception of individuation (according to which distinct instances of specifically the same form can only be distinct on account of the distinct parcels of matter they inform), it follows that there can be only one separate intellect shared by all humans. This conception, of course, raises a host of philosophical and theological problems, which invited both the official censure of the several condemnations mentioned in the General Introduction, and the severe philosophical and theological criticisms of the Averroistic position. One of the main critics was Aquinas, who, in the last question of selection number 27, provides precisely the sort of argument that Siger at the end of the previous selection admits he has no answer for.

But Aquinas was also treading a fine line in his own solution to the problem. Rejecting the Augustinian thesis of the plurality of substantial forms as metaphysically untenable (because, he argued in accordance with the doctrine of his *De Principiis Naturae* ("On the Principles of Nature"), a substantial form makes a thing actually existent absolutely speaking, and so any other form the thing can have can only be its accident making it actual in some respect), Aquinas has to say that the intellective soul is *both* the substantial form of the body *and* a subsistent entity, having its own operation in which it does not communicate with the body. But how is this possible? After all, if the human soul is the form of the body, then it is a material form: for it to be *is* for it to inform matter. On the other hand, if it is a subsistent form, then it has to be an immaterial form: for it to be *is not* for it to inform matter. Can there possibly be a middle ground between these apparently diametrically opposed characterizations? The answer is yes, if we consider that it is quite possible for the soul to have the same act of being that is the being of the body (and which is the same as the life of a living human being) as long as the soul informs the body, and to retain this same act

---

1   For a detailed discussion of this argument, along with another argument for the immateriality of the intellect in Aquinas, see G. Klima, "Aquinas's Proofs of the Immateriality of the Intellect from the Universality of Thought," *Proceedings of the Society for Medieval Logic and Metaphysics*, <http://www.fordham.edu/gsas/phil/klima/SMLM/PSMLM1.pdf>, 1 (2001), pp. 19–28. See also Robert Pasnau's comments and a rejoinder in the same volume, pp. 29–36 and pp. 37–44, respectively.

of being after its separation from the body, provided we allow the possibility that the being of the soul is merely contingently, but not necessarily, identical with the being of the body. But Aquinas' arguments from the proper, immaterial operation of the intellective soul are designed to establish precisely this conclusion, namely, that the existence that the soul has in the body is also the existence that properly belongs to the soul itself, whence the soul *can* have this same act of existence whether in or without the body.

It is the same position that is defended by John Buridan in the question presented here from his questions on Aristotle's *De Anima*. The important difference between Aquinas' and Buridan's approaches, however, is that Buridan takes this position to be established by faith alone.[2]

The selections of the next section present a sampling of general metaphysical considerations, which prepare the ground for the selections of the last section in this part, which deal with God's existence and what is supposed to be knowable about God by reason alone.

The brief selections from Avicenna are those passages that spelled out the most fundamental idea for practically all medieval thinkers in thirteenth-century metaphysics: the moderate realist conception of how common natures exist individuated both in the particulars that instantiate them and in the individual minds that can nevertheless comprehend them in abstraction from their individuating conditions. Acknowledging the formal unity of these instances (both in the mind and in the particulars) of the same common nature, without, however, ascribing independent existence and numerical unity to this nature, is nothing but the affirmation of the idea of "pervasive formal unity" discussed in the General Introduction.

It is this fundamental idea, among other things, that is articulated in careful detail in Aquinas' "metaphysical gem," his *De Ente et Essentia* ("On Being and Essence"), reproduced here in full. Aquinas' succinct, yet comprehensive, discussion takes us through his entire metaphysical system. Of particular importance are his discussions of the various sorts of metaphysical composition in created substances, contrasted with the absolute simplicity of God, his lucid exposition of Avicenna's idea of common nature in its absolute consideration and as it exists in singular substances and singular minds, and, especially, his famous arguments for the real distinction of essence and existence in creatures and the real identity of the same in God.

The importance of this idea will be evident in connection with the selections of the last section of this part, dealing with proving the existence of God, and spelling out the infinite differences between God and His creatures. So, the last selection of this section, presenting Buridan's arguments for the real identity of essence and existence also in creatures (an idea already present in the thirteenth century, in Siger of Brabant, Godfrey of Fontaines, and Henry of Ghent, among others), quite clearly indicates the sort of metaphysical challenges Aquinas' conception has to face in a different conceptual framework that would *not* spell out the distinction between Creator and creatures in terms of Aquinas' thesis of the real distinction of essence and existence in creatures.

The first short selection of the last section, from Augustine's *De Trinitate* ("On Trinity"), illustrates Augustine's conception of divine simplicity and presents his solution to the

---

2   For an excellent, thorough discussion of the finer details of Buridan's position see J. Zupko, "On Buridan's Alleged Alexandrianism: Heterodoxy and Natural Philosophy in Fourteenth-Century Paris," *Vivarium* 42/1 (2004), pp. 42–57.

problem of how certain predications can come to be and cease to be true of God without His change (which is excluded by His simplicity).

The next set of selections presents Anselm's arguments concerning the existence and nature of God, from both his *Monologion* and his *Proslogion*, along with selections from his debate with Gaunilo over the latter argument.

Finally, the last set of selections from Aquinas's *Summa Theologiae* presents some key texts from his natural theology concerning the provability of God's existence (containing his criticism of Anselm's approach), his actual proofs of God's existence, and some of his considerations concerning how we can meaningfully talk about God, despite our inability to comprehend His essence.

There is a sharp contrast between Aquinas' and Anselm's approaches to the same issues, despite some fundamental agreements between them. Aquinas finds Anselm's *a priori* approach in his *Proslogion* unpersuasive, because he clearly sees, just as Gaunilo did, that the mere linguistic understanding of Anselm's description of God as that than which nothing greater can be conceived cannot provide a logical short-cut to the requisite conception of God without which Anselm's reasoning cannot work.[3] Thus, Aquinas opted for his *a posteriori* approach, which, however, is very intimately tied to his Aristotelian physical and metaphysical principles that can be open to attack from many different angles, especially from different conceptual frameworks.

Nevertheless, the fundamental idea of these arguments is still quite appealing to many philosophers who have seriously engaged with Aquinas' thought. For if anything and every-thing in the world depends for its existence on something, and everything in the world is just a receiver, transformer, and transmitter of the energy needed for its own sustenance and for the sustenance of those it sustains, then it seems a plausible idea that anything in this world can exist only if there is a genuine, ultimate source of this energy, which itself does not need any sustenance, and which, therefore, is not something in this world. Aquinas' thesis of the real distinction between the existence and essence of creatures and the identity of the same in God was devised precisely to provide the metaphysical grounds for this idea, the idea of the radical dependency of everything in this world for its existence on something that cannot be a thing in this world.

---

3   For a detailed analysis of Anselm's argument and Aquinas's reaction along these lines, see G. Klima, "Saint Anselm's Proof," in G. Hintikka (ed.), *Medieval Philosophy and Modern Times* (Dordrecht: Kluwer Academic Publishers, 2000), pp. 69–88.

Hylomorphism, Causality, Natural Philosophy

19

Thomas Aquinas on the Principles of Nature

Chapter 1

Note that something can be, even if it is not, while something [simply] is. That which [only] can be [but is not] is said to be in ~~potentiality~~, whereas that which already exists is said to be in ~~actuality~~. But there are two kinds of being. There is ~~the essential or substantial being of the thing~~, as for a man to be, and this is just *to be*, without any qualification. The other kind of being is ~~accidental being~~, as for a man to be white, and this is [not just *to be*, but] *to be somehow.*[1]

It is with respect to both kinds of being that something is in potentiality. For something is in potentiality toward being a man, as the sperm and the menstrual blood; and something is in potentiality toward being white, as a man. Both that which is in potentiality in respect of substantial being and that which is in potentiality in respect of accidental being can be said to be matter, as the sperm can be said to be the matter of man and the man the matter of whiteness. But they differ in that the matter that is in potentiality in respect of substantial being is called ~~matter *from which* [something is made~~ – *materia ex qua*], while that which is in potentiality in respect of accidental being is called ~~matter *of which* [something is made~~ – *materia in qua*].[2]

---

1   The contrast in the Latin is that between *esse*, to be, absolutely speaking, and *esse aliquid*, literally, to be something. But since Aquinas' point here is the contrast between the substantial being of a thing on account of which it exists as a substance of some kind and its accidental being on account of which it is in a way, say, as being of such and such a shape, size, color, etc., the idea is better brought out in English by contrasting being absolutely with being somehow.

2   The literal rendering of the distinction in Latin (between *materia ex qua* and *in qua*, i.e., matter "from which" and "in which" something is made, respectively) would not be as helpful as the existing English distinction between matter that a thing is "made *from*" and matter that it is "made *of*." The former member of the existing distinctions in both languages indicates the transient matter of a thing, that *from* which it is made through some substantial transformation of this matter. This is how we say that bread is made *from* flour. But we cannot say that the bread is made *of* flour. The latter construction indicates the permanent matter of the thing, which is actually present in the constitution of the thing as long as the thing exists. This is how we say that a statue is made *of* bronze (but, again, a bronze statue is made *from* tin and copper).

Again, properly speaking, what is in potentiality toward accidental being is called a subject, while that which is in potentiality toward substantial being is properly called matter. And it is significant that what is in potentiality toward accidental being is called a subject, for we say that an accident is in a subject, while of a substantial form we do not say that it is in a subject.[3]

So, matter differs from subject in that a subject does not have being from what comes to it, as it has complete being in itself. For example, a man does not have his being [absolutely speaking] from his whiteness. Matter, however, does have its being from what comes to it, for matter in itself does not have complete being, but incomplete [i.e., merely potential] being. Therefore, form gives being to matter, absolutely speaking, but the subject gives being to the accident, even if sometimes one term is taken for the other, i.e. "matter" for "subject," and vice versa.

Again, just as everything that is in potentiality can be called matter, so everything from which something has being, whether accidental or substantial being, can be called a form; just as a man, who is white in potentiality, will be actually white on account of whiteness, and the sperm, which is a man in potentiality, will be actually a man on account of the soul. And since form makes something actual, form is also called actuality. That which makes something actual in accidental being is accidental form, and that which makes something actual in substantial being is substantial form.

Since generation is motion toward form, to these two kinds of form there correspond two kinds of generation: to substantial form there corresponds generation absolutely speaking, while to accidental form there corresponds generation with qualification. For when the substantial form is introduced, something is said to come to be, without further qualification. But when an accidental form is introduced, we do not say that something comes to be, without qualification, but that something comes to be this; just as when a man becomes white, we do not say that he comes to be, absolutely speaking, but that he comes to be white. And to these two kinds of generation there correspond two kinds of corruption, namely corruption in an absolute sense, and corruption with qualification. Generation and corruption absolutely speaking are only in the category of substance, while those with qualification are in the other categories.[4]

3 This is an allusion to Aristotle's doctrine in the *Categories*, where he distinguishes substance and accident in terms of *not being in* or *being in* a subject. Aquinas' point here is that strictly speaking it is only an accident that can be said to be in a subject, namely, in an actually existing substance that has its actual substantial being whether it actually has this accident or not. A substantial form, by contrast, cannot exist in a subject in this strict sense, for what it informs cannot have actual substantial existence without this form, since it has this actual existence precisely on account of actually having this form. Accordingly, a substantial form is not an accident, although it is not a complete substance either: it is a substantial part of a complete substance, along with the matter of this substance it informs.

4 Again, this is an allusion to Aristotle's doctrine of the *Categories*. Substantial change takes place only in the category of substance, i.e., with respect to substantial forms signified by terms falling into the logical category of substance. Accidental changes take place with respect to accidental forms signified by terms classified under one or the other of the categories of accidents. In his *Physics*, Aristotle also argues that primarily there is accidental change only in the categories of quantity (augmentation or diminution), quality (alteration), and place (locomotion). All other accidental changes take place on account of these primary changes: for example, the relational changes of becoming unequal or dissimilar obviously take place on account of the quantitative or qualitative change in one or the other of the things that started out as equal or similar.

And since generation is a kind of mutation from non-being into being, and corruption, conversely, should be from being to non-being, generation starts not from just any kind of non-being, but from a non-being that is a being in potentiality: for example, a statue is generated from bronze, which can be a statue, but is not actually a statue.

So, for generation three things are required: a being in potentiality, which is matter, non-being in actuality, which is privation, and that by which the thing will be actual, namely form. For example, when, from bronze, a statue is formed, the bronze, which is in potentiality toward the form of the statue, is matter; its shapelessness is called privation; and its shape, on account of which it is called a statue, is its form, though not its substantial form, for the bronze was already actual even before the introduction of this form or shape, and its existence does not depend on this shape, but is an accidental form. For all artificial forms are accidental, because art works only on what is supplied by nature already in complete existence.

Chapter 2

So, there are three principles of nature, namely matter, form, and privation, of which one is *that to which* generation proceeds, namely form, and the other two are *that from which* generation proceeds. Therefore, matter and privation are the same in their subject, but differ in their concepts. For the very same thing that is bronze is shapeless before the advent of the form; but it is for different reasons that it is called bronze and shapeless.

Therefore privation is called a principle not *per se* [on its own account] but *per accidens* [by coincidence], namely, because it coincides with matter, just as we say that this is *per accidens*: the doctor builds a house, for he builds not on account of being a doctor, but as a builder, who happens to be a doctor.

But there are two kinds of accidents: namely necessary [accident], which is not separated from its subject, as risibility[5] from man, and not necessary [accident], for example, whiteness, which can be separated from man.[6] Therefore, although privation is a principle *per accidens*, it does not follow that it is not required for generation, because matter is never stripped of privation; for insofar as it is under one form, it has the privation of another and, conversely, as in fire there is the privation of the form of air.[7]

---

5 "Risible": capable of laughter. See "John Buridan on the Predicables" (selection no. 8, n. 1 above).

6 This is an allusion to Porphyry's doctrine in his *Isagoge*, where he distinguishes inseparable and separable accidents. For although accidents may or may not belong to the same subject without the corruption of that subject according to Porphyry's definition, some accidents are naturally inseparable from their subjects, although their subjects can be conceived to exist without those accidents (so, in their case the "may" in the Porphyrian definition should be understood as mere logical possibility, as opposed to some genuine natural potentiality).

7 Privation is the *logically necessary* starting point of any coming-to-be (for if the thing already had the opposite form, then it could not *come* to have that form). Yet privation merely coincides with the principle that renders change *naturally possible*, namely, matter. For an amorphous lump of bronze *is able to* become a statute through its own change *not* on account of the fact that it does not have the shape of the statue (for otherwise everything that does not have that shape, say, an angel or the square root of two, would have to be able to do so), but on account of its *natural ability* to take on and preserve that shape. So, the *per se* principle of this change (that on account of which it can occur) is the bronze, which is coincidentally (*per accidens*), but logically necessarily lacking the shape it will take on when it is shaped into a statue.

We should know that even if generation proceeds from non-being, we do not say that its principle is negation, but that it is privation, for a negation does not determine its subject. For that it does not see can [truly] be said also of a non-being, as [when we say that] a chimera does not see, and also of a being that is naturally incapable of having sight, as [when we say that] a rock does not see. But a privation can be said only of a determinate subject, in which the opposite habit is naturally apt to occur, for example, only those things can be said to be blind that are naturally apt to see [but actually lack sight].

And since generation does not proceed from non-being absolutely speaking, but from a non-being in some subject, and not in just any kind of subject, but in a determinate subject (for it is not from just any kind of non-being that fire is generated, but from that kind of non-fire in which the form of fire is apt to come to be), we say that privation is a principle.

But it differs from the others in that the other two are principles both of being and of coming to be. For in order that a statue is generated there has to be bronze, and in the end there has to be the form of the statue, and, further, when the statue already exists, these two also have to exist. However, privation is only the principle of coming to be, but not of being, for while the statue is still coming to be, it is necessary that the statue does not yet exist. For if it already existed, it would not be coming to be, for what is still coming to be does not yet exist, apart from processes. But when the statue already exists, there is no privation of the shape of the statue, for affirmation and negation cannot stand together, and similarly neither can privation and habit.

Again, privation is a principle *per accidens*, as was explained above, and the other two are principles *per se*. From what has been said it is clear, then, that matter differs from form and privation in its concept. For matter is that in which form and privation are thought to be, as it is in the bronze that form and formlessness are thought to be.

Sometimes matter is named with privation, and sometimes without it. For example, the concept of bronze, when it is the matter of the statue, does not imply privation: for when I call something bronze, this does not imply that it is shapeless or formless. On the other hand, the concept of flour does imply the privation of the form of bread, for when I call something flour, this does signify a shapelessness or formlessness opposite to the form of bread.

And since in the process of generation matter or the subject remains, but privation or what is composed of matter and privation does not, that matter which does not imply privation in its concept is permanent, while that matter which does is transient.

We should know that some matter has some form, for example, the bronze, which is matter in respect of the statue, but bronze itself is composed of matter and form; wherefore bronze is not called prime matter, for it has matter. But that matter which is thought of without any kind of form or privation as subject to all forms and privations is called *prime matter*, because there is no other matter before it. And this is also called *hyle*.

Now, since [any] definition and cognition is [obtained] by form, prime matter cannot be cognized or defined in itself, only by comparison, as when we say that prime matter is that which is to all forms and privations as bronze is to the form of the statue and to the lack of this form. And this matter is called prime matter without qualification.

For something can [also] be called *prime* matter *in respect of a genus*, as water is the prime matter of all liquids. But it is not *prime matter* without qualification, for it is composed of matter and form, so it has matter prior to it.

We have to know that prime matter, as well as form, is not generated (or corrupted), for every generation proceeds to something from something. That *from which* generation proceeds is matter, and that *to which* generation proceeds is form. Therefore, if either matter or form were generated, then matter would have matter and form would have form, and so on, *in infinitum*. So, properly speaking, only the composite substance is generated.

We also have to know that matter is said to be numerically one in all things. But something is said to be numerically one in two ways. First, that is said to be numerically one which has one determinate form, for example Socrates; but prime matter is not said to be numerically one in this way, for in itself it does not have any form. Second, a thing can also be said to be numerically one because it lacks those dispositions which make things numerically different, and it is in this way that matter is said to be numerically one.

We should know that although matter does not have in its nature some form or privation, as in the concept of bronze neither shape nor the lack of some shape is included; nevertheless, matter is never stripped of form or privation, for sometimes it is under one form, while sometimes it is under another. But it can never exist in itself, because on account of its very concept it does not have any form, whence it does not have actual existence (since something can have actual existence only through its form), but it exists only potentially. So nothing in actual existence can be called prime matter.

Chapter 3

From what has been said it is clear, then, that there are three principles of nature, namely matter, form, and privation. But these three are insufficient for generation, for nothing drives itself into actuality, for example a chunk of bronze, which is in potentiality to become a statue, does not make itself into an actual statue, but it needs an agent that brings out the form of the statue from potentiality to actuality. And the form would not bring itself from potentiality into actuality either (and I am speaking here about the form of the thing being generated, which we call the end of the generation), for the form does not exist until it has come to be, but what is acting is already existing during the process of generation. So, it is necessary to have another principle beside matter and form, namely, something that acts, and this is called the efficient or moving cause, or the agent or the principle of motion. And since, as Aristotle says in the second book of his *Metaphysics*, whatever acts does so only intending something, there has to be also a fourth [principle], namely that which is intended by the agent, and this is called the end.

We have to know, however, that every agent, natural as well as voluntary, intends some end. But from this it does not follow that all agents recognize this end, or deliberate about the end. For to recognize the end is necessary only for those agents whose acts are not determined, but which can have alternatives for [their] action, namely, voluntary agents, who have to recognize their ends by which they determine their actions. However, the actions of natural agents are determined, so it is not necessary that they elect the means to an end. And this is what Avicenna illustrates with his example of the guitar player who does not need to deliberate the plucking of the strings, as these are determined for him, for otherwise there would be delays between the single sounds, which would result in dissonance.

Now a voluntary agent rather appears to deliberate than a natural agent. So, [since even a voluntary agent may act without deliberation,] it follows by *locus a maiori*[8] that it is

8 Aquinas alludes here to a dialectical topic (a form of probable argument discussed by Aristotle in his *Topics*, his logical work on probable reasoning). The *locus a maiori apparentia* (the topic from greater appearance) relies on the following maxim (a general observation that licenses a probable inference): if a thing that is more likely to have an attribute than another does not have it, then the other does

possible for a natural agent to intend some end without deliberation. And this kind of intending an end is nothing but having a natural inclination toward it.

From what has been said, then, it is clear that there are four kinds of causes, namely, material, efficient, formal, and final. And although the terms "principle" and "cause" can be used interchangeably, as is stated in the fifth book of the *Metaphysics*, in the *Physics* Aristotle distinguished four causes and three principles. For [there] he took causes to comprise both extrinsic and intrinsic ones. Now matter and form are said to be intrinsic to the thing, for they are constituent parts of the thing; but the efficient and the final cause are said to be extrinsic, for they are outside of the thing. But [in this passage of the *Physics*] he took only the intrinsic causes to be principles. On the other hand, privation is not counted among the causes, for privation is a *per accidens* principle, as we said. So, when we speak about the four causes, we mean the *per se* causes, but also *per accidens* causes are reduced to the *per se* ones, for whatever is *per accidens* is reduced to what is *per se*.

But even if in the first book of his *Physics* Aristotle takes intrinsic causes for principles, nevertheless, as he says in the eleventh book of his *Metaphysics*, properly speaking the extrinsic causes are principles and the intrinsic causes that are parts of the thing are elements, and both can be called causes. But sometimes these terms are used interchangeably. For every cause can be called a principle and every principle can be called a cause, though the concept of cause seems to add something to that of principle in its ordinary sense, for whatever is first can be called a principle,[9] whether there results some existence from it or not. For example, a craftsman can be called the principle of a knife, as from his work there results the being of the knife. But when something turns from black to white, then we can say that blackness is the principle [beginning] of this change – and generally speaking everything from which some change begins can be called a principle – still, from this blackness there did not result the being of whiteness. But only that first thing is called a cause from which there follows the being of a posterior thing; so we say that a cause is something from the being of which there follows the being of something else.

For this reason, that first thing from which the motion starts cannot be called a cause *per se*, even if it is a principle, whence privation is counted among principles, but not among causes, for privation is that from which generation starts. But [privation] can also be called a cause *per accidens*, insofar as it coincides with matter, as was explained earlier.

However, only those things are properly called elements that are causes of which the thing is composed, which are properly material, and not just any material causes, but only those of which the thing is primarily composed. We do not say, for example, that his limbs are the elements of a man, for the limbs themselves are also composed of others; but we do say

not have it either. The maxim, therefore, licenses the inference from the lack of an attribute in something that would be more likely to have it, i.e., concerning which there would be a greater appearance (*maior apparentia*) that it would have this attribute, to the lack of the same attribute in something else that is less likely to have it. For example, if a math teacher assigns a problem to his students that even he cannot solve, his students can argue that they should not be expected to solve it, relying on this form of argument. For in this case there is a greater appearance that the teacher should be able to solve the problem, based on his greater knowledge and experience. But if he cannot solve it, then the maxim licenses the conclusion that his students (who are less likely to solve a problem than he is) cannot solve it either. Likewise, if voluntary agents can intend something without deliberation, then involuntary agents can also intend something without deliberation.

9   In its ordinary, common, sense, the Latin word *principium* from which the English word 'principle' derives simply denotes the beginning or first member of any series of items.

that earth and water are elements, for these are not composed of other bodies, but it is from them that all natural bodies are primarily composed. Therefore Aristotle in the fifth book of the *Metaphysics* says that an element is something from which a thing is primarily composed, is in the thing, and is not divided according to form.

The first part of this definition, namely, "something from which a thing is primarily composed," is evident from what has been just said. The second part, namely, "is in the thing," is put here to distinguish elements from that kind of matter which is totally corrupted in generation. For example, bread is the matter of blood, but blood is not generated, unless the bread from which it is generated passes away; so the bread does not remain in the blood, whence bread cannot be said to be an element of blood. But elements somehow have to remain, since they do not pass away, as it is said in the book *On Coming To Be and Passing Away*. The third part, namely, that an element is not divided according to form, is meant to distinguish an element from those things that have parts different in form, i.e., in species, as, for example, a hand, the parts of which are flesh and bones, which are different in species. But an element is not divided into parts that differ in species, as water, of which every part is water. For it is not required for something to be an element that it should be indivisible in quantity, but it is sufficient, if it is not divisible according to species; but if something is indivisible also in this way, then it is also called an element, as letters are called the elements of expressions. So it is clear that "principle" covers more than "cause," and "cause" more than "element." And this is what the Commentator says in commentary on the fifth book of the *Metaphysics*.

Chapter 4

Having seen that there are four genera of causes, we have to know that it is not impossible for the same thing to have several causes, as for a statue, the causes of which are both the bronze and the sculptor, but the sculptor as efficient, while the bronze as its matter. Nor is it impossible for the same thing to be the cause of contraries. For example, the pilot can be the cause both of the salvation and of the sinking of the ship, but of the one by his presence, while of the other by his absence. We also have to know that it is possible that something be both cause and effect in respect of the same thing, but not in the same way: for walking is the cause of health as its efficient, but health is the cause of walking as its end: for we take a walk sometimes for the sake of our health. Again, the body is the matter of the soul, while the soul is the form of the body. Also, the efficient is said to be the cause of the end, for the end comes to be by the operation of the agent, but the end is the cause of the efficient, insofar as the agent operates only for the sake of the end. Whence the efficient is the cause of the thing that is the end, say, health; but it does not cause the end to be the end; as the doctor causes health, but he does not cause health to be the end. On the other hand, the end is not the cause of the thing that is the efficient, but is the cause for the efficient to be efficient: for health does not cause the doctor to be a doctor (and I am speaking about the health that is produced by the operation of the doctor), but it causes the doctor to be efficient, so the end is the cause of the causality of the efficient, for it causes the efficient to be efficient, and similarly, it causes matter to be matter and form to be form, for matter does not receive form, except for the sake of the end, and form does not perfect matter, except for the sake of the end. Whence it is said that the end is the cause of all causes, for it is the cause of the causality of all causes. For matter is said to be the cause of form, insofar as the form exists only in matter; and similarly, form is the cause of matter, insofar as matter has actual existence only by the form. For matter and form are correlatives, as is said in the second book of *Physics*. They are related to the composite substance, however, as parts and as simple [components] to the composite.

But since every cause insofar as it is a cause is naturally prior to its effect, we should know that something is called "prior" in two ways, as Aristotle says in the sixteenth book of his *On Animals*. And on account of this diversity something can be called both prior and posterior in respect of the same thing, and both cause and effect. For something is said to be prior to something else in respect of generation and time, and again, in respect of substance and completion. Now since the operation of nature proceeds from what is imperfect to what is perfect and from what is incomplete to what is complete, what is imperfect is prior to what is perfect in respect of generation and time, but what is perfect is prior in completion. So we can say that a man is prior to a boy in substance and perfection, but the boy is prior to the man in generation and time. But although among generable things that which is imperfect is prior to what is perfect, and potentiality is prior to act (considering the same thing that is imperfect prior to becoming perfect, and is in potentiality prior to becoming actual), nevertheless, absolutely speaking, what is actual and perfect is necessarily prior: for what reduces that which is in potentiality to actuality is in actuality, and what perfects the imperfect, is itself perfect. Now matter is prior to form in generation and time: for that to which something is coming is prior to what is coming to it. Form, however, is prior to matter in perfection, since matter has no complete existence, except by the form. Similarly, the efficient is prior to the end in generation and time, for it is from the efficient that motion starts toward the end. But the end is prior to the efficient, insofar as it is efficient, in substance and completion, for the action of the efficient is completed only by the end. So these two causes, namely, matter and the efficient, are prior in generation; but the form and the end are prior in perfection.

And we should note that there are two kinds of necessity: absolute necessity and conditional necessity. Absolute necessity proceeds from those causes that are prior in generation, which are matter and the efficient: for example, the necessity of death derives from matter and the disposition of the contrary components of the body; and this is called absolute, because it cannot be impeded. And this type of necessity is also called the necessity of matter. Conditional necessity, on the other hand, proceeds from those causes that are posterior in generation, namely, form and the end. For example, we say that conception is necessary, if a man is to be generated; and this is conditional, for it is not absolutely necessary for this woman to conceive, but under this condition, namely, that if a man is to be generated. And this is called the necessity of the end.

We should also know that three causes can coincide, namely the form, the end, and the efficient, as is clear in the generation of fire. For fire generates fire, so fire is the efficient, insofar as it generates; again, fire is form, insofar as it makes actual that was previously potential, and again, it is the end, insofar as it is intended by the agent, and insofar as the operation of the agent is terminated in it. But there are two kinds of ends, namely the end of generation and the end of the thing generated, as is clear in the generation of a knife. For the form of the knife is the end of its generation; but cutting, which is the operation of the knife, is the end of the thing generated, namely of the knife. Now the end of generation sometimes coincides with two of the above-mentioned causes, namely, when something is generated by something of the same species, as when man generates man, and an olive tree generates an olive tree. But this may not be thought to apply to the end of the thing generated.

We should know, however, that the end coincides with the form numerically, for it is numerically the same item that is the form of the generated thing and that is the end of the generation. But with the efficient it does not coincide numerically, but can coincide specifically. For it is impossible for the maker and the thing made to be numerically the same, but they can be the same specifically. For example, when a man generates a man, then the man generating and the man generated are numerically different, but are specifically the same. However, matter does not coincide with the others, because matter, since it is a being in potentiality, is by its very nature imperfect, while the other causes, since they are actual, are by their nature perfect; but what is perfect and what is imperfect never coincide.

Chapter 5

Having seen that there are four kinds of causes, namely, efficient, material, formal, and final, we have to know that each of these kinds is divided in various ways. For some causes are called prior and some are called posterior, as when we say that the art of medicine and the doctor are both causes of health, but the art is the prior, while the doctor is the posterior cause; and similar distinctions apply in the case of the formal cause and the other kinds of causes.

Note here that in our inquiry we always have to go back to the first cause, as when we ask: Why is he healthy? The answer is: because the doctor cured him. And then, further: How did he cure him? The answer is: by his knowledge of medicine. And we should know that it is the same thing to say that a cause is posterior and that it is proximate, or that a cause is prior and that it is remote. So these two divisions of causes, namely, into prior vs. posterior and into proximate vs. remote, signify the same. But we should know that the more universal cause is always called the remote cause and the more specific cause is called the proximate cause. For example, we say that the proximate form of man is what his definition signifies, namely rational, mortal animal, but his more remote form is animal and the even more remote one is substance. For all superiors are forms of the inferiors. Similarly, the proximate matter of the statue is bronze, while the more remote is metal and the even more remote one is body.[10]

Again, some causes are *per se*, others are *per accidens*. A *per se* cause of a thing is its cause insofar as it is such, as the builder [insofar as he is a builder] is the cause of the house, or the wood [insofar as it is wood] is the matter of the bench. A cause *per accidens* is one that coincides with the cause *per se*, as when we say that the doctor is building. For the doctor is a cause *per accidens* of the building, because he is building not insofar as he is a doctor, but insofar as he coincides with the builder. And the situation is similar in all other cases.

Again, some causes are simple, some are composite. Something is called a simple cause, when it is named only by the name of the *per se* cause, or only by the name of the *per accidens* cause, as when we say that the builder is the cause of the building, and similarly when we say that the doctor is the cause of the building. But a cause is called composite,

10 Although Aquinas exemplifies his claim in the case of formal and material causes, the same type of correlation between priority and universality can be observed in the case of efficient causes as well: the more remote, that is, prior cause is always more universal (i.e., acting in virtue of a more universal form, and so affecting a more extensive class of particulars). Therefore, if there is an absolutely first efficient cause, then it has to be the most universal cause, i.e., the absolutely universal cause of all beings (other than itself) as such.

165

AQUINAS ON THE PRINCIPLES OF NATURE

when we name it by the name of both, as when we say that the builder-doctor is the cause of the building.

But, according to Avicenna's exposition, something can also be called a simple cause, if it is a cause without the addition of anything else, as bronze is the cause of the statue, for the statue is made of bronze without the addition of any other matter, or when we say that the doctor causes health, or the fire causes heat. We have a composite cause, however, when several things need to come together to constitute the cause; for example, one man cannot be the cause of the movement of a ship [by towing it], but many can, or one stone cannot be the matter of a house, but many stones can.

Again, some causes are actual causes, others are potential. An actual cause is one that is actually causing the thing, as the builder when he is actually building, or the bronze, as the statue is actually being made of it. A potential cause, on the other hand, is what is not actually causing the thing, but can cause it, as the builder, when he is actually not building. And we should know that the actual cause and its effect should exist at the same time, so that if one of them exists, then the other has to exist too.[11] For if the builder is actually working, then he has to be building, and if the act of building actually takes place, then the builder actually has to be working. But this is not necessary in the case of merely potential causes.

We should know, further, that a universal cause is compared to a universal effect and a singular cause is compared to a singular effect. For example, we say that a builder is the cause of a building in general, but also that this builder is the cause of this building in particular.

Chapter 6

We should also know that we can speak about the agreements and differences of the principles in terms of the agreements and differences of what they are the principles of. For some things are numerically identical, as Socrates and this man, pointing to Socrates; some things are numerically different, and specifically the same, as Socrates and Plato, who are both human, but are numerically distinct. Again, some things differ specifically, but are generically the same, as a man and a donkey, which both belong to the genus of animals; still others are the same only analogically, as substance and quantity, which do not agree in some genus, but agree only analogically: for they agree only in that they are beings. But being is not a genus, because it is not predicated univocally, but analogically.

To understand this better, we have to know that it is in three different ways that something can be predicated of several things: univocally, equivocally, and analogically. Something is predicated univocally if it is predicated by the same name and according to the same concept or definition, as "animal" is predicated of a man and a donkey, because both [man and donkey] are said to be animals and both are animated sensible substances, which is the definition of animal. Something is predicated equivocally if it is predicated of several

11   An efficient cause of a thing is its actual cause only as long as it actually generates the thing, if it is a generative cause, or as long as it actually sustains the actual being of the thing, if it is a preservative cause. According to the medieval conception, it is in this latter sense that God, the Creator, is the actual efficient cause of his creatures continuously sustaining their existence in the ongoing act of continuous creation (*creatio continua*), without which creatures would simply fall into nothing, just as the lights go out if the power is turned off. It is this conception that allows the inference from the actual existence of creatures to the actual existence of the Creator, i.e., God.

things by the same name, but according to different concepts, as "dog" is predicated both of the barking animal and of the constellation, which agree only in this name but not in the definition or signification of this name: for what is signified by a name is its definition, as is stated in the fourth book of the *Metaphysics*. Finally, something is predicated analogically if it is predicated of several things, the concepts of which are different, but are related to the same thing. For example, "healthy" is said of the body of animals and of urine and of food, but it does not signify the same in all these cases. For it is said of urine, insofar as it is a sign of health, of the body, insofar as it is the subject of health, and of food, insofar as it is the cause of health; but all of these concepts are related to one and the same end, namely, health. For sometimes those that agree analogically, i.e., proportionally, or in some comparison or similitude, are related to the same end, as is clear in the previous example, but sometimes they are related to the same agent; for example, when "medical" is predicated of someone who operates by the knowledge of medicine, as a doctor, or without it, as a nurse, or when it is said of some medical instrument, always in relation to the same agent, namely the art of medicine. Again, sometimes they are related to the same subject, as when "being" is predicated of substance, of quality, of quantity, and of the other categories. For it is not entirely the same concept according to which a substance is said to be a being, and a quantity, and the rest, but all these are said to be beings only in relation to substance, which is the subject of all of them. So "being" is said primarily of substance, and only secondarily of the rest. Whence "being" is not a genus, for no genus is predicated primarily and secondarily of its species, but "being" is predicated analogically. And this is what we said, namely, that substance and quantity differ generically, but they are the same analogically.

Therefore, of those things that are numerically the same, also the form and matter are numerically the same, as Tully's and Cicero's. Of those things, however, that are specifically the same, but numerically distinct, also the matter and form are numerically distinct, but specifically the same, as Socrates' and Plato's. Likewise, of those things that are generically the same, also the principles are generically the same: as the soul and the body of a donkey and of a horse differ specifically, but are the same generically. Again, in a similar manner, of those that agree only analogically, also the principles agree only analogically. For matter and form or potentiality and actuality are the principles both of substance and of the other categories. But the matter of substance and that of quantity, and similarly their forms, differ generically, and agree only analogically or proportionally in that the matter of substance is to substance as the matter of quantity is to quantity. But just as substance is the cause of other categories, so the principles of substance are the principles of the rest.

Thomas Aquinas On the Mixture of the Elements

It is customarily a point of doubt among many people how the elements exist in a mixed [body].

[Avicenna's Theory[1]]

Now it seems to some that when the active and passive qualities of the elements are somehow reduced to an intermediate through alteration, the substantial forms of the elements remain. For if they do not remain, there will seem to be a kind of corruption of the elements and not a mixture.

Again, if the substantial form of a mixed body is the act of matter without presupposing the forms of simple bodies, then the simple bodies of the elements will lose their definition (*rationem*). For an element is that of which something is primarily composed, and exists in it and is indivisible according to species. But if the substantial forms [of the elements] are taken away, the mixed body will no longer be composed of simple bodies in such a way that they remain in it.

But it is impossible for this [view] to be so. For it is impossible for matter to take on diverse forms of the elements in the same way. If therefore the substantial forms of the elements are going to be preserved in a mixed body, it will be necessary for them to inhere in different parts of matter. Now it is impossible to get diverse parts of matter without quantity's being already understood in the matter. For if quantity is taken away, the indivisible substance remains, as is clear from *Physics* I [3 185^{b}16].[2] But a physical body is constituted out of matter, existing under quantity, and an advening substantial form. Therefore, the diverse parts of matter, subsisting through the forms of the elements, take on the aspect (*rationem*) of several bodies. Now it is impossible for [a physical body] to be many bodies at once. Therefore,

---

1 Avicenna, *Sufficientia*, I.6, (Venice, Bonetus Locatellus for Octavianus Scotus, 1508; photoreprint, Frankfurt am Main: Minerva, 1961), fol. 17va; *Metaphysica*, VIII.2 (ibid., fol. 98ra). See also Avicenna's view as reported by Averroës, *In De generatione et corruptione*, I, comm. 90, in *Aristotelis Opera cum Averrois commentariis*, 10 vols in 13 (Venice: Juntas, 1562–1574; photoreprint, Frankfurt am Main: Minerva, 1962), vol. 5, fol. 370k; *In De caelo*, III, comm. 67 (Juntas ed., vol. 5, fols. 226d–227h).

2 See also Aristotle, *Physics* I.7 189^{b}30–191^{a}22.

the four elements will not exist in each part of the mixed body. And so [if they do exist,] there will not be a true mixture but [only a mixture] according to sensation, as happens when bodies come together that are insensible because of their smallness.

Furthermore, every substantial form requires a proper disposition in matter, without which it cannot exist. Hence alteration is the way to generation and corruption. Now it is impossible for the proper disposition that is required for the form of fire and that which is required for the form of water to come together in the same thing. For fire and water are contraries in accordance with such dispositions; but it is impossible for contraries to be in exactly the same thing at once. Therefore, it is impossible that the substantial forms of fire and water should be in the same part of the mixed [body]. Therefore, if the mixed [body] should come to be while the substantial forms of the simple bodies remain, it follows that it is not a true mixture but only [a mixture] for sensation when the parts, insensible because of their smallness, are as it were placed next to one another.

[Averroës' Theory[3]]

But some people, wishing to avoid both these arguments, fell into an even greater inconsistency. For in order to distinguish a mixture from a corruption of the elements, they said that the substantial forms of the elements do remain in the mixed [body] somehow. But again, in order not to be compelled to say it is a mixture [only] for sensation and not in truth, they claimed that the forms of the elements do not remain in their fullness in the mixed [body], but are reduced to a certain intermediate. For they say that the forms of the elements admit of more and less and have a contrariety toward one another. But since this is plainly inconsistent with the common view and with the statements of Aristotle, who says in the *Categories* [5 3^{b}24 & 3^{b}33–34] that nothing is the contrary of substance, and that it does not admit of more and less, [therefore] they go further and say that the forms of the elements are the most imperfect inasmuch as they are closer to prime matter. Hence they are intermediate between substantial and accidental forms. And so, insofar as they approach the nature of accidental forms they can admit of more and less.

Now this position can be refuted in many ways. First, because it is entirely impossible for there to be anything intermediate between substance and accident; it would be something intermediate between affirmation and negation. For it is peculiar to an accident that it be in a subject, but to a substance that it not be in a subject. Now substantial forms are in matter, to be sure, but not in a subject. For a subject is a "this something." A substantial form, on the other hand, is what *makes* a "this something". But it does not presuppose it.

Again, it is ridiculous to say there is an intermediate between things that are not in one genus, as is proved in *Metaphysics* X [9 1057^{a}19–20 & 1057^{a}33–^{b}1]. For an intermediate and its extremes must be in the same genus. Therefore, nothing can be an intermediate between substance and accident.

Next, it is impossible for the substantial forms of the elements to admit of more and less. For every form admitting of more and less is divisible accidentally, insofar namely as a subject can participate [in] it either more or less. But there can be continuous motion with respect to what is divisible [either] by itself or accidentally, as is clear in *Physics* VI [5 234^{b}10–20]. For there is change of location, and increase and decrease with respect to quantity and place, which are by themselves divisibles, while there is alteration with respect

---

3   Averroës, *In De caelo*, III, comm. 67 (Juntas ed., vol. 5, fols. 226d–227h).

to qualities that admit of more and less, like hot and white. Therefore if the forms of the elements admit of more and less, both the generation and the corruption of the elements will be a continuous motion, which is impossible. For there is no continuous motion except in three categories, namely, quantity, quality and place, as is proved in *Physics* V [3–4 225^{b}7–9 & 226^{a}24–^{b}10].

Furthermore, every difference in substantial form varies the species. But [as for] what admits of more and less, what is more differs from what is less, and is in a certain way contrary to it, like more white and less white. Therefore if the form of fire admits of more and less, [then] when it is made more or made less it will vary the species and [will] not be the same form but another one. This is why the Philosopher says in *Metaphysics* VIII [3 1043^{b}36–1044^{a}2] that just as among numbers the species is varied by addition and subtraction, so among substances.

[Aquinas' Own Theory]

Therefore, we must find another way whereby a true mixture will be kept intact and yet the elements not be totally corrupted but somehow remain in the mixed [body]. Thus we must consider that the active and passive qualities of the elements are contraries to one another and admit of more and less. Now from contrary qualities admitting of more and less an intermediate quality can be constituted that may have the flavor of the nature of both extremes, like pale between white and black and tepid between hot and cold. So therefore, when the perfections (*excellentiis*) of the elementary qualities are relaxed, a kind of intermediate quality is constituted out of them that is the proper quality of the mixed body, yet differs in diverse [mixed bodies] according to the diverse proportion of the mixture. And this quality is the disposition proper to the form of the mixed body, just as a simple quality [is] to the form of a simple body. Therefore, just as the extremes are found in the intermediate, which participates [in] the nature of both, so the qualities of simple bodies are found in the proper quality of a mixed body. Now of course the quality of a simple body is other than its substantial form. Nevertheless, it acts in virtue of the substantial form. Otherwise heat would only make [something] hot, but the substantial form [for which heat is the proper disposition in matter] would not be drawn into act through [heat's] power, since nothing acts outside its species.

So therefore the powers of the substantial forms of simple bodies are preserved in mixed bodies. Thus the forms of the elements are in mixed [bodies] not actually but virtually. And this is what Aristotle says in *On Generation* I [10 327^{b}29–31]: "Therefore they do not remain actually – that is, the elements in the mixed [body] – as body and white do. Neither is either or both of them corrupted. For their power is preserved."

Giles of Rome on the Errors of the Philosophers

Here Begin the Errors of the Philosophers Aristotle, Averroës, Avicenna, Algazel, Alkindi, and Rabbi Moses (Maimonides), Compiled by Brother Giles of the Order of St. Augustine

And a compilation of Aristotle's errors is placed first.

Chapter I

As it is the case that many wrong conclusions follow from one faulty statement, so the Philosopher has drawn many errors from one faulty principle.

1. For he believed nothing to be disposed in some condition in which it previously was not, except it came to be that way through a preceding motion. He held, moreover, that there is no novelty except where there is change, taken properly. Because, therefore, every change taken properly is a terminus of motion, there can be no novelty without a preceding motion. Now from this principle he concluded that motion never began to be; since if motion began, the motion was new. But nothing is new except through some preceding motion. Therefore there was motion before the first motion, which is a contradiction.

2. Further: he erred because he posited time never to have begun. Now time always follows on motion, if, therefore, motion never began, neither did time. Moreover, it seemed to him that the principle of time involved a special difficulty. For since an instant is always the end of the past and the beginning of the future, a first instant cannot be given, because there was a time before every instant, and before any assigned time there was an instant. Time, therefore, did not begin, but is eternal.

3. Further: because of what has already been stated, he was forced to posit a mobile to be eternal and the world to be eternal. For as one cannot give a time without motion, and motion without a mobile, if time and motion are eternal, the mobile will be eternal, and so the world would never begin. All of this is clear from Book VIII of the *Physics*.

4. Further: he was forced to posit the heavens to be ungenerated and incorruptible, and never to have been made but always to have been. For since among the varieties of motion only the circular is continuous – as is clear from Book VIII of the *Physics* – if any motion is eternal, the circular will be eternal. And since circular motion is proper to the heavens – as is shown in Book I *On the Heavens and the Earth* – it then follows that the heavens are uncreated and that they were never made. Moreover, he had a special reason why the heavens never began: because whatever has the power to be forever in the future, always had the power to be in the past. And since the heavens will never cease to be, they did not begin to be.

5. Further: since, according to him, whatever comes about comes from pre-existent matter, he concluded that there could not be another world. Hence, God could not make another world, since this one is constructed from all the matter there is. This error also is found in Book I, *On the Heavens and the Earth*.

6. He held further that generation in this sublunary world would never end, and that it never began. For corruption precedes and follows every generation, and generation precedes and follows every corruption. Because of this, since a corruption has preceded any generation, while some generation has preceded a corruption, it is impossible for generation and corruption to have had a beginning; nor is it possible for them to cease to be, since a corruption follows any generation, and a generation follows any corruption. If, therefore, either generation or corruption were to cease, there would be a generation after the final generation, and a corruption after the final corruption. Moreover, that a corruption precedes and follows generation, he proved by way of motion. For something is not generated except because something is corrupted; and so corruption precedes generation and also follows it, since every generable is corruptible, and every corruptible will be corrupted of necessity. Thus also generation precedes corruption, because nothing is corrupted except it was previously generated; and generation follows because the corruption of one thing is the generation of another. However, this error – that generation and corruption neither begin nor end – can be found in Book I, and more expressly in Book II, *On Generation and Corruption*.

7. Further: since generation in this sublunary world is brought about through the sun, he was forced to maintain that the sun – to quote him – "will never cease to generate plants and animals." This is clear from Book I, *On Plants*.

8. Further: since, according to his posited principle, there is no novelty without a preceding motion, he erred in maintaining that something new could not proceed immediately from God. This is clear in Book II of his *On Generation and Corruption*, where he says that "the same thing, remaining the same, always makes the same."

9. Further: he was constrained to deny the resurrection of the dead. That he held it as erroneous that the dead should rise again, is clear from Book I, *On the Soul*. Also, in Book VIII of the *Metaphysics* he held that the dead cannot return to life except through many intermediaries; and if one does return, it does not return numerically the same, because things which have lost substance do not return numerically the same, as is said at the end of Book II, *On Generation and Corruption*.

Now if someone were to wish to excuse Aristotle on the ground that he is speaking in a naturalistic sense, this would not do: because he believed that nothing new could proceed from God immediately, but that every novelty comes about by way of motion and natural operation.

10. Further: since he believed that nothing new could occur except by way of motion and through the operation of nature, he believed – as appears in Book I of the *Physics* where he argues against Anaxagoras – that an intellect which wants to separate passions and accidents

from substance is, to quote him, "an intellect seeking the impossible." On this account it seems to follow that God cannot make an accident without a subject.

11. Further: since by way of motion the generation of one thing never occurs unless there is the corruption of another; and since one substantial form is never introduced unless another is expelled; and since the matter of all things possessing matter is the same; it follows that there are not more substantial forms in one composite than there are in another. Indeed, to one who would consistently pursue this line of reasoning, it would appear that there is but one substantial form in every composite; and this seems to be the Philosopher's view. Hence, in Book VII of the *Metaphysics*, in the chapter "On the Unity of Definition," he holds the parts of a definition not to be one, as he says, "because they are *in* one," but rather because they *define* one nature.

Now if he means here one composite nature consisting in many forms, then his view can be maintained; but if he means one simple nature, and that there is only one form in such a composite, it is false.

12. Further: he posited that where there is still water, or a sea, at some time it was there dry, and conversely; because time does not cease but is eternal, as is clear from Book I of *Meteors*. Hence, he also had to say, necessarily, that one cannot posit a first man or a first rainfall.

13. Further: since an intelligence is unable to move something unless it is itself actually moving; and since intelligences are posited to be in the best state when they are moving something; he said there were as many angels, or as many intelligences, as there are orbs. This is quite clear from Book XII of the *Metaphysics*.

Divine Scripture, however, contradicts this, saying: "thousands of thousands tended to Him, and ten-thousand times a hundred-thousand stood before Him."

Chapter II
In which the Errors of Aristotle Are Restated In Sum

These, therefore, are all of his errors in sum, namely:
1. That motion did not begin.
2. That time is eternal.
3. That the world did not begin.
4. That the heavens are not created.
5. That God could not make another world.
6. That generation and corruption neither began nor will end.
7. That the sun will always cause generation and corruption in this sublunary world.
8. That nothing new can proceed immediately from God.
9. That the resurrection of the dead is impossible.
10. That God cannot make an accident without a subject.
11. That there is but one substantial form in any composite.
12. That one cannot posit a first man or a first rainfall.
13. That there is no way in which two bodies can be in the same place.
14. That there are as many angels as there are orbs – because from this it follows that there are only 55 or 57.

Now certain men wanted to excuse the Philosopher's position on the eternity of the world. But this attempt cannot hold up, since he insists upon the aforesaid principle so as to demonstrate philosophical truths. Indeed, he almost never wrote a book of philosophy where he did not employ this principle.

Again, aside from the above-mentioned errors, some men wanted to impute to him the view that God knows nothing outside Himself, so that this sublunary world is not known to Him – citing as reason for this view the words which are found in Book XII of the *Metaphysics*, in the chapter "The Opinion of the Fathers." But that they do not understand the Philosopher, and that this is not his intention, is clear from what is said in the chapter "On Good Fortune," where he says that God, known through Himself, is the past and the future. Moreover, other errors, with which we are not concerned as they arise from an improper understanding of Aristotle, are attributed to him.

Chapter III
In which Is Refuted the Statement which Is Fundamental for All the Philosopher's Errors

Now all of his errors, if one investigates subtly, follow from this position: that *nothing new comes into being except there be a preceding motion*. This is, therefore, false: because God is the First Agent, and being a non-instrumental agent, He will be able to produce a thing without a preceding motion. Now an agent by nature is an instrumental agent; but because it is of the nature of an instrument that it move the moved, motion is of necessity presupposed in its action. The making, therefore, in the production of a first agent can be without such motion. Creation, therefore, is not motion, because motion presupposes a mobile. Creation, in truth, presupposes nothing; nor is creation properly a change, because all change is a terminus of motion; but, as is commonly held, it is a simple procession of things from the first agent. Therefore, whatever is argued by way of motion against the beginning of the world, or against that which is held by faith, is wholly sophistical.

Chapter IV
A Compilation of the Errors of Averroës

Now the Commentator agrees in all the errors of the Philosopher. Indeed, he spoke even more ironically and with greater pertinacity than the Philosopher against those who posited the world to have begun. He is to be argued against incomparably more than against the Philosopher, because he more directly impugns our faith, holding to be false that which could not contain falsity as it is based upon the First Truth.

1. He went beyond the Philosopher's errors because he scorned all law, as is clear from Book II and XI of the *Metaphysics*, where he mocks the law of the Christians, or our Catholic law, and even the Saracen law, because they too posit the creation of things and that something can be created from nothing. He mocks also in the beginning of Book III of the *Physics*, where he holds that some men, because of the contrary assertion of the laws, are led to deny self-evident principles – as when they deny that nothing can be created out of nothing. Indeed, what is worse, he derisively calls us, and others who hold the law, "talkers," as if we were babblers and irrational wanderers. And also in Book VIII of the *Physics* he scorns the laws; while the "talkers" in law he calls "willers," because they assert that something can have being after wholly non-being. Indeed, he calls this dictum "a will," as if it were arbitrarily established only, and completely lacking in reason. And not only once or twice, but many times in the same Book VIII he exclaims in a similar manner against the laws asserting the creation.

2. He erred further, saying in Book VII of the *Metaphysics* that no immaterial thing transmutes a material thing except through the mediation of an intransmutable body. Because of this, it follows that an angel cannot move one stone here in the sublunary world. In a certain sense this does follow from the Philosopher's position, however the Philosopher did not himself expressly take this position.

3. He erred further, saying in Book XII of the *Metaphysics* that the potency in the production of something could not be in the agent alone, scorning John the Christian who maintained this view. Indeed, Averroës' view is opposed to truth and the Saints, because in made things the whole principle of the made thing lies in the potency of the maker.

4. Further: he erred by saying in the same Book XII that no agent can immediately produce diverse and contrary things. And by saying this he scorns the speakers in the three laws: namely, the law of the Christians, Saracens and Moors – because they all asserted this.

5. Further: he erred, saying in Book XII that all intellectual substances are eternal and pure acts, having no admitted potency. But he was himself constrained by truth to contradict this opinion in Book III of *On the Soul*, where he says that "no form is absolutely free from potency except the first form"; for, as he himself adds, all "other forms are diversified in essence and quiddity."

6. Further: he erred saying in Book XII that God is neither solicitous, nor does He have care, nor does He provide for individuals existing in the sublunary world. For, as he says, "this is neither permissible to, nor consonant with, Divine Goodness."

7. He erred further, denying a Trinity to be in God, saying in Book XII that some men "held a Trinity to be in God, but they sought by this device to be evasive and to really say that there are three Gods and one God; still, they don't even know how to be evasive properly, because when substance is numbered, the aggregate will still be one through the one added intention."

Because of this, according to him, if God were three and one, it would follow that He would be a composite, which is contradictory.

8. Further: he erred because he said that God did not know particulars since they are infinite. This is clear from his comment in the chapter "The Opinion of the Fathers."

9. Further: he erred because he denied that all which occurs in the sublunary world is guided by Divine Solicitude or Divine Providence. For according to him, some things, as he puts it "occur owing to the necessity of matter" and without the guidance of such Providence.

But this is opposed to the Saints; because nothing that occurs here is completely independent of the aforesaid Guidance, since all that we see here is either brought about, or permitted, by Divine Providence.

10. Further: he erred because he posited that there was numerically one intellect in all. This is clear from Book III of *On the Soul*.

11. Further: since it follows from the position just stated that the intellect is not the form of the body, Averroës therefore concluded in the same Book III that the term "act" is applied equivocally to the intellect and to other forms. Because of this, he was constrained to say that man is not placed in a species through his possession of an intellective soul, but rather through his possession of a sensitive soul.

12. Further: reasoning from this principle, he concluded that from the union of the intellective soul and the body there is not constituted some third thing; and that from such a soul and body there no more arises a unity, than there arises such a unity from the union of the mover of the heavens and the heavens.

Chapter V
In which the Aforesaid Errors Are Restated In Sum

These are all the errors in which the Commentator goes beyond those of the Philosopher:

1. That no law is true, although it may be useful.

2. That an angel can move nothing immediately except it be a heavenly body.

3. That an angel is a pure act.

4. That in no made thing does the whole principle of the making lie in the potency of the maker.

5. That from no agent can there proceed diverse things simultaneously.

6. That God has no providence over some particulars.

7. That there is no trinity in God.

8. That God does not know singulars.

9. That something can proceed from the necessity of matter without the guidance of Divine Providence.

10. That the intellective soul is not multiplied with the multiplication of bodies, but is numerically one.

11. That man is placed in a species by his possession of a sensitive soul.

12. That a thing no more becomes one through the union of the intellective soul and the body, than does such a unity arise from the conjoining of the mover of the heavens and the heavens.

Chapter VI
A Compilation of the Errors of Avicenna

1. Now Avicenna also seems to have erred in that he posited but one form in a composite. This is clear from section II of his *Metaphysics*, in the chapter "Concerning the Division of Corporeal Substances," where he maintains that the generic form is not made specific by some extrinsic agency – through which is implied that the specific form is not any essence beyond the essence of the generic form.

2. Further: he erred in positing the eternity of motion. Indeed, he held motion to be eternal. Hence, he says in Book IX of his *Metaphysics*, in the chapter "Concerning the Active Property of the First Principle," that: "it is clear that motion does not become after having not been, except through something that was; and that which was, did not begin to be except through a motion contingent upon that other motion." Hence, affirming the Philosopher's fundamental position that nothing is in a new state except through a preceding motion, he held that motion did not begin, because then there would be motion before the first motion.

3. He erred further, maintaining that matter is presupposed in every new production. For this reason he says in the same chapter that "that which was not, cannot be, except it be preceded by receptive matter." Hence, he denies that something new could begin to be after nothingness, since – as he says himself – in nothingness there can be no "hour of ending, and hour of beginning," nor indeed, any temporal distinction whatsoever.

4. Further: he maintained that nothing contingent could proceed from a non-contingent God. Hence, he says in the same chapter that if something contingent proceeded immediately from God through His nature, He would be changed in nature; if through His intention, His intention would be changed; and if through His will, His will would be changed.

Indeed, what is worse, he calls heretics all those who say that God precedes creation by a priority of duration, because by saying this, according to him, they deny freedom of will to God, since if God did not immediately produce the creation, He would not have full freedom of action, but rather He was compelled to await the time and the hour to act.

5. Further: he erred in positing the eternity of time. Indeed, motion could not be eternal unless time were eternal. He says, indeed, in the already-cited chapter, that the motion of the heavens has no beginning as respects duration, but rather as respects their having a principal agent. Now as motion of this kind is caused by a soul, as he himself says, and because a soul and a body make an animal, he concluded "that the heavens were an animal obedient to God."

Now all of the aforesaid errors took their origin in that he did not clearly see the mode in which God acts according to the order of His wisdom. God, indeed, could have made the world prior to when He made it; but that He did not do this was not caused by His awaiting something in the future upon which to initiate His action, but rather because He had arranged it that way according to His wisdom. Nor is it proper for motion to precede in order that something proceed immediately from God, as has been pointed out above in the place where the Philosopher's views were set forth.

6. Further: he erred in respect of the process of things from the first principle. For not only did he posit the products of the first principle to have eternally proceeded from it, but he also held that from the first principle nothing proceeds immediately except it be numerically one – as the first intelligence. This is clear from Book IX of his *Metaphysics* in the chapter, "Concerning the Order of Intelligences and Souls." Hence, in the same chapter, he posits that "neither bodies, nor the forms which are the perfection of bodies, are the first effects of the first principle itself."

7. Further: reasoning from the above, he continued in error, in that he says that the souls of the celestial bodies were produced by intelligences or by angels, and that one intelligence was produced by another.

8. He said further, that the celestial bodies were produced by souls and that they were produced through the mediation of their forms. From this position, it follows that the intelligences are the creators of the celestial souls, and the celestial souls are the creators of bodies, and that the higher intelligence is the creator of the lower intelligence.

9. Further: he held that our souls were produced by the last intelligence, upon which depends the governance of our souls and, consequently, our beatitude. Now this is clearly stated in the afore-mentioned chapter of the above-cited book.

10. He erred further with regard to the animation of the heavens. For he held the heavens to be animated. The soul of the heavens, he said, is not only an appropriate mover, as the Philosopher and the Commentator maintain, but that one thing is produced by the union of the soul of the heavens and the heavens, just as one thing is produced by the union of our soul and our body.

But this is in opposition to Damascene, who says in Book II, Chapter VI, that the heavens are inanimate and insensible.

11. He erred further as regards the giving of forms. For he posited all forms to be from the giver of forms, as from the lowest intelligence. This is clear from that which is said in Book IX of his *Metaphysics*, in the chapter "Concerning the Disposition of Generation of the Elements."

But this is opposed to Augustine, who held the angels to induce no forms except through the furnishing of semen.

Moreover, he also held that our souls direct matter with respect to the reception of forms, as is clear from what he says in Book VI, *On Natural Things*. He believed enchantment to be true, in that the soul can be active not only in its own body, but also in an alien body.

12. Further: he erred in holding that there could be no evil in the intelligences, contradicting Scripture, where it is written that "in His angels He found depravity." But that this was his position is clear from what is said in Book IX of his *Metaphysics*, in the chapter, "On Showing How Things Are Contained under Divine Judgment."

13. He erred further as concerns the Divine Cognition, holding God could not know singulars in their proper form. This is clear from the last chapter in Book VIII of his *Metaphysics*.

14. Further: he erred concerning the Divine Attributes, holding that God's knowledge, and other of His perfections, are not something to be attributed positively to Him, but are rather to be attributed to Him only by negation.

But this is opposed to the Saint's way, according to whom such perfections are more truly in God than in us, and that God truly is whatever it is better to be than not to be.

15. He erred further with respect to the number of intelligences, positing there to be as many angels as there are orbs. Hence, he agrees with the Philosopher's dictum that the angels are about forty in number, since he believed that there were that many orbs. This position is set forth by him in Book IX of the *Metaphysics*, in the chapter, "How Actions Proceed from Higher Principles."

16. He erred further regarding prophecy. Now he spoke correctly with reference to prophecy when he said that a prophet is nobler than a non-prophet, because the prophet hears Divine Words, and because he sees, or at least can see, "angels transfigured before him in a form which can be seen." But he spoke badly when he held prophecy to be natural, and because he maintained that prophecy is delivered to us according to the order which our soul has with respect to supercelestial souls and the last intelligence.

17. He erred further with respect to orisons, alms and litanies. He spoke correctly when he maintained such to be of efficacy to man in that God has concern for things; but he strayed badly when he held such things to be subsumed under the order of nature.

This is false, since such things as direct us to supernatural beatitude are subsumed under the order of grace. That this error was deliberate on Avicenna's part, is clear from Book X of his *Metaphysics* in the chapter "Concerning Aspirations and Orisons."

18. Further: he erred concerning our beatitude, holding it to depend upon our works. Now from his position it follows that our beatitude consists in the contemplation of the last intelligence, as is clear from Book X of his *Metaphysics*, in the chapter "Concerning the Cult of God and its Utility."

Still other errors can be imputed to him, but either they take their origin from those cited above, or they are reducible to them.

Chapter VII
In which the Afore-Mentioned Errors of Avicenna Are Restated In Sum

These are all the errors of Avicenna:
1. That there is but one substantial form in a composite.
2. That motion is eternal.

3. That nothing comes from nothing.

4. That contingency cannot proceed immediately from the non-contingent.

5. That time never had a beginning.

6. That a plurality of things cannot proceed immediately from the first principle.

7. That from one intelligence, another intelligence either proceeds or is created.

8. That from the intelligences, the souls of the heavens either proceed or are created.

9. That from the soul of the heavens there proceeds the supercelestial bodies.

10. That from the last intelligence, our souls proceed.

11. That a single entity comes about from the union of the soul of the heavens and the heavens, just as from the union of our soul and body.

12. That the forms in this world are induced by the last intelligence and not by proper agents.

13. That bewitchment is something beyond the mere apprehension of the soul.

14. That the soul, through its imagination, is operative in alien bodies.

15. That there cannot be evil in the angels.

16. That God does not know singulars in their proper form.

17. That the attributes of God do not correspond positively to anything.

18. That there are as many intelligences as there are orbs.

19. That prophecy is natural.

20. That alms, litanies and orisons are subsumed under the natural order. On this account Avicenna appears to hold that whatever occurs here in this world, occurs necessarily; and also that he who fully knows the motion of the supercelestial beings, and the order of the spiritual substances, can foretell the future.

21. That our beatitude depends upon our works.

22. That our beatitude consists in the cognition of the last intelligence.

22

Selections from
the Condemnation of 1277

Condemnation of 219 Propositions

Stephen, by divine permission unworthy servant of the church of Paris, sends greetings in the Son of the glorious Virgin to all those who will read this letter.

We have received frequent reports, inspired by zeal for the faith, on the part of important and serious persons to the effect that some students of the arts in Paris are exceeding the boundaries of their own faculty and are presuming to treat and discuss, as if they were debatable in the schools, certain obvious and loathsome errors, or rather *vanities and lying follies* [Ps. 39:5], which are contained in the roll joined to this letter. These students are not hearkening to the admonition of Gregory, "Let him who would speak wisely exercise great care, lest by his speech he disrupt the unity of his listeners," particularly when in support of the aforesaid errors they adduce pagan writings that – shame on their ignorance – they assert to be so convincing that they do not know how to answer them. So as not to appear to be asserting what they thus insinuate, however, they conceal their answers in such a way that, while wishing to avoid Scylla, they fall into Charybdis. For they say that these things are true according to philosophy but not according to the Catholic faith, as if there were two contrary truths and as if the truth of Sacred Scripture were contradicted by the truth in the sayings of the accursed pagans, of whom it is written, *I will destroy the wisdom of the wise* [I Cor. 1:19; cf. Isa. 29:14], inasmuch as true wisdom destroys false wisdom. Would that such students listen to the advice of the wise man when he says: *If you have understanding, answer your neighbor; but if not, let your hand be upon your mouth, lest you be surprised in an unskillful word and be confounded* [Ecclus. 5:14].

Lest, therefore, this unguarded speech lead simple people into error, we, having taken counsel with the doctors of Sacred Scripture and other prudent men, strictly forbid these and like things and totally condemn them. We excommunicate all those who shall have taught the said errors or any one of them, or shall have dared in any way to defend or uphold them, or even to listen to them, unless they choose to reveal themselves to us or to the chancery of Paris within seven days; in addition to which we shall proceed against them by inflicting such other penalties as the law requires according to the nature of the offense.

By this same sentence of ours we also condemn the book *De Amore*, or *De Deo Amoris*, which begins with the words, *Cogit me multum*, and so on, and ends with the words, *Cave, igitur, Galtere, amoris exercere mandata*, and so on, as well as the book of geomancy that begins with the words, *Existimaverunt Indi*, and so on, and ends with the words, *Ratiocinare ergo super eum invenies*, and so on. We likewise condemn the books, scrolls, and leaflets dealing with necromancy, or containing experiments in fortunetelling, invocations of devils or incantations endangering lives, or in which these and similar things evidently contrary to the orthodox faith and good morals are treated. We pronounce the sentence of excommunication against those who shall have taught the said scrolls, books, and leaflets, or listened to them, unless they reveal themselves to us or to the chancery of Paris within seven days in the manner described earlier in this letter; in addition to which we shall proceed to inflict such other penalties as the gravity of the offense demands.

Given in the year of the Lord 1276, on the Sunday on which *Laetare Jerusalem* is sung at the court of Paris.

1. That there is no more excellent state than to study philosophy.
2. That the only wise men in the world are the philosophers.

[. . .]

4. That one should not hold anything unless it is self-evident or can be manifested from self-evident principles.
5. That man should not be content with authority to have certitude about any question.
6. That there is no rationally disputable question that the philosopher ought not to dispute and determine, because reasons are derived from things. It belongs to philosophy under one or another of its parts to consider all things.

[. . .]

8. That our intellect by its own natural power can attain to a knowledge of the first cause.
– This does not sound well and is erroneous if what is meant is immediate knowledge.
9. That we can know God by His essence in this mortal life.
10. That nothing can be known about God except that He is, or His existence.

[. . .]

13. That God does not know things other than himself.
14. That God cannot know contingent beings immediately except through their particular and proximate causes.
15. That the first cause does not have science of future contingents. The first reason is that future contingents are not beings. The second is that future contingents are singulars, but God knows by means of an intellectual power, which cannot know singulars. Hence, if there were no senses, the intellect would perhaps not distinguish between Socrates and Plato, although it would distinguish between a man and an ass. The third reason is the relation of cause to effect; for the divine foreknowledge is a necessary cause of the things foreknown. The fourth reason is the relation of science to the known; for even though science is not the cause of the known, it is determined to one of two contradictories by that which is known; and this is true of divine science much more than of ours.

16. That the first cause is the most remote cause of all things. – This is erroneous if so understood as to mean that it is not the most proximate.

17. That what is impossible absolutely speaking cannot be brought about by God or by another agent. – This is erroneous if we mean what is impossible according to nature.

18. That what is self-determined, like God, either always acts or never acts; and that many things are eternal.

[. . .]

20. That God of necessity makes whatever comes immediately from Him. – This is erroneous whether we are speaking of the necessity of coercion, which destroys liberty, or of the necessity of immutability, which implies the inability to do otherwise.

[. . .]

22. That God cannot be the cause of a newly-made thing and cannot produce anything new.

23. That God cannot move anything irregularly, that is, in a manner other than that in which He does, because there is no diversity of will in Him.

24. That God is eternal in acting and moving, just as He is eternal in existing; otherwise He would be determined by some other thing that would be prior to Him.

25. That God has infinite power, not because He makes something out of nothing, but because He maintains infinite motion.

26. That God has infinite power in duration, not in action, since there is no such infinity except in an infinite body, if there were such a thing.

27A.[1] That the first cause cannot make more than one world.

28. That from one first agent there cannot proceed a multiplicity of effects.

[. . .]

30. That the first cause cannot produce something other than itself, because every difference between maker and made is through matter.

[. . .]

33. That the immediate effect of the first being has to be one only and most like unto the first being.

34. That God is the necessary cause of the first intelligence, which cause being posited, the effect is also posited; and both are equal in duration.

[. . .]

38. That the intelligences, or separated substances, which they say are eternal, do not have an efficient cause properly speaking, but only metaphorically, in so far as they have a cause

---

1   Items numbered 'A' refer to the theses of Aquinas.

conserving them in existence; but they were not newly made, because then they would be mutable.

39. That all the separated substances are coeternal with the first principle.

40. That everything that does not have matter is eternal, because that which was not made through a change in matter did not exist previously; therefore it is eternal.

[. . .]

42A. That God cannot multiply individuals of the same species without matter.

43A. That God could not make several intelligences of the same species because intelligences do not have matter.

[. . .]

50A. That if there were any separated substance that did not move some body in this sensible world, it would not be included in the universe.

[. . .]

52A. That the separated substances, in so far as they have a single appetite, do not change in their operation.

53A. That an intelligence or an angel or a separated soul is nowhere.

54A. That the separated substances are nowhere according to their substance. – This is erroneous if so understood as to mean that substance is not in a place. If, however, it is so understood as to mean that substance is the reason for being in a place, it is true that they are nowhere according to their substance.

55A. That the separated substances are somewhere by their operation, and that they cannot move from one extreme to another or to the middle except in so far as they can will to operate either in the middle or in the extremes. – This is erroneous if so understood as to mean that without operation a substance is not in a place and that it does not pass from one place to another.

[. . .]

61. That since an intelligence is full of forms, it impresses these forms on matter by using the heavenly bodies as instruments.

[. . .]

63. That the higher intelligences impress things on the lower, just as one soul impresses things on another and even on a sensitive soul; and that through such an impression a spellbinder is able to cast a camel into a pitfall just by looking at it.

64. That God is the necessary cause of the motion of the higher bodies and of the union and separation occurring in the stars.

[. . .]

66. That God could not move the heaven in a straight line, the reason being that He would then leave a vacuum.

67. That the first principle cannot produce generable things immediately because they are new effects and a new effect requires an immediate cause that is capable of being otherwise.

68. That the first principle cannot be the cause of diverse products here below without the mediation of other causes, inasmuch as nothing that transforms, transforms in diverse ways without being itself transformed.

69. That God cannot produce the effect of a secondary cause without the secondary cause itself.

[. . .]

73. That the heavenly bodies are moved by an intrinsic principle which is the soul, and that they are moved by a soul and an appetitive power, like an animal. For just as an animal is moved by desiring, so also is the heaven.

[. . .]

76. That the intelligence moving the heaven influences the rational soul, just as the body of the heaven influences the human body.

[. . .]

79. That if the heaven stood still, fire would not burn flax because God would not exist.

80. That the reasoning of the Philosopher proving that the motion of the heaven is eternal is not sophistic, and that it is surprising that profound men do not perceive this.

[. . .]

82. That if in some humor by the power of the stars such a proportion could be achieved as is found in the seed of the parents, a man could be generated from that humor; and thus a man could be adequately generated from putrefaction.

83. That the world, although it was made from nothing, was not newly-made, and, although it passed from nonbeing to being, the nonbeing did not precede being in duration but only in nature.

84. That the world is eternal because that which has a nature by which it is able to exist for the whole future has a nature by which it was able to exist in the whole past.

85. That the world is eternal as regards all the species contained in it, and that time, motion, matter, agent, and receiver are eternal, because the world comes from the infinite power of God and it is impossible that there be something new in the effect without there being something new in the cause.

86. That eternity and time have no existence in reality but only in the mind.

87. That nothing is eternal from the standpoint of its end that is not eternal from the standpoint of its beginning.

[. . .]

89. That it is impossible to refute the arguments of the Philosopher concerning the eternity of the world unless we say that the will of the first being embraces incompatibles.

[. . .]

91. That there has already been an infinite number of revolutions of the heaven, which it is impossible for the created intellect but not for the first cause to comprehend.

92. That with all the heavenly bodies coming back to the same point after a period of thirty-six thousand years, the same effects as now exist will reappear.

[. . .]

96. That beings depart from the order of the first cause considered in itself, although not in relation to the other causes operating in the universe. – This is erroneous because the order of beings to the first cause is more essential and more inseparable than their order to the lower causes.

[. . .]

99. That there is more than one prime mover.

100. That, among the efficient causes, if the first cause were to cease to act, the secondary cause would not, as long as the secondary cause operates according to its own nature.

101. That no agent is in potency to one or the other of two things; on the contrary, it is determined.

102. That nothing happens by chance, but everything comes about by necessity, and that all the things that will exist in the future will exist by necessity, and those that will not exist are impossible, and that nothing occurs contingently if all causes are considered. – This is erroneous because the concurrence of causes is included in the definition of chance, as Boethius says in his book *On Consolation*.

[. . .]

110A. That forms are not divided except through matter. – This is erroneous unless one is speaking of forms educed from the potency of matter.

[. . .]

112. That the elements are eternal. They were nevertheless newly produced in the disposition that they now possess.

[. . .]

115A. That God could not make several numerically different souls.

116A. That individuals of the same species differ solely by the position of matter, like Socrates and Plato, and that since the human form existing in each is numerically the same, it is not surprising that the same being numerically is in different places.

117. That the intellect is numerically one for all, for although it may be separated from this or that body, it is not separated from every body.

118. That the agent intellect is a certain separated substance superior to the possible intellect, and that it is separated from the body according to its substance, power, and operation and is not the form of the human body.

[. . .]

122. That from the sensitive and intellectual parts of man there does not result a unity in essence, unless it be a unity such as that of an intelligence and a sphere, that is, a unity in operation.

123. That the intellect is not the form of the body, except in the manner in which a helmsman is the form of a ship, and that it is not an essential perfection of man.

[. . .]

126. That the intellect, which is man's ultimate perfection, is completely separated.

[. . .]

129. That the substance of the soul is eternal, and that the agent intellect and the possible intellect are eternal.

[. . .]

131. That the speculative intellect is simply eternal and incorruptible; with respect to this or that man, however, it is corrupted when the phantasms in him are corrupted.

[. . .]

133. That the soul is inseparable from the body, and that the soul is corrupted when the harmony of the body is corrupted.

[. . .]

135. That the separated soul is not alterable, according to philosophy, although according to the faith it is altered.

136. That the intellect can pass from body to body, in such a way that it is successively the mover of different bodies.

[. . .]

138. That there was no first man, nor will there be a last; indeed, the generation of man from man always was and always will be.

[. . .]

140. That the agent intellect is not united to our possible intellect, and that the possible intellect is not united to us substantially. And if it were united to us as a form, it would be inseparable.

141. That the possible intellect is nothing in act before it understands, because in the case of an intelligible nature, to be something in act is to be actually understanding.

[. . .]

143. That a man is said to understand to the same extent that the heaven is said to understand, or to live, or to move of itself, that is, because the agent performing these actions is united to him as mover to moved and not substantially.

[. . .]

146A. That the fact that we understand less perfectly or more perfectly comes from the passive intellect, which he says is a sensitive power. – This statement is erroneous because it asserts that there is a single intellect in all men or that all souls are equal.

147A. That it is improper to maintain that some intellects are more noble than others because this diversity has to come from the intelligences, since it cannot come from the bodies; and thus noble and ignoble souls would necessarily belong to different species, like the intelligences. – This is erroneous, for thus the soul of Christ would not be more noble than that of Judas.

[. . .]

150. That that which by its nature is not determined to being or nonbeing is not determined except by something that is necessary with respect to itself.

151. That the soul wills nothing unless it is moved by another. Hence the following proposition is false: the soul wills by itself. – This is erroneous if what is meant is that the soul is moved by another, namely, by something desirable or an object in such a way that the desirable thing or object is the whole reason for the movement of the will itself.

[. . .]

154. That our will is subject to the power of the heavenly bodies.

[. . .]

156. That the effects of the stars upon free choice are hidden.

157. That when two goods are proposed, the stronger moves more strongly. – This is erroneous unless one is speaking from the standpoint of the good that moves.

158. That in all his actions man follows his appetite and always the greater appetite. – This is erroneous if what is meant is the greater in moving power.

159. That the appetite is necessarily moved by a desirable object if all obstacles are removed. – This is erroneous in the case of the intellectual appetite.

160. That it is impossible for the will not to will when it is in the disposition in which it is natural for it to be moved and when that which by nature moves remains so disposed.

161. That in itself the will is undetermined to opposites, like matter, but it is determined by a desirable object as matter is determined by an agent.

162A. That the science of contraries alone is the cause for which the rational soul is in potency to opposites, and that a power that is simply one is not in potency to opposites except accidentally and by reason of something else.

163A. That the will necessarily pursues what is firmly held by reason, and that it cannot abstain from that which reason dictates. This necessitation, however, is not compulsion but the nature of the will.

[. . .]

165. That after a conclusion has been reached about something to be done, the will does not remain free, and that punishments are provided by law only for the correction of ignorance and in order that the correction may be a source of knowledge for others.

166. That if reason is rectified, the will is also rectified. – This is erroneous because contrary to Augustine's gloss on this verse from the Psalms: *My soul hath coveted to long*, and so on [Ps. 118:20], and because according to this, grace would not be necessary for the rectitude of the will but only science, which is the error of Pelagius.

167. That there can be no sin in the higher powers of the soul. And thus sin comes from passion and not from the will.

168. That a man acting from passion acts by compulsion.

169A. That as long as passion and particular science are present in act, the will cannot go against them.

[. . .]

172. That happiness is had in this life and not in another.

[. . .]

174. That after death man loses every good.

[. . .]

177. That raptures and visions are caused only by nature.

[. . .]

180. That the Christian law impedes learning.

181. That there are fables and falsehoods in the Christian law just as in others.

182. That one does not know anything more by the fact that he knows theology.

183. That the teachings of the theologian are based on fables.

[. . .]

188. That it is not true that something comes from nothing or was made in a first creation.

189. That creation is not possible, even though the contrary must be held according to the faith.

[...]

191. That the natural philosopher has to deny absolutely the newness of the world because he bases himself on natural causes and natural reasons, whereas the faithful can deny the eternity of the world because he bases himself on supernatural causes.

[...]

200. That no other virtues are possible except the acquired or the innate.

[...]

216. That a philosopher must not concede the resurrection to come, because it cannot be investigated by reason. – This is erroneous because even a philosopher must *bring his mind into captivity to the obedience of Christ* [cf. II Cor. 10:5].

[...]

23

John Buridan and the Impetus Theory of Projectile Motion

BOOK VIII, QUESTION 12. 1. It is sought whether a projectile after leaving the hand of the projector is moved by the air, or by what it is moved.

It is argued that it is not moved by the air, because the air seems rather to resist, since it is necessary that it be divided. Furthermore, if you say that the projector in the beginning moved the projectile and the ambient air along with it, and then that air, having been moved, moves the projectile further to such and such a distance, the doubt will return as to by what the air is moved after the projectile ceases to move. For there is just as much difficulty regarding this (the air) as there is regarding the stone which is thrown.

Aristotle takes the opposite position in the eighth [book] of this work (the *Physics*) thus: "Projectiles are moved further after the projectors are no longer in contact with them, either by antiperistasis, as some say, or by the fact that the air having been pushed, pushes with a movement swifter than the movement of impulsion by which it (the body) is carried towards its own [natural] place." He determines the same thing in the seventh and eighth [books] of this work (the *Physics*) and in the third [book] of the *De caelo*.

2. This question I judge to be very difficult because Aristotle, as it seems to me, has not solved it well. For he touches on two opinions. The first one, which he calls "antiperistasis," holds that the projectile swiftly leaves the place in which it was, and nature, not permitting a vacuum, rapidly sends air in behind to fill up the vacuum. The air moved swiftly in this way and impinging upon the projectile impels it along further. This is repeated continually up to a certain distance. . . . But such a solution notwithstanding, it seems to me that this method of proceeding was without value because of many experiences (*experientie*).

The first experience concerns the top (*trocus*) and the smith's mill (i.e. wheel – *mola fabri*) which are moved for a long time and yet do not leave their places. Hence, it is not necessary for the air to follow along to fill up the place of departure of a top of this kind and a smith's mill. So it cannot be said [that the top and the smith's mill are moved by the air] in this manner.

The second experience is this: A lance having a conical posterior as sharp as its anterior would be moved after projection just as swiftly as it would be without a sharp conical posterior. But surely the air following could not push a sharp end in this way, because the air would be easily divided by the sharpness.

The third experience is this: a ship drawn swiftly in the river even against the flow of the river, after the drawing has ceased, cannot be stopped quickly, but continues to move for a long time. And yet a sailor on deck does not feel any air from behind pushing him. He feels only the air from the front resisting [him]. Again, suppose that the said ship were loaded with grain or wood and a man were situated to the rear of the cargo. Then if the air were of such an impetus that it could push the ship along so strongly, the man would be pressed very violently between that cargo and the air following it. Experience shows this to be false. Or, at least, if the ship were loaded with grain or straw, the air following and pushing would fold over (*plico*) the stalks which were in the rear. This is all false.

3. Another opinion, which Aristotle seems to approve, is that the projector moves the air adjacent to the projectile [simultaneously] with the projectile and that air moved swiftly has the power of moving the projectile. He does not mean by this that the same air is moved from the place of projection to the place where the projectile stops, but rather that the air joined to the projector is moved by the projector and that air having been moved moves another part of the air next to it, and that [part] moves another (i.e., the next) up to a certain distance. Hence the first air moves the projectile into the second air, and the second [air moves it] into the third air, and so on. Aristotle says, therefore, that there is not one mover but many in turn. Hence he also concludes that the movement is not continuous but consists of succeeding or contiguous entities.

But this opinion and method certainly seems to me equally as impossible as the opinion and method of the preceding view. For this method cannot solve the problem of how the top or smith's mill is turned after the hand [which sets them into motion] has been removed. Because, if you cut off the air on all sides near the smith's mill by a cloth (*linteamine*), the mill does not on this account stop but continues to move for a long time. Therefore it is not moved by the air.

Also a ship drawn swiftly is moved a long time after the haulers have stopped pulling it. The surrounding air does not move it, because if it were covered by a cloth and the cloth with the ambient air were withdrawn, the ship would not stop its motion on this account. And even if the ship were loaded with grain or straw and were moved by the ambient air, then that air ought to blow exterior stalks toward the front. But the contrary is evident, for the stalks are blown rather to the rear because of the resisting ambient air.

Again, the air, regardless of how fast it moves, is easily divisible. Hence it is not evident as to how it would sustain a stone of weight of one thousand pounds projected in a sling or in a machine.

Furthermore, you could, by pushing your hand, move the adjacent air, if there is nothing in your hand, just as fast or faster than if you were holding in your hand a stone which you wish to project. If, therefore, that air by reason of the velocity of its motion is of a great enough impetus to move the stone swiftly, it seems that if I were to impel air toward you equally as fast, the air ought to push you impetuously and with sensible strength. [Yet] we would not perceive this.

Also, it follows that you would throw a feather farther than a stone and something less heavy farther than something heavier, assuming equal magnitudes and shapes. Experience shows this to be false. The consequence is manifest, for the air having been moved ought to sustain or carry or move a feather more easily than something heavier. . . .

4. Thus we can and ought to say that in the stone or other projectile there is impressed something which is the motive force (*virtus motiva*) of that projectile. And this is evidently better than falling back on the statement that the air continues to move that projectile. For

the air appears rather to resist. Therefore, it seems to me that it ought to be said that the motor in moving a moving body impresses (*imprimit*) in it a certain impetus (*impetus*) or a certain motive force (*vis motiva*) of the moving body, [which impetus acts] in the direction toward which the mover was moving the moving body, either up or down, or laterally, or circularly. *And by the amount the motor moves that moving body more swiftly, by the same amount it will impress in it a stronger impetus.* It is by that impetus that the stone is moved after the projector ceases to move. But that impetus is continually decreased (*remittitur*) by the resisting air and by the gravity of the stone, which inclines it in a direction contrary to that in which the impetus was naturally predisposed to move it. Thus the movement of the stone continually becomes slower, and finally that impetus is so diminished or corrupted that the gravity of the stone wins out over it and moves the stone down to its natural place.

This method, it appears to me, ought to be supported because the other methods do not appear to be true and also because all the appearances (*apparentia*) are in harmony with this method.

5. For if anyone seeks why I project a stone farther than a feather, and iron or lead fitted to my hand farther than just as much wood, I answer that the cause of this is that the reception of all forms and natural dispositions is in matter and by reason of matter. *Hence by the amount more there is of matter, by that amount can the body receive more of that impetus and more intensely* (intensius). *Now in a dense and heavy body, other things being equal, there is more of prime matter than in a rare and light one. Hence a dense and heavy body receives more of that impetus and more intensely, just as iron can receive more calidity than wood or water of the same quantity.* Moreover, a feather receives such an impetus so weakly (*remisse*) that such an impetus is immediately destroyed by the resisting air. *And so also if light wood and heavy iron of the same volume and of the same shape are moved equally fast by a projector, the iron will be moved farther because there is impressed in it a more intense impetus, which is not so quickly corrupted as the lesser impetus would be corrupted. This also is the reason why it is more difficult to bring to rest a large smith's mill which is moving swiftly than a small one, evidently because in the large one, other things being equal, there is more impetus.* And for this reason you could throw a stone of one-half or one pound weight farther than you could a thousandth part of it. For the impetus in that thousandth part is so small that it is overcome immediately by the resisting air.

6. From this theory also appears the cause of why the natural motion of a heavy body downward is continually accelerated (*continue velocitatur*). For from the beginning only the gravity was moving it. Therefore, it moved more slowly, but in moving it impressed in the heavy body an impetus. This impetus now [acting] together with its gravity moves it. Therefore, the motion becomes faster; and by the amount it is faster, so the impetus becomes more intense. Therefore, the movement evidently becomes continually faster.

[The impetus then also explains why] one who wishes to jump a long distance drops back a way in order to run faster, so that by running he might acquire an impetus which would carry him a longer distance in the jump. Whence the person so running and jumping does not feel the air moving him, but [rather] feels the air in front strongly resisting him.

Also, since the Bible does not state that appropriate intelligences move the celestial bodies, it could be said that it does not appear necessary to posit intelligences of this kind, because it would be answered that God, when He created the world, moved each of the celestial orbs as He pleased, and in moving them He impressed in them impetuses which moved them without His having to move them any more except by the method of general influence whereby He concurs as a co-agent in all things which take place; "for thus on the seventh day He rested from all work which He had executed by committing to others the actions and the passions in turn." And these impetuses which He impressed in the celestial bodies were not decreased nor corrupted afterwards, because there was no inclination of the celestial bodies for other movements. Nor was there resistance which would be corruptive or repressive of that impetus. But this I do not say assertively, but [rather tentatively] so that I might seek from the theological masters what they might teach me in these matters as to how these things take place. . . .

7. The first [conclusion] is that that impetus is not the very local motion in which the projectile is moved, because that impetus moves the projectile and the mover produces motion. Therefore, the impetus produces that motion, and the same thing cannot produce itself. Therefore, etc.

Also since every motion arises from a motor being present and existing simultaneously with that which is moved, if the impetus were the motion, it would be necessary to assign some other motor from which that motion would arise. And the principal difficulty would return. Hence there would be no gain in positing such an impetus. But others cavil when they say that the prior part of the motion which produces the projection produces another part of the motion which is related successively and that produces another part and so on up to the cessation of the whole movement. But this is not probable, because the "producing something" ought to exist when the something is made, but the prior part of the motion does not exist when the posterior part exists, as was elsewhere stated. Hence, neither does the prior exist when the posterior is made. This consequence is obvious from this reasoning. For it was said elsewhere that motion is nothing else than "the very being produced" (*ipsum fieri*) and the "very being corrupted" (*ipsum corumpi*). Hence motion does not result when it *has been* produced (*factus est*) but when it *is being* produced (*fit*).

8. The second conclusion is that that impetus is not a purely successive thing (*res*), because motion is just such a thing and the definition of motion [as a successive thing] is fitting to it, as was stated elsewhere. And now it has just been affirmed that that impetus is not the local motion.

Also, since a purely successive thing is continually corrupted and produced, it continually demands a producer. But there cannot be assigned a producer of that impetus which would continue to be simultaneous with it.

9. The third conclusion is that that impetus is a thing of permanent nature (*res nature permanentis*), distinct from the local motion in which the projectile is moved. This is evident from the two aforesaid conclusions and from the preceding [statements]. And it is probable (*verisimile*) that that impetus is a quality naturally present and predisposed for moving a body in which it is impressed, just as it is said that a quality impressed in iron by a magnet moves the iron to the magnet. And it also is probable that just as that quality (the impetus) is impressed in the moving body along with the motion by the motor; so with the motion it is remitted, corrupted, or impeded by resistance or a contrary inclination.

10. And in the same way that a luminant generating light generates light reflexively because of an obstacle, so that impetus because of an obstacle acts reflexively. It is true, however, that other causes aptly concur with that impetus for greater or longer reflection. For example, the ball which we bounce with the palm in falling to earth is reflected higher than a stone, although the stone falls more swiftly and more impetuously (*impetuosius*) to the earth. This is because many things are curvable or intracompressible by violence which are innately disposed to return swiftly and by themselves to their correct position or to the disposition natural to them. In thus returning, they can impetuously push or draw

something conjunct to them, as is evident in the case of the bow (*arcus*). Hence in this way the ball thrown to the hard ground is compressed into itself by the impetus of its motion; and immediately after striking, it returns swiftly to its sphericity by elevating itself upward. From this elevation it acquires to itself an impetus which moves it upward a long distance.

Also, it is this way with a cither cord which, put under strong tension and percussion, remains a lone time in a certain vibration (*tremulatio*) from which its sound continues a notable time. And this takes place as follows: As a result of striking [the chord] swiftly, it is bent violently in one direction, and so it returns swiftly toward its normal straight position. But on account of the impetus, it crosses beyond the normal straight position in the contrary direction and then again returns. It does this many times. For a similar reason a bell (*campana*), after the ringer ceases to draw [the chord], is moved a long time, first in one direction, now in another. And it cannot be easily and quickly brought to rest.

This, then, is the exposition of the question. I would be delighted if someone would discover a more probable way of answering it. And this is the end.

Augustine on the Soul

On the Customs of the Catholic Church
[= *De moribus ecclesiae catholicae*], I, 4, 6, PL 32, col. 1313.

Therefore, let us ask what is better than man. That of course will be hard to find out, unless we first consider and discuss what man himself is. I do not think a definition of man is now demanded of me. What seems to be asked of me at this point is rather the following: since there is almost universal consensus – or at least it is agreed on between me and those I am now dealing with, and that suffices – that we are composites of soul and body, what [then] is the man himself? Is he both of the things I [just] mentioned, or the body alone, or the soul alone? For although soul and body are two things, and neither would be called a "man" if the other did not exist (for neither would the body be a man if the soul did not exist, nor in turn would the soul be a man if a body were not animated by it), nevertheless it can happen that one of these should be regarded as the "man" and called [such]. Therefore, what do we call the "man"? [Is he] soul and body, like a "team" [of horses] or a centaur? [Is he] the body alone, which is being *used* by a soul that rules it, like a "lantern", [which is] not the flame and the container together but only the container, although we *call* it [a lantern] because of the flame? [Or] do we call nothing but the soul the "man", but *on account of* the body it rules, just as we call a "rider" not the horse and the man together but only the man, yet [only] insofar as he is suited to governing the horse? It is hard to decide this issue. Or if it is easy to figure out, [in any case] it requires a long explanation. We do not have to accept and take on that job and delay [here]. For whether both, or only the soul, takes the name of "man", the best thing for the man is not what is best for the body. Rather what is best for the soul and body together, or for the soul alone, that is best for the man.

    I, 27, 52, PL 32, col. 1332.
    Therefore man, as he appears to man, is a rational, mortal and earthly soul using a body.

On the Size of the Soul
[= *De quantitate animae*], 13, 22, PL 32, col. 1048.

The De quantitate animae *is a dialogue between Augustine and Evodius. In the present passage, Augustine is speaking.*

. . . But if you want to define the mind for yourself, and so ask what the mind is, it is easy for me to reply. For it seems to be to be a certain substance, partaking in reason, and fitted to ruling the body.

On Music
[= De musica], VI, 5, 9–10, PL 32, cols. 1168–1169.

The De musica is a dialogue between a "Master" and a "Disciple". The Master does all the talking in this passage.

Master. I will say directly what I think. Either follow me, or even go ahead [of me] if you can, if you notice that I am delaying or hesitating. For I do not think this body is animated by a soul except by the intention of the maker. Neither do I suppose [the soul] undergoes anything from [the body], but rather acts on [the body] and in it, as if [the body were] subjected by divine order to [the soul's] domination. Yet sometimes [the soul] operates with ease, sometimes with difficulty, according as the bodily nature yields to it more or less, in proportion to its merits. Therefore, whatever corporeal things are imposed on the body or hurled against it from outside, they produce something in the body itself but not in the soul. [The body] either resists its task or else agrees with it. And so, when [the soul] struggles against the resisting body, and with difficulty forces the matter subjected to [the soul] into the ways of its own task, it becomes more attentive because of the difficulty of the action. This difficulty, when it does not pass unnoticed, is called "sensing" because of the attention. And this is called "trouble" or "labor". But when what is introduced or applied [to the body] is agreeable, [the soul] easily turns all of [the body], or as much as is needed of it, to the paths of its own task. And this action of [the soul], by which it conjoins its body to an agreeable external body, does not pass unnoticed, because it is carried out more attentively on account of that extraneous factor. But, because of its agreeableness, it is sensed with pleasure. . . . And, lest I go on too long, it seems to me that when the soul senses in the body, it does not undergo anything from [the body], but rather acts more attentively in the midst of [the body's] passive processes [*passionibus*], and that these actions, whether they are easy because of an agreeableness or hard because of a disagreeableness, do not pass unnoticed by [the soul]. And all this is what is called "sensing".

On the Size of the Soul
[= De quantitate animae], 23, 41, PL 32, col. 1058.

Augustine. Pay attention, then. For I think sensation is that what the body undergoes does not pass unnoticed by the soul. . . . (10) Ibid., 25, 48, PL 32, cols. 1062–1063. *Augustine.* Now turn your mind to that definition of ours, and when you have considered it more expertly, fix it. For we had found that, although it was supposed to be the definition of sensation, it included something else that was not sensation. Hence [the definition] is not true when it is [logically] converted. For perhaps "Every sensation is a passive process of the body that does not pass unnoticed by the soul" is true, just as "Every man is a mortal animal" is true. But, just as "Every mortal animal is a man" is false, because beasts are also that, so [too] "Every passive process of the body that does not pass unnoticed by the soul is a sensation" is false. For my nails are now growing on me, and that does not pass unnoticed by my soul, since I know it. But I do not sense it. Rather I know it by inference. Therefore just as "rational" is added to the [above] definition of man to complete it, [and] when it is added, the beasts that were contained [in the definition] together [with man] are excluded, and we include nothing besides man, and every man, in such a [revised] definition, do you not suppose there is something to be added here too, by which the foreign element [our proposed definition of sensation] contains may be separated out and nothing understood in it except sensation, and every sensation? *Evodius.* I do suppose so, but I don't know what can be added. *A.* Every sensation is certainly a passive process of the body that does not pass unnoticed by the soul. But this proposition cannot be converted, because of that passive process of the body by which it either grows or shrinks while we know it – that is, so that it does not pass unnoticed by the soul. *E.* That's right. *A.* What? Is it through itself or through something else that this passive process does not pass unnoticed by the soul? *E.* Through something else, obviously. For it is one thing to see bigger nails, and another to know that they are growing. *A.* Therefore, since growing is itself a passive process that we do not come in contact with by any sense, while the size that we do sense is produced by that same passive process [but] is not that passive process, it is clear that we do not know such a passive process through itself, but through something else. If therefore it were *not* through something else that it did not pass unnoticed by the soul, would it not be sensed rather than inferred? *E.* I understand. *A.* So why do you doubt what is to be added to the definition? *E.* Now I see that [sensation] must be defined as follows, that "Sensation is a passive process of a body that *through itself* does not pass unnoticed by the soul." For both every sensation is like that, and everything like that, I think, is a sensation.

25

Averroës on the Immateriality of the Intellect

The Chapter on the Rational Faculty
[Commentary on *De Anima* 3.4–8]

(276) [429ª10] He said: Concerning that part of the soul whereby we have apprehensions, which is called intellect and comprehension, [and] whether it is separate from the rest of the faculties of the soul in location and in intention or only in intention without being separate in place, we first ought to investigate the intention, [meaning that] whereby this part is separate from the rest of the soul's faculties: what and how is it? – that is, what is conceptualization and how is it accomplished?

(277) We say that, if conceptualization exists among the passive faculties comparable to sensation, as appears to be its nature, then either its being affected by an intelligible object resembles the passivity whereby the senses are affected by sensible objects, or it is more remote than that true passivity of the senses, such that nothing of the intention of passivity which is in the senses will be found in it. For the passivity of the senses, even if it does not have the intention of true passivity – which is a change of subject concomitant with the reception [of the object] – does contain a measure of change. We say that this faculty – that which receives intelligible objects – must be completely unaffected; that is, it must be unreceptive to the change that occurs to faculties which are affected by virtue of their commingling with the subject in which they are found. [This,] so that the rational faculty will have only the receptive aspect of the intention of passivity and will be potentially similar to the object which it thinks, while not being the object itself. This faculty may be described by way of comparison; for its relation to intelligible objects is like that of the sensory faculty toward sensible objects, except that the faculty which receives sensible objects is mixed, to a degree, with the subject in which it is found, whereas this faculty must be completely unmixed with any material form. For, this faculty, which is called the hylic intellect, if it is to think all things – that is, receive the forms of all things – cannot be mixed with any one form; that is, it cannot be mixed with the subject in which it is found, as the other material faculties are.

(278) If the rational faculty were mixed with any form, then one of two things would have to occur: either the form of the subject with which it was mixed would impede the forms

this faculty would receive, or it would change them – that is, it would change the form being received. Were this so, the forms of things would not exist in the intellect as they really are – that is, the forms existing in the intellect would be changed into forms different from the actual forms. If, therefore, the nature of the intellect is to receive the forms of things which have retained their natures, it is necessary that it be a faculty unmixed with any form whatsoever.

(279) This is what Anaxagoras wanted [to convey] in saying, reportedly, that the intellect has to be unmixed in order to have knowledge, for, if [a form] were to manifest itself in the intellect, it would prevent the appearance of a different form or change it. That is, if any form were to be manifested in this disposition, one of two things would have to occur: either that form would prevent us from knowing a different form which we want to know, since [the intellect's] knowledge of a form is reception of it; or the [first form] would change the [other form] when it received it.

(280) This being the case with this intellect, its nature is nothing other than disposition only – that is, the potential intellect is solely disposition, not something in which disposition exists. Although this disposition is in a subject, since it is not mixed with the subject, the subject does not serve as an intellect in potentiality. This is the opposite of what obtains with other material faculties in which the subject is a substance – either composite (that is, something composed of form and matter) or simple (the first matter).

(281) This is Aristotle's concept of the passive intellect, according to the interpretation of Alexander. The other commentators, however, take Aristotle's statement that the hylic intellect has to be unmixed to mean that it is a disposition which exists in a separate substance – this, since the hylic intellect ought to be a substance, and [since] disposition by itself is neither a substance nor part of something. It is, rather, one of the concomitants of matter, and material causes are part of something material. In general, disposition is a distinguishing characteristic of matter, and it is impossible for disposition to be found in one genus and its subject in another – that is, that which is disposed to receive something intelligible must be an intellect. According to Alexander's approach, however, the potential intellect is nothing other than disposition only, its subject being from another genus: either a part of the soul, or the soul in its entirety.

(282) However, this view [of the other commentators] also entails an absurd position: that there should be a separate substance, the existence of which occurs in disposition and potentiality. This [is absurd] because potentiality is one of the properties of material objects. Another absurd position is also entailed [in this view], for the first perfection of the intellect would be eternal and the last [would be] generated and corruptible. Moreover, if man is generated and corruptible in his first perfection, this [later] perfection would have to be so, too.

(283) Once I gave these statements their due measure of doubt, it became apparent that, in one sense, the intellect is a disposition free of material forms, as Alexander said; and, in another sense, it is a separate substance attired with this disposition – that is, this disposition found in man is attached to this separate substance by virtue of the latter's conjunction with man. It is not the case that this disposition is something existing in the nature of this separate substance, as the commentators think; nor is it a pure disposition, as Alexander thinks. Proof that it is not purely a disposition is had in that we find that the hylic intellect apprehends this disposition devoid of the forms and apprehends the forms, making it possible thereby to think of privations – that is, by virtue of apprehending its essence devoid of forms. This being the case, necessarily, that which apprehends this disposition and the forms which obtain in it is other than the disposition.

(284) It has thus been explained that the hylic intellect is something composed of the disposition found in us and of an intellect conjoined to this disposition. As conjoined to the disposition, it is a disposed intellect, not an intellect in act; though, as not conjoined to this disposition, it is an intellect in act; while, in itself, this intellect is the Agent Intellect, the existence of which will be shown later. As conjoined to this disposition, it is necessarily an intellect in potentiality which cannot think itself but which can think other than itself (that is, material things), while, as not conjoined to the disposition, it is necessarily an intellect in act which thinks itself and not that which is here (that is, it does not think material things). We shall clarify this more fully later, once it is clear that two functions exist in our soul, one of which is the producing of intelligibles and the other is the receiving of them. By virtue of producing intelligibles, it is called agent, while, by virtue of receiving them, it is called passive, though in itself it is one thing.

(285) Both approaches to the hylic intellect have thus been explained to you – that of Alexander and that of the others – and it will have become clear to you that the truth, which is the approach of Aristotle, is a combination of both views, in the manner we have mentioned. For, by our position as stated, we are saved from positing something substantively separate as a certain disposition, positing [instead] that the disposition found in it is not due to its [own] nature but due to its conjunction with a substance which has this disposition essentially – namely, man – while, in positing that something here is associated incidentally with this disposition, we are saved from [considering] the intellect in potentiality as a disposition only. Having clarified this, we may now return to commenting in detail on everything which Aristotle says on these issues.

(286) [429^{a}24] Aristotle said: As this is the nature of the intellect, that it is only a disposition, it is unmixed with the body – that is, unmixed with any form. Were it mixed with the body, it would be either a tempered form, whether hot or cold, or it would have a corporeal organ, like the sense. However, it has nothing of this sort, and it is therefore not mixed with the body. This being the case, they spoke well who said that soul is the place of forms – except that this is not true for all the soul, but for the intellect only. Nor is the thinking faculty [in question] equivalent to the forms as perfected, but as in potentiality.

(287) Proof that the impassivity found in the intellect is not the same as that found in the sense – that is, that impassivity in the intellect is greater than in the sense – lies in the fact that, once the senses experience a strong object of sensation, they are not able to sense something inferior to it after having disengaged from it. For example, whoever has looked at the sun is not able to look at what is below it, the reason being that the eye is affected and influenced by a strong object of sensation whereas the opposite occurs to the intellect – that is, when it disengages from considering a strong intelligible, its consideration of an inferior one is [rendered] easier and better. The reason for this is that the sensory faculty is mixed with its subject to a certain degree, while the rational faculty is entirely unmixed.

(288) The intellect is said to be potential in two ways. One is like that which is said of habitual notions and forms – namely, that they have the potentiality to act by themselves, as a sage is said to be able to learn, speculate, and deduce things by himself; while the second way [in which the intellect is said to be potential] is like that which is said of passive faculties – for example, the student who is said to be potentially wise, though being unable to realize this by himself but, rather, through [the assistance] of others. This, then, is the difference between active and passive potentialities.

(289) [429^{b}10] He said: As a particular individual is one thing and its essence another – for example, a particular [quantity of] water is [one] thing and its essence is something else, and

similarly with many things (though not with all, for the existence and essence of simple things are one and the same) – it is necessary that these two intentions be apprehended [either] by two different faculties, each one being apprehended separately, or by one faculty, though one which has two different aspects. This, once it is realized that the essence and form of an object are other than the thing which has the form; for we apprehend the essence and form of an object by means of the intellect, whereas we apprehend an individual instance of this essence by means of the sense. Moreover, it is by means of the intellect that we apprehend that a particular essence is in a given individual – that is, in the matter of that form. Thus, if that matter has an essence which exists in the object, it is the intellect which appreciates this.

(290) Aristotle has compared this state of the intellect to a bent line. That is, he has compared the intellect's grasp of form to a straight line and its grasp that the form is in a substrate to a bent line. The substrate is either in physical entities, the intellect perceiving it by means of the sense, or in mathematical entities, three things being perceived by the intellect: form, the substrate of the form, and the being of the form in a substrate. The reason for this is that the substrates of the forms of mathematical entities are objects of the intellect, not of the sense, contrary to the situation which obtains with a physical object.

(291) [429ᵇ22] He said: One might be puzzled by the previous statement that the hylic intellect is simple and unaffected, whereas conceptualization is said to be subsumed in the category of affected faculties. This [is a problem] because it is thought that active and passive things are those which share the same matter; but, if the intellect is immaterial, how can it be acted upon?

(292) Another problem is whether or not the intellect itself is intelligible when in act. It is considered that one of two things should occur if the intellect were to think itself in thinking other things: Either all things would be actual intellects and intelligibles, or the intellect itself or something in it would be in potentiality – that is, it would have an intention which would become an actual intelligible once the intellect abstracted it, being potentially intelligible before that.

(293) Both statements are absurd, however; and we say in answer to the first problem that the intention of affection used above vis-à-vis the intellect is more general than that predicated of other things. The only intention of affection in the intellect is receptivity, without there occurring any change whatsoever, either in that which receives or in that which is received. Moreover, one should not believe that the subject of this receptivity is anything other than a disposition to receive the intelligible, and it is not anything in actuality before it is perfected by the intelligible. As Aristotle has said, [the intellect] resembles the disposition for receiving writing which is found in a tablet – that is, just as that disposition found on the surface of the tablet is not mixed with the tablet, so that the tablet's reception of writing can be [pure] passivity, such is the situation of the intellect with the intelligible.

(294) The second problem is resolved in saying that the intellect thinks itself in the same manner that it thinks all intelligibles, except that, in the latter case, that which thinks them is other than that which is thought, whereas it thinks itself insofar as that which thinks it and that which is thought are one and the same thing, both being intellect. It is in this way that speculative knowledge can be said to be the same as its object – that is, both that which apprehends and that which is apprehended are knowledge. One ought, however, to believe that Aristotle's statement concerning the identity in every respect of intellect and intelligible obtains fully [only] with respect to separate objects, whereas this identity is incidental,

as it were, in our intellect. That is, since the essence of man's intellect is nothing other than thinking objects which are external to itself, it happens to think itself when it thinks the objects external to it. However, its essence is nothing more than thinking things external to it, unlike [the intellects of] separate entities which do not think things external to themselves.

(295) [430ᵃ10] He said: That which concerns the intellect has to correspond to physical entities. In every genus of generated physical entities, we find one thing which corresponds to the recipient and another to the agent. The former is that which is potentially all the things found in that genus, the latter that which actualizes them, its relation in nature being like that of art to matter. Accordingly, these two differentia – namely, an agent and a passive intellect – have to exist in the intellect, and thus there will be an intellect in us which is intellect with respect to [its ability to] receive every intelligible, and an intellect in us with respect to [its ability to] actualize every intelligible.

(296) The relation of this intellect to intelligibles is in one respect like that of light to colors. As it is light which renders colors actual after their having been potential, and which gives the pupil of the eye that through which it can receive colors – namely, transparency – so this intellect is that which actualizes intelligibles and brings them forth, and it is that which gives the hylic intellect that through which it receives intelligibles (that is, something which resembles the transparency of sight, as has previously been explained).

(297) It is clear that, in one respect, this intellect is an agent and, in another, it is a form for us, since the generation of intelligibles is a product of our will. When we want to think something, we do so, our thinking it being nothing other than, first, bringing the intelligible forth and, second, receiving it. The individual intentions in the imaginative faculty are they that stand in relation to the intellect as potential colors do to light. That is, this intellect renders them actual intelligibles after their having been intelligible in potentiality. It is clear, from the nature of this intellect – which, in one respect, is form for us and, in another, is the agent for the intelligibles – that it is separable and neither generable nor corruptible, for that which acts is always superior to that which is acted upon, and the principle is superior to the matter. The intelligent and intelligible aspects of this intellect are essentially the same thing, since it does not think anything external to its essence. There must be an Agent Intellect here, since that which actualizes the intellect has to be an intellect, the agent endowing only that which resembles what is in its substance.

(298) [430ᵃ20] He said: In the individual, the potential intellect is prior in time, whereas, in absolute terms, the intellect in actuality is prior to that which is in potentiality in two senses of priority simultaneously: in time and in causation. This Agent Intellect, our final form, does not think at one time and not at another, nor does it exist at one time and not at another; it is, rather, unceasing, and will not cease. Thus, when separated from the body, it is immortal, necessarily. While it is this very intellect which thinks the intelligibles here when it is joined to the hylic intellect, it is not able to think anything here when it is separated from the hylic intellect. Therefore, we do not remember after death all that we knew when the intellect was conjoined with the body. Thus, when conjoined to us, the intellect thinks the intelligibles which are here, while when separated from us, it thinks itself. Whether it thinks itself while conjoined to us is a question which we will investigate later.

26

Siger of Brabant
On the Intellective Soul

[handwritten note:] is the intellective soul multiplied in accord w/ indiv. human bodies or is there a single intellect for all men?

[Chapter VII: Whether the Intellective Soul Is Multiplied in Accord with the Multiplication of Human Bodies]

As to the seventh point raised above, viz. whether the intellective soul is multiplied in accord with the multiplication of human bodies, it must be carefully considered insofar as such pertains to the philosopher and can be grasped by human reason and experience, by seeking the mind of the philosophers in this matter rather than the truth since we are proceeding philosophically. For it is certain according to that truth which cannot deceive that intellective souls are multiplied with the multiplication of human bodies. However, certain philosophers have thought otherwise.

According to philosophy, then: 1. A nature which is separated from matter in its being is not multiplied with the multiplication of matter. But according to the Philosopher the intellective soul enjoys being which is separated from matter, as we have already seen. Therefore, it should not be multiplied either with the multiplication of matter or with the multiplication of human bodies.

This reasoning is confirmed as follows. To differ in species, as man differs from ass, is to differ by reason of form. But to differ in number while belonging to the same species, as horse differs from horse, is to differ by reason of matter. For the form of horse is found in different parts of matter. Because of this it is asserted that what exists apart from any principle causing number or difference or multiplication lacks number, difference, and multiplication. But if the intellective soul enjoys being which is separated from matter then it exists apart from any principle that causes difference and number and multiplication of individuals within a species. Therefore, there do not seem to be many intellective souls within the same species.

2. No nature that subsists in itself and exists apart from matter and is thus individuated of itself can admit of numerically distinct individuals. But the intellective soul subsists in itself and exists apart from matter and is thus individuated of itself. Therefore it cannot admit of plurality of individuals within the same species.

Proof for the major: If it were of the essence of man to be this man or to be Socrates, just as there could not be many men each of whom would be Socrates or this man, neither could there be many men [at all]. Now if man subsisted in himself and apart from singulars, he would be individuated of his essence. Therefore every form that subsists in itself and has no materiality is individuated of its essence. And since nothing individuated can be common to many, no form enjoying being independently from matter can be common to many individuals. According to this reasoning, then, there is numerically only one intelligence in each species of intelligences separated from matter, a point on which all the philosophers have agreed. Wherefore, in holding that the ideas and species of material things are separated from matter, Plato posited only one individual per species.

[...]

But someone might say that since there is an intellective soul in me, God can make another like it and thus there will be more than one. To this it is to be replied that God cannot make that which is self-contradictory and repugnant. In like manner, God cannot produce many men, each of whom would be Socrates. For then he would make them to be many men and one man, many men and not many men, one man and not one man. But if the intellective soul is individuated of its essence and subsistent in itself and thus like Socrates, to make another intellective soul identical in species with one now existing would be to make it different from and the same as the first one. For in things separated from matter the individual is the species itself. Therefore, another individual within the species would be something contrary under that individual, which is impossible.

3. Something white can be divided into parts not because it is white but because it is quantified and continuous. But if there were something white that was neither quantified nor continuous, it would not be divisible into many white things. Nor would a separate and subsistent whiteness be divisible into many whitenesses. Just as that which is white is divisible into many white things because it is quantified and continuous, so too, if numerically distinct white things are actually found within the same species this is because of the actual division of the quantified and continuous thing in which the whiteness is present. From this it is argued that a nature whose being is separated from the quantified and continuous in such fashion that it is neither quantified nor continuous nor exists in anything quantified or continuous is unable to admit of many individuals within the same species, because of the absence of a cause to multiply and render distinct the various individuals of that nature within that species. But the intellective soul exists apart from the quantified and continuous and is not itself quantified or continuous as the Philosopher [Aristotle] proves in De anima I. . . . Therefore, since the intellect exists apart from the quantified and continuous and is not itself quantified and continuous, it will not admit of many individuals within one species. For such plurality and multiplication arises by division of that which is continuous.

4. The Philosopher [Aristotle] says in Metaphysics XII, that if there were many individuals [heavens] of the same species there would be many first movers of the same species. And he notes that then the first mover would have matter because that which is one in species but many in number has matter. But if the intellect is impassible, and shares nothing in common with anything else, and is separated from the body and a potency without matter, as the Philosopher holds, then that same Philosopher would not be likely to think that it is one in species and many in number but rather that it is only one in number.

5. According to the mind of the Philosopher an infinity of men have already existed. But if intellective souls are multiplied with the multiplication of human bodies, the Philosopher would have to hold that souls are infinite in number, which does not seem to be the case.

In the light of the above we must consider what kind of thing can be multiplied and pre-dicated of numerically different members of the same species. And we must also determine how the various members of a species differ and in what respects.

Concerning the first point: It is to be noted that nothing that is singular and individuated can be multiplied into or predicated of many individuals within the same species. For then the singular and the universal would not differ. And since a subsistent form is numerically one and singular of its nature, it is clear that it cannot be multiplied into many individuals within the same species or predicated of them. That which is composed of form and determined matter as existing in this place or that is singular, like the entity named Socrates. Therefore, for the same reason Socrates can neither be multiplied into many nor predicated of them. Nor can the same material form as received in determined matter be multiplied into many or predicated of many. And in general, since everything that exists does so as a singular (granted that certain things may be understood or spoken of universally), no being viewed as it exists can be multiplied into many individuals within its species or predicated of them. Only a material form considered in the abstract or something composed of form and indetermined matter, as that which is signified by composite universals such as man or horse, can be multiplied into many within the same species and predicated of them.

Concerning the second point: It is to be said or understood that two individuals of the same species do not differ in form. As found in them form is not divided according to its substance. Of itself the matter of this individual is not divided from the matter of that individual. Rather one individual differs from another of the same species through this, that one possesses its form under determined dimensions or under a determined position as located here, while the other possesses the form of its species as located there. The form as found in the two individuals is not rendered other by diversity according to the form itself and its substance, for such diversity of form results in difference in species. Rather both individuals possess the one form, which is undivided as form. Nor should anyone wonder at us for saying that the form in each individual is one by that unity which follows upon its substance and yet that it is found here and elsewhere. When we understand a form to be one by the unity that follows upon its substance we do not have in mind something taken individually, but rather according to species, since a material form is not individuated of itself. It is not impossible for that which is one in species to be found in different individuals and to occupy different positions, thus being found here and elsewhere. . . . And just as form found in individuals is not divided as form either directly or by way of consequence, so too, neither is matter. It is not divided of itself, but is divided because quantified things are located here and elsewhere.

But there are weighty arguments according to which the intellective soul must be multiplied with the multiplication of human bodies, and authorities can also be cited for this view. Thus Avicenna, Algazel, and Themistius maintain this. Themistius also holds that the agent intellect, taken as illuminating and as illuminated, is multiplied even though there is only one [supreme] illuminating intellect. All the more so does he mean that the possible intellect is multiplied.

Again, there are arguments for this view. If there were only one intellect for all men, when one knows then all would know. And one would not know while another did not. If to ima-gine is not the same as to understand, granted that the man who understands has phantasms, which the ignorant man lacks, this will not account for the fact that he knows more than the other. For the intellect in which actual understanding takes place is no more his than the ignorant man's, unless the position is changed.

For the sake of discussion someone might say that the one man knows and the other does not for this reason: that the act of intellection takes place by reason of one unique agent or one unique intellect operating in the man who knows, but not in the man who does not. Thus we described above how man understands or how the act of understanding may be attributed to man himself, namely, because the action of an agent united to matter is attributed to the whole composite. In the act of understanding the intellect unites itself to the one who knows and not to the one who does not know because it derives knowledge from the phantasms [of the knower]. Thus one man knows while another remains ignorant, not because the act of imagining on the part of one is greater than the act of understanding on the part of the other, nor because the intelligible species is found in the body of one rather than in the body of the other (for it exists apart), nor because they use different intellects in understanding (as the present position maintains), but because the act of understanding takes place by reason of the intellect, which is united to the body of one in operating but not to the body of the other.

But if someone should say this, then the argument may be developed in another way. Operations may be distinguished either by reason of the agent, or by reason of the time at which they occur. Thus if both you and I see the same object at the same time, the acts of sight are different [by reason of the agent]. If someone sees a white and a black object with one and the same eye, the acts of sight are different by reason of the object. If I see something white and then after some time see the same white object, the acts of sight differ by reason of time. Therefore, if two men understand the same intelligible object at the same time and if this takes place by means of one and the same intellect, this man's act of understanding will be the same as that man's act of understanding, which seems absurd.

Again, the Philosopher holds that the intellect is in potency to intelligible species and receptive of these species and is itself without species. But if there is only one intellect then it will always be filled with species and thus there will be no need for the agent intellect. Therefore, because of these difficulties and certain others, I acknowledge that I myself have been in doubt for quite some time both as to what should be held in the light of natural reason about this point and as to what the Philosopher thought about it. In such doubt one must hold fast to the faith, which surpasses all human reasoning.

27

Thomas Aquinas on the Nature and Powers of the Human Soul

Summma Theologiae

Part I, Question 75. The Soul's Nature

The first of these inquiries breaks up into seven problems:

1. whether the soul is corporeal;
2. whether the human soul is something which subsists;
3. whether the souls of brutes subsist;
4. whether the soul is the man, or whether, rather, man is not a compound of soul and body;
5. whether the soul is compounded of matter and form;
6. whether the human soul can pass away;
7. whether the soul is the same sort of thing as an angel.

Article 1. Whether the soul is corporeal (physical)

The first point:[1] 1. There are reasons for thinking that the soul is something corporeal. For the soul causes change in a body. But there is no cause of change which is not subject to change. For one thing, it does look as though nothing can bring on change without being changed itself, since nothing can give what it has not got; things that are not hot do not heat. And for another, if anything were an unchanged cause of change, it would give rise to an effect unendingly uniform in manner, as is proved in Aristotle's *Physics*.[2] But this is not what we observe in animal behaviour, which derives from soul. So the soul is not an unchanged cause of change. Now every cause of change that is subject to change is corporeal. Consequently the soul must be corporeal.

2. Besides, all knowledge comes through some likeness. But there can be no likeness between a body and a non-bodily thing. Accordingly, unless the soul were corporeal it could not know corporeal things.

---

1 Cf. *CG* II, 65. *In De Anima* II, *lect.* 1.
2 *Physics* VIII, 6. 259b32–260a1; 10. 267b3.

3. Again, there has to be some contact between the cause of change and the thing changed, yet contact is only between bodies. Since the soul moves the body, it must therefore be some sort of body.

On the other hand we have Augustine's remark that the soul *is said to be simple in relation to the body, because it is not extended quantitatively through the various parts of the body.*[3]

Reply: Inquiry into the nature of the soul presupposes an understanding of the soul as the root principle of life in living things within our experience. We speak of living things as 'animate', and of non-living things as 'inanimate'. Now the chief manifestations of life are the two activities of knowledge and movement. Philosophers of old, unable to transcend imagination, supposed that some body was the source, for they held bodies alone to be real things; that which was not a body was not anything at all.[4] And so they maintained that the soul was some sort of body.

Though we could show the error of this view in many different ways, let us employ just one line of reasoning, at once very accessible and certain, by which it becomes plain that the soul is not corporeal. It is obvious that not every principle of vital activity is a soul. Otherwise the eye would be a soul, since it is a principle of sight; and so with the other organs of the soul. What we call the soul is the root principle of life. Now though something corporeal can be some sort of principle of life, as the heart is for animals, nevertheless a body cannot be the root principle of life. For it is obvious that to be the principle of life, or that which is alive, does not belong to any bodily thing from the mere fact of its being a body; otherwise every bodily thing would be alive or a life-source. Consequently any particular body that is alive, or even indeed a source of life, is so from being a body of such-and-such a kind. Now whatever is actually *such*, as distinct from *not-such*, has this from some principle which we call its actuating principle. Therefore a soul, as the primary principle of life, is not a body but that which actuates a body. Much as heat, as the source of the heating process, is not the body heated, but a certain actuation of it.

Hence: 1. Granted that what changes is changed from outside, and that this process cannot be prolonged through an infinite regress, we must assert that not every cause of change is subject to causal influx from outside. Since all change is a passage from potentiality to actuality, the cause of change gives what it has to the subject of change to the precise extent that it actuates it. But as shown in the *Physics*,[5] there is a wholly unchangeable cause of change, which does not undergo change either from itself or from elsewhere. And such a source of change can produce a perpetually uniform pattern of effect. But there is another change-inducing agent which, while not essentially changeable, is changeable because of attendant conditions, and on this account does not give rise to a uniform pattern of effect. Such is a soul. Then there is another source of change which is of itself essentially changeable, namely, a body. Since the cosmologists of antiquity reckoned that nothing incorporeal existed, they held that every cause of change was itself subject to change, that the soul is essentially changeable, and something corporeal.[6]

2. A likeness of the thing known does not need to be actually present in the nature of the knower. If there be something that passes from being capable of knowing to actually

---

3   *De Trinitate* VI, 6. PL 42, 929.

4   Cf. 1a. 50, 1.

5   *Physics* VIII, 5. 258b4–9.

6   St Thomas's source here is *De Anima* I, 2. 403b29f.

knowing, then the likeness of the thing known need not be in the nature of the knower in actuality. It is enough if it is potentially in the knower, as colour is potentially in the retina, not actually. So there is no need for an actual likeness of corporeal things to be in the nature of the soul; it merely needs to have a capacity for such likenesses. But because the ancient cosmologists could not see the distinction between actuality and potentiality, they held that the soul must be a body in order to know a bodily thing. And to explain how it could know all bodily things they held that it was compounded of the elements of all physical things.[7]

3. There are two kinds of contact, quantitative and causal. According to the first kind of contact, bodies are touched only by bodies, but according to the second a body can be touched by an incorporeal agent acting upon it.

Article 2. Whether the human soul is something which subsists

The second point:[8] 1. There are reasons for saying that the human soul is not something which subsists. For what subsists is said to be 'this particular thing'. But the soul is not 'this particular thing'; only the compound of soul and body can be said to be that. Hence the soul is not something subsisting.

2. Besides, whatever subsists can be described as acting. But the soul is not described as acting; because, to quote the *De Anima*,[9] to speak of the soul sensing or understanding would be like speaking of it weaving or building. Hence the soul is not something which subsists.

3. Besides, if the soul were something subsisting, there would be some activity of the soul without the body. But it has no activity without the body, not even the act of understanding; for understanding does not take place without images, and there are no images apart from the body. Hence the soul is not something which subsists.

On the other hand we have what Augustine says, *Whoever sees the nature of the mind to be both substantial and incorporeal can see that those who hold it to be corporeal make the mistake of committing it to the things without which they cannot think of any nature,*[10] namely the pictures they form of bodily things. The human mind is incorporeal in nature, and indeed substantial: it is something which subsists.

Reply: The principle of the act of understanding, which is called the soul of man, must of necessity be some kind of incorporeal and subsistent principle. For it is obvious that man's understanding enables him to know the natures of all bodily things.[11] But what can in this way take in things must have nothing of their nature in its own, for the form that was in it by nature would obstruct the knowledge of anything else. For example, we observe how the tongue of a sick man with a fever and bitter infection cannot perceive anything sweet, for everything tastes sour. Accordingly, if the intellectual principle had in it the physical nature of any bodily thing, it would be unable to know all bodies. Each of them has its own determinate nature. Impossible, therefore, that the principle of understanding be something bodily.

And in the same way it is impossible for it to understand through and in a bodily organ, for the determinate nature of that bodily organ would prevent knowledge of all bodies. Thus

7 Cf. 1a. 84, 2c.
8 Cf. *De potentia* III, 9, 11. *In De Anima* III, lect. 7. *Q. de anima* I, 14. *De spiritualibus creaturis* 2.
9 *De Anima* I, 4. 408b9–18.
10 *De Trin.* X, 7. PL 42, 979.
11 Cf. 1a. 84, 7.

if you had a colour filter over the eye, and had a glass vessel of the same colour, it would not matter what you poured into the glass, it would always appear the same colour.

The principle of understanding, therefore, which is called mind or intellect, has its own activity in which body takes no intrinsic part. But nothing can act of itself unless it subsists in its own right. For only what actually exists acts, and its manner of acting follows its manner of being. So it is that we do not say that heat heats, but that something hot heats. Consequently the human soul, which is called an intellect or mind, is something incorporeal and subsisting.

Hence: 1. This particular thing can be taken two ways. First, it can refer to anything which subsists; again, it can be taken to refer to something subsisting in the full integrity of its nature, according to its type. Now the first sense of the phrase excludes its being an inhering accident or a form which can exist only when materialized. The second sense of the phrase excludes also the kind of incompleteness which pertains to a part. A hand can be considered to be 'this particular thing' in the first sense, because it subsists, but not in the second, because it is part of a thing. For it is the whole compound of body and soul that is described as 'this particular thing'.

2. Aristotle, in this passage, was expressing the views of those who held that intellectual understanding was a case of physical change; he was not expressing his own views, as is clear from the context.[12]

But you could well say that while nothing acts with an activity truly its own unless it has existence in its own right, nevertheless something which exists in its own right, even if it is only a part, can be described as something, provided it is not inhering as an accident or a material constituent of something else. But we describe a thing as subsistent in the most proper sense, or subsisting *per se*, when it is not inhering in the manner mentioned, or is not a part. And in this sense an eye or hand cannot be described as subsisting *per se*, nor in consequence as acting *per se*. For this reason the activities of parts are attributed to the whole through the parts. For we speak of a man seeing with his eye or feeling with his hand, but not in the same sense as when we speak of something hot heating by reason of its heat; for strictly speaking heat in no sense heats. It can be said, therefore, that the soul understands just as the eye sees; but it is much better to say that the man understands with his soul.

3. The body is necessary for the activity of the intellect, not as the organ through which it acts, but in order to supply it with its object; for images stand in relation to the intellect as colour in relation to sight. This dependence on body does not show that the intellect is non-subsistent; no more than the fact that it requires exterior sense-objects for sensation shows that an animal is not a subsisting thing.

Part I, Question 76. The Soul's Union with the Body

Next we must consider the union of the soul with the body. This raises eight problems:

1. whether the intellective principle is united to the body as its form;
2. whether there are as many intellective principles as there are human bodies, or whether there is one intellect for all men;
3. whether in the body whose form is the intellective principle there is some other soul;

12 *De Anima* I, 4. 408a34.

4. whether there is in it some other substantial form;
5. what kind of body the intellective principle informs;
6. whether it is united to such a body by means of some other body;
7. or by means of some accidental disposition;
8. whether the whole soul is in every part of the body.

Article 1. Whether the intellective principle is united to the body as its form

The first point:[13] 1. There are reasons for holding that the intellective principle is not united to the body as its form. For Aristotle, understanding is separate,[14] and not the act of any body. Hence it is not united to a body as its form.

2. Besides, every form is limited by the matter it informs; otherwise there would be no need for proportion between matter and form. If, then, intellect were united to the body as its form, it would follow, since every body has a limited nature, that the intellect would have a limited nature. In which case its knowledge would not extend to all things, in the manner explained above.[15] But this is against the very notion of understanding. Therefore the intellect is not united to a body as its form.

3. Besides, whenever a receptive capacity is an actuality of some body, it receives form in its material individuality, for the form must be received according to the recipient's manner of receiving. But the form of something understood is received by the understanding, not materially and individually, but rather immaterially and according to its universality. Otherwise the intellect would, like sense, know only singulars, not immaterial and universal forms. Therefore the intellect is not united to the body as its form.

4. Besides, power to act and activity pertain to the same subject; the thing that can do is the same as the thing that does. But intellectual activity is not bodily, as we saw above.[16] So intellectual power is not a power of some body. But no power can be more immaterial and simple than the thing it is a power of. So the substance of the intellect is not the form of the body.

5. Besides, what has being of itself is not united to the body as its form. For form is that by which something is, and so the form's being is not something it cannot not have. But the intellectual principle has being of itself, and is something subsisting, as we said above.[17] So it is not united to the body as its form.

6. Besides, what belongs to a thing by virtue of what it is always belongs to it. But it belongs to form by virtue of what it is to be united to matter; for by its essence, not by some accident, it actuates matter, otherwise matter and form would not constitute something substantially one, but rather something merely accidentally one. And therefore form cannot exist without its proper matter. But since, as we showed,[18] the intellectual principle is incorruptible, it remains after the body's corruption, not united to a body. Therefore the intellectual principle is not united to the body as its form.

---

13 Cf. *CG* II, 56–7, 59, 68. *De spiritualibus creaturis* 2. *Q. de anima* 1 & 2. *De unitate intellectus. In De Anima* II, *lect.* 4, 111, *lect.* 7.

14 *De Anima* III, 4. 429a24–7.

15 1a. 75, 2.

16 Loc. cit.

17 Loc. cit.

18 1a. 75, 6.

On the other hand, for Aristotle, logical differentiation of species depends on real formative principles.[19] But the difference constitutive of man is *rationality*, said of man by virtue of his intellective principle. So the intellectual principle is the form of man.

Reply: The intellect, as the source of intellectual activity, is the form of the human body. For the prime endowment by virtue of which anything acts is the form of that to which the activity is attributed, as health is the prime endowment by virtue of which the body is made healthy, and knowledge is the prime endowment by virtue of which the soul knows, and health, therefore, is the form of the body and knowledge of the soul. And the reason for this is that what a thing actually does depends on what it actually has to give; a thing acts precisely by virtue of its actuancy. Now it is obvious that the soul is the prime endowment by virtue of which a body has life. Life manifests its presence through different activities at different levels, but the soul is the ultimate principle by which we conduct every one of life's activities; the soul is the ultimate motive factor behind nutrition, sensation and movement from place to place, and the same holds true of the act of understanding. So that this prime factor in intellectual activity, whether we call it mind or intellectual soul, is the formative principle of the body. And this is how Aristotle proves it in the *De Anima*.[20]

Should anyone wish to maintain that the intellective soul is not the form of the body, he would have to find some way of making the act of understanding an act of this particular person. For each is conscious that it is he himself that understands. Now an action is attributed to somebody in three ways, as Aristotle shows.[21] For a thing is said to cause or act either through its whole self, as when a doctor heals; or through a part of itself, as when a man sees with his eyes; or *per accidens*, as when we say that a white man is building, his whiteness having nothing directly to do with the fact that he is building. When, then, we say that Socrates or Plato understands, it is obviously not attributed to him *per accidens*, for it is attributed to him in virtue of the fact that he is a man, which belongs to him by his essence. So we must either say that Socrates understands through his whole self, as Plato held, saying that man is an intellective soul,[22] or else we must say that the understanding is a part of Socrates. Now the first of these alternatives is untenable, as shown above,[23] on the grounds that one and the same man perceives himself both to understand and to have sensations. Yet sensation involves the body, so that the body must be said to be part of man. It remains, therefore, that the intellect whereby Socrates understands is a part of Socrates, in such wise that the intellect is in some way united to the body of Socrates.

Now Averroës, the Commentator, says that this union takes place through the automatic intelligibility of the mind's contents.[24] But to say mind is to say two distinct powers, the receptive understanding, and the imagination with its dependence on the nervous system. And thus the receptive understanding is joined to the body of this man or that through the automatic intelligibility of the mind's contents. But such joining or linking is not enough to make the activity of the intellect an activity of Socrates. This is obvious if we compare the

---

19   *Metaphysics* VIII, 2. 1043a2–20.
20   *De Anima* II, 2. 414a4–19.
21   *Physics* V, 1. 224a21–34.
22   1 *Alcibiades* 25. 129E–130.
23   1a. 75, 4.
24   *De Anima* III, comm. V, 5.

process of sensation, as Aristotle does before going on to consider the process of understanding. For as sense-images are to understanding, says the *De Anima*,[25] so are colours to sight. Therefore, as colours, with their seeableness, are to sight, so sense-images, with their intelligibility, are to the receptive understanding. Now it is obvious that while being seen the colours remain in the wall, and that consequently the activity called seeing is not attributed to the wall; the wall is the seen not the seer. And likewise, from the mere fact that sense-images, in their intelligibility, are received into the receptive understanding, it does not follow that Socrates does the understanding, merely because he has the images in him; all that follows is that he or his sense-images are understood.

Now some have sought to assert that the understanding is linked to the body as its motor, so that understanding and body form a unit to which the activity called understanding can be attributed. This is meaningless on many counts, however.[26] In the first place, the understanding moves the body only by virtue of a drive which itself presupposes intellectual activity. It is wrong to say that Socrates understands something because he is moved into action by his understanding. The truth is the reverse of this: Socrates is moved into action by his understanding because he understands something.

In the second place, consider the fact that Socrates is a particular individual whose unity of nature and essence is a compound unity, matter plus form. In that case, if the understanding is not the formative principle it must be something not belonging to Socrates' essence, and thus the understanding will be related to the whole Socrates as motor to thing moved. But understanding is not an activity that effects changes in things the way an activity like heating does; the act of understanding is something completely within the intellect. So understanding cannot be attributed to Socrates merely because he is acted on by understanding.

In the third place, the activity of a moving agent is attributed to the thing it moves in one case only, when it uses it as an instrument, as when a carpenter imparts his motions to his saw. Therefore if understanding were to be attributed to Socrates on the ground that it was the activity of some agent acting on him, it would follow that he was said to understand because being used for understanding. This is incompatible with the Philosopher's contention that understanding takes place without physical instrumentality.[27]

In the fourth place, grant that the action of a part may be attributed to the whole, as the action of the eye is said to be the action of the man, nevertheless such an action is never attributed to another part of the same whole (except by metonymy). We do not say the hand sees because the eye sees. If, then, Socrates and the power of understanding form a single whole in the manner in question, the activity of the understanding cannot be attributed to Socrates. Indeed, if Socrates is a whole composed by uniting the understanding with the rest of the things that go to make up Socrates, and yet the understanding is united to the rest only as their motor, it would follow that Socrates is not properly speaking one thing, that Socrates as Socrates does not have an existence of his own. A being exists as being one.

The only explanation left is the one Aristotle gives: each man understands because his intellective principle is his formative principle. So it is clear from the very activity of the understanding that the intellectual principle is united to the body as its form.

The same thing can be shown from the nature of man as a species. Each thing's nature declares itself through its activities. Now the activity peculiar to man is understanding; it is

---

25   *De Anima* III, 5. 430a10–17; 7. 431a14–17.

26   Also *Phædrus* 30, 250c. *Timæus* 15, 43–4. *Laws* X, 8–9. 898–9.

27   *De Anima* III, 4. 429a24–7.

by this that he transcends all animals. Hence it was that Aristotle fixed on this activity, as the most human of human activities, as the ultimate constituent perfecting human happiness.[28] It is natural therefore that the power behind this activity should determine the kind of being man is. But everything has its species determined by its formative principle. So we are left with this, that the intellective principle is the formative principle determining man as a species.

Yet we should bear in mind that the nobler a form is, the more it dominates physical matter and the less it is immersed in it, and the more it transcends it in activity and permanent power to act. We note, for instance, that the form of a chemical compound has activities which do not belong to the elements it is composed of. And the more valuable the form, the more its powers are found to exceed those of elementary particles of matter, as vegetable life has operations metals do not have, and sense-life has operations vegetable life does not have. Now the human soul stands at the top of the scale. Hence its powers so transcend the material world that it has an activity and a permanent power to act to which material forces contribute nothing. This is the power we call the understanding.

Note, though, that even if someone were to claim that the soul is compounded of matter and form, he could still on no account say that the soul was the form of the body. For since form is actuality, while matter is mere potentiality, there is no way for something compounded of matter and form to be in its entirety the formative principle of some other thing. But if it is formative by virtue of something in it, then we call the formative part the animating principle or soul and that of which it is the form the basic living or animated thing, as was said above.[29]

Hence: 1. It must be observed, with Aristotle,[30] that the loftiest natural form, at which the study of natural philosophy culminates, that is to say, the human soul, is at once non-material yet im-mattered. He argues that *man and the sun generate man from matter*. Man is non-material in respect of his intellectual power because the power of understanding is not the power of an organ the way sight is of the eye, for understanding is an activity that cannot be exercised through a bodily organ as sight is. Yet it is material to the extent that the soul it is a power of is the form of the body and the term of human generation. Accordingly he says that the understanding is *separate* because it is not the power of a bodily organ.

2 & 3. For man to be able to understand everything through his intellect, including non-material things and universal concepts, it is enough that the power of understanding is not a bodily act.

4. The human soul, being so lofty, is not a form immersed in physical matter or wholly swallowed up by it. So nothing prevents it from having some non-bodily activity, even though the soul's essence is to inform a body.

5. That act of being, in which it itself subsists, the soul communicates to physical matter; this matter and the intellectual soul form a unity such that the act of being of the compound whole is the soul's act of being. This does not happen in other forms which are non-subsistent. And for this reason the human soul continues in its act of being when the body is destroyed, whereas other souls do not.

6. It belongs to the very essence of the soul to be united to a body, just as it belongs to a light body to float upwards. And just as a light body remains light when forcibly displaced,

28 *Ethics* x, 7. 1177a12–19.

29 1a. 75, 5.

30 *Physics* ii, 2. 194b8–15.

and thus retains its aptitude and tendency for the location proper to it, in the same way the human soul, remaining in its own existence after separation from the body, has a natural aptitude and a natural tendency to embodiment.

Article 2. Whether there are as many intellectual principles as there are human bodies

The second point:[31] 1. There are reasons for thinking that there are not as many intellectual principles as there are human bodies, but rather one intellect in all men. For no non-material substance is multiplied as individuals within the same species. But the human soul is a non-material substance, for it is not compounded of matter and form, as was shown above.[32] So there are not many souls in one species. Now all men are of a single species. Therefore there is a single intellective principle for all.

2. Besides, when a cause is taken away, its effect will be too. Therefore if the number of souls depended on the number of bodies, the consequence would seem to be that on removal of the bodies there would no longer be many souls but one. Now this is heresy, since it would abolish the different rewards and punishments allotted to individuals.

3. Again, if my intellect differs from your intellect, then my intellect has its individuality and yours does too. Individuals differ numerically but agree in kind. But what a thing receives it receives on its own terms. So the presence of things in my understanding and in yours would differ according to our different individualities. But this goes against the very nature of intellect, which lifts universally valid notions clear of encumbering particulars.

4. Again, the thing understood is in the understanding actually at work. So if my intellect is different from yours, what is understood by me must be different from what is understood by you. And so what is understood will have numerical individuality and will be understood only potentially, and it will be necessary to abstract whatever common content there is in our separate minds (in any group of things, no matter how diverse, there is always some intelligible aspect common to all of them). But this goes against the very notion of intellect, since it does not seem to distinguish it from imagination. So the only alternative seems to be one power of understanding for all men.

5. Again, when a learner learns from a teacher, it cannot be said that the knowledge of the teacher begets the knowledge in the learner, because that would make out that knowledge is an active cause like heat, which is obviously untrue. It would seem, then, that the same individual bit of knowledge that is in the teacher gets into the learner, and this could not happen unless they both have the same intellect. So it seems that there is one intellect in both learner and teacher, and this goes for all men.

6. Besides, Augustine says, *Were I to say there were many human souls I would laugh at myself.*[33] Now the soul must be a unity above all in the field of understanding. So there is one intellect in all men.

On the other hand Aristotle says that as universal causes have universal effects, in the same way particular cases are related to their own particular effects.[34] But just as it is absurd

---

31 Cf. 1 *Sent.* 8, 5, 2 ad 6; 11, 17, 2, 1. *CG* II, 73, 75. *De spiritualibus creaturis* 9. *Q. de anima* 3. *Compend. theol.* 85. *De unitate intellectus.*

32 1a. 75, 5.

33 *De quantitate animæ* 32. PL 32, 1075.

34 *Physics* II, 3. 195b25–8.

to postulate one kind of soul for different kinds of animals, so it is impossible that one individual intellective soul should ensoul different individuals.

Reply: It is absolutely impossible for there to be one intellect operating in all men.

This would be quite clear if, as Plato thought, the man is the intellect.[35] For it would follow that if Socrates and Plato were one intellect they would be one man, distinguished from one another only by extrinsic factors. The distinction between them would be like the distinction between a man with his tunic on and the same man with his hat on, which is silly.

But the same impossibility holds if, as Aristotle thought, the intellect is a part or power of the soul that makes man what he is.[36] For a number of diverse individual things can no more have one form than they can have one existence, since form gives existence.

But however the union of the intelligence with the individual man is conceived, the thesis in question is impossible. For it is obvious that if you have one principal agent and two instruments you can speak of one agent but you must speak of more than one action; thus if a man touches things with both hands there is one toucher but two touches. If, on the other hand, you have one instrument and several principal agents, you will speak of many agents but one action; thus if several haul a boat by the same rope, there are many haulers but one haul. And if there is one principal agent and one instrument you will speak of one agent and one action; thus when a workman uses a hammer there is one hammerer and one hammering. Now it is obvious that however the intellect may be united or linked with this man or that, it enjoys a position as principal in relation to man's other faculties; the sense powers obey the understanding and minister to it. So then, if we were to postulate distinct intellects but one sense-power in two men – two men with one seeing eye, for instance – there would be more than one person seeing, even though there were only one visual faculty in act. (The thesis then fails.) If, though, the intellect is one, however diverse its instruments, then Socrates and Plato cannot but be one understander. And if we add to this that the understanding (gerund) done by the understanding (noun) does not take place in an organ, it will further follow that there is one action as well as one agent – I am speaking, of course, with respect to any one given object of understanding.

However, my intellectual activity might differ from yours thanks to our different sense-images, that is, because the image of a stone in me was one thing and its image in you another. This could be the case, provided the mere sense-image, in its individuality in me as distinct from you, were what informs the recipient understanding; for the same agent produces different actions according to the different qualities it has, as for instance there are different objects of its sight. But the sense-image is not what informs the recipient understanding; what is intelligible to the receptive understanding is the idea latent in the images, from which it is abstracted. And the intellect, from diverse images of one kind of thing, abstracts only one intelligible idea. This is plain in any one man. There can be many images of stones in his mind, but from all of them he gets one intelligible idea of what it is to be a stone; through this idea, one man's intellect in one act grasps the nature 'stone' despite the variety of images. So that if there were one intellect in all men the various sense-images in this man and that could not give rise to different acts of understanding attributable to this man and that respectively, the way Averroes imagines.[37] We are left with the fact that

---

35 1 *Alcibiades* 25. 129E–30. cf 1a. 75, 4.

36 *De Anima* II, 2 & 3. 414a4–19 & 29–32.

37 *In De Anima*. III, 5, 5.

it is absolutely impossible and incongruous to posit one single power of understanding among all men.

Hence: 1. Although the intellective soul, like an angel, is not constituted out of matter, none the less it does, unlike an angel, inform matter. Hence there are many souls of one species due to material differentiation, but there simply cannot be many angels of one species.

2. A unit, metaphysically speaking, is what has one existence. Hence whether there can be many of a thing depends on whether many such things can *be*. Now it is obvious that the intellectual soul's very existence involves embodiment as a body's form and yet, when the body goes, the intellectual soul continues to exist. By the same token, there are many souls because there are many bodies, yet when the bodies disappear, the many souls continue to exist.

3. The fact that the knower is an individual and his knowledge an individual piece of knowledge does not preclude it from being knowledge of something universal. Otherwise, since disembodied intelligences are subsistent and consequently have their own particular existence, they would not be able to understand universally valid truths. But if the knower and the form he knows by are material, this prevents knowledge of anything universally valid. For as all activity depends on the energy previously informing the agent, as heating depends on something being hot, so knowledge depends on what manner of form the knower knows by. Now it is obvious that a nature shared by many is distinguished and multiplied among them according to their material individuation. If, therefore, the form that accounts for knowledge is material, immersed in matter as its proper condition, such a form of knowledge will reflect the nature of the species or general category of the thing known only in so far as this is immersed in the abrupt individuality of the particular case, and hence the fact that the nature can be shared will not be known. If indeed the form is abstracted from the individual material conditions, it will be a reproduction of the nature without the things that individuate it when shared by many, and thus something universally valid will be known. On this point, it is of no consequence whether there is one human intelligence or many, for even if there were one only, it would have to be a certain particular one, and so would the form by which it understood anything.

4. Whether human intelligence is one thing or many, the thing it understands is one thing. For what is understood is in the understanding not in its physical being, but in a reproduction of it. *What is in the mind*, says the *De Anima, is not the stone but the intelligibility of the stone.*[38] Nevertheless the stone is what is understood, not its intelligibility (except in the case where the intellect is reflecting on its own processes), otherwise knowledge would be of ideas, not things. Now it is possible for many things to share the likeness of one same thing in many ways. And since knowledge involves a likening of the knower to the known, it follows that the same thing can be known by different knowers. This is clear at the level of sensation, for many can see the one patch of colour according to different reproductions of it. And so too many intelligences understand the same thing understood.

But in Aristotle's opinion,[39] sense and intellect differ in that a thing is sensed just as it is in its individuality outside the sensing soul, whereas the nature of a thing, while indeed it is extra-mental, does not exist in the mind in the same manner as it exists outside of it. For the nature as shareable by many is understood regardless of its individual features in the concrete. Now it does not have this sort of existence outside the mind. Plato, though,

38 *De Anima* III, 8. 431b28–432a3.
39 Ibid. 432a3–14.

maintained that a thing understood does have the same sort of existence outside the mind as it does in the understanding.[40] For he posited matterless natures of things.

5. It is not the same identical knowledge in the learner and the teacher. The process will be explained below.[41]

6. Augustine did not understand souls to be many in the sense that there are many distinct kinds of soul.

40   Cf. 1a. 84, 1; 85, 1.
41   1a. 117, 1.

28

John Buridan on the Immateriality of the Soul

Q.4 Fourth, it is asked whether the human intellect is a form inhering in the human body.

It is argued that it is, on the authority of Alexander and the Catholic faith.

The opposite is argued on the authority of the Commentator. The opinion of the Commentator was that the intellect does not inhere in the body although it is present to it,[1] just as Aristotle supposed that an intelligence is present to a celestial sphere, or that God is present to the world.[2] For although an intelligence is indivisible and not inherent, it is supposed to be immediately present to the entire sphere and to each and every part of it, just as God is present to the entire world and to each and every part of it. And so the Commentator says that the human intellect, an indivisible and unique existent, is immediately present to each and every man, even though it inheres in none of them.

And there are in this connection the Commentator's probable arguments.

The first is that no form inheres in matter if it is not derived from a material potentiality. But the human intellect is not derived from a material potentiality, as the Commentator says.[3] Therefore, etc.

His second argument is that there is a unique intellect for all men, for it is, as he says, everlasting, and everlasting things are not multiplied by the number of corruptible things.[4] But that which is unique and undivided does not inhere in a plurality of things, distinct in place and with parts outside parts, and human bodies are of this sort. Therefore, etc.

Again, the intellect is assumed to be indivisible (also according to the faith), because it is not materially extended, since it is not educed from a material potentiality. However, such an indivisible would not inhere in a divisible subject, and the human body is of this sort. Therefore, etc.

This argument can be set out deductively as follows: if an indivisible existing intellect inheres in a divisible body, it must be that it inheres in either (1) each and every part of

1 Cf. Averr. *In De an.* III.5; Crawford *Averrois Cordubensis Commentarium magnum in Aristotelis De anima libros*, ed. F. Stuart Crawford (CCAA: Versio Latina, vol. 6, 1), Cambridge, MA, 1953. pp. 401–4, ll. 449–500.

2 Cf. Arist. *Metaph.* XII.7.1072b20–1; XII.10.1075a11–16.

3 Averr. *In De an.* III.5; Crawford, pp. 404–5, ll. 501–20.

4 Averr. *In De an.* III.5: Crawford, pp. 406–7, ll. 556–96.

that body or (2) some part and not in another. If it is said that it inheres in one part and not in another, this is manifestly false, since it could not be consistently attributed to each part and quantity of the body. But if it is said that it inheres in the entire body, that is, in each and every part of it, it is certain that this will be in keeping with the body as a whole, since the intellect is not divisible.

And from this, many absurdities appear to follow.

The first is that the same thing would as a whole be moved and at rest simultaneously, and since resting is the same as not being moved, the same thing would be moved and not moved simultaneously, which implies a contradiction. The consequence is obvious. Suppose that your foot is at rest and your hand is moving. In that case, the same thing which, considered as a whole, is in your hand would be moved with the motion of your hand (since otherwise, it would not be continuous with your hand and in your hand) and, insofar as it is continuous with your foot, at rest in your foot, for it remains continuous in the same place, i.e., the place occupied by your foot. Therefore, your intellect, the same indivisible existent, would be moved and at rest simultaneously, since it would be moved in your hand and at rest in your foot.

But the absurdity grows, because it would follow that the same thing would be moved as a whole by contrary motions simultaneously: if you move your one hand to the right and the other to the left, or the one lower and the other higher, there is another inconsistency because it follows that the same thing would be apart from itself, which is impossible. The consequence holds, since the hand is apart from the foot, and so that which is wholly in the hand would be separate from that which is wholly in the foot as a whole.

Third, it would follow that your foot would understand, because the intellect, considered as a whole, would be present in it, and consequently, so would the act of understanding.

Fourth, it would follow that your foot would be a man, because there must be a composite of body and entire human substantial form for there to be an actual man, since a substantial form must actually exist as a particular entity. And your foot would be this kind of thing, since the intellect is the substantial form of the entire man.

Fifth, it would follow that a substantial form would move from subject to subject, which is plainly absurd. The consequence holds because through change, some parts of the body pass away and others come to be, and so the same intellect that was previously in the parts that have passed away would later be in those that have come to be.

Nevertheless, the Commentator's opinion is false, which is why I advance the opposite thesis: namely, that your intellect, by which you understand, inheres in your body or your matter.[5]

First, this thesis must be firmly upheld on the basis of the Catholic faith.

Second, this thesis must also be upheld by natural arguments, leaving the Catholic faith aside, just as a pagan philosopher would uphold it. My proof is that I think a pagan philosopher would follow the opinion of Alexander. More will be said about this later.

There are, however, natural arguments that the soul inheres in the human body.

The first is that otherwise, the soul would not belong to the essence of a man, or a man would not be a single something essentially. Both appear false. That is why it was adequately

---

5   Or possibly, 'without your matter [*sine materia tua*]'. For this ambiguity in the manuscripts, see Jack Zupko, "On Buridan's Alleged Alexandrianism: Heterodoxy and Natural Philosophy in Fourteenth-Century Paris," *Vivarium* 42 1 (2004), 47 n. 11.

argued in the preceding question that the intellect must be an intrinsic part of the substance of a man.[6]

The second argument is that one would assume either that there is a unique intellect for all men or that there are as many intellects as there are men. But both are obviously absurd. The first absurdity is that it is assumed to be unique, as we will see shortly.[7] And I also state that if the intellect is not inherent, there must not be one for me and another for you because suppose that they are A (yours) and B (mine). Then, since they would not inhere in us, they must have the same nature, and would be no more movable in keeping with your motion than they would mine. Therefore, intellect A would be no closer or more proximate to you than intellect B is to me, and vice versa – i.e., before either of us understood anything. Therefore, natural reason would not tell us that A is any more your intellect than mine.

The third argument is close to the preceding: Socrates' intellect is either moved from place to place with Socrates, or not. If you reply that this [i.e., that the intellect would be moved from place to place with Socrates] does not seem like a natural thing to say because it does not inhere in him (for no means could be given by which this might occur either by touch or impulse, nor could it be said how the intellect would be bound to Socrates' body, given that it is continuously moved with Socrates' body), this will not do, especially before Socrates understands anything. But if you say that it would not be moved from place to place with Socrates, then he would be apart from his own intellect, and so he could not understand through himself [per ipsum], unless you were to say that this intellect is everywhere by immediacy, as we speak of God. And then only one intellect would need to be assumed, since it would be just as close to me as it would be to you, especially before either of us understood anything. Therefore, I could understand through it just as well as you could, and so it would be a fiction to posit one for you and another for me. That is why the Commentator believed that it is unique[8] – a conclusion that will be disproved later.[9]

The fourth argument is that human reason, leaving the faith aside, or even [assuming] the faith, would not say that your intellect exists before you do unless it is assumed to be everlasting and unique, as the Commentator thought. But if it comes into existence in time, this would be either by creation – which natural reason, leaving the faith aside, does not consider – or by natural generation, in which case it would be educed from a material potentiality and inherent in the body. Therefore, everyone should assent to this conclusion, as long as men live in this world, whether they count themselves among the faithful or not.

For this reason, it seems to me that we must note that natural reason, leaving the faith and supernatural action aside, dictates that these [six characteristics], or their opposites, obtain as regards every form: being (1) inherent in matter; (2) educed from a material potentiality; (3) materially extended (4) numerically many (rather than unique and undivided by bodies that are separate and at a distance from one another); (5) generated; and (6) corruptible. Now Alexander thought that all of these are true as regards the human intellect, and others deny them all the same. But our position, based on faith, is that they do not follow from one another by necessity: i.e., we accept the [bodily] inherence and multiplication of the intellect, but deny that it is educed from the potentiality of matter and extended. And we also assume (1) that it is made in a supernatural way, i.e., by means of creation rather than natural

6   See Buridan, *Questions on Aristotle's De anima*[3], III. 3.
7   i.e. ibid. III.5.
8   Averr. *In De an.* III.5; Crawford, p. 401, ll. 424–5.
9   i.e. in Buridan, *Questions on Aristotle's De anima*[3], III.5.

generation; (2) that it is not strictly speaking corruptible, i.e., corruptible by natural means (although it can be annihilated); and (3) that it will never be annihilated.

To the Commentator's arguments, however, the person of faith would respond in one way and Alexander in another.

For to the first, the person of faith would deny the major and Alexander the minor.

As for the second argument, the person of faith and Alexander would both deny that there is a unique intellect belonging to all men. More will be said about this later.[10]

To the third argument, Alexander would deny that the intellect is indivisible, and so the absurdities raised against its being indivisible would not apply to him. But the person of faith grants that it is indivisible.

And so to the first counter-instance, it is replied that the intellect is not moved and at rest at the same time, since that would be contradictory, as the argument shows. But it is granted that the intellect is moved in the hand and at rest in the foot simultaneously. Therefore, it is simultaneously moved in the hand and not moved in the foot. But this is not a contradiction. For this reason, 'The intellect is at rest in the foot; therefore, it is at rest' does not follow, since 'The intellect is not moving in the foot; therefore, it is not moving' also does not follow. And when it is said that it is moved by contrary motions, we can speak of this just as we speak of the body of Christ in the consecrated host when one priest carries the body of Christ to the right and another to the left, for the body of Christ is moved neither in itself nor by a motion inhering in it, just as the magnitude of the host does not inhere in it. So in the same way, the intellect is moved neither in itself, nor by a motion inhering in it. If, however, something is denominated by contrary motions, there is no absurdity, since it does not follow from this that contraries exist in the same thing at the same time. For just as it is not absurd for the same thing to be in different places apart from each other (as will be discussed in reply to the next argument), so it is not absurd for the same thing to be moved to those places simultaneously, since those motions do not inhere in it, nor are they commensurably related to it.

To the second counter-instance, it is said that the intellect is not apart from itself because it does not exist in the hand or foot commensurably, given that it is not extended by the extension of the hand or foot. And it is not absurd for the same thing to be wholly and incommensurably in different places apart from each other, although this would be by supernatural means, as the body of Christ is simultaneously in paradise and on the altar: the body of Christ in the host on the altar is not on that account said to be apart from itself for it is not commensurate with the magnitude of the host, but exists in each and every part of it, although those parts are separate from each other. And so in a similar fashion, the intellect is somehow in the hand and foot, though in neither commensurably, since it is not extended in either of those members.

To the third counter-instance, we would not think it absurd to say that your foot understands as a partial understanding [partiale intelligens]. But I call that which is part of another understanding a 'partial understanding', and that which understands but which is not part of another understanding, a 'total understanding'. For this reason, neither the intellect nor some part of a man, but only the [entire] man himself, is a total understanding.

To the fourth counter-instance, it will be said that nothing is called a man or an animal in familiar and ordinary speech except the whole substance, i.e., that which is not part of another substance. Nor is any substance strictly called a particular thing, whether by its

10   i.e. ibid.

substantial form or in another manner (especially where living things are concerned), unless it is a whole substance. And this is better treated in another place.[11]

To the final counter-instance, it will be said that the way in which the intellect inheres in the human body is not natural but supernatural. And it is certain that God could supernaturally not only form what has not been educed from a material potentiality, but also separate what has been so educed from its matter, conserve it separately, and put it in some other matter. Why, then, wouldn't this be possible as regards the human intellect?

11   Cf. Arist. *Metaph.* VIII.3.1043a29–b5; Buridan, *Questions on Aristotle's De anima*³, II.7; Peter Gordon Sobol, "John Buridan on the Soul and Sensation: An Edition of Book II of his Commentary on Aristotle's Book of the Soul, with an Introduction and a Translation of Question 18 on Sensible Species," Ph.D. diss., Indiana University, pp. 92–104.

Avicenna on Common Nature

The first two passages below are translated from the Latin text in Avicenna, *Opera*, tr. Dominic Gundissalinus (Venice: Bonetus Locatellus for Octavianus Scotus, 1508). Unless there is a modern critical edition, this 1508 edition is the one usually cited. The last three passages are translated from the Latin text in *Avicenna Latinus, Liber de philosophia prima sive scientia divina*, ed. S. Van Riet, 2 vols (Louvain: E. Peeters; Leiden: E. J. Brill, 1977, 1980). For these last three passages, I have also given the folio reference to the 1508 edition.

Logica, III, folio 12ra

Animal is in itself a certain something, and it is the same whether it is sensible or is understood in the soul. But in itself it is neither universal nor is it singular. For if it were universal in itself, so that animality from the fact that it is animality would be universal, it would be necessary that no animal be singular. Rather, every animal would be universal. If, on the other hand, animal from the fact that it is animal were singular, it would be impossible for there to be more than one singular, namely, the very singular to which animality is due. And it would be impossible for another singular to be an animal.

Now animal in itself is a certain something, understood in the mind that it be animal. And according as it is understood to be animal, it is nothing but animal only. If, on the other hand, beyond this it is understood to be universal or singular, or anything else, then beyond this, namely, that which is animal, there is understood a certain something that happens to animality.

Metaphysica V, 1, ed. Van Riet, II,
p. 228, lines 31–6; 1508 edn, folio 86va

Horsehood, to be sure, has a definition that does not demand universality. Rather it is that to which universality happens. Hence horsehood itself is nothing but horsehood only. For in itself it is neither many nor one, neither is it existent in these sensibles nor in the soul, neither is it any of these things potentially or actually in such a way that this is contained under the definition of horsehood. Rather [in itself it consists] of what is horsehood only.

p. 231, lines 74–81; 1508 edn, folio 86vb

Hence, if someone should ask whether the humanity that is in Plato, insofar as it is humanity, is other than that which is in Socrates, and we say no, as we must, we will not have to agree with him when he says, "Therefore, this one and that one are the same in number", because the negation was absolute and we understood in it that that humanity, insofar as it is humanity, is humanity only. But insofar as it is other than the humanity that is in Socrates, that is something extraneous. On the other hand, he did not ask about humanity except insofar as it is humanity.

p. 233, line 36–p. 234, line 44; 1508 edn, folio 87ra

Now animal can be considered by itself, although it is together with what is other than it. For its essence is together with what is other than itself. Therefore, its essence belongs to it by itself, but its being together with what is other than it is something that happens to it, or something that accompanies its nature, like *this* animality, or humanity. Therefore, this consideration, ["insofar as it is animal",] precedes in being both the animal that is this individual because of its accidents, and also the universal that is in these sensibles and is intelligible, as the simple precedes the composite, and as a part the whole. For from this being there is neither genus nor species nor individual, neither one nor many. Rather from this being there is animal only, and man only.

Thomas Aquinas On Being and Essence

Prologue

Because a small error in the beginning grows enormous at the end, as the Philosopher remarks in Book 1 of *On the Heavens and the World*,[1] and being and essence are the first things to be conceived by our understanding, as Avicenna declares in Book 1 of his *Metaphysics*,[2] in order to avoid falling into error about them, and to reveal their difficulties, we should see what are signified by the names of being and essence, how these are found in various things, and how they are related to the logical intentions[3] of genus, species, and difference.

And since we need to arrive at the cognition of simple components from the cognition of what they compose, and from those that are posterior to those that are prior, so that the discussion may suitably progress from the easier subjects, we should proceed from the signification of the name of being to the signification of the name of essence.[4]

---

1   Aristotle, *De Caelo*, lb. 1, c. 5, A271; *Commentary* of St. Thomas, lc. 9.

2   Avicenna, *Metaphysica*, lb. 1, c. 6.

3   The "logical intentions" are second-order concepts (*secundae intentiones*) whereby we conceive of first-order concepts [*primae intentiones*], which in turn are concepts whereby we conceive of things that are not concepts. For example, by means of the first-order concepts of humans and of dogs we conceive of human beings and of dogs, which are not concepts. But by means of the second-order concept of species we conceive of the first-order, specific concepts of humans, dogs, donkeys, etc., and by means of the second-order concept of genus we conceive of the generic concepts of animals, plants, elements, etc.

4   This passage is a neat expression of Aquinas's general Aristotelian epistemological stance. We should start with the things with which we are more familiar, namely, the things given in our everyday experience, which are, nevertheless, metaphysically posterior to their simple components. But through the careful conceptual analysis of these things we may arrive at the understanding of their simple metaphysical constituents, which will then enable us to see how these constituents can be found even in things beyond our everyday experience.

Chapter 1. The Meanings of the Names of Being and Essence[5]

We should know that, as the Philosopher says in Book 5 of the *Metaphysics*, something is said to be a being [*ens per se*][6] in two different senses: in one sense, [only] those things [are called beings] that are sorted into the ten categories; in the other sense [calling something a being] signifies the truth of a proposition. And the difference between the two is that in the second sense everything can be said to be a being of which a [true] affirmative proposition can be formed, even if it posits nothing in reality; it is in this way that privations and negations are said to be beings, for we say that an affirmation *is* the opposite of negation, and that there *is* blindness in an eye. But in the first sense only that can be said to be a being which posits something in reality.[7] Therefore, blindness and the like are not beings in the first sense. So, the name "essence" [*essentia*] is not derived from "being" [*ens*] in the second sense (for some things are said to be beings in this sense although they do not have an essence, as is clear in the case of privations), but from "being" as it is used in the first sense. This is why the Commentator remarks in the same passage: "'Being' in the first sense signifies the substance of the thing."[8]

And since, as has been said, beings in this sense are sorted into the ten categories; "essence" has to signify something that is common to all natures on account of which various beings fall under the diverse genera and species, as for example humanity is the essence of man, and so on for the rest. And because that by which a thing is constituted in its proper genus or species is what we signify by the definition indicating what [*quid*] this thing is, philosophers changed the name of essence into the name "quiddity" [*quidditas*], and this is what the Philosopher often calls "what something was to be" [*quod quid erat esse*], that

---

5   The division of the text into seven chapters follows the Boyer edition, used for this translation ("Opusculum *De ente et essentia*, introductione et notis auctum," ed. C. Boyer, Textus et Documenta, Series Philosophica, 5: Pontificia Universitas Gregoriana (Rome, 1933)). The chapter titles are added by the translator.

6   Aristotle, *Metaphysics*, Bk. 5, c. 7, 1017a22–3; *Commentary* of St. Thomas, lc. 7. In the passage to which Aquinas refers, Aristotle contrasts "coincidental being" (*ens per accidens*) with "non-coincidental being" [*ens per se*]. A coincidental being is something identified on the basis of merely coincidental features, on account of which it would belong to two different categories; for example, a tall musician, described as such, is a merely coincidental being, described in terms of a quantity (height) and a quality (a capacity to play music). So, the person conceived and described in this way is a merely coincidental being, an *ens per accidens*. On the other hand, the same person considered merely as a human being, as such, is not described in coincidental terms, so, the person considered in this way is an *ens per se*. Obviously, the distinction itself is not a real distinction between two different sorts of things, but a mere distinction of reason between different ways of conceiving of the same thing.

7   This, initially puzzling, distinction between the two main senses of the term "being" is what is often referred to as the distinction between "real being" (*ens reale*) and "being of reason" (*ens rationis*) (sometimes also referred to as "being as true" (*ens ut verum*)). The distinction will at once be less puzzling, if it is read in its proper context, i.e., the "inherence theory of predication" and the corresponding theory of signification, assumed here by Aquinas, without any preliminary explanation. For detailed analyses of this distinction along these lines, see G. Klima, "The Semantic Principles Underlying Saint Thomas Aquinas's Metaphysics of Being," *Medieval Philosophy and Theology*, 5 (1996), pp. 87–141; "Aquinas' Theory of the Copula and the Analogy of Being," *Logical Analysis and History of Philosophy*, 5 (2002), pp. 159–76; "The Changing Role of *Entia Rationis* in Medieval Philosophy: A Comparative Study with a Reconstruction," *Synthese* 96 (1993), pp. 25–59.

8   Averroës, *In Metaph.*, lb. 5, com. 14.

is to say, that on account of which something is what it is. It is also called "form," because "form" signifies the determinate character [*certitudo*] of every thing, as Avicenna says in Book 2 of his *Metaphysics*.[9] It is also called "nature," taking "nature" in the first of the four senses assigned to it by Boethius in his *On Two Natures*,[10] namely, in the sense in which a nature is said to be that which can in any way be apprehended by the intellect. For a thing is intelligible only on account of its essence and definition; and it is also in this sense that the Philosopher in Book 5 of the *Metaphysics* says that every substance is a nature. But the name "nature" taken in this way seems to signify the essence of a thing insofar as it is related to the thing's proper operation, since nothing is deprived of its proper operation. The name "quiddity," on the other hand, is derived from the fact that it is signified by the definition; but it is called "essence" [*essentia*], because it is that through which and in which a thing has its being [*esse*].

Chapter 2. The Essence of Material Substances

But because a substance is said to be a being primarily and without qualification, whereas an accident is a being only secondarily and, as it were, with qualification, only a substance has an essence in a strict and true sense, while an accident has it only somehow, with qualification.

Some substances are simple, others are composite, and both sorts have their essence, but the simple ones in a more genuine and excellent way, just as they have a more excellent way of being. For they are the cause of the composite ones; at least this is true of the first, simple substance, which is God.

However, since the essences of these substances are quite hidden from us, we should begin with the essences of composite substances, so that our discussion may more suitably proceed from the easier subjects.

In composite substances, therefore, form and matter are known [components],[11] as are soul and body in man. But it cannot be said that one of these alone should be called the essence of the thing. That matter alone is not the essence of the thing is clear, because the thing is knowable through its essence, and it is on account of its essence that it falls under its proper species and genus; but its matter is not the principle of cognition of the thing, and it is not on account of its matter that a thing is determined to be in its proper genus or species, but that on account of which it actually exists. However, the form of a thing alone cannot be said to be its essence either, even if some people want to make this claim.[12] For on the basis of what has been said so far it is clear that the essence of a thing is what its definition signifies. But the definition of things of nature contains not only form, but matter as well; otherwise natural definitions would not differ from mathematical

---

9   Avicenna, *Metaph.*, 1, 6; 2, 2.

10   *De persona et duabus naturis*, c. 1. Migne Patrologia Latina (ML), 64, 1341.

11   Matter and form are the obviously given metaphysical components of any material substance, as it is clear from the hylomorphic analysis of physical change, provided by Aquinas in his *On the Principles of Nature*.

12   In particular, Averroës and his followers made this claim against Avicenna. Aquinas sides with Avicenna on the issue. Cf. Aquinas, *In Metaphysica*, lb. 7, lc. 9, n. 1467; *In Quattuor Libros Sententiarum Petri Lombardi* (*SN*) 4, d. 44, q. 1, a. 1b, resp. 2.

definitions.[13] And it cannot be said that matter is included in the definition of a natural substance as something added to its essence, or as something existing outside of its essence, for this sort of definition is proper to accidents, which do not have perfect essence, and therefore they have to receive in their definition their subject, which is outside their essence.[14] It is clear, therefore, that essence comprises both matter and form.

Nevertheless, it cannot be said that "essence" signifies a relation between matter and form, or something superadded to these, because that would necessarily be an accident or extrinsic to the thing, and the thing would not be known on account of it, none of which can apply to an essence. For by the form, which is the actuality of matter, matter is made into an actual being and *this* [particular] thing [*hoc aliquid*]. Therefore, whatever supervenes does not give actual being to matter absolutely speaking, but it makes it actual in some respect, just as accidents do, as whiteness makes something actually white. So, when a form of this sort is acquired, the thing is not said to be generated absolutely speaking, but only in some respect.

What remains, therefore, is that the name "essence" in composite substances signifies what is composed of matter and form. And Boethius agrees with this position in his *Commentary on the Categories*, when he says that *ousia* signifies something composite; for *ousia* signifies the same for the Greeks as "essence" does for us, as he says in his *On Two Natures*. Avicenna also says that the quiddity of composite substances is the composition of matter and form itself.[15] And even Averroës declares in his *Commentary* on Book 7 of the *Metaphysics*: "the nature that the species of generable and corruptible things have is a certain intermediary, that is, composed of matter and form."[16]

And reason agrees with this as well, for the act of being [*esse*] of a composite substance is neither of the form alone, nor of matter alone, but of the composite itself; and the essence is that on account of which the thing is said to be. Therefore, the essence, on account of which the thing is denominated a "being," cannot be the form alone or the matter alone, but has to be both, although it is the form that causes this act of being in its own way. We can see also in cases of other things composed of several principles that the thing is not denominated on account of only one of those principles that constitute it, but on account of what comprises both, as is clear in the case of flavors: for sweetness is caused by the action of warmth spreading wetness, and although in this way warmth causes sweetness, still, a body is not denominated sweet on account of its warmth, but on account of its flavor, which comprises both warmth and wetness.[17]

---

13   For example, the geometrical definition of a sphere would not differ from the natural definition of a pearl. But even if all pearls are essentially spherical (more or less), they also essentially consist of layers of crystallized calcium carbonate held together by conchiolin, which is why not all spherical bodies are pearls.

14   This point is discussed in more detail in c. 7 below, considering the definition of "pugness," which is necessarily a curvature of a nose, but in and of itself is the curvature only, having to have a nose as its subject. Cf. also n. 67 below.

15   Avicenna, *Metaph.*, 5, 5.

16   Averroës, *In Metaph.*, 7, 7, com. 27.

17   The example, based on the somewhat obscure Aristotelian doctrine of how the composite qualities of mixed bodies can be derived from the interaction of the simple active and passive qualities of the four elements, is not very illuminating to us. But the point is clear, and can, in fact, be illustrated by another, more familiar example: punch flavor is caused by mixing various fruit juices (and maybe some rum). Still, a punch-flavored cake or scoop of ice cream is not denominated by any of the components, but by the composite flavor resulting from the mixture.

However, since the principle of individuation is matter, from this it may appear to follow that the essence, which comprises both matter and form, is only particular and not universal, from which it would further follow that universals would not have definitions, if an essence is something that the definition signifies.

And for this reason we should know that matter considered in just any way is not the principle of individuation, but only designated matter is. And by *designated matter* I mean matter considered under determinate dimensions. This matter is not included in the definition of man as such, but it would be included in Socrates' definition, if Socrates had a definition. The definition of man, on the other hand, includes non-designated matter; for the definition of man does not include this bone or this flesh, but bones and flesh absolutely, which are the non-designated matter of man.[18]

Chapter 3. The Composition of Material Substances

In this way it is clear that the essence of man and the essence of Socrates differ only as designated and non-designated, and this is why the Commentator declares in his *Commentary on Book 7 of the Metaphysics*: "Socrates is nothing other than animality and rationality, which are his quiddity."[19] It is also in the same way that the essence of the genus and the essence of the species differ as designated and non-designated, although the manner of designation is different in the two cases. For the designation of the individual with respect to the species takes place through matter determined by dimensions, whereas the designation of the species regarding the genus occurs through a constitutive difference, which is taken from the form of the thing.

But the determination or designation of the species with respect to the genus is not through anything in the essence of the species that would in no way be in the essence of the genus; rather, whatever is in the species is also in the genus indeterminately. For if an animal were not the same as the whole that is a man, but only a part of it, then *animal* would not be predicated of *man*, for no integral part is predicated of its whole.

We can see how this happens if we consider how *body*, insofar as it is taken to be a part of an animal, differs from *body*, insofar as it is taken to be a genus; for it cannot be a genus in the sense in which it is an integral part. The name "body," therefore, can be taken in several senses. For a body, insofar as it is in the genus of substance, is said to be a body because it has a nature on account of which three dimensions can be designated in it; while

---

18   It is important to note here that the difference between designated and non-designated matter is, again, not a difference between two different kinds of entities, but rather a difference between two different ways of considering the same kind of entity; that is to say, the distinction between designated and non-designated matter is not a real distinction, but a distinction of reason. All matter in reality is designated matter, i.e., concrete chunks of matter existing under the determinate dimensions of the individual bodies they constitute. But just as the individuals can be considered in a universal manner, disregarding their individuating features, so their matter can be considered generally, not as this or that particular chunk of matter. And it is obvious that it is only matter considered in this way that can be signified by the definition of the species (the definition that signifies the specific essence of each individual), for it is clear that the definition of man, for example, cannot signify the flesh and bones of Socrates as *this* particular matter belonging to Socrates, for otherwise all men (i.e., all individuals having the essence signified by this definition) ought to have Socrates' flesh and bones, which is clearly absurd. Cf. n. 26 below.

19   Averroës, *In Metaph.*, 7, c. 5, com. 20.

the three designated dimensions themselves are the body which is in the genus of quantity. But it happens that something that has some perfection also reaches a further perfection, as is obvious in the case of man, who has a sensitive nature and beyond that also an intellective one. Likewise, to the perfection of a thing's having a form on account of which three dimensions can be designated in it, a further perfection can be added, such as life, or something like that. The name "body," therefore, can signify something which has a form from which there follows the designatability of three dimensions exclusively, namely, in such way that from that form no further perfection would follow, but if something is added, then it is beyond the signification of "body" in this sense. And in this sense the body will be an integral and material part of an animal, for in this way the soul will be beyond the signification of the name "body," and it will be superadded to the body itself, so that the animal will be constituted from these two, namely, from the soul and the body, as its parts.

But the name "body" can also be taken to signify some thing that has a form on account of which three dimensions can be designated in it, whatever that form may be, whether it may give rise to some further perfection or not. And in this sense *body* will be a genus of *animal*, because *animal* contains nothing that is not contained implicitly in *body*. For the soul is not another form than that on account of which in that thing three dimensions can be designated;[20] and so when it was said that a body is something that has a form on account of which three dimensions can be designated in it, this form was understood to be *any* form, regardless of whether it is animality or lapideity [rock-ness] or anything else of this sort. And in this way the form of *animal* is implicitly contained in the form of *body*, insofar as *body* is its genus.

There is a similar relationship between *man* and *animal*. For if "animal" only named a thing that has the perfection of sensing and moving on account of an intrinsic principle *with the exclusion* of any further perfection, then any further supervening perfection would be related to *animal* as to a part, and not as implicitly contained in the notion of *animal*. And in this way *animal* would not be a genus. But it *is* a genus insofar as it signifies a certain thing whose form can give rise to sensation and motion, no matter what sort of form it is, whether it is a sensitive soul only or a soul that is sensitive and rational as well. In this way, therefore, the genus indeterminately signifies the whole that is in the species, for it does not signify only matter.

Likewise, the difference signifies the whole and not only form; and even the definition signifies the whole, as does the species, but in different ways. For the genus signifies the whole as a certain denomination determining what is material in the thing without determining its proper form; and the genus is taken from matter, although it is not matter. Hence it is clear that something is said to be a body because it has the perfection that three dimensions can be designated in it, which is a perfection that is related as something material to the further perfections. The difference, on the other hand, is a certain determination taken from a determinate form without having some determinate matter in its primary notion, as is clear in the case of *animate*, namely, something that has a soul [*anima*], for this does not determine

---

20   This is an important expression of Aquinas's famous, and in his time very controversial, thesis of the unity of substantial forms. For a detailed discussion of this passage, see G. Klima, "Man = Body + Soul: Aquinas's Arithmetic of Human Nature," in B. Davies (ed.), *Thomas Aquinas: Contemporary Philosophical Perspectives*, Oxford: Oxford University Press, pp. 257–73. For more discussion of the thesis and its history, see D. A. Callus, "Forms, Unicity and Plurality of," in *New Catholic Encyclopedia*, New York: McGraw-Hill; 1967–79.

what sort of thing it is, whether a body or something else. This is why Avicenna says[21] that the genus is not understood in the difference as a part of its essence, but only as something outside its essence, just as their subject is not part of the understanding of attributes [*passiones*]; and so the genus is not predicated of the difference *per se*, as the Philosopher remarks in Book 3 of the *Metaphysics* and Book 4 of the *Topics*,[22] except, perhaps, in the way the subject is predicated of the attribute. But the definition and the species comprise both, namely, the determinate matter designated by the name of the genus and the determinate form designated by the name of the difference.

And from this it is clear why the genus, difference, and species are analogous to matter, form, and the composite in nature, although they are not identical with them. For the genus is not matter, but is taken from matter as signifying the whole, and the difference is not form, but is taken from the form as signifying the whole. Therefore, we say that man is a rational animal, but not that man is *composed of* animal and rational, as we say that man is *composed of* body and soul. For man is said to be composed of soul and body, as a third thing constituted by two things, neither of which is identical with it. For a man is neither soul nor body. But if *man* is somehow said to consist of *animal* and *rational*, then it will not be a third thing constituted by two other things, but rather a third concept constituted by two other concepts. For the concept of *animal* does not determine the specific form expressing the nature of the thing, because it is material with respect to the ultimate perfection; and the concept of the difference *rational* consists in the determination of the specific form; and the concept of the definition or species is constituted by these two concepts. Therefore, just as a thing constituted by others cannot be said to be any of those that constitute it, so a concept cannot be said to be any of the concepts that constitute it; for we do not say that the definition is the genus or the difference.

Although the genus signifies the entire essence of the species, still, the several species in the same genus do not have to have the same essence; for the unity of the genus stems from its indetermination or indifference. However, this does *not* happen in such a manner that what the genus signifies is some numerically one nature in the diverse species having some other thing supervening on it, namely, the difference determining it, as the form determines matter that is numerically one; *rather*, this happens because the genus signifies some form, but not determinately this or that form, which in turn is determinately expressed by the difference; however, this [determinately expressed form] is nothing else but what was indeterminately signified by the genus.[23] And this is why the Commentator says in his *Commentary* on Book 12 of the *Metaphysics* that prime matter is said to be one on account of the removal of all forms, but the genus is one on account of the community of the form signified.[24] So, it is clear that the addition of the difference, which removes the indetermination that was the cause of the unity of the genus, yields essentially diverse species.

And since, as has been said, the nature of the species is indeterminate with respect to the individual, just as the nature of the genus is with respect to the species, therefore, just as

---

21   Avicenna, *Metaph.*, 5, 6.

22   Aristotle, *Metaph.*, 3, 3, 998b24; St. Thomas's *Commentary*, lc. 7; *Topics*, 4, 2, 122b20; 6, 6, 144a32.

23   So, "animal" indeterminately signifies the animality of Socrates and the animality of his dog. But Socrates' animality is nothing else but his humanity, which is determinately signified by the difference "rational," and his dog's animality is nothing else but his "caninity" (dogginess), which is determinately signified by the proper specific difference of dogs (whatever that is).

24   Averroës, *In Metaph.*, 12, com 14.

the genus, insofar as it is predicated of the species, contains[25] in its signification everything that is determinately in the species, although indistinctly, so the species, insofar as it is predicated of the individual, has to signify everything that is essentially in the individual, although indistinctly; and this is how the essence of the species is signified by the name "man"; therefore, "man" is predicated of Socrates. However, if the nature of the species is signified with the exclusion of designated matter, which is the principle of individuation, then it is related to the individual as its part, and this is how it is signified by the name "humanity"; for "humanity" signifies that on account of which a man is a man. But designated matter is not that on account of which a man is a man, and so it is not contained in any way among the things from which a man has it that he is a man. Since, therefore, "humanity" includes in its understanding *only* those things from which a man has it that he is a man, it is clear that designated matter is excluded or cut off from its signification. And since a part is not predicated of the whole, this is why "humanity" is not predicated of a man or of Socrates.[26] This is why Avicenna remarks that the quiddity of the composite [substance] is not the composite [substance], although the quiddity itself is composite; just as humanity, even if it is composite, nevertheless, is not a man, but it has to be received in something, which is designated matter.

But, as has been said, the designation of the species regarding the genus is by means of forms, whereas the designation of the individual regarding the species is by means of

25   We get this translation by amending the text with the addition of the obviously missing verb "continet."

26   That is to say, the propositions: "A man is a humanity" and "Socrates is a humanity" are false. This is an expression of Aquinas' metaphysical claim that a material substance cannot be identical with its essence, but its essence is its part that is really distinct both from the whole and from the other part of the same individual, namely, its designated matter. Note that the real distinction between the specific essence and the designated matter of the same individual is not the same as the real distinction between the matter and substantial form of the same individual, although both distinctions are based on the materiality of the individual in question. These are two different ways of conceptually "carving up" the same individual. (This does not have to mean, however, that the parts thus distinguished are not really distinct: just because we can conceptually distinguish the left half and the right half, as well as the top half and the bottom half of a body, it does not mean that these parts are not really distinct regardless of whether we distinguish them or not.) The (prime) matter and substantial form of the same individual are distinguished on account of the analysis of substantial change: the prime matter of a thing is what takes on a new substantial form when the thing ceases to be, and a new thing comes to be from it, say, when hydrogen turns into helium in a nuclear fusion, or when a living being dies and turns into a corpse. Therefore, the form so distinguished excludes this matter from its notion. But the essence signified by the definition, as we could see above, does not exclude matter in general, but only *this* designated matter in particular (see n. 18 above), and only when it is signified exclusively, by the abstract form of the name of the species, as by the name "humanity." So, this essence, as signified by this term, is a formal component of the whole substance, received in, and individuated by, the designated matter of this substance. But this formal component is not exactly the same as the substantial form which is received in prime matter, for this formal component comprises both matter and form considered in general, excluding only what individuates them, namely, this designated matter, which is why this formal component, the essence, is also referred to as "the form of the whole" (*forma totius*), to distinguish it from "the form of the part" (*forma partis*), which is the form referred to in the other division, distinguishing substantial form and prime matter. So, an individual material substance, say, Socrates (disregarding his accidents) = substantial form (*forma partis*) + prime matter = essence (*forma totius*) + designated matter. Besides these two divisions of Socrates, there is a third one, not coinciding with either of these two, according to which Socrates = body + soul.

matter; therefore, the name signifying that from which the nature of the genus is taken *with the exclusion* of the determinate form that perfects the species has to signify the material part of the whole, as for example the body is the material part of man; while the name signifying that from which the nature of the species is taken, *with the exclusion* of designated matter, has to signify the formal part. So, humanity is signified as a sort of form, and is said to be the form of the whole [*forma totius*], but not, as it were, as something added over and above the essential parts, namely, form and matter, as the form of a house is added over and above its integral parts, but rather it is a form that is a whole, namely, comprising both matter and form, however, with the exclusion of those things that are apt to designate matter.[27]

In this way it is clear that the essence of man is signified both by the name "man" and by the name "humanity," but differently, as has been said. For the name "man" signifies it as a whole, namely, insofar as it does not exclude the designation of matter, but contains it implicitly and indistinctly, just as we said the genus contains the difference. And this is why the name "man" is predicated of the individuals. But the name "humanity" signifies it as a part, because it contains in its signification only what pertains to a man insofar as he is a man, and excludes all designation of matter; therefore it is not predicated of individual humans. And for this reason, the name "essence" is sometimes found to be predicated of a thing, for it is said that Socrates[28] is a certain essence; and sometimes it is negated, when we say that Socrates' essence is not Socrates.

Chapter 4. The Essence of Material Substance and the Logical Intentions

Having seen what is signified by the name "essence" in material substances, we should see how it is related to the notions of genus, species, and difference. Now, since that to which the notion of genus, species, or difference applies is predicated of this designated individual,[29] the notion of a universal, that is, of genus or species, cannot apply to essence insofar as it is signified as a part, for example, by the name "humanity" or "animality." And this is why Avicenna says that rationality is not a difference, but the principle of a difference;[30] and for the same reason, humanity is not a species, nor is animality a genus. Likewise, one cannot say that the notion of genus or species applies to essence insofar as it is something existing outside the singulars, as the Platonists believed; for in this way the genus and species would not be predicated of this individual; for it cannot be said that Socrates is something that is separate from him; and neither would that separate thing be of any use in the cognition of this singular. Therefore, it remains that the notion of genus or species applies to essence insofar as it is signified as a whole, for example, by the names "man" or "animal," as it implicitly and indistinctly contains all that is in the individual.

But a nature or essence so taken can be considered in two ways. In one way, according to its proper notion; and this is its absolute consideration. And in this way nothing is true

27 "Those things that are apt to designate matter" are the dimensions of the material substance, whereby it occupies its location in space, as distinct from other bodies.

28 Correcting the text's "Socratis" to "Socrates."

29 This is because according to the "canonical" definitions of Porphyry in his *Isagoge* (which was often referred to as *Praedicabilia*), all universals are "predicables," i.e., items that can be predicated of several individuals.

30 Avicenna, *Metaph.*, 5, 6.

of it except what pertains to it on account of what it is; therefore, if anything else is attributed to it, then the attribution is false. For example, to a man, on account of being a man, it pertains to be rational and animal and anything else that is in his definition; to be white or black, however, and anything else that is not involved in the notion of humanity does not pertain to a man on account of being a man. Therefore, if it is asked whether this nature considered in this way can be said to be one or many, neither alternative should be accepted, because both are outside of the understanding of humanity, and either can pertain to it. For if plurality were included in its understanding, then it could never be one, although it is one insofar as it is in Socrates. Likewise, if unity were included in its notion and understanding, then Socrates and Plato would have [numerically] one and the same nature, and it could not be multiplied in several things.[31] In the other way nature is considered according to its existence in this or that thing. And in this way something can be predicated of it accidentally [per accidens], on account of the thing in which it is. For example, it is said that a man is white, because Socrates is white, although this [i.e., being white] does not pertain to a man on account of being a man.

This nature has two sorts of existence [esse]: one in the singulars, another in the soul, and accidents follow upon this nature on account of each. And in the singulars it has several acts of existence [esse] according to the diversity of singulars. But the nature itself, according to its proper, that is absolute, consideration, does not have to have any of these. For it is false to say that the nature of man as such should have existence in this singular, for then it could never exist outside this singular [i.e., in another singular]; likewise, if it pertained to [the nature of] man as such *not* to exist in this singular, then it would never exist in this singular. But it is true to say that to [the nature of] man as such it does not pertain that it should exist in this singular or in that one or in the soul. It is clear, therefore, that the nature of man absolutely considered abstracts from all existence, without, however, excluding any of them.[32] And it is the nature considered in this way that is predicated of all the individuals [that have this nature].[33]

Nevertheless, one cannot say that the notion of universals applies to natures taken in this way; for the concept of universals includes unity and community,[34] but neither of these applies to human nature according to its absolute consideration. For if community were understood

31 This is why it is useful to think of this "common nature," i.e., the essence of any thing considered absolutely, as the common information content informing several individuals in its several instances, just as the common information content of a book is multiplied in its several copies, or the same genetic information is multiplied and reproduced in several generations of individual living things.
32 So the common nature as such is indifferent to any act of being and so to any mode of being, which is why it can exist in any appropriate singular subject in different ways, i.e., as the common information content of all these singulars, it can exist encoded in different media, whether in the soul or in the actual individuals, just as the same song, for example, can be encoded in magnetic or optical media, or as actual vibrations of the air, i.e., actual sounds.
33 Clearly, the predicate of the sentence "Socrates is a man" attributes to Socrates only what pertains to the nature signified by it according to its absolute consideration. For knowing that this sentence is true, we know that Socrates is a rational animal, and that he is a sensitive living body, etc., namely, whatever is involved in being a man as such, but we certainly do not know whether he is black or white, short or tall, handsome or ugly, etc., anything that does not pertain to human nature according to its actual consideration.
34 For according to one formulaic definition, *universale est unum commune multis*, a universal is [something] one common to many.

to be implied in the concept of man, then there would have to be community in anything in which there is humanity; but this is false, since there is no community in Socrates, but whatever is in him is individuated. Similarly, it cannot be said that the notion of genus or species applies to human nature insofar as it exists in individuals; for in the individuals human nature does not have the sort of unity according to which it is some single thing pertaining to all [of the same nature], which the notion of universals requires.

It remains, therefore, that the notion of species applies to human nature insofar as it exists in the intellect. For human nature itself exists in the intellect abstracted from all individuating conditions, whence it is uniformly related to all individuals [of this nature] outside the soul, being equally a similitude of all, and thus leading to the cognition of all, insofar as they are humans. And since it has this sort of relation to all individuals [of this nature], the intellect forms the notion of species and attributes to it,[35] and this is why the Commentator remarks in his commentary on Book 1 of *On the Soul* that it is the intellect that produces universality in things;[36] Avicenna also makes the same point in his *Metaphysics*.[37]

Now, although this nature as understood is universal, insofar as it is compared to the things outside the soul, for it is one similitude of them all, nevertheless, insofar as it exists in this or in that intellect, it is some particular species actually understood [*species intellecta*]. And from this it is easy to see the error of the Commentator who, in his commentary on Book 3 of *On the Soul*, on the basis of the universality of the form understood, wanted to conclude that there is a single intellect for all human beings; for that form is not universal in its existence that it has in the intellect, but insofar as it is a similitude of things, just as if there were a corporeal statue representing several people, it is obvious that the image or shape of the statue would have its own singular act of existence [*esse*], insofar as it would exist in this matter, but it would be common, insofar as it would be a common representation of several things.

Since human nature is predicated of Socrates according to its absolute consideration, and that it is a species does not pertain to it according to its absolute consideration, but it is one of the accidents it acquires on account of its being in the intellect, the name "species" is not predicated of Socrates, so that one could say "Socrates is a species." But this would have to be the case if the notion of species pertained to [the nature of] man on account of the being

---

35   "For it is not necessary that if this is a man and that is a man, then they should have the same humanity, just as there is no numerically one whiteness in two white things; rather, all that is needed is that one should be similar to the other in that this one has a humanity just as does the other; whence the intellect, taking humanity not insofar as it is the humanity of this one, but insofar as it is humanity, forms an intention common to all." *SN* 2 d. 17, q. 1, a. 1. Cf. "The individuation of the common nature in corporeal and material things comes from the corporeal matter contained under determinate dimensions; whereas a universal is abstracted from this sort of matter and from the individuating material conditions. Therefore, it is clear that a similitude of a thing received in a sense [organ] represents the thing insofar as it is singular, while received in the intellect, it represents the thing on account of its universal nature; and this is why the senses cognize singulars, and the intellect universals, and that the sciences concern the latter." *In De Anima*, II, lc. 12. Cf. *In Post.*, II, lc. 20. Cf. G. Klima, "The Medieval Problem of Universals," *The Stanford Encyclopedia of Philosophy* (Winter 2004 edn), ed. Edward N. Zalta, <http://plato.stanford.edu/archives/win2004/entries/universals-medieval/>.

36   Averroës, *In De Anima*, 1, com. 8: "one should not believe that the definitions of genera and species are definitions of general things existing outside the soul; rather, they are definitions of particular things, but the intellect produces universality in them."

37   Avicenna, *Metaph.*, 5, 2: "Universality exists only in the soul."

it has in Socrates, or according to its absolute consideration, namely, insofar as he is a man, for whatever pertains to a man insofar as he is a man is predicated of Socrates. Nevertheless, "to be predicated" pertains to a genus *per se*, for it is included in its definition.[38] For predication is something completed by the action of the judgment-forming intellect, but having some foundation in reality, namely the unity of those [things] of which one is predicated of the other. Therefore, the notion of predicability can be included in the definition of the intention that is the genus, and this is likewise completed by an act of the intellect. Still, that to which the intellect attributes the intention of predicability (predicating it of something else), is not the intention of genus, but rather that to which the intellect attributes the intention of genus, as it is signified by the name "animal."[39]

It is clear, therefore, how essence is related to the notion of species; for the notion of species is not one of those [attributes] that pertain to it according to its absolute consideration, nor is it one of those accidents that follow upon it on account of the existence it has outside the soul, such as whiteness or blackness, but it is one of those accidents that follow upon it on account of the existence it has in the intellect; and it is also in the same way that the notion of genus or difference applies to it.

Chapter 5. On the Essence of Immaterial Substances

Now it remains to be seen how essence is found in separate substances, namely, in the soul, in the intelligences [i.e., angels], and the first cause [i.e., God]. Although everybody acknowledges the simplicity of the first cause, nevertheless, some people want to introduce the composition of matter and form in the intelligences and the soul. This position originates from Avicebron, the author of the book called *The Fountain of Life*. But this contradicts the common teaching of philosophers, who called them substances separate from matter, and proved them to be without any matter whatsoever. The most powerful demonstration of this claim proceeds from their ability to understand.

It is clear that forms are not actually intelligible, unless they are separated from matter and its [individuating] conditions, and they are not rendered actually intelligible, except by the power of an intelligent substance, insofar as it receives them and works on them. Therefore, an intelligent substance has to be immune from matter in every way, so that it neither has matter as its part, nor does it exist as a form impressed in matter, as is the case with material forms.

And it cannot be said that intelligibility is impeded not by just any sort of matter, but only by corporeal matter. For if this feature, namely, that it impedes intelligibility, pertained only to corporeal matter as such, then matter would have to have this feature from the corporeal form, since matter is called corporeal only insofar as it is informed by the corporeal form.[40] But this cannot be the case, because the corporeal form itself is actually intelligible, just as

---

38   For according to the definition of Porphyry, a genus is something that can be predicated of several specifically different things in response to the question "What is this?".

39   That is to say, although the above-mentioned definition of the term "genus" includes that a genus is predicable, still, this definition does not state it of the intention of genus (expressed by the term "genus") that it is predicable, but of that to which the term "genus" (as well as its definition) applies, namely, to a generic concept, such as the concept expressed by the term "animal." Cf. *ST* 1 q. 85, a. 2, ad 2, included in section 10 of this volume.

40   "The corporeal form" (*forma corporalis*) Aquinas is talking about here is the form of corporeity [*corporeitas*], the form signified by the name "body" (*corpus*).

any other form that is abstracted from matter. Therefore, in the soul or in the intelligences there is no composition of matter and form in any way, so that they could be understood to have matter in the same sense in which corporeal substances do. But there is the composition of form and existence [*esse*] in them. Whence in the commentary on the ninth proposition of *The Book of Causes* it is stated that an intelligence is something having form and existence; and "form" is taken there for the quiddity or the simple nature itself.

And it is easy to see how this can be the case. For if two things are related in such a way that one of them is the cause of existence of the other, then the cause can exist without the other, but not conversely. But this is the relationship between matter and form, because form gives existence to matter; therefore, matter cannot exist without a form, but it is not impossible for a form to exist without matter. For a form, insofar as it is a form, does not have to depend on matter, but if one finds forms that cannot exist without matter, this happens to be the case because of their distance from the first principle, which is the first, pure actuality. So, those forms that are the closest to the first principle are forms subsisting without matter, for the whole genus of forms does not require matter, as has been said, and forms of this sort are the intelligences; so, the essences or quiddities of these substances do not have to be other than their form itself.

The difference, therefore, between the essence of a simple substance and that of a composite substance is that the essence of a composite substance is not only the form, but it comprises both form and matter, whereas the essence of a simple substance is its form only. And this gives rise to two other differences.

The first is that the essence of a composite substance can be signified either as a whole or a part, which results from the designation of matter, as has been explained. Therefore, the essence of a composite thing is not predicated in every way of the composite thing itself, for we cannot say that a man is his own quiddity.[41] But the essence of a simple thing, which is its form, can only be signified as a whole, for there is nothing there apart from the form, so there is nothing that could receive the form. Therefore, no matter how we consider the essence of a simple substance, it is predicated of the simple substance. This is why Avicenna says that the quiddity of a simple substance is the simple substance itself, for there is nothing else [in the simple substance] to receive it.

The second difference is that the essences of composite things, since they are received in designated matter, are multiplied by the division of designated matter, whence in their case it happens that there are numerically distinct things in the same species. However, since the essence of a simple thing is not received in matter, in their case there cannot be this kind of multiplication; therefore, in the case of these substances, there cannot be several individuals in the same species, but there are as many species as there are individuals, as Avicenna expressly claims.[42]

However, these substances, although they are only forms without matter, are not simple in every way, so that they would be pure actuality, but they are mixed with potentiality, which is clear from the following.

41   The essence of the composite thing is not predicated of it as it is signified exclusively, by means of an abstract term (say, "humanity"), but it *is* predicated of the thing as it is signified non-exclusively, by means of a concrete term (say, "man"). But the essence of a simple thing is predicated of the thing whether it is signified by a concrete term (say, "angel") or by an abstract term (say, "angelity"). So, while it is true that Socrates is a man, it is not true that Socrates is a humanity; but it is true that Gabriel is an angelity just as well as it is true that Gabriel is an angel. Compare the end of c. 3.

42   Avicenna, *Metaph.*, 5, 5.

Whatever is not included in the understanding of an essence or quiddity is coming to it from outside, entering into composition with the essence; for no essence can be understood without its parts. But every essence can be understood without even thinking about its existence, for I can understand what a man or a phoenix is, and not know whether it actually exists in the nature of things.[43] Therefore, it is clear that existence is distinct from essence, unless, perhaps, there is a thing whose quiddity is its own existence. And this thing would have to be unique and the first [being]. For something can only be multiplied either by the addition of some difference, as the nature of the genus is multiplied in the species, or on account of the reception of a form in diverse pieces of matter, as the nature of the species is multiplied in several individuals, or on account of one of the things multiplied being separate and the other received in something; for example, if there were some separate warmth, then it would be separate from a non-separate warmth [i.e., the warmth of a warm body] on account of its separation itself. However, if there were a thing that is existence only, so that it would be subsistent existence itself [*ipsum esse subsistens*], then this existence would not receive the addition of a difference, for then it would no longer be existence only, but existence and some form besides; and even less would it be receptive of the addition of matter, for then it would already be not subsistent, but material existence. Therefore, it remains that there can only be one thing that is its own existence. And so, in any other thing, the existence of the thing has to be other than its quiddity or nature or form. Therefore, the intelligences have to have existence besides their form, which is why it was said that an intelligence is form and existence.

Now, everything that a thing has[44] is either caused in it by its own principles, as the ability to laugh in man, or it comes to the thing from an external source, as the light in the air is coming from the sun. But the existence of a thing cannot be caused by its form or quiddity itself (I mean, as by an efficient cause), for then a thing would be its own cause, and would bring itself into existence, which is impossible. Therefore, all such things, namely, those that have their existence as something distinct from their nature, have to have their existence from something else. However, since everything that is through something else [*per aliud*] is reduced to what is through itself [*per se*] as its first cause, there has to be something that is the cause of existence for everything, since it is existence only. For otherwise the series of causes would go to infinity, since every thing that is not existence only has a cause for its existence, as has been said. It is clear, therefore, that an intelligence is both form and existence, and that it has its existence from the first being that is existence only; and this is the first cause, which is God.

---

43   Despite modern presumptions to the contrary, Aquinas did not take a phoenix to be a merely fictitious, mythical bird by definition. Cf. G. Klima, "On Kenny on Aquinas on Being: A Critical Review of *Aquinas on Being* by Anthony Kenny," feature review in *International Philosophical Quarterly*, 44 (2004), pp. 567–80. So, for Aquinas, the phoenix is rather the illustration of a real, yet ephemeral natural phenomenon, much like a lunar eclipse or a rainbow, of which we may have the scientific definition (and thus we may know perfectly well its real essence, as opposed to merely knowing the meaning of its name), and yet we may not know whether its real essence is presently actualized in any actually existing individual.

44   "Everything that a thing has" is implicitly contrasted with "what a thing *is*," i.e., what a thing is by its essence. For of course what a thing *is* by its essence is not *caused* in the thing either by intrinsic or by extrinsic principles. This is the reason why God, who *is* existence, is absolutely *uncaused*, whereas everything that merely *has* existence has to have it *caused* by something.

Everything that receives something from something else is in potentiality with respect to what it receives and the latter is its actuality. Therefore, the quiddity or form that is the intelligence has to be in potentiality with respect to the existence it receives from God, while the existence received is its actuality. And in this way there is potentiality and actuality in the intelligences, although not form and matter, unless equivocally. Thus, also to undergo [change], to receive, to be a subject, and the like, which appear to pertain to things on account of their matter, equivocally apply to intellectual substances and to corporeal ones, as the Commentator remarks in Book 3 of On the Soul.[45] And since, as has been said, the quiddity of an intelligence is the intelligence itself, its quiddity or essence is what itself is, and its existence received from God is that by which it subsists in the nature of things. For this reason, these substances are said to be composed of that *from which* something is [*ex quo est*] and *that which* is [*quod est*], or that which exists [*id quod est*] and existence [*esse*], as Boethius declares.[46]

And since intelligences have potentiality and actuality, it is not difficult to see how there can be a multitude of intelligences, which would be impossible if they had no potentiality whatsoever. This is why the Commentator says in his commentary on Book 3 of On the Soul that if we did not know the nature of the possible intellect, then we could not discover the multitude of separate substances.[47] So, they are distinguished by the different degrees of potentiality and actuality, so that a superior intelligence, which is closer to the first, has more actuality and less potentiality, and so on for the rest. And this series is completed in the human soul, which is at the lowest grade among intellectual substances. Therefore, the possible intellect is related to intelligible forms as prime matter (which is at the lowest grade among sensible beings) is related to sensible forms, as the Commentator remarks in his commentary on Book 3 of On the Soul.[48] And for this reason the Philosopher compares it to a clean slate on which nothing is written.[49] Therefore, since among other intellectual substances it has the greatest amount of potentiality, it is so close to material substances that it attracts a material thing to share its existence, so that from the soul and the body there results a single existence in one composite thing; although that existence, insofar as it is the existence of the soul, is not dependent on the body.[50] Therefore, after this form, which is the soul, we find other forms that have even more of potentiality and are closer to matter, so that they have no existence without matter. But even among these we find some order and degrees down to the forms of elements that are the closest to matter. So these do not even have any operation except what is demanded by the active and passive qualities and those that dispose matter to receive form.[51]

---

45   Averroës, *In De Anima*, 3, com. 14.

46   Boethius, *De hebdom*. ML 64, col. 1311 C.

47   Averroës, *In De Anima*, 3, com. 5.

48   Averroës, *In De Anima*, 3, com. 5.

49   Aristotle, *De Anima*, 3, c. 4, 429b31.

50   Besides his thesis of the unity of substantial forms, this is Aquinas' most fundamental metaphysical rationale for his uncompromising position on the substantial unity of body and soul, markedly distinguishing his philosophical anthropology from all forms of dualism both before him (Plato, Augustine, medieval Augustinians) and after him (Descartes, and post-Cartesian philosophy up to the present day), as well as from materialism.

51   This is an allusion to Aristotle's doctrine in his "On Coming to Be and Passing Away" (*De Generatione et Corruptione*), according to which each of the four elements is characterized by a pair of active and passive qualities (active: hot, cold; passive: wet, dry), which account for the material dispositions of all natural bodies, based on the various proportions of the elements that make them up.

Chapter 6. An Overview of the Essences of Substances in Relation to Logical Intentions

Having seen these points, it should be clear how essence is found in various things. Among substances, there are three ways of having their essence: for there is something, namely, God, whose essence is his own existence; and for this reason there are philosophers who say that God does not have a quiddity or essence, because his essence is not something other than his existence. And from this it follows that he is not in a genus. For everything that is in a genus has to have its essence *besides* its existence, since the quiddity or nature of their genus or species is not distinguished on account of the nature of those things of which these are the genus or species, but existence is diverse in the diverse things.[52]

Nevertheless, if we say that God is existence only, we still do not have to fall into the error of those who stated that God is that universal existence whereby each and every thing formally exists.[53] For the existence that is God is of such a condition that nothing can be added to it; therefore, it is distinct from every other existence by its own purity itself.[54] And for this reason, in the commentary of the ninth proposition of *The Book of Causes* it is stated that the first cause, which is existence only, is individuated through its own pure

---

52   This argument is stated in a very condensed form in the text, so it needs some explication. The idea is that if there are several things in the same genus or species, then they are obviously not distinguished by their generic or specific nature, since they belong to the same genus or species precisely on account of sharing *the same* generic or specific nature. Therefore, since they *are* nevertheless distinct, they have to be distinct on account of their distinct acts of existence (which in turn are distinct, of course, on account of the relevant principles of specification and individuation, namely, on account of the specific differences of different species in the same genus, and the distinct parcels of designated matter of the different individuals in the same species). So, if the generic or specific nature of several things in the same genus or species *is not* the reason why they are distinct, but their existence *is*, then the generic or specific nature of these things must be distinct from their existence. That is to say, if something is in a genus or a species, then its existence must be distinct from its essence, whence if the existence of something is *not* distinct from its essence, then it is *not* in a genus or a species. Therefore, divine nature cannot fall under any specific or generic concept, which means that divine nature cannot have a quidditative definition (which would have to contain at least a generic concept); all we can have is several partial characterizations of divine essence, which, however, is ultimately inexhaustible and incomprehensible by means of our finite concepts. Cf. *ST* 1 q. 3, a. 5, the third argument in the body of the article.

53   This was the pantheistic error of the Amalricians (Lat. *Almarici, Almariani, Amauriani*), the followers of Amalric of Bena (in French, Amaury de Bène or de Chartres, in Latin, *Almaricus, Amalricus, Amauricus*), a professor at the University of Paris, who died between 1204 and 1207. The Amalricians managed to establish a secret sect (allegedly devoted to ritualistic orgies, in the name of *everything* being divine), which was discovered and eradicated by the authorities in 1210. Their leaders, after refusing to recant, were burned at the stake, and their teachings were officially condemned (in 1210 in Paris, when Amalric's bones were exhumed and buried in non-consecrated ground, and again in 1215, at the Fourth Lateran Council).

54   In Roland-Gosselin's edition – "Le *De ente et essentia* de S. Thomas d'Aquin. Texte établi d'après les manuscrits parisiens. Introduction, notes et études historiques," ed. M. D. Roland-Gosselin, Bibliothèque thomiste, 8, J. Vrin (Paris: Le Saulchoir/Kain, 1926) – this sentence is completed by the following: *sicut si esset quidam color separatus, ex ipsa sua separatione esset aliud a colore non separato* – "just as if there were a separate color, then it would be distinct from a non-separate color by its very separation." But Boyer finds this addition inauthentic.

goodness. The common existence [*esse commune*],[55] however, just as it does not *include* in its understanding the addition of anything, does not *exclude* from its understanding any addition; for otherwise, [if such an addition *were excluded* from its understanding, then] no single thing in which something is added to the thing's existence could be understood to exist.

Likewise, although God is existence only, this does not mean that he should lack other perfections or excellences; rather, he has all perfections of all kinds, and for this reason he is said to be perfect absolutely speaking,[56] as the Philosopher and the Commentator assert in Book 5 of the *Metaphysics*.[57] But he has all these perfections in a more excellent manner than any other thing, for in him they are one, and in others they are diverse. And the reason for this is that he has all these perfections on account of his simple existence; just as, if there were someone who on account of a simple quality could perform the operations of all qualities, then in that simple quality he would have all qualities, so too does God have all perfections in his existence itself.[58]

In the second way, essence is found in created intellectual substances, in which existence is other than essence, although that essence is there without matter. Therefore, their existence is not subsistent, but received [in their essence], and so it is finite and delimited to the capacity of the receiving nature. But their nature or quiddity is subsistent, not received in some matter. And this is why it is stated in *The Book of Causes*[59] that the intelligences are infinite from below and finite from above; for they are finite with regard to their existence that they receive from above, but they are not finite from below, for their forms are not delimited to the capacity of some matter receiving them. And for this reason in their case there is no multitude of individuals in the same species, as has been declared, except in the case of the human soul, on account of the body with which it is united. And although its individuation is temporarily dependent on the body with regard to its beginning (for it cannot acquire an individuated act of existence, except in the body that it makes actual), nevertheless, it does not have to lose its individuation with the removal of the body. For once it has separate existence (after it has acquired individuated existence because it was made the form of *this* body), that existence always remains individuated.[60] And this is why

---

55   *esse commune* – existence as conceived by means of our common concept of existence.

56   As opposed to being a perfect this and a not-so-perfect that, as we can say of a man that he is, for example, a perfect lover but a not-so-perfect husband, or vice versa.

57   Aristotle, *Metaph.*, 5, c. 16, 1021b30; Averroës, com. 21; *Commentary* of St. Thomas, lc. 21.

58   Another (necessarily imperfect) analogy might be that just as he who has a Swiss army knife has all the tools of a toolbox in his pocket, so does God have all perfections in his existence.

59   *Liber de Causis*, lc. 16. Cf. lc. 4 and 5.

60   Obviously, if there are two souls already possessing their individual acts of existence on account of the fact that one of them is the form of this body and the other is the form of that body, then, if they continue existing after losing the bodies they actually inform, they do not have to merge into one soul. Indeed, merging into one would be precisely the loss of their individual existence, contrary to the assumption that each individually survives the loss of its body. To be sure, this is an assumption Aquinas does not prove here, he merely answers a possible objection on the basis of this assumption. But he does provide serious metaphysical arguments for the immateriality and the consequent immortality of the soul elsewhere, for example, in his *Questions on the Soul* (*Quaestio Disputata de Anima*), qq. 2 and 14. Cf. *SN* 3, d. 5, q. 3, a. 2, d. 22, q. 1, a. 1; *SN* 2, d. 19, a. 1, *SN* 4, d. 50, q. 1, a. 1; *Questiones Quodlibetales* (*QDL*) X, q. 3, a. 2; *Summa contra Gentiles* (*ScG*), II. 79–81; *ST* 1, q. 75, a. 4, a. 6; *Comp. Theol.*, c. 84. For a detailed discussion of Aquinas' arguments for the immateriality of the soul, see

Avicenna says that the individuation and multiplication of souls are dependent on the body, as far as their beginning is concerned, but not with regard to their end.[61] And since in these substances their quiddity is not the same as their existence, they can be sorted into categories; whence they have genera, species, and differences, although their proper differences are hidden from us. For their essential differences are unknown to us even in the case of sensible substances, whence we signify those through accidental differences that stem from the essential ones, as a cause is signified through its effect, as when being bipedal is taken to be the difference of man. But the proper accidents of immaterial substances are also unknown to us; therefore, we cannot signify their [essential] differences either in themselves or through accidental differences.

We should know, nevertheless, that genus and difference cannot be taken in the same way in those substances and in sensible substances. For in the case of sensible substances, their genus is taken from what is material in the thing, whereas the difference is taken from what is formal in it; this is why Avicenna says in the beginning of his book *On the Soul* that among things composed of matter and form, the form "is a simple difference of that which it constitutes."[62] But not in the sense that the form is the difference itself, but in the sense that it is the principle of the difference, as he also says in his *Metaphysics*;[63] and this sort of difference is said to be *simple difference*, for it is taken from what is a part of the quiddity, namely, from the form. Since, however, immaterial substances are simple quiddities, in their case the difference cannot be taken from a part of the quiddity, but [it has to be taken] from the whole quiddity. And this is why Avicenna remarks at the beginning of his book *On the Soul* that a simple difference "pertains only to those species whose essences are composed of matter and form."[64]

Likewise, their genus is taken from their whole essence, but in a different manner. For one separate substance agrees with another in immateriality; but they differ in their grade of perfection, in accordance with their being farther away from potentiality and being closer to pure actuality. Therefore, their genus is taken from that which pertains to them insofar as they are immaterial, such as their intellectuality or some such feature; but their difference is taken from their grade of perfection, which, however, is unknown to us. Yet, these differences do not have to be accidental, just because they correspond to greater or lesser perfection, which does not diversify species. For the grade of perfection in receiving specifically the same form does not diversify the form, as something whiter and something less white [do not differ specifically] on account of participating in the same nature of whiteness [to different degrees]; but the diverse grades of perfection among the forms or natures themselves do diversify the species; as nature proceeds stepwise from plants to animals, among which there are some intermediaries between animals and plants according to the Philosopher in his *On Animals*.[65] Again, intellectual substances do not have to be classified

G. Klima, "Aquinas' Proofs of the Immateriality of the Intellect from the Universality of Thought," *Proceedings of the Society for Medieval Logic and Metaphysics*, <http://www.fordham.edu/gsas/phil/klima/SMLM/PSMLM1.pdf>, 1 (2001), pp. 19–28. (See also Robert Pasnau's comments and my rejoinder in the same volume, pp. 29–36 and pp. 37–44, respectively.)

61   Avicenna, *De Anima*, 5, 3.
62   Ibid., 1, 1.
63   Avicenna, *Metaph.*, 5, 5.
64   Avicenna, *De Anima*, 1, 1.
65   Aristotle, *Hist. Animal.*, 8, c. 1, 588b4–6.

in terms of two real differences; for this cannot be done with all things, as the Philosopher says in Book 11 of his *On Animals*.[66]

In the third way, essence is found in substances composed of matter and form, in which existence is received and finite, both because they have their existence from something else and because their nature or quiddity is received in designated matter. And so they are finite both from above and from below; and in their case, because of the division of designated matter, it is already possible to have several individuals in the same species. And we have already discussed earlier how the essences of these substances are related to the logical intentions.

Chapter 7. The Essences of Accidents

Now it remains to be seen how essence is found in accidents; for we have explained how it is found in all substances. And since, as has been said, an essence is what is signified by a definition, accidents have to have their essence in the way they have a definition. But they have an incomplete definition, for they cannot be defined unless their subject is included in their definition, and this is because they do not have their existence separately from their subject, but, just as from form and matter there results a substantial act of existence [*esse substantiale*] when they are united, so from an accident and its subject there results an accidental act of existence [*esse accidentale*], when the accident comes to the subject. And for this reason even a substantial form does not have a complete essence, (and neither does matter); for in the definition of a substantial form one has to include that of which it is the form, and so its definition has to be framed with the addition of something that is outside its genus, similarly to the definition of an accidental form; therefore, the natural scientist, who considers the soul only insofar as it is the form of a natural body, includes the natural body in the definition of the soul.[67]

But there is an important difference between substantial and accidental forms. For just as a substantial form does not have its existence separately from that which it informs, neither does that which it informs, namely, matter. Therefore, their union results in that act of existence [*esse*] in which the thing itself subsists, and they yield something that is one *per se*.[68] Therefore, their union yields a certain essence; and so the form, although considered in itself not a complete essence, is nevertheless a part of a complete essence. But that which is informed by an accident is in itself a complete being, subsisting in its own existence, which

---

66 Aristotle, *Part. Animal.*, 1, c. 2, 642b5–7.

67 The soul is defined by Aristotle as the first actuality (i.e., the substantial form, as opposed to an accidental form, which would be a second or secondary actuality) of an organic natural body. Therefore, since no form is a body and no body is a form (because a body has to be a composite of matter and form), the definition of the soul includes something that is outside its genus, which means that this definition contains something that is outside the essence or quiddity of the soul, given that the quiddity of anything is what is signified by its quidditative definition strictly speaking, consisting of genus and difference. Accordingly, this "naturalist" definition of the soul is not its quidditative definition strictly speaking. Perhaps, a strict metaphysical definition could be: the soul is a vivifying substantial form. But of course this definition would apply even to the living subsisting forms of separate substances (and at least analogically even to God), whence it cannot be regarded as a definition in natural science, which only deals with the material universe.

68 Aquinas is talking here about something that is one *per se*, say, a man, as opposed to something that is one *per accidens*, i.e., by mere coincidence, say, a man who happens to be a teacher. Cf. n. 6 above.

naturally precedes the supervening accident. Therefore, the supervening accident does not cause by its union with the thing that act of existence in which the thing subsists, i.e., that on account of which the thing is a *per se* being, but it causes a certain secondary act of existence, without which the subsisting thing can be understood to exist, just as anything that is primary can be understood without what is secondary.[69] Therefore, an accident and its subject do not yield something that is one *per se*, but something that is one *per accidens* [by coincidence].[70] Therefore, from their union there does not result some essence, as does from the union of matter and form; and for this reason an accident is neither a complete essence nor a part of a complete essence, but just as it is a being with some qualification [*secundum quid*], so too, it only has essence with some qualification.

However, in any genus, that which maximally and most truly exemplifies its kind is the cause of those that do so to a lesser degree, as fire, which is ultimately hot, is the cause of heat in all hot things, as stated in Book 2 of the *Metaphysics*;[71] therefore, substance, which is the first in the kind of all beings, and which maximally and most truly has essence, has to be the cause of accidents, which participate in the nature of being only secondarily and with qualification [*secundum quid*]. But this happens in various ways. Since matter and form are the parts of substance, some accidents primarily stem from form, others from matter. But there is a certain form whose existence [*esse*] is not dependent on matter, as the intellectual soul, whereas matter only has existence through form. So some accidents stemming from the form do not communicate with matter, such as thinking, which does not take place in

---

69   For Aquinas, this is the fundamental difference between substantial and accidental forms: the act of being of a substantial form is the same as the act of being of the thing informed by it, whereas the act of being of an accidental form is distinct from the act of being of the thing it informs; therefore, it is logically impossible for a thing to exist without its substantial form, but it is logically possible for the thing to exist without its accidental form (even if it may *naturally* be impossible, as in the case of inseparable accidents). It is also worth noting that from this claim it is very easy to prove Aquinas' thesis of the unity of substantial forms. For suppose a substance s has two distinct substantial forms, f and g. Since f and g are supposed to be two distinct entities, they have to have two distinct acts of existence, e_f and e_g. But if both f and g are supposed to be substantial forms of s, then their acts of existence would have to be identical with the same act of existence of s, e_s, which is impossible (because if $e_f = e_s$ and $e_s = e_g$, then $e_f = e_g$, contrary to our assumption). Therefore, if both f and g are substantial forms of s, then f = g, for any f and g, i.e., s can have at most one substantial form (and if s exists, then it has to have at least one, whence it has to have exactly one). Also, equivalently, if s has two forms, one of which is a substantial form, then the other has to be an accidental form, as Aquinas usually argues.

70   Subject and accident, having two distinct acts of being, are two entities, which, however, coincide, insofar as the act of being of the accident is also the act of being of the subject, although not its primary but secondary act. For the being of, say, Socrates' wisdom is nothing but Socrates' being wise, since for Socrates' wisdom to be is for Socrates to be wise (although it is not for Socrates to be, absolutely speaking (*simpliciter*), which is why the act of being of the wisdom of Socrates is only a secondary act of being of Socrates, namely, an act of being with qualification (*secundum quid*)).

71   Aristotle, *Metaph.*, 2, c. 1, 993b24–6. Again, the example is illuminating only with the assumption of Aristotelian physics, where it is assumed that the heat of hot things other than fire is the result of participating in the heat of fire on account of having fire in their composition, whereas fire itself is maximally hot, because it is hot by its own nature and not by participation. But regardless of the example, the idea is clear: something that has a property essentially, and not by participation, has this property maximally and most truly and causes this property to be present to a lesser degree in all those things that have it by participation.

a corporeal organ,[72] as the Philosopher proves in Book 3 of *On the Soul*.[73] There are others stemming from the form, however, that do communicate with matter, such as sensing, but no accident stems from matter without communicating with the form.

But among the accidents stemming from matter there is some further diversity. For some accidents stem from matter in relation to the specific form, as, for example, the masculine and feminine gender in animals, whose diversity is reduced to matter, as stated in Book 10 of the *Metaphysics*; therefore, after removing the form of the animal, these accidents do not stay behind, except equivocally. Others, however, stem from matter in relation to the generic form; and so, after removing the specific form, these still stay behind in matter; as the skin color of a black man, which stems from the mixture of elements and not from the soul, remains in him after death.[74]

And since each and every [material] thing is individuated by matter, and is placed in a genus or species through its form, the accidents that stem from matter are the accidents of the individual, according to which individuals of the same species differ from each other. But accidents that stem from form are the characteristic attributes [*propriae passiones*] of the genus or the species; therefore, they can be found in all individuals that share the nature of genus or species, as for example the ability to laugh [*risibile*][75] arises from the form in man, because laughter stems from some apprehension of the human soul.

We should also know that accidents sometimes are caused by the essential principles [i.e., matter and form] in perfect actuality, as heat in fire, which is always actually hot, but sometimes they are caused only as a certain capacity, which is completed by an external agent, as the transparency of the air, which is completed by an external shining body;[76] and in the case of such accidents, the capacity itself is an inseparable accident, but its completion, which comes from an external principle that is outside the essence of the thing or does not enter the constitution of the thing, is separable, such as motion and the like.

72   According to Aquinas, we do not think with our brain. The brain merely supplies highly processed sensory information for the intellect to form its concepts and do its thinking with those concepts on its own, relying on the brain merely for this information input, but not for carrying out the thinking process itself. But this input *is* needed for proper mental functioning, which is why brain injuries lead to mental impairment.

73   Aristotle, *De Anima*, 3, c. 4, 429b4; *Commentary* of St. Thomas, lc. 7.

74   To be sure, consistently with Aquinas' thesis of the unity of substantial forms, even these accidents cannot remain *numerically* the same (since this accident is *this* accident on account of pertaining to this substance; so if *this* substance is gone, then *this* accident cannot remain either). However, they can remain in the sense that the new substance resulting from the corruption of another will have *specifically* the same, but *numerically distinct* accidents on account of the disposition of matter of the old substance, which determines what sort of substance with what kinds of accidents can result in a natural process of the corruption of the old substance. But Aquinas merely contrasted here accidents that remain merely equivocally (since being male or female can be said of a dead body only equivocally) with accidents that remain univocally (since being black or white applies in the same sense to a dead body as well as to a living body).

75   This is the stock example of a specific, yet non-essential, characteristic [*proprium*], as introduced by Porphyry. As Aquinas' subsequent remark makes clear, the "laughter" of chimpanzees does not count as laughter in the sense intended here, which is the specifically human kind of laughter that is supposed to come forth from a sudden realization of something inherently funny, as in getting the point of a political joke (which certainly does not happen with chimpanzees).

76   For the air is not actually transparent, i.e., one cannot actually see through it, unless it is actually illuminated, i.e., light actually passes through it.

We should know, however, that in the case of accidents, genus, species, and difference are taken in a different manner from the case of substances. For in the case of substances, from the substantial form and matter conjoined in one nature, there results something that is one *per se*, which properly falls into the category of substance;[77] therefore, in the case of substances, their concrete names, which signify the composite, are properly said to be in this category as species and genera, as are the names "man" and "animal." But matter and form are not in this way in this category, except by reduction, as principles are said to be in a category. However, from an accident and its subject there does not result something that is one *per se*, whence they are *not* conjoined in one nature to which the intention of genus or species could be attributed. Therefore, the concrete names of accidents, such as "white [thing]" [*album*] or "educated [person]" [*musicum*], do not fall under the categories as species and genera, except by reduction, only insofar as [the species and genera of accidents] are signified by the corresponding abstract names, such as "whiteness" [*albedo*] and "education" [*musica*]. And since accidents are not composed of matter and form, their genus cannot be taken from their matter and their difference from their form, as is the case with composite substances, but their first genus has to be taken from their mode of existence [*modus essendi*], insofar as "being" is predicated in different, primary and secondary, senses in the ten categories, as for example quantity is said to be [a being] insofar as it is a measure of substance [i.e., of what is a being in the primary sense], and quality [is said to be a being] insofar as it is a disposition of substance, and so on, as the Philosopher explained in Book 4 of the *Metaphysics*.[78]

Their differences, on the other hand, are taken from the diversity of the principles causing them. And since its proper attributes are caused by the proper principles of the subject, in the definition of an accident defined in the abstract form (in the form in which it is properly in a category), in the place of the difference one has to include its subject, as for example, pugness is defined as the curvature of a nose. But it would have to be the other way around if it were defined in the concrete form. For in that case their subject is included in their definition as their genus; since then they would be defined similarly to material substances, in the case of which the nature of the genus is taken from their matter, as we say that a pug is a curved nose.

The case is similar if one accident is the principle of another, as for example actions, passions, and quantities are the principles of relations, and this is the basis of the Philosopher's classification of relations in Book 5 of the *Metaphysics*.[79] However, since the proper principles of accidents are not always obvious, sometimes we take the differences of accidents from their effects, as when we take "concentrative" [*congregativum*] and "dispersive" [*disgregativum*] to be the differences of colors, which are caused by the abundance or paucity of light, causing the various species of colors.[80]

---

77 I am following here Roland-Gosselin's reading, noted by Boyer in his n. 122, according to which it is the thing that is *per se* one (and not its nature, as Boyer's reading would have it), that properly falls into the category of substance. To be sure, the nature of a substance is also in the category of substance, insofar as it is signified by all substantial predicates of the thing. But those predicates are predicated of the thing, and not of its nature, although they are predicated of the thing on account of its having this nature signified by these predicates.

78 Aristotle, *Metaph.*, 4, c. 2, 1002b5–7; *Commentary* of St. Thomas, lc. 1. Cf. also *In Meta.*, Bk. 5, lc. 9.

79 Aristotle, *Metaph.*, 5, c. 15, 1020b26; *Commentary* of St. Thomas, lc. 17.

80 Cf. Aquinas, *Commentary on the Metaphysics*, lb. 10, lc. 9, n. 11: "We should take into consideration, however, that *concentrative* and *dispersive of sight* are not the true constitutive differences of *white*

In this way, therefore, it is clear how essence and existence are in substances and in accidents, how they are in the composite and simple substances, and how the logical intentions are found in all, except in the First Principle, which is of infinite simplicity, to which therefore the notion of genus or species does not apply, and so neither does a definition because of its simplicity, in which let there be the end and consummation of this discussion. Amen.

and *black*, but rather their effects. But in place of differences, we can take their signs, just as substantial forms or differences are sometimes designated by means of accidents. For the dispersion of sight results from the vehemence of light, the abundance of which causes whiteness. And the concentration of sight comes from the contrary cause." The problem with this illustration, of course, is that Aquinas never tells us what he means by the "concentration" (or "gathering," "bringing together") and "dispersion" (or "scattering," etc.) of sight. One might think that "dispersion of sight" is something like the dazzling of sight by some bright white light, and the "concentration of sight," accordingly, is whatever the opposite effect of the lack of light is, but we can only guess. However, the theoretical point is clear: one may indicate unknown essential differences by means of known accidents caused by these differences, as when Lavoisier, giving Cavendish's "inflammable air" the name "hydrogen" (meaning "water-maker") in 1783, indicated the unknown difference of hydrogen (its atomic number) by means of its characteristic effect of producing water when burned in air. A similar illustration is often used by Aquinas with reference to the (mistaken, but to a barefoot medieval monk very plausible) etymology of the name *lapis* ("rock") as *laedens pedem* ("something that hurts the foot"). In this case also, the unknown difference on account of which a material substance is a rock is indicated by some well-known (indeed, painfully obvious) effect it has.

John Buridan on Essence and Existence

In the eighth question we ask whether essence and existence are the same in every thing. And in this question by "essence" I mean the thing itself, and thus the question is whether a rose is the same as for the rose to be [*rosam esse*], or a man is the same as for a man to be [*hominem esse*], etc.

And we first argue that these are not the same. The reason is that I can think of a rose or of thunder without thereby thinking that there is a rose or thunder. Therefore, these are not the same. And likewise, I can have scientific knowledge of roses or thunder, and yet I may not know whether there is a rose or whether there is thunder. Therefore, if one of these is known and the other is unknown to me, then it follows that the one is not the same as the other.

Again, names and definitions signify essences, but they do not signify existence or non-existence, as it is stated in Book 1 of the *Posterior Analytics*. And this is so because they signify without time; therefore, essence and existence are not the same.

Furthermore, the questions "What is it?" and "Is it?" are very different, as it is clear from Book 2 of the *Posterior Analytics*. But they differ only because of the difference between essence and existence, namely, because the question "What is it?" asks about the essence or quiddity of a thing and the question "Is it?" asks about its existence.

Again, nothing is an accident of itself. But its existence is an accident of a thing, for it is an accident of a rose that it exists or it does not exist, since a rose may or may not exist. Therefore, a rose is not its existence.

Again, if essence and existence were the same in all things, then it would follow that the intelligences [angels] would be just as simple as God, which is false, as is clear from Book 12 of the *Metaphysics*. And the consequence is clear because they are not composed of matter and form, or of quantitative parts, or degrees, whence no sort of composition can be assigned in them any more than in God, unless they are composed of essence and existence. And this is proved by the arguments of Avicenna: if the essence and existence of a rose were the same, then it would be tautologous to say that a rose exists, and it would be no different from saying that a rose is a rose, except only verbally [*non/nisi solum secundum vocem*], which is absurd.

Again, the predication "A rose exists" would be quidditative, and not denominative, just as this is quidditative, "A rose is a rose." But the consequent is false; because the proposition

"A rose exists" is accidental and contingent, whence it can be false; therefore, it does not seem to be quidditative.

The opposite opinion is said by the Commentator to be Aristotle's in the present fourth book, where he says that a man is the same as an existing man and one man; and by "existing man" Aristotle seems to understand a man's existence.

Again, you should know that older philosophers [*antiqui*], including St. Thomas [Aquinas], stated that in every being other than God there is a composition of essence and existence. And thus existence has to differ somehow from essence, for which reason only God is absolutely simple.

Others even said that existence and non-existence are some accidental modes that pertain accidentally to essence, and so with generation an essence acquires existence and by corruption it acquires non-existence. Thus, some people claimed essences to be perpetual, although these modes are successively attributed to essences, as when we sometimes say that a rose exists and sometimes that it does not, and so these people admitted quidditative predications to be true even when the thing does not exist. And perhaps this was the opinion of the cardinal who issued the bull that the proposition "A man is an animal" or even "A horse is an animal" is necessary because of the inclusion of terms, and would be true even if God annihilated all horses. But Grosseteste [*Lincolniensis*] in his *Commentary* on Book 2 of the *Posterior Analytics* seems to be of the contrary opinion; for he says that everything that is predicated of God predicates or signifies God's simple essence, but existence predicated of anything other than God predicates or signifies its dependence from God, and this dependence, as he says, causes no multiplicity in the dependent thing.

And I say with Grosseteste and the Commentator that for each and every thing, the thing itself and for the thing to exist are the same, so that essence does not differ from existence, or existence from essence. And this can be proved as follows.

One cannot say that a rose is different from its existence, unless one says that its existence is a distinct mode added to it and acquired by generation, and that its quiddity or essence is eternal, as held by the above-mentioned opinion. But this entire position is impossible; therefore, etc. The major proposition appears obvious, because it was precisely this point [namely, that existence is an accidental mode added to the eternal essence of the thing] and nothing else that the arguments brought up at the beginning of this question appeared to argue for, and which moved these people to posit the distinction between essence and existence. But the minor proposition, namely, that this position is impossible, is proved as follows. First, it would follow that we would not need to posit prime matter. For that is posited only because the subject undergoing transmutation has to remain in both termini of the change, but then that subject would be the quiddity or essence, now existing, now not-existing, and so we would not need to posit matter. In the second place, it would follow that in a dead body there would remain humanity, although it is on account of humanity that something is a man; therefore, a dead body would still be a man, which is false. And the first consequence is proved, because humanity can be nothing but the essence or quiddity of man that remains after the corruption of a human being, and it would either be separate or it would remain in the matter of the cadaver. If it were to remain in the matter of the cadaver, then we have what we wanted to prove. If it is said that it remains separately from matter, then this would amount to positing the Ideas of Plato, which Aristotle refuted. And the argument I made about man and humanity can be made about horse and equinity or a stone and its quiddity. Arguing about these would actually lead to greater absurdity, because we concede that the human soul is separable, which someone would perhaps claim to be man's quiddity.

Furthermore, such additional modes of existence would be posited entirely in vain. For if its existence would be a mode added to a thing, say, to a rose, acquired through its substantial generation, then the same difficulties that we had concerning the rose would at once recur concerning that existence. Because just as the rose can exist and can not exist, so that mode can exist and can not exist as well, and I would be able to think of that mode without thinking that it exists, indeed, perhaps thinking that it does not exist. For I would be able to think of the existence which existed when Aristotle existed, and yet whatever it was, I understand that he now does not exist. Hence it is clear that such an additional mode would do nothing for preserving definitions.

Again, Aristotle seems to indicate here an argument that the Commentator explicates in the following manner. That which would persist if a rose persisted, excluding everything that is additional to the rose, does not differ from the rose. But if the rose alone persisted in this way, then it would still exist, because it obviously entails a contradiction to claim that something persists and yet it does not exist. And if the rose existed, then its existence would exist as well; therefore, its existence is not different from it.

Again, as it has been said about existence and unity, they are generated by the same generation and corrupted by the same corruption. This is because the same generation that generates a rose generates its existence, for generation proceeds from the non-existence to the existence of the thing; therefore, etc.

But for the sake of answering the objections it seems that we should say in this question that essence and existence differ in their concepts. For the name "rose" and this name or expression "that a rose exists" are imposed from different concepts. Therefore, when it is said that I think of a rose, while I do not think that it exists, this I concede. But from this it does not follow that, therefore, that a rose exists differs from the rose; what follows is only that it is according to different concepts or on different accounts that the rose is thought of in terms of the name "rose" and the expression "that a rose exists."

But you will argue by means of the following expository syllogism: "This rose I understand, and this rose is the same as for this rose to exist; therefore, this rose to exist I understand." And I accept the entire syllogism. Thus, I concede that it is impossible that rose for you to understand, unless that rose to exist you also understand. But this consequence is not valid: "That rose to exist I understand; therefore, I understand that rose to exist." Here you need to know that we recognize, know, or understand things according to determinate and distinct concepts, and we can understand one thing according to one concept and ignore it according to another; therefore, the terms following such verbs as "understand" or "know" appellate [i.e., obliquely refer to] the concepts according to which they were imposed [to signify], but they do not so appellate their concepts when they precede these verbs. It is for this reason that you have it from Aristotle that this consequence is not valid: "I know Coriscus, and Coriscus is the one approaching; therefore, I know the one approaching." And this is because to know the one approaching is to know the thing according to the concept according to which it is called the one approaching. Now, although I know Coriscus, it does not follow, even if he is the one approaching, that I recognize him under the concept according to which I know him to be approaching. But this would be a valid expository syllogism: "Coriscus I know; and Coriscus is the one approaching; therefore, the one approaching I know." Therefore, the situation is similar in the case under consideration: I understand a rose, but I do not understand a rose to exist, although a rose to exist I understand. The same applies to the other case: I concede that I have scientific knowledge about roses and thunder in terms of several conclusions, yet, I do not have scientific knowledge about roses or thunder in terms of the conclusion that a rose or thunder exists.

Again, in response to the other objection the same point can be conceded concerning signification that was conceded concerning understanding, because names are imposed to signify by means of acts of understanding [*intellectiones*, i.e., concepts] of things. Therefore, the name "rose" signifies a rose, but does not signify a rose to exist, although this rose it signifies and this rose to exist it signifies as well [because this rose and for this rose to exist are the same], and the same goes for definitions.

Again, I say that the existence of a rose is not an accident of the rose, but the predicate "exists" is certainly an accidental predicate of the subject "rose"; therefore, the proposition "a rose exists" is contingent, and can be false. But the same applies to the proposition "a rose is a rose," for it would be false, if there were no roses. And when it is said that a rose can not exist, I concede this and even further that a rose can not be a rose. Because when no rose exists, its quiddity does not exist and it does not persist.

To the other objection I reply that God is absolutely simple, for he is neither composed of parts, nor can he be composed with another thing. But the intelligences [angels], although they are not composed of parts, nevertheless, they can be composed with accidents; for they understand or can understand by acts of understanding [*intellectiones*] added to them, which is not the case with God; but this sort of simplicity will be discussed in greater detail in Book 12 of this work.

The other arguments from Avicenna are solved in terms of mere conceptual difference, as they were solved in connection with existence and unity, etc.

God's Existence and Essence

32

Augustine on Divine Immutability

On the Trinity

Book V

Chapter 2. God the Only Unchangeable Essence

3. He is, however, without doubt, a substance, or, if it be better so to call it, an essence, which the Greeks call οὐσία. For as wisdom is so called from the being wise, and knowledge from knowing; so from being[1] comes that which we call essence. And who is there that is, more than He who said to His servant Moses, "I am that I am"; and, "Thus shall thou say unto the children of Israel, He who is hath sent me unto you"?[2] But other things that are called essences or substances admit of accidents, whereby a change, whether great or small, is produced in them. But there can be no accident of this kind in respect to God; and therefore He who is God is the only unchangeable substance or essence, to whom certainly being itself, whence comes the name of essence, most especially and most truly belongs. For that which is changed does not retain its own being; and that which can be changed, although it be not actually changed, is able not to be that which it had been; and hence that which not only is not changed, but also cannot at all be changed, alone falls most truly, without difficulty or hesitation, under the category of being.

[. . .]

Chapter 4. The Accidental Always Implies Some Change in the Thing

5. That which is accidental commonly implies that it can be lost by some change of the thing to which it is an accident. For although some accidents are said to be inseparable, which in Greek are called ἀχώριστα, as the color black is to the feather of a raven; yet the feather loses that color, not indeed so long as it is a feather, but because the feather is not always. Wherefore the matter itself is changeable; and whenever that animal or that feather ceases to be, and the whole of that body is changed and turned into earth, it loses certainly that

---

1   *Esse.*
2   Ex. 3: 14.

color also. Although the kind of accident which is called separable may likewise be lost, not by separation, but by change; as, for instance, blackness is called a separable accident to the hair of men, because hair continuing to be hair can grow white; yet, if carefully considered, it is sufficiently apparent, that it is not as if anything departed by separation away from the head when it grows white, as though blackness departed thence and went somewhere and whiteness came in its place, but that the quality of color there is turned and changed. Therefore there is nothing accidental in God, because there is nothing changeable or that may be lost. But if you choose to call that also accidental, which, although it may not be lost, yet can be decreased or increased, – as, for instance, the life of the soul: for as long as it is a soul, so long it lives, and because the soul is always, it always lives; but because it lives more when it is wise, and less when it is foolish, here, too, some change comes to pass, not such that life is absent, as wisdom is absent to the foolish, but such that it is less; – nothing of this kind, either, happens to God, because He remains altogether unchangeable.

Chapter 5. Nothing is Spoken of God According to Accident, But According to Substance or According to Relation

6. Wherefore nothing in Him is said in respect to accident, since nothing is accidental to Him, and yet all that is said is not said according to substance. For in created and changeable things, that which is not said according to substance, must, by necessary alternative, be said according to accident. For all things are accidents to them, which can be either lost or diminished, whether magnitudes or qualities; and so also is that which is said in relation to something, as friendships, relationships, services, likenesses, equalities, and anything else of the kind; so also positions and conditions,[3] places and times, acts and passions. But in God nothing is said to be according to accident, because in Him nothing is changeable; and yet everything that is said, is not said, according to substance. For it is said in relation to something, as the Father in relation to the Son and the Son in relation to the Father, which is not accident; because both the one is always Father, and the other is always Son: yet not "always," meaning from the time when the Son was born [natus], so that the Father ceases not to be the Father because the Son never *ceases* to be the Son, but because the Son was *always* born, and never began to be the Son. But if He had begun to be at any time, or were at any time to cease to be, the Son, then He would be called Son according to accident. But if the Father, in that He is called the Father, were so called in relation to Himself, not to the Son; and the Son, in that He is called the Son, were so called in relation to Himself, not to the Father; then both the one would be called Father, and the other Son, according to substance. But because the Father is not called the Father except in that He has a Son, and the Son is not called Son except in that He has a Father, these things are not said according to substance; because each of them is not so called in relation to Himself, but the terms are used reciprocally and in relation each to the other; nor yet according to accident, because both the being called the Father, and the being called the Son, is eternal and unchangeable to them. Wherefore, although to be the Father and to be the Son is different, yet their substance is not different; because they are so called, not according to substance, but according to relation, which relation, however, is not accident, because it is not changeable.

[. . .]

---

3 *Habitus*.

Chapter 16. What Is Said of God in Time, Is Said Relatively, Not Accidentally

17. Nor let it trouble us that the Holy Spirit, although He is co-eternal with the Father and the Son, yet is called something which exists in time; as, for instance, this very thing which we have called Him, a thing that has been given. For the Spirit is a gift eternally, but a thing that has been given in time. For if a lord also is not so called unless when he begins to have a slave, that appellation likewise is relative and in time to God; for the creature is not from all eternity, of which He is the Lord. How then shall we make it good that relative terms themselves are not accidental, since nothing happens accidentally to God in time, because He is incapable of change, as we have argued in the beginning of this discussion? Behold! to be the Lord, is not eternal to God; otherwise we should be compelled to say that the creature also is from eternity, since He would not be a lord from all eternity unless the creature also was a servant from all eternity. But as he cannot be a slave who has not a lord, neither can he be a lord who has not a slave. And if there be any one who says that God, indeed, is alone eternal, and that times are not eternal on account of their variety and changeableness, but that times nevertheless did not begin to be in time (for there was no time before times began, and therefore it did not happen to God in time that He should be Lord, since He was Lord of the very times themselves, which assuredly did not begin in time): what will he reply respecting man, who was made in time, and of whom assuredly He was not the Lord before he was of whom He was to be Lord? Certainly to be the Lord of man happened to God in time. And that all dispute may seem to be taken away, certainly to be your Lord, or mine, who have only lately begun to be, happened to God in time. Or if this, too, seems uncertain on account of the obscure question respecting the soul, what is to be said of His being the Lord of the people of Israel? since, although the nature of the soul already existed, which that people had (a matter into which we do not now inquire), yet that people existed not as yet, and the time is apparent when it began to exist. Lastly, that He should be Lord of this or that tree, or of this or that corn crop, which only lately began to be, happened in time; since, although the matter itself already existed, yet it is one thing to be Lord of the matter (*materiæ*), another to be Lord of the already created nature (*naturæ*).[4] For man, too, is lord of the wood at one time, and at another he is lord of the chest, although fabricated of that same wood; which he certainly was not at the time when he was already the lord of the wood. How then shall we make it good that nothing is said of God according to accident, except because nothing happens to His nature by which He may be changed, so that those things are relative accidents which happen in connection with some change of the things of which they are spoken. As a friend is so called relatively: for he does not begin to be one, unless when he has begun to love; therefore some change of will takes place, in order that he may be called a friend. And money, when it is called a price, is spoken of relatively, and yet it was not changed when it began to be a price; nor, again, when it is called a pledge, or any other thing of the kind. If, therefore, money can so often be spoken of relatively with no change of itself, so that neither when it begins, nor when it ceases to be so spoken of, does any change take place in that nature or form of it, whereby it is money; how much more easily ought we to admit, concerning that unchangeable

---

4   "Matter" denotes the material as created *ex nihilo*: "nature" the material as formed into individuals. In this reference, Augustine speaks of "the nature of the soul" of the people of Israel as existing while "as yet that people existed not" individually – having in mind their race-existence in Adam.

substance of God, that something may be so predicated relatively in respect to the creature, that although it begin to be so predicated in time, yet nothing shall be understood to have happened to the substance itself of God, but only to that creature in respect to which it is predicated? "Lord," it is said, "Thou hast been made our refuge."[5] God, therefore, is said to be our refuge relatively, for He is referred to us, and He then becomes our refuge when we flee to Him; pray does anything come to pass then in His nature, which, before we fled to Him, was not? In us therefore some change does take place; for we were worse before we fled to Him, and we become better by fleeing to Him: but in Him there is no change. So also He begins to be our Father, when we are regenerated through His grace, since He gave us power to become the sons of God.[6] Our substance therefore is changed for the better, when we become His sons; and He at the same time begins to be our Father, but without any change of His own substance. Therefore that which begins to be spoken of God in time, and which was not spoken of Him before, is manifestly spoken of Him relatively; yet not according to any accident of God, so that anything should have happened to Him, but clearly according to some accident of that, in respect to which God begins to be called something relatively. When a righteous man begins to be a friend of God, he himself is changed; but far be it from us to say, that God loves any one in time with as it were a new love, which was not in Him before, with whom things gone by have not passed away and things future have been already done. Therefore He loved all His saints before the foundation of the world, as He predestinated them; but when they are converted and find Him; then they are said to begin to be loved by Him, that what is said may be said in that way in which it can be comprehended by human affections. So also, when He is said to be wroth with the unrighteous, and gentle with the good, they are changed, not He: just as the light is troublesome to weak eyes, pleasant to those that are strong; namely, by their change, not its own.

5   Ps. 90: 1.
6   John 1: 12.

33

Anselm of Canterbury on God's Existence

Monologion

1. That of all the Things that Exist, There Is One that Is the Best, Greatest and Supreme

Of all the things that exist, there is one nature that is supreme. It alone is self-sufficient in its eternal happiness, yet through its all-powerful goodness it creates and gives to all other things their very existence and their goodness. Now, take someone who either has never heard of, or does not believe in, and so does not know, this – this, or indeed any of the numerous other things which we necessarily believe about God and his creation. I think that they can, even if of average ability, convince themselves, to a large extent, of the truth of these beliefs, simply by reason alone. Now, since this could be done in several ways, I will set down here the one that I consider to be the most readily available. For, given that all desire only what they think is good, anyone can easily avail himself of the following opportunity: he can at any time turn the mind's eye to look for the source of the things that are good – things that one would not want unless one judged them to be good. In this way, then, guided by reason, he may make rational progress towards what he, unreasonably, does not know.

But if I say something along the way that greater authority does not teach, then I wish it to be taken in the following way: it is, indeed, reached as a necessary conclusion from reasoning which seems right to me. Nevertheless, it is not thereby asserted as necessary without qualification. Rather I assert it as possible – for the present at least.

Anyone, then, can quite easily ask himself the following question: 'Given that there is such an uncountable number of good things, the sheer multiplicity of which is simply a datum of bodily sense as well as something we perceive by means of the rational mind – given this, are we to believe that there is some one thing through which all good things whatsoever are good? Or do different goods have their existence through different things?' Quite certain, indeed, and clear to all who are willing to see, is the following: take some things that are said to be (say) X, and relative to each other are said to be less, more, or equally X. It is through this X that they are said to be so, and this X is understood as the very same thing in the various cases and not something different in each case (whether X is considered to be in them equally or not equally). Take, for example, some things that are said, relative to each other, to be, either equally, or more, or less just. They cannot be understood to be just except through justice, and justice is not something different in each of the various cases. Therefore, since it is certain that all good things when compared with each other are either equally or not equally good, necessarily all good things are good through something, and this something is understood to be the same thing in each of various good things.

Different good things may none the less appear to be called good through different things. Thus a horse may appear to be called good through one thing, because it is strong, and through something else, because it is swift. For it seems to be called good through strength and good through speed, and yet strength and speed do not seem to be the same thing. And if the horse is good because it is strong and swift, how come the thief that is swift and strong is bad? Rather, it is the case that the swift and strong thief is bad because he does harm, and the strong and swift horse is good because it is beneficial. (And indeed ordinarily nothing is thought to be good except on the grounds either of what is beneficial, e.g. health and what makes for it – or of what is excellent, e.g. beauty and what contributes to it.) Now, the reasoning above is irrefutable. Necessarily, therefore, everything beneficial or excellent is, if it is truly good, good through that same one thing, through which all good things necessarily are good, whatever that thing may be. And who would doubt that that through which all things are good is a great good?

Because, then, it is that through which every good thing is good, it is good through itself. It therefore follows that all the other good things are good through something other than what they themselves are, while this thing alone is good through itself. But nothing that is good through something other than itself is equal to or greater than that good which is good through itself. The one thing, therefore, that is good through itself is the one thing that is supremely good. For the supreme is that which so overtops the others that it has no equal and no superior. But what is supremely good is also supremely great. There is therefore one thing that is supremely good and supremely great, and this is of all the things that exist, the supreme.

[. . .]

Proslogion

2.   That God Truly Exists

Well then, Lord, You who give understanding to faith, grant me that I may understand, as much as You see fit, that You exist as we believe You to exist, and that You are what we believe You to be. Now we believe that You are something than which nothing greater can be thought. Or can it be that a thing of such a nature does not exist, since 'the Fool has said in his heart, there is no God' [Ps. 13: 1; 52: 1]? But surely, when this same Fool hears what I am speaking about, namely, 'something-than-which-nothing-greater-can-be-thought', he understands what he hears, and what he understands is in his mind, even if he does not understand that it actually exists. For it is one thing for an object to exist in the mind, and another thing to understand that an object actually exists. Thus, when a painter plans beforehand what he is going to execute, he has [the picture] in his mind, but he does not yet think that it actually exists because he has not yet executed it. However, when he has actually painted it, then he both has it in his mind and understands that it exists because he has now made it. Even the Fool, then, is forced to agree that something-than-which-nothing-greater-can-be-thought exists in the mind, since he understands this when he hears it, and whatever is understood is in the mind. And surely that-than-which-a-greater-cannot-be-thought cannot exist in the mind alone. For if it exists solely in the mind, it can be thought to exist in reality also, which is greater. If then that-than-which-a-greater-cannot-be-thought exists in the mind alone, this same that-than-which-a-greater-*cannot*-be-thought is that-than-which-a-greater-*can*-be-thought. But this is obviously impossible. Therefore there is absolutely no doubt that something-than-which-a-greater-cannot-be-thought exists both in the mind and in reality.

3.   That God Cannot Be Thought Not To Exist

And certainly this being so truly exists that it cannot be even thought not to exist. For something can be thought to exist that cannot be thought not to exist, and this is greater than that which can be thought not to exist. Hence, if that-than-which-a-greater-cannot-be-thought can be thought not to exist, then that-than-which-a-greater-cannot-be-thought is not the same as that-than-which-a-greater-cannot-be-thought, which is absurd. Something-than-which-a-greater-cannot-be-thought exists so truly then, that it cannot be even thought not to exist.

   And You, Lord our God, are this being. You exist so truly, Lord my God, that You cannot even be thought not to exist. And this is as it should be, for if some intelligence could think of something better than You, the creature would be above its Creator and would judge its Creator – and that is completely absurd. In fact, everything else there is, except You alone, can be thought of as not existing. You alone, then, of all things most truly exist and therefore of all things possess existence to the highest degree; for anything else does not exist as truly, and so possesses existence to a lesser degree. Why then did 'the Fool say in his heart, there is no God' [Ps. 13: 1; 52: 1] when it is so evident to any rational mind that You of all things exist to the highest degree? Why indeed, unless because he was stupid and a fool?

4.   How 'the Fool said in his heart' What Cannot Be Thought

How indeed has he 'said in his heart' what he could not think; or how could he not think what he 'said in his heart', since to 'say in one's heart' and to 'think' are the same? But if he really (indeed, since he really) both thought because he 'said in his heart' and did not 'say in his heart' because he could not think, there is not only one sense in which something is 'said in one's heart' or thought. For in one sense a thing is thought when the word signifying it is thought; in another sense when the very object which the thing is is understood. In the first sense, then, God can be thought not to exist, but not at all in the second sense. No one, indeed, understanding what God is can think that God does not exist, even though he may say these words in his heart either without any [objective] signification or with some peculiar signification. For God is that-than-which-nothing-greater-can-be-thought. Whoever really understands this understands clearly that this same being so exists that not even in thought can it not exist. Thus whoever understands that God exists in such a way cannot think of Him as not existing.

   I give thanks, good Lord, I give thanks to You, since what I believed before through Your free gift I now so understand through Your illumination, that if I did not want to *believe* that You existed, I should nevertheless be unable not to *understand* it.

5. That God Is Whatever It Is Better To Be than Not To Be and that, Existing through Himself Alone, He Makes All Other Beings from Nothing

What then are You, Lord God, You than whom nothing greater can be thought? But what are You save that supreme being, existing through Yourself alone, who made everything else from nothing? For whatever is not this is less than that which can be thought of; but this cannot be thought about You. What goodness, then, could be wanting to the supreme good, through which every good exists? Thus You are just, truthful, happy, and whatever it is better to be than not to be – for it is better to be just rather than unjust, and happy rather than unhappy.

[. . .]

15. How He Is Greater than Can Be Thought

Therefore, Lord, not only are You that than which a greater cannot be thought, but You are also something greater than can be thought. For since it is possible to think that there is such a one, then, if You are not this same being something greater than You could be thought – which cannot be.

16. That This Is the 'Inaccessible Light' in which He 'Dwells'

Truly, Lord, this is the inaccessible light in which You dwell. For truly there is nothing else which can penetrate through it so that it might discover You there. Truly I do not see this light since it is too much for me; and yet whatever I see I see through it, just as an eye that is weak sees what it sees by the light of the sun which it cannot look at in the sun itself. My understanding is not able [to attain] to that [light]. It shines too much and [my understanding] does not grasp it nor does the eye of my soul allow itself to be turned towards it for too long. It is dazzled by its splendour, overcome by its fullness, overwhelmed by its immensity, confused by its extent. O supreme and inaccessible light; O whole and blessed truth, how far You are from me who am so close to You! How distant You are from my sight while I am so present to Your sight! You are wholly present everywhere and I do not see You. In You I move and in You I have my being and I cannot come near to You. You are within me and around me and I do not have any experience of You.

[. . .]

22. That He Alone Is what He Is and Who He Is

You alone then, Lord, are what You are and You are who You are. For what is one thing as a whole and another as to its parts, and has in it something mutable, is not altogether what it is. And what began [to exist] from non-existence, and can be thought not to exist, and returns to non-existence unless it subsists through some other; and what has had a past existence but does not now exist, and a future existence but does not yet exist – such a thing does not exist in a strict and absolute sense. But You are what You are, for whatever You are at any time or in any way this You are wholly and forever.

And You are the being who exists in a strict and absolute sense because You have neither past nor future existence but only present existence; nor can You be thought not to exist at any time. And You are life and light and wisdom and blessedness and eternity and many suchlike good things; and yet You are nothing save the one and supreme good, You who are completely sufficient unto Yourself, needing nothing, but rather He whom all things need in order that they may have being and well-being.

Pro Insipiente (On Behalf of the Fool) [by Gaunilo]

6

For example: they say that there is in the ocean somewhere an island which, because of the difficulty (or rather the impossibility) of finding that which does not exist, some have called the 'Lost Island'. And the story goes that it is blessed with all manner of priceless riches and delights in abundance, much more even than the Happy Isles, and, having no owner or inhabitant, it is superior everywhere in abundance of riches to all those other lands that men inhabit. Now, if anyone tell me that it is like this, I shall easily understand what is said, since nothing is difficult about it. But if he should then go on to say, as though it were a logical consequence of this: You cannot any more doubt that this island that is more excellent than all other lands truly exists somewhere in reality than you can doubt that it is in your mind; and since it is more excellent to exist not only in the mind alone but also in reality, therefore it must needs be that it exists. For if it did not exist, any other land existing in reality would be more excellent than it, and so this island, already conceived by you to be more excellent than others, will not be more excellent. If, I say, someone wishes thus to persuade me that this island really exists beyond all doubt, I should either think that he was joking, or I should find it hard to decide which of us I ought to judge the bigger fool – I, if I agreed with him, or he, if he thought that he had proved the existence of this island with any certainty, unless he had first convinced me that its very excellence exists in my mind precisely as a thing existing truly and indubitably and not just as something unreal or doubtfully real.

[. . .]

Reply to Gaunilo

3

You claim, however, that this is as though someone asserted that it cannot be doubted that a certain island in the ocean (which is more fertile than all other lands and which, because of the difficulty or even the impossibility of discovering what does not exist, is called the 'Lost Island') truly exists in reality since anyone easily understands it when it is described in words. Now, I truly promise that if anyone should discover for me something existing either in reality or in the mind alone – except 'that-than-which-a-greater-cannot-be-thought' – to which the logic of my argument would apply, then I shall find that Lost Island and give it, never more to be lost, to that person. It has already been clearly seen, however, that 'that-than-which-a-greater-cannot-be-thought' cannot be thought not to exist, because it exists as a matter of such certain truth. Otherwise it would not exist at all. In short, if anyone says that he thinks that this being does not exist, I reply that, when he thinks of this, either he thinks of something than which a greater cannot be thought, or he does not think of it. If he does not think of it, then he does not think that what he does not think of does not exist. If, however, he does think of it, then indeed he thinks of something which cannot be even thought not to exist. For if it could be thought not to exist, it could be thought to have a beginning and an end – but this cannot be. Thus, he who thinks of it thinks of something that cannot be thought not to exist; indeed, he who thinks of this does not think of it as not existing, otherwise he would think what cannot be thought. Therefore 'that-than-which-a-greater-cannot-be-thought' cannot be thought not to exist.

[. . .]

5

As for the other objections you make against me on behalf of the Fool, it is quite easy to meet them, even for one weak in the head, and so I considered it a waste of time to show this. But since I hear that they appear to certain readers to have some force against me, I will deal briefly with them.

First, you often reiterate that I say that that which is greater than everything exists in the mind, and that if it is in the mind, it exists also in reality, for otherwise that which is greater than everything would not be that which is greater than everything. However, nowhere in all that I have said will you find such an argument. For 'that which is greater than everything' and 'that-than-which-a-greater-cannot-be-thought' are not equivalent for the purpose of proving the real existence of the thing spoken of. Thus, if anyone should say that 'that-than-which-a-greater-cannot-be-thought' is not something that actually exists, or that it can possibly not exist, or even can be thought of as not existing, he can easily be refuted. For what does not exist can possibly not exist, and what can not exist can be thought of as not existing. However, whatever can be thought of as not existing, if it actually exists, is not that-than-which-a-greater-cannot-be-thought. But if it does not exist, indeed even if it should exist, it would not be that-than-which-a-greater-cannot-be-thought. But it cannot be asserted that 'that-than-which-a-greater-cannot-be-thought' is not, if it exists, that-than-which-a-greater-cannot-be-thought, or that, if it should exist, it would not be that-than-which-a-greater-cannot-be-thought. It is evident, then, that it neither does not exist nor can not exist or be thought of as not existing. For if it does exist in another way it is not what it is said to be, and if it should exist [in another way] it would not be [what it was said to be].

However it seems that it is not as easy to prove this in respect of what is said to be greater than everything. For it is not as evident that that which can be thought of as not existing is not that which is greater than everything, as that it is not that-than-which-a-greater-cannot-be-thought. And, in the same way, neither is it indubitable that, if there is something which is 'greater than everything', it is identical with 'that-than-which-a-greater-cannot-be-thought'; nor, if there were [such a being], that no other like it might exist – as this is certain in respect of what is said to be 'that-than-which-a-greater-cannot-be-thought'. For what if someone should say that something that is greater than everything actually exists, and yet that this same being can be thought of as not existing, and that something greater than it can be thought, even if this does not exist? In this case can it be inferred as evidently that [this being] is therefore not that which is greater than everything, as it would quite evidently be said in the other case that it is therefore not that-than-which-a-greater-cannot-be-thought? The former [inference] needs, in fact, a premiss in addition to this which is said to be 'greater than everything'; but the latter needs nothing save this utterance itself, namely, 'that-than-which-a-greater-cannot-be-thought'. Therefore, if what 'that-than-which-a-greater-cannot-be-thought' of itself proves concerning itself cannot be proved in the same way in respect of what is said to be 'greater than everything', you criticize me unjustly for having said what I did not say, since it differs so much from what I did say.

If, however, it can [be proved] by means of another argument, you should not have criticized me for having asserted what can be proved. Whether it can [be proved], however, is easily appreciated by one who understands that it can [in respect of] 'that-than-which-a-greater-cannot-be-thought'. For one cannot in any way understand 'that-than-which-a-greater-cannot-be-thought' without [understanding that it is] that which alone is greater than everything. As, therefore, 'that-than-which-a-greater-cannot-be-thought' is understood and is in the mind, and is consequently judged to exist in true reality, so also that which is greater than everything is said to be understood and to exist in the mind, and so is necessarily inferred to exist in reality itself. You see, then, how right you were to compare me with that stupid person who wished to maintain that the Lost Island existed from the sole fact that being described it was understood.

Thomas Aquinas on God's Existence and Simplicity

Summa Theologiae

Part I, Question 2. Does God Exist?

With respect to this question there are three points of inquiry:

1. Is it self-evident that God exists?
2. Can we demonstrate that God exists?
3. Does God exist?

Article 1. Is it self-evident that God exists?

1. It seems that 'God exists' is self-evidently true. For we say that things are self-evident to us when we know them by nature, as by nature we know first principles. But as Damascene observes when beginning his book, 'the knowledge that God exists is implanted by nature in everybody'.[1] So, 'God exists' is self-evidently true.

2. Moreover, a proposition is self-evident if we perceive its truth immediately upon perceiving the meaning of its terms – a characteristic of first principles of demonstration (according to Aristotle).[2] For example, when we know what wholes and parts are, we know at once that wholes are always bigger than their parts. But once we understand the meaning of the word 'God', we immediately see that God exists. For the word means 'that than which nothing greater can be signified'. So, since what exists in thought and fact is greater than what exists in thought alone, and since, once we understand the word 'God', he exists in thought, he must also exist in fact. It is, therefore, self-evident that God exists.

3. Again, it is self-evident that truth exists, for even denying so would amount to admitting it. If there were no such thing as truth, it would be true that there is no truth. So, something

---

1 *On the Orthodox Faith* 1.1. *PG* 94.789.
2 *Posterior Analytics* 1.2, 72a7–8.

is true and, therefore, there is truth. But God is truth itself: 'I am the way, the truth, and the life.'[3] So, it is self-evident that God exists.

On the contrary, as Aristotle's discussion of first principles makes clear, nobody can think the opposite of what it self-evident.[4] But we can think the opposite of the proposition 'God exists.' For 'the fool' in the Psalms 'said in his heart: "There is no God."'[5] So, it is not self-evident that God exists.

Reply: A proposition can be self-evident in two ways: (a) in itself, though not to us, and (b) both in itself and to us. For a proposition is self-evident when its predicate forms part of its subject's definition (thus, for example, it is self-evident that human beings are animals since being an animal is part of the meaning of 'human being'). And if everyone knows the essence of the subject and predicate, the proposition will be self-evident to everybody. This is clearly the case with first principles of demonstration, which employ common terms known to all of us (such as 'being' and 'non-being', 'whole' and 'part', and the like). But if some people do not know the essence of its subject and predicate, then a proposition, though self-evident in itself, will not be so to them. This is why Boethius can say that 'certain notions are self-evident and commonplaces only to the learned, as, for example, that only bodies can occupy space'.[6]

So, I maintain that the proposition 'God exists' is self-evident in itself, for, as I shall later show,[7] its subject and predicate are identical since God is his own existence. But, because we do not know what God is, the proposition is not self-evident to us and needs to be demonstrated by things more known to us, though less known as far as their nature goes – that is, by God's effects.

Hence:

1.   Knowledge that God exists is not implanted in us by nature in any clear or specific way. Admittedly, we naturally know what we naturally desire, and we naturally desire happiness, which is to be found only in God. But this is not to know unequivocally that there is a God any more than to be aware of someone approaching is to be aware of Peter (even if it is really Peter who is approaching). Many, in fact, believe that the ultimate good that will make us happy is riches, or pleasure, or some such thing.

2.   Someone hearing the word 'God' may very well not understand it to mean 'that than which nothing greater can be thought'. Indeed, some people have believed God to be something material. And even if someone thinks that what is signified by 'God' is 'that than which nothing greater can be thought', it does not follow that the person in question thinks that what is signified by 'God' exists in reality rather than merely as thought about. If we do not grant that something in fact exists than which nothing greater can be thought (and nobody denying the existence of God would grant this), the conclusion that God in fact exists does not follow.

---

3   John 14: 6.
4   *Metaphysics* 4.3, 1005b11; *Posterior Analytics* 1.10, 76b23–7.
5   Psalms 13: 1. The numbering of the Psalms follows that of the Latin Vulgate.
6   *How Substances Are Good in Virtue of their Existence without Being Substantial Goods* (*De Hebdomadibus*). PL 64.1311.
7   1a 3.4.

3.   It is self-evident that there is truth in general. But it is not self-evident to us that there is a First Truth.

Article 2. Can we demonstrate that God exists?

1. It seems that we cannot demonstrate[8] that God exists. For it is an article of faith that God exists, and we cannot demonstrate matters of faith since demonstration causes knowledge while faith, as St Paul says, is concerned with 'the unseen'.[9] So, it is impossible to demonstrate that God exists.

2. Moreover, the middle term[10] in a demonstration is what something is. But, as Damascene tells us, we do not know what God is, only what he is not.[11] So, we cannot demonstrate that God exists.

3. Again, if we could demonstrate God's existence, the demonstration would have to proceed by reference to his effects. But God and his effects are incommensurable, for God is infinite and his effects finite, and the finite cannot measure the infinite. So, since a cause cannot be demonstrated by effects that are incommensurate with it, it does not seem possible to demonstrate that God exists.

On the contrary, St Paul tells us that 'the invisible things of God can be clearly seen, being understood from what he has made'.[12] And if that is right, then we must be able to demonstrate that God exists from what he has made, for that something exists is the first thing we need to know about it.

Reply: There are two kinds of demonstration. One kind, 'demonstration why' something is so, argues from cause to effect and proceeds by means of what is unqualifiedly first. The other, 'demonstration that' something is so, argues from effect to cause and proceeds by means of what is first so far as we are concerned (for when an effect is more apparent to us than its cause, we come to know the cause through its effect). But, in cases where the effect is better known to us, any effect of a cause demonstrates that the cause exists, for effects depend on causes and can occur only if their causes exist. So, from effects that we know we can demonstrate what in itself is not self-evident to us, namely, that God exists.

Hence:

1.   The truths about God that St Paul says we can know by our natural powers of reasoning (that God exists, for example) are not articles of faith.[13] They are presupposed by them. For faith presupposes natural knowledge, just as grace does nature, and just as all perfections presuppose that which they perfect. But there is nothing to stop people from accepting on faith some demonstrable truth that they cannot personally demonstrate.

2.   When we demonstrate a cause from its effect, the effect takes the place of what the cause is in the proof that the cause exists, especially if the cause is God. For, when proving

---

8   i.e. prove by deducing from known premises.

9   Hebrews 11: 1.

10   The term in an Aristotelian syllogism that lets one link the subject of one premise with the predicate of another. Thus in the argument 'S is P, all Ps are Qs, so S is Q', the middle term is 'P'.

11   *On the Orthodox Faith* 1.4. PG 94.800.

12   Romans 1: 20.

13   Romans 1: 19–20.

that something exists, the middle term is not what the thing is (we cannot even ask what it is until we know that it exists) but what we are using the name of the thing to mean. But when demonstrating from effects that God exists, we are able to start from what the word 'God' means, for, as I shall later explain,[14] what we predicate of God is derived from these effects.

3. Effects can give comprehensive knowledge of their cause only when they are commensurate with it. But, as I have said, any effect can make it clear that a cause exists. So, God's effects can serve to demonstrate that God exists, even though they cannot help us to know him comprehensively for what he is.

Article 3. Does God exist?

1. It seems that there is no God. For if one of two contraries were infinite, the other would be completely destroyed. But by the word 'God' we understand a certain infinite good. So, if God existed, nobody would ever encounter evil. But we do encounter evil in the world. So, God does not exist.

2. Moreover, anything that can be caused by few principles is not caused by many. But it seems that we can fully account for everything we observe in the world while assuming that God does not exist. Thus we explain natural effects by natural causes, and intentional effects by human reasoning and will. So, there is no need to accept that God exists.

On the contrary, Exodus represents God as saying, 'I am who am.'[15]

Reply: There are five ways in which we can prove that there is a God.

The first and most obvious way is based on change. It is certain, and clear to our senses, that some things in the world undergo change. But anything in process of change is changed by something else. For nothing can be undergoing change unless it is potentially whatever it ends up being after its process of change – while something causes change in so far as it is actual[16] in some way. After all, to change something is simply to bring it from potentiality to actuality, and this can only be done by something that is somehow actual: thus fire (actually hot) causes wood (able to be hot) to become actually hot, and thus it changes and modifies it. But something cannot be simultaneously actually x and potentially x, though it can be actually x and potentially y (something actually hot, for instance, cannot also be potentially hot, though it can be potentially cold). So, something in process of change cannot itself cause that same change. It cannot change itself. Necessarily, therefore, anything in process of change is changed by something else. And this something else, if in process of change, is itself changed by yet another thing; and this last by another. But there has to be an end to this regress of causes, otherwise there will be no first cause of change, and, as a result, no subsequent causes of change. For it is only when acted upon by a first cause that intermediate causes produce change (if a hand does not move the stick, the stick will not move

---

14   1a 13.1ff.

15   Exodus 3: 14.

16   Aquinas's claim is that causes cause due to a property they have, not one they lack. When we say that the pilot's absence caused the shipwreck, then, Aquinas would parse this more precisely by saying that what caused the shipwreck was the storm and the hidden reef, but the pilot's absence permitted these causes to operate.

anything else). So, we are bound to arrive at some first cause of change that is not itself changed by anything, which is what everybody takes God to be.

The second way is based on the notion of efficient causation.[17] We find that there is an order of efficient causes in the observable world. Yet we never observe, nor ever could, something efficiently causing itself. For this would mean that it preceded itself, which it cannot do. But an order of efficient causes cannot go back infinitely. For an earlier member in it causes an intermediate, and the intermediate causes a last (whether the intermediate be one or many). If you eliminate a cause, however, you also eliminate its effect. So, there cannot be a last cause, nor an intermediate one, unless there is a first. If there is no end to the series of efficient causes, therefore, and if, as a consequence, there is no first cause, there would be no intermediate efficient causes either, and no last effect, which is clearly not the case. So, we have to posit a first cause, which everyone calls 'God'.

The third way is based on the possible and the necessary, and it runs as follows. Some of the things we encounter are able to be or not to be, for we find them generated and perished (and, therefore, able to be or not to be). But not everything can be like this. For something that is capable of not being at some time is not. So, if everything is able not to be, at some time there was nothing in the world. But if that were true, there would be nothing even now, for something that does not exist is only brought into being by something that does exist. Therefore, if nothing existed, nothing could have begun to exist, and nothing would exist now, which is patently not the case. So, not everything is the sort of thing that is able to be or not to be. There has got to be something that must be. Yet a thing that must be either does or does not have a cause of its necessity outside itself. And, just as we must stop somewhere in a series of efficient causes, so we must also stop in the series of things which must be and owe this to something else. This means that we are forced to posit something which is intrinsically necessary, owing its necessity to nothing else, something which is the cause that other things must be.

The fourth way is based on the gradations that we find in things. We find some things to be more and less good, more and less true, more and less noble, and so on. But we speak of various things as being more or less F in so far as they approximate in various ways to what is most F. For example, things are hotter and hotter the closer they approach to what is hottest. So, something is the truest and best and most noble of things, and hence the most fully in being.[18] For, as Aristotle says, the truest things are the things most fully in being.[19] But when many things possess some property in common, the one most fully possessing it causes it in the others. To use Aristotle's example, fire, the hottest of all things, causes all other things to be hot. So, there is something that causes in all other things their being, their goodness, and whatever other perfection they have, and we call this 'God'.

The fifth way is based on the governance of things. For we see that some things that lack intelligence (i.e. material objects in nature) act for the sake of an end. This is clear from the fact that they always, or usually, act in the same way so as to achieve what is best (and therefore reach their goal by purpose, not by chance). But things lacking intelligence tend to a goal only as directed by one with knowledge and understanding. Arrows, for instance, need archers. So, there is a being with intelligence who directs all natural things to ends, and we call this being 'God'.

17   Causation in the usual sense.
18   *Metaphysics* 2.1, 993b30.
19   *Metaphysics* 2.1, 993b25.

Hence:

1.   As Augustine says, 'Since God is supremely good, he would not permit any evil at all in his works, unless he were sufficiently powerful and good to bring good even from evil.'[20] So, it belongs to the limitless goodness of God that he permits evils to exist and draws good from them.

2.   Since nature acts for definite ends under the direction of a higher cause, its effects must be traced to God as the first of all causes. Similarly, even things done intentionally must be traced back to a higher cause than human reasoning and will, for these are changeable and lacking. And, as I have said, we must trace all such things back to a first cause that cannot change and is intrinsically necessary.

Part I, Question 3. God's Simplicity

Having recognized that something exists, we still have to investigate the way in which it exists, so that we may come to understand what it is that exists. But we cannot know what God is,[21] only what he is not. We must therefore consider the ways in which God does not exist rather than the ways in which he does. So, now I consider:

> First, the ways in which God is not;
> second, the ways in which we know him;
> third, the ways in which we describe him.

The ways in which God is not will become apparent if we rule out everything unfitting to him, such as being composite, changing, and the like. So, I shall ask:

First, about God's simplicity, thus ruling out composition.[22] And because simplicity implies imperfection and incompleteness in the material world, I shall then ask:

> second, about God's perfection;
> third, about his limitlessness;
> fourth, about his unchangeableness;
> fifth, about his oneness.

About the first of these questions there are eight points of inquiry:

1.   Is God a body? Is he, that is to say, composed of extended parts?
2.   Is he composed of form and matter?

---

20   *A Handbook on Faith, Hope and Love (Enchiridion)* 11. PL 40.236.
21   According to Aquinas, we know that God necessarily satisfies many descriptions – that he is omnipotent, omniscient, etc. But God satisfies these because he is divine. For Aquinas these descriptions do not tell us what it is to be divine; it is not the case that to be divine is to be omniscient, omnipotent, etc. Deity is some property other than any of these. Aquinas's claim here is that we cannot intellectually grasp this property. We can know what it is to be omniscient or to be human, but we cannot know what it is to be divine.
22   Literally consisting of or having been put together from parts. We usually think of parts as concrete things from which other concrete things are assembled. But the same thing can consist completely of different sorts of parts: books, say, of both quarks and molecules. Aquinas thinks that concrete things consist completely of concrete parts, but also abstract ones – essences, accidents, and the like.

3. Is he composed of 'whatness' (essence or nature) and subject?
4. Is he composed of essence and existence?
5. Is he composed of genus and difference?
6. Is he composed of substance and accidents?
7. Is there any way in which he is composite, or is he altogether simple?
8. Does he enter into composition with other things?

Article 1. Is God a body composed of extended parts?

1. It would seem that God is a body. For a body is something with three dimensions, and sacred Scripture ascribes three dimensions to God: 'He is higher than heaven and what will you do? He is deeper than hell and how will you know? His measure is longer than the earth and broader than the sea.'[23] So, God is a body.

2. Moreover, everything with shape is a body, for shape is characteristic of extended things as such. But God seems to have a shape, for in Genesis we read, 'Let us make human beings in our image and likeness',[24] where 'image' means 'figure' or 'shape' as in Hebrews: 'who is the brightness of his glory, and the figure [that is to say, image] of his substance'.[25] So, God is a body.

3. Moreover, anything with bodily parts is a body. But Scripture ascribes bodily parts to God, saying in Job, 'Have you an arm like God?',[26] and in the Psalms, 'The eyes of the Lord are towards the righteous'[27] and 'the right hand of the Lord does valiantly'.[28] So, God is a body.

4. Moreover, only bodies can assume postures. But Scripture ascribes certain postures to God: thus Isaiah 'saw the Lord sitting',[29] and says that 'the Lord stands to judge'.[30] So, God is a body.

5. Again, nothing can be the starting-point or finishing-point of a spatial movement unless it is a body or bodily. But Scripture refers to God as the finishing-point of a spatial movement ('Come to him and be enlightened')[31] and as a starting-point ('Those that depart from you shall be written in the earth').[32] So, God is a body.

On the contrary, John writes: 'God is spirit.'[33]

Reply: God is in no way a body, and we can show this in three ways.

First, no body causes change without itself being changed, as can be shown inductively. But I have shown above that God is the unchanging first cause of change.[34] So, God is clearly not a body.

23 Job 11: 8–9.
24 Genesis 1: 26.
25 Hebrews 1: 3.
26 Job 40: 4.
27 Psalms 33: 16.
28 Psalms 117: 16.
29 Isaiah 6: 1.
30 Isaiah 3: 13.
31 Psalms 33: 6.
32 Jeremiah 17: 13.
33 John 4: 24.
34 1a 2.3.

Second, the first being must of necessity be actual and in no way potential. For, although in any one thing that passes from potentiality to actuality, the potentiality temporally precedes the actuality, actuality, absolutely speaking, precedes potentiality, for nothing can be changed from a state of potentiality to one of actuality except by something actual. Now we have seen that the first being is God.[35] So, there can be no potentiality in God. In bodies, however, there is always potentiality, because the extended is as such divisible. So, God cannot be a body.

Third, God is the most noble of beings, as is clear from what I have already said.[36] But a body cannot be the most noble of beings. For bodies are either living or non-living, and living bodies are clearly the more excellent. Yet a living body is not alive simply in virtue of being a body (otherwise all bodies would be living); it is alive because of some other principle (in our case, the soul). Such a principle will be more excellent than body as such. So, God cannot be a body.

Hence:

1.   As I remarked earlier, sacred Scripture uses bodily metaphors to convey truth about God and spiritual things.[37] So, in ascribing three dimensions to God they are using bodily extension to signify the extent of God's power: depth, for example, signifies his power to know what is hidden; height, the loftiness of his power above all other things; length, the lasting quality of his existence; breadth, the universality of his love. Or there is Dionysius's explanation of depth as the incomprehensibility of God's essence, length as the penetration of all things by God's power, and breadth as the boundless reach of God's guardianship enveloping all things.[38]

2.   We say that human beings are in God's image, not because they have bodies, but because of their superiority to other animals. And this is why Genesis, after saying, 'Let us make human beings in our image and likeness', adds, 'that they may have dominion over the fishes of the sea',[39] and so on. Human beings owe this superiority to reason and intellect. So, they are in God's image because of their intellect and reason, which are incorporeal.

3.   The Scriptures ascribe bodily parts to God by a metaphor drawn from their functions. Eyes, for example, see; so, when we attribute an 'eye' to God it refers to his power of seeing things in an intelligible rather than a sensory manner. And similarly with other parts of the body.

4.   The ascribing of posture to God is again simply metaphor. He is said to be sitting, for instance, because of his unchangeableness and authority. He is said to be standing because his might triumphs in the face of all opposition.

5.   One approaches God, and one draws away from him, not by bodily movement, since he is everywhere, but by movement of the heart. In this context, 'approaching' and 'drawing away' are metaphors that picture being moved in spirit as if it were like being moved in space.

---

35   1a 2.3.
36   1a 2.3.
37   1a 1.9.
38   *The Divine Names* 9.5. PG 3.913.
39   Genesis 1: 28.

Article 2. Is God composed of form[40] and matter[41]?

1. God seems to be composed of form and matter. For since soul is the form of the body,[42] anything with a soul is composed of matter and form. But the Scriptures ascribe soul to God; thus in Hebrews we find quoted, as if from the mouth of God, 'my righteous one shall live by faith, and if he shrinks back my soul will have no pleasure in him'.[43] So, God is composed of matter and form.

2. Moreover, according to Aristotle, anger, joy, and the like, are passions of something made up of parts.[44] But the Scriptures ascribe such passions to God: 'the anger of the Lord,' says the psalm, 'was kindled against his people'.[45] So, God is composed of matter and form.

3. Again, matter is what makes a thing an individual. But God seems to be an individual, not something predicable of many individuals. So, God is composed of matter and form.

On the contrary, since having dimensions is one of the primary properties of matter, anything composed of matter and form must be a body. As I have shown, however, God is not a body.[46] So, he is not composed of matter and form.

Reply: God cannot contain matter.

First, because matter is potential, while God, as I have shown, is sheer actuality with no potentiality.[47] So, God cannot be composed of matter and form.

Second, in things composed of form and matter, their form gives them perfection and goodness. Such composite things therefore only participate in goodness, for matter participates in form. But the first and best good (i.e. God) does not participate in goodness, for being good by essence is prior to being good by a kind of participation.[48] So, God cannot be composed of matter and form.

Third, all agents act in virtue of their form, so the way in which they are agents will depend on the type of form they have. What is primarily and essentially an agent must therefore be primarily and intrinsically form. Yet God is the primary agent, since, as I have explained, he is the first efficient cause.[49] So, God is essentially form and is not composed of matter and form.

---

40 A real attribute 'in' the thing. Aquinas thinks of forms as abstract constituents, as particular as their bearers: Socrates' humanity is something abstract that is 'in' and particular to Socrates. Forms are either substantial or accidental. For any x, x' substantial form is that in x which made x' matter (q.v.) become and/or makes it be actually x' kind of thing. The substantial form of water, for instance, is a structure which makes of a group of atoms an instance of the kind *water molecule*. A form is accidental just if it is not substantial. A form may be, for example, a shape, a structure, a power, a quality or a soul.

41 That which 'bears' or 'receives' forms. For any x, x' matter is the stuff of which x is made, the parts of which x is composed, or most generally that which was potentially x and became actually x.

42 For Aquinas, for any x, x' form is that in x which made (or makes) x' matter (q.v.) become (or be) actually x' kind of thing. Every soul is a form: a dog's soul is that in the dog which made and makes its matter a living canine body, and so a dog. But not every form is a soul. Water has a form but no soul.

43 Hebrews 10: 38.

44 *On the Soul* 1.1, 403a3ff.

45 Psalms 105: 40.

46 1a 3.1.

47 1a 3.1.

48 Something 'participates in' a form just if it bears the form and is not identical with it.

49 1a 2.3.

Hence:

1.   Scripture ascribes soul to God by a metaphor drawn from its activity. For since soul is the seat of volition in us, we call what is pleasing to God's will 'pleasing to his soul'.

2.   Scripture ascribes anger and the like to God by a metaphor drawn from their effects. For it is characteristic of anger that it stimulates us to requite wrong. Divine retribution is therefore metaphorically called 'anger'.

3.   The forms of material things are individualized by matter, which cannot be predicable of a subject since it is itself the first underlying subject – though a form as such (unless something interferes) can be received by many things. But a form which cannot be received in matter, and is self-subsisting, is individualized just because it cannot be received in a subject, and God is such a form. So, it does not follow that there is matter in God.

Article 3. Is God composed of 'whatness' (that is, essence[50] or nature) and subject?[51]

1. It seems that God is not the same as his essence or nature. For nothing is in itself. But we say that God's essence or nature (his divinity) is in God. So, it seems that God must differ from his essence or nature.

2. Moreover, effects resemble their causes, for what a thing does reflects what it is. But individual created things are other than their natures (a particular human being, for instance, is not humanity). So, it seems that God is not divinity.

On the contrary, we speak of God not only as living but as life: 'I am the way, the truth and the life.'[52] But divinity bears the same relationship to God as life does to the living. So, God is divinity itself.

Reply: God is the same as his essence or nature.

We shall understand this when we note that things composed of matter and form cannot be the same as their natures or essences. For essence or nature in these things includes only what falls within the definition of a species – as humanity includes what falls within the definition of human being, for this makes us to be human and is what humanity signifies (i.e. what makes human beings to be human beings). But we do not define the species of anything by the matter and properties peculiar to it as an individual. We do not, for example, define human beings as things that have *this* flesh and *these* bones, or are white, or black, or the like. *This* flesh and *these* bones, and the properties peculiar to them, belong indeed to *this* human being, but not to its nature. Individual human beings therefore possess something that human nature does not, and particular human beings and their nature are not, therefore, altogether the

---

50   For any x, x′ having its essence makes x the kind of thing it is, and so is that which makes true the answer to the question 'what is x?' Things acquire their essences by acquiring their substantial forms: a water molecule acquires its essence, *being water*, by coming to host the distinctive structure of a water molecule. Aquinas thinks of essences as abstract constituents, as particular as their bearers: Socrates' humanity is something abstract that is 'in' and particular to Socrates.

51   Subject: that which receives or bears an essence. When hydrogen and oxygen atoms come to make up a water molecule, the atoms are the subject that receives the essence (that is, come to be structured as water molecules are) and the resulting water is the subject that bears the essence.

52   John 14: 6.

same thing. 'Human nature' names the formative element in human beings; for what gives a thing definition is formative with respect to the matter that gives it individuality.

However, the individuality of things not composed of matter and form cannot derive from this or that individual matter. So, the forms of such things must be intrinsically individual and themselves subsist as things. Such things are therefore identical with their natures.

In the same way, then, God, who, as I have said, is not composed of matter and form,[53] is identical with his own divinity, his own life, and with whatever else is similarly predicated of him.

Hence:

1.   When we talk about simple things we have to use the composite things from which our knowledge derives as models. So, when talking about God we use concrete nouns to signify his subsistence (since the subsistent things with which we are familiar are composite), and we use abstract nouns to express his simplicity. Therefore, when we talk of divinity, or life, or something of that sort, residing in God, we should not attribute the diversity that this implies to God himself, but to the way in which we conceive of him.

2.   God's effects resemble God as far as they can, but not perfectly. This failure in resemblance is due to the fact that they can represent only by many what, in itself, is simple and one. As a result they are composite and cannot, therefore, be identified with their natures.

Article 4. Is God composed of essence and existence?

1. It seems that essence and existence are not the same when it comes to God. If they were, there would be nothing added to God's existence. But existence to which nothing is added is existence in general (the existence that is predicated of everything), and, if essence and existence are the same in God, the word 'God' would mean 'existence in general' (the existence we can predicate of everything). But this is not so. As the book of Wisdom says, 'they gave the incommunicable name to wood and stones'.[54] So, God's existence is not his essence.

2. Moreover, as I said earlier, we can know that God exists, but we cannot know what he is.[55] So, God's existence is not the same as what God is – his essence or nature.

On the contrary, Hilary writes, 'Existence is not an accident in God; it is subsisting truth.'[56] So, what subsists in God is his existence.

Reply: I have shown that God is his own essence.[57] That he is also his own existence can be shown in a number of ways.

First, what belongs to a thing over and above its essence must be caused: either from the principles of the essence itself, as accidents peculiar to a particular species (as the sense of humour characteristic of human beings derives from human nature), or from an external cause (as heat in water derives from some fire). So, if the existence of something is other than its essence, it must derive from the thing's essence, or it must have an external cause.

53   1a 3.2.
54   Wisdom 14: 21.
55   1a 2.2.
56   St Hilary of Poitiers (*c.* 315–*c.* 368), *On the Trinity* 8. PL 10.208.
57   1a 3.3.

But it cannot be caused by the principles of the thing's essence, for nothing of which the existence is derived can bring itself into being. If a thing's existence differs from its essence, therefore, its existence must be caused by something other than the thing in question. But this cannot be so in God's case, for, as we have seen, he is the first efficient cause.[58] So, we cannot say that God's existence is something other than his essence.

Second, existence is what makes every form or nature actual (which is why we only express the actuality of goodness or human nature by speaking of them as existing). So, when a nature is not what amounts to existence as such, then, it must exist potentially. Now, as I have shown, God does not contain potentialities.[59] In him, therefore, essence cannot differ from existence, and existence is his essence.

Third, anything on fire, without being fire itself, participates in fire. Similarly, anything existing, without being 'existence as such', participates in existence. Now, God and his essence are the same, as I have shown.[60] And if God is not 'existence as such' (if existence is not what his essence amounts to), then he only participates in existence and will not therefore be the primary existent, which he clearly is. So, God is not only his own essence, but also his own existence.

Hence:

1. We can understand 'something to which nothing is added' in two ways. We can take it as implying that further addition is excluded by definition (as reason is excluded by definition from irrational animals). We can also take it as implying that further addition is just not included in the definition (as reason is not included in the definition of animals in general, though neither is it excluded). Understood in the first way, divine existence is existence without addition. Understood in the second way, existence without addition is existence in general.

2. We use the verb 'to be' in two ways: to signify the act of existence, and to signify the mental uniting of predicate to subject which constitutes a proposition. Now, we cannot know what God's act of existence amounts to any more than we can know his essence. But we can know God's being in the second sense in so far as we know ourselves to be speaking truly when we say that God exists. As I have said, we know that we are speaking truly here because of God's effects.[61]

Article 5. Is God composed of genus and difference?

1. It seems that God does belong to a genus. For the definition of a substance ('something self-subsistent') is most fully applicable to God. So, God belongs to the genus of substance.

2. Moreover, any measure must belong to the same genus as the things it measures (lengths are measured by length, and numbers by number). But it seems from what Averroës says that God is the measure of all substances.[62] So, God must belong to the genus of substance.

On the contrary, a genus is logically prior to the things that exemplify it. But nothing is prior to God in either reality or understanding. So, God does not belong to a genus.

---

58   1a 2.3.
59   1a 3.1.
60   1a 2.3.
61   1a 2.2, especially *ad* 2.
62   Ibn Rushd, also known as Averroes (1126–98), *Commentary on Aristotle's Metaphysics* 10.7.

Reply: There are two ways of belonging to a genus: strictly and without qualification, as do the species that fall under a genus; and by way of reduction, as principles and privations do. For example, unity and the point are reduced to the genus of quantity as principles of quantity; and blindness, like all other defects, is reduced to the genus of its corresponding. But God belongs to a genus in neither of these ways.

We can show that he cannot be a species within a genus in three ways.

First, because we define species by differentiating some generic notion. Such differentiation is always based on some actualization of the potentiality that gave rise to the generic notion. Thus sense-life, envisaged in the concrete, gives rise to the notion of animal (an animal being something that lives by sense-perception), while mental life gives rise to the notion of a reasoning creature (a creature which lives by its mind). But the mind-life of human beings realizes potentialities of their sense-life. And we see the like in other cases. So, since realization of potentialities does not occur in God, he cannot be a species within a genus.

Second, since the genus of something states what the thing is, a genus must express a thing's essence. But God's essence is to exist, as I have shown.[63] So, the only genus to which God could belong would be the genus of being. Aristotle, however, has shown that there is no such genus: for genera are differentiated by factors not already contained within those genera, and no differentiating factor could be found that did not already exist (it could not differentiate if it did not exist).[64] So, we are left with no genus to which God could belong.

Third, all members of a genus share one essence or nature: that of the genus stating what they are. As existing things, however, they differ, for some particular horse is not some particular man, and this man is not that man. So, when something belongs to a genus, its nature, or what it is, must differ from its existence. As I have shown, though, this difference does not exist in God.[65] God, therefore, clearly cannot be a species within a genus.

And this shows why we cannot assign either genus or difference to God, nor define him, nor demonstrate anything of him except by means of his effects; for definitions are composed of genus and difference, and demonstration depends upon definition.

It is also clear that God does not belong mediately to a genus by initiating or generating it. For anything that initiates a genus in such a way that it mediately belongs to it is ineffective outside that genus: only the point generates extension, and only unity generates number. But God initiates everything that is, as I shall later show.[66] So, he does not initiate any particular genus so as to belong to it.

Hence:

1. The word 'substance' does not mean baldly that which exists of itself, for existence is not a genus, as I have shown. Rather, 'substance' means 'that which is possessed of an essence such that it will exist of itself, even though to exist is not its essence'. So, it is clear that God does not belong to the genus of substance.

2. This argument supposes that like is measured by like. Strictly speaking, however, God is not like anything, though he is called the measure of all things in as much as the closer things come to God the more fully they exist.

---

63   1a 3.4.
64   *Metaphysics* 3.3, 998b22.
65   1a 3.4.
66   1a 44.1.

Article 6. Is God composed of substance[67] and accidents?[68]

1. It seems that there are accidents in God. For Aristotle says that 'substance is never accidental to anything'.[69] So, something that is accidental in one thing cannot be the substance of another. The fact that heat, for example, is an accidental form of some things proves that it cannot be the substantial form of fire. But wisdom, power, and the like, which we ascribe to God, are accidents in us. So, there are accidents in God.

2. Moreover, in every genus there is a principal member. But there are many genera of accidents. So, if the principal members of these genera are not in God, there will be many other principal members besides God; and this does not seem right.

On the contrary, every accident is an accident of some subject. But God cannot be a subject, since, as Boethius says, 'no simple form can be a subject'.[70] So, there cannot be accidents in God.

Reply: What I have already said makes it clear that accidents cannot exist in God.

First, because accidents realize some potentialities of their subject, since an accident is a mode in which the subject achieves actuality. But, as I have said, we must entirely rule out potentiality from God.[71]

Second, because God is his own act of existence, and as Boethius says, 'you may add to an existent, but you cannot add to existence itself'[72] (just as a hot thing may have other properties besides being hot – such as whiteness – but heat itself cannot be otherwise than hot).

Third, because what exists by nature is prior to what is accidental, so that if God is the absolutely prime existent, nothing can exist in him by accident. Nor can there be accidents existing in him by nature (as, for example, people have a sense of humour by nature). For such accidents derive from a subject's essential nature. But there is nothing derived in God. All derivation starts from him. It therefore follows that God contains no accidents.

Hence:

1. As I shall explain later, we do not ascribe power and wisdom to God and to us in the same sense.[73] So, it does not follow that accidents exist in God as they do in us.

2. Since substance is prior to accidents, the principles of accidents are reducible to the principles of substance as to something prior. And although God is not first in the genus of substance, he is still first with respect to all being, transcending all genera.

---

67   A concrete particular thing that bears attributes.

68   Accidents: attributes (forms) that are not essences or substantial forms. Aquinas thinks of accidents as abstract constituents, as particular as their bearers: Socrates' weight is something abstract that is 'in' and particular to Socrates. As Aquinas sees it, all real accidents are either quantities (which make true answers to questions in the 'how much?' family), qualities (which make true answers to questions in the 'how is it?' or 'what is it like?' families) or relations (which make true answers to questions about how things are related).

69   *Physics* 1.3, 186b1–4.

70   *On the Trinity* 2. PL 64.1250.

71   1a 3.1.

72   *How Substances Are Good in Virtue of Their Existence without Being Substantial Goods* (*De Hebdomadibus*). PL 64.1311.

73   1a 13.5.

Article 7. Is there any way in which God is composite, or is he entirely simple?

1. It seems that God is not entirely simple. For the things that derive from God resemble him: thus everything deriving from the first being exists, and everything deriving from the first good is good. But nothing deriving from God is entirely simple. So, God is not entirely simple either.

2. Moreover, we should ascribe whatever is better to God. But, in the world with which we are familiar, composite things are better than simple ones: compounds are better than elements, for example, and elements are better than their constituent parts. So, we should not assert that God is altogether simple.

On the contrary, Augustine says that God is truly and absolutely simple.[74]

Reply: There are many ways of showing that God is entirely simple.

First, relying on what I have already said, God is not composed of extended parts (since he is not a body), nor of form and matter, nor does he differ from his own nature, nor his nature from his existence. Nor can we distinguish in him genus and difference, nor substance and accidents. It is therefore clear that God is in no way composite. Rather, he is entirely simple.

Second, everything composite is subsequent to its components and dependent on them. But God, as I have shown, is the first of all beings.[75]

Third, everything composite is caused; for elements diverse of themselves do not combine unless made to do so by a cause. As I have said, though, God is not caused since he is the first efficient cause.[76]

Fourth, in any composite there is a realizing of potentialities such as cannot occur in God: for either the potentialities of one component are realized by another, or, at any rate, all the components together are potentially the whole.

Fifth, we cannot predicate anything composite of its own component parts. This is obvious in composites made up of different parts, for no part of a man is a man, and no part of a foot is a foot. And although in composites made up of similar parts certain ways of describing the whole apply also to the parts (every bit of air, for example, is air, and every drop of water is water), other ways do not (thus if a unit of water occupies two cubic feet, no part of it will do so). So, in all composites there is some element that is not the composite itself. Now, even if we grant that a thing possessed of a form may contain something that is not itself (e.g. that a white thing contains elements not included in the concept of whiteness), in the form itself there is nothing other than itself. But God is form itself, indeed existence itself. So, he can in no way be composite. And this was what Hilary was pointing out when he said, 'God, being power, is not made up of things that are weak; and, being light, is not pieced together from things that are darkness.'[77]

Hence:

1. Things deriving from God resemble him as effects resemble a primary cause. But it is in the nature of an effect to be composite in some way, because even at its simplest its existence differs from its essence, as I shall later explain.[78]

74 *On the Trinity* 4.4–8. PL 42.927–9.

75 1a 2.3.

76 1a 2.3.

77 *On the Trinity* 7. PL 10.223.

78 1a 50.2, *ad* 3.

2.   In the world with which we are familiar composite things are better than simple ones, because created perfection is found in many things, not just one. But divine perfection is found in one simple thing, as I shall shortly show.[79]

Article 8. Does God enter into composition with other things?

1. It seems that God does enter into composition with other things. For Dionysius declares that 'the existence of everything is the divine nature, which is beyond being'.[80] But the existence of everything enters into the composition of each. So, God enters into composition with other things.

2. Moreover, God is a form, for Augustine says that 'the Word of God' (which is God) 'is unformed form'.[81] But form is a component of things. So, God must be a component of something.

3. Again, things which exist without differing are identical. But God and prime matter[82] exist without differing and are, therefore, completely identical. Yet prime matter enters into the composition of things. So, God must do so too. – To prove the middle step in this argument: things that differ do so by certain differentiating factors, and must therefore be composite. But God and prime matter are altogether simple and, therefore, they are identical.

On the contrary, Dionysius says that 'nothing can touch God, nor is there any union with him by mingling part with part'.[83]

Reply: On this point three mistakes have been made. As we learn from Augustine, some people have held that God is the soul of the world.[84] We can include with these people those who said that God is the soul of the outermost heaven.[85] Others have said that God is the form of all things – the reputed view of Amaury of Bène and his followers. The third mistake was the really stupid thesis of David of Dinant – that God is prime matter. All these opinions are clearly wrong. God cannot enter into composition with anything in any way, whether as a formal principle or as a material one.

First, because God is the first efficient cause of things, as I have already said.[86] But the form of an effect, though specifically similar to its efficient cause (e.g. people beget people),

---

79   1a 4.2, *ad* 1.

80   *The Celestial Hierarchy* 4.1. PG 3.177.

81   Sermons 38. PL 38.662.

82   The ultimate receiver of all attributes. Suppose with Aquinas that there are four elements – earth, air, fire and water – and that some earth can change into some water. If this is one body of stuff changing, rather than being replaced by another body of stuff, something must be there throughout that first bears the attribute of being earth and then bears the attribute of being water. But if earth and water are *elements*, they are ultimate kinds of chemical matter: they are not made up of some more fundamental chemical stuff. Aquinas infers that there is a more basic kind of matter than chemical elements, and he calls it prime matter. Since for Aquinas every physical thing is composed of elements, for Aquinas, every physical thing contains prime matter.

83   *The Divine Names* 2.5. PG 3.643.

84   *The City of God* 7.6. PL 41.199.

85   Aquinas accepted Aristotle's cosmology, in which the earth was surrounded by a series of crystalline spheres, the heavens.

86   1a 2.3.

is not numerically identical with the efficient cause. Matter and efficient causes are neither numerically nor specifically identical, for matter is in potentiality while efficient causes are actual.

Second, since God is the first efficient cause, efficient activity belongs to him primarily and essentially. But a component is not an efficient cause primarily and essentially. Thus a hand does not act. Rather, human beings act by means of their hands, and it is fire which warms by virtue of its heat. So, God cannot be a component of anything.

Third, no part of something composite can be the first being. Nor can the matter or form of composite things (their first parts) be the first among beings. For matter is in potentiality, and potentiality is unqualifiedly secondary to actuality, as I have shown.[87] Again, form, when a part of something composite, is a form which participates in something. Now something that participates in x is posterior to that which is essentially x.

For example, the fire that is in things that are on fire is posterior to that which is by nature fire. But I have already shown that God is the primary being, without qualification.[88]

Hence:

1. Dionysius means that God's nature is the existence of all things by efficient causality and as an exemplar, not by its essence.
2. The Word is not a component form but an exemplary one.[89]
3. Simple things do not differ from one another because of differences. That is the case only with composites. Hence, although the factors 'rational' and 'irrational' differentiate people and horses, these factors themselves do not require further factors to differentiate them one from another. Strictly speaking, therefore, simple things are not *different*, but *diverse*. According to Aristotle, things that are diverse are absolutely distinct, but things that are different are different in some respect.[90] Strictly speaking, then, God and prime matter are not *different* but *diverse*. So, it does not follow that they are identical.

Part I, Question 13. Talking about God

Having considered how we know God, I now turn to consider how we speak of him, for we speak of things as we know them. Here there are twelve points of inquiry:

1. Can we use any words to refer to God?
2. Do we predicate of God substantially?[91]
3. Do we predicate of God literally, or must we always do so metaphorically?
4. Are the many terms we predicate of God synonyms?
5. Are words we use both of God and of creatures used univocally or equivocally?
6. Given that we actually use them analogically, do we predicate them primarily of God or of creatures?
7. In speaking of God, can we use words that imply temporal succession?

87 1a. 3.1.
88 1a 2.3.
89 The prototype or model in accordance with which things are made.
90 *Metaphysics* 10.3, 1054b24.
91 i.e. do words in the category of substance express God's nature when used to describe him?

8. Is 'God' the name of a nature or of a certain activity?

9. Is the name 'God' peculiar to God or not?

10. When it is used of God, of what shares in divinity, and of what is merely supposed to do so, is it used univocally or equivocally?

11. Is 'The One who Is' the most appropriate name for God?

12. Can we formulate affirmative propositions about God?

Article 1. Are any words suitable for talking about God?

1. It seems that no words are suitable for talking about God. For Dionysius says, 'of him there is no naming nor any opinion',[92] and we read in Proverbs, 'What is his name or the name of his son if you know?'[93]

2. Moreover, nouns are either abstract or concrete. But concrete nouns are inappropriate to God because he is altogether simple; and we can rule out abstract nouns because they do not signify a complete subsistent thing. So, we can predicate no term of God.

3. Again, a noun signifies something as coming under some description; verbs and participles signify it as enduring in time; pronouns signify it as being pointed out or as being in some relationship. None of these is appropriate to God: he has no qualities or accidental attributes; he is non-temporal; and he cannot be pointed to because he is not available to the senses; moreover he cannot be referred to by relative pronouns since the use of these depends on the previous use of some other referring term such as a noun, participle or demonstrative pronoun. So, there is no way of referring to God.

On the contrary, in Exodus we read, 'The Lord is a great warrior; His name is Almighty.'[94]

Reply: Aristotle says that spoken words are signs for thoughts, and thoughts are likenesses of things.[95] So, words refer to things indirectly through thoughts. We can therefore designate something in so far as we can know it intellectually. Now, I have already shown that we cannot see God's essence in this life.[96] We only know him from creatures. We think of him as their source, and then as surpassing them all and as lacking anything that is merely creaturely. So, we can designate God from creatures, though the words we use do not express that divine essence as it is in itself. In this they differ from a term like 'human being', which is intended to express by its meaning the essence of human being as it is – for the meaning of 'human being' is given by a definition of human being which expresses its essence, for the nature that a name signifies is the definition.

Hence:

1. We say that God has no name, or is beyond naming, because his essence is beyond what we understand of him and the meaning of the names we use.

2. Since we come to know God from creatures, and since this is how we come to refer to him, the expressions we use to name him signify in a way that is appropriate to the

---

92 *The Divine Names* 1. PG 3.593.

93 Proverbs 30: 4.

94 Exodus 15: 3.

95 *On Interpretation* 1.1, 16a3.

96 1a 12.4.

material creatures we ordinarily know. Among such creatures the complete subsistent thing is always a concrete union of form and matter; for the form itself is not a subsistent thing, but that by which something subsists. Because of this the words we use to signify complete subsistent things are concrete nouns which are appropriate to composite subjects. When, on the other hand, we want to speak of the form itself we use abstract nouns which do not signify something as subsistent, but as that by which something is: 'whiteness', for example, signifies that by which something is white.

Now God is both simple, like a form, and subsistent, like something concrete. So, we some-times refer to him by abstract nouns (to indicate his simplicity) while at other times we refer to him by concrete nouns (to indicate his subsistence and completeness) – though neither way of speaking measures up to his way of being, for in this life we do not know him as he is in himself.

3.   To signify something as coming under some description is to signify it as subsisting in a certain nature or definite form. I have already said that the reason we use concrete nouns for God is to indicate his subsistence and completeness;[97] it is for the same reason that we use nouns signifying a thing under some description. Although they imply temporal succession, we can use verbs and participles of him because his eternity includes all time. Just as we can understand what is both simple and subsistent only as though it were composite, so we can understand and speak of the simplicity of eternity only after the manner of temporal things. It is composite and temporal things that we ordinarily and naturally understand. We can use demonstrative pronouns of God in so far as they point, not to something seen, but to something understood, for so long as we know something, in whatever way, we can point it out. So, just as nouns and participles and demonstrative pronouns can signify God, so can relative pronouns.

Article 2. Do we predicate any term of God substantially?

1. It seems that we predicate no term of God substantially. For John Damascene says, 'The words used of God must signify not what he is substantially but what he is not, or his rela-tionship to something else, or something that follows from his nature or activity.'[98]

2. Moreover, Dionysius says, 'You will find a chorus of holy teachers seeking to distin-guish clearly and laudably the divine processions in the naming of God.'[99] This means that the words which the holy teachers use in praising God differ according to his different causal acts. But to speak of something's causal activity is not to speak of its essence. So, such words are not predicated of God substantially.

3. Again, we designate things to the extent that we understand them. But in this life we do not understand God's substance (what God is). So, we cannot predicate anything of him substantially (we cannot say what he is).

On the contrary, Augustine says, 'To be God is to be strong, to be wise, or whatever else we say of his simplicity in order to signify his substance.'[100] So, all such terms signify God's substance.

---

97   See the reply to objection 2 in the present article.
98   *On the Orthodox Faith* 1.9. PG 94.835.
99   *The Divine Names* 1. PG 3.589.
100   *On the Trinity* 6.4. PL 42.927.

Reply: It is clear that the problem does not arise for negative terms or for words which express the relationship of God to creatures. These obviously do not express what he is but rather what he is not or how he is related to something else – or, better, how something else is related to him. The question is concerned with words like 'good' and 'wise' which are neither negative nor relational terms, and about these there are several opinions.

Some have said that sentences like 'God is good', though they sound like affirmations, are in fact used to deny something of God rather than to assert anything. Thus, for example, when we say that God is living we mean that he is not like something inanimate, and likewise for all such propositions. This was the view of the Rabbi Moses.[101]

Others said that such sentences are used to signify the relation of God to creatures, so that when we say 'God is good' we mean that God is the cause of goodness in things, and likewise in other such propositions.

Neither of these views seems plausible, however, for three reasons.

First, on neither view can there be any reason why we should use some words about God rather than others. God is just as much the cause of bodies as he is of goodness in things. So, if 'God is good' means no more than that God is the cause of goodness in things, why not say 'God is a body' since he is the cause of bodies? Likewise, we could also say 'God is a body' because we want to deny that he is merely potential being like prime matter.

Second it would follow that everything we say of God is true only in a secondary sense, as when we say that medicine is 'healthy', meaning merely that it causes health in the one who takes it. But it is the living body that we call healthy in a primary sense.

Third, this is not what people want to say when they talk about God. When people speak of the 'living God' they do not simply want to say that God is the cause of our life, or that he differs from a lifeless body.

So, we must find some other solution to the problem: that such words do say what God is (they are predicated of him in the category of substance),[102] but they fail adequately to represent what he is. The reason for this is that we speak of God as we know him, and since we know him from creatures we can only speak of him as they represent him. Any creature, in so far as it possesses any perfection, represents God and is like him, for he, being simply and universally perfect, has pre-existing in himself the perfections of all his creatures, as I have already noted.[103] But a creature is not like God as it is like another member of its species or genus. It resembles him as an effect may in some way resemble a transcendent cause although failing to reproduce perfectly the form of the cause – as in a certain way the forms of inferior bodies imitate the power of the sun. I explained this earlier when I was dealing with God's perfection.[104] So, words like 'good' and 'wise' when used of God do signify something that God really is, but they signify it imperfectly because creatures represent God imperfectly.

So, 'God is good' does not mean the same as 'God is the cause of goodness' or 'God is not evil'. It means that what we call 'goodness' in creatures pre-exists in God in a higher way. Thus God is not good because he causes goodness. Rather, goodness flows from him because he is good. As Augustine says, 'Because he is good, we exist.'[105]

---

101 Moses Maimonides (1138–1204), *Guide for the Perplexed* 1.58.
102 They express his nature.
103 1a 4.2.
104 1a 4.3.
105 *On Christian Doctrine* 1.32. PL 34.32.

Hence:

1.   Damascene is saying that these words do not signify what God is since none of them express completely what he is; but each signifies imperfectly something that he is, just as creatures, represent him imperfectly.

2.   Sometimes the reason why a word comes to be used is quite different from the meaning of the word. Take, for example, the Latin word *lapis* (stone). Speakers of Latin derive the word from *laedens pedem* (what hurts a foot). However, it is not used to mean 'what hurts a foot', but to refer to a particular kind of physical object. Otherwise everything that hurts a foot would be a stone. In the case of words used of God we may say that the reason they came to be used derives from his causal activity, for our understanding of him, and our language about him, depends on the different perfections in creatures which represent him, however imperfectly, in his various causal acts. Nevertheless, we do not use these words to signify his causal acts. 'Living' in 'God is living' does not mean the same as 'causes life'. We use the sentence to say that life pre-exists in the source of all things, though in a higher way than we can understand or signify.

3.   In this life we cannot understand God's essence as it is in itself. But we can do so in so far as the perfections of his creatures represent it. And this is how the words we use can signify it.

Article 3. Can we say anything literally about God?

1. It seems that we cannot use any word literally of God. For, as I have said, we take every word we use when talking about God from our speech about creatures.[106] But we use such words metaphorically of God, as when we call him a 'rock' or a 'lion'. So, we only speak metaphorically when talking about God.

2. Moreover, we do not use a word literally of something if it would be more accurate not to use it than to use it. But according to Dionysius it would be truer to say that God is not good or wise or any such thing than to say that he is.[107] So, we say none of these things literally of God.

3. Again, we apply the names of bodily things to God only metaphorically, for he is incorporeal. But all such names imply corporeal conditions, for they signify temporal succession and composition of matter and form, which belong to the material world. So, we use such words only metaphorically of God.

On the contrary, Ambrose says, 'Some names clearly show forth what is proper to divinity, and some express the luminous truth of the divine majesty, but there are others which we predicate of God metaphorically and through a certain likeness.[108] So, we do not use all words of God metaphorically. We use some of them literally.

Reply: As I have said, we know God from the perfections that flow from him to creatures,[109] and these perfections certainly exist in him in a more excellent way than they do in them. Yet we understand such perfections as we find them in creatures, and as we understand

---

106   1a 13.1.
107   *The Celestial Hierarchy* 2. PG 3.41.
108   *On Faith* 2, prol. PL 16.583.
109   1a 13.2.

them so we use words to speak of them. Thus we have to consider two things in the words we use to attribute perfections to God: first, the perfections themselves that are signified (goodness, life, and the like); second, the way in which they are signified. As far as the perfections signified are concerned, we use the words literally of God, and in fact more appropriately than we use them of creatures, for these perfections belong primarily to God and only secondarily to other things. But so far as the way of signifying these perfections is concerned, we use the words inappropriately, for they have a way of signifying that is appropriate to creatures.

Hence:

1.   Some words that signify what has come forth from God to creatures do so in such a way that part of the meaning of the word is the imperfect way in which creatures share in God's perfection. Thus it is part of the meaning of 'stone' that it is a material thing. We can use such words of God only metaphorically. There are other words, however, that simply mean certain perfections without any indication of how these perfections are possessed – words, for example, like 'being', 'good', 'living', and so on, and we can use words like these literally of God.

2.   The reason why Dionysius says that such words are better denied of God is that what they signify does not belong to God in the way that they signify it, but in a higher way. In the same passage he therefore says that God is beyond every substance and life.[110]

3.   These words imply bodily conditions not in what they mean but in the way in which they signify it. But the ones that are used metaphorically have bodily conditions as part of what they mean.

Article 4. Are all the words we predicate of God synonymous?

1. It seems that all the words we apply to God are synonymous. For synonyms are words that mean exactly the same thing. But whatever words we apply to God refer to exactly the same reality in God, for his goodness, and his wisdom, and such-like are identical with his essence. So, all these expressions are synonyms.

2. Moreover, if someone should argue that, although they signify the same thing, they do so from different points of view, there is an answer we can give: that it is useless to have different points of view which do not correspond to any difference in the thing viewed.

3. Again, something that can only be described in one way is more perfectly one than something that can be described in many ways. But God is supremely one. So, he is not describable in many ways, and the many things we say about him all have the same meaning: they are synonymous.

On the contrary, piling up synonyms adds nothing to the meaning: 'clothing garments' are just the same as 'garments'. So, if everything we say about God is synonymous it would be inappropriate to speak of 'the good God' or anything of the kind. Yet Jeremiah says, 'Most strong, mighty and powerful, your name is Lord of armies.'[111]

---

110   *The Celestial Hierarchy* 2. PG 3.41.

111   Jeremiah 32: 18.

Reply: The words we use to speak of God are not synonymous. This is clear enough in the case of words we use to deny something of him, or to speak of his causal relation to creatures. Such words differ in meaning according to the different things we wish to deny of him, or the different effects to which we are referring. But it should be clear from what I have previously said[112] that even the words that signify what God is (though they do it imperfectly) also have distinct meanings.[113]

What we mean by a word is the concept we form of what the word signifies. Since we know God from creatures, we understand him through concepts appropriate to the perfections that creatures receive from him. What pre-exists in God in a simple and unified way is divided among creatures as many and varied perfections. The many perfections of creatures correspond to one single source which they represent in varied and complex ways. Thus the different and complex concepts that we have in mind correspond to something altogether simple which they enable us imperfectly to understand. Thus the words we use for the perfections we attribute to God, though they signify what is one, are not synonymous, for they signify it from many different points of view.

1. So, the solution to the first objection is clear. Synonyms signify the same thing from the same point of view. Words that signify the same thing that is thought of in different ways do not, properly speaking, signify the same, for words only signify things by way of thoughts, as I noted above.[114]

2. The many different points of view are not baseless and pointless, for they all correspond to a single reality which each represents imperfectly in a different way.

3. It belongs to the perfection of God's unity that what is many and diverse in others should in him be unified and simple. That is why he is one thing described in many ways, for our minds learn of him in the many ways in which he is represented by creatures.

Article 5. Do we use words univocally or equivocally of God and creatures?

1. It seems that words used both of God and of creatures are used univocally. The equivocal is based on the univocal as the many is based on the one. A word such as 'dog' may be used equivocally of the animals that bark and of something in the sea [i.e. dogfish], but only because it is first used univocally (of the things that bark); otherwise there would be nowhere to start from and we should go back for ever. Now some causes are univocal because their effects have the same name and description as themselves – what is generated by human beings, for example, is also a human being. But some causes are equivocal, as is the sun when it causes heat, for the sun itself is only equivocally hot. Since, therefore, the equivocal is based on the univocal it seems that the first agent upon which all others are based must be a univocal one. So, we univocally predicate the terms that we use of God and of creatures.

2. Moreover, there is no resemblance between things that are only equivocally the same. But according to Genesis there is a resemblance between creatures and God: 'Let us make

112   1a 13.2.
113   1a 13.1 and 2.
114   1a 13.1.

human beings in our own image and likeness.[115] So, it seems we can say something univocally of God and creatures.

3. Again, as Aristotle says, the measure must be of the same order as the thing measured.[116] But God is the first measure of all beings, as Aristotle also says. So, God is of the same order as creatures and something can therefore be said univocally of both.

On the contrary, the same word when used with different meanings is used equivocally. But no word when used of God means the same as when it is used of a creature. 'Wisdom', for example, means a quality when it is used of creatures, but not when it is applied to God. So, it must have a different meaning, for we have here a difference in the genus which is part of the definition. The same applies to other words. So, we must use all of them equivocally when we apply them to both God and creatures.

Furthermore, God is more distant from any creature than any two creatures are from each other. Now there are some creatures so different that we can say nothing univocally of them (when they differ in genus, for example). Much less, therefore, can we say anything univocally of creatures and God. Everything we say of them we must say equivocally.

Reply: It is impossible to predicate anything univocally of God and creatures. Every effect that falls short of the power of its agent cause represents it inadequately, for it is not the same kind of thing as its agent cause. Thus what exists simply and in a unified way in the cause will be divided up and take various different forms in such effects – as the simple power of the sun produces many different effects in things on earth. In the same way, as I said earlier, all the perfections which in creatures are many and various pre-exist in God as one.[117]

The words denoting perfections that we use in speaking of creatures all differ in meaning and each one signifies a perfection as something distinct from all others. Thus when we say that a man is wise, we signify his wisdom as something distinct from the other things about him – his essence, for example, his powers, or his existence. But when we use 'wise' when talking about God we do not intend to signify something distinct from his essence, power or existence. When we predicate 'wise' of a human being we, so to speak, circumscribe and define the limits of the aspect of human beings that it signifies. But this is not so when we predicate 'wise' of God. What it signifies in him is not confined by the meaning of our word but goes beyond it. So, it is clear that we do not use 'wise' in the same sense of God and people, and the same goes for all other words. So, we cannot use them univocally of God and creatures.

Yet although we never use words in exactly the same sense of creatures and of God, we are not merely equivocating when we use the same word, as some have said, for if this were so we could never argue from statements about creatures to statements about God – any such argument would be invalidated by the Fallacy of Equivocation.[118] That this does not happen we know not merely from the teachings of the philosophers who prove many things about God but also from the teaching of St Paul, for he says, 'The invisible things of God are made known by those things that are made.'[119]

---

115 Genesis 1: 26.
116 *Metaphysics* 10.1, 1053a24.
117 1a 13.4.
118 The following argument commits this fallacy – all pigs are kept in pens, pens are something to write with, therefore all pigs are kept in something to write with. The premises do not imply the conclusion – that is, the argument is invalid – because 'pen' has a different sense in its two occurrences.
119 Romans 1: 20.

So, we must say that words are used of God and of creatures in an analogical way, in accordance with a certain order between them. We can distinguish two kinds of analogical or proportional uses of language. First, there is the case of one word being used of two things because each of them has some order or relation to a third thing. Thus we use the word 'healthy' of both medicine and urine because each of these has some relation to health in animals, the former as a cause, the latter as a symptom of it. Second, there is the case of the same word used of two things because of some relation that one has to the other – as 'healthy' is used of medicine and animals because the former is the cause of health in the latter.

In this way some words are used neither univocally nor purely equivocally of God and creatures, but analogically, for we cannot speak of God at all except in the language we use of creatures, as I have said. So, whatever we say of both God and creatures we say in virtue of the order that creatures have to God as to their source and cause, in which all the perfections of things pre-exist most excellently.

This way of using words lies somewhere between pure equivocation and simple univocity, for the word is neither used in the same sense, as with univocal usage, nor in totally different senses, as with equivocation. The several senses of a word used analogically signify different relations to some one thing, as 'healthy', said of urine, indicates health in an animal, and as when it signifies a cause of that health when predicated of medicine.

1. Even if it were the case that equivocal predications are based on the univocal, the same cannot be true when it comes to agent causation. A non-univocal efficient cause is causal with respect to an entire species – as the sun accounts for there being any people. A univocal cause, on the other hand, cannot be the universal cause of the whole species (otherwise it would be the cause of itself, since it is a member of that same species) but is the particular cause that this or that individual should be a member of the species. So, a universal cause, which must be prior to a particular cause, is non-univocal. Such a cause, however, is not wholly equivocal even though it is not univocal, for then there would be absolutely no resemblance between it and its effects. We could call it an analogical cause, and this would be parallel to the case of speech, for all univocal predications are based on one non-univocal, analogical predicate, that of being.

2. The resemblance of creatures to God is an imperfect one, for as I have said, they do not even share a common genus.[120]

3. God is not a measure proportionate to what is measured. So, it does not follow that he and his creatures belong to the same order.

The two arguments in the contrary sense do show that words are not used univocally of God and creatures. But they do not show that they are used equivocally.

Article 6. Do we predicate words primarily of God or of creatures?

1. It seems that the words we use of God apply primarily to creatures. For we speak of things as we know them since, as Aristotle says, words are signs for things as understood.[121] But we know creatures before we know God. So, our words apply to creatures before they apply to God.

---

120   1a 4.3.

121   *On Interpretation* 1.1, 16a3.

2. Dionysius says that 'the language we use about God is derived from what we say about creatures'.[122] But when a word such as 'lion' or 'rock' is transferred from a creature to God it is used first of the creature. So, such words apply primarily to a creature.

3. Words used of both God and creatures are used of him in that he is the cause of all things, as Dionysius says.[123] But what we say of something in a causal sense applies to it only secondarily – as 'healthy' applies primarily to a living animal and only secondarily to the medicine that causes its health. So, we apply such words primarily to creatures.

On the contrary, we read in Ephesians, 'I bend my knees to the Father of our Lord Jesus, from whom all fatherhood in heaven and on earth is named';[124] and the same seems to apply to other words used of God and creatures. So, we use these words primarily of God.

Reply: Whenever a word is used analogically of many things, it is used of them because of some order or relation they have to some central thing.[125] In order to explain an extended or analogical use of a word it is necessary to mention this central thing. Thus you cannot explain what you mean by 'healthy' medicine without mentioning the health of the animal of which it is the cause. Similarly you must understand 'healthy' as applied to an animal before you can understand what is meant by 'healthy urine', which is a symptom of that health. The primary application of the word is to the central thing that has to be understood first. Other applications will be more or less secondary in so far as they approximate to this use.

Thus all words used metaphorically of God apply primarily to creatures and secondarily to God. When we use them of God they signify merely a certain likeness between God and a creature. When we speak metaphorically of a meadow as 'smiling' we only mean that it shows at its best when it flowers, just as people show at their best when they smile: there is a likeness between them. In the same way, if we speak of God as a 'lion', we only mean that, like a lion, he is mighty in his deeds. It is obvious that the meaning of such a word as applied to God depends on and is secondary to the meaning it has when used of creatures.

This would be the case for non-metaphorical words too if they were only used to express God's causality, as some have supposed. If, for example, 'God is good' meant the same as 'God is the cause of goodness in creatures' the word 'good' as applied to God must be defined in terms of what it means when applied to creatures; and hence 'good' would apply primarily to creatures and secondarily to God.

But I have already shown that words of this sort do not only say how God is a cause.[126] They also say what he is essentially. When we say that he is good or wise we do not simply mean that he causes wisdom or goodness, but that he possesses these perfections eminently. So, we should conclude that from the point of view of what the words mean they are used primarily of God and derivatively of creatures, for what the words mean (the perfections they signify) flows from God to creatures. But from the point of view of our use of the words we apply them first to creatures because we know them first. That

122 *The Divine Names* 1. PG 3.596.
123 *Mystical Theology* 1. PG 3.1000.
124 Ephesians 3: 14–15.
125 *Metaphysics* 4.7, 1012a23.
126 1a 13.2.

is why, as I have mentioned already, they have a way of signifying that is appropriate to creatures.[127]

1.   This is valid so far as our first application of the words is concerned.

2.   Words used of God metaphorically are not in the same case as the others, as I have said.[128]

3.   This objection would be valid if all words were used to express God's causality and not to say what he is, as 'healthy' expresses the causality of a medicine and not what it consists in.

Article 7. In speaking of God, do we use words that imply temporal succession?

1. It seems that we do not apply to God words that imply temporal succession, even when we are speaking of his relation to creatures. It is generally agreed that such words signify what God is in himself. Thus Ambrose says that 'Lord' indicates his power,[129] but this is the divine substance, and 'creation' indicates his action, but this is his essence. God, however, is not temporal but eternal. So, we do not apply these words to him in a temporal sense but as applicable from eternity.

2. Moreover, whatever is true of something in a temporal sense can be said to be made (as, for example what is white has been made white). But nothing in God is made. So, we say nothing of him in a temporal sense.

3. Moreover, if the reason why we use words of God in a temporal sense were that such words imply a relation to creatures, then the same would be true of every word that implied such a relation. But we apply some of these as from eternity. We say, for example, that God knew and loved creatures from eternity – 'I have loved you with an everlasting love.'[130] So, all other words, such as 'Lord' or 'Creator', are applicable from eternity.

4. Moreover, these words signify a relation, and this must therefore be a reality in God or in the creature alone. It cannot, however, be only in the creature, for if this were so, we would call God 'Lord' in virtue of the opposite relation existing in the creature. But we name nothing from its opposite. The relation, therefore, must be something real in God. Yet, since he is beyond time, it cannot be temporal. So, it seems that we do not use such words of God in a temporal sense.

5. Moreover, we call something relative in virtue of some relationship it has. For instance, we refer to someone as 'lord' because of the lordship he has, just as we call something white because of its whiteness. If, therefore, the relation of lordship were something that God did not really have but were merely a way of thinking of him, it would follow that God is not truly Lord, which is clearly false.

6. Again, when the two terms of a relationship are not of the same order, one may exist without the other – for example, the knowable can exist without knowledge, as we read in the *Categories*.[131] But in the case of relations between God and creatures, the two terms are not of the same order, and so something could be said relatively of God even though

127   1a 13.3.
128   See the body of the present article.
129   *On Faith* 1.1. PL 16.553.
130   Jeremiah 31: 3.
131   *Categories* 7, 7b30.

creatures did not exist. In this way words like 'Lord' and 'Creator' can apply to God from eternity and are not used in a temporal sense.

On the contrary, Augustine says that the relative term 'Lord' is applicable to God in a temporal sense.[132]

Reply: Some words that imply a relation to creatures are said of God in a temporal sense and not as applicable from eternity.

In order to explain this we must first say something about relations.

Some have said that being related to something is never a reality in nature – that it is something created by our way of thinking about things. But this is false because some things do have a natural order or relation to others. Since, whenever we can say of x that it is related to y, we can also say of y that it is related to x, there are three possibilities here.

Sometimes both what we say of x and what we say of y is true of them not because of any reality in them, but because they are being thought of in a particular way. When, for instance, we say that something is identical with itself, the two terms of the relation only exist because the mind takes one thing and thinks of it twice, thus treating it as though it has a relation to itself. Similarly, any relation between a thing and nothing is set up by the mind treating 'nothing' as though it were a term. The same is generally true of all relations that are set up as part of our thinking – the relation of *being a species of a certain genus*, for instance.

In the second case both what we say of x and what we say of y is true of them because of some reality in x and y. They are related because of something that belongs to both – quantity, for example, as with the relations of *being bigger than* and *being smaller than*, *being double* and *being half*, and so forth. It is the same with the relations that result from causal activity as *being what is changed by* and *being what changes*, *being father of* and *being son of*, and so forth.

In the third case the truth about x that it is related to y is due to something real in x, but the truth about y that it is related to x is not due to anything real in y. This happens when x and y are not of the same order. Take, for example, the relation of *being knowable by* and *knowing* (whether we mean knowledge by the senses or by the mind). When x is knowable by y, x is not in and by itself something knowable. In so far as it exists in its own right it lies outside the order of knowledge. So, while the relation of *knowing* x is a reality in the senses or mind of y – for knowing is what makes a real difference to these – *being knowable by* y is not a reality in x. Thus Aristotle says that we call some things relative not because they are related to others but because others are related to them.[133] We say that one side of a column is the right side because it is on the right side of some animal; the relation of *being on the right of* is real in the animal but not in the column.

Now, since God is altogether outside the order of creatures (because they are ordered to him but not he to them), it is clear that being related to God is a reality in creatures, but being related to creatures is not a reality in God. We say it about him because of the real relation in creatures. So it is that when we speak of his relation to creatures we can apply words implying temporal sequence and change, not because of any change in him but because of a change in the creatures; just as we can say that a column has changed from being on

---

132   *On the Trinity* 5.16. *PL* 42.922.
133   *Metaphysics* 5.15, 1021a29.

my left to being on my right, not through any alteration in the column, but simply because I have turned around.

1.   Some relative words signify a relationship, others signify that on account of which there is a relationship. Thus 'lord' says nothing more about a lord except that he stands in some relationship. To be a lord precisely is to be related to a servant – the same is true of words like 'father', 'son', and so forth. Other relative words, however, such as 'mover' and 'moved', 'head' and 'being headed', signify something on account of which there is a relationship. Some of the words we use of God are of the first kind and some of the second. 'Lord', for instance, signifies nothing but a relation to creatures, though it presupposes something about what God is, for he could not be lord without his power, which is his essence. Others such as 'Saviour' or 'Creator' which refer directly to God's activity, which is his essence, are of the second kind and signify something on account of which God has a relationship. But we use both sorts of word of him in a temporal sense in so far as they convey expressly or by implication a relation to creatures. We do not predicate them temporally in so far as they signify directly or indirectly the divine essence.

2.   Relations that we attribute to God in a temporal sense are not real in him but belong to him as a way of speaking of him and with no real change in him. The same is true of any becoming that we attribute to him – as when we say, 'Lord, you have become a refuge for us.'[134]

3.   Thinking is not something we do to other things, but remains within us; and the same is true of willing. So, we apply from eternity expressions signifying relations that ensue from God's thinking and willing. When, however, they signify relations that ensue from acts which, according to our way of thinking about God, proceed from him to external effects, they can be used of him in a temporal sense. This is the case with words like 'Creator' and 'Saviour'.

4.   God's temporal relations to creatures are in him only because of our way of thinking of him, but the opposite relations of creatures to him are realities in the creatures. It is quite admissible to attribute a relation to God because of something that takes place in a creature, for we cannot express a reality in creatures without talking as though there were also matching relations in God. So, we say that God is related to a creature because the creature is related to him – just as, according to Aristotle, we say that the knowable is related to knowledge because knowledge is related to it.[135]

5.   God is related to creatures in so far as creatures are related to him. Since the relation of subjection to God is really in the creature, God is really Lord. It is the relationship of lordship in him that is supplied by our minds, not the fact of his being the Lord.

6.   When we ask whether the terms of a relation are of the same order or not, we are not asking about the things that are said to be related but about the meaning of the relative words used. If one entails the other, and vice versa, then they are of the same order – as with being double and being half of or with being father of and being son of. If, however, one entails the other, but not vice versa, then they are not of the same order. This is the case with knowing and being knowable by. For x to be knowable by y it is not necessary that y should be knowing x; it is sufficient that it should have the power to know x. Thus 'being knowable' signifies intelligibility as something prior to actual knowledge. If, however, we

---

134   Psalms 89: 1.
135   *Metaphysics* 5.15, 1021a30.

take 'being knowable' to mean being actually here and now intelligible, then it coincides with the actual exercise of knowledge, for a thing cannot be so known unless someone is knowing it. In a parallel way, although God is prior to creatures (as being knowable is prior to knowing) since 'x is lord of y' and 'y is subject to x' entail each other, *being lord of* and *being subject to* are of the same order. So, God was not lord until he had a creature subject to him.

Article 8. Is 'God' the name of a nature?

1. It seems that 'God' is not the name of a nature. For Damascene says that 'God' (θεός) is derived from θέειν, which means 'to take care of' or 'to foster all things'; or else from αἴθειν, which means 'to burn' – for our God is a fire burning up all wickedness; or from θεᾶσθαι, which means 'to consider all things'.[136] All the verbs mentioned here signify activity. So, 'God' signifies an activity, not a nature.

   2. Moreover, we name things in so far as we know them. But we do not know God's nature. So, the term 'God' cannot signify what that is.

On the contrary, Ambrose says that 'God' is the name of a nature.[137]

Reply: The reason why we use a word to mean something is not always what the word is used to mean. We come to understand what a thing is from its properties or activities, and we often derive our name for the sort of thing something is from some property or activity of it. For example, speakers of Latin derive the word 'rock' (*lapis*) from something it does – hurting the foot (*laedens pedem*). Yet the word 'rock' signifies what a rock is in itself, not what it does. On the other hand, though, we do not name things we know in themselves (e.g. cold, heat, whiteness, and so on) from anything else. In their cases the reason why we use the word to mean something is the same as what it is used to mean.

   Now, God is not known to us in his own nature, but through his activity or effects; so, as I have said, we can derive the language we use in speaking of him from these.[138] 'God' is therefore the name of an activity, for it is an activity of God that leads us to use it – the word is derived from his universal providence: everyone who uses the word 'God' has in mind one who cares for all things. Thus Dionysius says, 'the Deity is what watches over all things in perfect providence and goodness'.[139] But, although derived from this activity, the word 'God' is used to signify the divine nature.

   1. Everything John Damascene says here refers to divine Providence, which is what makes us use the word 'God' in the first place.
   2. The meaning of the name we give to something depends on how much of its nature we understand from its properties and effects. Since from its properties we can understand what a stone is in itself, the word 'stone' signifies the nature of the stone as it is in itself. Its meaning is the definition of a stone, in knowing which we know what a stone is; for 'what a word means is the definition'.[140] But from God's effects we do not come to understand

136 *On the Orthodox Faith* 1.9. PG 94.835, 838.
137 *On Faith* 1.1. PL 16.553.
138 1a 13.1.
139 *The Divine Names* 12. PG 3.969.
140 *Metaphysics* 4.7, 1012a23.

what God's nature is in itself, so we do not know what God is. We know him, as I have noted, only as being excellent, as being causal, and as lacking in anything merely creaturely.[141] It is in this way that the word 'God' signifies the divine nature: it is used to mean something that is above all that is, and that is the source of all things and is distinct from them all. This is how those that use it mean it to be used.

Article 9. Is the name 'God' peculiar to God alone?

1. It seems that 'God' is not peculiar to God, but can be used of other things. For whatever shares in what a name signifies can share in the name. But I have just said that 'God' signifies the divine nature,[142] which, according to 2 Peter, is something that can be communicated to others: 'He has bestowed upon us precious and very great promises . . . that by this we may become partakers of God's nature.'[143] So, 'God' may be applied to others besides God.

2. Furthermore, only proper names are altogether incommunicable. But 'God' is a common noun, not a proper name, as is clear from the fact that it can be used in the plural, as in the psalm: 'I have said that you are gods.'[144] So, 'God' is applicable to many things.

3. Again, as I have said, the name 'God' is applied to God because of an activity.[145] But other words that we use of God because of his activities (e.g. 'good', 'wise', and the like) are all applicable to many things. So, 'God' is as well.

On the contrary, we read in Wisdom, 'They gave the incommunicable name to sticks and stones',[146] and the reference is to God's name. So, the name 'God' is incommunicable.

Reply: A name may be used of many things in two ways, either properly or by metaphor. It is properly used of many when the whole of what it means belongs to each of them; it is used metaphorically when some part of what it means belongs to each. The word 'lion', for example, properly speaking, applies only to the things that have the nature it signifies, but it is also applied metaphorically to other things that have something of the lion about them. The courageous or the strong can be spoken of in this way as 'lions'.

To understand which names, properly speaking, apply to many things we must first recognize that every form that is instantiated by an individual either is or at least can be thought of as being common to many. Human nature can be thought of, and in fact is, common to many in this way. The nature of the sun, on the other hand, can be thought of as being, but in fact is not, common to many. The reason for this is that the mind understands such natures in abstraction from individual instances; hence whether it be in one individual or in many is irrelevant to our understanding of the nature itself. Given that we understand a nature we can always think of it as being in many instances.

An individual, however, from the very fact of being individual, is divided from all others. Hence a word that is used precisely to signify an individual cannot be applicable to many in fact, nor can it be thought of as applicable to many. It is impossible to think that there could be many of some particular individual. Hence no proper name is properly speaking

---

141   1a 12.12.
142   1a 13.8.
143   2 Peter 1: 4.
144   Psalms 81: 6.
145   1a 13.8.
146   Wisdom 14: 21.

communicable to many, though it may be communicable through some resemblance – as a man may metaphorically be called 'an Achilles' because he has the bravery of Achilles.

But consider the case of forms which are instantiated not by being the form of an individual, but by themselves (inasmuch as they are subsistent forms). If we understood these as they are in themselves, it would be clear that they are not common to many in fact and also cannot be thought of as being common to many – except perhaps by some sort of resemblance as with individuals. In fact, however, we do not understand such simple self-subsistent forms as they are in themselves. We have to think of them on the model of the composite things that have their forms in matter. For this reason, as I said earlier, we apply to them concrete nouns that signify a nature as instantiated in an individual.[147] Thus the nouns we use to signify simple subsistent natures are grammatically the same as those we use to signify the natures of composite things.

Now, as I have said, we use 'God' to signify the divine nature,[148] and, since this nature cannot have more than one instance,[149] it follows that, from the point of view of what is in fact signified, the word cannot be used of many, though it can mistakenly be thought of as applying to many – rather as someone who mistakenly thought there were many suns would think of 'sun' as applying to many things. Thus we read in Galatians, 'You were slaves to gods who by nature were not gods',[150] and a gloss says, 'not gods by nature but according to the opinion of human beings.'[151]

Nevertheless the word 'God' does have several applications, though not in its full meaning. It is applied metaphorically to things that share something of what it means. Thus 'gods' can mean those who by resembling God share in some way in the divine, as in the psalm: 'I say you shall be gods.'[152]

If, however, a name were given to God, not as signifying his nature but referring to him as something distinct, regarding him as an individual, such a proper name would be altogether incommunicable and in no way applicable to others – perhaps the Tetragrammaton[153] was used in this way among the Hebrews: it would be as though someone were to use the word 'Sun' as a proper name designating this individual.

1. God's nature can be communicated to others only in the sense that they can share in God's likeness.

2. 'God' is a common noun and not a proper name because it signifies the divine nature in the concrete, though God himself is neither universal nor particular. We do not, however, name things as they are in themselves but as they are to our minds. In fact, the name 'God' is incommunicable, rather as I said of 'Sun'.[154]

3. We apply words like 'good' and 'wise' to God because of the perfections that flow from God to creatures. They do not signify God's nature; rather, they signify these perfections absolutely speaking. So, not only can we think of them as applicable to many things;

147 1a 13.1, *ad* 2.
148 1a 13.8.
149 1a 11.3.
150 Galatians 4: 8.
151 Interlinear gloss. *PL* 192.139.
152 Psalms 81: 6.
153 The four Hebrew letters that spell out God's personal name.
154 See the body of the present article.

they actually are so. But we apply the word 'God' to him because of the activity peculiar to him which we constantly experience, and we use it to signify his nature.

Article 10. Is the name 'God' used in the same sense of God, of what shares in divinity and of what is merely supposed to do so?

1. It seems for three reasons that 'God' is used univocally of what has the divine nature, what shares in this nature, and what is supposed to have it. For when we do not have the same meaning for the same word we cannot contradict each other. Equivocation eliminates contradiction. But when Catholics say 'The idol is not God', they contradict pagans who say 'The idol is God.' So, 'God' is being used univocally by both.

2. Furthermore, an idol is supposed to be God, but is not so in fact, just as the enjoyment of the delights of the flesh is supposed to be felicity, but is not so in fact. But the word 'happiness' is used univocally of this supposed happiness and of true happiness. So, 'God' must also be used univocally of the supposed and the real God.

3. Again, words are used univocally if they have the same meaning. But when Catholics say there is one God they understand by 'God' something almighty, to be revered above all things. But pagans mean the same when they say that their idol is God. So, the word is used univocally in the two cases.

On the contrary, what is in the mind is a sort of picture of what is in reality, as *On Interpretation* says.[155] But when we say 'That is an animal', both of a real animal and of one in a picture, we are using the word equivocally. So, 'God' used of the real God and of what is thought to be God is used equivocally. Furthermore, we cannot mean what we do not understand. But pagans do not understand the divine nature. So, when they say, 'The idol is God', they do not mean true divinity. Yet when Catholics say that there is only one God they mean this. So, Catholics and pagans do not use the term 'God' univocally. They predicate it equivocally of the true God and of what is supposed to be God.

Reply: In the three meanings listed above, 'God' is used neither univocally nor equivocally but analogically. When a word is used univocally it has exactly the same meaning in each application. When it is used equivocally it has an entirely different meaning in each case. But when it is used analogically its meaning in one sense is to be explained by reference to its meaning in another sense. Thus to understand why we call accidents 'beings' we have to understand why we call substances beings. Likewise, we need to know what it means for animals to be healthy before we can understand what expressions like 'healthy urine' or 'healthy medicine' mean. For healthy urine indicates a state of health, and healthy medicine makes animals healthy.

It is the same with the case I am now considering. For we have to refer to the use of 'God' as meaning the true God in order to explain its use as applied to things that share in divinity or which are supposed to be gods. When we say that something is a 'god' by sharing in divinity we mean that it shares in the nature of the true God. Similarly, when we say that an idol is a god, we take 'god' to mean something that people suppose to be the true God. So, it is clear that while 'God' is used with different meanings, one of these meanings is involved in all the others and the word is therefore used analogically.

---

155   *On Interpretation* 1, 16a5.

1. We say that a word has different uses not because we can use it in different statements but because it has different meanings. Thus 'man' has one meaning and one use whatever it is predicated of, whether truly or falsely. It would be said to have several uses if we meant it to signify different things – if, for instance, one speaker used it to signify a man and another to signify a stone or something else. Thus it is clear that Catholics,[156] when they say that an idol is not God, are contradicting pagans who affirm that it is God, for both are using 'God' to signify the true God. When pagans say 'The idol is God' they are not using 'God' to mean that which is merely supposed to be God. If they were, they would be speaking truly, as Catholics do when they sometimes use the word in that way (cf. 'All the gods of the pagans are demons').[157]

2, 3. We can make the same reply to the second and third objections. For these have to do with the different statements we can make with a word, not with a difference in meaning.

4. As to the fourth argument which takes the opposite point of view: the word 'animal' is not used wholly equivocally of a real animal and an animal in a picture. Aristotle uses the word 'equivocal' in a broad sense to include the analogical,[158] thus he sometimes says that 'being', which is used analogically, is used equivocally of the different categories.

5. Neither Catholics nor pagans understand the nature of God as he is in himself, but both know him as in some way causing creatures, as surpassing them and as set apart from them, as I have said.[159] In this way when pagans say 'The idol is God' they can mean by 'God' just what Catholics mean when they declare, 'The idol is not God.' People who knew nothing whatever about God would not be able to use 'God' at all, except as a word whose meaning they did not know.

Article 11. Is 'The One who Is' the most appropriate name for God?

1. It seems that 'The One who Is' is not the most appropriate name for God. For the name 'God' cannot be shared, as I have said.[160] But 'The One who Is' is a name that can be shared. So, it is not the most appropriate name for God.

2. Dionysius says, 'To call God good is to show forth all that flows from him.'[161] But what is supremely characteristic of God is to be the source of all things. So, the most appropriate name for God is 'The Good' rather than 'The One who Is'.

3. Every name of God seems to imply a relation to creatures – for we only know God from creatures. But 'The One who Is' implies no such relation. So, it is not the most appropriate name for God.

On the contrary, we read in Exodus that when Moses asked, 'If they ask me, "What is his name?" what shall I say to them?,' the Lord replied, 'Say this to them, "The One who Is has sent me to you." '[162] So, 'The One who Is' is the most appropriate name for God.

156 Aquinas used this to refer to all Western Christians, and in this particular use it might simply refer to Christians.
157 Psalms 95:5.
158 *Categories* 1, 1a1.
159 1a 12.12.
160 1a 13.9.
161 *The Divine Names* 3. *PG* 3.680.
162 Exodus 3:13 and 14.

Reply: There are three reasons for regarding 'The One who Is' as the most appropriate name for God.

First, because of its meaning; for it does not signify any particular form, but existence itself. Since the existence of God is his essence, and since this is true of nothing else (as I have shown),[163] it is clear that this name is especially fitting for God, for we name everything by its form.

Second, because of its universality. All other names are either less general or, if not, they at least add some nuance of meaning which restricts and determines the original sense. In this life our minds cannot grasp what God is in himself; whatever way we have of thinking of him is a way of failing to understand him as he really is. So, the less determinate our names are, and the more general and simple they are, the more appropriately do we apply them to God. That is why Damascene says, 'The first of all names used of God is "The One who Is", for he comprehends all in himself, he has his existence as an ocean of being, infinite and unlimited.'[164] Any other name selects some particular aspect of the being of the thing, but 'The One who Is' fixes on no aspect of being but stands open to all and refers to God as to an infinite ocean of being.

Third, 'The One who Is' is the best name for God because of its tense. For it signifies being in the present, and it is especially appropriate to predicate this of God – for his being knows neither past nor future, as Augustine says.[165]

1. 'The One who Is' is more appropriate than 'God' because of what makes us use the name in the first place, that is, his existence, because of the unrestricted way in which it signifies him, and because of its tense, as I have just said.[166] But when we consider what we use the word to mean, we must admit that 'God' is more appropriate, for we use this to signify the divine nature. Even more appropriate is the Tetragrammaton which is used to signify the incommunicable and, if we could say such a thing, the individual substance of God.

2. 'The Good' is a more fundamental name for God is so far as he is a cause. But it is not more fundamental simply speaking, for to be comes before being a cause.

3. God's names need not necessarily imply a relation to creatures. It is enough that they should come to be used because of the perfections that flow from God to creatures, and of these the primary one is existence itself, from which we get the name 'The One who Is'.

Article 12. Can we formulate affirmative propositions about God?

1. It seems that we cannot formulate affirmative propositions about God. For Dionysius says, 'Negative propositions about God are true, but affirmative ones are vague.'[167]

2. Moreover, Boethius says, 'A simple form cannot be a subject.'[168] But God is a simple form to the highest degree, as I have already shown.[169] So, he cannot be a subject. But affirmative propositions are about their subjects. So, we cannot formulate such propositions about God.

163   1a 3.4.
164   *On the Orthodox Faith* 1.9. PG 94.836.
165   *On the Trinity* 5.2. PL 42.912.
166   See the body of the present article.
167   *The Celestial Hierarchy* 2. PG 3.140.
168   *On the Trinity* 2. PL 64.1250.
169   1a 3.7.

3. Again, we fall into error when we understand something as different from the way it is. Now God is altogether without composition in his being, as I have proved.[170] So, since every affirmative act of the intellect understands an object as composite, it would seem that we cannot truly formulate affirmative propositions about God.

On the contrary, what is of faith cannot be false. But some affirmative propositions are matters of faith, as, for example, that God is three and one, and that he is almighty. So, we can formulate true affirmative propositions about God.

Reply: In every true affirmative proposition, although the subject and predicate signify what is in fact in some way the same thing, they do so from different points of view. This is so both in propositions that express an accidental predication and in those that express an essential predication. After all, in 'The man is a white thing' it is clear that 'man' and 'white thing' refer to the same object but differ in meaning, since what it is to be a man is not the same as what it is to be a white thing. But it is also true for a statement such as 'human beings are animals'. That which is human is truly an animal: in one and the same thing we find the sensitive nature because of which we call it an animal and the rational nature because of which we call it a human being.

There is even a difference in point of view between subject and predicate when they have the same meaning, for when we put a term in the subject place we think of it as referring to something, whereas in the predicate place we think of it as saying something about the thing, in accordance with the saying 'we understand predicates formally (as meaning a form), and we understand subjects materially (as referring to what has the form)'.

The difference between subject and predicate represents two ways of looking at a thing, while the fact that they are put together affirmatively indicates that it is one thing that is being looked at. Now, God, considered in himself, is altogether one and simple, yet we think of him through a number of different concepts because we cannot see him as he is in himself.

But although we think of him in these different ways we also know that to each corresponds a single simplicity that is one and the same for all. We represent the different ways of thinking of God in the difference of subject and predicate. We represent his unity by bringing them together in an affirmative statement.

1.   Dionysius says that what we assert of God is vague (or, according to another translation, 'incongruous') because no word used of God is appropriate to him in its way of signifying, as I have observed.[171]

2.   Our minds cannot understand subsisting simple forms as they are in themselves. We understand them in the way that we understand composite things, in which there is the subject of a form and something that exists in that subject. And so we apprehend a simple form as if it were a subject, and we attribute something to it.

3.   In the sentence, 'We fall into error when we understand something as different from the way it is', 'different from' can refer either to the thing understood or the way of understanding. Taken in the former sense the proposition means that we are mistaken when we understand something to be different from what it is. That is true, but it is irrelevant when it comes to our present concern, for when we formulate propositions about God we do not say that he has any composition. We understand him to be simple. But if we take 'different

170   1a 3.7.
171   1a 13.6.

from' to apply to the way of understanding, then the proposition is false, for the way of understanding is always different from the way the thing understood is. It is clear, for example, that our minds non-materially understand material things inferior to them; not that they understand them to be non-material, but that we have a non-material way of understanding. Similarly when our minds understand simple things superior to them we understand them in our own way, that is on the model of composite things; not that we understand the simple things to be composite, but that composition is involved in our way of understanding them. So, the fact that our statements about God are composite does not make them false.

Part III

Practical Philosophy

Introduction

Practical philosophy deals with our fundamental normative and evaluative principles, especially with regard to human action and character. Accordingly, in medieval philosophy it comprises philosophical ethics and moral theology (given their inextricable theoretical connections), as well as foundational issues in political and legal thought. The vast medieval literature is represented in this part by four major, "perennial" aspects of medieval thought on the subject, i.e., such considerations that are still quite directly relevant to our thinking on the same issues. The first section presents the characteristic medieval conception of the metaphysical foundation of objective value (and thus of objective value-judgments), which can be briefly referred to as "the idea of the convertibility of being and goodness." The second section deals with issues of the freedom of the will, insofar as it is principally free acts of the will that embody moral goodness or evil. The third section presents two competing conceptions on the issue of the ultimate human good, i.e., human happiness. Finally, the fourth section deals with the foundational issues of legal theory, insofar as laws of human society are supposed to regulate human conduct in the interest of the common good.

The first section begins with two selections from Augustine. The first, from his *Enchiridion* (literally, "Handbook" – a brief summary of the basic tenets of the Catholic faith), explains the fundamental idea of the convertibility of being and goodness: everything there is, insofar as it is, is good (and, of course, everything that is good, insofar as it is good, is). This is the Neoplatonic idea that rescued the young Augustine's thought from the clutches of Manicheism (a dualistic religion founded by the prophet Mani in the third century, teaching that everything in the world is the result of the battle between two equally powerful ultimate principles of good and evil, light and darkness, which in some form or other was very influential among Christians of Augustine's time), and made him realize how it can provide an answer to *the problem of evil*. For although Manicheism provides an easy answer to the question of the origin of evil in the world (as resulting from the intrusion of darkness into the realm of light), it obviously goes against the orthodox Christian idea of divine omnipotence (identifying God with light, and Satan with darkness). But if one embraces the orthodox Christian idea of God, then the problem inevitably arises: how can there be evil in the creation of an omnipotent, omniscient, and loving God?

The idea of the convertibility of being and goodness provides at least part of the solution of the problem. For if God brings His creation out of nothing by giving being to every thing, then, by the very same act, He provides each creature with its own goodness, endowing it with the perfections allowed and demanded by its nature. (Of course, creatures cannot receive perfections that are not allowed by their nature: a rock cannot have life, a plant cannot have human intelligence, and an ant or a human being cannot have the perfection of divine nature.) Since creatures are necessarily of limited perfection, they cannot have the absolute *immutable perfection* of divine nature, and so they cannot have all possible perfections allowed and demanded by their nature all the time. Hence, necessarily, time and again they can become defective, falling short of their possible perfection, i.e., they may become plagued by some natural evil, such as illness, or some other natural defect, in general, some *privation*, the lack of some perfection that they could and ought to have by their nature. But these defects are not caused by God, indeed, as Augustine argues, they are not caused properly speaking by anything. Defects cannot directly be caused by an *efficient* cause (that by its activity gives being and hence goodness); they can only have a *deficient* cause, i.e., one that fails to produce its proper effect (as, for example, a birth defect is the result of some genetic deficiency).

This, however, does not mean that *nobody* is responsible for *any* evil occurring in God's creation, as Augustine explains in the next selection from his *De Civitate Dei* ("City of God"). Although natural defects cannot be blamed on anyone, *voluntary* defects *are* to be blamed on those agents who are able to choose between good and evil on account of their free will. Thus, moral evil, for which voluntary agents are duly held responsible, originates in a specific sort of defect, namely, the defective use, or rather abuse, of their God-given free will, when they deliberately subject themselves to some inordinate desire, choosing what they ought not to choose. By contrast, therefore, moral goodness consists in the proper direction of the will, which is realized when a voluntary, rational agent is acting rationally, desiring and choosing what it ought to desire and choose according to right reason. So, moral evil, and its opposite, moral goodness, in this framework simply turn out to be specific cases of metaphysical evil and goodness, namely, the lacking (*privatio*) or having (*habitus*) of the proper direction of the will.

The subsequent two selections in this section from Boethius and Aquinas, respectively, provide a more detailed, sophisticated analysis of the same fundamental idea of the convertibility of being and goodness that these authors approach already armed with the conceptual apparatus of Aristotelian logic and metaphysics. Boethius' *De Hebdomadibus*, reproduced here in full, is a rather enigmatic short treatise seeking the solution to a problem raised in its subtitle (or alternative title): *How is it possible that substances are good in that they are, although they are not substantially good?* According to one tradition, the question was raised by a friend and disciple, John the Deacon (who was to become Pope John I), in connection with one of the theses of a larger work, now lost, called *Hebdomades*, so called after the arrangement of its treatises into groups of seven (in Greek, *hebodmades*), imitating Plotinus' *Enneades*, the treatises of which were organized into groups of nine (in Greek, *enneades*), by Plotinus' disciple, Porphyry (the author of *Isagoge*, referred to in the first part of this volume).

In any case, Aquinas certainly found Boethius' answer to the question, in terms of distinguishing God from creatures on the basis of the metaphysical composition of creatures (in particular, the composition of their essence with their existence) as opposed to divine simplicity, to be a "perfect match" to his own ideas on the same issue (although it is debated in the modern literature whether Boethius actually did mean what Aquinas takes him to mean).[1] It is no wonder, therefore, that Aquinas wrote a detailed running commentary on Boethius' work. But that commentary would have been too long for the purposes of this anthology.

However, the brief question from Aquinas' *Summa Theologiae* presented here, which explicitly draws on Boethius' doctrine, provides a very clear, succinct discussion of the main concern that quite naturally arises in connection with the interpretation of the very idea of the convertibility of being and goodness.

The issue can be put in the following way. It seems to be one thing for something to exist and another for it to be good. For obviously not everything that exists is good. Therefore, "being" and "good" do not seem to be convertible terms. Aquinas' response carefully distinguishes what these terms – or rather the concepts they express – signify, namely, the act of existence of the thing, from the conditions of their predicability without qualification, on account of their difference in connotation. The concept of being merely signifies the actuality of the thing of which it is true. The concept of goodness, however, connotes the perfection of the thing, i.e., it signifies not only the actuality of its substantial being, but also the actuality of all those superadded qualities that make the thing perfect in its kind. The thing, therefore, can be called a being absolutely speaking merely on account of the actuality of its substantial being. (And it can be said to be a being in a certain respect or it can be said to be somehow on account of its further, accidental actualities.) But it cannot be called good, absolutely speaking, merely for the reason that it exists, absolutely speaking, for it can be called good only if it has all those superadded perfections in actuality that are needed for its goodness, absolutely speaking. Without those perfections, the thing can be said to be good only with respect to its substantial being, i.e., insofar as it exists at all or with respect to some of the perfections it actually has. However, just because something has existence, absolutely speaking, it does not mean that it is good, absolutely speaking, even if it has some goodness in it, namely, at least its existence. As a result, even if it is not true, absolutely speaking, that anything that exists is good, it *is* true that anything that exists absolutely speaking *is* good with some qualification, namely, insofar as it exists.[2]

The second section of this part is devoted to considerations of the primary source of the specifically moral good and evil, namely, *free will*. Again, the enormous medieval literature on the freedom of the will, and especially its relation to the theological issues of divine providence, predestination, and grace in the salvation history of individual humans and mankind as a whole (as it was first sketched out in Augustine's monumental *De Civitate Dei*) can hardly even be touched on in this introductory survey of medieval philosophy. These selections are therefore merely meant to call attention to some distinctive features of medieval thought on the more directly philosophical aspects of the issue of free will, although, as will be obvious even from these short selections, the philosophical considerations in this area in medieval philosophy are almost always inextricably bound up with theological considerations.

The first selection is Augustine's famous description of his agony right before his conversion, often referred to as Augustine's discussion of the "divided will" or "two wills," on account

---

1   For a detailed discussion of the issue see Ralph McInerny, *Boethius and Aquinas* (Washington, DC: The Catholic University of America Press, 1990).

2   The further intricacies of the idea, along with its profound metaphysical and theological implications are amply discussed in an excellent collection of modern essays: Scott MacDonald (ed.), *Being and Goodness: The Concept of the Good in Metaphysics and Philosophical Theology* (Ithaca, NY: Cornell University Press, 1991).

of his philosophical puzzlement over his state of mind at that time. Whether the will is free is not a question for Augustine; he is never bothered by issues of causal determinism: for him, the human soul by its very nature is an autonomous agent, which is certainly influenced, but is never fully determined, by external causes. What puzzles and deeply disturbs him, therefore, is rather when he finds himself unable to want something, indeed, unable to want something that he wants himself to want (namely, his full commitment to chastity and religious life in general): "The mind commands the body and is instantly obeyed; the mind commands itself, and meets with resistance," as he says. He finds the explanation for this "bizarre situation" in a "sickness of the mind," when it is divided against itself, not being able to fully commit to what it sees it ought to do. This "sickness" is in fact the only genuine, intrinsic hindrance to the freedom of the will, which therefore can only be fully possessed if the mind regains its integrity, when it is cured of this sickness by committing itself to what it ought to do with the aid of the grace of God.

The selection from *Consolatione Philosophiae* contains Boethius' equally famous and enormously influential discussion of the issue of the compatibility of the freedom of the will and divine providence, another potential constraint on the freedom of the will. The problem, very briefly, is this: if God foreknows what I will do tomorrow, as He certainly does, given His omniscience, then tomorrow I cannot but do what He now knows I will do. But if I will *have to* do it, then I have no choice, so my will is not free. Boethius' ingenious solution, in terms of distinguishing absolute and conditional necessity, as well as his subtle discussion of divine eternity, served as the starting point for all later discussions of the problem.

The next selection reproduces in full Anselm's short treatise "On Free Will." Perhaps the most peculiar thing about Anselm's discussion to the modern reader is the idea, already present in Augustine, but most fully expounded here, that the freedom of the will does not require several alternative possibilities among which the will could choose. On this conception, even if the will cannot choose anything except what it actually does, it is still free, provided that choosing this one possible choice is still the result of autonomously choosing what one ought to do. Indeed, the perfect freedom of the will is exercised precisely when it can only choose what it ought to choose, for it is morally (not physically) incapable of making a sinful choice. This is the freedom of saints, good angels, and God. So it is no wonder that several centuries later, even in a radically different philosophical setting, the will endowed with this sort of autonomy would be called "the holy will" by Immanuel Kant.[3]

So, the freedom of the will consists in its autonomy, or self-determination, which is fully exercised when the will chooses what it ought to choose according to right reason. But should this mean, then, that it is reason that determines what the will ought to choose? In other words, is reason a power superior to the will? The last selection of this part presents Henry of Ghent's negative answer to this question, carefully arguing for the Augustinian "voluntaristic" position, as opposed to the Aristotelians' (especially, Aquinas') perceived "intellectualism."

The selections of the next section are meant to illustrate the "internal" debate of the Aristotelians, contrasting the Averroist philosophers' view of "immanent" happiness achievable in this life through Boethius of Dacia's short treatise on the supreme good with the theologians' conception of "transcendent" happiness achievable only in the beatific vision, through the selected articles of Aquinas' *Summa Theologiae*. It is to be noted, though,

---

3 For a more detailed discussion of the issue along these lines, see Gergely Klima, "The Primal Choice: An Analysis of Anselm's Account of Free Will," *Sapientia et Doctrina* 1/2 (2004), pp. 5–13.

that the philosophers' "immanent" conception ultimately targets the same transcendent object, namely, the contemplation of the divine essence, but in a way that is thought to be achievable in this life.

A similar balancing act – which, as we could see, is typical in practically all aspects of medieval thought – between immanence and transcendence can be observed in the last two selections, dealing with some foundational issues in medieval legal thought. For medieval thinkers, legality, or legal justice, just like morality, is in no way a matter of convention, even if the actual implementation of its objective standards in a society is always dependent on the actual social circumstances. As we can see from the selections from Aquinas' *Summa Theologiae*, the implementation of the norms of legality through legislation results in positive law, i.e., the laws posited by the legislative authority of society. However, what justifies the legality or justice of this positive legislation is natural law, inherent in the demands of securing the common good of human society. And this common good is the precondition of the flourishing of individual humans in society, the needs of which in turn are determined by human nature as such.

It is quite important to notice here the dynamic aspect of Aquinas' thought, often ignored in contemporary discussions of natural law (as the foundation of basic human rights). Precisely because positive law is merely the temporal implementation of the unchanging norms of natural law, positive law cannot remain static in a changing society, but needs to be adjusted in accordance with the changing social circumstances. For what is a just positive norm in one situation may become unjust simply on account of the changes in society. Although Aquinas is certainly not a revolutionary, he is definitely committed to the idea of revising positive legislation precisely on account of the unchanging demands of justice in a changing society.

But all of these considerations concerning natural law and positive law presuppose in a theological context the clarification of the relationships between the natural and supernatural sources of the unchanging norms of justice, namely, natural law and divine law (including, for example, the precepts of the Ten Commandments or the Two Precepts of Charity: cf. Matthew 22: 37–40). The last selection, from John Duns Scotus, presents the Subtle Doctor's highly nuanced view on the issue, arguing that in some sense even the Ten Commandments can be regarded as pertaining to natural law, in stark contrast to later views, which would see in the divine law nothing but the possibly arbitrary commandments of a supreme, absolute monarch. However, that conception already points away from the highest achievements of typically medieval thought, which was always in search of a harmonious continuity and balance between immanence and transcendence, the natural and supernatural aspects of human life.

Goodness and Being

35

Augustine on Evil as the Privation of Goodness

Enchiridion

Chapter 10. The Supremely Good Creator Made All Things Good

By the Trinity, thus supremely and equally and unchangeably good, all things were created; and these are not supremely and equally and unchangeably good, but yet they are good, even taken separately. Taken as a whole, however, they are very good, because their *ensemble* constitutes the universe in all its wonderful order and beauty.

Chapter 11. What is Called Evil in the Universe is But the Absence of Good

And in the universe, even that which is called evil, when it is regulated and put in its own place, only enhances our admiration of the good; for we enjoy and value the good more when we compare it with the evil. For the Almighty God, who, as even the heathen acknowledge, has supreme power over all things, being Himself supremely good, would never permit the existence of anything evil among His works, if He were not so omnipotent and good that He can bring good even out of evil. For what is that which we call evil but the absence of good? In the bodies of animals, disease and wounds mean nothing but the absence of health; for when a cure is effected, that does not mean that the evils which were present – namely, the diseases and wounds – go away from the body and dwell elsewhere: they altogether cease to exist; for the wound or disease is not a substance, but a defect in the fleshly substance, – the flesh itself being a substance, and therefore something good, of which those evils – that is, privations of the good which we call health – are accidents. Just in the same way, what are called vices in the soul are nothing but privations of natural good. And when they are cured, they are not transferred elsewhere: when they cease to exist in the healthy soul, they cannot exist anywhere else.

Chapter 12. All Beings Were Made Good, But Not Being Made Perfectly Good, are Liable to Corruption

All things that exist, therefore, seeing that the Creator of them all is supremely good, are themselves good. But because they are not, like their Creator, supremely and unchangeably good, their good may be diminished and increased. But for good to be diminished is an evil, although, however much it may be diminished, it is necessary, if the being is to continue, that some good should remain to constitute the being. For however small or of whatever kind the being may be, the good which makes it a being cannot be destroyed without destroying the being itself. An uncorrupted nature is justly held in esteem. But if, still further, it be incorruptible, it is undoubtedly considered of still higher value. When it is corrupted, however, its corruption is an evil, because it is deprived of some sort of good. For if it be deprived of no good, it receives no injury; but it does receive injury, therefore it is deprived of good. Therefore, so long as a being is in process of corruption, there is in it some good of which it is being deprived; and if a part of the being should remain which cannot be corrupted, this will certainly be an incorruptible being, and accordingly the process of corruption will result in the manifestation of this great good. But if it do not cease to be corrupted, neither can it cease to possess good of which corruption may deprive it. But if it should be thoroughly and completely consumed by corruption, there will then be no good left, because there will be no being. Wherefore corruption can consume the good only by consuming the being. Every being, therefore, is a good; a great good, if it can not be corrupted; a little good, if it can: but in any case, only the foolish or ignorant will deny that it is a good. And if it be wholly consumed by corruption, then the corruption itself must cease to exist, as there is no being left in which it can dwell.

Chapter 13. There Can Be No Evil Where There is No Good; And an Evil Man is an Evil Good

Accordingly, there is nothing of what we call evil, if there be nothing good. But a good which is wholly without evil is a perfect good. A good, on the other hand, which contains evil is a faulty or imperfect good; and there can be no evil where there is no good. From all this we arrive at the curious result: that since every being, so far as it is a being, is good, when we say that a faulty being is an evil being, we just seem to say that what is good is evil, and that nothing but what is good can be evil, seeing that every being is good, and that no evil can exist except in a being. Nothing, then, can be evil except something which is good. And although this, when stated, seems to be a contradiction, yet the strictness of reasoning leaves us no escape from the conclusion. We must, however, beware of incurring the prophetic condemnation: "Woe unto them that call evil good, and good evil: that put darkness for light, and light for darkness: that put bitter for sweet, and sweet for bitter."[1] And yet our Lord says: "An evil man out of the evil treasure of his heart bringeth forth that which is evil."[2] Now, what is evil man but an evil being? for a man is a being. Now, if a man is a good thing because he is a being, what is an evil man but an evil good? Yet, when we accurately distinguish these two things, we find that it is not because he is a man that he is an evil, or because he is wicked that he is a good; but that he is a good because he is a man, and an evil because he is wicked. Whoever, then, says, "To be a man is an evil," or, "To be wicked is a good," falls under the prophetic denunciation: "Woe unto them that call evil good, and good evil!" For he condemns the work of God, which is the man, and praises the defect of man, which is the wickedness. Therefore every being, even if it be a defective one, in so far as it is a being is good, and in so far as it is defective is evil.

1 Isa. 5: 20.
2 Luke 6: 45.

36

Augustine on the Origin of Moral Evil

City of God

Book XII

Argument – Augustine first institutes two inquiries regarding the angels; namely, whence is there in some a good, and in others an evil will? and, what is the reason of the blessedness of the good, and the misery of the evil? Afterwards he treats of the creation of man, and teaches that he is not from eternity, but was created, and by none other than God.

Chapter 1. That the Nature of the Angels, Both Good and Bad, Is One and the Same

It has already, in the preceding book, been shown how the two cities originated among the angels. Before I speak of the creation of man, and show how the cities took their rise so far as regards the race of rational mortals I see that I must first, so far as I can, adduce what may demonstrate that it is not incongruous and unsuitable to speak of a society composed of angels and men together; so that there are not four cities or societies, – two, namely, of angels, and as many of men, – but rather two in all, one composed of the good, the other of the wicked, angels or men indifferently.

That the contrary propensities in good and bad angels have arisen, not from a difference in their nature and origin, since God, the good Author and Creator of all essences, created them both, but from a difference in their wills and desires, it is impossible to doubt. While some steadfastly continued in that which was the common good of all, namely, in God Himself, and in His eternity, truth, and love; others, being enamored rather of their own power, as if they could be their own good, lapsed to this private good of their own, from that higher and beatific good which was common to all, and, bartering the lofty dignity of eternity for the inflation of pride, the most assured verity for the slyness of vanity, uniting love for factious partisanship, they became proud, deceived, envious. The cause, therefore, of the blessedness of the good is adherence to God. And so the cause of the others' misery will be found in the contrary, that is, in their not adhering to God. Wherefore, if when the question is asked, why are the former blessed, it is rightly answered, because they adhere to God; and when it is asked, why are the latter miserable, it is rightly answered, because they do not adhere to God, – then there is no other good for the rational or intellectual creature save God only. Thus, though it is not every creature that can be blessed (for beasts, trees, stones, and things of that kind have not this capacity), yet that creature which has the capacity cannot be blessed of itself, since it is created out of nothing, but only by Him by whom it has been created. For it is blessed by the possession of that whose loss makes it miserable. He, then, who is blessed not in another, but in himself, cannot be miserable, because he cannot lose himself.

Accordingly we say that there is no unchangeable good but the one, true, blessed God; that the things which He made are indeed good because from Him, yet mutable because made not out of Him, but out of nothing. Although, therefore, they are not the supreme good, for God is a greater good, yet those mutable things which can adhere to the immutable good, and so be blessed, are very good; for so completely is He their good, that without Him they cannot but be wretched. And the other created things in the universe are not better on this account, that they cannot be miserable. For no one would say that the other members of the body are superior to the eyes, because they cannot be blind. But as the sentient nature, even when it feels pain, is superior to the stony, which can feel none, so the rational nature, even when wretched, is more excellent than that which lacks reason or feeling, and can therefore experience no misery. And since this is so, then in this nature which has been created so excellent, that though it be mutable itself, it can yet secure its blessedness by adhering to the immutable good, the supreme God; and since it is not satisfied unless it be perfectly blessed, and cannot be thus blessed save in God, – in this nature, I say, not to adhere to God, is manifestly a fault.[1] Now every fault injures the nature, and is consequently contrary to the nature. The creature, therefore, which cleaves to God, differs from those who do not, not by nature, but by fault; and yet by this very fault the nature itself is proved to be very noble and admirable. For that nature is certainly praised, the fault of which is justly blamed. For we justly blame the fault because it mars the praiseworthy nature. As, then, when we say that blindness is a defect of the eyes, we prove that sight belongs to the nature of the eyes; and when we say that deafness is a defect of the ears, hearing is thereby proved to belong to their nature; – so, when we say that it is a fault of the angelic creature that it does not cleave to God, we hereby most plainly declare that it pertained to its nature to cleave to God. And who can worthily conceive or express how great a glory that is, to cleave to God, so as to live to Him, to draw wisdom from Him, to delight in Him, and to enjoy this so great good, without death, error, or grief? And thus, since every vice is an injury of the nature, that very vice of the wicked angels, their departure from God, is sufficient proof that God created their nature so good, that it is an injury to it not to be with God.

Chapter 2. That There is No Entity[2] Contrary to the Divine, Because Nonentity Seems to Be that Which is Wholly Opposite to Him Who Supremely and Always Is

This may be enough to prevent any one from supposing, when we speak of the apostate angels, that they could have another nature, derived, as it were, from some different origin,

1 *Vitium*: perhaps "fault," most nearly embraces all the uses of this word.
2 *Essentia*.

and not from God. From the great impiety of this error we shall disentangle ourselves the more readily and easily, the more distinctly we understand that which God spoke by the angel when He sent Moses to the children of Israel: "I am that I am."[3] For since God is the supreme existence, that is to say, supremely is, and is therefore unchangeable, the things that He made He empowered to be, but not to be supremely like Himself. To some He communicated a more ample, to others a more limited existence, and thus arranged the natures of beings in ranks. For as from *sapere* comes *sapientia*, so from *esse* comes *essentia*, – a new word indeed, which the old Latin writers did not use, but which is naturalized in our day,[4] that our language may not want an equivalent for the Greek οὐσία. For this is expressed word for word by *essentia*. Consequently, to that nature which supremely is, and which created all else that exists, no nature is contrary save that which does not exist. For nonentity is the contrary of that which is. And thus there is no being contrary to God, the Supreme Being, and Author of all beings whatsoever.

Chapter 3. That the Enemies of God Are So, Not by Nature, But by Will, Which, as It Injures Them, Injures a Good Nature; For if Vice Does Not Injure, It Is Not Vice

In Scripture they are called God's enemies who oppose His rule, not by nature, but by vice; having no power to hurt Him, but only themselves. For they are His enemies, not through their power to hurt, but by their will to oppose Him. For God is unchangeable, and wholly proof against injury. Therefore the vice which makes those who are called His enemies resist Him, is an evil not to God, but to themselves. And to them it is an evil, solely because it corrupts the good of their nature. It is not nature, therefore, but vice, which is contrary to God. For that which is evil is contrary to the good. And who will deny that God is the supreme good? Vice, therefore, is contrary to God, as evil to good. Further, the nature it vitiates is a good, and therefore to this good also it is contrary. But while it is contrary to God only as evil to good, it is contrary to the nature it vitiates, both as evil and as hurtful. For to God no evils are hurtful; but only to natures mutable and corruptible, though, by the testimony of the vices themselves, originally good. For were they not good, vices could not hurt them. For how do they hurt them but by depriving them of integrity, beauty, welfare, virtue, and, in short, whatever natural good vice is wont to diminish or destroy? But if there be no good to take away, then no injury can be done, and consequently there can be no vice. For it is impossible that there should be a harmless vice. Whence we gather, that though vice cannot injure the unchangeable good, it can injure nothing but good; because it does not exist where it does not injure. This, then, may be thus formulated: Vice cannot be in the highest good, and cannot be but in some good. Things solely good, therefore, can in some circumstances exist; things solely evil, never; for even those natures which are vitiated by an evil will, so far indeed as they are vitiated, are evil, but in so far as they are natures they are good. And when a vitiated nature is punished, besides the good it has in being a nature, it has this also, that it is not unpunished.[5] For this is just, and certainly everything

---

3   Ex. 3: 14.

4   Quintilian calls it *dura*.

5   With this may be compared the argument of Socrates in the *Gorgias*, in which it is shown that to escape punishment is worse than to suffer it, and that the greatest of evils is to do wrong and not be chastised.

just is a good. For no one is punished for natural, but for voluntary vices. For even the vice which by the force of habit and long continuance has become a second nature, had its origin in the will. For at present we are speaking of the vices of the nature, which has a mental capacity for that enlightenment which discriminates between what is just and what is unjust.

Chapter 4. Of the Nature of Irrational and Lifeless Creatures, which in their own Kind and Order Do Not Mar the Beauty of the Universe

But it is ridiculous to condemn the faults of beasts and trees, and other such mortal and mutable things as are void of intelligence, sensation, or life, even though these faults should destroy their corruptible nature; for these creatures received, at their Creator's will, an existence fitting them, by passing away and giving place to others, to secure that lowest form of beauty, the beauty of seasons, which in its own place is a requisite part of this world. For things earthly were neither to be made equal to things heavenly, nor were they, though inferior, to be quite omitted from the universe. Since, then, in those situations where such things are appropriate, some perish to make way for others that are born in their room, and the less succumb to the greater, and the things that are overcome are transformed into the quality of those that have the mastery, this is the appointed order of things transitory. Of this order the beauty does not strike us, because by our mortal frailty we are so involved in a part of it, that we cannot perceive the whole, in which these fragments that offend us are harmonized with the most accurate fitness and beauty. And therefore, where we are not so well able to perceive the wisdom of the Creator, we are very properly enjoined to believe it, lest in the vanity of human rashness we presume to find any fault with the work of so great an Artificer. At the same time, if we attentively consider even these faults of earthly things, which are neither voluntary nor penal, they seem to illustrate the excellence of the natures themselves, which are all originated and created by God; for it is that which pleases us in this nature which we are displeased to see removed by the fault, – unless even the natures themselves displease men, as often happens when they become hurtful to them, and then men estimate them not by their nature, but by their utility; as in the case of those animals whose swarms scourged the pride of the Egyptians. But in this way of estimating, they may find fault with the sun itself; for certain criminals or debtors are sentenced by the judges to be set in the sun. Therefore it is not with respect to our convenience or discomfort, but with respect to their own nature, that the creatures are glorifying to their Artificer. Thus even the nature of the eternal fire, penal though it be to the condemned sinners, is most assuredly worthy of praise. For what is more beautiful than fire flaming, blazing, and shining? What more useful than fire for warming, restoring, cooking, though nothing is more destructive than fire burning and consuming? The same thing, then, when applied in one way, is destructive, but when applied suitably, is most beneficial. For who can find words to tell its uses throughout the whole world? We must not listen, then, to those who praise the light of fire but find fault with its heat, judging it not by its nature, but by their convenience or discomfort. For they wish to see, but not to be burnt. But they forget that this very light which is so pleasant to them, disagrees with and hurts weak eyes; and in that heat which is disagreeable to them, some animals find the most suitable conditions of a healthy life.

Chapter 5. That in All Natures, of Every Kind and Rank, God Is Glorified

All natures, then, inasmuch as they are, and have therefore a rank and species of their own, and a kind of internal harmony, are certainly good. And when they are in the places assigned to them by the order of their nature, they preserve such being as they have received. And those things which have not received everlasting being, are altered for better or for worse, so as to suit the wants and motions of those things to which the Creator's law has made them subservient; and thus they tend in the divine providence to that end which is embraced in the general scheme of the government of the universe. So that, though the corruption of transitory and perishable things brings them to utter destruction, it does not prevent their producing that which was designed to be their result. And this being so, God, who supremely is, and who therefore created every being which has not supreme existence (for that which was made of nothing could not be equal to Him, and indeed could not be at all had He not made it), is not to be found fault with on account of the creature's faults, but is to be praised in view of the natures He has made.

Chapter 6. What the Cause of the Blessedness of the Good Angels Is, and What the Cause of the Misery of the Wicked

Thus the true cause of the blessedness of the good angels is found to be this, that they cleave to Him who supremely is. And if we ask the cause of the misery of the bad, it occurs to us, and not unreasonably, that they are miserable because they have forsaken Him who supremely is, and have turned to themselves who have no such essence. And this vice, what else is it called than pride? For "pride is the beginning of sin."[6] They were unwilling, then, to preserve their strength for God; and as adherence to God was the condition of their enjoying an ampler being, they diminished it by preferring themselves to Him. This was the first defect, and the first impoverishment, and the first flaw of their nature, which was created, not indeed supremely existent, but finding its blessedness in the enjoyment of the Supreme Being; whilst by abandoning Him it should become, not indeed no nature at all, but a nature with a less ample existence, and therefore wretched.

If the further question be asked, What was the efficient cause of their evil will? there is none. For what is it which makes the will bad, when it is the will itself which makes the action bad? And consequently the bad will is the cause of the bad action, but nothing is the efficient cause of the bad will. For if anything is the cause, this thing either has or has not a will. If it has, the will is either good or bad. If good, who is so left to himself as to say that a good will makes a will bad? For in this case a good will would be the cause of sin; a most absurd supposition. On the other hand, if this hypothetical thing has a bad will, I wish to know what made it so; and that we may not go on forever, I ask at once, what made the *first* evil will bad? For that is not the first which was itself corrupted by an evil will, but that is the first which was made evil by no other will. For if it were preceded by that which made it evil, that will was first which made the other evil. But if it is replied, "Nothing made it evil; it always was evil," I ask if it has been existing in some nature. For if not, then it did not exist at all; and if it did exist in some nature, then it vitiated and corrupted it, and injured it, and consequently deprived it of good. And therefore the evil will could not exist in an

---

6 Eccles. 10: 13.

evil nature, but in a nature at once good and mutable, which this vice could injure. For if it did no injury, it was no vice; and consequently the will in which it was, could not be called evil. But if it did injury, it did it by taking away or diminishing good. And therefore there could not be from eternity, as was suggested, an evil will in that thing in which there had been previously a natural good, which the evil will was able to diminish by corrupting it. If, then, it was not from eternity, who, I ask, made it? The only thing that can be suggested in reply is, that something which itself had no will, made the will evil. I ask, then, whether this thing was superior, inferior, or equal to it? If superior, then it is better. How, then, has it no will, and not rather a good will? The same reasoning applies if it was equal; for so long as two things have equally a good will, the one cannot produce in the other an evil will. Then remains the supposition that that which corrupted the will of the angelic nature which first sinned, was itself an inferior thing without a will. But that thing, be it of the lowest and most earthly kind, is certainly itself good, since it is a nature and being, with a form and rank of its own in its own kind and order. How, then, can a good thing be the efficient cause of an evil will? How, I say, can good be the cause of evil? For when the will abandons what is above itself, and turns to what is lower, it becomes evil – not because that is evil to which it turns, but because the turning itself is wicked. Therefore it is not an inferior thing which has made the will evil, but it is itself which has become so by wickedly and inordinately desiring an inferior thing. For if two men, alike in physical and moral constitution, see the same corporal beauty, and one of them is excited by the sight to desire an illicit enjoyment while the other steadfastly maintains a modest restraint of his will, what do we suppose brings it about, that there is an evil will in the one and not in the other? What produces it in the man in whom it exists? Not the bodily beauty, for that was presented equally to the gaze of both, and yet did not produce in both an evil will. Did the flesh of the one cause the desire as he looked? But why did not the flesh of the other? Or was it the disposition? But why not the disposition of both? For we are supposing that both were of a like temperament of body and soul. Must we, then, say that the one was tempted by a secret suggestion of the evil spirit? As if it was not by his own will that he consented to this suggestion and to any inducement whatever! This consent, then, this evil will which he presented to the evil suasive influence, – what was the cause of it, we ask? For, not to delay on such a difficulty as this, if both are tempted equally and one yields and consents to the temptation while the other remains unmoved by it, what other account can we give of the matter than this, that the one is willing, the other unwilling, to fall away from chastity? And what causes this but their own wills, in cases at least such as we are supposing, where the temperament is identical? The same beauty was equally obvious to the eyes of both; the same secret temptation pressed on both with equal violence. However minutely we examine the case, therefore, we can discern nothing which caused the will of the one to be evil. For if we say that the man himself made his will evil, what was the man himself before his will was evil but a good nature created by God, the unchangeable good? Here are two men who, before the temptation, were alike in body and soul, and of whom one yielded to the tempter who persuaded him, while the other could not be persuaded to desire that lovely body which was equally before the eyes of both. Shall we say of the successfully tempted man that he corrupted his own will, since he was certainly good before his will became bad? Then, why did he do so? Was it because his will was a nature, or because it was made of nothing? We shall find that the latter is the case. For if a nature is the cause of an evil will, what else can we say than that evil arises from good or that good is the cause of evil? And how can it come to pass that a nature, good though mutable, should produce any evil – that is to say, should make the will itself wicked?

Chapter 7. That We Ought Not to Expect to Find Any Efficient Cause of the Evil Will

Let no one, therefore, look for an efficient cause of the evil will; for it is not efficient, but deficient, as the will itself is not an effecting of something, but a defect. For defection from that which supremely is, to that which has less of being, – this is to begin to have an evil will. Now, to seek to discover the causes of these defections, – causes, as I have said, not efficient, but deficient, – is as if some one sought to see darkness, or hear silence. Yet both of these are known by us, and the former by means only of the eye, the latter only by the ear; but not by their positive actuality,[7] but by their want of it. Let no one, then seek to know from me what I know that I do not know; unless he perhaps wishes to learn to be ignorant of that of which all we know is, that it cannot be known. For those things which are known not by their actuality, but by their want of it, are known, if our expression may be allowed and understood, by not knowing them, that by knowing them they may be not known. For when the eyesight surveys objects that strike the sense, it nowhere sees darkness but where it begins not to see. And so no other sense but the ear can perceive silence, and yet it is only perceived by not hearing. Thus, too, our mind perceives intelligible forms by understanding them; but when they are deficient, it knows them by not knowing them; for "who can understand defects?"[8]

Chapter 8. Of the Misdirected Love Whereby the Will Fell Away from the Immutable to the Mutable Good

This I do know, that the nature of God can never, nowhere, nowise be defective, and that natures made of nothing can. These latter, however, the more being they have, and the more good they do (for then they do something positive), the more they have efficient causes; but in so far as they are defective in being, and consequently do evil (for then what is their work but vanity?), they have deficient causes. And I know likewise, that the will could not become evil, were it unwilling to become so; and therefore its failings are justly punished, being not necessary, but voluntary. For its defections are not to evil things, but are themselves evil; that is to say, are not towards things that are naturally and in themselves evil, but the defection of the will is evil, because it is contrary to the order of nature, and an abandonment of that which has supreme being for that which has less. For avarice is not a fault inherent in gold, but in the man who inordinately loves gold, to the detriment of justice, which ought to be held in incomparably higher regard than gold. Neither is luxury the fault of lovely and charming objects, but of the heart that inordinately loves sensual pleasures, to the neglect of temperance, which attaches us to objects more lovely in their spirituality, and more delectable by their incorruptibility. Nor yet is boasting the fault of human praise, but of the soul that is inordinately fond of the applause of men, and that makes light of the voice of conscience. Pride, too, is not the fault of him who delegates power, nor of power itself, but of the soul that is inordinately enamored of its own power, and despises the more just dominion of a higher authority. Consequently he who inordinately loves the good which any nature possesses, even though he obtain it, himself becomes evil in the good, and wretched because deprived of a greater good.

7 *Specie.*
8 Ps. 19: 12.

37

Boethius on Being and Goodness

De Hebdomadibus

[Prologue]

You ask that I should set out and explain a little more clearly the obscurity of that question from our hebdomads which concerns the way in which substances are good in virtue of the fact that they have being when they are not substantial goods. And you say that this should be done because the method of writings of this sort is not known to all. Now I myself am your witness how eagerly you have embraced these things before. But I contemplate the hebdomads on my own for myself and keep my thoughts in my memory rather than share them with any of those who, out of perversity and impudence, permit nothing to be composed without jest and laughter. Therefore, do not object to the obscurities associated with brevity which, since they are a faithful guardian of a secret, have the advantage of speaking only with those who are worthy. For that reason I have put forward first terms and rules on the basis of which I will work out all the things that follow, as is usually done in mathematics (and other disciplines also).

[The Axioms]

[I.] A conception belonging to the common understanding is a statement that anyone approves once it has been heard. There are two types of these. One type is common in the sense that it belongs to all men – e.g., if you propose: "If you take away equals from two equals, what remain are equals," no one who understands it denies it. The other type belongs only to the learned, even though it comes from such conceptions as belong to the common understanding – e.g., "Things which are incorporeal are not in a place," and others that the learned but not the uneducated acknowledge.

[II.] Being and that which is are different. For being itself does not exist yet, but that which is exists and is established when it has taken on the form of being.

[III.] That which is can participate in something, but being itself participates in no way in anything. For participation comes about when something already exists; but something exists when it has assumed being.

[IV.] That which is can have something besides what it itself is; but being itself has nothing besides itself mixed into it.

[V.] Being something *merely* and being something *in virtue of the fact that it has being* are different. For an accident is signified in the former case, a substance in the latter.

[VI.] Everything that participates in being so that it exists participates in something else so that it is something. Hence, that which is participates in being so that it exists; but it exists so that it might participate in anything else whatever.

[VII.] Every simple has its being and that which is as one.

[VIII.] For every composite, being and it itself are different.

[IX.] Every difference is discord, but likeness is to be sought. And what seeks another is itself shown to be naturally the same sort as that very thing which it seeks.

These things that we have set down to begin with, therefore, are enough. A careful interpreter of the reasoning will fit each one to its arguments.

[The Question]

Now the question is of this sort. Things which exist are good. For the common view of the learned holds that everything which exists tends toward good. But everything tends toward its like. Therefore, the things which tend toward good are themselves good. But we have to ask how they are good, by participation or by substance?

If by participation, they are in no way good in themselves. For what is white by participation is not white in itself in virtue of the fact that it itself has being. And the same applies to other qualities. Therefore, if they are good by participation, they are in no way good in themselves. Therefore, they do not tend toward good. But that was granted. Therefore, they are not good by participation but by substance.

Now for those things the substance of which is good, what they are are good.[1] But that which they are they have from [their] being. Therefore, their being is good; and therefore, the being itself of all things is good. But if [their] being is good, those things which exist are good in virtue of the fact that they have being, and, for them, being is the same as being good. Therefore, they are substantial goods because they do not participate in goodness.

But if being itself is good in their case, there is no doubt that since they are substantial goods, they are like the first good. And hence, they will be this good itself, for nothing is like it besides it itself. It follows from this that all things which exist are God, which is an impious claim. Therefore, they are not substantial goods, and hence being is not good in their case. Therefore, they are not good in virtue of the fact that they have being. But neither do they participate in goodness, for then they would in no way tend toward good. Therefore, they are in no way good.

---

1   The awkward English in this sentence reflects what seems to me to be Boethius's use of painstakingly precise Latin terminology. The Latin text of the short argument in which this claim occurs is: "*Quorum vero substantia bona est,* ID QUOD SUNT BONA SUNT; *id quod sunt autem habent ex eo quod est esse. Esse igitur ipsorum bonum est.*" The emphasized clause is the cause of the awkward English. Boethius's understanding of the expression *id quod sunt* in this passage seems to me to be the following. He takes *id quod est* to signify the essence of a thing ('that which it is' or 'what it is' – notice that this use of *id quod est* is different from its use in the Axioms). Since many things share one essence, Boethius uses *id quod sunt* ('that which they are,' 'what they are'). But there are many such essences, and Boethius wants to claim that all of these are good; hence the last plural verb: *bona sunt.*

[The Solution]

A solution of the following sort can be offered to this question. There are many things that, although they cannot be separated in actuality, nevertheless are separated in the mind and in thought. For example, although no one separates a triangle (or other [geometric figures]) from the underlying matter in actuality, nevertheless, distinguishing it in the mind, one examines the triangle itself and its essential character apart from matter. Therefore, let us remove from our mind for a little while the presence of the first good. (That it does exist is, of course, certain on the basis of the view of the learned and the unlearned and can be known from the religions of barbarian races.) Therefore, having removed this for a little while, let us suppose that all things which are good exist. And let us consider how those things could be good if they had not flowed down from the first good.

From this point of view I observe that, in their case, that they are good and what they are are different. For let one and the same good substance be supposed to be white, heavy, and round. Then that substance itself, its roundness, its color, and its goodness would all be different, for if these items were the same as the substance itself, heaviness would be the same as color, [color] as good, and good as heaviness. But nature does not allow this. Therefore, in their case, being and being something would be different; and then they would indeed be good but they would not have [their] being itself as good. Therefore, if they did exist in any way, then they would not be from the good and they would be good and they would not be the same as good; but, for them, being and being good would be different.

But if they were nothing else at all except good, neither heavy nor colored nor extended in spatial dimension nor were there any quality in them excepting only that they were good, then it would seem that they are not [merely] things but the source of things. Nor would "they" seem [so], but rather "it" would seem [so], for there is one and only one thing of this sort that is only good and nothing else.

But because they are not simple they cannot exist at all unless that thing which is only good willed that they exist. Therefore, they are said to be good because their being flowed from the will of the good. For the first good, because it is, is good in virtue of the fact that it is.[2] But a second good, because it flowed from that whose being itself is good, is itself also good. But the being itself of all things flowed from that which is the first good and which is such that it is properly said to be good in virtue of the fact that it is. Therefore, their being itself is good, for it is then in it [– that is to say, the first good].

In this the question has been resolved. For although they are good in virtue of the fact that they have being, nevertheless they are not like the first good. For it is not just in any way whatever in which things have being that their being itself is good, but because the being itself of things cannot exist unless it has flowed down from the first being, i.e., the good. Therefore, [their] being itself is good and it is not like that from which it has being. For [the first good] is good in virtue of the fact that it is in whatever way it is, for it is not anything other than good. But [a second good] could perhaps be good but it could not be good in virtue of the fact that it has being unless it were from [the first good]. For then it would per-haps participate in good; but they could not have being itself, which they would not have from the good, as good. Therefore, when the first good is removed from them in the mind

2 In this sentence I translate the phrase *in eo quod est* with 'in virtue of the fact that it is' rather than the usual 'in virtue of the fact that it has being' because Boethius is talking here about the first good, which is simple and therefore cannot be said to *have* properties.

and in thought, these things could not be good in virtue of the fact that they have being, even though they could be good. And since they could not exist in actuality unless that which truly is good had produced them, their being is good, and that which flowed from the substantial good is not like it. And if they had not flowed from it, they could not be good in virtue of the fact that they have being, even though they could be good – this is because they would be both other than the good and not from the good, while that thing is itself the first good and is being itself and the good itself and being good itself.

[Objections and Replies]

And will it not also be necessary that white things are white in virtue of the fact that they have being, since those things that are white have flowed from the will of God so that they are white? Not at all. For being and being white are different in their case because of the fact that he who produced them so that they exist is indeed good but not white. Therefore, it followed from the will of the good that they are good in virtue of the fact that they have being. But it did not follow from the will of what is not white that the essential character such that a thing is white in virtue of the fact that it has being belongs to it; for they have not flowed down from the will of the white. And so, because he who willed those things to be white was not white, they are white *merely*. But because he who willed those things to be good was good, they are good *in virtue of the fact that they have being*.

Therefore, according to this reasoning, must not all things be just since he is just who willed them to exist? No indeed. For being good has to do with essence, but being just with an act. In him, however, being is the same as acting, and therefore being good is the same as being just. But, for us, being is not the same as acting, for we are not simple. For us, therefore, being good is not the same as being just; but, for us, all [and only] the things in virtue of which we have being are the same.[3] Therefore, all things are good [but] not also just.

Further, good is of course general, but just is specific, and a species does not descend into all [the members of its genus]. Therefore, some things are just, some another [species of good], [but] all things are good.

---

3   The phrase I have translated 'in virtue of which we have being' is *in eo quod sumus*. Except for the fact that the verb is in the first person plural, it is the same phrase as the phrase that I have translated consistently throughout as 'in virtue of the fact that it has being (they have being)' [*in eo quod est (sunt)*]. Maintaining consistency in the present passage would lose the sense.

Thomas Aquinas on the Convertibility of Being and Goodness

Summa Theologiae

Part I, Question 5. On Goodness in General

Article 1. Whether being and goodness are the same in reality?

Objection 1. It appears that goodness is different from being in reality. For Boethius says in his *De Hebdomadibus* [PL 64, 1312]: "I observe that it is one thing that things are good and it is another that they are." Therefore, being and goodness are different in reality.

Objection 2. Further, nothing gives form to itself. "But something is said to be good on account of [goodness] giving form to being," according to the commentary on the *Book of Causes* [XIX]. Therefore, goodness differs from being in reality.

Objection 3. Further, goodness can have degrees, but being cannot. Therefore goodness differs from being in reality.

On the contrary, Augustine says [*De Doctrina Christiana* I, 32. PL 34, 32] that "inasmuch as we exist we are good."

I answer that goodness and being are the same in reality; they only differ in their concepts. And this should be obvious from the following. The concept of being good consists in being desirable; this is why the Philosopher says in bk. 1 of the *Ethics* [*Nicomachean Ethics* I, 1, 1094a3] that good is what everything desires. But it is evident that everything is desirable insofar as it is perfect, for everything desires its own perfection. On the other hand, everything is perfect to the extent that it has reached actuality; so it is obvious that everything is good inasmuch as it is, for being is the actuality of every thing, as is clear from what was said earlier [Ia. 3, 4; 4, 1, ad 3]. Therefore, it is clear that goodness and being are the same in reality, but the concept of goodness implies desirability, which is not implied by the concept of being.

Reply to Objection 1. To the first objection, therefore, we have to say that although goodness and being are the same in reality, since they differ in their concept, it is not in the same way that something is said to be good and that something is said to be, without qualification.

Since the concept of being properly speaking implies actuality, and actuality is properly opposed to sheer potentiality, something is said to be, without qualification, on account of that by which it is primarily distinguished from something that is merely in potentiality. And this is the substantial being of each and every thing. Therefore, it is on account of its substantial being that anything is said to be, without qualification. On the other hand, it is on account of further, superadded actualities that something is said to be somehow, as to be white means to be somehow, for being white does not remove sheer potentiality absolutely speaking, because it just renders something that already is in actuality to be somehow. But being good implies perfection, which is desirable, and therefore refers to what is an end. So that thing is said to be good without qualification which has its ultimate perfection. But a thing that does not have the ultimate perfection that it ought to have (even if it does have some perfection insofar as it actually exists) is not said to be perfect without qualification, nor do we call it good without qualification, but only with some qualification. So, on account of its primary act of being, which is its substantial being, something is said to be without qualification; but on that account it is said to be good with qualification, i.e., insofar as it is a being. On the other hand, on account of its ultimate actuality something is said to be with qualification, but on that account it is said to be good without qualification. Therefore, what Boethius said, namely that it is one thing for something to be, and it is another for it to be good, should be understood as concerning a thing's being and its being good absolutely speaking, without qualification. For on account of its primary actuality [i.e., its substantial being] something is a being, absolutely speaking, but on account of its ultimate actuality [i.e. its ultimate perfection] a thing is good, absolutely speaking. On the other hand, on account of its primary actuality the thing is good somehow [i.e., insofar as it exists at all], while on account of its ultimate perfection the thing is somehow, [i.e., with qualification].

Reply to Objection 2. Goodness is said to give form insofar as goodness is taken absolutely, for ultimate actuality.

Reply to Objection 3. Again, goodness has degrees in the thing's superadded actualities, as in knowledge or virtue.

Freedom of the Will

39

Augustine on the "Divided Will"

Confessions

Book VIII. Conversion

5, 10. . . . It was no iron chain imposed by anyone else that fettered me, but the iron of my own will. The enemy had my power of willing in his clutches, and from it had forged a chain to bind me. The truth is that disordered lust springs from a perverted will; when lust is pandered to, a habit is formed; when habit is not checked, it hardens into compulsion. These were like interlinking rings forming what I have described as a chain, and my harsh servitude used it to keep me under duress.

A new will had begun to emerge in me, the will to worship you disinterestedly and enjoy you, O God, our only sure felicity; but it was not yet capable of surmounting that earlier will strengthened by inveterate custom. And so the two wills fought it out – the old and the new, the one carnal, the other spiritual – and in their struggle tore my soul apart.

[. . .]

8, 19. Within the house of my spirit the violent conflict raged on, the quarrel with my soul that I had so powerfully provoked in our secret dwelling, my heart, and at the height of it I rushed to Alypius with my mental anguish plain upon my face. "What is happening to us?" I exclaimed. "What does this mean? What did you make of it? The untaught are rising up and taking heaven by storm, while we with all our dreary teachings are still groveling in this world of flesh and blood! Are we ashamed to follow, just because they have taken the lead, yet not ashamed of lacking the courage even to follow?" Some such words as these I spoke, and then my frenzy tore me away from him, while he regarded me in silent bewilderment. Unusual, certainly, was my speech, but my brow, cheeks and eyes, my flushed countenance and the cadences of my voice expressed my mind more fully than the words I uttered.

Adjacent to our lodgings was a small garden. We were free to make use of it as well as of the house, for our host, who owned the house, did not live there. The tumult in my breast had swept me away to this place, where no one would interfere with the blazing dispute I had engaged in with myself until it should be resolved. What the outcome would be you knew, not I. All I knew was that I was going mad, but for the sake of my sanity, and dying that I might live, aware of the evil that I was but unaware of the good I was soon to become. So I went out into the garden and Alypius followed at my heels; my privacy was not infringed by his presence, and, in any case, how could he abandon me in that state? We sat down as far as possible from the house. I was groaning in spirit and shaken by violent anger because I could form no resolve to enter into a covenant with you, though in my bones I knew that this was what I ought to do, and everything in me lauded such a course to the skies. It was a journey not to be undertaken by ship or carriage or on foot, nor need it take me even that short distance I had walked from the house to the place where we were sitting; for to travel – and more, to reach journey's end – was nothing else but to want to go there, but to want it valiantly and with all my heart, not to whirl and toss this way and that a will half crippled by the struggle, as part of it rose up to walk while part sank down.

20. While this vacillation was at its most intense many of my bodily gestures were of the kind that people sometimes want to perform but cannot either because the requisite limbs are missing, or because they are bound and restricted, or paralyzed through illness, or in some other way impeded. If I tore out my hair, battered my forehead, entwined my fingers and clasped them round my knee, I did so because I wanted to. I might have wanted to but found myself unable, if my limbs had not been mobile enough to obey. So then, there were plenty of actions that I performed where willing was not the same thing as being able; yet I was not doing the one thing that was incomparably more desirable to me, the thing that I would be able to do as soon as I willed, because as soon as I willed – why, then, I would be willing it! For in this sole instance the faculty to act and the will to act precisely coincide, and the willing is already the doing. Yet this was not happening. My body was more ready to obey the slightest whim of my soul in the matter of moving my limbs, than the soul was to obey its own command in carrying out this major volition, which was to be accomplished within the will alone.

9, 21. How did this bizarre situation arise, how develop? May your mercy shed light on my inquiry, so that perhaps an answer may be found in the mysterious punishments meted out to humankind, those utterly baffling pains that afflict the children of Adam. How then did this bizarre situation arise, how develop? The mind commands the body and is instantly obeyed; the mind commands itself, and meets with resistance. When the mind orders the hand to move, so smooth is the compliance that command can scarcely be distinguished from execution; yet the mind is mind, while the hand is body. When the mind issues its command that the mind itself should will something (and the mind so commanded is no other than itself), it fails to do so. How did this bizarre situation arise, how develop? As I say, the mind commands itself to will something: it would not be giving the order if it did not want this thing; yet it does not do what it commands.

Evidently, then, it does not want this thing with the whole of itself, and therefore the command does not proceed from an undivided mind. Inasmuch as it issues the command, it does will it, but inasmuch as the command is not carried out, it does not will it. What the will is ordering is that a certain volition should exist, and this volition is not some alien thing, but its very self. Hence it cannot be giving the order with its whole self. It cannot be identical with that thing which it is commanding to come into existence, for if it were whole and entire it would not command itself to be, since it would be already.

This partial willing and partial non-willing is thus not so bizarre, but a sickness of the mind, which cannot rise with its whole self on the wings of truth because it is heavily burdened by habit. There are two wills, then, and neither is the whole: what one has the other lacks.

10, 22. Some there are who on perceiving two wills engaged in deliberation assert that in us there are two natures, one good, the other evil, each with a mind of its own. Let them perish from your presence, O God, as perish all who talk wildly and lead our minds astray. They are evil themselves as long as they hold these opinions, yet these same people will be good if they embrace true opinions and assent to true teaching, and so merit the apostle's commendation, You were darkness once, but now you are light in the Lord. The trouble is that they want to be light not in the Lord but in themselves, with their notion that the soul is by nature divine, and so they have become denser darkness still, because by their appalling arrogance they have moved further away from you, the true Light, who enlighten everyone who comes into the world. I warn these people, Take stock of what you are saying, and let it shame you; but once draw near to him and be illumined, and your faces will not blush with shame.

When I was making up my mind to serve the Lord my God at last, as I had long since purposed, I was the one who wanted to follow that course, and I was the one who wanted not to. I was the only one involved. I neither wanted it wholeheartedly nor turned from it wholeheartedly. I was at odds with myself, and fragmenting myself. This disintegration was occurring without my consent, but what it indicated was not the presence in me of a mind belonging to some alien nature but the punishment undergone by my own. In this sense, and this sense only, it was not I who brought it about, but the sin that dwelt within me as penalty for that other sin committed with greater freedom;[1] for I was a son of Adam.

23. Moreover, if we were to take the number of conflicting urges to signify the number of natures present in us, we should have to assume that there are not two, but many. If someone is trying to make up his mind whether to go to a Manichean conventicle or to the theater, the Manichees declare, "There you are, there's the evidence for two natures: the good one is dragging him our way, the bad one is pulling him back in the other direction. How else explain this dithering between contradictory wills?" But I regard both as bad, the one that leads him to them and the one that lures him back to the theater. They, on the contrary, think that an inclination toward them can only be good.

But consider this: suppose one of our people is deliberating, and as two desires clash he is undecided whether to go to the theater or to our church, will not our opponents too be undecided what attitude to take? Either they will have to admit that it is good will that leads a person to our church, just as good as that which leads to theirs the people who are initiated into their sacred rites and trapped there – and this they are unwilling to admit; or they will conclude that two evil natures and two bad minds are pitted against each other within one person, in which case their habitual assertion of one good and one evil nature will be erroneous; or, finally, they will be brought round to the truth and no longer deny that when a person is deliberating there is but one soul, thrown into turmoil by divergent impulses.

24. When, therefore, they observe two conflicting impulses within one person, let them stop saying that two hostile minds are at war, one good, the other evil, and that these derive from two hostile substances and two hostile principles. For you are true, O God, and so you chide and rebuke them and prove them wrong. The choice may lie between two impulses that are both evil, as when a person is debating whether to murder someone with poison

---

1   That is, by Adam. Augustine uses the comparative to suggest a relative freedom enjoyed by Adam, superior to our own but short of perfect freedom. He was to spell out the distinction later in *Correction and Grace* XII, 33 between *posse non peccare* (the ability not to sin, Adam's privilege), and *non posse peccare* (the perfection of freedom in heaven).

or a dagger; whether to annex this part of another man's property or that, assuming he cannot get both; whether to buy himself pleasure by extravagant spending or hoard his money out of avarice; whether to go to the circus or the theater if both performances are on the same day – and I would even add a third possibility: whether to go and steal from someone else's house while he has the chance, and a fourth as well: whether to commit adultery while he is about it. All these impulses may occur together, at exactly the same time, and all be equally tempting, but they cannot all be acted upon at once. The mind is then rent apart by the plethora of desirable objects as four inclinations, or even more, do battle among themselves; yet the Manichees do not claim that there are as many disparate substances in us as this.

The same holds true for good impulses. I would put these questions to them: Is it good to find delight in a reading from the apostle? To enjoy the serenity of a psalm? To discuss the gospel? To each point they will reply, "Yes, that is good." Where does that leave us? If all these things tug at our will with equal force, and all together at the same time, will not these divergent inclinations put a great strain on the human heart, as we deliberate which to select? All are good, but they compete among themselves until one is chosen, to which the will, hitherto distracted between many options, may move as a united whole. So too when the joys of eternity call us from above, and pleasure in temporal prosperity holds us fast below, our one soul is in no state to embrace either with its entire will. Claimed by truth for the one, to the other clamped by custom, the soul is torn apart in its distress.

11, 25. Such was the sickness in which I agonized, blaming myself more sharply than ever, turning and twisting in my chain as I strove to tear free from it completely, for slender indeed was the bond that still held me. But hold me it did. In my secret heart you stood by me, Lord, redoubling the lashes of fear and shame in the severity of your mercy, lest I give up the struggle and that slender, fragile bond that remained be not broken after all, but thicken again and constrict me more tightly. "Let it be now," I was saying to myself. "Now is the moment, let it be now," and merely by saying this I was moving toward the decision. I would almost achieve it, but then fall just short; yet I did not slip right down to my starting-point, but stood aside to get my breath back. Then I would make a fresh attempt, and now I was almost there, almost there . . . I was touching the goal, grasping it . . . and then I was not there, not touching, not grasping it. I shrank from dying to death and living to life, for ingrained evil was more powerful in me than new-grafted good. The nearer it came, that moment when I would be changed, the more it pierced me with terror. Dismayed, but not quite dislodged, I was left hanging.

26. The frivolity of frivolous aims, the futility of futile pursuits, these things that had been my cronies of long standing, still held me back, plucking softly at my garment of flesh and murmuring in my ear, "Do you mean to get rid of us? Shall we never be your companions again after that moment . . . never . . . never again? From that time onward so-and-so will be forbidden to you, all your life long." And what was it that they were reminding me of by those words, "so-and-so," O my God, what were they bringing to my mind? May your mercy banish such memories far from me! What foul deeds were they not hinting at, what disgraceful exploits! But now their voices were less than half as loud, for they no longer confronted me directly to argue their case, but muttered behind my back and slyly tweaked me as I walked away, trying to make me look back. Yet they did slow me down, for I could not bring myself to tear free and shake them off and leap across to that place whither I was summoned, while aggressive habit still taunted me: "Do you imagine you will be able to live without these things?"

27. The taunts had begun to sound much less persuasive, however; for a revelation was coming to me from that country toward which I was facing, but into which I trembled to cross. There I beheld the chaste, dignified figure of Continence. Calm and cheerful was her manner, though modest, pure and honorable her charm as she coaxed me to come and hesitate no longer, stretching kindly hands to welcome and embrace me, hands filled with a wealth of heartening examples. A multitude of boys and girls were there, a great concourse of youth and persons of every age, venerable widows and women grown old in their virginity, and in all of them I saw this that this same Continence was by no means sterile, but the fruitful mother of children conceived in joy from you, her Bridegroom. She was smiling at me, but with a challenging smile, as though to say, "Can you not do what these men have done, these women? Could any of them achieve it by their own strength, without the Lord their God? He it was, the Lord their God, who granted me to them. Why try to stand by yourself, only to lose your footing? Cast yourself on him and do not be afraid: he will not step back and let you fall. Cast yourself upon him trustfully; he will support and heal you." And I was bitterly ashamed, because I could still hear the murmurs of those frivolities, and I was still in suspense, still hanging back. Again she appealed to me, as though urging, "Close your ears against those unclean parts of you which belong to the earth and let them be put to death. They tell you titillating tales, but have nothing to do with the law of the Lord your God."

All this argument in my heart raged only between myself and myself. Alypius stood fast at my side, silently awaiting the outcome of my unprecedented agitation.

12, 28. But as this deep meditation dredged all my wretchedness up from the secret profundity of my being and heaped it all together before the eyes of my heart, a huge storm blew up within me and brought on a heavy rain of tears. In order to pour them out unchecked with the sobs that accompanied them I arose and left Alypius, for solitude seemed to me more suitable for the business of weeping. I withdrew far enough to ensure that his presence – even his – would not be burdensome to me. This was my need, and he under-stood it, for I think I had risen to my feet and blurted out something, my voice already choked with tears. He accordingly remained, in stunned amazement, at the place where we had been sitting. I flung myself down somehow under a fig-tree and gave free rein to the tears that burst from my eyes like rivers, as an acceptable sacrifice to you. Many things I had to say to you, and the gist of them, though not the precise words, was: "O Lord, how long? How long? Will you be angry for ever? Do not remember our age-old sins." For by these I was conscious of being held prisoner. I uttered cries of misery: "Why must I go on saying, 'Tomorrow . . . tomorrow'? Why not now? Why not put an end to my depravity this very hour?"

29. I went on talking like this and weeping in the intense bitterness of my broken heart. Suddenly I heard a voice from a house nearby – perhaps a voice of some boy or girl, I do not know – singing over and over again, "Pick it up and read, pick it up and read." My expression immediately altered and I began to think hard whether children ordinarily repeated a ditty like this in any sort of game, but I could not recall ever having heard it anywhere else. I stemmed the flood of tears and rose to my feet, believing that this could be nothing other than a divine command to open the Book and read the first passage I chanced upon; for I had heard the story of how Antony had been instructed by a gospel text. He happened to arrive while the gospel was being read, and took the words to be addressed to himself when he heard, "Go and sell all you possess and give the money to the poor: you will have treasure in heaven. Then come, follow me" [Matt. 19: 21]. So he was promptly converted to you by this plainly divine message. Stung into action, I returned to the place

where Alypius was sitting, for on leaving it I had put down there the book of the apostle's letters. I snatched it up, opened it and read in silence the passage on which my eyes first lighted: "Not in dissipation and drunkenness, nor in debauchery and lewdness, nor in arguing and jealousy; but put on the Lord Jesus Christ, and make no provision for the flesh or the gratification of your desires" [Rom. 13: 13–14]. I had no wish to read further, nor was there need. No sooner had I reached the end of the verse than the light of certainty flooded my heart and all dark shades of doubt fled away.

30. I closed the book, marking the place with a finger between the leaves or by some other means, and told Alypius what had happened. My face was peaceful now. He in return told me what had been happening to him without my knowledge. He asked to see what I had read: I showed him, but he looked further than my reading had taken me. I did not know what followed, but the next verse was, "Make room for the person who is weak in faith." He referred this text to himself and interpreted it to me. Confirmed by this admonition he associated himself with my decision and good purpose without any upheaval or delay, for it was entirely in harmony with his own moral character, which for a long time now had been far, far better than mine.

We went indoors and told my mother, who was overjoyed. When we related to her how it had happened she was filled with triumphant delight and blessed you, who have power to do more than we ask or understand, for she saw that you had granted her much more in my regard than she had been wont to beg of you in her wretched, tearful groaning. Many years earlier you had shown her a vision of me standing on the rule of faith; and now indeed I stood there, no longer seeking a wife or entertaining any worldly hope, for you had converted me to yourself. In so doing you had also converted her grief into a joy far more abundant than she had desired, and much more tender and chaste than she could ever have looked to find in grandchildren from my flesh.

Boethius on Divine Providence and the Freedom of the Will

The Consolation of Philosophy

Book V

Chapter 2. Philosophy argues that rational natures must necessarily have free will

"I have listened carefully and agree that chance is as you say. But, within this series of connected causes, does our will have any freedom, or are the motions of human souls also bound by the fatal chain?"

"There is free will," Philosophy answered, "and no rational nature can exist which does not have it. For any being, which by its nature has the use of reason, must also have the power of judgment by which it can make decisions and, by its own resources, distinguish between things which should be desired and things which should be avoided. Now everyone seeks that which he judges to be desirable, but rejects whatever he thinks should be avoided. Therefore, in rational creatures there is also freedom of desiring and shunning.

"But I do not say that this freedom is the same in all beings.

"In supreme and divine substances there is clear judgment, uncorrupted will, and effective power to obtain what they desire. Human souls, however, are more free while they are engaged in contemplation of the divine mind, and less free when they are joined to bodies, and still less free when they are bound by earthly fetters. They are in utter slavery when they lose possession of their reason and give themselves wholly to vice. For when they turn away their eyes from the light of supreme truth to mean and dark things, they are blinded by a cloud of ignorance and obsessed by vicious passions. By yielding and consenting to these passions, they worsen the slavery to which they have brought themselves and are, as it were, the captives of their own freedom. Nevertheless, God, who beholds all things from eternity, foresees all these things in his providence and disposes each according to its predestined merits."

Chapter 3. Boethius contends that divine foreknowledge and freedom of the human will are incompatible

"Now I am confused by an even greater difficulty," I said.

"What is it?" Philosophy answered, "though I think I know what is bothering you."

"There seems to be a hopeless conflict between divine foreknowledge of all things and freedom of the human will. For if God sees everything in advance and cannot be deceived in any way, whatever his Providence foresees will happen, must happen. Therefore, if God foreknows eternally not only all the acts of men, but also their plans and wishes, there cannot be freedom of will; for nothing whatever can be done or even desired without its being known beforehand by the infallible Providence of God. If things could somehow be accomplished in some way other than that which God foresaw, his foreknowledge of the future would no longer be certain. Indeed, it would be merely uncertain opinion, and it would be wrong to think that of God.

"I cannot agree with the argument by which some people believe that they can solve this problem. They say that things do not happen because Providence foresees that they will happen, but, on the contrary, that Providence foresees what is to come because it will happen, and in this way they find the necessity to be in things, not in Providence. For, they say, it is not necessary that things should happen because they are foreseen, but only that things which will happen be foreseen – as though the problem were whether divine Providence is the cause of the necessity of future events, or the necessity of future events is the cause of divine Providence. But our concern is to prove that the fulfillment of things which God has foreseen is necessary, whatever the order of causes, even if the divine foreknowledge does not seem to make the occurrence of future events necessary. For example, if a man sits down, the opinion that he is sitting must be true; and conversely, if the opinion that someone is sitting be true, then that person must necessarily be sitting. Therefore, there is necessity in both cases: the man must be sitting and the opinion must be true. But the man is not sitting because the opinion is true; the opinion is true because the sitting came before the opinion about it. Therefore, even though the cause of truth came from one side, necessity is common to both.

"A similar line of reasoning applies to divine foreknowledge and future events. For even though the events are foreseen because they will happen, they do not happen because they are foreseen. Nevertheless, it is necessary either that things which are going to happen be foreseen by God, or that what God foresees will in fact happen; and either way the freedom of the human will is destroyed. But of course it is preposterous to say that the outcome of temporal things is the cause of eternal foreknowledge. Yet to suppose that God foresees future events because they are going to happen is the same as supposing that things which happened long ago are the cause of divine Providence. Furthermore, just as when I know that a thing is, that thing must necessarily be; so when I know that something will happen, it is necessary that it happen. It follows, then, that the outcome of something known in advance must necessarily take place.

"Finally, if anyone thinks that a thing is other than it actually is, he does not have knowledge but merely a fallible opinion, and that is quite different from the truth of knowledge. So, if the outcome of some future event is either uncertain or unnecessary, no one can know in advance whether or not it will happen. For just as true knowledge is not tainted by falsity, so that which is known by it cannot be otherwise than as it is known. And that is the reason why knowledge never deceives; things must necessarily be as true knowledge knows them to be. If this is so, how does God foreknow future possibilities whose existence is uncertain? If He thinks that things will inevitably happen which possibly will not happen, He is deceived. But it is wrong to say that, or even to think it. And if He merely knows that they may or may not happen, that is, if He knows only their contingent possibilities, what is such knowledge worth, since it does not know with certainty? Such knowledge is no better than that expressed by the ridiculous prophecy of Tiresias: 'Whatever I say will either be or not be.' Divine Providence would be no better than human opinion if God judges as men do and knows only that uncertain events are doubtful. But if nothing can be uncertain to Him who is the most certain source of all things, the outcome is certain of all things which He knows with certainty shall be.

"Therefore, there can be no freedom in human decisions and actions, since the divine mind, foreseeing everything without possibility of error, determines and forces the outcome of everything that is to happen. Once this is granted, it is clear that the structure of all human affairs must collapse. For it is pointless to assign rewards and punishment to the good and wicked since neither are deserved if the actions of men are not free and voluntary. Punishment of the wicked and recognition of the good, which are now considered just, will seem quite unjust since neither the good nor the wicked are governed by their own will but are forced by the inevitability of predetermination. Vice and virtue will be without meaning, and in their place there will be utter confusion about what is deserved. Finally, and this is the most blasphemous thought of all, it follows that the Author of all good must be made responsible for all human vice since the entire order of human events depends on Providence and nothing on man's intention.

"There is no use in hoping or praying for anything, for what is the point in hope or prayer when everything that man desires is determined by unalterable process? Thus man's only bonds with God, hope and prayer, are destroyed. We believe that our just humility may earn the priceless reward of divine grace, for this is the only way in which men seem able to communicate with God; we are joined to that inaccessible light by supplication before receiving what we ask. But if we hold that all future events are governed by necessity, and therefore that prayer has no value, what will be left to unite us to the sovereign Lord of all things? And so mankind must, as you said earlier, be cut off from its source and dwindle into nothing."

[. . .]

Chapter 6. Philosophy solves the problem of providence and free will by distinguishing between simple and conditional necessity

"Since, as we have shown, whatever is known is known according to the nature of the knower, and not according to its own nature, let us now consider as far as is lawful the nature of the Divine Being, so that we may discover what its knowledge is. The common judgment of all rational creatures holds that God is eternal. Therefore let us consider what eternity is, for this will reveal both the divine nature and the divine knowledge.

"Eternity is the whole, perfect, and simultaneous possession of endless life. The meaning of this can be made clearer by comparison with temporal things. For whatever lives in time lives in the present, proceeding from past to future, and nothing is so constituted in time that it can embrace the whole span of its life at once. It has not yet arrived at tomorrow, and it has already lost yesterday; even the life of this day is lived only in each moving, passing moment. Therefore, whatever is subject to the condition of time, even that which – as Aristotle conceived the world to be – has no beginning and will have no end in a life coextensive with the infinity of time, is such that it cannot rightly be thought eternal. For it does not comprehend and include the whole of infinite life all at once, since it does not embrace the future which is yet to come. Therefore, only that which comprehends and possesses the whole plenitude of endless life together, from which no future thing nor any past thing is absent, can justly be called eternal. Moreover, it is necessary that such a being be in full possession of itself, always present to itself, and hold the infinity of moving time present before itself.

"Therefore, they are wrong who, having heard that Plato held that this world did not have a beginning in time and would never come to an end, suppose that the created world is coeternal with its Creator. For it is one thing to live an endless life, which is what Plato ascribed to the world, and another for the whole of unending life to be embraced all at once as present, which is clearly proper to the divine mind. Nor should God be thought of as older than His creation in extent of time, but rather as prior to it by virtue of the simplicity of His nature. For the infinite motion of temporal things imitates the immediate present of His changeless life and, since it cannot reproduce or equal life, it sinks from immobility to motion and declines from the simplicity of the present into the infinite duration of future and past. And, since it cannot possess the whole fullness of its life at once, it seems to imitate to some extent that which it cannot completely express, and it does this by somehow never ceasing to be. It binds itself to a kind of present in this short and transitory period which, because it has a certain likeness to that abiding, unchanging present, gives everything it touches a semblance of existence. But, since this imitation cannot remain still, it hastens along the infinite road of time, and so it extends by movement the life whose completeness it could not achieve by standing still. Therefore, if we wish to call things by their proper names, we should follow Plato in saying that God indeed is eternal, but the world is perpetual.

"Since, then, every judgment comprehends the subjects presented to it according to its own nature, and since God lives in the eternal present, His knowledge transcends all movement of time and abides in the simplicity of its immediate present. It encompasses the infinite sweep of past and future, and regards all things in its simple comprehension as if they were now taking place. Thus, if you will think about the foreknowledge by which God distinguishes all things, you will rightly consider it to be not a foreknowledge of future events, but knowledge of a never changing present. For this reason, divine knowledge is called providence, rather than prevision, because it resides above all inferior things and looks out on all things from their summit.

"Why then do you imagine that things are necessary which are illuminated by this divine light, since even men do not impose necessity on the things they see? Does your vision impose any necessity upon things which you see present before you?"

"Not at all," I answered.

"Then," Philosophy went on, "if we may aptly compare God's present vision with man's, He sees all things in his eternal present as you see some things in your temporal present. Therefore, this divine foreknowledge does not change the nature and properties of things; it simply sees things present before it as they will later turn out to be in what we regard as the future. His judgment is not confused; with a single intuition of his mind He knows all things that are to come, whether necessarily or not. Just as, when you happen to see simultaneously a man walking on the street and the sun shining in the sky, even though you see both at once, you can distinguish between them and realize that one action is voluntary, the other necessary; so the divine mind, looking down on all things, does not disturb the nature of the things which are present before it but are future with respect to time. Therefore, when God knows that something will happen in the future, and at the same time knows that it will not happen through necessity, this is not opinion but knowledge based on truth.

"If you should reply that whatever God foresees as happening cannot help but happen, and that whatever must happen is bound by necessity – if you pin me down to this word 'necessity' – I grant that you state a solid truth, but one which only a profound theologian can grasp. I would answer that the same future event is necessary with respect to God's knowledge of it, but free and undetermined if considered in its own nature. For there are two kinds of necessity: one is simple, as the necessity by which all men are mortals; the other is conditional, as is the case when, if you know that someone is walking, he must necessarily be walking. For whatever is known, must be as it is known to be; but this condition does not involve that other, simple necessity. It is not caused by the peculiar nature of the person in question, but by an added condition. No necessity forces the man who is voluntarily walking to move forward; but as long as he is walking, he is necessarily moving forward. In the same way, if Providence sees anything as present, that thing must necessarily be, even though it may have no necessity by its nature. But God sees as present those future things which result from free will. Therefore, from the standpoint of divine knowledge these things are necessary because of the condition of their being known by God; but, considered only in themselves, they lose nothing of the absolute freedom of their own natures.

"There is no doubt, then, that all things will happen which God knows will happen; but some of them happen as a result of free will. And, although they happen, they do not, by their existence, lose their proper natures by which, before they happened, they were able not to happen. But, you may ask, what does it mean to say that these events are not necessary, since by reason of the condition of divine knowledge they happen just as if they were necessary? The meaning is the same as in the example I used a while ago of the sun rising and the man walking. At the time they are happening, they must necessarily be happening; but the sun's rising is governed by necessity even before it happens, while the man's walking is not. Similarly, all the things God sees as present will undoubtedly come to pass; but some will happen by the necessity of their natures, others by the power of those who make them happen. Therefore, we quite properly said that these things are necessary if viewed from the standpoint of divine knowledge, but if they are considered in themselves, they are free of the bonds of necessity. In somewhat the same way, whatever is known by the senses is singular in itself, but universal as far as the reason is concerned.

"But, you may say, if I can change my mind about doing something, I can frustrate Providence, since by chance I may change something which Providence foresaw. My answer is this: you can indeed alter what you propose to do, but, because the present truth of Providence sees that you can, and whether or not you will, you cannot frustrate the divine knowledge any more than you can escape the eye of someone who is present and watching you, even though you may, by your free will, vary your actions. You may still wonder, however, whether God's knowledge is changed by your decisions, so that when you wish now one thing, now another, the divine knowledge undergoes corresponding changes. This is not the case. For divine Providence anticipates every future action and converts it to its own present knowledge. It does not change, as you imagine, foreknowing this or that in succession, but in a single instant, without being changed itself, anticipates and grasps your changes. God has this present comprehension and immediate vision of all things not from the outcome of future events, but from the simplicity of his own nature. In this way, the problem you raised a moment ago is settled. You observed that it would be unworthy of God if our future acts were said to be the cause of divine knowledge. Now you see that this power of divine knowledge, comprehending all things as present before it, itself constitutes the measure of all things and is in no way dependent on things that happen later.

"Since this is true, the freedom of the human will remains inviolate, and laws are just since they provide rewards and punishments to human wills which are not controlled by necessity. God looks down from above, knowing all things, and the eternal present of his vision concurs with the future character of our actions, distributing rewards to the good and punishments to the evil. Our hopes and prayers are not directed to God in vain, for if they are just they cannot fail. Therefore, stand firm against vice and cultivate virtue. Lift up your soul to worthy hopes, and offer humble prayers to heaven. If you will face it, the necessity of virtuous action imposed upon you is very great, since all your actions are done in the sight of a Judge who sees all things."

41

Anselm of Canterbury on Free Will

On Free Will

Chapters

1.   That the power of sinning does not pertain to free will

Student. Since free will seems to be repugnant to grace, predestination and God's foreknowledge, I want to understand freedom of will and know whether we always have it. For if 'to be able to sin and not to sin' is due to free will, as some are accustomed to say, and we always have it, why do we sometimes need grace? But if we do not always have it, why is sin imputed to us when we sin without free will?

Teacher. I do not think free will is the power to sin or not to sin. Indeed if this were its definition, neither God nor the angels, who are unable to sin, would have free will, which it is impious to say.

S. But what if one were to say that the free will of God and the angels is different from ours?

T. Although the free will of men differs from the free will of God and the angels, the definition of freedom expressed by the word ought to be the same. For although one animal differs from another either substantially or accidentally, the definition attached to the word 'animal' is the same for all. That is why we must so define free will that the definition contains neither too little nor too much. Since the divine free will and that of the good angels cannot sin, to be able to sin does not belong in the definition of free will. Furthermore, the power to sin is neither liberty nor a part of liberty. Pay attention to what I am going to say and you will fully understand this.

S. That is why I am here.

T. Which free will seems more free to you, that which so wills that it cannot sin, such that it can in no way be deflected from the rectitude constituted by not sinning, or that which can in some way be deflected to sinning?

S. I do not see why that which is capable of both is not freer.

T. Do you not see that one who is as he ought to be, and as it is expedient for him to be, such that he is unable to lose this state, is freer than one who is such that he can lose it and be led into what is indecent and inexpedient for him?

S. I think there is no doubt that this is so.

T. And would you not say that it is no less doubtful that to sin is always indecent and harmful.

S. No one of healthy mind would think otherwise.

T. Therefore a will that cannot fall from rectitude into sin is more free than one that can desert it.

S. Nothing seems to me more reasonable to say.

T. Therefore, since the capacity to sin when added to will diminishes liberty, and its lack increases it, it is neither liberty nor a part of liberty.

S. Nothing is more obvious.

2.   Both the angel and man sinned by this capacity to sin and by free will and, though they could have become slaves of sin, sin did not have the power to dominate them

T. What is extraneous to freedom does not pertain to free will.

S. I can contest none of your arguments, but I am not a little swayed by the fact that in the beginning both the angelic nature and ours had the capacity to sin, since without it, they would not have sinned. Wherefore, if by this capacity, which is alien to free will, both natures sinned, how can we say they sinned by free will? But if they did not sin by free will, it seems they sinned necessarily. That is, they sinned either willingly or necessarily. But if they sinned willingly, how so if not by free will? And if not by free will, then indeed it seems that they sinned necessarily.

And there is something else that strikes me in this ability to sin. One who can sin, can be the slave of sin, since 'he who commits sin, is the slave of sin' [John 8: 34]. But he who can be the slave of sin, can be dominated by sin. How was that nature created free then, and what kind of free will is it that can be dominated by sin?

T. It was through the capacity to sin willingly and freely and not of necessity that ours and the angelic nature first sinned and were able to serve sin, yet they cannot be dominated by sin in such a way that they and their judgement can no longer be called free.

S. You must expand on what you said since it is opaque to me.

T. The apostate angel and the first man sinned through free will, because they sinned through a judgement that is so free that it cannot be coerced to sin by anything else. That is why they are justly reprehended; when they had a free will that could not be coerced by anything else, they willingly and without necessity sinned. They sinned through their own free will, though not insofar as it was free, that is, not through that thanks to which it was free and had the power not to sin or to serve sin, but rather by the power it had of sinning, unaided by its freedom not to sin or to be coerced into the servitude of sin.

What seemed to you to follow does not, namely, that if will could be a slave to sin it could be dominated by sin, and therefore neither it nor its judgement are free. But this is not so. For what has it in its power not to serve cannot be forced by another to serve, although it can serve by its own power: for as long as the power uses that which is for serving and not that which is for not serving, nothing can dominate it so that it should serve. For if the rich man is free to make a poor man his servant, as long as he does not do so, he does not lose the name of freedom nor is the poor man said to be able to be dominated or, if this is said, it is said improperly, for this is not in his power but in another's. Therefore nothing prevents either angel or man from being free prior to sin or from having had free will.

3.   How free will is had after they have made themselves slaves of sin and what free will is

S. You have satisfied me that nothing certainly prevents this prior to sin, but how can they retain free will after they have made themselves slaves of sin?

T. Although they subjected themselves to sin, they were unable to lose natural free will. But now they cannot use that freedom without a grace other than that which they previously had.

S. I believe that, but I want to understand it.

T. Let us first consider the kind of free will they had before sin when they certainly had free will.

S. I am ready.

T. Why do you think they had free will: to attain what they want or to will what they ought and what is expedient for them to will?

S. The latter.

T. Therefore they had free will for the sake of rectitude of will. As long as they willed what they ought, they had rectitude of will.

S. That is so.

T. Still to say that they had free will for the sake of rectitude of will is open to doubt unless something is added. So I ask: How did they have free will for the sake of rectitude of will? To take it without any giver when they did not yet have it? To receive what they did not have when it was given to them? To abandon what they received and to get it back again after they had let it go? Or to receive it in order to keep it always?

S. I do not think they had the liberty for the sake of rectitude without a giver, since there is nothing they have that they have not received. We should not say that they had liberty to receive from a giver what they previously did not have, because we ought not to think that they were made without right will. Although it should not be denied that they had the freedom to receive this rectitude, if they abandon it it would be restored to them by the original giver. We often see men brought back from injustice to justice by heavenly grace.

T. It is true as you say that they can receive the lost rectitude if it is restored, but we are asking about the freedom they had before they sinned, since without any doubt they had free will then, and not about what no one would need if he had never abandoned the truth.

S. I will now respond to the other things you asked me. It is not true that they had liberty in order to abandon that rectitude, because to abandon the rectitude of the will is to sin, and we showed above that the power to sin is not liberty nor any part of it. They do not receive liberty in order to take on again a rectitude they had abandoned, since such rectitude is given in order that it might never be lost. The power of receiving again what is lost would bring about negligence in retaining what is had. It follows then that freedom of will was given to the rational nature in order that it might retain the rectitude of will it has received.

T. You have responded well to what was asked, but we must still consider for what purpose a rational nature ought to retain that rectitude, whether for the sake of the rectitude itself, or for the sake of something else.

S. If that liberty were not given to such a nature in order that it might preserve rectitude of will for the sake of rectitude, it would not avail for justice. Justice seems to be the retention of rectitude of will for its own sake. But we believe that free will is for the sake of justice. Therefore without a doubt we should assert that the rational nature receives liberty solely to preserve rectitude of will for its own sake.

T. Therefore, since all liberty is a capacity, the liberty of will is the capacity for preserving rectitude of the will for the sake of rectitude itself.

S. It cannot be otherwise.

T. So it is now clear that free judgement is nothing other than a judgement capable of preserving the rectitude of will for the sake of rectitude itself.

S. It is indeed clear. But as long as will has that rectitude it can preserve what it has. But how, after it has lost it, can it preserve what it does not have? In the absence of the rectitude that can be preserved, there is no free will capable of preserving it. For it does not avail for preserving what is not had.

T. But even if the rectitude of will is absent, the rational nature still has undiminished what is proper to it. I think we have no power sufficient unto itself for action, and yet when those things are lacking without which our powers can scarcely be led to act, we are no less said to have them insofar as they are in us. Just as no instrument suffices of itself to act, and yet when the conditions for using the instrument are wanting, it is not false to say that we have the instrument to do something. What you may observe in many things, I will show you in one. No one having sight is said to be incapable of seeing a mountain.

S. Indeed, one who cannot see a mountain, does not have sight.

T. He who has sight has the power and means of seeing a mountain. And yet if the mountain were absent and you said to him, 'Look at the mountain,' he would answer, 'I cannot, because it is not there. If it were there, I could see it.' Again, if the mountain were there and light absent, he would say that he could not see the mountain, meaning that without light he cannot, but he could if there were light. Again, if the mountain and light are present to one with sight but there is something blocking sight, as when one closes his eyes, he would say that he cannot see the mountain, although if nothing blocked sight, he could without any doubt see the mountain.

S. Everyone knows these things.

T. You see, then, that the power of seeing a body is (1) in the one seeing in one sense and (2) in another sense in the thing to be seen, and in yet another sense in the medium, which is neither the seeing nor the thing to be seen; and with respect to what is in the medium, there we must distinguish between (3) what helps and (4) what does not impede, that is, when nothing that can impede does impede.

S. I plainly see.

T. Therefore these powers are four, and if one of them is lacking the other three singly or together cannot bring it off; yet when the others are absent we do not deny either that he who has sight or the means or the power of seeing can see, or that the visible can be seen to be seen, or that light can aid sight.

4. How those who do not have rectitude have the power to preserve it

The fourth power is improperly so called. That which can impede sight, is said to give the power of seeing only because by being removed it does not impede. The power to see light [properly] consists in only three things because that which is seen and that which aids are the same. Is this not known to all?

S. Indeed it is unknown to none.

T. If then the visible thing is absent, or in the dark, or if those having sight have shut or covered their eyes, so far as we are concerned we have the power to see any visible thing. What then prevents us from having the power to preserve rectitude of will for its own sake, even if that rectitude is absent, so long as reason whereby we can know it and will whereby we can hold it are in us? It is in these – reason and will – that freedom of will consists.

S. You have put my mind at rest that this power of preserving rectitude of will is always in a rational nature, and that this is the power of free will in the first man and the angel, nor could rectitude of will be taken away from them unless they willed it.

5. That no temptation forces one to sin unwillingly

S. But how can the judgement of will be free because of this power, given the fact that often and without willing it a man who has right will is deprived of his own rectitude under the force of temptation?

T. No one is deprived of this rectitude except by his own will. One who acts unwillingly is said to act against what he wills; and no one is deprived of this rectitude against his will. But a man can be bound unwillingly, because he does not wish to be bound, and is tied up unwillingly; he can be killed unwillingly, because he can will not to be killed; but he cannot will unwillingly, because one cannot will to will against his will. Every willing person wills his own willing.

S. How can one be said to lie unwillingly when he lies to avoid being killed, something he only does willingly? For just as he unwillingly lies, so he unwillingly wills to lie. And he who wills unwillingly to lie, is not willing that he wills to lie.

T. Perhaps then he is said to lie unwillingly because he so wills the truth that he will only lie to save his life, and he wills the lie for the sake of life and not for the sake of the lie itself, since he wills the truth; and thus he lies both willingly and unwillingly. For to will something for its own sake, e.g. as we will health for its own sake, is different from will-ing something for the sake of something else, as when we will to drink absinthe for the sake of health. Perhaps with respect to these two kinds of willing one could be said to lie both willingly and unwillingly. He is said to lie unwillingly because he does not will it in the way he wills the truth, but that does not conflict with my view that no one unwillingly abandons rectitude of will. He wills to abandon it by lying for the sake of his life, according to which he does not unwillingly abandon it but wills to in the sense of will of which we now speak. That is, willing to lie for the sake of his life, not willing to lie for its own sake. Therefore either he certainly lies unwillingly, because he must either be killed or lie unwill-ingly, that is, he is not willingly in the anguish because either of these will necessarily come about. For although it is necessary that he be either killed or lie, yet it is not necessary that he be killed, because he can escape death if he lies, nor is it necessary for him to lie, because he could not lie and be killed. Neither of these is determinately necessary, because both are in his power. Therefore although he either lies or is killed unwillingly, it does not follow that he lies unwillingly or is killed unwillingly.

There is another argument frequently given to show why someone is said to do something unwillingly, against his grain and necessarily, yet does not want to. What we do not do because we can only do it with difficulty, we say we cannot do and necessarily turn away from. And what we can abandon only with difficulty we say we do unwillingly and necessarily. In this way, one who lies lest he be killed, is said to lie against his will, not willingly, and of necessity, given that he cannot avoid the falsehood without the penalty of death. He who lies in order to save his life is improperly said to lie against his will, because he willingly lies, and he is improperly said to will to lie against his will, because he wills it precisely by willing it. For just as when he lies he wills himself to lie, so when he wills to lie, he wills that willing.

S. I cannot deny what you say.

T. Why then not say that free will is that which another power cannot overcome without its assent?

S. Can we not for a similar reason say that the will of a horse is free because he only serves his appetite willingly?

T. It is not the same. For in the horse there is not the will to subject himself, but natu-rally, always and of necessity he is the slave of sense appetite, whereas in man, as long as his will is right, he does not serve nor is he subject to what he ought not to do, nor can he be diverted from that rectitude by any other force, unless he willingly consents to what he ought not to do, which consent does not come about naturally or of necessity as in the horse, but is clearly seen to be from itself.

S. You have taken care of my objection about the horse; let us go back to where we were.

T. Would you deny that every free being is such that it can only be moved or prevented willingly?

S. I do not see how I could.

T. Tell me how right will prevails and how it is conquered.

S. To will the preservation of rectitude for its own sake is for it to prevail, but to will what it ought not is for it to be conquered.

T. I think that temptation can only stop right will or force it to what it ought not to will willingly, such that it wills the one and not the other.

S. I do not see any way in which that could be false.

T. Who then can say that the will is not free to preserve rectitude, and free from temp-tation and sin, if no temptation can divert it save willingly from rectitude to sin, that is, to willing what it ought not? Therefore when it is conquered, it is not conquered by another power but by itself.

S. That demonstrates what has been said.

T. Do you see that from this it follows that no temptation can conquer right will? For if it could, it would have the power to conquer and would conquer by its own power. But this cannot be, since the will can only be conquered by itself. Wherefore temptation can in no way conquer right will, and it is only improperly said to conquer it. For it only means that the will can subject itself to temptation, just as conversely when the weak is said to be able to be conquered by the strong, he is said to be *able*, not by his own power but by another's, since it only means that the strong has the power to conquer the weak.

6. How our will, although it seems powerless, is powerful against temptations

S. Although you were to make subject to our will all the forces fighting against it and contend that no temptation can dominate it in such a way that I cannot counter your assertions, none the less I cannot agree that there is no impotence in the will, something nearly all experience when they are overcome by violent temptation. Therefore, unless you can reconcile the power that you prove and the impotence that we feel, my mind will not be at rest on this matter.

T. In what does the impotence of which you speak consist?

S. In the fact that I cannot adhere to rectitude with perseverance.

T. If you do not adhere because of impotence, you are turned away from rectitude by an alien force.

S. I admit it.

T. And what is this force?

S. The force of temptation.

T. This force does not turn the will from rectitude unless it wills what the temptation suggests.

S. That is so. But by its very force temptation prompts it to will what it suggests.

T. But how can it force willing? Because it can will only with great trouble or because it can in no way not will?

S. Although I have to admit that sometimes we are so oppressed by temptations that we cannot without difficulty manage not to will what they suggest, still I cannot say that they ever so oppress us that we can in no way not will what they inspire.

T. I do not see how that could be said. For if a man wills to lie in order that he not suffer death and live a little longer, who would say that to will not to lie is impossible for him in order that he might avoid eternal death and live eternally? So you should not doubt that the impotence in preserving rectitude, which you say is in our will when we consent to temptation, is a matter of difficulty rather than impossibility. We often say that we cannot do something, not because it is impossible for us, but because we can do it only with difficulty. This difficulty does not destroy freedom of will. Temptation can fight against a will that does not give in but cannot conquer it against its will. In this way I think we can see how the power of the will as established by true arguments is compatible with the impotence our humanity experiences. For just as difficulty does not in any way destroy the freedom of will, so that impotence, which we assign to will because it can retain its rectitude only with difficulty, does not take away from the power to persevere in rectitude.

7.   How it is stronger than temptation even when it succumbs to it

S. I am unable to deny what you prove but at the same time I cannot absolutely say that will is stronger than temptation when it is conquered by it. For if the will to preserve rectitude were stronger than the impetus of temptation, the will in willing what it keeps would be stronger as temptation is more insistent. For I do not otherwise know myself to have a more or less strong will except insofar as I more or less strongly will. Wherefore when I will less strongly than I ought because of the temptation to do what I ought not, I do not see how temptation is not stronger than my will.

T. I see that the equivocation of 'will' misleads you.

S. I would like to know this equivocation.

T. 'Will' is said equivocally much as 'sight' is. For we say that sight is an instrument of seeing, that is, a ray proceeding from the eyes whereby we sense light and the things that are in the light; and we also call sight the work of this instrument when we use it, that is, vision. In the same way the will means both the instrument of willing which is in the soul and our turning will to this or that as we turn sight to see different things. And this use of the will, which is the instrument of willing, is also called will, just as sight means both the use of sight and that which is the instrument of seeing. We have sight which is the instrument of seeing, even when we do not see, but the sight which is its work is only had when we see. So too will, namely the instrument of willing, is always in the soul even when it does not will something, as when it sleeps, but we only have the will that is the work of this instrument when we will something. Therefore what I call the instrument of willing is always one and the same whatever we will; but that which is its work is as many as the many things that we will. In this way sight is always the same whatever we see, or even in the dark or with closed eyes, but the sight which is its work and which is named vision is as numerous as are the things seen.

S. I see clearly and I love this distinction with respect to will, and I can see how I fell into error through deception. But do continue what you began.

T. Now that you see that there are two wills, namely the instrument of willing and its work, in which of the two do you find the strength of willing?

S. In that which is the instrument of willing.

T. If therefore you know a man to be strong, when he is holding a bull that was unable to escape and you saw the same man holding a ram who was able to free itself from his grasp, would you think him less strong in holding the ram than in holding the bull?

S. I would indeed judge him to be equally strong in both but that he did not use his strength equally in the two cases. For he acted more strongly with the bull than with the ram. But he is strong because he has strength and his act is called strong because it comes about strongly.

T. Understand that the will that I am calling the instrument of willing has an inalienable strength that cannot be overcome by any other force, but which it uses sometimes more and sometimes less when it wills. Hence it in no way abandons what it wills more strongly when what it wills less strongly is offered, and when what it wills with greater force offers itself it immediately drops what it does not will equally. And then the will, which we can call the action of this instrument, since it performs its act when it wills something, is said to be more or less strong in its action since it more or less strongly occurs.

S. I must admit that what you have explained is now clear to me.

T. Therefore you see that when a man, under the assault of temptation, abandons the rectitude of will that he has, he is not drawn away from it by any alien force, but he turns himself to that which he more strongly wills.

8. That not even God can take away the rectitude of will

S. Can even God take away rectitude from the will?

T. This cannot happen. God can reduce to nothing the whole substance that he made from nothing, but he cannot separate rectitude from a will that has it.

S. I am eager to have the reason for an assertion I have never before heard.

T. We are speaking of that rectitude of will thanks to which the will is called just, that is, which is preserved for its own sake. But no will is just unless it wills what God wants it to will.

S. One who does not will that is plainly unjust.

T. Therefore to preserve rectitude of will for its own sake is, for everyone who does so, to will what God wants him to will.

S. That must be said.

T. Should God remove this rectitude from anyone's will, he does this either willingly or unwillingly.

S. He could not do so unwillingly.

T. If then he removes this rectitude from someone's will he wills to do what he does.

S. Without any doubt.

T. But then he does not want the one from whom he removes this rectitude to preserve the rectitude of will for its own sake.

S. That follows.

T. But we already said that to preserve in this way the rectitude of will is for one to will what God wants him to will.

S. Even if we had not said it, it is so.

T. Hence if God were to take from something that rectitude of which we have so often spoken, he does not will one to will what he wants him to will.

S. An inevitable and impossible consequence.

T. Therefore nothing is more impossible than that God should take away the rectitude of will. Yet he is said to do this when he does not impede the abandonment of this rectitude. On the other hand, the devil and temptation are said to do this or to conquer the will and to remove from it the rectitude it has when they offer something or threaten to take away something that the will wants more than rectitude, but there is no way they can deprive it of that rectitude as long as the will wants it.

S. What you say is clear to me and I think nothing can be said against it.

9. That nothing is more free than right will

T. You can see that there is nothing freer than a right will since no alien power can take away its rectitude. To be sure, if we say that, when it wills to lie lest it lose life or safety, it is forced by the fear of death or torment to desert the truth, this is not true. It is not forced to will life rather than truth, but since an external force prevents it from preserving both at the same time, it chooses what it wants more – of itself that is and not unwillingly, although it would not of itself and willingly be placed in the necessity of abandoning both. It is not less able to will truth than safety, but it more strongly wills safety. For if it now should see the eternal glory which would immediately follow after preserving the truth, and the torments of hell to which it would be delivered over without delay after lying, without any doubt it would be seen to have a sufficiency for preserving the truth.

S. This is clear since it shows greater strength in willing eternal salvation for its own sake and truth for the sake of reward than for preserving temporal safety.

10.   How one who sins is a slave of sin, and that it is a greater miracle when God restores rectitude to one who has abandoned it than when he restores life to the dead

T. The rational nature always has free will because it always has the power of preserving rectitude of will for the sake of rectitude itself, although sometimes with difficulty. But when free will abandons rectitude because of the difficulty of preserving it, it is afterward the slave of sin because of the impossibility of recovering it by itself. Thus it becomes 'a breath that goes forth and returns not' [Ps. 77: 39], since 'everyone who commits sin is a slave of sin' [John 8: 34]. Just as no will, before it has rectitude, can have it unless God gives it, so when it abandons what it has received, it cannot regain it unless God restores it. And I think it is a greater miracle when God restores rectitude to the will that has abandoned it than when he restores life to a dead man. For a body dying out of necessity does not sin such that it might never receive life, but the will which of itself abandons rectitude deserves that it should always lack it. And if one gave himself over to death voluntarily, he does not take from himself what he was destined never to lose, but he who abandons the rectitude of will casts aside what he has an obligation to preserve always.

S. I do indeed see what you mean by slavery, whereby he who commits sin becomes the slave of sin, and of the impossibility of recovering abandoned rectitude unless it be restored by him who first gave it, and I see that all those to whom it has been given ought to battle ceaselessly to preserve it always.

11.   That this slavery does not take away freedom of will

S. But this opinion does much to depress me because I had thought myself to be a man sure to have free will always. So I ask that you explain to me how this slavery is compatible with what we said earlier. For it seems the opposite of liberty. For both freedom and slavery are in the will, thanks to which a man is called free or a slave. But if he is a slave, how can he be free, and if free, how can he be a slave?

T. If you think about it carefully you will see that when the will does not have the rectitude of which we speak, it is without contradiction both slave and free. For it is never within its power to acquire the rectitude it does not have, although it is always in its power to preserve what it once had. Because it cannot return from sin, it is a slave; because it cannot be robbed of rectitude, it is free. But from its sin and slavery it can return only by the help of another, although it can depart from rectitude only by itself. But neither by another or by itself can it be deprived of its freedom. For it is always naturally free to preserve rectitude if it has it, even when it does not have what it might preserve.

S. This suffices to show me that freedom and slavery can be in one and the same man without contradiction.

12.   Why a man who does not have rectitude is called free because if he had it no one could take it from him, and yet when he has rectitude he is not called a slave because if he loses it he cannot regain it by himself

S. I very much want to know why one who has not rectitude is called free because when he has it no one can take it from him, and yet when he has rectitude he is not called a slave because he cannot regain it by himself if he lose it. In fact, because he cannot by himself come back from sin, he is a slave; because he cannot be robbed of rectitude he is called free, and just as no one can take it from him if he has it, so he can never himself regain it if he does not have it. Wherefore, just as he always has this freedom, it seems that he should always have this slavery.

T. This slavery is nothing other than the powerlessness not to sin. For whether we say this is powerlessness to return to rectitude or powerlessness of regaining or again having rectitude, man is not the slave of sin for any other reason than that, because he cannot return to rectitude or regain and have it, he cannot not sin. For when he has that same rectitude, he does not lack the power not to sin. Wherefore when he has that rectitude, he is not the slave of sin. He always has the power to preserve rectitude, both when he has rectitude and when he does not, and therefore he is always free.

As for your question why he is called free when he does not have rectitude, since it cannot be taken from him by another when he has it, and not called slave when he has rectitude because he cannot regain it by himself when he does not have it, this is as if you were to ask why a man when the sun is absent is said to have the power to see the sun because he can see it when it is present and when the sun is present is said to be powerless to see the sun because when it is absent he cannot make it present. For just as, even when the sun is absent, we have in us the sight whereby we see it when it is present, so too when the rectitude of will is lacking to us, we still have in us the aptitude to understand and will whereby we can preserve it for its own sake when we have it. And just as when nothing is lacking in us for seeing the sun except its presence, we only lack the power to make it present to us, so only when rectitude is lacking to us, do we have that powerlessness which its absence from us brings about.

S. If I ponder carefully what was said above when you distributed the power of seeing into four powers, I cannot doubt this now. So I confess the fault of doubting it.

T. I will pardon you now only if in what follows you have present to mind as needed what we have said before, so that there is no necessity for me to repeat it.

S. I am grateful for your indulgence, but you will not wonder that after having heard only once things of which I am not in the habit of thinking, they are not all always present in my heart to be inspected.

T. Tell me now if you have any doubt about the definition of free will we have given.

13.   That the power of preserving the rectitude of will for its own sake is a perfect definition of free will

S. There is still something that troubles me. For we often have the power of preserving something which yet is not free because it can be impeded by another power. Therefore when you say that freedom of will is the power of preserving rectitude of will for the sake of rectitude itself, consider whether perhaps it should be added that this power is free in such a way that it can be overwhelmed by no other power.

T. If the power of preserving the rectitude of will for the sake of rectitude itself could sometimes be found without that liberty that we have succeeded in seeing clearly, your proposed addition would be fitting. But since the foregoing definition is perfected by genus and difference such that it can contain neither more nor less than what we call freedom, nothing should be added or subtracted from it. For 'power' is the genus of liberty. When 'of preserving' is added it separates it from every power which is not one of preserving, such as the power to laugh or walk. By adding 'rectitude' we separate it from the power of preserving gold and whatever else is not rectitude. By the addition of 'will' it is separated from the power of preserving the rectitude of other things, such as a stick or an opinion.

By saying that it is 'for the sake of rectitude itself' it is distinguished from the power of preserving rectitude for some other reason, for example for money, or just naturally. A dog preserves rectitude of will naturally when it loves its young or the master who cares for it. Therefore since there is nothing in this definition that is not necessary to embrace the free judgement of a rational creature and exclude the rest it sufficiently includes the one and excludes the other, nor is our definition too much or lacking anything. Does it not seem so to you?

S. It seems perfect to me.

T. Tell me then if you wish to know anything else of this freedom which is imputed to one having it whether he uses it well or badly. For our discourse is concerned only with that.

14.   The division of this freedom

S. It now remains to divide this freedom. For although this definition is common to every rational nature, there is a good deal of difference between God and rational creatures and many differences among the latter.

T. There is a free will that is from itself, which is neither made nor received from another, which is of God alone; there is another made and received from God, which is found in angels and in men. That which is made or received is different in one having the rectitude which he preserves than in one lacking it. Those having it are on the one hand those who hold it separably and those who hold it inseparably. The former was the case with all the angels before the good were confirmed and the evil fell, and with all men prior to death who have this rectitude.

What is held inseparably is true of the chosen angels and men, but of angels after the ruin of the reprobate angels and of men after their death. Those who lack rectitude either lack it irrecoverably or recoverably. He who recoverably lacks it is one of the men in this life who lack it although many of them do not recover it.

Those who lack it irrecoverably are reprobate angels and men, angels after their ruin and men after this life.

S. You have satisfied me with God's help on the definition of liberty such that I can think of nothing to ask concerning such matters.

Henry of Ghent on the Primacy of the Will

Quodlibetal Questions

Quodlibet I, Question 14

Is the will a higher power than the intellect, or the intellect a higher power than the will?

There follows a treatment of questions that pertain both to the separated soul and to the soul joined to the body. One of these concerned the comparison of its two principal powers to each other, namely, whether the will is a higher power than the intellect or the intellect is a higher power than the will. The other five were concerned with the comparison of their actions.

With regard to the first question, it was argued that the intellect would be a higher power, because the Philosopher says this in the tenth book of the *Ethics*.[1] According to him, practical reason is the first mover in things to be done by the will.[2] Moreover, Augustine says in chapter twenty two of *Against Faustus*: Without a doubt in actions of the soul, contemplation, which belongs to the intellect, is preeminent.[3] Moreover, in his reason man is formed anew according to the image of God.[4] Finally, that which directs is higher than that which it directs and the judgment of the intellect directs the will.

Against this view is the fact that the will is the first mover of itself and other things in the whole kingdom of the soul, and such a power is higher.[5]

<The Solution>

To this we must say that, since the powers of the soul of themselves are hidden from us and unknown to us, just as the substance of the soul is, we have to seek, in a way appropriate

1   Cf. Aristotle, *Nicomachean Ethics* X, 7, 1177b30–1178a2.
2   Cf. Aristotle, *Nicomachean Ethics* I, 13, 1102b28.
3   Cf. Augustine, *Against Faustus* (*Contra Faustum*) XXII, 27: *CSEL* XXV, 621. Where the citation is not exact, as in the present case, I have omitted quotation marks.
4   Cf. 2 Co 3:18 and Col 3:10.
5   Early in the thirteenth century, William of Auvergne had drawn an extended comparison of the will to the king or emperor over the other powers of the soul; cf. his *De anima* c. II, pt. 15, in *Opera omnia* (Orléans-Paris, 1674), vol. II, pp. 85f.

to us, all knowledge concerning them from what is subsequent to them. Hence, we have to judge the preeminence of one power over another from those things that are subsequent to the powers and that provide us a way of coming to know the powers. These are three: habit, act, and object. We must say that the power whose habit, act, and object are superior to the habit, act and object of another is without qualification superior to that other power.

Now it is the case that the habit, act, and object of the will are utterly superior to the act, habit, and object of the intellect. Hence, we must say that the will is absolutely superior to the intellect and is a higher power than it.

The position we have taken is clear because the characteristic habit of the will which carries it toward the good by an act of true love is the habit of charity. By it, according to Augustine, we love God in himself and the neighbor in God and because of God.[6] But the highest habit of the intellect is wisdom by which we contemplate God and things eternal, according to Augustine in book fourteen of *The Trinity*.[7] The Apostle states well the degree by which the habit of charity is superior to every habit of wisdom and knowledge, when he says in chapter thirteen of the First Letter to the Corinthians, "If I speak with the tongues of men and of angels and do not have charity," and so on.[8]

The degree by which the act of the will, which is to will or to love, surpasses the act of the intellect, which is to know or to have knowledge, is obvious from two comparisons: first, from the comparison of one act to the other, second, from the comparison of each of them in terms of how the subject of the act is perfected by its object.

What we are aiming at is clear from the first comparison. For, as Augustine says in book twelve of *On Genesis*, and the Philosopher says in book three of *The Soul*, "The agent and the mover are always more noble than that upon which they act."[9] But the will is the universal and first mover in the whole kingdom of the soul and superior to and first mover of all other things to their end, as will be seen below. For, as Anselm says in *Likenesses*, "It moves reason and all the powers of the soul."[10] And as Augustine says in book three of *Free Choice*, "The mind itself is first subject to the intention of the mind; then the body which it governs, and thus it moves any member to activity."[11] Hence, the will commands reason to consider, to reason, and to deliberate when it wills and about what topics it wills, and it likewise makes it to stop. The intellect does not command or move the will in any such way, as will become clear further on, when we say more about their comparison.

From the second comparison, what we are aiming at is likewise clear. For by the action of the will the will itself is perfected by the very reality that is loved as it exists in itself, because by its action the will is inclined toward the reality itself. But by the action of intellect the intellect is perfected by the thing known as it exists in the intellect. By its action the intellect draws into itself the reality known, while by its action the will transfers itself to the object willed for its own sake so that it may enjoy it. For this reason, as Dionysius says in chapter four of *The Divine Names*, by its action the intellect likens itself to the reality known, but the will transforms itself into the object willed.[12] It is much more perfect and lofty to be

6   Cf. Augustine, *On Christian Doctrine (De doctrina christiana)* I, xxii, 21: CC XXXII, 17–18.

7   Cf. Augustine, *On the Trinity (De trinitate)* XIV, i, 3ff.: CC L/A, 422ff.

8   1 Co 13: 1ff.

9   Cf. Augustine, *The Literal Interpretation of Genesis (De Genesi ad litteram)* XII, 16: CSEL XXVIII, 402, and Aristotle, *On the Soul (De anima)* III, 5, 430a18–19.

10   Pseudo-Anselm, *Likenesses (De similitudinibus)* 2: PL CLIX, 605C.

11   Augustine, *Free Choice (De libero arbitrio)* III, xxv, 75: CC XXIX, 320.

12   Cf. Pseudo-Dionysius, *The Divine Names (De divinis nominibus)* IV, #4: PG III, 711C–D.

transformed into the good as it is in itself according to its own nature than to be made like the true as it is in the knower in the manner of the knower and thus in an inferior manner. Accordingly, Augustine says in the eleventh book of *The Trinity*, "When we know God, his likeness comes to be in us, but a likeness of an inferior degree, because it is in an inferior nature."[13] Hence, the activity of the will is far more perfect and lofty than the activity of the intellect to the degree that love and esteem for God is better than knowledge of God. Even if with respect to those things that are less than the soul the opposite is the case, namely, that the action of the intellect is higher than the will, because the knowledge of bodily things in the soul is higher and more noble than the love of them, this only makes the intellect to be more noble than the will in a certain respect. But the first relation and comparison makes the will to be higher without qualification. For the first goodness and the first truth are the essential and primary objects of the intellect and the will; other things are objects of the intellect and the will in comparison to them secondarily and in a certain respect. In the same way, in other things something true or good is true or good in some respect in comparison to the first truth and first goodness, since by nature it does not have the character of true or good except through an impression of the first truth and goodness, as will have to be explained elsewhere. Thus the will seeks something good by reason of some participation that thing has in the first goodness and the intellect knows something true only by reason of some participation that thing has in the first truth. Accordingly, it is more natural for the will to be perfected by the first goodness than by anything else and for the intellect to be perfected by the first truth than by anything else. For this reason the will and the intellect cannot perfectly come to rest in the enjoyment of any good or in the knowledge of any truth until the first goodness and the first truth are attained. In accord with this, Augustine says in the beginning of *The Confessions*, "You have made us for yourself, and our heart is restless until it rests in you."[14] Hence, since everything should be judged to be unqualifiedly more of a certain kind in comparison to that which is more without qualification and more in terms of its nature, as the Philosopher says in the first book of *Posterior Analytics*,[15] the act of the will should be judged unqualifiedly better than the intellect and absolutely so, since it is unqualifiedly better than it in comparison to its first object. This agrees with the thought of the Philosopher in the *Topics*: "If the best in this genus is better than the best in that genus, then the former is better than the latter without qualification."[16]

Next, that the object of the will is superior to the object of the intellect is obvious, because the object of the will, which is the good without qualification, has the character of an end without qualification and of the ultimate end. The object of the intellect, which is the true, has the character of a good of something, for example, of the intellect. Thus it has the character of an end subordinate to another end and ordered to the other end as to the ultimate end. For, when there are many particular ends, they are all included under some one end, and all the powers which have divers ends are subordinated to some one power whose end is the ultimate one, as is stated in the beginning of the *Ethics*.[17] In accord with this, then, the intellect is completely subordinated to the will. And in this way, as in all active potencies ordered to an end, that potency which regards the universal end always moves

---

13   Augustine, *The Trinity* (*De trinitate*) IX, xi, 16: CC L, 307.

14   Augustine, *The Confessions* (*Confessiones*) I, i, 1: CC XXVII, 1.

15   Cf. Aristotle, *Posterior Analytics* I, 2, 72a29–30.

16   Aristotle, *Topics* III, 2, 52c.

17   Cf. Aristotle, *Nicomachean Ethics* I, 1, 1094a6–10, 18–19.

and impels to activity the other potencies which regard particular ends and regulates them, as the master art regulates the other arts in a city, as is stated in the beginning of the *Ethics*,[18] so the will moves the reason and directs it to activity, as well as all the powers of the soul and members of the body.

It must, then, be said that the will is absolutely the higher power in the whole kingdom of the soul and thus higher than the intellect.

\<With Regard to the Arguments\>

It is easy to reply to the objections raised against this position.

To the first objection, with regard to what the Philosopher says in book six of the *Ethics*, one should say that his comparison is literally understood with regard to those potencies in which there are the other intellectual habits, and thus nothing from that statement applies to the will.

To the second objection, that practical reason is what moves first, one should say that something is said to move in two senses. In one way, metaphorically, by proposing and revealing an end toward which one should move. Practical reason moves in this way, and in this way it moves the person who wills; it does not, properly speaking, move the will, which is moved by the person who wills. Nor does reason, properly speaking, move in this sense; rather, it is the object that of itself moves reason to know and, thereby, in revealing itself as good, it metaphorically moves the person who wills to desire it. For the good as known moves the person who wills, but reason itself as knowing does not move the will. In another way, something is said to move another in the manner of an agent and one impelling the other to act. In this way the will moves the reason, and this is more truly to move.

To the third objection that contemplation holds the first rank in the actions of the soul, one should admit that it is true, but this has nothing to do with the will, since he was speaking about the relation of the active and the contemplative life. Of these the one is ruled by speculative reason which is the higher; the other is ruled by practical reason which is lower. But both are ruled by the will which is above both of them.

To the fourth objection, that the image is formed anew in reason, one should say that it is true, but not the whole truth. For part of the image, and the perfecting part, pertains to the will. For this reason the mental word in which the perfect character of the image shines forth, is, according to Augustine, "knowledge along with love."

To the fifth objection, that what directs is superior to what it directs, one should say that there is one who directs with authority, as a lord directs a servant; he is the higher. In that way the will directs the intellect. Or, one directs another by way of service, as a servant directs a master in carrying a light before him at night so that the master does not stumble. Such a director is inferior, and in this way the intellect directs the will. Hence, the will can withdraw the intellect from directing and knowing when it wills, as a master can withdraw a servant.

---

18   Cf. Aristotle, *Nicomachean Ethics* I, 1, 1094a4–5, 9–10.

Virtues and Happiness

43

Boethius of Dacia on the Supreme Good, or on the Life of the Philosopher

Since in every kind of being there is a supreme possible good, and since man too is a certain species or kind of being, there must be a supreme possible good for man, not a good which is supreme in the absolute sense, but one that is supreme for man. The goods which are accessible to man are limited and do not extend to infinity. By means of reason we will seek to determine what the supreme good is which is accessible to man.

The supreme good for man should be his in terms of his highest power, and not according to the vegetative soul, which is also found in plants, nor according to the sensitive soul, which is also found in animals and from which their sensual pleasures arise. But man's highest power is his reason and intellect. For this is the supreme director of human life both in the order of speculation and in the order of action. Therefore, the supreme good attainable by man must be his by means of his intellect. Therefore, men who are so weighed down by sense pleasures that they lose intellectual goods should grieve. For they never attain their supreme good. It is insofar as they are given to the senses that they do not seek that which is the good of the intellect itself. Against these the Philosopher protests, saying: "Woe to you men who are numbered among beasts and who do not attend to that which is divine within you!"[1] He calls the intellect that which is divine in man. For if there is anything divine in man, it is right for it to be the intellect. Just as that which is best among all beings is divine, so also that which is best in man we call divine.

Moreover, one power of the human intellect is speculative and the other is practical. This is clear from this fact, that man theorizes concerning certain objects of which he is not the active cause, e.g., eternal things, and about others he acts under the direction of the intellect in choosing some fitting means whenever any human act is in question. From this, then, we know that these two intellectual powers are present in man. But the supreme good accessible to man in terms of the power of his speculative intellect is knowledge of what is true and delight in the same. For knowledge of what is true gives delight. An intelligible object

---

1 M. Grabmann, "Die Opuscula De Summo Bono sive De Vita Philosophi und De Sompniis des Boetius von Dacien," *Mittelalterliches Geistesleben*, II (1936), 200–24: 209, n. 18, notes that this statement cannot be found in the writings of Aristotle.

gives delight to the one who knows it. And the more wondrous and noble the intelligible object and the greater the power of the apprehending intellect to perfectly comprehend, the greater the intellectual delight. One who has tasted such delight spurns every lesser pleasure, such as that of sense. The latter is, in truth, less, and is more base. And the man who chooses such pleasure is, because of that pleasure, more base than one who chooses the former.

It is because of this, because the object known gives delight to the one who knows, that the Philosopher [Aristotle] in Book XII of the *Metaphysics* maintains that the first intellect enjoys the most pleasurable life.[2] For since the first intellect is the most powerful in understanding and the object which it knows is the noblest, its essence itself – for what nobler object can the divine intellect have than the divine essence? – therefore, it has the life of greatest delight. No greater good can befall man in terms of his speculative intellect than knowledge of the universality of beings, which come from the first principle and, by means of this, knowledge of the first principle insofar as such is possible, and delight in it. Therefore, our conclusion above follows: that the supreme good accessible to man by means of his speculative intellect is knowledge of what is true in individual cases, and delight in the same.

Likewise, the supreme good accessible to man in terms of his practical intellect is the doing of good, and delight in the same. For what greater good can befall man in terms of his practical intellect than to choose the fitting means in human action and to delight therein?

For no man is just unless he takes delight in acts of justice. The same must be said of the acts of the other moral virtues. From what has been said one can evidently conclude that the supreme good open to man is to know the true, to do the good, and to delight in both.

And because the highest good possible for man is happiness, it follows that human happiness consists in knowing the true, doing the good, and taking delight in both. The military profession is prescribed in a state by the lawmaker for this reason, that when enemies have been expelled, citizens may devote themselves to intellectual virtues in contemplating the true, and to moral virtues in doing good, and thus live a happy life. For the happy life consists in these two. This then is a greater good, which man can receive from God and which God can give to man in this life. With reason does a man desire a long life who desires it for this, to become more perfect in this good. He who shares more perfectly in that happiness which reason tells us is possible for man in this life draws closer to that happiness which we expect in the life to come on the authority of faith. And since so great a good is possible for man, as has been said, it is right for all human action to be directed toward that good, so as to attain it. For just as all actions as regards a certain law are right and proper when they tend toward the end of the law, and better the more closely they approach the end of the law, while actions which are opposed to the end of the law or which are weak or indifferent without either being opposed to the end of the law or in accord with it, while all such actions sin against the law to a greater or lesser degree as is clear from what has been said, the same is true in man himself. All designs and deliberations, all actions and desires of man which tend to this supreme good which is accessible to man according to the above, these are right and proper. When man so acts, he acts in accord with nature. For he acts for the sake of the supreme good, to which he is ordered by nature. And when he so acts he is properly ordered. For then he is ordered to his best and his ultimate end. But all actions of man which are not ordered to this good, or which are not such as to render man stronger and better disposed for actions which are ordered to this good, all such actions in man are sin.

---

2   Cf. Aristotle, *Metaphysics* XII, 1072b, 24.

Wherefore the happy man never does anything except works of happiness, or works by means of which he becomes stronger and better fitted for works of happiness. Therefore, whether the happy man eats or sleeps or is awake, he lives in happiness so long as he does those things by means of which he is rendered more capable of the works of happiness. Therefore, all acts of man which are not directed to this supreme good of man which has been described, whether they are opposed to it or whether they are indifferent, all such acts constitute sin in man to a greater or lesser degree, as is clear. The cause of all such acts is inordinate desire. It is also the cause of all moral evil. Moreover, inordinate desire in man is the cause which most greatly prevents him from attaining that which is desired naturally. For all men naturally desire to know. But only the smallest number of men, sad to say, devote themselves to the pursuit of wisdom. Inordinate desire bars the others from such a good. Thus we find certain men pursuing a life of laziness, others detestable sense pleasures, and others giving themselves to the desire for riches. So it is that all today are prevented by inordinate desire from attaining to their supreme good, with the exception of a very small number of men, men who should be honored.

I say they are to be honored because they despise sense desire and pursue the delight of reason and intellectual desire, striving to know truth. Again I say they are to be honored because they live in accord with nature. All lower powers found in man are for the sake of the highest power. Thus the nutritive power is there for the sake of the sensitive. For the sensitive power is a perfection of an animated body, and an animated body cannot live without food. But it is the nutritive power which changes and assimilates food. Therefore, it follows that the nutritive power exists in man for the sake of the sensitive. And the sensitive power is for the sake of the intellective since, in us, intelligibles are derived from things imagined. Wherefore, we understand with greater difficulty things which of themselves cannot be imagined by us. But imagination presupposes the senses. The proof of this is that one who imagines is also affected on the level of sense. Wherefore, according to the Philosopher, imagination or *fantasia* is a movement arising from an actual exercise of sense.[3] [Just as all lower powers in man are for the sake of the higher,] so too all operations of man's lower powers are for the sake of the operations of his highest power, the intellect. And if, among the operations of the intellective power, there is one which is best and most perfect, all others naturally exist for its sake. When a man performs such an operation, he enjoys the highest state possible for man.

Such men are the philosophers, who spend their lives in the pursuit of wisdom. Wherefore, all powers found in the philosopher operate according to the natural order, the prior for the sake of the posterior, the lower for the sake of the higher and more perfect. But all other men, who live according to lower powers and choose their operations and the delights found in such operations, are not ordered in accord with nature. They sin against the natural order. For man to turn away from the natural order is sin in man. Because the philosopher does not turn away from this order, for this reason he does not sin against the natural order. Morally speaking, the philosopher is virtuous for three reasons. *First*, because he recognizes the baseness of action in which vice consists and the nobility of action in which virtue consists. Therefore, he can more easily choose the one and avoid the other and always act according to right reason. He who so acts never sins. But such is not true of the ignorant man. It is difficult for him to act rightly. *Secondly*, because he who has tasted a greater delight despises every lesser delight. But the philosopher has tasted intellectual delight in theoretical consideration

---

3   Cf. *De anima* III, 429a, 1.

of the value of beings. This delight is greater than that of sense. Therefore, he despises sense pleasures. But many sins and vices consist in excessive sense pleasure. *Thirdly*, because there is no sin in understanding and theorizing. There is no possibility of excess and of sin in the order of supreme goods. But the action of the philosopher is such a contemplation of truth. Therefore, it is easier for the philosopher to be virtuous than for another. So it is that the philosopher lives as man was born to live, and according to the natural order.

Since in him the lower powers and their operations are for the sake of the higher powers and their operations, and all taken together for the highest power and that highest action, which is contemplation of truth and delight in the same, above all, the first truth, the desire to know will never be satisfied until the uncreated being is known. As the Commentator says, all men naturally desire to know about the divine intellect.

Desire for any knowable object is a kind of desire for the first knowable object. This is the proof. The closer beings are to the first knowable being, the more we desire to know them and the more we delight in thinking of them.

Therefore, by studying the caused beings which are in the world and their natures and relationships to one another, the philosopher is led to consider the highest causes of things. For a knowledge of effects leads to a knowledge of the cause. And in noting that higher causes and their natures are such that they must have another cause, he is led to a knowledge of the first cause. And because there is pleasure in speculative knowledge, and all the more so the nobler the object known, the philosopher leads a life of very great pleasure. The philosopher also knows and observes that it is necessary for this cause to be its own cause of being, that is to say, not to have another cause. For if there were nothing in the universe which was not caused by another, then there would be nothing at all. He also notes that this cause must be eternal and unchangeable, always remaining the same. For if it were not eternal then nothing whatsoever would be eternal. And again, since certain things in the world have begun to be, and since one being which begins to be cannot be a sufficient cause of another being which begins to be, as is evident, it clearly follows that all things in this world which begin to be must derive from an eternal cause. This cause is also unchangeable and always remains the same. For change is possible only in imperfect things. And if there is some most perfect being in the universe, it is right for this to be the first cause. The philosopher also notes that the entire being of the universe, with the exception of this first cause itself, must come from it and thus, that this first cause is the cause which produces beings and orders them to one another and maintains them in existence – certain ones in terms of their individual identity and without any kind of change (as the separated substances); certain ones according to their individual identity, but as subject to change (as the heavenly bodies); and certain ones in terms of their species alone (as those which are below the heavenly orbit, such as the lowest levels of beings). He also notes that just as all things derive from this first cause, so too, all things are ordered to it. For that being is the beginning of all things, the end of all things, and that through which all things are joined to their end, that being is the first being according to the philosophers and God the Blessed according to the holy men. Nevertheless, in this order there is great range. Those beings which are closest to the first principle are nobler and more perfect. Those which are farther removed from the first principle are lower and less perfect.

This first principle is to this world as the father of a family is to his household, as a commander to his army, and as the common good to the state. Just as the army is one because of the unity of its commander, and just as the good of the army is essentially in the commander and in others in terms of their relationship to him, so too, from the unity of this first principle derives the unity of the world, and the good of this world is essentially in this first principle and in other beings of this world, insofar as they participate in the first principle and are ordered to it. So it is that there is no good in any being in this world which is not a participation in the first principle.

Considering all these things, the philosopher is moved to wonder at this first principle and to love it. For we love that from which our goods derive, and we love that to the greatest degree from which our greatest goods derive.

Therefore, the philosopher, noting that all goods come to him from this first principle and are preserved for him insofar as they are preserved by this first principle, is moved to the greatest love for this first principle. This is in accord with right reason of nature and right reason of intellect. And since everyone takes delight in that which he loves and maximum delight in that which he loves to the maximum degree, and since the philosopher has the greatest love for this first principle, as has been indicated, it follows that the philosopher takes maximum delight in this first principle and in contemplating its goodness, and that this alone is right pleasure. This is the life of the philosopher. Whoever does not lead such a life does not live rightly. However, I call "philosopher" any man who lives according to the right order of nature and who has acquired the best and ultimate end of human life. And the first principle of whom we have spoken is the glorious and most high God, who is blessed forever and ever. Amen.

Thomas Aquinas on Happiness

Summa Theologiae

Part II/1, Question 2. On what constitutes human happiness

Article 7. Whether some good of the soul constitutes man's happiness?

Objection 1: It would seem that some good of the soul constitutes man's happiness. For happiness is some human good. But human goods are divided into the following three kinds: external goods, goods of the body, and goods of the soul. But happiness does not consist in external goods or in goods of the body, as was shown above (in articles 1–6). Therefore, it consists in goods of the soul.

Objection 2: Further, we love that for which we desire some good more than the good we desire for it: thus we love a friend for whom we desire money more than we love money. But human beings desire *all* sorts of goods for themselves. Therefore, they love themselves more than all other goods. Now happiness is what is loved above all, which is evident from the fact that all else is loved and desired for its sake. Therefore, happiness consists in some good of humans themselves. Not, however, in goods of the body; therefore, in goods of the soul.

Objection 3: Furthermore, perfection is something belonging to that which is perfected. But happiness is a perfection of man. Therefore happiness is something belonging to man. But it is not something belonging to the body, as shown above.[1] Therefore it is something belonging to the soul; and thus it consists in goods of the soul.

On the contrary, As Augustine says, "that which constitutes the life of happiness is to be loved for its own sake."[2] But man is not to be loved for man's own sake, but whatever is in man is to be loved for God's sake. Therefore happiness consists in no good of the soul.

---

1 *ST* 1–2 q. 2, a. 5.
2 *De Doctrina Christiana* I, 22.

I answer that we call something an end in two ways, as it was stated above:[3] the thing itself that we desire to attain, and its use, namely, the attainment or possession of that thing. Therefore, speaking about man's ultimate end as about the thing itself we desire as the ultimate end, it is impossible for man's ultimate end to be the soul itself or something belonging to it. Because the soul, considered in itself, is as something existing in potentiality: for it becomes actually knowing from being potentially knowing and actually virtuous from being potentially virtuous. Now since potentiality is for the sake of actuality as for its fulfillment, that which in itself is in potentiality cannot be the ultimate end. Therefore the soul itself cannot be its own ultimate end. Likewise, nothing belonging to the soul can be the ultimate end, whether power, habit, or act. For the good which is the ultimate end is the perfect good that fulfils desire. Now man's desire, that is, the will, is for the universal good. And any good inherent in the soul is a participated good, and consequently a particular good. Therefore none of these can be man's ultimate end.

But if we speak about man's ultimate end as the attainment or possession or any use of the thing desired as the end, then in this way the ultimate end is something of the human soul, since man attains happiness through the soul. Therefore, the thing itself which is desired as the end is that which constitutes happiness, and makes man happy; but the attainment of this thing is called happiness. Consequently, we must say that happiness is something belonging to the soul; but that which constitutes happiness is something outside the soul.

Reply to Objection 1: Inasmuch as that division includes all goods that man can desire, what is said to be a good of the soul is not only a power, a habit, or an act, but also an object of these, which is something external. And in this way nothing prevents us from saying that what constitutes happiness is a good of the soul.

Reply to Objection 2: As far as the proposed objection is concerned, happiness is loved above all, as the good that is desired; whereas a friend is loved as someone for whom some good is desired; and human beings love themselves in this way as well. Consequently, we do not have the same kind of love in both cases. Whether humans love anything more than themselves with the love of friendship, however, we shall have an occasion to inquire when we discuss charity.[4]

Reply to Objection 3: Happiness itself, since it is a perfection of the soul, is an inherent good of the soul; but that which constitutes happiness, namely, what makes man happy, is something outside his soul, as stated above.

Article 8. Whether any created good constitutes man's happiness?

Objection 1: It would seem that some created good constitutes man's happiness. For Dionysius says that Divine wisdom "unites the ends of first things to the beginnings of second things,"[5] from which we may gather that the summit of a lower nature touches the base of the higher nature. But man's highest good is happiness. Since, therefore, the angel is above man in the order of nature, as stated in the first part,[6] it seems that man's happiness consists in man somehow reaching the angel.

3   *ST* 1 q. 1, a. 8.
4   *ST* 2–2, qq. 23–7.
5   *De Divinis Nominibus* vii.
6   *ST* 1, q. 111, a. 1.

Objection 2: Further, the ultimate end of each thing consists in that in which it achieves its own perfection; therefore, the part is for the whole, as for its end. But the universe of creatures, which is called the macrocosm, is compared to man, who is called the microcosm,[7] as perfect to imperfect. Therefore man's happiness consists in the whole universe of creatures.

Objection 3: Further, human beings are made happy by what satisfies their natural desire. But the natural desire of human beings does not reach out to a good surpassing their capacity. Therefore, since man's capacity does not include that good which surpasses the limits of all creation, it seems that man can be made happy by some created good. Consequently, what constitutes man's happiness is some created good.

On the contrary, Augustine says:[8] "As the soul is the life of the body, so God is man's life of happiness, of whom it is written: 'Happy is the people whose God is the Lord'."[9]

I answer that, It is impossible for any created good to constitute man's happiness. For happiness is that perfect good which entirely satisfies one's desire; otherwise it would not be the ultimate end, if something yet remained to be desired. Now the object of the will, i.e. of man's desire, is what is universally good; just as the object of the intellect is what is universally true. Hence it is evident that nothing can satisfy man's will, except what is universally good. This is to be found, not in any creature, but in God alone, because every creature has participated goodness. Therefore, God alone can satisfy the will of man, according to the words of the *Psalms* (102:5): "Who satisfies your desire with good things." Therefore, God alone constitutes man's happiness.

Reply to Objection 1: The summit of man does indeed touch the base of the angelic nature, by a kind of likeness; but man does not rest there as in the ultimate end, but reaches out to the universal wellspring of goodness itself, which is the common object of happiness of all the blessed, being the infinite and perfect good.

Reply to Objection 2: If a whole is not the ultimate end, but ordained to a further end, then the ultimate end of a part of the whole is not the whole itself, but something else. Now the universe of creatures, to which man is compared as part to whole, is not the ultimate end, but is ordained to God, as to its ultimate end. Therefore the ultimate end of man is not the good of the universe, but God himself.

Reply to Objection 3: Some created good is not lesser than that good of which man is capable *as of something intrinsic* and inherent to him; but it is lesser than the good of which man is capable *as of an object*, which is infinite, whereas the participated good which is in an angel, or even in the whole universe, is a finite and restricted good.

---

7   *Physics* VIII, 2.
8   *De Civitate Dei* xix, 26.
9   *Psalms* 143: 15.

Divine Law, Natural Law, Positive Law

45

Thomas Aquinas on Natural Law and Positive Law

Summa Theologiae

Part II/1, Question 94. On the Natural Law

Article 1. Is the natural law a habit?

We thus proceed to the first inquiry. It seems that the natural law is a habit, for the following reasons:

Objection 1. "Three things belong to the soul: powers, habits, and emotions," as the Philosopher says in the *Ethics*.[1] But the natural law is neither a power of the soul nor an emotion. Therefore, the natural law is a habit.

Objection 2. Basil says that conscience, that is, *synderesis*, is "the law of our intellect,"[2] and we can only understand such regarding the natural law. But *synderesis* is a habit, as I maintained in the First Part.[3] Therefore, the natural law is a habit.

Objection 3. The natural law always abides in human beings, as I shall make clear later.[4] But human beings' reason, to which that law belongs, is not always thinking about the natural law. Therefore, the natural law is a habit, not an act.

On the contrary, Augustine says in his work *On the Marital Good* that "habits are the means whereby we do things when we need to."[5] But the natural law is not such, since that law belongs to infants and the damned, who cannot act by reason of its presence. Therefore, the natural law is not a habit.

I answer that we can speak about habits in two ways. We speak of them in one way in the strict sense and essentially, and then the natural law is not a habit. For I have said before that the

1 *Ethics* II, 5 (1105b20–21).
2 *On the Six Days of Creation*, homily 7, n. 5 (PG 29:157).
3 I, Q. 79, A. 12.
4 A. 6.
5 *On the Marital Good* 21 (PL 40:390).

natural law is constituted by reason,[6] just as propositions are works of reason. And what one does, and the means whereby one does it, are not the same. For example, one makes a fitting speech by means of the habit of grammar. Therefore, since habits are the means whereby one does things, the natural law cannot be a habit in the strict sense and essentially.

We can speak of habits in a second way as what we possess by reason of habits. For example, we call faith what we have by reason of the habit of faith. And so, as reason sometimes actually considers precepts of the natural law and sometimes only habitually possesses them, we can in the latter way say that the natural law is a habit. Just so, the indemonstrable first principles in theoretical matters are principles belonging to the habit of first principles, not the very habit.

Reply Objection 1. The Philosopher in the cited text is attempting to discover the genus of virtues. And since virtues are evidently sources of activity, he posits only things that are sources of human activity, namely, powers, habits, and emotions. But other things belong to the soul besides the latter three. For example, certain acts belong to the soul: willing to those willing, and things known to those knowing. And the natural properties of the soul, such as immortality and the like, belong to the soul.

Reply Objection 2. Basil calls *synderesis* the law of our intellect insofar as it is the habit that contains the precepts of the natural law, that is, the first principles of human actions.

Reply Objection 3. The argument of this objection reaches the conclusion that we possess the natural law in a habitual way, and we concede this.

Qualification to the argument in the section On the contrary. Sometimes, due to an impediment, one cannot make use of what one possesses habitually. For example, human beings cannot make use of habitual knowledge when they are asleep. And likewise, children cannot make use of habitual understanding of first principles, or even of the natural law, which they possess habitually, due to their immature age.

Article 2. Does the natural law include several precepts or only one?

We thus proceed to the second inquiry. It seems that that the natural law includes only one precept, not several, for the following reasons:

Objection 1. Law belongs to the genus of precept, as I have maintained before.[7] Therefore, if there were to be many precepts of the natural law, it would follow logically that there would also be many natural laws.

Objection 2. The natural law results from the nature of human beings. But human nature as a whole is one, although multiple regarding its parts. Therefore, either there is only one precept of the natural law because of the unity of the whole, or there are many precepts because of the many parts of human nature. And so even things that regard inclinations of concupiscible power will need to belong to the natural law.

Objection 3. Law belongs to reason, as I have said before.[8] But there is only one power of reason in human beings. Therefore, there is only one precept of the natural law.

6 I–II, Q. 90, A. 1, *ad* 2.
7 I–II, Q. 92, A. 2.
8 I–II, Q. 90, A. 1.

On the contrary, the precepts of the natural law in human beings are related to action as the first principles in scientific matters are related to theoretical knowledge. But there are several indemonstrable first principles of theoretical knowledge. Therefore, there are also several precepts of the natural law.

I answer that as I have said before,[9] the precepts of the natural law are related to practical reason as the first principles of scientific demonstrations are related to theoretical reason. For both the precepts of the natural law and the first principles to scientific demonstrations are self-evident principles. And we speak of things being self-evident in two ways: in one way as such; in a second way in relation to ourselves. We indeed speak of self-evident propositions as such when their predicates belong to the nature of their subjects, although such propositions may not be self-evident to those who do not know the definition of the subjects. For example, the proposition "Human beings are rational" is by its nature self-evident, since to speak of something human is to speak of something rational, although the proposition is not self-evident to one who does not know what a human being is. And so, as Boethius says in his work *On Groups of Seven*,[10] there are axioms or universally self-evident propositions, and propositions whose terms all persons know (e.g., "Every whole is greater than one of its parts" and "Things equal to the same thing are themselves equal") are such. But some propositions are self-evident only to the wise, who understand what the proposition's terms signify. For example, for those who understand that angels are not material substances, it is self-evident that angels are not circumscriptively in a place, something not evident to the uneducated, who do not understand the nature of angels.

And there is a priority regarding the things that fall within the understanding of all persons. For what first falls within our understanding is being, the understanding of which is included in everything that one understands. And so the first indemonstrable principle is that one cannot at the same time affirm and deny the same thing. And this principle is based on the nature of being and nonbeing, and all other principles are based on it, as the *Metaphysics* says.[11] And as being is the first thing that without qualification falls within our understanding, so good is the first thing that falls within the understanding of practical reason. And practical reason is ordered to action, since every efficient cause acts for the sake of an end, which has the nature of good. And so the first principle in practical reason is one based on the nature of good, namely, that good is what all things seek. Therefore, the first precept of the natural law is that we should do and seek good, and shun evil. And all the other precepts of the natural law are based on that precept, namely, that all the things that practical reason by nature understands to be human goods or evils belong to precepts of the natural law as things to be done or shunned.

And since good has the nature of end, and evil the nature of the contrary, reason by nature understands to be good all the things for which human beings have a natural inclination, and so to be things to be actively sought, and understands contrary things as evil and to be shunned. Therefore, the ordination of our natural inclinations ordains the precepts of the natural law.

First, for example, human beings have an inclination for good by the nature they share with all substances, namely, as every substance by nature seeks to preserve itself. And

9   I–II, Q. 91, A. 3.

10   *On Groups of Seven* (PL 64:1311). This work is otherwise known as *How Substances as Existing Things Are Good*.

11   Aristotle, *Metaphysics* III, 3 (1005b29–34).

regarding this inclination, means that preserve our human life and prevent the contrary belong to the natural law.

Second, human beings have more particular inclinations by the nature they share with other animals. And so the *Digest* says that things "that nature has taught all animals,"[12] such as the sexual union of male and female, and the upbringing of children, and the like, belong to the natural law.

Third, human beings have inclinations for good by their rational nature, which is proper to them. For example, human beings by nature have inclinations to know truths about God and to live in society with other human beings. And so things that relate to such inclinations belong to the natural law (e.g., that human beings shun ignorance, that they not offend those with whom they ought to live sociably, and other such things regarding those inclinations).

Reply Objection 1. All the precepts of the natural law, insofar as they relate to one first precept, have the nature of one natural law.

Reply Objection 2. All the inclinations of any part of human nature (e.g., the concupiscible and irascible powers), insofar as reason rules them, belong to the natural law and are traced to one first precept, as I have said.[13] And so there are many precepts of the natural law as such, but they share a common foundation.

Reply Objection 3. Reason, although as such one power, ordains everything that concerns human beings. And so the law of reason includes everything that reason can rule.

Article 3. Do all virtuous acts belong to the natural law?

We proceed thus to the third inquiry. It seems that not all virtuous acts belong to the natural law, for the following reasons:

Objection 1. It belongs to the nature of law that law be ordained for the common good, as I have said before.[14] But some virtuous acts are ordained for the private good of an individual, as is particularly evident in the case of acts of the virtue of moderation. Therefore, not all virtuous acts are subject to the natural law.

Objection 2. All sins are contrary to certain virtuous acts. Therefore, if all virtuous acts belong to the natural law, it seems that all sins are consequently contrary to nature. And yet we say this in a special way about some sins.

Objection 3. Everybody agrees about things that are in accord with nature. But not everybody agrees about virtuous acts, for things that are virtuous for some are vicious for others. Therefore, not all virtuous acts belong to the natural law.

On the contrary, Damascene says in his work *On Orthodox Faith* that "virtues are natural."[15] Therefore, virtuous acts are also subject to the natural law.

I answer that we can speak about virtuous acts in two ways: in one way as virtuous; in a second way as we consider such acts in their own species. Therefore, if we are speaking about virtuous acts as virtuous, then all virtuous acts belong to the natural law. For I have said

12   Justinian, *Digest* I, title 1, law 1.
13   In the body of the article.
14   I–II, Q. 90, A. 2.
15   *On Orthodox Faith* III, 14 (PG 94:1045).

that everything to which human beings are inclined by their nature belongs to the natural law.[16] But everything is by its nature inclined to the activity that its form renders fitting. For example, fire is inclined to heat things. And so, since the rational soul is the specific form of human beings, everyone has an inclination from one's nature to act in accord with reason. And this is to act virtuously. And so in this regard, all virtuous acts belong to the natural law, since one's own reason by nature dictates that one act virtuously.

But if we should be speaking about virtuous acts as such and such, namely, as we consider them in their own species, then not all virtuous acts belong to the natural law. For we do many things virtuously to which nature does not at first incline us, but which human beings by the inquiry of reason have discovered to be useful for living righteously.

Reply Objection 1. Moderation concerns the natural desires for food and drink and sex, which desires are indeed ordained for the natural common good, just as other prescriptions of the natural law are ordained for the common moral good.

Reply Objection 2. We can call the nature proper to human beings the nature of human beings. And so all sins, insofar as they are contrary to reason, are also contrary to nature, as Damascene makes clear in his work *On Orthodox Faith.*[17] Or else we can call the nature common to human beings and other animals the nature of human beings. And so we speak of certain particular sins being contrary to nature. For example, the sexual intercourse of males, which we specifically call the sin contrary to nature, is contrary to the sexual union of male and female, and such sexual union is natural for all animals.

Reply Objection 3. The argument of this objection is valid regarding virtuous acts as such and such. For then, because of the different conditions of human beings, some acts may be virtuous for some persons, as proportionate and suitable for them, which are nonetheless wicked for other persons, as disproportionate for them.

Article 4. Is the natural law the same for all human beings?

We thus proceed to the fourth inquiry. It seems that the natural law is not the same for all human beings, for the following reasons:

Objection 1. The *Decretum* says that "the natural law is contained in the [Old] Law and the Gospel."[18] But what is contained in the Law and the Gospel is not in the common possession of all, since Rom. 10:16 says: "Some do not heed the Gospel." Therefore, the natural law is not the same for all human beings.

Objection 2. "We call things in accord with law just," as the *Ethics* says.[19] But the same work says that nothing is so universally just that it is not otherwise for some.[20] Therefore, even the natural law is not the same for all human beings.

Objection 3. Things to which human beings' nature inclines them belong to the natural law, as I have said before.[21] But nature inclines different human beings to different things. For

16   A. 2.
17   *On Orthodox Faith* II, 4 and 30 (PG 94:876, 976).
18   Gratian, *Decretum* I, dist. 1, preface.
19   Aristotle, *Ethics* V, 1 (1129b12).
20   Ibid. V, 7 (1134b32).
21   AA. 2, 3.

example, nature inclines some to desire pleasures, others to desire honors, others to desire other things. Therefore, the natural law is not the same for all human beings.

On the contrary, Isidore says in his *Etymologies:* "The natural law is common to all nations."[22]

I answer that things to which nature inclines human beings belong to the natural law, as I have said before,[23] and one of the things proper to human beings is that their nature inclines them to act in accord with reason. And it belongs to reason to advance from the general to the particular, as the *Physics* makes clear.[24] And regarding that process, theoretical reason proceeds in one way, and practical reason in another way. For inasmuch as theoretical reason is especially concerned about necessary things, which cannot be otherwise disposed, its particular conclusions, just like its general principles, are true without exception. But practical reason is concerned about contingent things, which include human actions. And so the more reason goes from the general to the particular, the more exceptions we find, although there is some necessity in the general principles. Therefore, truth in theoretical matters, both first principles and conclusions, is the same for all human beings, although some know only the truth of the principles, which we call universal propositions, and not the truth of the conclusions. But truth in practical matters, or practical rectitude, is the same for all human beings only regarding the general principles, not regarding the particular conclusions. And not all of those with practical rectitude regarding particulars know the truth in equal measure.

Therefore, the truth or rectitude regarding the general principles of both theoretical and practical reason is the same for all persons and known in equal measure by all of them. And the truth regarding the particular conclusions of theoretical reason is the same for all persons, but some know such truth less than others. For example, it is true for all persons that triangles have three angles equal to two right angles, although not everybody knows this.

But the truth or rectitude regarding particular conclusions of practical reason is neither the same for all persons nor known in equal measure even by those for whom it is the same. For example, it is correct and true for all persons that they should act in accord with reason. And it follows as a particular conclusion from this principle that those holding goods in trust should return the goods to the goods' owners. And this is indeed true for the most part, but it might in particular cases be injurious, and so contrary to reason, to return the goods (e.g., if the owner should be seeking to attack one's country). And the more the particular conclusion goes into particulars, the more exceptions there are (e.g., if one should declare that entrusted goods should be returned to their owners with such and such safeguards or in such and such ways). For the more particular conditions are added to the particular conclusion, the more ways there may be exceptions, so that the conclusion about returning or not returning entrusted goods is erroneous.

Therefore, we should say that the natural law regarding general first principles is the same for all persons both as to their rectitude and as to knowledge of them. And the natural law regarding particulars, which are, as it were, conclusions from the general principles, is for the most part the same for all persons both as to its rectitude and as to knowledge of it. Nonetheless, it can be wanting in rather few cases both as to its rectitude and as to knowledge of it. As to rectitude, the natural law can be wanting because of particular obstacles,

---

22 *Etymologies* V, 4 (*PL* 82:199).

23 AA. 2, 3.

24 Aristotle, *Physics* I, 1 (184a16–27).

just as natures that come to be and pass away are wanting in rather few cases because of obstacles. And also as to knowledge of the natural law, the law can be wanting because emotions or evil habituation or evil natural disposition has perverted the reason of some. For example, the Germans of old did not consider robbery wicked, as Caesar's *Gallic Wars* relates,[25] although robbery is expressly contrary to the natural law.

Reply Objection 1. We should not understand the cited statement to mean that all the matters included in the Law and the Gospel belong to the natural law, since the Law and the Gospel transmit to us many things above nature. Rather, we should understand the statement to mean that the Law and the Gospel completely transmit to us the things that belong to the natural law. And so Gratian, after saying that "the natural law is contained in the Law and the Gospel," immediately adds by way of example: "And everyone is thereby commanded to do unto others what one wishes to be done to oneself."

Reply Objection 2. We should understand the cited statement of the Philosopher regarding things just by nature as conclusions derived from general principles, not as the general principles. And such conclusions are correct for the most part and are wanting in rather few cases.

Reply Objection 3. As the power of reason in human beings rules and commands other powers, so reason needs to direct all the natural inclinations belonging to other powers. And so it is universally correct for all persons to direct all their inclinations by reason.

Article 5. Can the natural law vary?

We thus proceed to the fifth inquiry. It seems that the natural law can vary, for the following reasons:

Objection 1. A gloss on Sir. 17:9, "He [God] supplied them with instruction and the law of life," says: "He wanted the [Old] Law to be written in order to correct the natural law."[26] But what is corrected is changed. Therefore, the natural law can vary.

Objection 2. The killing of innocent human beings as well as adultery and theft are contrary to the natural law. But God altered these precepts. For example, God on one occasion commanded Abraham to slay his innocent son, as Gen. 22:2 relates. And God on another occasion commanded the Jews to steal vessels the Egyptians had lent them, as Ex. 12:35–36 relates. And God on another occasion commanded Hosea to take a fornicating wife, as Hos. 1:2 relates. Therefore, the natural law can vary.

Objection 3. Isidore says in his *Etymologies* that "the common possession of all property and the same freedom for all persons belong to the natural law."[27] But we perceive that human laws have altered these prescriptions. Therefore, it seems that the natural law can vary.

On the contrary, the *Decretum* says: "The natural law originates with rational creatures. It does not vary over time and abides without change."[28]

I answer that we can understand the mutability of the natural law in two ways. We can understand it in one way by things being added to it. And then nothing prevents the natural law

25 Julius Caesar, *Gallic Wars* VI, 23.
26 *Glossa ordinaria*, on Sir. 17:9 (PL 109:876; 113:1201).
27 *Etymologies* V, 4 (PL 82:199).
28 Gratian, *Decretum* I, dist. 5, preface.

changing, since both divine law and human laws add to natural law many things beneficial to human life.

We can understand the mutability of the natural law in a second way by way of subtraction, namely, that things previously subject to the law cease to be so. And then the natural law is altogether immutable as to its first principles. And as to its secondary precepts, which we said are proper proximate conclusions, as it were, from the first principles,[29] the natural law is not so changed that what it prescribes is not for the most part completely correct. But it can be changed regarding particulars and in rather few cases, due to special causes that prevent observance of such precepts, as I have said before.[30]

Reply Objection 1. We say that written law has been given to correct the natural law either because the written law supplements what the natural law lacked, or because the natural law in the hearts of some regarding particulars had been corrupted insofar as they thought that things by nature evil were good. And such corruption needed correction.

Reply Objection 2. All human beings, without exception, both the innocent and the guilty, die when natural death comes. And God's power indeed inflicts such natural death on human beings because of original sin, as 1 Sam. 2:6 says: "The Lord causes death and life." And so, at the command of God, death can without any injustice be inflicted on any human being, whether guilty or innocent.

Likewise, adultery is sexual intercourse with another man's wife, whom the law handed down by God has allotted to him. And so there is no adultery or fornication in having intercourse with any woman at the command of God.

And the argument is the same regarding theft, which consists of taking another's property. One does not take without the consent of the owner (i.e., steal) anything that one takes at the command of God, who is the owner of all property.

Nor is it only regarding human affairs that everything God commands is owed to him. Rather, regarding things of nature, everything God does is also in one respect natural, as I said in the First Part.[31]

Reply Objection 3. We speak of things belonging to the natural law in two ways. We speak of them belonging in one way because nature inclines us to them. For example, one should not cause injury to another. We speak of them belonging in a second way because nature did not introduce the contrary. For example, we could say that it belongs to the natural law that human beings are naked, since nature did not endow them with clothes, which human skill created. And it is in the latter way that we say that "the common possession of all property and the same freedom for all persons" belong to the natural law, namely, that the reason of human beings, not nature, introduced private property and compulsory servitude. And so the natural law in this respect varies only by way of addition.

Article 6. Can the natural law be excised from the hearts of human beings?

We thus proceed to the sixth inquiry. It seems that the natural law can be excised from the hearts of human beings, for the following reasons:

---

29 A. 4.
30 Ibid.
31 I, Q. 105, A. 6, *ad* 1.

Objection 1. A gloss on Rom. 2:14, "When the Gentiles, who do not have the law," etc., says: "The law of righteousness, which sin had wiped out, is inscribed on the inner human being renewed by grace."[32] But the law of righteousness is the natural law. Therefore, the natural law can be wiped out.

Objection 2. The law of grace is more efficacious than the law of nature. But sin destroys the law of grace. Therefore, much more can the natural law be wiped out.

Objection 3. What law establishes is rendered just, as it were. But human beings have established many things contrary to the natural law. Therefore, the natural law can be excised from the hearts of human beings.

On the contrary, Augustine says in his *Confessions*: "Your law is inscribed on the hearts of human beings, and indeed no wickedness wipes it out."[33] But the law inscribed on the hearts of human beings is the natural law. Therefore, the natural law cannot be wiped out.

I answer that as I have said before,[34] there belong to the natural law, indeed primarily, very general precepts, precepts that everyone knows, and more particular, secondary precepts, which are like proximate conclusions from first principles. Therefore, regarding the general principles, the natural law in general can in no way be excised from the hearts of human beings. But the natural law is wiped out regarding particular actions insofar as desires or other emotions prevent reason from applying the general principles to particular actions, as I have said before.[35]

And the natural law can be excised from the hearts of human beings regarding the other, secondary precepts, either because of wicked opinions, just as errors in theoretical matters happen regarding necessary conclusions, or because of evil customs or corrupt habits. For example, some did not think robbery a sin, or even sins against nature to be sinful, as the Apostle also says in Rom. 1:24–28.

Reply Objection 1. Sin wipes out the natural law regarding particulars but not in general, except perhaps regarding secondary precepts of the natural law, in the way I mentioned.[36]

Reply Objection 2. Although grace is more efficacious than nature, nature is nonetheless more essential to human beings and so more abiding.

Reply Objection 3. The argument of this objection is valid regarding the secondary precepts of the natural law, contrary to which some lawmakers have passed wicked statutes.

Part II/1, Question 97. On Revision of Laws

Article 1. Should human law be revised in any way?

We thus proceed to the first inquiry. It seems that human law should be revised in no way, for the following reasons:

---

32   *Glossa ordinaria*, on Rom. 2:14 (*PL* 114:476); Peter Lombard, *Glossa*, on Rom. 2:14 (*PL* 191:1345).
33   *Confessions* II, 4 (*PL* 32:678).
34   AA. 4, 5.
35   I–II, Q. 77, A. 2.
36   In the body of the article.

Objection 1. Human law is derived from the natural law, as I have said before.[37] But the natural law remains immutable. Therefore, human law ought to remain immutable.

Objection 2. Measures ought to be most permanent, as the Philosopher says in the *Ethics*.[38] But human law is the measure of human actions, as I have said before.[39] Therefore, human law ought to remain without change.

Objection 3. It belongs to the nature of law to be just and upright, as I have said before.[40] But things once upright are always upright. Therefore, things once law ought always to be law.

On the contrary, Augustine says in his work *On Free Choice*: "Temporal law, although just, can be justly revised over time."[41]

I answer that as I have said before,[42] human law is a dictate of reason directing human actions. And so there can be two reasons why laws may be rightly revised: one, indeed, regarding reason; the second regarding human beings, whose actions laws regulate. One reason indeed regards reason, since it seems to be natural for reason to advance step-by-step from the imperfect to the perfect. And so we perceive, regarding theoretical sciences, that the first philosophers transmitted imperfect doctrines that later philosophers corrected. So also is this the case in practical matters. For the first lawmakers, who strove to discover things useful for the human community but were unable of themselves to contemplate everything, instituted imperfect laws that were deficient in many respects. And later lawmakers revised those laws, establishing laws that could fail to serve the commonweal in fewer cases.

And regarding human beings, whose actions laws regulate, laws can be rightly revised to suit the changed conditions of human beings, and different things are expedient for human beings according to their different circumstances. Just so, Augustine in his work *On Free Choice* poses this example:

> If a people should be well-tempered and serious and most diligently mindful of the commonweal, a law is rightly framed that permits such a people to choose magistrates to administer the commonwealth. Then, if the same people, corrupted over time, sell their votes and entrust their governance to scoundrels and criminals, the power to bestow offices is rightly taken away from such a people, and the power to bestow the offices falls to the choice of a few good persons.[43]

Reply Objection 1. The natural law is a participation in the eternal law, as I have said before,[44] and so the natural law remains immutable. And the natural law has this immutability from the immutability and perfection of the divine reason that establishes human nature. But human reason is mutable and imperfect.

And besides, the natural law consists of universal precepts that always abide, while laws established by human beings consist of particular precepts that regard different situations that arise.

37 I–II, Q. 95, A. 2.
38 *Ethics* V, 5 (1133a25).
39 I–II, Q. 90, AA. 1, 2.
40 I–II, Q. 90, A. 2.
41 *On Free Choice* I, 6, n. 14 (PL 32:1229).
42 I–II, Q. 91, A. 3.
43 *On Free Choice* I, 6, n. 14 (PL 32:1229).
44 I–II, Q. 91, A. 2; Q. 96, A. 2, *ad* 3.

Reply Objection 2. Measures ought to be as permanent as possible. But there cannot be anything altogether immutably permanent in mutable things. And so human laws cannot be altogether immutable.

Reply Objection 3. We predicate upright of material things in an absolute sense, and so they stay upright as far as it is in their power. But we speak of the rectitude of laws in relation to the commonweal, to which the same things are not always duly proportionate, as I have said before.[45] And so such rectitude changes.

Article 2. Should human laws always be revised for something better?

We thus proceed to the second inquiry. It seems that human laws should always be revised for something better, for the following reasons:

Objection 1. Human reason devises human laws, just as it devises human skills. But prior rules regarding other skills are modified for better rules. Therefore, we should also do the same regarding human laws.

Objection 2. We can provide for the future from things of the past. But many unsuitable things would result if human laws were not revised by adding better provisions, since the laws of antiquity were unsophisticated in many respects. Therefore, it seems that laws should be revised as often as something better presents itself to be made law.

Objection 3. Human laws are framed for the particular actions of human beings. But regarding such actions, we can gain complete knowledge only by experience, which "takes time," as the *Ethics* says.[46] Therefore, it seems that better things can occur over time and should be enacted as laws.

On the contrary, the *Decretum* says: "It is foolish and rather detestably shameful to allow the traditions of our forefathers to be modified."[47]

I answer that as I have said,[48] human laws are revised insofar as their revision serves the commonweal. But the very revision of laws, considered as such, involves some detriment to the commonweal. For custom avails very much for the observance of laws, since we regard things done contrary to common custom, even if those things be in themselves slight, as rather serious. And so the binding force of law is diminished when laws are revised, since custom is removed. And so human laws should never be revised unless the commonweal gains in one respect as much as it loses in the other. And such indeed is the case either because a very great and very clear benefit results from the new law, or because there is a very great necessity due either to the fact that the existing law is clearly unjust, or to the fact that observance of the existing law is most harmful. And so the Jurist says that "in establishing new laws, the benefit of departing from laws long perceived as just ought to be evident."[49]

---

45   In the body of the article.
46   *Ethics* II, 1 (1103a16).
47   Gratian, *Decretum* I, dist. 12, c. 5.
48   A. 1.
49   *Digest* I, title 4, law 2.

Reply Objection 1. The rules relating to skills derive their efficacy only from reason, and so prior rules should be revised whenever a better reason presents itself. But "laws have their greatest power from custom," as the Philosopher says in the *Politics*.[50] And so we should not rush to revise laws.

Reply Objection 2. The argument of this objection rightly concludes that laws should be revised. But they should be revised for the sake of a great benefit or necessity, not for the sake of any betterment, as I have said.[51]

Reply Objection 3. The same argument applies to this objection.

Article 3. Can customs obtain the force of law?

We thus proceed to the third inquiry. It seems that customs cannot obtain the force of law or abolish laws, for the following reasons:

Objection 1. Human law is derived from the natural law and the divine law, as is evident from what I have said before.[52] But human customs cannot alter the natural law or the divine law. Therefore, they also cannot alter human law.

Objection 2. Moral good cannot come out of many wicked acts. But those who first begin to act contrary to a law act wickedly. Therefore, many such acts do not produce something morally good. But law is something morally good, since law regulates human actions. Therefore, customs cannot abolish laws so that the customs obtain the force of law.

Objection 3. Framing laws belongs to public persons, whose business it is to govern a community, and so private persons cannot make law. But customs flourish through the acts of private persons. Therefore, custom cannot obtain the force of law so as to abolish laws.

On the contrary, Augustine says in a letter: "We should consider the customs of God's people and the prescriptions of our ancestors as laws. And as those who disobey God's laws should be punished, so also should those who condemn the Church's customs."[53]

I answer that all laws come from the reason and will of lawmakers: the divine and natural laws, indeed, from the reasonable will of God, and human laws from human wills regulated by reason. But the deeds of human beings as much as their words indicate their reason and will regarding things to be done. For example, everyone seems to desire as good what one carries out in deed. And human words evidently alter and also explain laws insofar as the words explain the internal movements and thoughts of human reason. And so also even acts, especially when repeated so as to constitute custom, can alter and explain laws, and cause things to obtain the force of law, namely, insofar as repeated external acts most effectively manifest internal movements of the will and the thoughts of reason. For things done repeatedly seem to proceed from deliberate judgments of reason. And so custom both has the force of law and abolishes law and interprets law.

---

50   *Politics* II, 5 (1269a20–24).
51   In the body of the article.
52   I–II: Q. 93, A. 3; Q. 95, A. 2.
53   *Letter 36*, to Casulanus (PL 33:136).

Reply Objection 1. The natural law and the divine law come from the divine will, as I have said.[54] And so only divine authority, not customs that come from the will of human beings, can alter those laws. And so no custom can obtain the force of law in opposition to the divine and natural laws, as Isidore says in his *Synonyms*: "Let custom yield to authority; let law and reason prevail over wicked customs."[55]

Reply Objection 2. Human laws are wanting in particular cases, as I have said before.[56] And so one can sometimes act outside the law, namely, in cases in which the laws are wanting, and yet the actions will not be morally evil. And when such instances are repeated because of alterations in human beings, then customs indicate that laws are no longer useful, just as it would be evident that laws are no longer useful if expressly contrary laws were to be promulgated. But if the same reason for which the original law was useful still persists, the law prevails over the custom, not the custom over the law. There may be an exception if the law seems useless simply because it is not "possible according to a country's customs," which was one of the conditions of law.[57] For it is difficult to destroy a people's customs.

Reply Objection 3. The people among whom a custom is introduced can be in two situations. For if a people is free, that is, self-governing, the consent of the whole people, which custom indicates, counts more in favor of a particular legal observance than the authority of its ruler, who only has the power to frame laws insofar as the ruler acts in the name of the people. And so the whole people can establish laws, but individual persons cannot.

But if a people should not have the free disposition to frame laws for itself or to abolish laws imposed by a higher power, the very customs prevailing in such a people still obtain the force of law insofar as those who have the power to impose laws on the people tolerate the customs. For rulers thereby seem to approve what the customs introduce.

Article 4. Can the people's rulers dispense subjects from human laws?

We thus proceed to the fourth inquiry. It seems that the people's rulers cannot dispense subjects from human laws, for the following reasons:

Objection 1. Laws are established "for the commonweal," as Isidore says.[58] But the common good should not be cast aside for the private convenience of a particular person, since "the good of the people is more godlike than the good of one human being," as the Philosopher says in the *Ethics*.[59] Therefore, it seems that no one should be dispensed to act contrary to the people's common law.

Objection 2. Dt. 1:17 commands those with authority over others: "You shall listen to the lowly as well as the mighty, nor shall you regard who anyone is, since your judgment is God's." But to grant to one what is denied to all seems to be regard for who the person is. Therefore, the people's rulers cannot give such dispensations, since this is contrary to a precept of the divine law.

---

54 In the body of the article.
55 *Synonyms* II, n. 80 (*PL* 83:863).
56 I–II, Q. 96, A. 6.
57 I–II, Q. 95, A. 3.
58 *Etymologies* II, 10 (*PL* 82:131); V, 3 (*PL* 82:199).
59 *Ethics* I, 2 (1094b9–10).

Objection 3. Human law, if just, needs to be in accord with the natural and divine laws; otherwise, it would not "be fitting for religion" or "be suitable for training," which are prerequisites of law, as Isidore says.[60] But no human being can dispense anyone from the divine and natural laws. Therefore, neither can any human being dispense someone from a human law.

On the contrary, the Apostle says in 1 Cor. 9:17: "Dispensation has been entrusted to me."

I answer that dispensing, properly speaking, signifies allotting common goods to individuals. And so we also call the heads of households dispensers, since they with due weight and in due measure distribute to each member of their households both duties and things necessary for living. Therefore, we also say regarding any political community that one dispenses, since that one in a way ordains how individuals should fulfill a general precept. And a precept generally for the convenience of the community may sometimes be unsuitable for a particular person or in a particular case, either because it would prevent something better, or because it would even bring about some evil, as is evident from what I have said before.[61] But it would be most dangerous to commit this to the discretion of each individual, except, perhaps, when there is a clear and present danger, as I have said before.[62] And so those empowered to rule a people have the power to dispense from human laws that rest on the rulers' authority, namely, as regards persons or situations in which the law is wanting, to grant permission not to observe precepts of the law.

But if rulers should grant this permission at their mere whim, without the persons or situations warranting it, they will be unfaithful or unwise dispensers. Rulers will be unfaithful dispensers if they do not aim at the common good, and they will be unwise dispensers if they ignore the reason for granting dispensations. And so the Lord says in Lk. 12:42: "Who, do you think, is the faithful and wise dispenser that a master sets over his household?"

Reply Objection 1. One ought not to be dispensed from observing general laws at the prejudice of the common good. Rather, dispensations should be granted for the purpose of benefiting the common good.

Reply Objection 2. There is no regard for who persons are if unequal things are dispensed to persons who are unequal. And so when the condition of persons requires that special things be reasonably accorded them, there is no regard for who the persons are if special favors are granted them.

Reply Objection 3. The natural law as consisting of general precepts, which are never wanting, cannot be dispensed. But human beings sometimes dispense from other precepts of the natural law, which are quasi-conclusions from the general precepts (e.g., dispensing from the obligation to repay loans owed to traitors, or the like).

But every human being is subject to the divine law as private persons are subject to public law. And so, as only rulers or their representatives can dispense from human laws, so only God or his special representatives can dispense from precepts of the divine law.

---

60 *Etymologies* II, 10 (*PL* 82:131); V, 3 (*PL* 82:199).
61 I–II, Q. 96, A. 6.
62 Ibid.

John Duns Scotus on Natural Law and Divine Law

The Decalogue and the Law of Nature
(*Ordinatio* III, suppl., dist. 37)

In regard to the thirty-seventh distinction [of Bk. III] I ask: Do all of the commandments of the decalogue belong to the law of nature?

[Arguments pro and con]

For the negative view:

[1] In those things which pertain to the law of nature it does not seem God can dispense; but he has done so in some matters that run counter to precepts of the decalogue; therefore, etc. Proof of the major premise: What pertains to the law of nature is either a practical principle known immediately from its terms or necessary conclusions that follow from such principles. In either case they possess necessary truth. Therefore, God cannot make them false. Hence, he cannot make what they say is good to be anything but good, or what they say must be avoided to be anything but evil, and thus he cannot make what is illicit licit. Proof of the minor premise: To kill, to steal, to commit adultery, are against the precepts of the decalogue, as is clear from Exodus [20: 13]: "You shall not kill" [etc.]. Yet God seems to have dispensed from these. This is clear in regard to homicide from Genesis 22, regarding Abraham and the son he was about to sacrifice; or for theft from Exodus 11: [2] and [12: 35] where he ordered the sons of Israel to despoil the Egyptians, which despoilment is taking what belongs to another without the owner's consent, which is the definition of theft. As for the third, there is Hosea 1: "Make children of fornications."

[2] Furthermore, the Apostle says to the Romans 7: [7]: "It was only through the law that I came to know sin. I should never have known what evil desire was unless the law had said: 'You shall not covet.'" But what is known from the law of nature is recognized as something to be done or not to be done, even though it is not written, just as what is known naturally in theoretical matters would still be known naturally, even if it were not revealed.

[3] Besides, the law of nature is obligatory for every state in which man finds himself, because it is known what such a nature must do and must not do. But the decalogue was not obligatory in every state, for instance, in the state of innocence, for the law had not yet been promulgated, nor did it seem to oblige before it was given.

For the opposite view:

In the beginning of the *Decrees* [*of Gratian*, in dist. 6], the first gloss "Illis omnino."

And look in the canonical epistle of John, ch. 2 [vv. 3–7]: "The way we can be sure of our knowledge of him is to keep his commandments, because whoever keeps his word, truly has the love of God been made perfect in him. The man who claims, 'I have known him,' without keeping his commandments is a liar. It is no new commandment I write to you, but an old one which you had from the start." This for the negative view.

[Body of the question]

[View of others] One view here claims that the whole decalogue pertains to the law of nature and explains it in some such way as this. The law of nature is a law proceeding from first principles known to hold for actions; these are seminal practical principles known from their terms. The intellect is naturally inclined to their truth because of their terms, and the will is naturally inclined to assent to what they dictate. From such principles everything in the decalogue follows either mediately or immediately. For all that is commanded there has a formal goodness whereby it is essentially ordered to man's ultimate end, so that through it a man is directed towards his end. Similarly everything prohibited there has a formal evil which turns one from the ultimate end. Hence, what is commanded there is not good merely because it is commanded, but commanded because it is good in itself. Likewise, what is prohibited there is not evil merely because it is prohibited, but forbidden because it is evil. On this view, then, it seems the reply to the first argument should be that God simply cannot dispense from such cases, for what is unlawful of itself cannot, it seems, become licit through any will. For instance, killing is an evil act, from the fact that it is directed against such and such a person, for instance, a neighbor. Then given this situation, it will always be evil, and so no willing extrinsic to what are the circumstances of the case can make killing good. And then one would have to explain away those texts where God seems to have given a dispensation. One way of doing this is to claim that though a dispensation could be granted to an act that falls under a generic description [like killing in general], it could never be given insofar as it is prohibited according to the intention of the commandment [e.g., killing an innocent neighbor], and hence [killing an unjust aggressor, for example] would not be against the prohibition. Put another way, an act that is inordinate cannot become well ordered, but an act insofar as it violates a prohibition is inordinate. Therefore, it cannot be subject to dispensation insofar as it is against a prohibition.

[Refutation of this view] But these explanations, which come down to the same thing, do not seem to save what they were intended to save. For to dispense does not consist in letting the precept stand and permitting one to act against it. To dispense, on the contrary, is to revoke the precept or declare how it is to be understood. For there are two kinds of dispensations – one revokes the law, the other clarifies it.

My question then is this. Granted that all the circumstances are the same in regard to this act of killing a man except the circumstances of its being prohibited in one case and not prohibited in another, could God cause that act which is circumstantially the same, but performed by different individuals, to be prohibited and illicit in one case and not prohibited but licit in the other? If so, then he can dispense unconditionally, just as he changed the old law when he gave a new law. And he did this in regard to the ceremonial functions he required, not by letting the ceremonial precepts stand, but not requiring them to be observed, but rather by letting an act remain the same [e.g., eating only kosher food], but not requiring anyone to do this as he did before. This is also the way any legislator dispenses unconditionally when he revokes a precept of positive law made by himself. He does not allow the prohibited act or precept to remain as before, but removes the prohibition or makes what was formerly illicit now licit. But if God cannot cause this act [of killing], which under such and such circumstances was formerly prohibited, to be no longer prohibited, even under the same circumstances, then he can not make killing licit – but that he did so is clear in the case of Abraham and in many other instances.

Also, those propositions which are true by reason of their terms, whether they be immediately so or conclusions therefrom, have their truth value prior to any act of the will, or at least they would be true even if, to assume the impossible, no act of willing existed. Therefore, if those precepts of the decalogue or the practical propositions that could be formed from them possessed such necessity (e.g., if these were necessary: "No neighbor should be hated or killed," "Theft should never be committed," and the like), it would follow that apart from all volition the divine intellect would see such propositions as true of themselves, and then the divine will would necessarily agree with them or it would not be right, and thus one would have to assume God has practical knowledge [as regards creatures], which was denied in the first book in the question about praxis. It would also be necessary to assume that his will is necessarily determined in an unqualified sense in regard to willing things other than himself, the opposite of which was asserted to be the case also in the first book, dist. 2, where we discussed the fact that his will tends to nothing other than himself except contingently.

And even if you say that a created will must necessarily be conformed to these truths if it is to be right, this still does not say that the divine will wills in accord with them; rather because it wills accordingly, therefore they are true.

The proponent of this first view replies to the question [I raise] that reason proves the opposite [namely, that God cannot make an act with the same circumstances licit at one time but not at another], for when the divine intellect apprehends these terms [of the propositions in question] and can understand from them that the propositions are true, a truth they possess prior to any act of his will in regard to them, then in the second sign of nature, namely, when the will does act in regard to them, it has to will necessarily in conformity to that dictate and hence cannot will the opposite.

[Scotus' own opinion] To the question, then, I say that some things can be said to belong to the law of nature in two ways:

[1] One way is as first practical principles known from their terms or as conclusions necessarily entailed by them. These are said to belong to the natural law in the strictest sense, and there can be no dispensation in their regard, as the argument for the first opinion proves. It is to these that the canon of the *Decrees of Gratian* refers, where it is said that "the natural law begins from the very beginnings of rational creatures, nor does time change it, but it is immutably permanent" – and this I concede.

But this is not the case when we speak in general of all the precepts of the second table [of the decalogue]. For the reasons behind the commands and prohibitions there are not practical principles that are necessary in an unqualified sense, nor are they simply necessary conclusions from such. For they contain no goodness such as is necessarily prescribed for attaining the goodness of the ultimate end, nor in what is forbidden is there such malice as would turn one away necessarily from the last end, for even if the good found in these maxims were not commanded, the last end [of man as union with God] could still be loved and attained, whereas if the evil proscribed by them were not forbidden, it would still be consistent with the acquisition of the ultimate end.

But it is different with the precepts of the first table, because these regard God immediately as object. Indeed the first two, if they be understood in a purely negative sense – i.e., "You shall not have other gods before me" and "You shall not take the name of the Lord, your God, in vain," i.e., "You should show no irreverence to God" – belong to the natural law, taking law of nature strictly, for this follows necessarily: "If God exists, then he alone must be loved as God." It likewise follows that nothing else must be worshiped as God, nor must any irreverence be shown to him. Consequently, God could not dispense in regard to these so that someone could do the opposite of what this or that prohibits. (In support of this put the two authorities here that are found in Richard, ch. 5.)

The third commandment of the first table is that which concerns the observance of the Sabbath. It is affirmative insofar as it prescribes that some worship be given to God at a specific time, but so far as the specification to this or that time goes, it does not pertain to the law of nature strictly speaking. Similarly with the negative portion included therein, which forbids servile work for a definite time that would interfere with the worship to be shown to him. For such work is only prohibited because it impedes or keeps one from the cult that is commanded.

[A doubt] But there is some doubt whether this precept of observing the Sabbath pertains to the natural law strictly to the extent that it requires that at some definite time worship be shown to God. For if it does not, then God could dispense from it absolutely, so that a man for the entire duration of his life would never have to manifest any affection or love for God. This does not seem probable, for without some act of goodwill or love towards God as the ultimate end, one could not do anything simply good that would be needed to attain that end, and thus this person would never be bound to will anything that is simply good in an unqualified sense. For the same reason that excludes from strict natural law the need to show worship to God now, holds also for then [i.e., the Sabbath] and, by the same token, for any specific time. Therefore, strictly speaking, it is not clear how one could infer that a person is bound then or now to worship God and, by the same reasoning, how anyone is bound at some undefined time to do so, for no one is obliged to perform at some undefined time an act which he is not obligated to perform at some definite time when some opportunities for doing so present themselves.

But if this is strictly of the natural law, so that "God must be loved" follows necessarily from "God must not be hated" or some other such precept, then this argument from singular instances to a universal statement does not hold, but represents a fallacy of a figure of speech, even as does the converse, where one argues from several determinate instances to one indeterminate one. But if this third commandment is not strictly a matter of natural law, then it must be judged like the precepts of the second table of the decalogue.

[2] The other way in which things belong to the law of nature is because they are exceedingly in harmony with that law, even though they do not follow necessarily from those first practical principles known from their terms, principles which are necessarily grasped by any intellect understanding those terms. Now, it is certain that all the precepts of the second table also belong to the natural law in this way, since their rightness is very much in harmony with the first practical principles that are known of necessity. And in this way one has

to understand that statement in the *Decrees of Gratian*, dist. 6, canon 3: "The moral precepts pertain to the natural law, and therefore they show no evidence of having undergone any change." Note the gloss which says: "The law concerns change not as regards moral matters but only as regards those pertaining to ritual."

This distinction can be made clear by an example. Given the principle of positive law that life in a community or state ought to be peaceful, it does not follow from this necessarily that everyone ought to have possessions distinct from those of another, for peace could reign in a group or among those living together, even if everything was common property. Not even in the case of the infirm is private possession an absolute necessity; nevertheless, that such persons have their own possessions is exceedingly consonant with peaceful living, for the infirm care more about goods of their own than they do about common property, and would prefer rather that the common goods be assigned to them than that they be given to the community and its custodians for the common good, and so strife and disorder could occur. And it is this way, perhaps, with all positive laws, for although there is some one principle which serves as the basis for establishing these laws, still positive laws do not follow with simple [logical] necessity from the principle in question or explicate it as regards certain particular cases. Nevertheless, these explications are greatly in harmony with the first universal principle they clarify.

To put all we have said together, first we deny that all the commandments of the second table pertain strictly to the law of nature; second, we admit that the first two commandments belong strictly to the law of nature; third, there is some doubt about the third commandment of the first table; fourth, we concede that all the commandments fall under the law of nature, speaking broadly.

[An objection] Against the first of these, I argue: According to the Apostle to the Romans [13: 9]: "The commandments, 'You shall not commit adultery; you shall not murder . . .' and if there be any other commandments, they may all be summed up in this: 'You shall love your neighbor as yourself.'" Therefore, in this precept, "Love your neighbor," etc., are included the precepts of the second table. For the Apostle appears to prove this point expressly and thus seems to conclude "Whoever loves his neighbor fulfills the law." What the Savior says also proves this, for the major [of the argument] is found in Matthew 22: [40]: "On this depends the whole law and the prophets." But the love of neighbor follows necessarily from this necessary principle: "God must be loved." Therefore, all the precepts of the second table, from first to last, follow from the precepts of the first table. Hence, if those of the first table pertain strictly to the law of nature, because they are included in the first precept or principle, which does belong to the natural law in an unqualified sense, it follows that the precepts of the second table also belong strictly to that law, even though they are conclusions drawn from the same principle. – Proof of the assumption [that love of neighbor follows from love of God]: This is clear from what was said in dist. 28 of this third book, where it was proved in two ways. The perfect love of God is a well-ordered love and cannot be jealous, in the sense of being appropriated [to oneself alone], because love of the good of all as something belonging to oneself alone is inordinate. Now, the love of someone who does not want the beloved [i.e., God] to be loved by others is inordinate and imperfect. Hence, it follows that if God is to be loved perfectly and orderly, then the one loving God must will that his neighbor also love God; but in so willing, he is loving his neighbor. Indeed this is the only way in which our neighbor is loved out of [supernatural] charity, as is pointed out in the *Glosses*, therefore, etc.

[Solution] To this one can reply in three ways:

First, the precept "Love the Lord, your God," etc., is not simply of the natural law insofar as it is affirmative. However, insofar as it is negative, prohibiting the opposite, namely, "Do not hate God," it does pertain strictly to the natural law. Just when one is required to love God is not clear, however, as was pointed out in discussing the third commandment. Now, from the negative precept, it does not follow that one must want his neighbor to love God, although this would follow from the affirmative formulation, which is not clearly something belonging to the natural law strictly.

Second, one could reply that from this precept, "Love the Lord, your God," it does not follow that I ought to want my neighbor to love God. And when one insists that a perfect and well-ordered love is not a jealous one, I reply that I do not have to will that the common good pertain to another in such a way that [God] has to be loved by this other. For it is not necessary that I will this good for another, if God does not want to be the good of such [e.g., for one who dies hating God], as when he destines one [viz., the saint] and not the other [viz., the sinner], wishing to be the good of the former but not of the latter. The same argument holds for the maxim "Whoever loves perfectly, wishes the beloved to be loved," namely, by one whose friendship pleases the beloved. It is not certain from the law of nature that everyone is such that his love is accepted by the God who is loved or should be loved.

The third way of answering the objection is that even if it were strictly a matter of the natural law that our neighbor be loved in the way this was explained above, namely, that one must want the neighbor himself to love God, because this is what it means to love one's neighbor, the precepts of the second table still do not follow [logically] from this. For instance, that one must not kill him, so far as the good of his person is concerned; or that one must not want him to commit adultery, so far as the good of his partner is concerned; or that one must not want him to steal, so far as the goods of fortune that he uses are concerned; or that one must want him to show reverence to his parents, which consists not just in honoring them but also in supporting them. For it is possible for me to will that my neighbor love God and nevertheless not will that he preserve corporeal life or conjugal fidelity, and so on with the other precepts. Consequently, these two can coexist, viz., that I want my neighbor to love God as I ought to love him (which would be a kind of necessary conclusion from the practical principles) and still do not will him this or that good pertaining to the second table, since the latter is not a necessary truth.

And then one could say to the quotations from Paul and Christ that God has now explained [in the Scriptures] a higher love of neighbor that transcends that which is included in, or follows from, the principles of the law of nature. In other words, although the love of neighbor that can be inferred from principles of the law of nature only requires that we love him in himself, still the love of neighbor as explained [by Christ and Paul] includes willing him these other goods, or at least not wishing him the opposite evils, such as not wanting him to be deprived unjustly of corporeal life, or conjugal fidelity, or temporal goods, and the like. Hence it is true that love of neighbor fulfills the law, viz., in the way it has been explained that this law of love must be observed, although not in the way that love of neighbor follows from the first principles of natural law. In a similar fashion, the whole law – so far as the second table and the prophets are concerned – depends on this commandment: "Love your neighbor as yourself," again understanding this not as something that follows of necessity from the first practical principles of the law of nature, but as the Lawgiver intended the love of neighbor to be observed according to the precepts of the second table.

[Reply to the initial arguments]

[To 1] As for the initial arguments, the first is in my favor, for it proves that the precepts of the second table are not part of the natural law strictly speaking.

[To 2] To the second, I say that although God's existence could have been inferred by natural reason from principles known in themselves, nevertheless, for the ignorant people unskilled in intellectual matters, it would be known only from revealed law. Hence the Apostle to the Hebrews 11: [6] says: "Anyone who comes to God must believe that he exists" – understanding this to mean, if he neither had nor could have any other knowledge of God. Thus, even if some sin could be inferred to be against the law of nature, nevertheless to corrupt men it might not be known that their lusts were against the natural law, and therefore, it would have been necessary to explain – either by the law that was given, or in some other way – that such sins of lust are prohibited by the second table. One could concede that such things are not known *per se*.

[To 3] To the other, I say that in every state all the commandments have been observed and should be observed. In the state of beatitude, indeed, there will be the highest observance of the affirmative precepts and of the negative ones as well, except perhaps that alone of honoring parents, not because there will be any wish not to honor them, but because in heaven there will be no necessity of performing actions, at least so far as "honor" includes providing them with what is necessary to sustain life, for there no one will need such help. In the state of innocence also all were bound by these precepts, which were either prescribed interiorly in the heart of everyone or perhaps by some teaching given exteriorly by God and passed on by parents to their children, even though at that time nothing would have been written in a book. Nor need it have been, because they would have easily remembered it, and the people of those times had longer lives and were better endowed naturally than the people of a later age, at which time the weakness of the people required that the law be given and written down.

As to the point touched upon in the first argument about the children of Israel despoiling the Egyptians, it could be said that in this case God did not dispense them from the law "Do not steal," for they did not simply take away a thing belonging to another. Since God was the higher owner, he could have transferred the ownership of these things, even if the lower "owners" were unwilling. In this way Christ did not sin in allowing the demons to enter the pigs, which were immediately thrown into the sea; for he did not unjustly deprive their owner of his pigs. Another explanation could be this: the sons of Israel, by serving the Egyptians, deserved the things they took as wages, even though the Egyptians unjustly were unwilling to give them up. In such a case the superior judge could have compelled the Egyptians to do so, and since the Jews accepted these things which should have been theirs by permission of the same higher judge, they licitly and justly appropriated them.

As for the argument for the opposite viewpoint, the canon in question has to be understood of the law taken in a broad sense, and in this case it extends to the precepts of the second table.

Suggestions for Further Reading

GENERAL SURVEYS OF MEDIEVAL PHILOSOPHY

Armstrong, A. H., ed. 1970. *The Cambridge History of Later Greek and Early Medieval Philosophy.* Cambridge: Cambridge University Press.

Copleston, Frederick. 1950. *A History of Philosophy*, vol. 2: *Medieval Philosophy: From Augustine to Duns Scotus.* Westminster, MD: The Newman Press (many subsequent reprintings by various presses).

Copleston, Frederick. 1953. *A History of Philosophy*, vol. 2: *Late Medieval and Renaissance Philosophy.* Westminster, MD: The Newman Press (many subsequent reprintings by various presses).

Gilson, Étienne. 1955. *History of Christian Philosophy in the Middle Ages.* New York: Random House.

Gracia, Jorge J. E., and Timothy B. Noone, eds. 2003. *A Companion to Philosophy in the Middle Ages.* Blackwell Companions to Philosophy. Oxford: Blackwell.

Kenny, A. 2005. *A New History of Western Philosophy*, vol. 2: *Medieval Philosophy.* Oxford: Clarendon Press.

Kretzmann, Norman, et al., eds. 1982. *The Cambridge History of Later Medieval Philosophy: From the Rediscovery of Aristotle to the Disintegration of Scholasticism, 1100–1600.* Cambridge: Cambridge University Press.

Luscombe, David E. 1997. *History of Western Philosophy*, vol. 2: *Medieval Thought.* Oxford: Oxford University Press.

Marenbon, John. 1981. *From the Circle of Alcuin to the School of Auxerre: Logic, Theology and Philosophy in the Early Middle Ages.* Cambridge: Cambridge University Press.

Marenbon, John. 1983. *Early Medieval Philosophy (480–1150): An Introduction.* London: Routledge & Kegan Paul.

Marenbon, John. 1991. *Later Medieval Philosophy (1150–1350): An Introduction.* London: Routledge.

Marenbon, John, ed. 1998. *The Routledge History of Philosophy*, vol. 3: *The Middle Ages.* London: Routledge.

McGrade, A. S., ed. 2003. *The Cambridge Companion to Medieval Philosophy.* Cambridge: Cambridge University Press.

Spade, Paul Vincent. 2004. "Medieval Philosophy." *The Stanford Encyclopedia of Philosophy* (Fall 2004 edn), ed. Edward N. Zalta. <http://plato.stanford.edu/archives/fall2004/entries/medieval-philosophy/>.

SECONDARY LITERATURE ON MAJOR FIGURES

The primary literature is amply referenced in these works.

ANSELM OF CANTERBURY

Davies, Brian, and Brian Leftow, eds. 2004. *The Cambridge Companion to Anselm*. Cambridge: Cambridge University Press.
Hopkins, Jasper. 1972. *A Companion to the Study of St. Anselm*. Minneapolis: University of Minnesota Press.
Southern, R. W. 1990. *Saint Anselm: A Portrait in Landscape*. Cambridge: Cambridge University Press.

AUGUSTINE

Kretzman, Norman, and Eleonore Stump, eds. 2001. *The Cambridge Companion to Augustine*. Cambridge: Cambridge University Press.
Markus, R. A., ed. 1972. *Augustine: A Collection of Critical Essays*. Garden City, NY: Doubleday/Anchor Books.
Matthews, Gareth B., ed. 1999. *The Augustinian Tradition*. Berkeley: University of California Press.
Mendelson, Michael. 2000. "Saint Augustine." *The Stanford Encyclopedia of Philosophy* (Winter 2000 edn), ed. Edward N. Zalta. <http://plato.stanford.edu/archives/win2000/entries/augustine/>.

BOETHIUS

Chadwick, H. 1981. *Boethius: The Consolations of Music, Logic, Theology, and Philosophy*. Oxford: Oxford University Press.
Gibson, M., ed. 1981. *Boethius: His Life, Thought and Influence*. Oxford: Blackwell.
Marenbon, John. 2002. *Boethius*. New York: Oxford University Press.
Marenbon, John. 2005. "Anicius Manlius Severinus Boethius." *The Stanford Encyclopedia of Philosophy* (Summer 2005 edn), ed. Edward N. Zalta. <http://plato.stanford.edu/archives/sum2005/entries/boethius/>.

GILES OF ROME

Donati, Silvia. 2003. "Giles of Rome," in Jorge J. E. Gracia and Timothy B. Noone, eds, *A Companion to Philosophy in the Middle Ages*. Blackwell Companions to Philosophy. Oxford: Blackwell, pp. 266–71.
Lambertini, Roberto. 2004. "Giles of Rome." *The Stanford Encyclopedia of Philosophy* (Fall 2004 edn), ed. Edward N. Zalta. <http://plato.stanford.edu/archives/fall2004/entries/giles/>.

HENRY OF GHENT

Guldentops, Guy, and Carlos Steel, eds. 2003. *Henry of Ghent and the Transformation of Scholastic Thought*. Leuven: Leuven University Press.
Marrone, Steven P. 1985. *Truth and Scientific Knowledge in the Thought of Henry of Ghent*. Cambridge, MA: Medieval Academy.
Marrone, Steven P. 2001. *The Light of Thy Countenance: Science and Knowledge of God in the Thirteenth Century*. Leiden: Brill.
Vanhamel, W., ed. 1996. *Henry of Ghent. Proceedings of the International Colloquium on the Occasion of the 700th Anniversary of his Death (1293)*. Leuven: Leuven University Press.

JOHN BURIDAN

Freidmann, Russell L., and Sten Ebbesen, eds. 2004. *John Buridan and Beyond: Topics in the Language Sciences 1300–1700*. Copenhagen: The Royal Danish Academy of Sciences and Letters.

Klima, Gyula. 1999. "Buridan's Logic and the Ontology of Modes," in S. Ebbesen and R. L. Friedmann, eds, *Medieval Analyses in Language and Cognition*. Copenhagen: The Royal Danish Academy of Sciences and Letters, pp. 473–95.

Klima, Gyula. 2003. "John Buridan," in Jorge J. E. Gracia and Timothy B. Noone, eds, *A Companion to Philosophy in the Middle Ages*. Oxford: Blackwell, pp. 340–8.

Klima, Gyula. 2005. "The Essentialist Nominalism of John Buridan," *The Review of Metaphysics* 58, pp. 301–15.

Zupko, Jack. 1993. "Buridan and Skepticism," *Journal of the History of Philosophy* 31, pp. 191–221.

Zupko, Jack. 2001. "John Buridan on the Immateriality of the Intellect," *Proceedings of the Society for Medieval Logic and Metaphysics* 1, pp. 4–18.

Zupko, Jack. 2003. *John Buridan: Portrait of a 14th-Century Arts Master*. Notre Dame, IN: University of Notre Dame Press.

JOHN DUNS SCOTUS

Cross, Richard. 1999. *Duns Scotus*. Oxford: Oxford University Press.

Frank, William A., and Allan B. Wolter OFM. 1995. *Duns Scotus: Metaphysician*. Lafayette, IN: Purdue University Press.

Williams, Thomas. 2003. *The Cambridge Companion to Duns Scotus*. New York: Cambridge University Press.

JOHN OF SALISBURY

Guilfoy, Kevin. 2005. "John of Salisbury." *The Stanford Encyclopedia of Philosophy* (Fall 2005 edn), ed. Edward N. Zalta. <http://plato.stanford.edu/archives/fall2005/entries/john-salisbury/>.

Nederman, C. 2005. *John of Salisbury*. Authors of the Middle Ages. Tempe, AZ: Medieval and Renaissance Texts and Studies.

JOHN SCOTTUS ERIUGENA

Gersh, Stephen. 1978. *From Iamblichus to Eriugena*. Leiden: Brill.

McGinn, Bernard, and Willemien Otten, eds. 1994. *Eriugena: East and West*. Notre Dame, IN: University of Notre Dame Press.

Moran, Dermot. 1989. *The Philosophy of John Scottus Eriugena: A Study of Idealism in the Middle Ages*. Cambridge: Cambridge University Press.

O'Meara, John J. 1988. *Eriugena*. Oxford: Clarendon Press.

Otten, Willemien. 1991. *The Anthropology of Johannes Scottus Eriugena*. Leiden: Brill.

NICHOLAS OF AUTRECOURT

Dutton, B. D. 1996. "Nicholas of Autrecourt and William of Ockham on Atomism, Nominalism, and the Ontology of Motion." *Medieval Philosophy and Theology* 5, pp. 63–85.

Scott, Theodore K. 1971. "Nicholas of Autrecourt, Buridan, and Ockhamism," *Journal of the History of Philosophy* 9, pp. 15–41.

Thijssen, J. M. M. H. 1998. *Censure and Heresy at the University of Paris, 1: 200–1400*. Philadelphia: University of Pennsylvania Press.

Thijssen, Hans, "Nicholas of Autrecourt," *The Stanford Encyclopedia of Philosophy* (Winter 2001 edn), ed. Edward N. Zalta. <http://plato.stanford.edu/archives/win2001/entries/autrecourt/>.

PETER ABELARD

Brower, Jeff, and Kevin Guilfoy, eds. 2004. *The Cambridge Companion to Abelard*. New York: Cambridge University Press.

King, Peter. 2004. "Peter Abelard." *The Stanford Encyclopedia of Philosophy* (Fall 2004 edn), ed. Edward N. Zalta. <http://plato.stanford.edu/archives/fall2004/entries/abelard/>.

Luscombe, David. 1969. *The School of Peter Abelard*. Cambridge: Cambridge University Press.

SIGER OF BRABANT

Dales, Richard C. 1991. *Medieval Discussions of the Eternity of the World*. Leiden: Brill.

Dales, Richard C. 1995. *The Problem of the Rational Soul in the Thirteenth Century*. Leiden: Brill.

Dodd, Tony. 1998. *The Life and Thought of Siger of Brabant*. Lewiston, Queenstown, and Lampeter: Edwin Mellen Press.

THOMAS AQUINAS

Davies, Brian. 1992. *The Thought of Thomas Aquinas*. Oxford: Clarendon Press.

Davies, Brian, ed. 2002. *Thomas Aquinas: Contemporary Philosophical Perspectives*. Oxford: Oxford University Press.

Haldane, John, ed. 2002. *Mind, Metaphysics, and Value in the Thomistic and Analytic Traditions*. Notre Dame, IN: University of Notre Dame Press.

Kenny, Anthony. 1993. *Aquinas on Mind*. New York: Routledge.

Kenny, Anthony. 2002. *Aquinas on Being*. Oxford: Clarendon Press.

Kretzmann, Norman, and Eleonore Stump, eds. 1993. *The Cambridge Companion to Aquinas*. Cambridge: Cambridge University Press.

McInerny, Ralph. 2004. *Aquinas*. Cambridge: Polity.

Pasnau, Robert, and Christopher Shields, 2004. *The Philosophy of Aquinas*. Boulder, CO: Westview.

Stump, Eleonore. 2003. *Aquinas*. London: Routledge.

WILLIAM OF OCKHAM

Adams, Marilyn McCord. 1987. *William Ockham*, 2 vols. Notre Dame, IN: University of Notre Dame Press.

Panaccio, Claude. 2004. *Ockham on Concepts*. Ashgate Studies in Medieval Philosophy. Aldershot: Ashgate.

Spade, Paul Vincent, ed. 1999. *The Cambridge Companion to Ockham*. Cambridge: Cambridge University Press.

Spade, Paul Vincent. 2002. "William of Ockham," *The Stanford Encyclopedia of Philosophy* (Fall 2002 edn), ed. Edward N. Zalta. <http://plato.stanford.edu/archives/fall2002/entries/ockham/>.

SECONDARY LITERATURE ON SUBJECT AREAS

PART I. LOGIC AND EPISTEMOLOGY

Ashworth, E. Jennifer. 1974. *Language and Logic in the Post-Medieval Period*. Synthese Historical Library, vol. 12. Dordrecht: D. Reidel.

Ashworth, E. Jennifer. 1977. *The Tradition of Medieval Logic and Speculative Grammar: A Bibliography*. Toronto: Pontifical Institute of Mediaeval Studies.

Broadie, Alexander. 1993. *Introduction to Medieval Logic*, 2nd edn. Oxford: Oxford University Press.

Bubacz, Bruce. 1981. *St. Augustine's Theory of Knowledge: A Contemporary Analysis*. Lewiston, Queenstown, and Lampeter: Edwin Mellen Press.

SUGGESTIONS FOR FURTHER READING

Holopainen, Toivo J. 1996. *Dialectic and Theology in the Eleventh Century*. Leiden: Brill.

Klima, Gyula. 1993. "The Changing Role of *Entia Rationis* in Medieval Philosophy: A Comparative Study with a Reconstruction," *Synthese* 96, pp. 25–59.

Klima, Gyula. 1996. "The Semantic Principles Underlying Saint Thomas Aquinas's Metaphysics of Being," *Medieval Philosophy and Theology* 5, pp. 87–141.

Klima, Gyula. 2004. "The Medieval Problem of Universals," *The Stanford Encyclopedia of Philosophy* (Winter 2004 edn), ed. Edward N. Zalta. <http://plato.stanford.edu/archives/win2004/entries/universals-medieval/>.

Pasnau, Robert. 1997. *Theories of Cognition in the Later Middle Ages*. Cambridge: Cambridge University Press.

Pasnau, Robert. 1999. "Divine Illumination," *The Stanford Encyclopedia of Philosophy* (Fall 2002 edn), ed. Edward N. Zalta. <http://plato.stanford.edu/archives/fall2002/entries/illumination/>.

Pironet, Fabienne. 1997. *The Tradition of Medieval Logic and Speculative Grammar: A Bibliography (1977–1994)*. Turnhout: Brepols.

Read, Stephen. 2002. "Medieval Theories: Properties of Terms," *The Stanford Encyclopedia of Philosophy* (Spring 2002 edn), ed. Edward N. Zalta. <http://plato.stanford.edu/archives/spr2002/entries/medieval-terms/>.

Schmidt, R. W. 1966. *The Domain of Logic According To Saint Thomas Aquinas*. The Hague: Martinus Nijhoff.

Spade, Paul V. 1982. "The Semantics of Terms," in Norman Kretzmann, Anthony Kenny, and Jan Pinborg, eds, *The Cambridge History of Later Medieval Philosophy*. Cambridge: Cambridge University Press, pp. 188–96.

Tweedale, Martin M. 1999. *Scotus vs. Ockham: A Medieval Dispute over Universals*, 2 vols. Lewiston, Queenstown, and Lampeter: Edwin Mellen Press.

PART II. PHILOSOPHY OF NATURE, PHILOSOPHY OF THE SOUL, METAPHYSICS

Callus, D. A. 1967. "Unicity and Plurality of Forms," *New Catholic Encyclopedia*. New York: McGraw-Hill, pp. 1967–79.

Cross, Richard. 2003. "Medieval Theories of Haecceity," *The Stanford Encyclopedia of Philosophy* (Fall 2003 edn), ed. Edward N. Zalta. <http://plato.stanford.edu/archives/fall2003/entries/medieval-haecceity/>.

Gracia, Jorge J. E. 1984. *Introduction to the Problem of Individuation in the Early Middle Ages* (2nd edn 1988). Munich and Washington, DC: Philosophia Verlag and Catholic University of America Press.

Gracia, Jorge J. E., ed. 1994. *Individuation in Scholasticism: The Later Middle Ages and the Counter-Reformation*. SUNY Series in Philosophy. Albany: State University of New York Press.

Grant, Edward. 1977. *Physical Science in the Middle Ages*. New York: Cambridge University Press.

Grant, Edward, and John E. Murdoch. 1987. *Mathematics and its Applications to Science and Natural Philosophy in the Middle Ages*. Cambridge: Cambridge University Press.

Holscher, Ludger. 1986. *The Reality of the Mind: Augustine's Philosophical Arguments for the Human Soul as a Spiritual Substance*. London: Routledge & Kegan Paul.

Klima, Gyula. 1998. "*Ancilla Theologiae* vs. *Domina Philosophorum*: Thomas Aquinas, Latin Averroism, and the Autonomy of Philosophy," in J. Aertsen and A. Speer, eds, *What Is Philosophy in the Middle Ages? Proceedings of the Tenth International Congress of Medieval Philosophy* (SIEPM). Berlin: Walter de Gruyter, pp. 393–402.

Klima, Gyula. 2000a. "Thomas of Sutton on the Nature of the Intellective Soul and the Thomistic Theory of Being," in J. Aertsen, et al., eds, *Nach der Verurteilung von 1277. Philosophie und Theologie an der Universität von Paris im letzten Viertel des 13. Jahrhunderts*. Miscellanea Mediaevalia 28. Berlin and New York: Studien und Texte, pp. 436–55.

Klima, Gyula. 2000b. "Saint Anselm's Proof: A Problem of Reference, Intentional Identity and Mutual Understanding," in G. Hintikka, ed., *Medieval Philosophy and Modern Times*. Dordrecht: Kluwer Academic Publishers, pp. 69–88.

Klima, Gyula. 2000c. "Aquinas on One and Many," *Documenti e Studi sulla Tradizione Filosofica Medievale (An International Journal on the Philosophical Tradition from Late Antiquity to the Late Middle Ages of the Società Internazionale per lo Studio del Medioevo Latino)* 11, pp. 195–215.

Klima, Gyula. 2002. "Man = Body + Soul: Aquinas's Arithmetic of Human Nature," in Brian Davies, ed., *Thomas Aquinas: Contemporary Philosophical Perspectives*. Oxford: Oxford University Press, pp. 257–73 (slightly revised reprint of a 1997 paper).

Knuuttila, S. 2001. "Necessities in Buridan's Natural Philosophy," in J. M. M. H. Thijssen and Jack Zupko, eds, *The Metaphysics and Natural Philosophy of John Buridan*. Leiden: Brill, pp. 65–76.

MacDonald, Scott. 1984. "The Esse/Essentia Argument in Aquinas's *De ente et essentia*," *Journal of the History of Philosophy* 22, pp. 157–72.

Pasnau, Robert. 2002. *Thomas Aquinas on Human Nature: A Philosophical Study of "Summa Theologiae" 1a 75–89*. Cambridge: Cambridge University Press.

Thijssen, J. M. M. H., and Jack Zupko, eds. 2001. *The Metaphysics and Natural Philosophy of John Buridan*, Leiden: Brill.

Wippel, John. 2000. *The Metaphysical Thought of Thomas Aquinas: From Finite Being to Uncreated Being*. Washington, DC: Catholic University of America Press.

PART III. PRACTICAL PHILOSOPHY

Evans, Gillian R. 1982. *Augustine on Evil*. Cambridge: Cambridge University Press.

Fay, Thomas A. 1993. "The Development of St. Thomas' Teaching on the Distinction Between Primary and Secondary Precepts of Natural Law," *Doctor Communis*, 46, pp. 262–72.

Finnis, John. 1980. *Natural Law and Natural Rights*. Oxford: Clarendon Press.

Finnis, John. 1998. *Aquinas: Moral, Political, and Legal Theory*. Oxford: Oxford University Press.

Holopainen, Taina M. 1991. *William Ockham's Theory of the Foundations of Ethics*. Helsinki: Luther Agricola Society.

Kenny, Anthony. 1969. "Divine Foreknowledge and Human Freedom," in A. Kenny, *Aquinas: A Collection of Critical Essays*. South Bend, IN: University of Notre Dame Press.

Kent, Bonnie. 1995. *Virtues of the Will: The Transformation of Ethics in the Late Thirteenth Century*. Washington, DC: Catholic University of America Press.

Kent, Bonnie. 2001. "Augustine's Ethics," in E. Stump and N. Kretzmann, eds, *The Cambridge Companion to Augustine*. Cambridge: Cambridge University Press, pp. 205–33.

Kent, Bonnie. 2003a. "The Moral Life," in A. S. McGrade, ed., *The Cambridge Companion to Medieval Philosophy*. Cambridge: Cambridge University Press, pp. 231–53.

Kent, Bonnie. 2003b. "Rethinking Moral Dispositions: Scotus on the Virtues," in T. Williams, ed., *The Cambridge Companion to Duns Scotus*. Cambridge: Cambridge University Press, pp. 352–76.

Klima, Gergely. 2004. "The Primal Choice: An Analysis of Anselm's Account of Free Will," *Sapientia et Doctrina* 2, pp. 5–13.

Lee, Patrick. 1998. "Is Thomas's Natural Law Theory Naturalist?," *American Catholic Philosophical Quarterly* 4, pp. 567–87.

MacDonald, Scott. 1988. "Boethius's Claim That All Substances Are Good," *Archiv für Geschichte der Philosophie* 70, pp. 245–79.

MacDonald, Scott. 1989. "Augustine's Christian-Platonist Account of Goodness," *New Scholasticism* 63, pp. 485–509.

MacDonald, Scott, ed. 1991. *Being and Goodness*. Ithaca, NY: Cornell University Press.

Pope, Stephen J., ed. 2002. *The Ethics of Aquinas*. Washington, DC: Georgetown University Press.

Saarinen, Risto. 1994. *Weakness of the Will in Medieval Thought: From Augustine to Buridan*. Leiden: Brill.

Williams, Thomas, and Sandra Visser. 2001. "Anselm's Account of Freedom," *Canadian Journal of Philosophy* 31, pp. 221–44.

Index

CPSIA information can be obtained at www.ICGtesting.com
Printed in the USA
LVOW132350131211

259256LV00003B/7/P

9 781405 135658